The Scandinavian Character of Anglian England in the pre-Viking Period

John Hines

BAR British Series 124
1984

B.A.R.

122 Banbury Road, Oxford OX2 7BP, England

GENERAL EDITORS

A.R. Hands, B.Sc., M.A., D.Phil.
D.R. Walker, M.A.

B.A.R. -124,1984 : 'The Scandinavian Character of Anglian England in
the Pre-Viking Period'.

Price £ 20.00 post free throughout the world. Payments made in
currency other than sterling must be calculated at the current rate
of exchange. Cheques should be made payable to B.A.R. and sent
to the above address.

ISBN 0 86054 254 8

For details of all BAR publications in print please write to the
above address. Information on new titles is sent regularly on
request, with no obligation to purchase.

Volumes are distributed direct from the publisher. All BAR prices
are inclusive of postage by surface mail anywhere in the world.

Printed in Great Britain

CONTENTS

Note: All figures and plates are reproductions at the scale
      of 1:1 unless otherwise indicated.

PREFACE

This book contains, in essence, my doctoral thesis, which was submitted under the same title under the Faculty of Anthropology and Geography at Oxford University in 1983. I should like to take this opportunity of thanking my examiners on that occasion, David Brown of the Ashmolean Museum, and Ulla Lund Hansen of the Forhistorisk-Arkæologisk Institutt, Copenhagen University, for their work in the task of examining the thesis, for their encouragement to me to publish its contents, and for a number of improvements which they helpfully suggested.

There are two major changes to the thesis text in the following book which should be noted here, both of which are intended to make the work easier to follow. In Chapter 2 the forms of clasps of Classes B and C in England and Scandinaivia are now numbered in one series covering both areas (Forms B 1-20, C 1-3), rather than in separate English and Scandinavian series as before. In Chapter 3, on square-headed brooches, the former use of abbreviated forms of the names of the find spots to identify individual brooches (e.g. Dart for Dartford, Kent) was felt to be too awkward overall, and the brooches are now referred to in the course of the text by the full name of their find spot, without the county, followed by a grave- or group-number if applicable. The systems used here are intended to supersede those found in the thesis.

Some apology may also be made for the fact that more illustrations might helpfully have been provided with the text than will be found. A work dealing with the archaeology of a large area of England and Scandinavia in the 5th. to 8th. centuries involves the discussion of a great volume of material, and this compels some selectivity in the provision of illustrations. In general, I have sought to illustrate that material which is not adequately illustrated in other publications which one would expect to be generally accessible in the libraries of British and European institutions such as universities and museums: e.g. Leeds's Corpus of Early Anglo-Saxon Great Square-Headed Brooches, Hougen's The Migration Style of Ornament in Norway, Mackeprang's De Nordiske Guldbrakteater, Åberg's Den nordiska folkvandringstidens kronologi and The Anglo-Saxons in England, etc. I would hope that it should be unnecessary for a reader to surround himself with piles of arcane publications in order to comprehend the central argument of the thesis, or, as is hoped will be the case, to employ the new classifications proposed for the clasps and Anglo-Saxon square-headed brooches.

I owe a great debt of gratitude to Dr Martin Welch of University College London for patiently and diligently proof-reading the word-processed text of this publication and in the course of this for providing a number of valuable corrections and comments. Responsibility for errors which have escaped remains, of course, my own. I wish finally to thank Sabina Thompson for her work in setting up the text on the word-processor.

ACKNOWLEDGEMENTS

I was occupied in the preparation of my thesis from October 1979 to July 1983. During this time I was a member of Keble College, Oxford, and also spent some time at the Historisk Museum, Universitetet i Bergen, Norway (August 1981 - May 1982), and at Københavns Universitet, Denmark (June - September 1982). Financial support came from a Major State Studentship from the Department of Education and Science, a Senior Scholarship at Keble College, and Research Scholarships from the Norwegian Utenriksdepartment and Danish Undervisningsministeriet, to all of whom I am most grateful.

It would have been impossible to complete - to the extent that it _is_ complete - the task attempted in this study without the helpful co-operation of a great many people associated with my college, and with universities and museums all over England and Scandinavia and in northern Europe. Simply to list some three hundred or more names would suggest that my debt to them was one of honour rather than true gratitude, and so I here offer my sincere thanks to all who have helped me in any way for their own contribution. Where possible and appropriate, due acknowledgement is made for specific contributions in the course of the text, appendices, lists and figures. Special and particular thanks are reserved, however, for my supervisor, Mrs S.C. Hawkes, for her constant interest in the work, and for never failing to provide help and encouragement when either or both were wanted.

Finally, I could never have been able to undetake and complete this work without the understanding, patience, and faith which my family and my wife, Pamela, have shown towards me and my studies. To them, I affectionately dedicate this work.

Museums contacted or visited and reference code for use within this work

England

The British Museum, London	BM
Maidstone Museum	Maidstone Mus
Barbican House, Lewes	Lewes Mus
Brighton Pavilion Museum	Brighton Mus
Surrey Archaeological Society Museum, Guildford	Guildford Mus
Ashmolean Museum	Ashmolean
Ipswich Museum	Ipswich Mus
Moyse's Hall Museum, Bury St. Edmunds	BSE Mus
Castle Museum, Norwich	Norwich Mus
Colchester and Essex Museum	Colchester Mus
University Museum of Archaeology and Anthropology, Cambridge	MAA Cam
City Museum, Peterborough	Peterborough Mus
Bedford Museum	BEDFM
Luton Museum	Luton Mus
Westfield Museum, Kettering	Kettering Mus
Central Museum, Northampton	N'pton Mus
Oundle School Museum	Oundle
County Museum, Warwick	Warwicks Mus
Coventry Museum	Coventry Mus
New Place Museum, Stratford-upon-Avon	Stratford Mus
City Museum, Worcester	Worcester Mus
Jewry Wall Museum, Leicester	Leicester Mus
Rutland County Museum, Oakham	RCM
Melton Mowbray Museum	Melton Mowbray Mus
Spalding Gentlemen's Society Museum	Spalding Gents' Soc Mus
Grantham Museum	Grantham Mus
City and County Museum, Lincoln	Lincoln Mus
Brewhouse Yard Museum, Nottingham	Nottingham Mus
Nottingham University Museum	Nottingham University Mus
Derby Museum	Derby Mus
Scunthorpe Museum	Scunthorpe Mus
Archaeological Museum, Kingston upon Hull	Hull Mus
Sewerby Hall Museum, Bridlington	Sewerby Hall Mus
Yorkshire Museum, York	Yorks Mus

West Germany

Schleswig-Holsteinisches Landesmuseum für Vor- und
    Frühgeschichte, Schloss Gottorf, Schleswig   KS

Denmark

Nationalmuseet København, afdeling 1	NMK
Sorø amts Museum	SAM
Fyens Stiftsmuseum, Odense	-
Vendsyssel Historiske Museum, Hjørring	VHM
Ålborg Historiske Museum	ÅHM
Viborg Stiftsmuseum	VSM
Kulturhistoriske Museum, Randers	KHM
Vejle Kulturhistoriske Museum	-
Ringkjøbing Museum	-
Den antikvariske samling i Ribe	-
Haderslev Museum	HM

Norway

Universitetets Oldsaksamling, Oslo	C
Arkeologisk museum i Stavanger	S
Historisk Museum, Bergen	B
Ålesund Museum	Å
Det Kongelige norske videnskabersselskabs Museet, Trondheim	T
Tromsø Museum	Ts

Sweden

Statens Historiska Museum, Stockholm	SHM
Stockholms Stadsmuseum	SSM
Göteborgs arkeologiska Museum	GAM
Skaraborgs läns Museum, Skara	SLM
Lunds universitets historiska Museum	LUHM
Västmanlands läns Museum	VLM
Sundsvall Museum	Sundsvall Mus
Jämtlands läns Museum	JLM

Abbreviations: Periodicals and Series

Aarb.	Aarbøger for nordisk Olddyndighed og Historie
AASRP	Associated Architectural Societies. Reports and Papers.
Ab.	Aarsberetning for Foreningen til norske fortidsminnesmerkers Bevaring
Acta Arch.	Acta Archaeologica (Copenhagen)
ANS.NNM	American Numismatic Society, New York. Numismatic Notes and Monographs
Ant. J.	Antiquaries' Journal
Ant. St.	Antikvariske Studier
Arch.	Archaeologia
Arch. Cant.	Archaeologia Cantiana
Arch. J.	Archaeological Journal
Arch. suisse	Archéologie suisse
ASE	Anglo-Saxon England
ASSAH	Anglo-Saxon Studies in Archaeology and History
Beds.A.J.	Bedfordshire Archaeological Journal
BMÅ	Bergen Museum Årbok
BRGK	Bericht der Römisch-Germanischen Kommission
C.Arch.	Current Archaeology
EAA	East Anglian Archaeology
EETS	Early English Text Society
FS	Frühmittelalterliche Studien
Fv	Fornvännen
Med.Arch.	Medieval Archaeology
NA	Nationalmuseets Arbejdsmark
P.C.A.S.	Proceedings of the Cambridge Antiquarian Society
P.S.A.	Proceedings of the Society of Antiquaries
P.S.A.S.	Proceedings of the Society of Antiquaries of Scotland
P.Sfk.I.A.N.H.	Proceedings of the Suffolk Institute for Archaeology and Natural History
SMÅ	Stavanger Museums Årbok
Sx.A.C.	Sussex Archaeological Collections
T.B.A.A.	Transactions of the British Architectural Association
UOÅ	Universitetets Oldsaksamling Årbok
VCH	Victoria County Histories
YAJ	Yorkshire Archaeological Journal
ÅUB	Årbok for Universitetet i Bergen

CHAPTER 1

INTRODUCTION

It is the purpose of this study to describe and to seek to explain certain parallels in the material culture found in two areas of land separated by a substantial tract of sea (the North Sea from east to west) within a specific period. The work thereby involves the investigation of the sources of a section of past English culture, and of its relationship to cultural practices and developments outside of England. To make progress along this road must make the basis for further studies or interpretations of early Anglo-Saxon culture more reliable. In the particular case considered here, positive progress should substantially and significantly expand the geographical and cultural frame of reference within which such studies and interpretations may confidently be made.

An essential concern of the study, then, is the spatial distribution of material culture, which may be represented by a selected but connected range of artefacts. The simple, basic questions to be asked and answered concern the origin of certain artefact-types and the geographical extension of their range, the dates and rate of their development and distribution, and what, subsequently, may be suggested to have been the mechanisms or modes of their changing range.

It would, however, be virtually impossible to examine this topic exclusively in such bare, materialistic terms. Questions concerning the ethnography of the earliest settlers of England are too tightly entangled with studies of early Anglo-Saxon material culture to be evaded or ignored here, and are a valuable extension to the scope and sophistication of artefact-based archaeology. The academic background to this present work shows a continuous engagement with these questions, especially in the influential work of E.T. Leeds (e.g. Leeds 1913, 1945). One part of the restricted geographical area on which the work in this study concentrates, Anglian England, is implicitly delimited to some extent by ethnographic factors. The results obtained through this research in terms of geographically restricted cultural relationship, and the form of cultural relationship between peoples living in different areas, ought to be compared with our inheritance of historical and archaeological studies and traditions on the ethnic identity of the English settlers and population in the period concerned.

The fundamental reference point for a consideration of the ethnography of the earliest Germanic settlers of England is of course Bede's description of the English invasion of Brittania (HE I.15). Bede names three gentes or populi, the Saxones, the Angli, and the Iutae/-i

1

(Saxons, Angles, and Jutes) as those primarily involved in the settlement. He indicates three discrete areas from which they came: the Saxons from "ea regione quae nunc Antiquorum Saxonum cognominatur" (the region which is now known as that of the Old Saxons), and the Angles from "illa patria quae Angulus dicitur ... inter provincias Iutarum et Saxonum" (that homeland which is called Angulus ... between the provinces of the Jutes and the Saxons). He also indicates who their descendants were, and, partly by implication, where they or their descendants were settled in England: the Jutes in Kent, the Isle of Wight, and a part of the mainland north of the Isle of Wight; the Saxons producing the East, South, and West Saxons, the men of Essex, Sussex, and Wessex; the Angles producing the East and Middle Angles, the Mercians, the Northumbrians (living north of the river Humber), and "other Anglian populi".

A later passage in Bede's history might suggest he knew a tradition of the participation of further nationes in the English settlement. Reviewing Ecgberht's missionary plans, he wrote:

> ... in Germania plurimas noverat esse nationes, a quibus Angli vel Saxones, qui nunc Brittaniam incolunt, genus et originem duxisse noscuntur ... Sunt autem Fresones, Rugini, Danai, Hunni, Antiqui Saxones, Boructuari.

> ... he knew there to be several nationes in Germany, from (amongst ?) whom the Angles and Saxons, who now live in Britain, are known to have derived their race and origin ... There are moreover the Frisians, the Rugians, the Danes, the Huns, the Old Saxons, and the Boruhtware.

(HE V.9)

Bede has already identified the Antiqui Saxones as a parent natio of some English settlers, but a careful reading of the text leaves it unclear whether the other groups were thought of as taking part in the settlement too. If we believe that Bede would have been careful to be consistent on this point in HE I.15 and V.9, then one would suppose not. We may therefore concentrate for now on the Angles, Saxons, and Jutes, although the other nationes Bede lists here return for consideration later in the study. One further early historical source to be considered is the 6th.-century Byzantine historian Procopius of Caesarea's muddled account of the island of Brittia, inhabited by the Angiloi, Phrissones, and Brittones, in a digression in his account of the Gothic Wars (Stenton 1943 pp.4-8). Of particular importance is the apparent report of Frisians amongst the settlers of Britain. But Procopius seems to have confused separate stories and sources. Brittia, he states, is not the same island as Brettania. Deriving the

2

Angiloi and Brettones from this island implies that
Procopius could have misrepresented a report reflecting
accurate details of Britain, but it would be equally
possible to interpret the "island" east of Brettania,
inhabited by Angiloi, and with a long wall running north-
south, as Jutland (cf. Neumann 1982), conflated in his
account with reports of Britain and Frisia, and those
areas' relationships with the Franks. Stenton's interpretation of Procopius may be true, and there may have been a
significant Frisian element amongst the settlers of
Britain. But it is Bede's account in HE I.15 that is the
more plausible primary reference point, and the vague
implications of Procopius's story can only be evaluated in
the light of and along with other evidence as potentially
modificatory of Bede's basic model.

Independent recognition of the Angles, Saxons, and
Jutes occurs in other early sources. Tacitus, writing in
his Germania towards the end of the 1st. century A.D.,
records the existence of the Anglii and Eudoses amongst a
group of nationes, a subdivision of the Suebi, who had in
common the worship of a goddess Nerthus (Germ 38-40).
These two names may confidently be identified with those of
Bede's Angli and Iutae. The credibility of Tacitus's
report is enhanced by the recording in much later Norse
literature of a fertility god Njǫrðr, a name certainly
descended from an earlier Nerthu-. The 5th.-century
historian Orosius numbers the Eduses amongst the groups
forming the army of the Germanic king Ariovistus in the
1st. century B.C. (Orosius VI.7), but this account may be
indirectly dependent on Tacitus. Orosius also tells of the
Saxones, a gens living in marshy land by the coast
(VIII.32). The terms Saxo and Saxones are recorded in a
number of Latin prose and poetic texts from the second half
of the 4th. and the 5th. centuries (cf. Lewis and Short
s.v. Saxo). The 5th-century Notitia Dignitatum lists
certain coastal military stations in Britain under the
command of a comes litoris Saxonici (Count of the Saxon
Shore), a title of uncertain age (Salway 1981 p.257).
Finally, the geographer Ptolemy, writing in the mid 2nd.
century in Greek, names three groups whose names appear to
be forms of those of the Angles, Saxons, and Jutes (Neumann
1982 pp.91-101; Stenton 1943 pp.11-13).

It can therefore be affirmed that groups of people
contemporaneously recognised as Angles, Saxons, and Jutes
did exist in 5th.-century Europe. Modern place-names
suggest approximate locations for them on the continent:
for the Saxons there is Saxony (German: -Sachsen), to the
north-east of this, across the river Elbe, is the region of
Angeln in Schleswig-Holstein, and north of Angeln is
Jutland (Danish: Jylland; German: Jütland). This agrees
perfectly with Bede's placing of Angulus between the
"provinces" of the Saxons and the Jutes. In the 2nd.
century, however, Ptolemy indicates that the Saxons were
located east of the Elbe.

3

Modern place-names, however, should be regarded only as a potentially helpful but untrustworthy guide to the possible 5th.-century locations of population groups. The most prominent place-name containing a Modern English derivative of the original form _Angli-_ is England, denoting more than the whole area said by Bede to have been settled by the Angles, Saxons, and Jutes. Modern English place-names are probably of most assistance in indicating areas once dominated by Saxons to the extent of bequeathing their name to them. The divisions of the East, South, and West Saxons have descended to us in the forms of Essex, Sussex, and Wessex, the former two surviving as county-names. The old county of Middlesex implies the location of a group of Middle Saxons between East and West Saxons, and the etymology of the place-name Surrey, south of the Thames from Middlesex, _super-ge_ (southern district), implies a connection, though not necessarily an ethnic one, of this area to Middlesex (Cameron 1961 p.54). An 11th.-century place-name supporting the location of Jutes on the mainland north of the Isle of Wight is _Ytene_ for the New Forest in Hampshire (Stenton 1943 p.23).

The extent to which Bede's ethnography of the English settlements accurately reflects the state of affairs in the 5th. century is historically doubtful. His ethnography is likely to be largely a rationalization of the information available to him in the late 7th. and 8th. centuries in the form of place-names, folk-names, and information concerning the areas of most immediate interest to kings of the various groups named Angles or Saxons in some form, and is thereby unlikely to reflect any complexities of the period of settlement. Nevertheless his presumed inference that folk-names derivative of certain group-names indicate some form of dominant presence of that group at some stage seems completely reasonable. The inference of ethnic backgrounds in this way would not, moreover, explain his statement that the Jutes became the men of Kent and the Isle of Wight ("Cantuari et Uictuarii"), which are folk-names containing surviving Roman and even pre-Roman forms, and we have Bede's own testimony on the various sources he used for early Kentish history, including "seniorum traditio ...", (the tradition of old men, HE Preface). Bede's account, then, is to be regarded as a valid basis for discussion. Besides his outline given in HE I.15 must be set the abundant historical evidence, in, for example, the remainder of HE and the _Anglo-Saxon Chronicle_, for the areas of most immediate concern to the kings of the Angles and the Saxons (cf. Chadwick 1906 pp.2-11). Perhaps the most significant point of this kind, which may be noted in the present context, is the interest of the West Saxon kings in the Thames Valley in the early period (Stenton 1943 pp.20-39), with the baptism of the West Saxon king Cynegils and the establishment of the first bishop to the West Saxons in Dorchester-on-Thames in the 630s (HE III.7).

We may claim therefore that we know that the three groups, Angles, Saxons, and Jutes, existed, and have some evidence for where they may have been located at certain periods. But one fundamental question is not directly tackled by the ancient authors who give evidence for these groups, namely, what precisely is implied by the name Angle, Saxon, or Jute. What sort of groups were they ? Were they characterized by cultural uniformity, genetic relationship, linguistic uniformity, political unity, geographical location, or by some combination of these ? Tacitus, for instance, variously indicates that a gens may have a coherent political structure below a leader (Germ 13, 25), while to some extent "individual gentes differ from one another in their institutions and practices" (Germ 27). The Chatti are distinguished both by physical attributes and distinctive customs (Germ 30-31). There also appears in Tacitus the notion, recurring in Orosius and Bede, that groups have their own particular territories (Germ 34). Tacitus's ethnography is descriptive rather than analytical, and no other ancient authority supplies this information. Our best-founded image of these groups, then, is probably one that accords with Clarke's proposition:

> Most tribes are polythetically homogeneous in race, culture and language, with the tribe within the intersect of these differently bounded sets
> (Clarke 1978 p.365)

In practical terms within the present context I take this to mean that we may look within the appropriate identified areas for, for example, a coalescence of "Saxon" culture, language, genetic relationship, and maybe political organisation too, but none of these features alone is to define or even be wholly restricted to the Saxon area, or is essential to the quality of Saxonitas.

Our knowledge of the material culture of the areas concerned far outstrips our knowledge of the genetic characteristics of the folk who lived or died there or their social organisation, and in the relevant period is considerably greater and more precise than our knowledge of the language. Modern criticism, reactions, and modifications to Bede's settlement ethnography therefore rely very heavily on the limited basis of material culture alone, and are valid only to the extent that the Angles, Saxons, and Jutes - and other groups - can be identified with particular culture groups. One could expect this to be only imperfectly the case (Clarke 1978 pp.363-408). But it makes the best and most comprehensive use of the diverse forms of evidence available to us to accept that there is likely to be a positive correlation between material culture and ethnic identity. Although the ethnographic conclusions that can be drawn from a study of material culture are restricted, it is fully justifiable to seek to improve understanding within these limits. The subject-matter of this study is therefore assessed to see how it affects the traditional picture of the settlement of England and early Anglo-Saxon England's overseas relationships.

Over a century of archaeological research in England and northern Europe has shown a fair measure of congruence between Bede's report of the settlement of England and the distribution of certain artefact-types or sub-types in England and on the continent (cf. Hills 1979 pp. 313-317). The principal features of this agreement should be familiar to all with any knowledge of Anglo-Saxon archaeology, but since the various divisions of the topic have been unevenly studied, and all continue to develop, it is appropriate to make a brief review here.

The connections between early Kent and Jutland have most recently emerged from obscurity. The evidence for these was recently summarized by S.C. Hawkes (Hawkes and Pollard 1981). Artefacts which imply some special relationship between these areas include pottery, relief, square-headed, and cruciform brooches, and bracteates. Myres described close parallels in pottery of various forms, both simple and unusual, between Kent and Jutland, and noted that similar pottery was also to be found in lesser quantities in Frisia (Myres 1969 pp.49, 95-97). The most substantial study of the connections between Kent and Jutland witnessed by the cruciform brooches is that of Hawkes (Hawkes and Pollard 1981 pp.322-324), made in the context of Reichstein's study of this brooch-type (Reichstein 1975). This is still regrettably brief. Certain points may be added to Hawkes's review. Further to the similarity she notes between the Lyminge cruciform brooch (Åberg 1926 fig.39) and a brooch from Nebstrup, Jutland, we may add that the headplate of the Lyminge brooch has a close parallel on a brooch from N.Møllegard in northern Jutland (VHM 11334*; Fig.1.1). The broad plain headplate wings of the cruciform brooches from Milton-next-Sittingbourne (Åberg 1926 figs.40-41) are highly reminiscent of those on cruciform brooches from Hjemsted, Jutland g.25 (HM 1004x195-196). The square decorative panel on the centre of the bow of one of these Milton-next-Sittingbourne brooches (op.cit. fig.41, where, unfortunately, it is very poorly illustrated) contains sunken rectilinear decoration, and may be compared to a similar feature on at least three Jutlandic brooches, two from Sejlflod, graves DY and IZ (Fig.1.2), and one from Grunderup (NMK C7431). Dubiously identified as cruciform brooches, but certain evidence of special connections between Kent and Jutland are the two brooches of Reichstein's Typ Oxbøl (Reichstein 1975 p.46). Reichstein's Typen Byrkje and Goutum would initially appear to be very closely related to the Kentish and Frisian examples of Typ Byrkje.

----

* For key to museum references see <u>Acknowledgements</u>.

6

The similar pots of Kent and Jutland are rather
vaguely dated by Myres to the 5th. century, and the mid
5th. century is the accepted starting date for the Kentish
cruciform brooches. About the same date can be assigned to
a Jutish Nydam-style relief brooch found near Canterbury,
Kt (Bakka 1958 p.9; Haseloff 1981 p.140). To the last
quarter of the 5th. century and the early 6th. can be
assigned the South Scandinavian influence that brought the
square-headed relief brooches to Kent (Bakka 1958;
Haseloff 1981 pp.18-173). To this same broad period can
be assigned the South Scandinavian influence which brought
in the gold bracteates (Hawkes and Pollard 1981; see
below, Chronological Conventions). Not every instance of
cultural influence is to be taken as direct evidence of
migration, of course, but the intimate connections between
the two areas are clear.

Kentish connections with the Isle of Wight are
archaeologically clear, although not particularly in the
form of specifically Jutish material (Arnold 1982 pp.97-
109). As yet there is only place-name and historical
evidence for the location of a related people, the
Meonware, on the mainland north of the Isle of Wight.

Excluding, for the moment, Frisia, the "Jutish"
material outside of England which comes to prominence in
comparison with finds from Kent is distributed mainly in
Jutland down to about the present Danish - West German
border (cf. Hawkes and Pollard 1981 fig.1; Myres 1969 map
7). Related examples of relief and cruciform brooches,
however, are rather more widely spread in South Scandinavia
from Jutland, eastwards over the Danish islands to southern
Sweden and the Baltic, and northwards to southern Norway.
It is, however, the southern limit of continental Jutish
culture that is of most immediate interest, and this is
considered further below.

A combination of dress-accessories and pottery-types
of apparently Saxon character can also be used to associate
areas of England with a particular area on the continent,
although in this case the resultant picture is only
partially in agreement with Bede. The north-eastern border
of the German land of Niedersachsen, along the river Elbe,
marks the clear border of a culture-province of the 4th.
and 5th. centuries which one may call Saxon. It is
distinguished, inter alia, by the occurrence of certain
supporting-arm brooches, relief decorated equal-armed
brooches, saucer brooches, and pottery with particular
forms of decoration. Comprehensive distribution maps of
saucer brooches (Böhme 1974 Karten 7-8) show these to
associate the area south and west of the Elbe with England,
as well as occurring farther west in the Low Countries.
This brooch-type is particularly predominant in England
south of the Thames (other than "Jutish" East Kent) and in
the Thames Valley (Welch 1983 pp 163-170), but, as Böhme's
maps show, also occurs to the north of this in Norfolk,

Cambridgeshire, Bedfordshire, and Northamptonshire. With
the exception of an example from Collingbourne, Wilts,
relief decorated equal-armed brooches have been found in
England only along the Thames Valley and in Cambridgeshire
and Bedfordshire (Böhme 1974 Karte 5), and the supporting-
arm brooches are found in much the same area (Evison 1977).
Features characteristic of the pottery south and west of
the Elbe in contrast to the areas on the other side of the
river include "standing arch" (stehende Bogen) decoration
and the related Buckelurnen (Myres 1969 pp.41-47). But,
like the "Saxon" brooches, such elements are found well to
the north of what we might expect to be the northern Saxon
border of Essex, Middlesex, and Wessex in England. Early
forms of the standing arch decoration occur in an area from
the Thames Valley to Humberside (Myres 1969 map 3; 1977
pp.28-31), while the Buckelurnen of the latter half of the
5th. century onwards occur in the same area, and in Sussex
and Surrey (Myres 1969 map 4a; 1977 pp.31-34). A further
largely Saxon-looking decorative motif, chevron-and-dot
decoration, also occurs predominantly in this area north of
the Thames (Myres 1977 pp.48-51).

To a limited extent this "Saxon" cultural presence in
England north of the Thames Valley and Essex may be the
result of initial Saxon influence on the southern areas
subsequently spreading northwards. A large proportion of
the saucer brooches, both cast and applied, from the
northerly area, are datable to the 6th. century. The great
disproportion in the volume of Saxon-type pottery in the
northerly area compared with that to the south is of
limited significance because the burial rite in the latter
area seems to have changed rapidly from cremation to
inhumation while cremation remained common in the north
(Leeds 1913 pp.57-58; Hills 1979 pp.316-317). But it is
not probable that this northerly extension of the Saxon
culture-province is entirely secondary in England. The
detailed evidence of the dates, internal development, and
distribution of the equal-armed and supporting-arm brooches
implies the opposite (Evison 1977). Areas reached by the
expanding Saxon culture-province in the 5th. century in
particular are likely to have seen the presence of persons
ethnically identifiable as Saxon, and Saxon settlement may
therefore be postulated well to the north of the later
borders of the West and East Saxon kingdoms in eastern
England, as well as in southern England as far east as the
Medway in Kent. Leeds indeed suggested that East Anglia
was a corridor for Saxon settlement of the Thames Valley
(Leeds 1933), but a more sophisticated hypothesis of the
relationship between these areas has recently been proposed
by S.C. Hawkes (Hawkes 1978).

Areas in England we would expect from Bede's account
to have been settled by Angles - East and Middle Anglia,
Lindsey, and even Northumbria - were thus subject to a
detectable Saxon cultural influence which may well be
evidence of a Saxon ethnic presence there. The

identification of the part which Bede's Angles played in
the settlement is perhaps the most problematic aspect of
ethnographic early Anglo-Saxon archaeology. On the
continent we may look for the Angles "inter provincias
Iutarum et Saxonum", that is, on the basis of the evidence
just reviewed, first and foremost in Schleswig-Holstein,
between the Elbe and the area of the present Danish-West
German border. A summary review of the archaeology of this
area in the relevant periods, and the problem of the
Angles, was produced some 30 years ago by Genrich (Genrich
1954) and the same issues have most recently been
considered by Neumann (Neumann 1982). Neumann argues in
detail that markedly differential archaeological remains of
the 3rd. to 5th. centuries fall north and south of a
political border of the same period marked by the ditch
Olgerdiget, fractionally to the north of the present
international border, and that this marks the border
between the Angles and the Jutes (cf. Neumann 1982
fig.36b). The burial rite south of the approximate line
between the putative Jutes and Angles is predominantly
cremation, while north of this line there is an abrupt
change to inhumation (Neumann 1982 pp.86-89). It is an
obvious consequence that cinerary urns should be of
particular importance in the search for "Anglian
characteristics" of this period.

Genrich in fact divided Schleswig-Holstein into three
ceramic Formenkreise, one "Östholsteinisch", one "Anglian",
and a "North Sea coast group". The archaeological basis
for this is unchallenged (Jankuhn 1979 pp.279-284).
Geographically the dividing line between the East Holstein
and Anglian groups appears to coincide with the river
Eider, while the North Sea coast group is, as the name
suggests, distributed down the western coast of Schleswig-
Holstein, an area largely separated from Angeln and East
Holstein by marsh-land. To the north, the Anglian ceramic
Formenkreis is concentrated in an area up to about the line
of the present international border, but is also well
represented in the southern, western, and central areas of
the island of Fyn (Genrich 1954 Karten 6-8). This especial
cultural association of Angeln with Fyn in these periods is
also attested by Mackeprang (Mackeprang 1943 pp.52-57, 83)
and Neumann (Neumann 1982 pp.88-90). It would, however, be
a mistake to believe that the pottery of the three
subdivisions in Schleswig-Holstein was particularly
distinctive, isolated, and unique. The North Sea coast
group in particular consists of forms with close parallels
to the north in Scandinavia and to the south-west in Saxony
(Genrich 1954 pp.30-31). In the Migration Period, pottery
of the Anglian group shows, according to Genrich, signs of
"ever stronger influence from Holstein", and pottery of
closely related forms is found as far north as Norway,
although not in large quantities relative either to the
volume from Schleswig-Holstein, or to the whole corpus of
Norwegian Migration Period pottery (Genrich 1954 p.30; cf.
Bøe 1931, esp. pp.141-151, 226-227; Slomann 1961).

Nevertheless, Myres has succeeded in identifying
certain features of early Anglo-Saxon pottery which would
appear to associate certain areas of England with the area
between the Elbe and the Danish border, and with the
Anglian _Formenkreis_ in particular. Especially
characteristic of continental Anglian pottery are urns with
relatively tall, steep, decorated necks, and decoration
very commonly taking the form of horizontal corrugation
(Genrich 1954 pp. 27ff.). Myres's corpus of English
pottery shows that very similar examples are concentrated
in Norfolk, and also distributed in Bedfordshire,
Lincolnshire, the Trent Valley,and Humberside (Myres 1977
pp.38-41). Amongst plain urns, the "larger high-
shouldered" type appears to associate the same areas of
England and the continent, although Myres also illustrates
an example from Mucking in Essex, on the Thames estuary
(Myres 1977 p.4, fig.14). Thus there are parallels between
the area of midland, eastern, and northern England and the
area of Schleswig-Holstein of the type that we would expect
from the ethnographic historical and archaeological
evidence already reviewed. It is possible that the Anglian
homeland so identified extends to include part of the
island of Fyn, while the inclusion of the easterly parts of
Holstein in it is doubtful. The presence of the North Sea
coast group in western Schleswig-Holstein should not be
allowed to confuse the issue. The finds constituting this
group are few (Genrich 1954 p.31). The scattered
connections they show to the north and south-west are
rather to be expected of a relatively marginal area of
settlement, and they certainly do not render the pottery of
this area "inter provincias Iutarum et Saxonum" hopelessly
mixed and impossible to characterize.

Partly as a result of the predominance of the
cremation rite, it is not very easy to identify regional
pecularities in the metalwork of the Anglian area,
particularly in the later 4th. and 5th. centuries. The
usual brooches in use there in this later period are
cruciform and small-long brooches (Genrich: _Fibeln mit
dreiläppige Kopfplatte_; cf. Genrich 1954 Taff.28-33).
The earlier cruciform brooches found in this area are
identified by Reichstein as belonging to types that are
generally widely distributed in northern Germany, in
Schleswig-Holstein, Niedersachsen, and Mecklenburg
(Reichstein 1975 pp.41-42, Karten 2-3), besides occasional
occurrences further west, and to the north in Scandinavia,
mostly in Denmark. It is clear that the earliest cruciform
brooches in England outside of Kent are to be associated
with these North German brooches rather than the early
Norwegian ones. Of Reichstein's "ältere" brooches, Typen
Dorchester and Pritzier include examples from Mildenhall,
Sfk, Dorchester, Oxon, and Nassington, N'hants. Typ Gross
Siemss, a "jüngere" type, includes a brooch from Glaston,
Leics, and two further English finds seem to belong to this
type rather than any other, from Colchester, Ex (Crummy et
al. 1981 pp.10-11), and Hockwold-cum-Wilton, Nfk (Fig.1.3).

A "späte" type distributed in the same wide area is Typ Krefeld-Gellep. Reichstein, however, gives too little evidence to positively associate two North German finds with the many English brooches of his "späte" Typ Stratford. There are two types described by Reichstein as "not reliably datable" which show a similar distribution, Typen St. John's College and Hjelmhede (Reichstein 1975 p.45, Taf.115). On traditional typological grounds (see below, Chronological Conventions) one would be inclined to align these with "jüngere" types such as Gross Siemss rather than date them later. Very similar to the examples of Typ Hjelmhede is a cruciform brooch not mentioned by Reichstein from Glentham, Lincs (Fig.1.4). Very similar again to this however is a brooch not from northern Germany but from Mejlby in northern Jutland (Fig.1.5), which was unclassified by Reichstein (Reichstein 1975 no.505). The Mejlby brooch is dated early in the 5th. century by association with a silver-sheet brooch. We may finally note the similarity in all details other than the headplate knobs between a brooch from Empingham I, Leics g.3 (Fig.1.6) and two brooches of the "jüngere" Typ Perdöhl from Mecklenburg and Niedersachsen (Reichstein 1975 Taf.73.1 & 3). The distribution of the five types placed in Reichstein's "ältere" and "jüngere" phases (early and middle 5th. century) is shown on Map 1.1. This demonstrates the association of a broad area north of the Thames with northern Germany in this period. It may not conclusively demonstrate a connection between Anglian England and Schleswig-Holstein, but that is the area of northern Germany where these brooches are most numerous, and the one area of northern Germany where all five types occur as in England.

Brooches classifiable in English terms as "small-long" remain as Leeds described them in the only substantial study made of this brooch type: "quite scarce" in continental Europe (Leeds 1945 p.5). Leeds divided the English small-long brooches into 5 main classes, 4 characterized by forms of the headplate, and the fifth by the "lozenge-shaped foot". Of these five main classes, those distinguished by Cross Potent and Cross Pattee headplates can be difficult to distinguish from one another in what Leeds regarded as their later forms (cf. Leeds 1945 figs.10-11, 14-16), and for further reasons which appear below may be best considered in tandem. A list of brooches recorded from outside England with features closely similar to those which define the major types of English small-long brooch is given in List 1.1. This list includes 13 brooches from Schleswig-Holstein and 6 from Niedersachsen and Nordrhein-Westfalen, 4 each from Jutland and southern Norway, and 1 each from Frisia and southern Sweden (Map 1.2). Of the Schleswig-Holstein examples, 6 have a Cross Potent headplate and 3 a Cross Pattee headplate, all from the Borgstedt cemetery. There is a good case for regarding Schleswig-Holstein as the area of origin of these forms. 4 of the brooches found in Niedersachsen, and 3 of the

Norwegian brooches, also show such forms, but in these areas, unlike in Schleswig-Holstein, such small-long brooches are a minority and unusual type (cf. Böhme 1974; Shetelig 1910), and to be regarded as intrusive. There is one example of this form from northern Jutland, a pair of brooches from Sejlflod g.Tr (ÅHM 669/1457-1458), and the brooch from Almenum, Frisia, shows a derivative example of this form (Boeles 1951 pl.XXV.6). In England the distribution of such forms is clearly concentrated in the eastern, midland, and northern areas north of the Thames Valley (Leeds 1945 figs.9, 12, 17), although a considerable number occur along the Thames Valley itself.

To the trefoil-headed small-long brooches of England, with an even more predominantly northern distribution than the Cross Pattee types (Leeds 1945 figs.6-7), Leeds could cite "nothing comparable" from overseas. However two brooches from Jutland (Figs.1.7-8) and one brooch from South-East Norway (Reichstein 1975 Taf.24.2) now seem to fill this gap. Two of these are classified by Reichstein as cruciform brooches (Reichstein 1975 nos.28 and 495) but their flat headplate knobs cast in one piece with the headplate, and spatulate feet are essentially indistinguishable from the features of trefoil-headed small-long brooches (cf. Leeds 1945 figs.4-5). The trefoil-headed small-long brooch is probably a late development from the cruciform brooch series, and may be partially independent of the _Fibeln mit dreiläppige Kopfplatte_, the Cross Potent and Pattee small-long brooches, whose earliest dates and origins are quite obscure. If this is so, the earliest stages of this form appear to be evidenced in southern Scandinavia.

The lozenge-foot occurs with headplate forms also found in England on three recorded examples from Schleswig-Holstein (e.g. Genrich 1954 Taff.33.2 & 7) and three from Saxony (e.g. Cosack 1982 Taff.31, 48). It would thus be difficult to claim that it was particularly characteristic of one region rather than the other, even though the small-long brooch _per se_ is more typical of the Angles than the Saxons (see above). Correspondingly, this element in England seems particularly well represented in the Thames Valley and southern England relative to the areas to the north (Leeds 1945 fig.24).

In fine, Schleswig-Holstein looks the most probable source of the small-long brooch with Cross Potent or Cross Pattee headplate, and such brooches in England are concentrated in an area north of and including the counties of Suffolk, Cambridgeshire, Bedfordshire, Northamptonshire, and Warwickshire (Leeds 1945 pp.88-96). Examples from this area out-number those from the Thames Valley and further south by about 11:1. This therefore has all the appearance of an example of Anglian cultural influence congruent with the settlement of Angles from Schleswig-Holstein in this more northerly part of England. The date of the earliest of these forms is obscure, but it would normally be placed later rather than earlier in the 5th. century (cf. Leeds 1945 pp.104-105, and below, Chronological Conventions). The trefoil-headed small-long brooches may either be a parallel development from the cruciform brooches in southern Scandinavia and England, or appear in England as a result of South Scandinavian influence. This issue is considered further in Chapter 5 of this study. These can be dated, at the earliest, to the last quarter of the 5th. century (see Chronological Conventions, below). The lozenge-foot provides evidence for no more than a general relationship of Anglo-Saxon England to Anglian and Saxon areas on the continent. The only other form of footplate on small-long brooches recorded outside of England is the spatulate form (as on Figs.1.7-8), also common in England.

One further, minor, dress-accessory may be mentioned here as seemingly illustrative of a particular relationship between Anglian England and the region between the provinces of the Jutes and the Saxons. These are model bucket pendants, of which I have recorded 13 English finds (List 1.2; Map 1.3; cf. Meaney 1981 pp. 166-168). Such pendants also occur in no less than 15 graves from the 4th.-century cemetery at Preetz, Kr. Plön, Schleswig-Holstein (Brandt 1960 p.31), apparently the only site where they occur as a typical and common item of female costume, although further isolated examples are known from Sörup and Thorsberger Moor in Schleswig-Holstein (Raddatz 1981 p.46), and Wehden in Niedersachsen (Meaney 1981 p.168). These too are dated to the 4th. century. There are also 3 examples from the Danish islands of Fyn and Sjælland (List 1.2), one of which, from Skyttemarksvej, Præstø, is again dated to the 4th. century by association with a swastika brooch. None of the English examples is positively dated early in the 5th. century, and some are to be dated to the 6th. Yet it seems inconceivable that so peculiar a form could have appeared in England other than as a result of direct influence from the Schleswig-Holstein/southern Denmark area some time between the late 4th. and the early 6th centuries.

A combination and concentration of Anglian pottery forms, cruciform brooches, certain small-long brooches, and pendants, help to distinguish the material culture of an area to the north of an approximate line from the mouth of the Stour on the east coast of England running almost due west to the valley of the Avon from the Jutishness of Kent, and the predominant Saxonness of the Thames Valley and the remainder of southern England. This may be attributed to a settlement of Angles such as history describes, and the earliest objects concerned here date from very early in the 5th century at least. The identification of this area as an "Anglian province of culture" is well established in archaeological literature (Leeds 1945; Vierck 1966). This area is positively marked by the presence or concentration of certain artefact-types: e.g. cruciform brooches (Leeds

1945 pp.69-73);   small-long brooches (Leeds 1945 pp.4-44);
annular brooches (Leeds 1945 pp.46-49), swastika brooches
(Leeds 1945 pp.51-53);   wrist-clasps (Brown III pp.362-364;
Leeds 1945 pp.53-61; Vierck 1966 pp.62-106); and scutiform
pendants and silver bracteates (Vierck 1966 pp.40-61).   Of
these, it is suggested that the concentration of cruciform
and small-long brooches is to some extent due to influence
from the continental Anglian homelands.

    However a distinctly "Sandinavian character" has been
noted in some of the other artefact-types listed above,
most clearly demonstrated so far in Vierck's work on the
wrist-clasps, scutiform pendants, and silver bracteates
(Vierck 1966*).   "Scandinavia" may be simply defined here
as the area to the north and north-east of what appears to
have been the Anglian homeland in Schleswig-Holstein and
south-eastern Fyn, and may virtually be identified with the
modern kingdoms of Denmark, Norway, and Sweden, and also
Finland.   Sources and parallels to these objects in England
seem best to be sought in Scandinavia, not in areas further
south.   Besides Vierck's thesis should be considered a
number of other archaeological studies which appear, or
claim, to uncover special parallels between Scandinavia and
England, particularly to material characteristic of this
"Anglian province of culture", notably Shetelig and Åberg
on cruciform brooches (Shetelig 1906;   Åberg 1953 p.30),
Leeds on square-headed brooches (Leeds 1949 pp.111-115),
and further work by Vierck on burial forms (Vierck 1973).

    It is such material that this study seeks to advance
the knowledge and understanding of: a range of artefact-
types or sub-types apparently distributed exclusively in
the "Anglian province of culture", which may be called
"Anglian England", and Scandinavia. From the state of the
subject which this study has as its starting-point, these
parallels seem to create a "Scandinavian character of
Anglian England" from the 5th. century onwards.   The
research work which follows in this study supplies much-
needed confirmation that this apparent Scandinavian
character of Anglian England is to a significant extent
real and not illusory, and shows that it would appear to be
the product of a complex web of relationships and contacts
associating these areas, and other areas of England and
northern Europe.

    Practical considerations compel one to select and
limit the material considered for a representation of this
topic. A priority is to study the relevant material in the
greatest useful detail, rather than to provide a survey
that is wide-ranging, but too shallow for persuasive
conclusions to be drawn.   Building on the foundations laid
----
* Regrettably, access to this study was restricted until
   late 1980.   The available copy in the Bodleian Library
   lacks figures, plates, and maps, and is marred by
   frequent inaccuracies in bibliographical references.

14

by Shetelig, Leeds, Åberg, and Vierck, and in accordance with one of the predominant themes of English Anglo-Saxon and continental Migration Period archaeology of the present century, this work concentrates on a range of dress-accessories - that is, fasteners and ornaments worn about the costume - which appear to have been worn mostly by women. The study of all the artefact-types selected proceeds with topics which have already been introduced to some extent in the literature of the subject that is available, or soon to be available. The particular contribution of this study is the more extensive evidence considered, and the new conclusions drawn or hypotheses formed about the history and developing distribution of these artefact-types, not the annexation of whole new fields of study to the central theme.

The main body of this study involves the detailed study of the following artefact-types:

Clasps
Square-headed brooches
Bracteates
Scutiform pendants
Cruciform brooches
Anglian equal-armed brooches
Annular brooches

Initially, the types are examined in turn. Firstly they are considered as types in isolation, in an attempt to identify the course of development of their forms, their chronology, their developing geographical distribution, and, if necessary, their developing functions. In certain cases this involves a considerable volume of preliminary study of the artefacts of the traditional classificational kind, in order to clarify our view of previously inadequately published material. Then each artefact-type is assessed to see what evidence (if any) it provides of Anglo-Scandinavian contacts or an Anglo-Scandinavian relationship falling within the limits of this study.

As will be seen, no single, simple answer to the question of what explains the Scandinavian character of Anglian England in this period is obtained, nor should one necessarily have been expected. The evidence accumulates to give a complex and variegated picture of cultural diffusion, represented by artefacts of this character, around the North Sea in the 5th and 6th centuries. The order in which the artefact-types are considered is not random. An attempt has been made to arrange them so that the evidence of those met earlier in the study supports or clarifies the evidence of those following after.

This close analysis of the material occupies Chapters 2 to 5. A full summary of the evidence of these predominantly Migration Period artefact-types is made in

Chapter 6, together with a discussion of the provisional conclusions drawn in the earlier chapters as to their modes of diffusion in the Anglian-Scandinavian area, assessed in the broader archaeological and historical context. Finally Chapter 7 extends consideration of the topic from the Migration Period, upon which Chapters 2 to 6 are principally focussed, to the lower chronological limit of this study, the inception of the Viking Period.

CHRONOLOGICAL CONVENTIONS

Chronology, the methods of dating the making, period of use, and deposit or loss of the objects of archaeological study, and the form in which those dates are expressed, can be a fraught and frustrating issue in the periods with which this thesis is concerned. Ambivalently, the rather broad range of the present work compounds the chronological problems in some respects and reduces them in others. A preliminary review of the state of chronological studies, and a statement of the chronological conventions to be used in the course of this work, will be made here. An attempt to build the work on as clear and explicit a basis as possible is self-justifying. It is hoped that a single introductory statement will minimise ad hoc chronological digressions in the discussion of particular finds in the course of the work and possible inconsistencies which could otherwise arise.

The "pre-Viking Period" of the title of this thesis is the period before the two historically recorded Scandinavian attacks on the English coast at the end of the 8th. century which signalled a dramatic change in the relationship of England and Scandinavia. These were in Dorset in ca.787 (ASC MS E s.a.787), and more famously on Lindisfarne in 793. Historical descriptions or studies of "Viking Age England" regularly start from these points (e.g. Stenton 1943 p.237; Wilson 1976 p.393; Loyn 1977 p.55). Such studies may recognize the existence of Anglo-Scandinavian contact previous to these events (e.g. Wilson op.cit.), or tread carefully in emphasizing that it was the attacks that were so startling to contemporary Englishmen, not necessarily merely the arrival of Scandinavians in itself (e.g. Loyn op.cit.). But the earlier Anglo-Scandinavian relationship remains unillustrated, and without better information one would often infer it to have been insignificant, if existent at all (cf. Loyn 1977 p.21ff.). To begin to illuminate the range and nature of this relationhip before this point is the goal of this thesis.

The lower chronological limit of this thesis is therefore defined by a historical period. The material upon which the thesis is based, however, is almost exclusively archaeological, and recognized archaeological and historical periods are not always the same. A review of the conventional terminology and definitions of archaeological periods in the centuries and areas with which this work is most concerned reveals a complex and not entirely satisfactory picture. The established sequences of periods, such as they are, for England (which is difficult to treat as a unit in the Anglo-Saxon period), Scandinavia, and western continental Europe, differ markedly.

In a number of respects the chronological situation is happiest and clearest in Scandinavia. The bulk of the following work concerns one established Scandinavian period, the Migration Period, which has recently been effectively defined by Bakka in an article whose main purpose was to examine the internal chronology of this period (Bakka 1973). The whole collection of artefact-types and art styles Bakka uses to distinguish phases within the Migration Period serve to characterize the period in general: bracteates of Types A-D; silver-sheet, relief, and cruciform brooches; the Sösdala and Nydam Styles, and Style I. The period is recognized under this name in Norway and Sweden (Norwegian: folkevandringstid), although in Denmark it usually goes under the name of the Early Germanic Iron Age (ældre germanske jernalderen).

The Scandinavian Migration Period is preceded by a period in which the culture of Scandinavia, as much of the rest of free Germany, was subject to Imperial Roman influence, even though these areas lay outside the Roman Empire. This period is known as the Roman Period (Swedish: romertid) or Roman Iron Age (Norwegian: romerske jernalderen. The archaeological definition of the boundary between the Roman Iron Age and the Migration Period has produced much fine and involved argumentation concerning the identification and definition of determinative artefact-types, and the relationship of archaeology and historical events (see, for example, Reichstein, Bakka, Slomann, and Stjernquist in Kossack and Reichstein 1977). The field of dispute, however, is relatively small, and in the present context the fine points of difference concerned are of no practical significance. It is therefore permissible to cut the Gordian knot by accepting Bakka's definition of the beginning of the Migration Period as the appearance of cruciform brooches of the Dorchester Type, as Bakka's definition of the leading characteristics of the period has been accepted, and his study is also accepted as the basis for closer dating within this period in Scandinavia. The transition from the Roman Iron Age to the Migration Period may be dated sometime within the last quarter of the 4th. century.

The archaeological period which succeeds the Migration Period in Scandinavia is rather diverse in character and name in different regions. The most significant common feature is the fact of a deep cultural change marking the end of the Migration Period right across Scandinavia. In Norway this later period is known as the Merovingian Period, in Sweden the Vendel Period, and in Denmark the Later Germanic Iron Age. The key developments marking the end of the Migration Period and the inception of its successor must of course be in those elements which are used to define the Migration Period. Bracteates of Types A-D cease, and bracteates themselves (of Type E) continue only on the island of Gotland. At this transitional point relief brooches are replaced by Scandinavian disc-on-bow brooches (Åberg 1924 pp.43-44), and Salin's Style I is supplanted by Salin's Style II. There are also further apparently contemporary critical changes in pottery, burial practices, and settlement sites, implying how deep and comprehensive a cultural change was involved. A date around the 560s is suggested for this transitional point, and is supported in detail below.

To standardize the terminology used in referring to Scandinavia, I propose to use the terms Roman Iron Age and Migration Period for the earliest two periods described above. References to the Roman Iron Age will mostly be to its "later" phase, that is broadly the 3rd. and 4th. centuries A.D. It is appropriate, however, to maintain the long-established distinctions between the Merovingian and Vendel Periods and Later Germanic Iron Age in Norway, Sweden, and Denmark respectively, and therefore each of these terms may be met with reference to the relevant material. A recognized archaeological Viking Period succeeds these periods across this whole area towards the end of the 8th. century - about the same time as the raids on England noted above - which again may be adequately defined by dress-accessories and art styles (cf. Petersen 1928; Wilson and Klindt-Jensen 1966). The culture of this period, however, lies largely outside the concerns of this thesis.

Continental Germanic finds, mostly from northern Germany and the Frankish Rhineland and Gaul also figure significantly in this thesis. The term "Migration Period" is a familiar one in German (Völkerwanderungszeit) and this, together with Roman Iron Age, may be used of northern Germany - principally of Saxony and Schleswig-Holstein - as corresponding to the same terms in Scandinavia. There are, of course, differences in the material characteristic of the Migration Periods in these two areas: silver-sheet brooches do not occur outside Scandinavia, and in northern Gemany some small-long, equal-armed, and saucer brooches may be added to the leading artefact-types (cf. Roeder 1930). Otherwise cruciform and square-headed (=relief) brooches, and Style I, are common to both areas.

A modern chronological scheme for Frankish finds has recently been outlined by Ament (Ament 1976; 1977). He does not use the term Migration Period, but instead defines a Merowingerzeit running from ca.450-720, divided into an "ältere" and a "jüngere" Merowingerzeit (AM and JM respectively), and subsequently into 6 phases. Although Ament's chronological scheme has not yet been fully published in all necessary detail, it supersedes the older chronological scheme of Böhner (Böhner 1958), and synthesizes independent studies of chronological sequences within limited find-contexts (v. Ament 1977 p.138 fn.13). Historically and archaeologically, Ament is able to begin his Merowingerzeit with the reign of Childeric (d.482), whose grave was discovered in the 17th. century in Tournai. The end of the Merowingerzeit he defines, with reservations, by the end of the Reihengräbersitte. Ament's Merowingerzeit is very different from the Norwegian Merovingian Period, and care should be taken not to confuse the two by observing the context in which the terms are used. Nevertheless Ament's terminology for the ältere and jüngere Merowingerzeit is used here where possible for Frankish finds.

The situation in England, however, is very unclear. No thorough and systematic periodizing of Anglo-Saxon archaeology seems ever to have been attempted, and a range of terms are in circulation - e.g. the "Early", "Pagan", "Middle", and "Late" Anglo-Saxon Periods - frequently meaning different things to different people and in different contexts. A historical Roman Period in Britain can be neatly terminated de facto with the removal of the legions by Constantine III in 407, and formally with the Rescript of Honorius in 410. Whether this historical period overlaps with the first archaeological Anglo-Saxon period is a matter of much discussion (cf. Hills 1979) but not of immediate concern here. The first Anglo-Saxon period is most commonly known as the Early or Pagan Anglo-Saxon Period, but it does not yet have defined and established archaeological characteristics and therefore there can be no clear line between this and a succeeding Middle or Late Anglo-Saxon Period.

It would be too ambitious to propose a comprehensive system of period division for Anglo-Saxon archaeology here. Indeed a complete system of this kind would not necessarily be helpful or appropriate: there is significant diversity between different regions in England, and archaeological material does not always fall nicely into periods. However there is one term I wish to establish provisionally for reference to Anglian England within the scope of this thesis - that is the Anglian English Migration Period. The term is justified by the correspondence between a definite Anglian English cultural period and both the Migration Period of Scandinavia and the northern German Völkerwanderungszeit referred to above. The period is characterized by the same dress-accessories, Type A-D bracteates, square-headed, cruciform, small-long, and saucer brooches, and by the later of Bakka's characteristic Migration Period art styles, Style I. In the course of this work it will appear that other artefact-types and art styles can be added to this list. Logically, as in Scandinavia, the end of this period is marked by radical changes in such artefact-types and art styles. Salin's Style II supplanted Style I, and the series of square-headed, cruciform, and small-long brooches came to an abrupt end.

For the present work, it is within the Migration Period that a regular system of conventions for the finer dating of finds and objects is required. For the most part, of course, it is Anglian English and Scandinavian finds that are concerned, but the occasional occurrence of imported continental material amongst these finds provides valuable opportunities to tie the Scandinavian and Anglian English chronologies in with external ones. The internal chronology of the Migration Period in Scandinavia is very much clearer than that in England. Norway in particular has produced an especially rich find material with a valuable number of find-associations preserved or recorded, and this was the basis of Bakka's study of Scandinavian chronology in the Migration Period referred to above. In the course of this study, Bakka (writing in Geman) divided the Scandinavian grave-finds into four consecutive <u>Stufen</u> (phases), <u>Völkerwanderungszeit Stufen I-IV</u> respectively. Assignment of a grave-find to a particular <u>Stufe</u> depends essentially on the presence in that find of particular forms of the artefact-types or art styles which were listed above to characterize the period as a whole. The system therefore concerns itself first and foremost with dress-accessories recovered from female graves. It is based upon the defensible assumption that these objects will usually have much the same age, having been in contemporary use on a single costume. Anomalies are liable to occur, but should not, in a rich find-material, distort the perception of a genuine sequence. Accordingly, objects associated in graves with the key types of Bakka's phases may, with due caution, be relatively dated within these <u>Stufen</u>.

The aspect of Bakka's system which is the most open to criticism in the light of more recently published research is the beginning of his final phase, <u>VWZ Stufe</u> IV. This begins with the appearance of Type D bracteates, for which Bakka suggested an absolute chronological date of ca.525. But articles by Malmer (in Kossack and Reichstein 1977) and S.C. Hawkes (Hawkes and Pollard 1981) have argued for a considerably earlier date for the first appearance of the D-bracteates. Malmer examined statistically the proportion of D-bracteates in hoards containing both bracteates and gold <u>solidi</u>, none of which contains coins dated later than 476, and argued that the substantial number of D-bracteates in these, and their absence in hoards containing later coins, supported the view that D-bracteates were already in production by ca.475. His study showed this earlier date to be possible, but not proven. Hawkes based her arguments on the newly-appreciated high degree of wear on the D-bracteates in the much-discussed grave D3 from Finglesham, Kt, for which burial a date of around 525-530 is accepted. Since these bracteates are so worn down they must have been made a good time before ca.525-530, and it was suggested that they could be as old as the square-headed brooch in the grave, which displays an early essay in Style I, and has an agreed date of ca.480. But to date the earliest D-bracteates contemporary with Finglesham D3 square-headed brooch would mean that Bakka's VWZ Stufe IV begins at exactly the same time as VWZ Stufe III, which he began with the first relief brooches with a plane/undivided foot, and the beginning of Style I. So early a date is contradicted by the associations of D-bracteates in Norwegian grave finds, albeit there are only two, and simultaneously by the existence of a clear and distinct Norwegian VWZ Stufe III with relatively plenteous finds of C-bracteates. This cannot properly be explained by a relatively late adoption of D-bracteates in Norway compared to Jutland and South Sweden, since one of the Norwegian grave finds (Rivjaland, Årdal, Rogaland; Bakka 1973 Taf.XVII) has an example, by no means an obviously late one, of Mackeprang's North-Jutish/West-Swedish group (Mackeprang 1952 pp.58-59), a group with much in common with the Jutish group of which the Finglesham D3 bracteates in question are members. Bakka's absolute date for the inception of VWZ Stufe IV appears untenable, and indeed he accepts an earlier date for some D-bracteates in a recent article in Myres's Festschrift (Myres fs. 1981). A greater period of overlap between the later Type C- and Type D-bracteates than Bakka originally allowed also seems probable. A date for the inception of the D-bracteates much closer to 500 than to 525 may be suggested. 475, however, seems too early. Although Haseloff is most cautious about attaching relative chronological significance to any of Style I's Stilphasen (Haseloff 1981 pp.174ff.) the style of the early D-bracteates, Haseloff's Style Phase D, requires some time to develop from the original Style I ornament of Style Phase A, found on certain Scandinavian relief brooches, e.g. from Tveitane, Brunlanes, Vestfold, Norway or the Danish Gummersmark brooch (Haseloff 1981 Taff. 14.1, and 23). Time alone is not the only factor which produces wear on objects as on the Finglesham D3 bracteates. What could be the effect on these pendants of incessant fingering by a particularly nervous, or even religious, owner ?

An earlier dating of the inception of the D-bracteates leads directly to a second problematic characteristic of Bakka's Stufe IV, the appearance of "late developments of Style I". This is not closely defined, and Haseloff's substantial work on Style I gives no obvious clue as to what this might mean. Since the D-bracteates are decorated in Style I of Haseloff's Style Phase D it seems likely that this is what Bakka had in mind, but Haseloff shows all Style Phases, other than the first examples of Style Phase A, to be to some extent in simultaneous use, and ornament of Style Phase D occurs on relief brooches belonging to

Nissen Meyer's Stadium 5, and _ipso facto_ to Bakka's VWZ
Stufe III.   Another form of animal ornament with a
groundwork of symmetry and interlace, regarded by Salin as
Style I, but newly redesignated by Haseloff as Style II
(Haseloff 1981 pp.222-230), is certainly a later
development, and may readily be accepted as a leading
characteristic of Stufe IV, although it is not clear that
this alone is what Bakka had in mind.

     The surest basis for assigning grave-groups to Stufe
IV is the presence of the late forms of relief brooches,
placed by Nissen Meyer in "Stadium 6".   D-bracteates may
also be used, although the consequences of their re-dating
in absolute terms for the relative-chronological sequence
is to imply a degree of overlap between VWZ Stufen III and
IV not originally countenanced by Bakka.   It is most
practical simply to accept this situation, which leaves the
system perfectly workable.   It is certainly preferable to
trying to compress VWZ Stufe III to the period ca.475-500
and postulating an abrupt transition from Type C to Type D
bracteates about the beginning of the 6th. century.   It is
also much simpler than attempting to remove the earlier D-
bracteates to leave a Stufe IV defined by later
developments of Style I (whatever those are), certain
relief brooches, later D-bracteates, and the absence of
cruciform brooches, thus commencing closer to Bakka's first
suggested date.

     Cruciform brooches play a key part in Bakka's system,
the appearance of particular forms marking the beginnings
of VWZ Stufen I and II respectively, and their total demise
marking the end of Stufe III. Bakka was writing before the
publication of Reichstein's extensive survey of cruciform
brooches (Reichstein 1975), but he knew Reichstein's work
and refers to it. Reichstein, however, does not explicitly
align his chronology of the Norwegian cruciform brooches
with Bakka's system, and a comparison must be made here.
On the basis of 81 closed grave-groups, Reichstein was able
to construct a sequence of cruciform brooches and their
associated finds, which could be divided into 8
"combination-groups", which could further be divided into 3
relative phases, "ältere", "jüngere", and "späte". Both
"Leitformen" (Types) and "Einzelformen" (unique forms) are
dated within this scheme.   Reichstein was further able to
observe certain typological trends in the development of
Norwegian cruciform brooches from the sequence (op.cit.
pp.66-72).   Cruciform brooches were divided by Bakka into
the "früheste", the "jüngere", and the "jüngste" forms. It
must be assumed that he intended these to correspond to
Reichstein's "ältere", "jüngere", and "späte" groups. But
there are discrepancies.   If we look at the objects
associated with Reichstein's "späte" types, we find that
these include a brooch from Lunde, Lista, Vest-Agder, that
is a classic example of the Nydam Style (Haseloff 1981
pp.12-16) and therefore belongs to Bakka's Stufe II.
Associated with a member of the somewhat diverse Typ

Tveitane-Hunn, which figures in both Reichstein's "ältere" and "jüngere" phases, is a bronze brooch with a rectangular headplate and rhomboidal footplate with stamped ornament, evidently a representation in cheaper material of the silver-sheet brooches of the same shape, which are to characterize VWZ Stufe I. The harmony between the phases of different brooch types and art styles is evidently not total, and indeed it would unreasonable to expect it to be so. This does not mean the irretrievable breakdown of Bakka's system, however. It would be possible to prioritize the developments amongst art styles and silver-sheet and relief brooches in marking the Stufen, and therefore place Reichstein's "jüngere" and "späte" cruciform brooches within two Stufen each, VWZ Stufen I and II, and VWZ Stufen II and III, respectively. Conversely the cruciform brooch phasing could be prioritized, and the art styles, silver-sheet and relief brooches adjusted into double-Stufen accordingly. These modifications seem unnecessarily complicated, and unnecessarily blunt the effectiveness of the system, if it is borne in mind that the great majority of Reichstein's "späte" cruciform brooches have perfectly acceptable VWZ Stufe III contexts as first defined by Bakka. A simpler approach therefore is to allow Bakka's original definitions to stand, and to treat only those grave-finds with discordant assemblages (in the system's terms) as lying on the cusp between the two Stufen they may be held to represent. It will not do to take the "latest" object in a group as decisive, as this provides a terminus post quem for the actual burial, not a relative-chronological placement of the whole dress-assemblage.

A double-Stufe is however of use in dating some of the Scandinavian cruciform brooches which Reichstein does not place in any phase but which on his typological grounds are clearly not "ältere" types and therefore may be located somewhere within VWZ Stufen II and III. We have, then, two phenomena not originally expressed in Bakka's system: grave-finds on the cusp between consecutive Stufen, and a double-Stufe. As will appear, this broader phase is of great use in tracing the history of certain objects. For ease of reference, Bakka's VWZ Stufen I-IV will be abbreviated as VWZ I, VWZ II, etc. in the following pages. A hyphen will be used to indicate the cusp between two Stufen, e.g. VWZ II-III, while an oblique stroke will indicate a double-Stufe, e.g. VWZ III/IV.

Bakka emphasized his belief that only with great difficulty could artefact-types or groups other than those upon which his system was already built be added to it. But there are groups of chronologically significant material outside of his system, and it is reasonable to see whether the evidence of these can be expressed in common terms with the forms already noted. Especially prominent in significance for the present work are various types of small bronze brooches, forms of which appear ultimately to have supplanted the cruciform brooches. These were the subject of a rather brief survey by Shetelig (Shetelig 1910). Amongst these are certain series which from their sources and parallels amongst more finely decorated brooches, and the evidence of their find-contexts, appear to belong at the broadest to the latter half of the Migration Period, VWZ III and IV (e.g. Shetelig 1910 figs.13, 15-28, 52-53, and 69-72). Not all, of course, are spread evenly over the whole of this period, but in the absence of a more advanced study than Shetelig's no closer dating can be offered.

Arguments are made in Chapter 2 for adding certain types of Scandinavian clasps to the reliable dating evidence by which whole find-assemblages can be relatively placed within this sytem. Two further classes of material of which chronological studies have been made, but which cannot be formally related to this system, are pottery (Bøe 1931), and weapons and weapon-sets (Fett 1938-40). Both these works have weaknesses, and, not surprizingly, are old-fashioned now: Fett lacks any basic discussion of chronological principles, and Bøe relies too heavily on pure typology. Both nevertheless contain valuable information, especially as these classes of material involve male graves in chronological studies far more than is possible under Bakka's system as published. An illustration of the potential of a modern re-assessment of such material is provided by Solberg (Solberg 1981). Recourse is occasionally made to the evidence of pottery and weapons in the following pages, and on such occasions attempts to relate this evidence to Bakka's system or to the absolute-chronological scale must be individually made in each case.

Although based of necessity on Norwegian grave-finds, Bakka's system is presented as a common Scandinavian system, and it is worth pausing to consider its applicability to Denmark and Sweden, and thereby occasionally to Finland. Until very recently the absence of a large number of closed inhumation burials of the relevant period providing a sufficiently rich find material has made a seriation of finds in these areas comparable to that created for the Norwegian cruciform brooches impossible. In Denmark, however, the excavation within the past four years of substantial late Roman Iron Age and Migration Period cemeteries at Sejlflod and Hjemsted in North and South Jutland respectively promises to change this state of affairs radically. But it is as yet to early to anticipate the results: the Hjemsted finds are being conserved and publication prepared; at the time of writing, the Sejlflod site is still under excavation (it is hoped to complete this in Autumn 1983). In Central Sweden too, the excavation of some 2,000 cremation burials since the beginning of the 1960s has given rise to a project to establish a chronological sequence for the Migration Period, but no results have as yet been published

(Ambrosiani et al. 1981). There is therefore as yet no adequate independent sequence with which to test or refine the Norwegian one. The similarities between Norwegian, Danish, and Swedish archaeological remains are, however, sufficient for one to accept the application of Bakka's system to these areas. Reichstein finds Norwegian cruciform brooch types of different phases in Denmark, allowing at least some finds there to be accurately placed under Bakka's system. The same applies to Sweden, where Reichstein is further able to establish two independent "späte" Swedish Types, in one case through association with these Norwegian brooches (Reichstein 1975 pp.72-74). There is no reason to suspect that occurrences of the Sösdala and Nydam Styles are not contemporary in each of these areas, or that parallel stages in the development of Style I reached different areas at significantly different times. Nissen Meyer produced a chronological sequence for the silver-sheet and relief brooches which covered all of these areas (Nissen Meyer 1934), although one may feel reservations about the synchronization of later Swedish with later Norwegian and Danish developments in anticipation of finer evidence eventually emerging from the Helgö material. The dating of the D-bracteates has already been discussed. On the grounds of design there is reason to believe that Jutish and West-Swedish types were in production for some time before any distinct Norwegian groups appeared. Since, however, D-bracteates occur in only two Norwegian grave-finds, one of these bracteates being an example of a North-Jutish/West-Swedish type, and none so far at all from Denmark and Sweden, this potential problem to all practical purposes disappears.

The applicability of Bakka's system to hoard-finds is a problem of especial relevance in the context of Denmark and Sweden. Bakka would include only grave-finds, since the same presumption of practical contemporaneity which is possible for most dress-accessories associated in individual graves is not permissible for the majority of hoards, particularly hidden (and unreclaimed) collections of valuable metals. The latest object in a hoard gives a terminus post quem for the hoard's deposition, but the age of the valuables hoarded may demonstrably vary extensively. However all hoards are not of the same type, and in the case of single sacrifices of war booty, as seems to have been the case at Ejsbøl Mose in South Jutland, for example (Ørsnes 1964), if suitable material is present, certain finds may be coupled to the system. In discussing finds from the excluded hoards too, for instance Høstentorp from Sjælland or Djurgårdsäng from southern Sweden, it is also useful to refer the latest object in the find, and sometimes other objects too, to the Stufe-system, rather than returning to a system of approximate absolute dates.

Bakka's Stufengliederung, with modifications and developments, thus forms the framework for chronological references for most Scandinavian finds in this study.

Unfortunately no equivalent exists for the finds from Anglian England. Here, on the whole, dates have traditionally been expressed in sometimes rather vague absolute-chronological terms: e.g. "early/late 6th. century", "second half of 5th. century", "about 500", and so on. Two forms of evidence in particular have formed the basis of dating Anglian English finds: cruciform brooches, for the most part following Åberg's old typological outline (Åberg 1926), and art styles, especially, of course, Style I, the chronology of which has now been thoroughly discussed by Haseloff, although his references to English examples are regrettably limited (Haseloff 1981). Supplementary schemes may be based, convincingly or not, upon such bases, e.g. Leeds's chronology of the square-headed brooches (Leeds 1949). Very occasionally, imported material in Anglian grave-finds, Kentish, Frankish, and even possibly Norwegian, provides firm datings for Anglian finds from external chronologies.

The publication of Reichstein's survey provides at least the opportunity for the dating of Anglian finds through cruciform brooches to be brought up to date. The results of this work are, however, rather disappointing as far as England is concerned, certainly when compared with Norway. The exclusion of the ill-defined "late" and "insular" forms, mostly, one supposes, "florid" cruciform brooches, leaves a substantial lacuna in the English material, and Vierck's promised work on the subject has not materialised. For the brooches he did deal with, Reichstein proposed two chronological fixed points, one early, with the famous Dorchester brooch at around 400, and one late, with a cruciform brooch from Little Wilbraham, Cambs g.133, associated with two Frankish radiate-head brooches of Kühn Type 21 (Kühn 1940). Reichstein dated these no more closely than "6th.-century", but the dating of this type has recently been discussed by Koch (Koch 1977 pp.48-49), and a comparison of her conclusions with the evidence of Werner and Böhner (Werner 1935; Böhner 1958) shows the dating of burials containing such brooches to the period ca.520-550 (=Ament's AM2) to be quite reliable. Around Little Wilbraham g.133 Reichstein established a series of 24 grave-finds linked by common artefact-types and cruciform brooch Types. He subsequently proposed the division of this sequence into two phases "späte" and "späteste", involving, in the sequence, 9 "späte" and 4 "späteste" Types. Between the Dorchester brooch and the "späte" forms, a number of "ältere", "ältere/jüngere", and "jüngere" examples were identified. Reichstein argued for the dating of the "späte" phase in the second half of the 5th. century, perhaps a short way into the 6th., with the "späteste" phase succeeding this in the 6th. century.

Reichstein's division of his sequence of chronologically contiguous grave-groups into "späte" and "späteste" groups must be treated with considerable caution. He himself described it as "somewhat hypothetical". Some grave-finds are grouped close together in the sequence on the basis only of sharing artefact-types which may have had particularly long lives: for instance certain small-long brooches, and the form of clasp numbered 14 in his Tabelle 7 (cf. Chapter 2). The seriation itself does not show substantially overlapping grave-finds cohering in distinct "combination-groups" or phases. The distinction between "späte" and "späteste" is produced by dividing the sequence into two at the point where the overlap between the two divisions is least. There is no imperative reason to disagree with Reichstein that the objects towards the "späte" side of the series look earlier on the whole than those towards the other, but some overlap of artefact-types between the two divisions appears in the table, and one ought to reckon with a substantial degree of overlap in chronological fact, unless any finer dating methods can be found for the brooches involved to produce a clearer, surer picture.

What absolute dates, then, may be put to these cruciform brooches ? Reichstein put the "späte" types largely in the second half of the 5th. century. Bakka's study gives the impression that "späte" forms in Scandinavia emerge from a period of creativity that also saw the appearance of Style I. There is no reason to date the English "späte" forms any earlier than this, and they share a number of typological developments characteristic of the Norwegian "späte" forms, e.g. the presence of half-round and decorated headplate knobs, a relatively broad headplate, and lappets and trapezoid or shovel-shaped terminals on the foot. A date of ca.475, Haseloff's date for the emergence of Style I, may therefore be preferred to the beginning of the English "späte" brooches to ca.450. From this date, the "späte" forms continue in use into the 6th century. Reichstein's statement that the square-headed brooch from Little Eriswell, Sfk g.28 with which one of these "späte" examples was associated looks undeveloped and ought to be dated to the 5th. century is unsupported and unfounded. The English square-headed brooches are studied in Chapter 3, below, and a 6th.-century date is supported there.

The "späteste" types are dated to the 6th. century by Little Wilbraham, Cambs g.133. To an extent these may have run parallel to and contemporary with the more florid types of cruciform brooch in England, those with more extensive and prominent animal ornament on the headplate knobs and foot, usually gilded and silvered, which are not discussed in Reichstein's work. The brooch from Holywell Row, Sfk g.16, for instance (Reichstein 1975 no. 853), shows marked similarities to a more florid example from Swaffham, Nfk g.6 (EAA 2 pl.IV), in overall size, design of the top knob, form of the bow, and form of the horse's head below the lappets. One could regard the Swaffham brooch as typologically descended from the Holywell Row type, but they could equally well be closely contemporary, the

27

differences between them being governed by taste and cost rather than time. In Morningthorpe, Nfk g.353, a pair of clasps of the same distinctive type as those in Holywell Row g.16 were associated with a cruciform brooch, bronze, not gilt, whose headplate knobs are of a similar florid form to those of the Swaffham brooch. The appearance of the "florid" brooches does not therefore necessarily mark the end of the "späteste" forms, which could continue down into the middle of the 6th. century. Towards the middle of the 6th. century, however, gilt, and usually silvered, square-headed and florid curciform brooches appear to have become especially common as the major central brooch in the Anglian dress-set, and this probably marks the close of the few, simpler, plainer forms that Reichstein deals with.

The inception of Reichstein's "späte" cruciform brooch forms in England has been set at ca.475. There is no solid evidence from which an approximate date for the termination of these forms can be directly drawn, but they continue into the 6th century, and overlap with the "späteste" forms, one of which appears to have been buried in the period 520-550. In this situation it is easiest to talk in round figures, and to attribute to the "späte" forms a period of use of about half a century, i.e. ca.475-525. In the same grossly simplified terms, the "späteste" types can be attributed a period of use in the first half of the 6th. century. To have these latter brooches covering a period of 50 years spreads out Reichstein's few "späteste" examples rather incongruously, but the round figure will err only on the side of caution, and the evidence is simply not available for finer adjustments.

Unfortunately even this rather clumsy chronological scheme involves relatively few of the Anglian English finds one would seek to date. There are a large number of grave-finds including cruciform brooches not included in Reichstein's corpus. Many he omitted, several of which do not obviously belong to the late and insular forms on which Vierck's work is awaited. There is also a good number of finds which have come to light since Reichstein made his survey. It is not usually easy to attribute these brooches to any of Reichstein's datable types, since he lays down no clear and followable classification procedure. To associate these brooches with the chronological results of Reichstein's work, one frequently finds oneself intuitively drawn back to comparing general similiarities of proportion, size of headplate, form of knobs, bow, lappets, horse's head and nostrils, etc. - in fact something very similar to the coarse Åberg-based typological dating methods which held sway in the 50 years between Åberg's study and Reichstein's. Nevertheless, together with Style I decorated objects, cruciform brooches remain the leading form of dating evidence for Anglian English grave-finds.

The outline of a phasing of the Anglian English 5th.- and 6th.-century grave-finds comparable to Bakka's for

Scandinavia has been sketched by Vierck (in Kossack and Reichstein 1977). Vierck proposed the division of the material into three phases. This study, however, is simply too brief, and, with the exception of the definition of the "bichrome style", too scant in the detailed exposition of the phases to be brought into formal use here. The definitions of the phases made by Vierck are not sufficiently internally comprehensive and externally exclusive. Phase 1, for instance, includes forms especially close to continental models, but is not, presumably, intended to include the occasional Frankish 6th.-century radiate-head brooches that appear in Anglian graves. The key to the succession of Phase 3 to Phase 2 appears to be the supplanting of earlier forms of Style I by the bichrome style, but where does one place an object carrying neither of these styles ? Is it acceptable to place the florid cruciform brooches discussed above, from Morningthorpe, Nfk g.353, and Swaffham, Nfk g.6, in Phases 2 and 3 respectively on the basis of the presence or absence of gilding and silver-plating or tinning alone ? The basic sequence Vierck points to is comprehensible, but requires much more substantial definition and demonstration. It is premature to establish a phasing of the Anglian English material without a proper, detailed discussion of the histories of the leading artefact-types involved. Only to a limited extent does Reichstein provide this for the cruciform brooches, and the results of this are thin as far as England is concerned. The chronology of the Anglian wrist-clasps, and the Anglo-Saxon square-headed brooches, are discussed in detail in the course of this study, substantially, even radically, revising chronologies previously proposed by Vierck (Vierck 1966) and Leeds (Leeds 1949) respectively. One might hope that the ubiquitous and varied small-long brooches would prove valuable chronological indicators, but Leeds's study (Leeds 1945) produced few concrete results, and no substantial advances have been made since. The Anglian saucer brooches may also provide valuable, as yet largely untapped, information. Whether any significant chronological evidence could ever be won from such generally simpler artefacts as girdle-hangers or annular brooches is open to doubt, but they should not be summarily dismissed. Ideally, a phasing of the Anglian grave-finds would eventually couple the furnishings of inhumation graves with the numerous cinerary urns. There is ultimately one profound objection to this sort of phasing of sequences of archaeological material: that it forces divisions on to what may with more historical accuracy be regarded as a continuum. The justification of the approach is its practicality. We lack the means to post gradual developments in the Migration Period art styles or artefact-types sufficiently accurately against the absolute-chronological scale to dispense with relative-chronological phasing.

A separate criticism may be made of the absolute datings Vierck proposed. In accepting without further discussion Morris's date of ca.430 for the beginning of Phase 1, Vierck is out of step with current views on the start of the Adventus Saxonum (cf. Hawkes 1978). At the other end of this period, a dating of ca.550-600 for the flourishing of the bichrome style is, I believe, too late. In Chapter 3, a case is made for the emergence of this style by about the 520s. Of more practical relative-chronological significance than the disappearance of all traces of the bichrome style is the disappearance of the objects on which it is first recognized and first flourishes (i.e. square-headed and florid cruciform brooches), that is, the end of the Migration Period, for which a date of ca.560-570 may be proposed.

It must now be accepted that the end of the Migration Period took place well before the end of the 6th. century. One of the key signs of the succession of the new cultural period over the Migration Period is the appearance of Salin's Style II. It is noted that Haseloff has recently re-defined Style II in terms of the patterns of composition rather than the forms of the animals parts (Haseloff 1981 pp.222-230), but while this complete re-application of the term "Style II" is justifiable in terms of art history in vacuo, it does spoil the point that Salin's Animal Style II, which is no less real and readily recognizable, appears simultaneously in both England and Scandinavia with those radical changes in artefact-types and forms which have already been noted as marking the end of the Migration Period. Early Style II as defined by Haseloff, however, must be regarded as a later Migration Period phenomenon, supplanting Haseloff's Style I on later Norwegian relief brooches and D-bracteates, and in some measure on late Anglo-Saxon square-headed brooches.

The best evidence we have for dating the emergence of Salin's Style II in absolute-chronological terms is from the continent. The transition from Style I to Style II can be observed there on a particular continental type of brooch, and has been thoroughly discussed by Haseloff (1981 pp.540-673). The dating of the manufacture of examples of these Fibeln vom kontinentalen Typ with Style I ornament is not aided by the precise points provided by coin-dated graves, but Haseloff indicates that it continued up to and around the middle of the 6th. century (pp.568, 586). A pair of brooches from Krepsau, Baden g.4 show marked tendencies towards the characteristic patterns of composition of Style II, but still belong to Salin's Style I in terms of the elements of the animal bodies. This grave is coin-dated by including the copy of a solidus of Justinian I dated to 555-565, and Haseloff argues for a dating of the brooches to ca.565 at the latest (pp.597-629). From Soest, Westfalen g.106, comes a pair of these continental brooches with unmistakable decoration of Salin's Style II, associated with a "slightly worn" solidus

of Justinian I, again struck between 555 and 565, and
mounted as a pendant. Like Haseloff we may regard the last
quarter of the 6th. century as the most probable burial
date, but the brooches show signs of wear too, and there is
no reason to suppose that they are significantly younger
tan the coin (pp.666-673, Taf.90). We may therefore follow
Haseloff in placing the emergence of Style II (in fact
Salin's Style II) somewhere around the 560s. There is
nothing amongst Werner's coin dated Austrasian graves to
contradict this (Werner 1935). A degree of overlap between
Styles I and II on the continent is not, of course,
unlikely. It is clear that a form of Style I was in use
amongst the Lombards in Italy as late as the 570s (Roth
1973 pp.9-51, 271f.). But this is of little relevance to
the history of Style I in western and northern Europe and
England, and indeed the late Lombardic Style I involves
certain motifs that are more reminiscent of Style II in
those areas than Style I, such as the ribbon-like animal
bodies with two framing bands filled with a row of
filigree-like pellets.

One grave-find which Haseloff did not admit as
evidence for the dating of the appearance of Salin's Style
II, but which cannot be ignored, is the "Arnegundis" grave
from Paris (Fleury and France-Lanord 1963). This was the
grave of a woman, wearing a finger ring with the
inscription ARNEGUNDIS and a monogram of the title regina,
in the basilica of St. Denis, and therefore clearly the
grave of a woman of royal rank. Some of her dress-fittings
were decorated in Salin's Style II. It has been suggested
that this is the grave of a wife of Lothar I, recorded by
Gregory of Tours as one AREGUND (gen. Aregundis, HF IV.3),
who, if she reached the age of the woman buried in St.
Denis, would have been buried about the period 565-570.
Clearly this interpretation of the find is not incompatible
with the evidence for the emergence of Style II given
above, although it might imply that the 550s at least were
a preferable date to the 560s. But the interpretation is
too dubious for the grave to be admitted as dating
evidence. Firstly the MSS of HF are unanimous in naming
the queen AREGUND, and the intrusive n on the ring is a
significant discrepancy, if not an insuperable one.
Secondly, even if Arnegund is an authentic variant of the
name of Lothar's queen, she was not necessarily the only
Merovingian regina ever to bear that name (although no
other is in fact recorded): the name of the mother of
King Chilperic may indeed have been considered a good name
to bestow on a royal baby girl for much of the latter half
of the 6th. century.

The 560s is a good approximate date for the adoption
of Salin's Style II on the continent. It therefore
provides us with a guide to the date when we might expect
this style to appear in Anglian England and Scandinavia,
although we cannot simply assume it to have been
contemporary in all areas. Unlike Scandinavia and

continental Europe, Anglian English metalwork in Style I shows few signs of a tendency towards the principles of composition that are characteristic of Style II, although pure non-zoomorphic interlace does occur, on certain square-headed brooches for instance (e.g. Leeds 1949 Group B1). Presumably, then, animal Style II was imported to Anglian England. In suggesting that this is best dated to about the 560s too, one is forced back on to the rather weak argument that there is no sign of the development of the styles anterior to Salin's Style II (e.g. Style I and non-zoomorphic interlace, and the bichrome style) any later in Anglian England than anywhere else. In Anglian England, Scandinavia, and continental Europe, the successive ascendencies of different art styles in the 6th. century, Style I, interlace, Style II, seem to proceed step-by-step, and there is no reason to suppose significant chronological discrepancies between the areas (cf. Speake 1980 pp. 23-37). Bakka's study of the Norwegian Migration Period (Bakka 1973) shows his belief that the adoption of Style II in Scandinavia, marking the end of the period, was contemporary with its adoption on the continent. It may be added in support of the date proposed for this cultural watershed, that a recent study of the Vendel graves, which mark the succession of the Vendel Period in Sweden, on quite independent grounds, has also dated the earliest of these graves to ca. 560 (Arrhenius 1980).

A summary of the major points made here is given in tabular form in Fig.1.9. This defines the limits for specific areas of such period-designations (e.g. Roman Iron Age, Migration Period, etc.) as will commonly be met with, with appropriate abbreviations. In the following text, Bakka's phases of the Scandinavian Migration Period will be referred to by the abbreviations given above and in the table, and, as far as possible, Ament's phasing of the Merowingerzeit will be used for the appropriate continental material, although supplementary reference may have to be made to chronological studies such as Werner 1935, Böhner 1958, and Koch 1977. In Anglian England, any form of close dating still has to be done in more or less broad absolute-chronological terms, and not in relative-chronological phases

GEOGRAPHICAL CONVENTIONS

The material dealt with in this study is drawn from an extensive geographical area. It is hoped that the following brief explanation of the conventional terms of reference for the areas most frequently referred to will be helpful for those unfamiliar with either Scandinavia or England, and will again allow such references in the main text to be consistently and concisely made.

The find-places of objects from England will normally be cited in the form find-place + county. The counties

referred to are the new counties established after local
government re-organization in the early 1970s. These
differ to some extent from those referred to in much of the
earlier literature concerned with the topic studied here.
Huntingdonshire and Rutland, for instance, are absorbed
into Cambridgeshire and Leicestershire respectively, and a
new county of Humberside has been formed out of northern
Lincolnshire and the East Riding of Yorkshire. Abbreviated
forms for the county names are regularly used and these
forms are explained below.

In Scandinavian archaeology, there are standard forms
for expressing a find-place. The full conventional form in
Denmark has four elements: the find-place; the sogn
(parish); the herred (district); and the amt (region).
Administrative re-organization has recently introduced new
names and boundaries for the amter, but archaeological
references adhere to the old system. For the sake of
brevity, the full four-element reference is not always
given here, especially when to do so would involve
unnecessary repetition. It is not unusual for a sogn to be
within a herred of the same name: such repetition may be
indicated in the find-place formula by the element do.
(=ditto). A list of abbreviated forms of the amt-names is
given below. Denmark is regularly abbreviated Dk.

The system of reference in Norway for a long time
comprised the three elements find-place (usually a farm-
name); prestegjeld or occasionally sogn (parish or sub-
parish); and fylke (region). A trend of secularization in
Norwegian archaeology has recently brought about the
modification of this form with the substitution of the
kommune (district) for the parish in the sequence. However
the majority of finds still have their find-places cited in
the old form in museum indices and catalogues, and there is
no readily-available hand-list for the translation of
prestegjeld into kommuner. Considerable confusion can
result: it is not immediately obvious to one unfamiliar
with Norwegian archaeology that Kvassheim, Ogna, Rogaland,
Kvassheim, Egersund, Rogaland, and Kvassheim, Hå, Rogaland,
are one and the same place. For the simple practical
reason that I have obtained most references in the terms of
the old (parish) system, and I have been unable to
translate them into the new (district) system, the old
system is normally used here. If, occasionally, the
kommune is cited rather than the prestegjeld then a k.
follows the name. Abbreviated forms of the names of the
fylker are listed below. Norway may be abbreviated N.

The usual Swedish system is similar to the old
Norwegian system, with three elements: find-place; socken
(parish); and landskap (region). This creates its own
problems, since a comprehensive map of Swedish parishes
seems to be unobtainable. Abbreviations for the names of
those Swedish landskap referred to are given below; Sweden
may be abbreviated S.

English Counties

Kt	Kent	Ex	Essex
GL	Greater London	Cambs	Cambridgeshire
ESx	East Sussex	Beds	Bedfordshire
WSx	West Sussex	N'hants	Northamptonshire
Sy	Surrey	Warwicks	Warwickshire
IoW	Isle of Wight	HW	Hereford & Worcestershire
Bucks	Buckinghamshire	Leics	Leicestershire
Berks	Berkshire	Lincs	Lincolnshire
Oxon	Oxfordshire	Notts	Nottinghamshire
Wilts	Wiltshire	Derbys	Derbyshire
Glos	Gloucestershire	Hu	Humberside
Sfk	Suffolk	N.Yorks	North Yorkshire
Nfk	Norfolk	Co.D	County Durham

Denmark (Dk): amter

Fr	Frederiksborg	Vi	Viborg
Kbh	København	Ra	Randers
Hol	Holbæk	År	Århus
So	Sorø	Sk	Skanderborg
Pr	Præstø	–	Vejle
Ma	Maribo	Rk	Ringkøbing
Od	Odense	–	Ribe
Sv	Svendborg	Had	Haderslev
Hj	Hjørring	Tø	Tønder
Th	Thisted	Åb	Åbenrå
Ål	Ålborg	Sø	Sønderborg

Norway (N): fylker

Øf	Østfold	Ro	Rogaland
Ak	Akershus	Ho	Hordaland
He	Hedmark	SFj	Sogn og Fjordane
Op	Opland	MR	Møre og Romsdal
Bu	Buskerud	ST	Sør-Trøndelag
Vf	Vestfold	NT	Nord-Trøndelag
Te	Telemark	No	Nordland
AA	Aust-Agder	Tr	Troms
VA	Vest-Agder		

Sweden (S): landskap

Bo	Bohuslän	Up	Uppland
Dls	Dalsland	Vml	Västmanland
Vg	Västergötland	Vä	Värmland
Hal	Halland	Gä	Gästrikland
Sk	Skåne	Drn	Dalarne
Bl	Blekinge	Hä	Hälsingland
Sm	Småland	Me	Medelpad
Ög	Östergötland	Jä	Jämtland
Sö	Södermanland	Got	Gotland
Nä	Närke	Öl	Öland

CHAPTER 2

CLASPS

Introduction

A glance at the distribution map (Map 2.1) shows plainly how Scandinavian clasps and Anglian wrist-clasps take a primary place in the investigation of the Scandinavian character of Anglian England in the pre-Viking period. A thorough investigation of the material which forms this map produces detailed results with which one can start to build up a picture of the relationship between Anglian England and Scandinavia in these centuries.

The clasps are a body of material which are rather poorly dealt with in published archaeological literature. The basis of such conventional classification as exists of the Scandinavian clasps as a whole are Rygh's figures 268-271; if Scandinavian clasps are classified by anything other than a verbal description it is normally done by comparison with the examples figured here. Blindheim (Blindheim 1946; 1947) produced some detailed and, at least as far as Norway was concerned, relatively comprehensive information about the use and distribution of the major forms of Scandinavian clasps, but seems to have seen no need to provide any formal classification. The excavation of a workshop producing ornate buttons for the most common form of Scandinavian clasp on the island of Helgö in the Mälaren area of central Sweden is of enormous importance for the study of this form of clasp in eastern Scandinavia, and a publication has appeared (K. Lamm in Helgö IV). But this illuminates just one portion of the material, emphasizing, in fact, the shadows which lie across most of the rest.

Baldwin Brown described and illustrated a number of English clasps in his survey of The Arts in Early England, and drew attention to their markedly Anglian distribution (Brown III pp.360-366). Leeds was more specific on the ethnic significance of the wrist-clasps found in England in the course of his short study of them (Leeds 1945 pp.53-61). In this work, Leeds proposed a classification of the wrist-clasps based on, as he himself said, a survey of the material that was "not ... exhaustive". His classification is in fact highly idiosyncratic, and of virtually no practical use. His classes a - e, for instance, are based on descriptions of the wrist-clasps' bars, but it is not always clear what the differences between classes is, or to which classes examples other than those few illustrated should be assigned. The "type" which Leeds describes as "simplest" and "most widespread" (form B 7 in England, below) is not designated a class at all.

A comprehensive study of the Anglian wrist-clasps and some Scandinavian counterparts was made in a chapter on "Sleeve-Clasps in Anglian England with their Scandinavian Prototypes" by Vierck in his B.Litt. thesis (Vierck 1966 pp.62-106). Here Vierck produced a complete classification of all the English examples known to him. He lists some 271 examples, a handful of which he considered "unclassifiable". This classification appears to be basically founded upon his perception of the typological relationship between the various English "Types", while in some respects his sub-groupings appear to be influenced by Leeds's division of the material. A critical assessment of the most substantial, and perhaps most significant, section of Vierck's classification (his Types I-VI) appears below in the introduction to English Class B.

The provision of a new classification of the English and Scandinavian clasps is wholly justifiable. It is suggested as a particular merit of the following work that for the first time the English and Scandinavian clasps are classified according to a common system. It is, of course, of significance in itself that they readily conform to such treatment, and common designations for common features makes the discussion of such points very much clearer. The field is open for the establishment of such a system: none, in effect, exists for Scandinavia, while Vierck's for England is inaccessible, practically unusable, leaves considerable room for improvement, and can only be extended to cover the Scandinavian material with considerable awkwardness.

A second major point is the very great increase here in the volume of material upon which the classification is based and which is analyzed to investigate the history and development of the clasps. While Vierck listed 31 examples of a certain type of clasp from Norway (Class A, below), this number is here increased to 63. The number of clasps known from Denmark has recently trebled, largely as a result fo the excavation of the cemeteries of Sejlflod and Hjemsted, the former of which is not yet completed. The number of English examples included is increased from under 300 in Vierck to almost 600.

Under the system established here the whole clasp corpus of England and Scandinavia is divided into three classes, Classes A, B, and C, on the basis of the distinctive elements of the composition of each clasp. These are detailed in the individual descriptions of each class below. No clasp is unclassifiable under this scheme. The only awkwardnesses that occur, involving no more than half-a-dozen cases out of well over a thousand, concern examples which in some respects join features of two classes. Each of these classes occurs in both England and Scandinavia, and the descriptions of the classes in either area are kept separate below. Classes B and C are further divided into a number of distinctive forms, designated

36

forms B 1, 2, 3, etc. Not all forms, however, are represented in both Scandinavia and England: forms B 2 and B 3, for instance, are at present known only from Scandinavia, while forms B 8-B 20, inclusive, seem as yet to be peculiarly English forms. A general overview of all classes and forms of clasps from Anglian England and Scandinavia is given in Fig. 2.1. In certain cases, particular types may be identified amongst the clasps of a certain form. Lists of the examples recorded in the survey are given in Lists 2.1 and 2.2.

In this chapter, the Scandinavian clasps are described first, in order in Classes A-C, followed by the English clasps in the same order. Chronological evidence for the classes, forms, or types is provided with their definition and description. A summary of the history of the artefact-type as a whole, and a preliminary consideration of its significance in the investigation of the relationship between Anglian England and Scandinavia, is made at the end of the chapter.

SCANDINAVIA

Class A (List 2.1)

Clasps of Class A are formed of a length of metal wire, the two ends of which are rolled up in opposite directions to form spirals. A length of wire is left between these two spirals which is pinched together and thus doubled-up between them, from which it projects to form either the hook- or the catch-element of the clasps (Fig. 2.2). Such clasps are often referred to as a "hook-and-eye" type in English, and correspondingly "hekter og maljer", etc., in Scandinavia.

There is no very great variety in the forms and composition of this class of clasp as represented by the known Scandinavian material. The metal used is normally silver, occasionally bronze. Very little decorative variation is found. Two Norwegian examples have the ends of the wire, and therefore the innermost rings of the spirals, beaded, from Åtland, Bakke, VA (C8715), and Hauge, Klepp, Ro (Magnus 1975 fig.43). A similar effect is achieved by twisting the ends of the wire on a few of the pieces in the Danish Høstentorp hoard (cf. Voss 1954 p.186). An unusual variant, with the wire flattened out to form a relatively broad band, is from Sejlflod, do., Fleskum, Ål, Dk g.FK. An example from Riskadal, Årdal, Ro (S2587) has a small domed silver stud in the centre of the spiral, and the clasps from Lovik, Dverberg, No, N (Sjøvold 1962 pp.97-98, pl.28-29) appear to have the same feature. It is possible that this stud may have had some obscure practical function, rather than simply being decorative.

The greatest and most significant single variable amongst the clasps of Class A is the size of their spirals. A measurement was taken on as many examples as possible of the diameter of the spiral from the point where the hook or catch-loop leaves it (cf. Fig.2.2). The Scandinavian material produced a range of measurements from 0.4 to 2.0 cm. The diameter is normally consistent for all four spirals of a single complete pair of clasps where these are all available for measurement, although variations of one or two millimetres may occur, more often when the diamter is relatively large (i.e. 1.3 cm. or more). In a number of cases it is not possible to record a certain diameter, because only one broken-off spiral is preserved in the find, with no remnant of its hook or catch. In these cases, however, it often appears likely that the break was made at the weak point of the spiral where the projecting hook or catch-element left it, and that the maximum diameter of the spiral preserved is a fair indication of its original diameter. Uncertain measurements of this kind are too few to make a great difference to the figures discussed below.

Another variable loosely related to that of the spirals' diameter is the number of turns made in the wire to form the spiral. In some cases the wire will only go through one complete turn before leaving the spiral to form the hook or catch (Fig. 2.3), while in others it can go through up to more than five complete turns. Obviously it is considerably easier to fit a relatively large number of turns in a spiral of a diameter approaching two centimetres than in one of only half-a-centimetre diameter. But there is a considerable degree of lassitude in the relationship of the diameter of a spiral to the number of turns it is composed of. The clasps found at Simmersted, Magstrup, Gram, Had, Dk (NMK df.22,25/46) included examples with spirals of up to 1.7 cm. diameter composed of only one turn. On the other hand, the piece from Orust, Röra, Bo, S (SHM 1472) had 2½ turns in a diameter of 0.7 cm., while the clasps from Sande, Gloppen, SFj, N (VJG fig.112) turned through 3½ circuits in the compass of 1 cm.

The average diameter of the spirals of Class A clasps appears to have increased steadily with time. A sufficient number of finds of Class A clasps in Scandinavia are reliably dated by find associations within the relative-chronological periods stated in the introductory chapter to make an apparently meaningful calculation of the average diameter of spirals and the range of diameters one can expect to meet within those periods. The dated finds within which a measurement of the diameter of the clasp-spirals has been obtainable are as follows:

Find	Museum Number	Dating evidence	Spiral Diameter (cm.)
Roman Iron Age			
Harpelev, Holme-Ostrup Pr, Dk g.2	NMK C28269 C28272 C28273	Pottery	0.5>0.6
Fraugde, do., Åsum, Od, Dk g.38/38A	NMK C8511	Returned-foot brooches; pottery; "sewing-needle"	0.4
Rosilde, Vindinge, do., Sv, Dk	NMK C13352 -C13355	Bow brooches	0.5>0.7
Hjemsted, Skærbæk, Hvidinge, Tø, Dk g.303	HM 1004 x 994-999, 1163	Silver-sheet brooch	0.6
Bredsätra, do., Öl, S	SHM 18406:1	"Sewing-needle"; beads	0.6

Average diameter of spirals: 0.55 cm.
Spiral diameter range   : 0.4 > 0.7 cm.

Find	Museum Number	Dating evidence	Spiral Diameter (cm.)
VWZ I (all Norway)			
Eidsten, Brunlanes, Vf	C19231 -40	Silver-sheet brooch	1.2>1.4
Roligheden, Hedrum, Vf	C14344	Silver-sheet brooch	1.2
Lunde, do., Te	C21648	Cruciform brooch (Reichstein 1975 no.54)	1.2
Fossevik, Evje, AA	C29487	Cruciform brooch (Reichstein 1975 no.62)	0.8
Foss, Lyngdal, VA	C21650	Silver-sheet brooch	1.3
Fosse indre, Alvesund, Ho	B11475	Cruciform brooch (Reichstein 1975 no.223)	0.6

Average diameter of spirals: 1.07 cm.
Spiral diameter range   : 0.6 > 1.4 cm.

Find	Museum Number	Dating evidence	Spiral Diameter (cm.)
VWZ II			
Tåstrupgård, Høje-Tåstrup Smørum, Kbh, Dk	NMK C26672	Relief brooch	1.5>1.7
Hjemsted, Skærbæk, Hvidinge, Tø, Dk g.93	HM 1004x99	Cruciform brooch	1.3
Erge, Klepp, Ro, N	S7131	Relief brooch	1.5
Hauge, Klepp, Ro, N	B2277	Relief brooch	1.3
Tu, Klepp, Ro, N	C21407	Relief brooch	1.4
Nygård, Hafslo, SFj, N	B6110	Cruciform brooch (Reichstein 1975 no.258)	1.7
Veiberg, Nordalen, MR, N	B7079	Cruciform brooch (Reichstein 1975 no.282)	0.7

Average diameter of spirals: 1.275 cm.
Spiral diameter range   : 0.7 > 1.7 cm.

Find	Museum Number	Dating evidence	Spiral Diameter (cm.)
VWZ III (all Norway)			
Ringdal, Hedrum, Vf	C13208	Cruciform brooch	1.6
Hæm, Sanda, Te	C10362	Cruciform brooch (Reichstein 1975 no.55)	1.7
Åtland, Bakka, VA	C8715	Style I ornamented mounts	1.4
Stallemo, Øvrebo, VA	C23141	Cruciform brooch	1.3
Slettebø, Bjerkreim, Ro	S5046	Cruciform brooch (Reichstein 1975 no.133)	1.3

Find	Museum Number	Dating evidence	Spiral Diameter (cm.)
Riskadal, Årdal, Ro	S2587	Cruciform brooch (Reichstein 1975 no.219)	1.6
Tu, Klepp, Ro	B2513	Cruciform brooch (Reichstein 1975 no.203)	1.1
Lyse, Høle, Ro	S2718	Cruciform brooch	1.3
Skeim, Aurland, SFj	B8552	Cruciform brooch	2.0

Average diameter of spirals: 1.48 cm.
Spiral diameter range   : 1.1 > 2.0 cm.

Where a single find contains more than one clasp-half or spiral which are identical both in spiral-diameter and the number of turns of which that spiral is made, these are only counted once for the purpose of calculating the average diameters. They may be considered as making up a single set of clasps. The grave-find from Tåstrupgård, however (VWZ II), contained the remains of at least 3 pairs of clasps with a spiral diameter of up to 1.7 cm. made up of between five-and-a-quarter and five-and-three-quarter turns of the wire, and one clasp-piece with the same diameter spiral made up of only four-and-a-quarter turns. These were considered sufficiently different for the measure to figure twice in the calculation of the average. Alternative approaches to calculating the average would not significantly affect the results obtained.

In broad outline, the chronological development of the Class A clasps' form is clear. The earliest forms, from the Roman Iron Age, have an average diameter of only 0.55 cm. Finds from VWZ I show an average of slightly over 1 cm., which increases in VWZ II by about 2 mm. It is interesting to note that clasps placed within Bakka's VWZ I on the basis of their association with very early cruciform brooches have a much smaller average diameter than those which are placed within this group through their associations with silver-sheet brooches, while the two Norwegian finds assigned to VWZ II on the basis of cruciform brooches bring down the average spiral diameter in that Stufe markedly. There is more than one possible explanation for this phenomenon, existing as it is in such few examples, but it certainly brings into question the validity of the relative phasing of the silver-sheet brooches and Reichstein's "ältere" and "jüngere" cruciform brooches.

Although there was a clear trend to increase the size of the spirals as time passed, there is no necessary, direct, and regular relationship between the diameter of spirals and the relative date of manufacture. The significant figures are those for the range of diameter measurements that one could expect to meet from a given chronological phase. It transpires that spiral diameters bertween 1.1 and 1.4 cm. could occur in any period from VWZ I to VWZ III, and nearly 50 per cent of the clasps I have been able to measure fall within this range. Nevertheless, in certain cases the sizes of the spirals may be considered as chronological evidence, albeit for a "broad" rather than a "narrow" dating. Spirals with diameters between 0.4 and 0.6 cm. have been recorded only from RIA and VWZ I. Spirals with diameters between 0.8 and 1.0 cm. have been recorded only from VWZ I and VWZ II. One may therefore infer that otherwise undatable clasp spirals with diameters falling within these ranges are likely to belong to the relevant broad phases, although the inference is only conditional.

With a chronology based on find associations and a supplementary chronology based on the size of the clasp-spirals, over 60 per cent of the recorded finds of Class A clasps from Scandinavia can be more or less closely relatively dated. This provides reasonably stable foundations for a description of the developing distribution of the class outside England.

The example from what would appear to be the earliest dated context is also the only find outside of England which could not properly be called Scandinavian. This is the fragmentary Class A clasp from grave 5 at Heiligenhafen, Kr. Oldenburg, Schleswig-Holstein, on the north-western coast of West Germany, facing the Danish islands (Raddatz 1962 p.99, fig.6). A dating of the grave is provided by the brooch it contained, dated by Schulze (Schulze 1977 pp.123 & 256, Kat.no.112, Gruppe 225) to the later 3rd. or early 4th. century.

The remaining finds of the Roman Iron Age, for all of which a 4th.-century date is suggested, are concentrated in southern Scandinavia, that is Denmark, Skåne, and Öland (Map 2.2). To the clasps whose diameter measurements were listed above may be added the find from g.55 at Simris, Sk, S (Stjernquist 1955 p.23, pl.XXIII.12) dated to this period by its associated pottery and the date-range of its whole cemetery context.

The distribution of clasps of this class dated to the first phase of the Migration Period (VWZ I) shows a marked shift northwards (Map 2.2). Norway comes within the range, with a group of finds in southern Vestfold (see list of measurements above), and other finds spread around the coast as far as Hordaland. A find more broadly dated to

1RIA/VWZ I extends the range of distribution north to Carlsborg, Allhelgona, Ög, S (SHM 15694). The scarcity of finds of Class A certainly from VWZ I from the southernmost part of Scandinavia should not lead us to suppose that the use of the class must have declined there in this period. There is no particular shortage of examples dated to later phases in this area, and there are three Danish examples which on the evidence of their spiral diameters probably belong to VWZ I/II, i.e. Nykirke, Nørvang h., Vejle, and Sejlflod graves NT and RD.

But it is Norway that is particularly productive of finds of Class A clasps dated to VWZ II and later (Map 2.3). The distribution of the class stretches as far north as Nordland, from whence the specially decorated Class A clasp from Lovik, Dverberg Hg.3, referred to above, may be dated to this period on the basis of its spiral-diameter, ca.1.5 cm., and its similarity to the clasp from Riskadal, Årdal, Ro, from a grave-find dated to VWZ III by a cruciform brooch. A second find from Arctic Norway is that from Bessebostad, Trondenes, Tr (Sjøvold 1962 p.104).

Finds of this class of clasp dated to the latest phase of the Migration Period in Scandinavia are strikingly difficult to establish. Only once are Class A clasps associated with D-bracteates, that is in the Djurgårdsäng hoard from Västergötland, Sweden. These are by no means particularly late D-bracteates, and one should recall the chronological problems concerning objects associated in hoards as opposed to ojects associated in grave-finds. A second find which might be considered to be relatively late is that from Bryne, Time, Ro, N (B5607). Here fragments of a clasp of this class were associated with a small bronze equal-armed brooch of a type which is generally late (Fig.2.4; cf. Shetelig 1910 pp.84-86). But no very precise dating can be made on the basis of this brooch, and it would appear from Shetelig's brief study that it could as well belong to VWZ III as VWZ IV.

In all, there is only slight reason to suspect that Class A clasps survived into VWZ IV, but one may speculate that in the future an example may be discovered firmly placed by association within that _Stufe_. But sooner or later within the course of VWZ IV, the class appears to have gone out of use.

It would appear that clasps of Class A were an almost exclusively female dress-accessory in Scandinavia. The matter of the sex of the wearer is, as shall be shown, of especial importance when the Scandinavian clasp material of all classes comes to be compared with the English, and it is therefore worth reviewing the problems concerning the sexing of graves in the Migration Period in some detail here. It is highly unusual in Scandinavia for adequate skeletal evidence to be found in an excavated grave to determine the sex of the occupant on osteological grounds.

The main basis for establishing sex therefore is the recovery of characteristically male or female grave goods.

Working from such material in an endeavour to analyze the sex of wearer of various forms of clasp, it seems the graves can be divided into five useful categories:

Almost certainly female (F):
   any one of - a pair of brooches or pins; 3 or more brooches and/or pins; 15 or more beads; pendants; and combination of individual items under (f), below.

Probably female (f):
   any one of - 2 unlike brooches; 10 or more beads; spindle-whorl; key; and fragments which appear to be reconstructable as objects listed under (F), above.

Almost certainly male (M):
   weapons, especially sword, spears, and shield-boss; also arrow-heads and axe.

Probably male (m):
   fragments which appear to be reconstructable as objects listed under (M), above.

Indeterminable:
   grave-finds not classifiable as any of the above.

This does not exhaust the possibilities of establishing sex on the basis of grave-goods. Grave-finds such as a pair of tweezers and bone gaming-pieces may be considered to be characteristically, though not exclusively, male, but the criteria listed here provide suitably comprehensive reliable evidence for the present purposes.

Of 79 certain grave-finds recorded from Scandinavia containing Class A clasps, 43 are almost certainly female graves and a further 13 probably female - in all just over 70 per cent of the known total of grave-finds. Only two finds can one believe to have come from mens' graves. One of these is the extremely early find in grave 5 at Heiligenhafen, Schleswig-Holstein. This grave included 3 iron arrow heads (Raddatz 1962 pp.97-99). The second is very dubious - a grave-find from Lyse, Høle, Ro, N (22722). The published catalogue of this (in SMÅ 1905) records "Halvdelen af en malje af elektron" (half of an "eye" of electrum), while the card index in the museum records "stykke av hekte av bronse" (piece of a "hook" of bronze), which would appear to refer to a clasp of Class A, but need not necessarily do so. Unfortunately I was unable to locate this object when I visited the museum in March-April 1982. Its grave associations included a single small bronze brooch, 2 beads, and an iron arrow head.

But this leaves over 25 per cent of the recorded
grave-finds for which the sex is indeterminable, a
substantial portion of the material. It is necessary to
attempt to decide how many of these are likely to have been
male or female respectively. If it be the case that the
proportion amongst the indeterminable graves is the same as
amongst the sexed graves, then the narrowest ratio between
female and male finds is 28:1, and at most only one of the
indeterminable graves is even likely to be a male. But
this is not an assumption that can so simply be made. It
is a belief that one commonly meets, particularly amongst
archaeologists in Norway, where the bulk of these grave-
finds come from, that Migration Period female graves are
very much more easily and frequently identified than their
male counterparts, presumably because brooches and other
characteristically female dress-accessories were more
willingly expended under the prevalent burial customs than
were the weapons that would charcaterize men. If this is
the case, and assuming that the respective tallies of male
and female graves from Migration Period Scandinavia ought
to be approximately equal, then it would follow that a
relatively high proportion of otherwise sexually
indeterminable graves, whether containing Class A clasps or
not, were originally male.

One method of estimating approximately how many of the
archaeologically indeterminable graves should be considered
to have been male burials is to quantify the disproportion
between the totals of apparently male and female burials
found, and then redress the balance by assuming an
appropriate number of indeterminable graves to have been
those of the more poorly represented sex.

Childrens' graves, where one might not expect to find
possibly adult dress-accessories such as clasps, present a
theoretical problem in the proportional re-allocation of
indeterminable graves for this purpose. Assume a sample of
100 graves, of which 40 are apparently female, 20
apparently male, and 40 indeterminable. Clearly, of these
remaining 40, about 10 should be female and 30 male. But
if of these 40 indeterminable graves, 12 produce clasps,
can one therefore apportion these in the same ratio: 3 to
the women, 9 to the men ? If it is the case that the 10
remaining female graves were girls too young to wear
clasps, then all 12 should be male. The ratio of child to
adult burials, and the extent of differences between
childrens' and adults' dress, are unknown factors. But, as
we shall see, this problem is very much greater in theory
than in practice here.

Another controlling statistic is the proportion of all
recognized female burials that contain clasps against the
proportion of all recognized male burials that contain
clasps, provided that the total number of either of these
is sufficiently large to be statistically valid. Such

figures are in fact used in the context of Class B clasps, below.

To count and sex all the burials recorded in Migration Period Scandinavia seemed too massive a task. I therefore decided to use that sample of the material represented by the grave-finds recorded in the published catalogues of material in the Historisk Museum, Bergen (nos. B1 - B12199, various publications 1866-1970). This collection includes virtually all the finds from the fylker of Hordaland and Sogn og Fjordane, together with sizeable collections of material from Vest-Agder, Rogaland, and Møre og Romsdal, and a few items from Nordland. These areas of western Norway together form the most productive area of finds in Migration Period Scandinavia. To produce statistics relevant to the study of the use of clasps I decided to count the graves recorded from the late Roman Iron Age and throughout the Migration Period. It is possible that the use of clasps did not reach the area until the Migration Period (see above), but not certain, and early graves involved do not substantially alter the balance of the figures. Counting in these graves allows one to admit graves dated only by pottery types which were current both in the lRIA and Migration Period (i.e. bucket-shaped pots, and pots of type Rygh 361). Adequately dating the relevant womens' graves is no particular problem, but more caution has to be taken wth mens' graves described as belonging to the "ældre Jernalderen" (earlier Iron Age) or "folkevandringstid" (Migration Period), especially in the older published lists. No "Vendel" or "Merovingian" Period is recognized between the Migration and Viking Periods until 1918. In general only those mens' graves are counted which are dated by pottery types such as those referred to above, or possibly dress-accessories such as brooches or clasps, until the weapons can be reliably dated by reference to Fett's Arms in Norway 400-600 A.D. (Fett 1938-40). In certain cases this is probably over-cautious, although where possible doubtful cases were carefully individually assessed.

Such problems leave a certain margin of possible error in the detailed tallies obtained, but the figures are valid as a guide to the relative ease of attributing graves to either sex. Excluding the briefly noted and as yet unpublished cemetery of Kvassheim, Egersund, Ro, slightly less than 400 graves from the period were counted. Of these almost precisely 50 per cent were sexually indeterminable. Remarkably, of the remainder, the numbers of male and female graves recorded were all but equal, about 100 of each. Some regional variation was noted: Sogn og Fjordane produced a relatively high proportion of male graves amongst the determinable burials, just under 60 per cent, a proportion offset by a relatively high number of female graves amongst the fewer finds from Vest-Agder and Rogaland.

Further use of these figures is made later (Class B, below). As regards Class A clasps one clear conclusion can be drawn. The massive majority of finds of these in female graves is not misleading. The only reliable find of a Class A clasp in a man's grave lies at one extreme of the material, both chronologically and geographically. It is possible that apart from this very earliest stage, Class A clasps were only ever worn by women.

The disappearance of skeletal material from so many of the inhumation graves, the disturbance of graves by one means or another, and the frequent lack of detailed plans of the precise placement of these clasps relative to other objects within graves, make the evidence for where upon the dress these fasteners were used rather thinner than one would hope. Nevertheless, in the earliest find, Heiligenhafen g.5, the clasp was under the wrist (Raddatz 1962 loc.cit.), and in the 4th.-century woman's grave from Rosilde, Vindinge, do., Sv, Dk, the clasps were described as being found "ved hofteregion og håndled" (by the hip-region and the wrist). The disposition of the clasps was well preserved and recorded in Hjemsted, Skærbæk, Hvidinge, Tø, Dk g.303, where the woman appears to have had 6 pairs of clasps in a row by either wrist, with her arms crossed over her body when lain in the grave (unpublished grave plan, HM). In the early find from Skåne, Simris g.55, the clasp was found around about the level of the waist (Stjernquist 1955), a feature repeated in several of the Sejlflod graves. The clasps from Stallemo, Øvrebo, VA, N were described as lying "nede ved håndleddene" (down by the wrists: in UOÅ 1943-44, C23141). On such evidence it has been concluded that these clasps are commonly wrist-clasps, fastening the slit in a sleeve of a garment by the wrist (Blindheim 1947 pp. 79-82; Vierck 1978 pp.247-248).

But it may not be assumed that this was the only dress-fastening for which these clasps were employed. The report of the grave-find from Eidsten, Brunlanes, Vf, N (C19231-40; Ab.1898 pp.88-92) indicates that these clasps may have been worn in a row fixing or joining a garment down the buried woman's front, from about the throat to about the waist. The oral report and lack of skeletal material mean that no definite conclusions can be drawn from the evidence, but it would appear that the linear layout of the objects was striking enough to impress the finder, and the detail of the disposition of the cruciform brooches in the grave is a credible one, which increases confidence in the reliability of the report. A warning against too readily identifying clasps found in the waist- or hip-region as probable wrist-clasps is provided by the grave-find from Skaim, Aurland, SFj, N (B8552, BMÅ 1934 H-a.r.2 pp.6-7). Two pairs of Class A clasps were found in such a position in this grave, but there was clear skeletal evidence that the arms of the dead woman, rather than stretching down to her middle, had been bent up away from here, underneath her head. The clasps were therefore interpreted as having belonged to "a purse or something similar".

It is not possible to draw any conclusions about how many joints in the dress were fastened by these clasps on the basis of the numbers of them found in individual graves. More than one pair of clasps could be used to make a single fastening as in Hjemsted g.303 (above). Nor is there good evidence for how many pairs of clasps were normally originally used on a single costume, and whether one can identify any such thing as a standard "set" of "sets" of clasps. The figures for the minimum number of pairs of clasps for which evidence now survives per inhumation grave are as follows:

Minimum number of pairs of clasps			Number of inhumation graves
1	...	...	19
2	...	...	18
3	...	...	2
4	...	...	5
5	...	...	1
6	...	...	2*
7	...	...	1
"several"	...	...	1

* Hjemsted g.303 is included here. 6 pairs of clasps physically survive, but the site notebook indicates that traces of another row of 6 pairs were seen.

Obviously one cannot suppose that the minimum number of clasps evidenced by the recovered material is the same as the number of clasps that originally belonged to the costume or went into the grave. That the highest tally is of graves where evidence for only one pair of clasps survives implies only that these clasps are vulnerable to the effects of time and inadequate methods of recovery and conservation. It is clear from the figures that an even number of pairs of clasps was more usual, which is consistent with the wearing of equal numbers of pairs by either wrist. Occasionally Class A clasps are found in graves with clasps of other classes: graves from Gjermo and Olde, Voss, Ho, N (B7607 and B1352 respectively) contained remains of at least one pair of Class A clasps, but three and two pairs respectively of all classes.

Class B (List 2.1)

Scandinavian clasps of Class B are defined primarily as clasps composed of two metal plates, one forming the hook-piece, the other the catch-piece. The hook-element is usually formed by bending down and backwards a tongue projecting from the metal plate, and the catch- element by

48

cutting a hole or slit of an appropriate size in the second plate. Occasionally, however, the hook- and catch-elements are formed by soldering suitably shaped pieces of metal on to the plates.

Scandinavian Class B clasps are subdivided into 7 forms (forms B 1-7) on the basis of the means by which these two plates are fixed to the garment for which they were fasteners. When the English developments of Class B clasps come to be discussed, certain of the elements used to fix the plates to the garment have to be used as primary criteria for the classification of the clasps concerned as Class B. The Scandinavian range of Class B clasps being less complex, this is not necessary for the present.

Form B 1 – Metal plates riveted to the garment with buttons

By far the most numerous single form of clasp in Scandinavia is form B 1, represented by over 100 finds from Norway, about 185 from Sweden and Gotland, over 25 from Denmark and Bornholm, the majority of which are from the cemetery at Sejlflod, and about 40 from Finland[*]. With this form, the plates are held fast on the underside of the garment by buttons, normally with round, often decorated heads, on shanks which pass through the cloth and holes in the metal plates, to be splayed out on the far side, forming a rivet sandwiching the cloth between the button-head and the plates (cf. Fig.2.1). This technique of fixing the plates to the garment may be supplemented by sewing the plates to the cloth too. A close examination of the clasps from the rich man's grave from Evebø, Gloppen, SFj, N (B4590; personal communication Bente Magnus) has revealed this feature. This practice provides an explanation for the occasional provision of more holes on the plate than there are, or is room for, rivet-buttons.

Of this basic form a great number of variations were produced by varying the size and occasional decoration of the plates, the number, size, and decoration of the buttons, and the materials of which these were made. The size of the clasp-halves ranges from particularly tiny examples, such as that from Roligheden, Hedrum, Vf, N (Fig.2.6), no larger than 7 x 6 mm., at one extreme, to a particularly large example from Veiem, Grong, NT, N (Farbregd 1980 fig.19), whose plate measures ca.8.5 x 1.3cm. at the other. The plate sometimes carries simple decoration in the form of a few incised lines. The

---

[*] The number for Finland is abstracted from two publications: K. Lamm in Helgö IV, and Kivikoski 1973. I have not yet had the opportunity to study these examples fully and so they cannot figure prominently in the following discussion. I understand there are also a small number of examples from Estonia and Latvia (personal communication K. Lamm).

diameter of the round button-heads may be as small as 4 mm.
(e.g. Laland, Klepp, Ro, N S1028), or as large as 2.9 cm.
(Folkare, By, Drn, S SHM 20811). Both buttons and plates
occur made of iron, silver, and bronze, although the latter
alloy is the commonest material. Both silver and bronze
button-heads may be gilded, and on more than one example
(e.g. the smith's grave, Vestly, Time, Ro, N S8635;
Sletten, Vanse, VA, N B4234) a repoussé decorated disc of
gold or silver gilt foil is applied to the head of the
button.

Amongst the most interesting variables between
different clasps of this one basic form are the decorative
shapes and ornamentation of the button-heads. Lamm's study
of the mould-finds from Helgö and comparable material
(Helgö IV pp. 70-131) displays the complexity of variation
that occurs within only a limited portion of the surviving
evidence. Both the heads and the sides of the button-heads
are liable to decoration, which may be cast, stamped, or
applied, and which includes both geometric and linear, and
anthropo- and zoomorphic designs. This is not the place to
pursue a discussion of the range of button types into the
welter of detail which would be possible. But since button
types can be used in a significant number of cases to date
finds in which chronological evidence were otherwise
lacking, this will be touched upon below.

The earliest examples of this form of clasp appear to
be those which occur on the island of Gotland, described by
Almgren and Nerman (Almgren and Nerman 1923 figs.413-415,
561-565; pp.78, 104-105, etc.). The former of these are
placed by these authors in their period V:1 (ca.250-350) on
the basis of associations variously with arrow-heads, a
shield-boss, and belt-fittings. The latter are assigned to
period V:2 (ca.350-400), principally through associations
with belt-fittings. It is noteworthy that the earliest
examples of form B 1, and thereby Class B, are broadly
contemporary with the earliest example of Class A, from
Heiligenhafen, Schleswig-Holstein (above). These early
examples display a considerable variety of form. Almgren
and Nerman's figs.413-414 already show the basically
rectangular plate form which becomes virtually standard in
the Migration Period. The form of plate elongated away
from the hook- and catch-elements, triangular or T-shaped,
as on Almgren and Nerman's figs.415 and 562, is an
interesting variant to which attention is drawn here in
anticipation of the future discussion of other forms and
classes of clasp. But already during period V:2 we can see
a distinct type of tiny clasp becoming common, with very
small hook- and catch-plates, riveted to the cloth with a
single button. Amongst the Gotlandic clasps which Nerman
assigned to the earlier part of the Migration Period, his
period VI:1 (Nerman 1935 figs.211-215), this type of clasp
is virtually the sole representative.

The corpus of form B 1 clasps from Denmark has recently undergone a dramatic and radical change with the excavation of a large number of Migration Period graves at Sejlflod, do., Fleskum, Ål, in North Jutland (Nielsen 1980 pp.83-103, esp. fig.18). While still incomplete, this excavation has increased the total known by 150 per cent. Since this site is still being excavated, it is not possible to provide here the comprehensive and detailed study of the Sejlflod clasp material which that material undoubtedly deserves. One find of especial importance, however, is Sejlflod g.FC, where a pair of the tiny type of clasps just noted from Gotland were found in association with a Haraldsted brooch, and therefore assignable to the later RIA. Two other graves of Sejlflod producing this type of clasp were graves Z and HP, but not with any decisive datable evidence. One find of a larger example of a form B 1 clasp from Englerup Mølle, Sigersted, Ringsted, So may be assigned to the later RIA by its cemetery context (SAM 180-181, personal communication Ulla Lund Hansen). So far as I know there is no evidence as yet from Denmark to challenge the identification of Gotland as the probable origin of the B 1 clasps. The next datable Danish find is from the Ejsbøl Mose deposit (Ørsnes 1964), a hook piece with a single button, and a similar single loose button, in gilt silver with very fine Nydam-style ornament, assignable to VWZ II.

The earliest reliably dated find in Norway is that from Roligheden, Hedrum, Vf, which contained the tiny silver B 1 clasps mentioned above, together with Class A clasps referred to in the previous section, and a silver-sheet brooch (Hougen 1967 fig.66). This find belongs within VWZ I, but not early within the Stufe. A second find to be dated to VWZ I is that from Holmegard, Holum, VA, which contained two early cruciform brooches (Reichstein 1975 no. 76). This find also contained a fragment of what looks like a form B 1 hook-plate, with holes for (at least) 3 button-rivets. Unfortunately the identification of this item as a clasp-piece may only be described as probable, and cannot be certain.

There is a small number of Norwegian finds for which an early date of VWZ I or even the RIA may be or has been proposed, but which tantalizingly lack absolutely solid dating bases. One of these is a grave-find from Ås, Sande, Vf (UOÅ 1956-57 pp.214-216 C29263) where 4 small silver buttons, apparently from the same type of tiny clasps as were found in the Roligheden grave, were found associated with a bronze bow brooch (Fig.2.7) and a pottery beaker with a close parallel in Bøe 1931 fig.142. This type of bronze bow brooch was briefly described by Shetelig (Shetelig 1910 pp.68-70) who pointed out that although the type derives from the later RIA, such forms continue well into the Migration Period. The beaker is of a type which Bøe suggested did not continue "down into the 5th. century". One could scarcely offer a close dating of the

51

grave on the basis of the pot, but there seems to be good reason to regard the Ås find as at least contemporary with the Roligheden find, and possibly earlier.

Comparable to the Ås find is a find from Øvstebø, Sandeid, Ro (S2258) in which 4 pairs of similar type of tiny clasps to those in the Roligheden grave were found in a row still on the textile, to form, in effect, a single dress-fastening, as illustrated in SMÅ 1900 pp.68-69 fig.3. Unfortunately these clasps appear now to be missing in the museum. They were associated with a bronze bow brooch, which, although incomplete, shows substantial similarities to that from the Ås grave-find (Fig.2.8). The find also included a handled-pot of type Rygh 361 which while not providing a close date for the grave, does not contradict a placing of the grave in about the same period as the Ås and Roligheden graves.

A particularly interesting find of buttons apparently from a form B 1 clasp is that from Haug 34 at Nordre Opstad, Tune, Øf (C31074). In this find were the catch-piece of a tiny silver clasp, again as in the Roligheden find, together with two larger, ornamented buttons, partially deformed by the heat of the funeral pyre (Fig.2.9). Other objects in this grave from which a date can be estimated are a number of bronze belt-mounts, and a pot. The belt-mounts have been published and discussed in a different context by Magnus (Magnus 1975 pp.38-40), who referred to Bullinger 1969 to date these Roman-looking belt-mounts to ca.350-410. The pot (UOÅ 1963-64 p.148, figure) is of a distinctive and unusual type for which Magnus accepts Bøe's dating in the second half of the 4th. century. In relative-chronological terms this cremation burial is to be placed in the period 1RIA/VWZ I - the absolute-chronological location of neither the grave nor the border between 1RIA and VWZ I are sure enough to propose the placing of the burial within either one of these phases. However ornamented buttons found in the grave may themselves be used as evidence for a dating of the grave as late as the other grave-goods would allow. They are silver, of 1.5 cm. diameter, and ornamented in relief, with the disc of the button divided into quadrants by a cross, within which quadrants are raised knobs for decoration. Similar, and quite possibly related, buttons have been found in graves from Skreia, Tjølling, Vf (Fig.2.10a) with a developed form of cruciform brooch (Fig.2.10b) to be placed in VWZ III, and Lunde, Vanse, VA (Fig.2.11), with the well-known Nydam-style brooch (Hougen 1967 fig.24) and a cruciform brooch (Reichstein 1975 no.105), belonging to VWZ II-III. There is, of course, no reason why the Opstad clasps should not be substantially earlier than the Skreia and Lunde examples. But to reduce the gap between these developed button-forms and those of Skreia and Lunde as much as possible provides the best possible fit of the Opstad buttons to the whole of the rest of the Scandinavian form B 1 clasp material.

Finds of B 1 clasps dated within VWZ II in Norway are also few. The grave from Lunde, Vanse, VA (B3543, just mentioned) contained besides the clasp buttons already discussed a second type of clasp button, with a stylized human profile head, which may be regarded as executed in the Nydam Style (Rygh 269). Clasp buttons which on minute investigation have proved to be absolutely identical with these (personal communication Bente Magnus) were found amonst what were probably more than one confused burials at Giskegjerde, Giskeøy, MR (B724). A third find apparently to be placed within VWZ II is the grave from Evebø, Gloppen, SFj (VJG pp.111-117). This is dated by the coin of Theodosius II (408-450) and the relief spiral-ornamented scabbard-mount.

It is only with finds dated within VWZ III and VWZ IV that finds of this clasp form become really numerous (Maps 2.4-5). A sufficient number of particular types of clasp button are consistently dated by grave associations to this period as a whole for one to confidently assign other examples of the same type to the same double-_Stufe_, even if associated evidence is lacking. It follows, of course, from Bakka's original division of the Migration Period that clasp buttons decorated in Style I should belong to VWZ III/IV, but it is still relevant to mention that such buttons do indeed produce no embarrassingly inappropriate early material amongst their associated finds, which include a D-bracteate, relief brooches, cruciform brooches, and other forms of small bronze brooch. Another important example of a dated button type is the type illustrated by Rygh, fig.268, a simple type with a plane button decorated with a stamped cross formed of 4 lentoid arms, which occurs both in Norway and Denmark. A less common, closely related variant has a three-armed triskele formed in the same way. Six examples of the former and one of the latter are dated to VWZ III/IV by grave associations with relief or small bronze brooches, while one of the latter, from Olde, Voss, Ho (B1352), is assigned to VWZ III by association with a cruciform brooch. On this basis, it seems reasonable to assign four further examples from Norway and two from Denmark to the broad phase VWZ III/IV. Finds dated thus are included on Map 2.5.

The predominance of the cremation process amongst graves producing remains of B 1 clasps in Sweden and Gotland in the Migration Period means that the general history of this form there in this period has to be inferred as much from circumstantial as from direct evidence. None of the earliest dated examples can be certainly placed as early as VWZ II. Two examples are associated with cruciform brooches which were not listed by Reichstein, but which on the basis of his work belong typologically to VWZ II/III: Raustad, Häggum, Vg (SHM 26214:15c:4/43), and Hillsta, Forsa, Hä (SHM 29500:3:IV). The cruciform brooches from the Raustad find are small, but have relatively broad headplates, short catchplates, and side-knobs cast-in-one with the rest of the brooch. The smaller of the two has full round knobs, the larger half-round. The clasps found in the grave were of much the same tiny type as those mentioned previously from Gotland and southern Norway, although of bronze not silver. Further examples of these tiny clasps occur in Sweden from Åsen, Kolbäck, Vml (SHM 19311) and Fornby, By, Drn (SHM 15468:4). The type itself, however, cannot be taken as evidence of a particularly early date. The type continues in use in Norway long enough to occur in the rich grave of Ommundrød, Hedrum, Vf (Dybsand 1955), to be placed at VWZ II-III. Yet it is impossible to believe that this form appears in Jutland in the RIA and southern Norway at about the beginning of the Migration Period having presumably spread there from Gotland, yet wholly by-passing southern Sweden. One may therefore reasonably hope that examples of B 1 clasps, probably of the tiny type, will eventually be found in the southern landskap of Sweden, well dated by association to the later Roman Iron Age and VWZ I.

In all, a useful relative-chronological date can be put to only slightly less than 40 per cent of Swedish and Gotlandic B 1 clasp finds, the core of which is done by find-association, the remainder by button type. Of 71 datable finds, all but 15 Gotlandic, and the 2 mainland finds described above, can be placed within VWZ III/IV. A number of these are associated with relief brooches, or smaller bronze or late equal-armed brooches. A good number of clasp buttons carry Style I animal ornament, and thus fall within VWZ III/IV. In 9 cases a distinctive domed button type is dated to VWZ III/IV by association either with Style I decorated buttons or other datable grave-goods.

The majority of Swedish form B 1 clasp buttons differ quite markedly from the forms normally met in Norway. The domed type, for instance, is unknown in Norway, and the average size of Swedish domed and Style I decorated buttons is considerably larger than Norwegian Style I buttons. The diameters of the Swedish examples average ca.2.2 cm., while only in exceptional cases do these Norwegian buttons measure as much as 2 cm. across; their average diameter is 1.7 cm. There are some indications that the divergence between Norway and Sweden was greater in the latter half of the Migration Period, VWZ III/IV, when to all appearances B 1 clasps were very much more numerous than in the first half of the Migration Period, although the failure definitely to identify any Swedish B 1 clasps of VWZ II or earlier makes this impression rather difficult to substantiate. Both Norway and Sweden were producing characteristic types in VWZ III/IV, types characteristic of the respective regions as well as the period. The tiny type of clasp of the Gotlandic, Raustad, and Roligheden finds mentioned above, however, which on the whole is relatively early, turns up with little variety of

54

form in Denmark, Norway, Sweden, and Gotland. But the commonest type of B 1 clasp from Sweden and Gotland, accounting for nearly half of all finds, has only plain bronze buttons on a more or less rectangular plate (cf. Nerman 1935 figs.526-535), and is to all practical purposes quite undatable.

The history of form B 1 clasps in Scandinavia may be summed up as follows. The form emerges in the late 3rd. or early 4th. century, and the evidence indicates that Gotland was its place of origin. It emerges at about the same time as Class A clasps first appear. During the 4th. century the form reaches Denmark, and around about the beginning of the Migration Period the form reaches southern Norway. Again, this is broadly the same time that Class A clasps appear there. Other than on Gotland, where no Class A clasps have been recorded, form B 1 seems everywhere to be in a minority in proportion to the numbers of Class A clasps found until VWZ III. From this point, form B 1 begins to dominate all other forms and classes numerically, in all areas except Denmark, where the few datable examples of Class A and form B 1 are almost equal. Examples from Denmark and Bornholm indicate that the development of the form there was largely a shadow of its development in Norway and Sweden, and many of the examples could be imported. In Norway and Sweden there are plenty of finds dated to VWZ IV, the last phase of the Migration Period, which Class A scarcely reaches. The end of form B 1 clasps is one of the features of the whole abrupt cultural change which was the end of the Migration Period.

Form B 2 - Metal plates riveted to the garment with a bar

With this form of clasp the individual buttons which formed the heads of the rivets by which the clasp-plates were fastened to cloth in form B 1 are "replaced" by a metal bar joining two (in practice: theoretically there could be more) rivet shafts. Numerically this is a small group of clasps. I have discovered only 5, possibly 6, examples (Figs.2.12-15). The doubtful example is reconstructable from burnt bronze fragments from grave 40 at Lilla Bjerges, Lau, Gotland (SHM 18703:34). In the case of three of the examples it seems to be particularly reasonable to talk of the bar "replacing" the buttons. On the examples from Sejlflod g.DD (Fig.2.12) and Älby, Ösmo, Sö, S (Fig.2.14) the bar is cast in the form of a row of buttons. The cast roundels beside the more bar-like element on the cast upper "bar" on the example from grave 7 at Kobbeå, Østerlars,. Bornholm (Fig.2.13a) may be interpreted in the same way. The Kobbeå clasps are the only example of this form where the "bar" is soldered on to rivets with flat heads much as the individual buttons of B 1 clasps; on the other finds the rivet shafts are cast-in-one with the bar.

The six possible examples here are quite diverse in appearance, but one further factor besides their essential form giving a degree of coherence to the "group" is their largely East Scandinavian distribution (Map 2.6). Two examples are from mainland Sweden, Jämtland and Södermanland, two or three from the Baltic islands of Gotland and Bornholm, and one from northern Jutland. This strengthens the possiblity of there being some true relationship between the known examples, rather than their each being coincidental, independent modifications of the B 1 form. Where and when the form could first have emerged, though, is difficult to say. Such datable associated grave-goods as there are point late in the Migration Period. The clasps from Brunflo, Jä, were found together with a small equal-armed brooch of this general date (cf. Åberg 1953 figs.69-76). A find from Stora Karlsö, Eksta, Got was placed by Nerman in his period VI:2, broadly the second half of the Migration Period (Nerman 1935 fig.540). Grave 7 from Kobbeå, Bornholm included a spear-head with domed oval bronze mounts (Fig.2.13) with several parallels in East Scandinavian contexts all dated to the Vendel rather than the Migration Period (Kivikoski 1973 p.78, fig.534; Nerman 1969 figs.561, 563, 569-70, 573, 1209, & 1217). The appearance of the Kobbeå clasp in such a late context must be considered a little freakish. The remaining finds do not have any useful datable associations.

Form B 3 – Metal plates fastened to the garment with buttons and a pin

Form B 3 is represented by only one find, but together with form B 4 (below) is of enormous importance for the comparative study of the English and Scandinavian clasp material. Form B 3 arises from a simple and practical modification of form B 1. The lower ends of the shafts of the buttons, instead of being flattened and spread out on the underside of the clasp-plates to form rivets, are formed into small loops, through which a metal rod is passed, thus pinning the plate and buttons and the cloth in between them together (Fig.2.16). The advantage of this is that the clasps can simply be removed from the garment to which they are attached merely by drawing the pin, without doing the irreparable damage to either the clasps or the garment that would be necessary to remove clasps of form B 1. Thus form B 3 clasps can be re-used on more than one costume, or could be removed in order to wash the garment.

The single find of B 3 clasps is the major man's grave from Ugulen, Hafslo, SFj, N (B6071 and 6092; de Lange 1909; Map 2.6). This grave produced four pairs of clasps, two pairs each of two different examples of B 3 clasps. The buttons on one of these (B6071p-q, B6092c) are decorated with Style I ornament; those on the second type (B6071o, B6092b) are plain except for bevelled edges. The

grave must be dated late in the Migration period. Besides
the use of Style I on the buttons, the grave contained a
weapon set which Fett considered partricularly late, and
dated to the second half of the 6th. century (Fett 1938-40
II pp.26-27). This date of Fett's should now be adjusted
into relative-chronological terms as the latter part of the
Migration Period: VWZ III or more probably VWZ IV. The
grave also contained a Buckelurne (de Lange 1909 fig.9),
which does not provide any independent dating evidence in
itself, but does not contradict a later Migration Period
date. The very size of the plates of these clasps also
argues for a late date: on the one type they measure 7.6 x
1.4 cm., on the other 6.5 x 0.9 cm. In very few dated finds
do the whole plates of B 1 clasps survive, so there is no
solid body of statistical evidence, especially after the
tiny type of clasps are discounted as misleading in the
present context. Average sizes have to be taken from
between one and five examples per Stufe, hardly a
satisfactory sample in the former (earlier) cases. For what
it is worth, the average dimensions of the plates of three
complete Norwegian examples of VWZ III are 4.6 x 1.0 cm.,
and of five examples of VWZ IV, 5.0 x 1.1 cm., while the
very few complete examples from earlier contexts are
considerably smaller. The figures imply, but do not prove,
a steady increase in the average dimensions of the plates
of Class B clasps. The Ugulen B 3 clasp-plates are
unusually large. These clasps can be dated to VWZ III/IV,
and more likely to VWZ IV than VWZ III.

Form B 4 - Metal plates fastened to the garment with a bar and a pin

This form of clasp stands formally in the same relationship
to form B 2 as form B 3 does to form B 1, namely instead of
forming a rivet to fasten bar, plate, and cloth together,
the whole assemblage is held together by a removable pin.
Like form B 3, form B 4 is represented by only one find
from western Norway (Map 2.6). Regrettably, it is
represented by only one incomplete example in this find.
The credit for recognizing its probable identity is
Vierck's (Vierck 1966 pp.67-68). The object in question is
from a cremation burial at Lunde, Høyland, Ro (VJG p.23;
Fig.2.17). Unfortunately, since this putative clasp has
been preserved in such a damaged state, presumably as a
result of the cremation process, some doubt must hover over
its identification. This identification is supported by two
points. Firstly it is clear that the bronze bar and iron
plate were bolted together by the same technique used on
the buttons and plates of the B 3 clasps and when the
object was assembled room would be left between bar and
plate for whatever the object was mounted on - the garment
if it were a clasp. Secondly, the Lunde object shows
striking and significant similarities to a form B 4 clasp
from England (cf. Figs.2.18-20). On these grounds, the
identification is accepted here.

Unfortunately the Lunde cremation-find is impossible to date closely. Shetelig, indeed, assigned the grave to the earlier Roman Iron Age on the basis of a similarity he perceived between the "clasp" and a Roman mount from South Shields, England, lacking any more useful dating evidence. The associated objects are a coarse and simple urn, and 6 hemispherical bone gaming pieces with 2 small concavities on the underside. For this assemblage, a Migration Period date can be accepted (Bøe 1931 p.14, and Ch.1 note 15). The affinities of the B 4 clasp to forms B 2 and B 3, both dated relatively late in the Migration Period, could imply that the Lunde clasp should also be considered late. Certainly the technical parallel between this object and the Ugulen B 3 clasps inclines one to presume as small as possible a chronological difference between the two examples. The geographical distance of the B 4 clasp from the B 2 group may suggest, however, that the use of the bar instead of buttons could have been independently developed in western Norway to produce the Lunde clasp. Further discussion of the chronology is postponed until the relevant English forms are discussed.

Form B 5 - Metal plates riveted to the garment with a decorative plate

A solitary find provides form B 5, Sejlflod, Dk g.DY (Fig.2.21). The clasps recovered from this grave show a number of fine and remarkable features. The clasp-plates are of silver and triangular in shape. The upper plate which fixes these to the cloth is also triangular, cast in silver with relief spiral ornament which should perhaps be more accurately described as the Sjörup Style than the Nydam Style (Haseloff 1981 pp.74-79), and gilt. The cast, ornamental character of the upper plates, and their triangular shape, are reminiscent of certain features to be met amongst Scandinavian Class C clasps (below).

Two items of evidence assist in dating these clasps: the art style of the upper plates, and the cruciform brooches the grave contained. The Sjörup Style is a late development of the Nydam Style and more likely to represent VWZ III than VWZ II. The cruciform brooches are not identifiable as any of Reichstein's datable types, but the feature of a plane, squared area on the crest of the bow appears to belong typologically to "späte" forms, again implying a dating in VWZ III.

Form B 6 - A cast form, derived from form B 1, fastened to the garment by sewing

Once again, form B 6 is represented by a single find from western Norway (Map 2.6). This is a grave-find from Lye, Time, Ro (S9510, SMÅ 1969 pp. 95-99). One pair of cast

bronze clasps were found (Fig.2.22). On either half of
these were two roundels, with a raised penannular outer rim
and concave centre part, with a gap in the middle crossed
by a small bar. Around this bar the clasps were sewn to
the cloth, and an amount of textile still adhered to the
hook-piece when the clasps were first found. There can be
little doubt that these roundels are design reproductions
of the buttons of form B 1 clasps. The small gap in the
raised rim of the roundels is reminiscent of a particular
type of "penannular" clasp button. An example of this type
is from the Ommundrød, Hedrum, Vf, N grave (Dybsand 1955
p.13, fig.5).

The dating of the Lye find is something of a puzzle.
The barrow (no.6c) also produced 6 brooches, 4 of bronze
and 2 of iron (Fig.2.22), 10 beads, bronze and iron
fragments, and many potsherds. The finds were haphazardly
scattered on the ground surface underneath the mound, upon
which surface there were also two separate burnt layers.
It seems likely that the objects do not all belong to a
single grave-find. The small square-headed brooch probably
belongs to VWZ III/IV (Shetelig 1910 pp.58-68). The iron
brooches and fragmentary bronze brooches are undatable. But
the barrow also produced two equal-armed brooches with
triangular end-plates. This type is discussed in detail in
Chapter 5, but it is generally considered to be
characteristic of RIA, especially examples with the double
pin-axis like these, although the form does survive into
the Migration Period. The typology of the clasps
themselves may also be taken as broad dating evidence. The
penannular button form, which it is suggested is copied on
the Lye clasps, occurs in three dated graves: Ommundrød,
Hedrum, Vf, N (VWZ II-III); Sejlflod, Dk. g.HT (VWZ III);
and Viken, Lovö, Up, S (VWZ III/IV). Form B 6 is derived
from form B 1, a form which, it has been argued, was not
especially well established in Norway until about the
beginning of VWZ III. Most importantly of all, the sewing
of the clasps to the garment around a bar dividing a hole
on the clasp is also found on a group of Norwegian Class C
clasps, discussed below. As will be seen, these can be
dated around the beginning of VWZ III. A similar date can
be proposed for the B 6 clasp. The discrepancy between
this date and the various apparent brooch dates is not so
great that the early brooches could not have survived in
use for an unusually long time, but the easiest explanation
is that the barrow at Lye covered two separate burials.

Form B 7 - Metal plates sewn to the garment

The minor forms of Class B clasps in Scandinavia are
represented by very few examples compared with over 350
examples of form B 1, and with form B 7 we reach a form of
which there are admittedly no certain examples at all.
Unless it is especially moulded as the B 6 clasp from Lye,
or hypothetically should survive with sufficient textile

still attached, there is no sure way of telling whether a Class B clasp plate with a number of holes in it and found without button or bar rivets was originally sewn to the garment, or fastened by buttons or a bar which have subsequently disappeared. Since the overwhelming majority of B 1 clasps are identified by buttons alone, and frequently no more than fragments of the plates survive (cf. form B 3, above) this uncertainty does not mean that a significant number of the clasps discussed under form B 1 could in fact properly belong under form B 7. One such, however, is the possible clasp-half from Holmegard, Holum, VA, N (C2646-80) discussed under form B 1 as possibly one of the earliest finds of that form in Norway. But given the overwhelming preponderance of form B 1 in Class B amonst Scandinavian clasps, and in the absence of other reasons to believe that these plates were sewn rather than riveted to the cloth, I have counted the Holmegard clasp, and two comparable finds from each of Sweden and Denmark, in with form B 1.

One find, however, that was withheld for description under form B 7 is from a grave at Øvre Haugland, Time, Ro, N (S9341; SMÅ 1967 pp.64-66; Map 2.6). This find produced the remains of at least two pairs of clasps, surviving as silver plates with a hole at either rounded end. No button rivets were recovered from the grave. In part these clasps distinguish themselves from the plates of clasps of B 1-4 by the apparent fine quality of the silver they are made of, although silver plates do occur amongst B 1 clasps, and the rounded ends of the Øvre Haugland plates can be paralleled there too. Amongst the five plates without buttons assigned to B 1 mentioned above, in four cases only the plate of one clasp-half was recovered, and in two of these cases some doubt remains as to whether these fragments really belong to clasps at all. In three cases the plates contained three or more holes, while only two are necessary to sew the clasp firmly to the cloth, and only two are ever found on corresponding sewn English examples of Class B. There is no doubt that the Øvre Haugland clasps are clasps, and in their case fragments of two catch-pieces, and apparently a piece of a hook-piece too, survived without any buttons surviving. The Øvre Haugland clasp-pieces have each only two holes. The case is not proven but the Øvre Haugland find is the most likely case there is of a Scandinavian clasp belonging to form B 7. The only dating evidence there is for this clasp is provided by pots with which it was found. These included two bucket-shaped pots, thickly decorated with stamped ornament including rows of circular beading, one with grooved lines in a rhythmical interlace. These indicate a relatively late date in the Migration Period. Two handled hollow-necked urns in the find with light incised chevron decoration are in complete accord with such a general date.

One final find to be considered under form B 7 for want of a better place to put it is an unusual clasp-half found at the settlement site of Dalshøj, Ibsker, Bornholm (Klindt-Jensen 1957 fig.147.13). This certainly looks like a clasp-half, a rectangular bronze plate, with a tongue bent over as a hook on one long edge, and a long slit, exactly like the catch-element on other examples of Class B clasp, by the other. The clasp could have been sewn to the cloth through the long slit, but it would have been very much simpler just to have sewn it through two holes. There is no parallel for this kind of slit as a means of fastening the clasp to the garment, if that is what it was.

* * * * * * *

Since Scandinavian Class B clasps are dominated by form B 1, and the few examples of minor forms can all be seen as derivative of form B 1, it is appropriate to examine the uses of Class B clasps as a whole, not individually for each form. Class A clasps appeared to have been worn almost exclusively by women, and to have been often, if not exclusively, used to fasten slits in the sleeves by the cuffs. For Class B clasps there is solid evidence for their regular use by both sexes, and in some cases better evidence for their employment in fastening different joints of the costume.

Several mens' graves containing clasps have already figured prominently in the descriptions of the various forms of Class B clasps. The ratio of mens' graves containing clasps to female graves containing clasps, and possible changes in this ratio either in time or by region, are matters of interest whose relevance will become apparent in the course of the comparison of English and Scandinavian clasp traditions. Apart from the earliest finds, those on Gotland assigned by Almgren and Nerman to period V:1, mens' graves containing clasps appear to be consistently in a minority. The Gotlandic graves of period V:1, it will be noted, are broadly contemporary with Heiligenhafen g.5, the only dependable example of a man buried wearing Class A clasps. In Norway the proportion of presumably mens' graves to female containing Class B clasps is 22:46; in Sweden (other than Gotland) 9:33. The numbers of indeterminable graves producing Class B clasps, however, are high - I have recorded 41 from Norway, and 109 from Sweden, thanks to the destructive character of the cremation practice. However it has already been shown, for western Norway at least, that it is not the case that a relatively high proportion of these indeterminable graves may have been men's graves (see above, Class A), and therefore the proportion of men to women wearing Class B clasps in the Migration Period may be fairly estimated as somewhere around 1:2 or 1:3. A further statistic gleaned from the survey of the graves recorded at the Historisk Museum, Bergen, was the proportion of all buried men and the proportion of all buried women who could be shown to have been wearing Class B clasps. For men the figure was slightly over 13 per cent, for woman over 26 per cent.

It is extremely difficult to detect changes in the proportion of men to women wearing Class B clasps over time, because the chronological system established by Bakka is built principally upon material which is characteristic of womens` graves, and it is rare for a man`s grave to contain material that can readily be translated into either Bakka`s relative-chronological terms, or into any other than very broad absolute-chronological terms. A great majority of mens` graves containing Class B clasps are therefore to practical purposes undatable. But it would appear that Class B clasps were worn by men throughout the whole period that Class B clasps were in use at all, and that the higher number of womens` graves producing these clasps cannot be explained either by the clasps going temporarily out of use amongst men, or permanently out of use amongst them earlier than amongst women. All three of the Gotlandic grave-finds assigned by Almgren and Nerman to period V:1 appear to have been mens` graves (Almgren and Nerman 1923 p.78). The early find from N.Opstad, Tune, Øf, N, discussed above, was a man`s grave. Further examples of Class B in mens` graves can be dated to VWZ I, VWZ II, VWZ III, and VWZ III/IV. Amongst the latest examples of the class in mens` graves may be mentioned the grave of Ugulen, Hafslo, SFj, N (see B 3, above), which cannot be certainly dated closer than VWZ III/IV, but has the appearance of falling late within this period. Where other dating evidence is lacking, Fett`s dating of mens` graves according to their weapon sets places a relatively high proportion of such graves also containing clasps in the second half of the Migration Period, the 6th. century as he called it (Fett 1938-40).

A survey of the evidence for where about the dress Class B clasps were used by women provides much the same picture as that which emerged for Class A clasps: convincing evidence for their use to fasten sleeves at the wrists, or possibly a little higher up the arm, and some evidence for their being worn centrally, fastening a garment in front of the upper half of the body. I have come across no new evidence for the use of Class B clasps on the sleeves to add to that of Blindheim (Blindheim 1947 pp.82-84), who provides diagrams of three graves from Hordaland illustrating this. For the employment of a single pair of clasps worn approximately centrally, there is the evidence of two relatively fully recorded graves from western Norway: Hauglum, Leikanger, SFj (B8045, BMÅ. 1929 no.3 pp.21-25) and Eikeland, Time, Ro (S9181, SMÅ 1965 pp.49-51, 59-78). In both graves remains of, or evidence for, only a single pair of clasps was found; both were inhumations, with the grave-goods generally in a good state of preservation. The Hauglum clasps were found "ubetydelig til høire" (fractionally to the right) of the grave`s long axis, about 40 cm. "below" the relief brooch, and 10 cm.

"above" the key-ring which should mark the waist- or belt-line. Myhre's plan of the Eikeland grave shows the recovered clasp to have been found roughly in between objects one would expect to be associated with the belt/waist region - knives and a ring brooch - and objects one would expect to be associated with the breast and shoulders - a pair of small brooches and a relief brooch (Myhre 1965 fig.2). From what one can gather of female costume in the Migration Period, the most likely explanation of single clasps worn thus centrally is as fasteners for a shawl or cape, or to gather the dress under the bosom, supplementary to the de luxe relief brooches (Blindheim 1947 pp.46-62, 78-79; Vierck 1978 pp.245-252).

Of course it is a possibility that even in such apparently well preserved and well excavated graves as these, a second pair of clasps has somehow gone missing. The number of womens' inhumation graves providing sure evidence for only one pair of clasps is higher than that providing evidence for two, or occasionally more, 27 having evidence of one, 16 having evidence of two pairs, but the former include graves from which only a single button has survived, so the chances of loss of full clasp-evidence from a grave must be reckoned significantly high. Womens' graves with evidence for the employment of more than two clasps are scarce. A grave at Nordre Braut, Klepp, Ro, N (S2451) produced two pairs of form B 1 clasps with plain bronze buttons and plates, and four extra buttons of the Rygh 268 form, evidence for a third pair of clasps. There is no record of where about the costume these clasps were situated. A similar state of affairs is found in a grave from Sletten, Vanse, VA, N (B4234), with two pairs of clasps with plain bronze buttons, plus one further plain bronze button of different dimensions to those on the above, and a further unusually large and elaborately ornamented button. The grave of Ommundrød, Hedrum, Vf, N (Dybsand 1955) produced two pairs of one type of B 1 clasp, three pairs of the tiny type of clasp, and two further pairs of Class C clasps, discussed below. The positions of these on the grave-plan unfortunately give no clear signs of where on the costume they were used.

One clear difference in the use of Class B clasps by men is their use by the ankles as well as the wrists, presumably to fasten up slits in the ends of the trouser-legs corresponding to slits by the cuffs of sleeves. One of the earliest Gotlandic finds, an inhumation from Vallstenarum, Vallstena (SHM 6595:17) showed very clearly a row of B 1 clasps along the calf of the leg reaching down to each ankle (Almgren and Nerman 1923 Textfig.124). Three further Swedish/Gotlandic finds illustrate the use of B 1 clasps by men both at the ankles and at the wrists, two graves from Havor, Hablingbo, Got, of Almgren and Nerman's period V:2 (SHM 8064:158, 171; Almgren and Nerman 1923 Textfig.222), and the splendid man's grave from Högom, Selanger, Me (Sundsvall Mus), dated to ca.500 A.D., indicating continuity of the habit from the RIA to the latter half of the Migration Period. A Migration Period Gotlandic man's grave with the clasps at the wrists only is that of Lilla Bjerges, Lau (Nerman 1935 p.14). From Norway possible evidence for two separate sleeved garments both with wrist-clasps is provided by the already mentioned graves of Evebø, Gloppen, SFj, and Ugulen, Hafslo, SFj (Blindheim 1947 pp.20, 84-85).

There are also examples from Norway of men's graves where a single pair of clasps is recorded, approximately centrally placed in front of the body's upper half. A grave at Røkke, Stjørdal, NT (T2566-72) produced one pair of clasps, recorded as lying "ved brystet" (by or on the chest). The smith's grave from Vestly, Time, Ro (S8635) produced the remains of one pair of clasps, which were interpreted as having fastened a belt (Møllerup 1960). There is, however, reason to doubt this suggestion. The Vestly clasp was found on fragments of a brick-woven band of a kind which normally formed the hem of a garment (cf. Blindheim 1947 pp.30-32). The clasp was also found in a very decayed state, and it is easy to believe that a second pair of clasps could have disappeared from the grave. According to their position in the grave, these clasps could as well have been wrist-clasps as belt-clasps.

Statistics of the minimum number of pairs of Class B clasps which can be affirmed for mens' inhumations graves, leaving aside the tiny type of clasps of which a large number are likely to perform the function of one of the more usual types of clasp, are illuminating. The figures for Norway and Sweden are as follows:

Minimum number			Total of graves
1	...	...	9
2	...	...	6
3	...	...	1
4	...	...	5
5	...	...	0
6	...	...	1
7/8	...	...	0
9	...	...	1
10	...	...	1

The high number of graves producing only one clasp may reflect a common use of a single clasp to fasten a garment such as a cape, or a belt, centrally, but probably reflects principally the poor chances of clasps surviving and being recovered. The high figure of 9 is provided by the early grave of Vallstenarum, Vallstena, Got (SHM 6595:17, see above) where all of these clasps were used to fasten slits in the ends of the trouser legs. The 6 pairs of clasps were recovered from the grave at Högom, Selanger, Me, S: 2 pairs of clasps were worn by each of the ankles, and one pair at each wrist. The peak at 4 is striking; presumably these 4 pairs could be used either as wrist-clasps on two separate sleeved garments, as in the Norwegian finds mentioned above, or at the wrists and at the ankles. Unfortunately the three remaining finds with 4 pairs, Veiem, Grong, NT, N (Farbregd 1980), and Viken, Lovö, Up, S graves 1 and 3 (J.P. Lamm 1972 pp.13-24, 30-44) did not show where these clasps had been used. The same applies to the grave that contained at least 3 pairs, Snartemo, Hægebostad, VA, N g.II (Hougen 1935 pp.2-4). It is clear that men regularly wore more pairs of Class B clasps about themselves than women did.

Class C (List 2.1; Map 2.7)

Class C is formed of a relatively small number of decorated cast clasps whose forms cannot be classified under Classes A and B, although they may be derived from them. All of the recorded Class C clasps in fact carry zoomorphic ornament, but I am reluctant to include this feature in the definition of the class, as it would be quite in order for a clasp to turn up with, for instance, Nydam-style spiral ornament, which would be best included under Class C rather than being treated as a class on its own (cf. form B 5, above). Scandinavian Class C has considerable internal coherence, and great significance in the Anglo-Scandinavian context.

Form C 1 - Epsilon-shaped clasps

a)   Denmark

The majority of Scandinavian Class C clasps can be grouped together as form C 1 on the basis of a fundamental epsilon-shaped form. One such example comes from Denmark, from the Høstentorp hoard from Sjælland (Voss 1954 fig.4). On this example the epsilon shape is made up of a broad slightly rounded band, in cast silver, ending in two symmetrically placed animal heads on either side of the catch-element. The epsilon shape in itself recalls the common outline of Class A clasps, and the form of broad, flattish band met on the Høstentorp clasp is also met on one example of Class A in Denmark, from Sejlflod g.FK (above). Consequently, it appears clear that form C 1 is derivative of Class A, a point independently supported by further features of Norwegian examples of form C 1. On the basis of its early Style I animal heads the Høstentorp clasp may be dated early within VWZ III.

b)   A Norwegian Group

A group of Norwegian clasps, which is clearly related to the Danish C 1 form, comprises three finds (List 2.1;

Figs.2.23-24). The epsilon shape made up of two roundels on the Ommundrød example (Dybsand 1955 fig.8), and the ridged moulding of these, persuasively indicates the source of this form in the wire spirals of Class A. The epsilon shape is modified and obscured on the other two representatives of this group, but nevertheless visible. A symmetrical placement of two animal heads on the ends of the epsilon, facing one another across the centre of each clasp-half, is common to these clasps. An obvious common feature is that all have two holes on either clasp-half crossed by a bar around which the clasp is to be sewn to the garment. This technique also occurred on the single representative of form B 6, a cast and plain clasp from Rogaland, assigned to Class B because of its obvious close relationship to form B 1. This relationship warns against too simple a derivation of form C 1 clasps directly from Class A.

Amongst the three clasps of this group, the Gitlevåg and Mellberg examples are obviously much more similar to one another than these two are to the third example (Figs.2.23-24). The Gitlevåg clasp, however, shows a very close relationship indeed to one of the brooches from the Ommundrød find (Dybsand 1955 fig.13). Taking, for instance, any of the three wings on the headplate of this brooch, there is great similarity between the execution of the heads and eyes of the beaked heads on both clasp and brooch, and absolute identity between the eyes or mask-element lying in between these beaked heads in both cases. Such identity suggests the same workshop or workman, and much the same date. One may therefore infer that all three of these examples are quite closely contemporary. The occurrence of a very early exercise in Style I in the animal in the centre of the Ommundrød brooch headplate, amongst other articles showing affinity to the Nydam Style, and therefore datable VWZ II (e.g. Dybsand 1955 fig.12), places the Ommundrød group at VWZ II-III, a date which is not modified by any other evidence for the other examples, and may be accepted for the group as a whole.

c)   A Gotlandic Example

Nygårds, Dalhem, Got   SHM 8409   Nerman 1935 Textfig.195, fig.541

A modified epsilon shape is visible on this object, rather similar to that on the Gitlevåg and Mellberg clasps. One also notes the symmetrical animal heads on the ends of the epsilon, although on this example facing in a different direction than on previously discussed C 1 clasps, and the ridged moulding which recalls wire-spirals. But no particular relationship between this example and any of the Norwegian or Danish examples is apparent. This was a single stray find, but may be dated to VWZ III/IV as it carries Style I animal ornament.

Form C 2 - Two finds from Västergötland

The tally of Class C clasps is completed by two finds from Västergötland (List 2.1; Fig.2.25). These two finds have in common:

a)   an elongated triangular shape, and a very marked curvature when viewed from the side

b)   Style I ornament

c)   their provenance in Västergötland (Map 2.7).

Clasps with triangular plates have already been noted in a a very early example of form B 1 from Gotland (Almgren and Nerman 1923 fig.415), and the single example of form B 5 from Sejlflod, Dk g.DY. Some form of relationship between the Swedish form C 2 clasps and the latter Danish find appears likely, but nothing has been discovered to link these with the early Gotlandic example.

It is unclear how the Swedish form C 2 clasps were fastened to whatever garment they were intended to fix. Neither carries holes or lugs by which they could be sewn; the photographs of the Grumpan examples show no traces of rivets on the underside* (Sutton Hoo 2 fig.395). The undersides of the Djurgårdsäng examples however carry certain traces which may be signs of two rivets per clasp-half which originally held them to the cloth, but it is by no means certain that this is what these marks represent (Fig.2.25). But the form C 2 clasps should not be confused with the B 5 example with its cast decorative upper plate and separate clasp-plates: on form C 2 the hook- and catch-elements are on the cast decorative plates.

The use of Style I ornament on these two examples dates them to VWZ III/IV. Both were from hoard-finds, the deposition of which should be dated within VWZ IV.

* * * * * * * * *

The Ommundrød form C 1 clasps were recovered from a woman's grave, but it is not possible to say where about the dress she was wearing them. Apart from this there is no evidence for any other Class C clasps as to which sex wore them, and where. One may even doubt whether the Grumpan C 2 clasps were necessarily dress-accessories at all.

----

*   I have unfortunately not been able to examine these objects personally.

67

Gusset Plates

To complete this survey of Scandinavian clasps, two very similar objects from western Norway (Map 2.17), which are not clasps themselves but adjuncts to clasps, must be described. These are examples of what is known in English as a gusset plate, a triangular-shaped mount, which, it appears, was fastened to the sleeve above the wrist-clasps, covering the end of the slit in the sleeve which those clasps fastened, and presumably strengthening and protecting it. The close similarity of the two Norwegian examples, from Giskegjerde, Giske, MR and Dalum, Sparbu, NT (Figs.2.26-27) is obvious, and one may therefore assume them to be closely contemporary. The Giskegjerde find does not have reliable associations, but the Dalum find is well dated to VWZ III (Bakka 1973 pp.67-68). Further discussion of these objects is postponed until they can be discussed in conjunction with the English examples.

ENGLAND

Class A

The definition of English Class A clasps is precisely the same as that of the Scandinavian (see above). In all I have recorded 20 finds of Class A clasps in England, 21 including a special form from Market Overton, Leics (List 2.2; Map 2.8).

In certain cases the examples found in England are quite indistinguishable from their Scandinavian counterparts, but amongst others certain noticeably English characteristics appear. The use of bronze wire rather than silver is markedly commoner in England, although Class A clasps of silver remain in a slight majority here. On average the English examples are considerably larger than the Scandinavian ones: the average spiral diameter is about 1.9 cm. in England, produced from spirals whose diameters range from 1.2 > 2.5 cm. (2.75 cm. on the special Market Overton clasps). The number of turns of the wire to form the spirals covers the same range in both areas. One particular English type however has the spiral formed of a single small first turn in the end of the wire, with a considerably larger diameter for subsequent turns, leaving the small first loop standing alone in the open centre of the spiral (e.g. Holywell Row, Sfk g.17, Fig.2.5). Other examples of this type are from Morningthorpe, Nfk g.396, Spong Hill, Nfk g.5, Wakerley, N'hants g.42, and Burrough Hill/Twyford, Leics. On some English examples, as on some Scandinavian, the ends of the wire are decorated by beading (e.g. Beeby, Leics, Leeds 1945 fig.33g). The special Market Overton form mentioned here is a unique form with the ends of the wire in the inner turns of the spiral flattened out and shaped, and decorated by stamps and gilding to form a stylized zoomorphic head (Clough et al. 1975 pl.7b).

Dating evidence for the English Class A clasps in the form of find-associations is reasonably satisfactory, covering one-third of the finds, and showing a nice consistency. The earliest-dated find would appear to be Sleaford, Lincs g.155, where fragmentary, but clearly relatively small Class A clasps were found in association with a cruciform brooch of Reichstein's Typ Stratford (Reichstein 1975 no.826 Taf.93.4-10), one of his "späte" forms, and threfore datable to the last quarter of the 5th. or the first quarter of the 6th century. Holywell Row, Sfk g.79 contained larger clasps associated with a cruciform brooch assigned by Reichstein to his "späteste" phase (Reichstein 1975 no.857 Taf.105); a number of other grave-finds with Class A clasps include cruciform brooches of very similar types and therefore datable within the same phase, broadly the early to middle 6th. century: Little Eriswell, Sfk g.33 (Hutchinson 1966 pl.IIIa), Morningthorpe, Nfk g.396, Beeby, Leics, and Welbeck Hill, Hu g.57. In Wakerley, N'hants g.42 clasps of this class were found with a particularly florid gilt bronze and silver-plated cruciform brooch, which I am inclined to date around the middle of the 6th. century. Three examples of this type with the "loose" central spiral are datable to the early to middle 6th. century, Morningthorpe, Spong Hill, and Wakerley, and one may consequently reasonably assign the two further examples, Holywell Row g.17 and Burrough Hill/Twyford, to the same date.

It would appear that the demise of Class A clasps in England was a consequence of the radical change in dress-style which is regarded as one of the marks of the end of the Migration Period in Anglian England. The dating and significance of these changes are discussed elsewhere in greater detail in the course of this work. It is interesting to note that this class was relatively flourishing in England at a time at which it apparently became extinct in its Scandinavian homeland. A steady increase in the average size of the clasp-spirals was noted in Scandinavia, a trend which would appear to have continued in England. The earliest English examples can probably be dated to the late 5th./early 6th. century, a period when the form was still common in Scandinavia (VWZ III). Besides Sleaford, Lincs g.155, Holywell Row, Sfk g.20 may be pointed out as an early looking specimen (Lethbridge 1931 fig.7B) on the basis of its size and form, although it lacks datable find-associations.

Class A clasps are quite widely and evenly distributed in Anglian England (Map 2.8). Some slight surprise may be expressed at the absence of the class amongst finds recorded from Cambridgeshire, and its scarcity in Northamptonshire. But the class could not be regarded as especially common anywhere, and these <u>lacunae</u> could as well be attributed to the chance nature of recovery as to regional variation.

It is generally accepted that English clasps of all classes were used exclusively by women as wrist-clasps. Accordingly I know of no English grave which produced more than 2 pairs of Class A clasps. Detailed evidence of the function of all clasps in England will be assembled and discussed later.

Class B

For Scandinavia, Class B was defined as clasps consisting fundamentally of two metal plates as hook- and catch-plates. The class was subdivided into a number of forms, on the basis principally of the means by which these plates were fastened to the garment, and the elements involved in this. Amongst these elements were buttons and bars, either riveted or pinned together with the plate. Notice was given that the definition of Class B would have to be developed for the classification of the English clasps. Within England, Class B is defined as clasps constructed of any of three basic elements, plates, bars, or buttons, alone, in combination, or in some form derivative of these.

As in Scandinavia, Class B is clearly the best represented class of clasps in England, with over 500 examples, over 90 per cent of the total recorded. But as the above definition of English Class B clasps implies, the class comprises a much more diverse and complex series of forms in England. Vierck divided the clasps of Class B into his groups I-VI, further subdivided into a total of 20 sub-groups (Vierck 1966 pp.62ff.). Leaving aside the problems in using Vierck's work already mentioned, his classification of clasps is unexceptionable in that he generally groups like with like, but his principle of classification was first and foremost his perception of the typological development of the English clasps from the Scandinavian models which he knew of. His classification presumes certain relationships between forms which are questionable or unproven, and a more objective division and ordering of the material is desirable. The contrastive features between clasps he used are variously and unsystematically their elements of composition, means of fixing to the garment, and decorative elements, which produces some insignificant divisions of the material (e.g. the permutation of "triangles" and "scallops" in his groups IIIa-c), obscuration of other potentially significant variants between clasps (e.g. between the purely decorative use of the bar on the clasps from Holywell Row, Sfk g.48 (Lethbridge 1931 fig.12.5) and its use as a fundamental element in other clasps of Vierck's group IIb, to which the former is added under his scheme), some puzzling collocations of material (e.g. his groups Va and b), and some unclassifiable clasps. Some important examples and forms do not occur at all in Vierck's study, a fact that is only partially explained by the increase in material available for study since the mid-60s.

In the following classification, the English Class B clasps are divided into 16 forms which represent the various permutations of the three basic elements listed under the definition of Class B, and the different means by which these clasps were fastened to the garment. Since certain of the basic elements occur on some clasps in a purely decorative function (e.g. the bar on form B 13, below), in some cases certain variants in decoration become decisive in differentiating specific forms. Thus form B 13 is not distinguished from form B 7 simply as rectangular plates with applied bars for decoration, but as rectangular plates with all forms of applied decorative items. The ordering of the forms may be subjective rather than controlled by a clearly defined formula; the order is that which seems most appropriate to me: firstly to begin with those forms which also appear in Scandinavia or have the closest Scandinavian counterparts, and then to describe first the simpler and then the more complex permutations of the basic elements. This division has at least the virtue of regularity, although any attempt to create order out of the anarchy of combinations of forms within Class B in England is likely to be misleading. Thus there may be a very close similarity between examples with the features "rectangular plate + bar", be the two soldered together, cast-in-one, or with the bar formed in repoussé, but each belongs to a different form in the following classification. It is intended that this classification should at least provide a clear guide to the range of forms occurring amongst English Class B clasps, and simultaneously take account of the broader Anglo-Scandinavian context to which these clasps belong. Within individual forms some sub-groups and types may be distinguished, either to illustrate further the range of variety of Class B clasps, or to indicate particular relationships between individual examples. Some of forms B 1-7, the forms which appear in Scandinavia, have not been found in England, while forms B 8-20 are developments of Class B as yet only known from England.

Form B 1 - Metal plates riveted to the garment with buttons

English form B 1 is the same as Scandinavian form B 1: rectangular metal plates fastened to the garment by button-rivets. Unlike Scandinavia the form is scarce in England; I have discovered only four certain examples (List 2.2; Figs.2.28-29; Map 2.9). No data providing a significantly close dating of the find-contexts of these examples is available.

All of the English examples have bronze plates, also the commonest material in Scandinavia. Undistinguished plain bronze buttons as found on the three East Anglian examples are also found widely in Scandinavia. The Staxton example is unique, however, in that "decayed enamel" is reported as found on the heads of the buttons. Enamelling does occur on clasps of other classes in England, and with other forms of metalwork, but never on any Scandinavian clasps.

Form B 4 - Metal plates fastened to the garment with a bar and a pin

As in Scandinavia, form B 4 in England consists of clasps where a plate and a bar are fastened together and to the garment by a removable pin, which sits on the underside of the plate when the clasp is assembled. This form is rare in England as it is in Scandinavia, represented by only two possible examples (List 2.2; Fig. 2.18; map 2.9). Both examples consist of T-shaped bronze bars, with similar plain areas and moulded decoration. The Sancton find also includes remains of the iron plates, and the iron pin which fastened these together with the bar. The form of the bar on these English examples differs from the one putative Scandinavian find, from Lunde, Høyland, Ro, N (see Scandinavian form B 4, above, and Fig.2.17), but the combination of a bronze bar, a pin, and iron plates on this and in England corroborates the identification of the Norwegian piece.

The example from Castle Acre, Nfk, is identical in all respects to the T-shaped bronze bar from Sancton, except in that there is no sign of perforation of the projections below this to receive the pin. It is therefore listed here with reservations. It could be an incompleted casting for the making of one of these clasps.

Little useful dating evidence is available for form B 4 in England. Sancton, Hu urn 180/1958 also included the burnt fragments of a small-long brooch with a square-headed headplate (Myres and Southern 1973 fig.25). This probably gives a terminus post quem for the cremation in the later 5th. century, but nothing closer.

Form B 7 - Rectangular plates with simple or no decoration only, sewn to the garment

Form B 7 is by far the commonest form of clasp found in England (List 2.2; Map 2.10). Being so numerous, the number of tiny fragmentary examples of this form is proportionally high too, so one must be cautious in putting an exact total to the individual examples known. Altogether, however, I have recorded about 235 individual examples, which, out of nearly 600 examples of clasps of all forms recorded in England, falls not far short of 40 per cent. The expansion of the definition of this form in England, compared to Scandinavia, requires a little clarification. The term "rectangular" should not be taken too strictly: a number of examples counted here have slightly rounded lines or angles, and a few are more trapezoid than rectangular. The term is used here to differentiate this form from clasps with deliberately shaped, decorative edges. By "simple decoration" is meant repoussé, stamped, or incised decoration executed on the plate itself; this is to be distinguished from clasps with rectangular plates with composite decoration in the form of decorative rivets (cf. form B 8) or applied plates, bars, or tubes, etc. (cf. form B 13, below).

Clasps of form B 7 are invariably of bronze. The major variations within this form are effected by different selections or permutations from the range of surface decoration just specified. The most common form of decoration is in the form of repoussé hemispherical bosses (Fig.2.35); about half the total number of B 7 clasps are decorated with these alone. Add to these the examples where repoussé bosses appear together with stamped decoration (Fig.2.36) and occasionally incised lines, and the total carrying repoussé decoration is about three-quarters of all B 7 clasps. B 7 clasps carrying stamped ornament alone are not particularly common, numbering about 23 examples, and are especially scarce north of the River Witham, with only 2 examples from Humberside (Welbeck Hill g.35, Fig.2.37; Driffield BC44) together with one of unknown provenance in Hull Museum. A combination of repoussé bosses and stamps is more common, occurring on over 50 examples, but again is scarce in the north. Relatively large numbers appear in the cemeteries of Sleaford, Lincs, and Willoughby-on-the-Wolds, Notts, but then only one from Welbeck Hill, Hu g.3, and one from Staxton, N. Yorks. Incised lines occur on only 5 examples. I have recorded over 30 plain, undecorated examples from the whole area covered by B 7 clasps. This figure may be a little too high as in some cases one has only a fragment of a clasp to deal with, in others corrosion may disguise some slight ornamentation, and in others it is possible that soldered decorative additions (belonging to form B 13) have disappeared without trace. But there need be no doubt that the plain variant is a genuine variant of this form. One final distinctive variant to be mentioned is that on which a decorative bar is modelled on the rectangular plate in repoussé. There are examples from Gt. Chesterford, Ex g.124, and Sleaford, Lincs g.124/125 (Fig.2.38). Holywell Row, Sfk g.70 (Lethbridge 1931 fig.18A.4) may be a third example. The paucity of examples of this type indicates it to be an occasional variant or copy of the variants of form B 13 (see below) consisting of a rectangular plate with applied decoration of a separate bar or tube.

A small number of B 7 clasps belong to sufficiently early find-contexts to suggest that the form could have emerged before the end of the 5th. century. One of these clasps was found in Sleaford, Lincs g.155, already described as the earliest-looking grave containing a Class A clasp in England on the basis of the cruciform brooch it contained (Reichstein 1975 no.826). Reichstein also identifies the fragmentary cruciform brooch from Lackford, Sfk urn 50/127, which also contained a somewhat unusual B 7 clasp (Lethbridge 1951 fig.14), as one of his "späte" forms, Typ West Stow Heath (Reichstein 1975 no.861). In Wakerley, N'hants g.1, a form B 7 clasp was associated with three cruciform brooches with close parallels amongst the many brooches of Reichstein's "späte" Typen Stratford and West Stow Heath. Finally, the cruciform brooch found with a form B 7 clasp in Welbeck Hill, Hu g.3 has features in common with both the "späte" Typ Holywell Row and the "späteste" Typ Little Wilbraham. Its headplate is of a form common to these two types. Immediately below the bow it has a plain plate with well-moulded, restrained profile animal-head lappets which are a feature of the earlier type rather than the later. However the contrary is the case with a spreading spatulate nose between the scroll-shape nostrils of the terminal head (cf. Reichstein 1975 pp.43-44). Since "späte" and "späteste" forms are thought to overlap in the first quarter of the 6th. century (see Chapter 1, Chronological Conventions), it might be best to date the brooch to this period.

Finds of form B 7 clasps clearly dated to the 6th. century are very much more plentiful. The majority of these are dated by cruciform brooches, i.e. Little Eriswell, Sfk g.9 (Hutchinson 1966 pl. Ia), Nassington, N'hants gg.28 and 31 (Leeds and Atkinson 1944 pl. XXVI, and XXVII), Little Wilbraham, Cambs g.32 (Neville 1852 pl.7), Sleaford, Lincs gg.143 and 158, and Willoughby-on-the-Wolds, Notts gg.3, 8, 61 (Nottingham Mus). Three are dated by association with square-headed brooches, Little Wilbraham, Cambs g.111 (Neville 1952 pl.2), Wakerley, N'hants g.50 (Plate 3.8), and Londesborough, Hu g.6. A particularly interesting case is that of Sleaford, Lincs g.216. A catch-piece in this grave is decorated with repoussé bosses and an unusual double-spiral stamp (Fig.2.36). The same stamp seems to have been used on an annular brooch in grave 80 at Sleaford, a grave dated to the first half of the 6th. century by a cruciform brooch very similar to Reichstein's Typ Nassington. An especially late date may be suggested for the find in Bergh Apton, Nfk g.7, which included what is argued in the next chapter to be a late example of one of the latest forms of Anglian square-headed brooch (EAA 7 figs.68-69).

Form B 7 clasps in Anglian England, then, appear to have remained in use up until the end of the dress-style to which clasps belonged at the end of the Migration Period. The date of the inception of the form is a little uncertain. Sleaford, Lincs g.155 looks like a 5th.-century grave group, but one could wish for more certain evidence of B 7 clasps in the 5th. century than the other graves noted above provide. One could worry inordinately about whether B 7 clasps came into use shortly before or shortly after 500, but the point is of considerable interest and significance in establishing both the form and the pace of the typological development of clasps in England, an issue that is taken up later.

Form B 8 - <u>Metal plates sewn to the garment, with decorative rivets, derived from form B 1</u>
           (List 2.2; Map 2.9)

Examples of form B 8 are slightly more numerous in England than the form which they appear to be typologically derivative of, form B 1. B 8 is a form in which the clasps consist of metal plates sewn to the cloth, but decorated with rivets which would seem to derive directly from form B 1.

Three miscellaneous examples of form B 8 are those from Glaston, Worlaby, and Staxton (Figs.2.30-31). The Glaston piece is rather enigmatic (Fig.2.30). A row of studs, without the usual rounded heads remaining, has been riveted, welded, or soldered into holes on bronze plates, with room behind for two perforations through which the plate may be sewn. Were it not for the room provided for the perforations by the breadth of the plate, one might suggest that this was originally a clasp of form B 1, with the buttons-heads filed off, and perforations drilled in order to transfer the clasp to a second garment. No close dating evidence is available for any of these examples.

A distinct type of form B 8 clasps is represented by examples from Girton, Cambs g.71 (Hollingworth and O'Reilly 1925 pl.II), Morningthorpe, Nfk g.208 (Fig.2.32), and Sancton, Hu urn 2012 (Fig.2.33). Here decorative rivets with circular heads at either end of the plate are joined by a decorative rivet with a rhomboidal head in between. The best dated of these examples is Morningthorpe g.208, which contained a cruciform brooch corresponding to Reichstein's "späteste" forms, and therefore probably dating the grave within the first half of the 6th. century. Three small-long brooches in Girton g.71 and urn 2012 from Sancton neither confirm nor contradict this broad dating of the form.

Form B 9 - <u>A cast type, derivative of the form B 8</u>

Form B 9 consists of three examples of a type of clasp that is a cast derivative of the distinctive type of form B 8 described immediately above (List 2.2; Fig.2.34; Map 2.9). All of these are of cast bronze, composed of two

discs and a rhombus.   Morningthorpe, Nfk g.48 contained no
useful dating material besides the clasp.   Londesborough,
Hu g.10, however, contained another form of clasp (see
below, form B 20), a cruciform brooch of Åberg's Group IV,
and a small-long brooch. The cruciform brooch is not listed
by Reichstein. It may, however, be broadly assigned to the
later 5th. or first half of the 6th. century. The affinity
of form B 9 with the type of form B 8 found in
Morningthorpe g.208 may suggest that a 6th.-century date is
more probable.

                    * * * * * * * *

     The typological relationship postulated here between
forms B 1, 8, and 9 in England is well supported, if not
actually confirmed, by the congruent distributions of these
forms (Map 2.9), concentrated around Norfolk and the
Humberside area.   It is interesting to note that specific
types, i.e. the ⬭⬭-type of form B 8 and form B 9 occur
in both of these geographically separated foci, implying
some special connection between them. This typological
relationship should be treated with the greatest caution as
dating evidence however.   A formal chronological sequence
B 1 -> B 8 -> B 9 does not of course date all examples of
these forms into three distinct, sequential phases.   A
rather vague dating of examples of forms B 8 and B 9 to the
first half of the 6th. century tells us nothing in any
meaningful detail about the date-range of form B 1 in
England.

Form B 10 - A metal bar fastened to the garment with a pin

This form is represented by a single clasp-half consisting
of a bar which itself is the hook-piece fastened to the
cloth with a pin;   there is no plate. The example is again
from Sancton, Hu (Fig.2.19).   The clasp-half and pin are
bronze.   Intrestingly this hook-piece forms a pair of
clasps with a catch-piece, again consisting of a bar alone,
but to be sewn to the garment through a lug, not pinned to
it (Fig.2.19).   This catch-piece has to be reckoned as a
different form (B 12, see below). No dating evidence
accompanies this find.

Form B 11 - Metal bars sewn directly to the garment

A single example representing this form is from Burgh
Castle, Nfk (List 2.2; Fig.2.20). Here are seen remains of
cast bronze T-shaped bars very similar to those forming the
upper part of the form B 4 clasps, but in this case
modified to form the hook- and catch-pieces in themselves,
not with any separate metal plates to form these.   In the
absence of any other evidence, it is most reasonable to

suppose that these bars were to be sewn direct to the garment, that is by taking the thread around the bars themselves. A distinction is made between bars sewn in this way, and those which have special lugs added to them so that they can be sewn to the cloth (see below, form B 12).

The pair of clasps from Burgh Castle have no closely datable find-context. The similarity of the bar with that of form B 4 implies that form B 11 is chronologically contiguous with that form. Unfortunately no very close dating of form B 4 was possible.

* * * * * * * *

It is striking that forms B 4, 10, and 11 continue the distribution pattern concentrated in the two areas of Norfolk and Humberside which was noted for forms B 1, 8, and 9 (Map 2.9).

Form B 12 - Metal bars sewn to the garment with lugs

Form B 12 comprises clasps formed of metal - invariably bronze - bars, which are cast with lugs by which they can be sewn to a garment, and usually have the elements making them into hook- or catch-pieces cast-in-one with them too. I have recorded 50 clasps belonging to this form altogether (List 2.2; Map 2.11). In consequence, it is helpful to distinguish certain sub-groupings and particular types within the clasps of this form.

Most form B 12 clasps are composed quite simply of a bronze bar, often decoratively divided by two moulded sections separating three plain sections, with two or three open lugs, or occasionally T-shaped spiggots, behind the plain sections for sewing (Figs.2.39-41). In certain cases the bar has no great breadth, and is relatively thick in cross-section (e.g. Glaston, Leics g.9, Fig.2.39), which form, together with the moulded decoration, is strongly reminiscent of the bars of forms B 4 and B 11 (Figs.2.18 & 20). Other bars are to differing degrees markedly broader and flatter (e.g. Driffield, Hu 11, Fig.2.41), a form which is close to that which is described below as a "cast plate/bar" (see below, forms B 19-20). The earliest find-contexts in which these clasps occur are represented by Girton, Cambs g.7 (Fox 1923 pl.XXXIV.1), a grave which included a cruciform brooch which Reichstein identifies as one of his "späte" types (Reichstein 1975 no.782). Little Wilbraham, Cambs g.168 also contained a pair of these clasps, together with a cruciform brooch which Reichstein considers an Einzelform (Reichstein 1975 no.795) and a small-long brooch. Reichstein places this grave amongst his "späte" group, but on the somewhat doubtful basis of the clasps plus the small-long brooch (op.cit. Tab.7).

Other examples found associated with cruciform brooches not listed by Reichstein, but which appear that they could as well belong to his "späte" as his "späteste" group, are Girton, Cambs g.39, and Glaston, Leics g.9. The cruciform brooch probably associated with a pair of clasps from Holdenby, N'hants, with flat profile animal heads attached to the top knob, as lappets, and on the horse's head's nose pieces, should fall within the "späteste" horizon. One notes that these Holdenby clasps are of the form with a broader, flatter bar (Fig.2.40).

A number of form B 12 clasps, however, are distinguished by having a decorative tail or knob in the middle of the back edge of the bar, that is the edge opposite to that on which the hook- or catch-element is. In certain cases the resultant T-shaped clasp is quite reminiscent of the T-shaped bars of forms B 4 and B 11 (Fig.2.43, cf. Figs.2.18 and 20), and a close relationship between the forms may be suggested. In other cases the tail or knob is more prominently shaped (Fig. 2.42), while it may be no different from the attachment lugs on the bar, other than being unperforated (e.g. Icklingham, Sfk g.25, Leeds 1945 fig.32e). Clasps of this particular shape are concentrated in East Anglia (Map 2.11), the furthest afield from there being an example from Fonaby, Lincs (Cook 1981 fig.27.56) with a relatively flat, broad bar, and no particularly close parallels in East Anglia. There is no reason to suppose that the date-range of this sub-group is any different to that of the majority group of B 12 clasps to which it stands so close. An example from Morningthorpe, Nfk g.97 is associated with a cruciform brooch which appears to have its closest parallels in Reichstein's Typ Holywell Row, a "späte" form, while the example from Icklingham g.25, cited above, was found with a cruciform brooch which Reichstein places amongst the "späteste" forms. The example from Linton Heath, Cambs g.30 (Fig.2.42) was associated with a Frankish radiate-head brooch virtually identical to one from Rittersdorf, Kr. Bitburg, West Germany g.15, dated by Böhner to his <u>Stufe</u> III (525-600, Böhner 1958 I p.84). Similar examples collected by Werner (Werner 1935) suggest that the burial should not be dated much after the middle of the 6th. century; it may be placed in Ament's AM II.

There remain a number of distinct but minor types to be noted under form B 12. One of these is represented by three examples from the area of Rutland and southern Lincolnshire. These are:

Glaston, Leics g.2 (Fig.2.44)
(probably) Ruskington, Lincs. Lincoln Mus
Sleaford, Lincs. Spalding Gents' Soc. Mus

These three are very similar indeed, consisting of a bronze bar, silvered in the centre, between two sunken, grooved, gilt rectangles. A cruciform brooch with a florid animal head on the headplate top knob in Glaston g.2 suggests a date in the first half of the 6th. century for this type.

Two similar clasps from Sleaford, Lincs g.116 (Leeds 1945 fig.32h) and West Stow, Sfk (Fig.2.45) may also be considered as variants of the same type. Here are a square at either end of the bar, decorated in relief with a cross with lentoid arms, with a rectangular section of the bar in between, T-shaped attachment-lugs behind the decorated squares, and a decorative "cap" on the top end of the bar. Sleaford g.116 contained a gilt and silver-plated florid cruciform brooch, suggesting a date around the middle of the 6th. century.

One final, rather florid example of form B 12 to be mentioned is Morningthorpe, Nfk g.253 (Fig.2.46). I have found no particularly close parallels to this piece. The grave also contained a cruciform brooch which looks to belong to the early 6th. century.

To sum up the apparent history for form B 12: the most usual forms, the simple type, and that with a decorative tail or knob, seem to occur first in England at the same time as cruciform brooches of Reichstein's "späte" types, and so the earliest examples of the form probably belong to the last quarter of the 5th. century. The form continues in use, however, right up into the middle of the 6th century, and one may suppose that it survived until wrist-clasps became obsolete with the dress-change at the end of the Migration Period. There is reason to believe that there was a tendency to flatten out and broaden the bars of the clasps with time, but no fine chronological distinctions may be based on this observation. The more elaborately decorated, minor types described here may also be considered a later development in the history of the form, although no more closely dated than within the 6th. century. The typological relationship of this form to other forms will be fully discussed later.

Form B 13 - Rectangular plates with applied decoration, sewn to the garment

This form of clasp has already been mentioned in the description of form B 7. The plates of B 13 clasps are much the same as the plates of B 7 clasps, always of bronze, and subject to certain limitations, liable to the same simple surface decoration. But they also carry separate, applied decorative items, usually soldered to the plates, but sometimes fixed with small rivets. Form B 13 is divided into three major and two minor sub-groups according to the form of the applied decoration. These sub-groups are designated B 13 a-e, and are individually discussed below.

a)   With applied bars

The most numerous sub-group of form B 13 is that consisting of rectanglar plates plus applied bars (List 2.2). These bars are generally much the same length as the plate they belong to, flat, with a rectangular cross-section, usually between 1 and 3 mm. thick, and 4 to 8 mm. wide. The bars carry quite a wide range of decoration. Some have two sunken areas of ribbed moulding separating three plain areas, in a form that must be related to the form of bars that is so common amongst B 12 clasps (e.g. Morningthorpe, Nfk g.24 Fig.2.47, cf. Figs.2.39-41). The bars may also carry incised lines, or stamped decoration, and the threefold division of the bar may be retained alongside these forms of decoration (e.g. Nassington, N'hants g.I, Leeds and Atkinson 1944 pl.XXIX.Ib; Churchover, Warwicks Fig.2.48). Faceted bars also occur. A rather interesting example in Morningthorpe, Nfk g.387, which was found in a grave with an annular brooch carrying the same decoration, the two artefact-types presumably belonging to a single suite (Fig.2.49 a-b).

The range of simple decoration of the plates of form B 13 is the same as that of form B 7 - repoussé bosses, stamps, incised lines, or none at all. However the proportions in which these forms of decoration occur are very different. Most common and equally common are variants with either plain plates, or with only stamped decoration on the plates, of which I have recorded about 30 examples each. Once again, however, the appearance of stamped plates is a rarity north of Sleaford, Lincs, and Willoughby-on-the-Wolds, Notts: 2 examples further north in Lincolnshire are from Fonaby, and Welton g.2. B 13 a clasps with repoussé decoration are distinctly few - I have found only 7 examples altogether, one combining bosses and stamps. The decoration of the plates with incised lines is again scarcer still.

The dating of form B 13 a clasps reproduces the same picture and the same major problems as B 7 - that is the problem of establishing how early the earliest examples are. There are four examples with cruciform brooches which could fall into either Reichstein's "späte" or "späteste" periods: Morningthorpe, Nfk gg.96 and 362, Girton, Cambs g.33 (Reichstein 1975 no.784), and Sewerby, Hu g.15. More examples are reliably dated into the 6th. century: Morningthorpe, Nfk g.133, and Staxton, N.Yorks by cruciform brooches, Little Eriswell, Sfk g.28, and Little Wilbraham, Cambs g.40 by square-headed brooches (see Chapter 3), and Bidford-on-Avon, Warwicks g.187 by a bronze "mount", apparently the detached knob of a florid cruciform brooch. It is probable that form B 13 a is entirely contemporary with form B 7.

b)   With applied tubes

A distinctive form is form B 13 b, with a hollow tube, formed of a rolled bronze plate, round in cross-section, put in the place of the bar of form B 13 a (Fig.2.50).   In some cases this tube carries a simple threefold decorative scheme reminiscent of the threefold division of the bars of B 12 and B 13 a (above).   Other examples have plain tubes (e.g. Holdenby, N'hants g.8, Fig.2.51). The latter example displays an unusual feature in that the hook-piece hooks up into the hollow tube of the catch-piece, not down into a slit by the front edge. I have recorded only 7 examples of form B 13 b (List 2.2;   but 8 if Gt. Chesterford, Ex g.66 (Fig.2.61) is included, cf. below, form B 17), and 4 examples of detached tubes being found with no evidence for the shape of the plate they were attached to. Three of the certain examples have plain plates, and four stamp-decorated plates.

The dating situation for B 13 b is again the same as for B 7 and B 13 a.   One find, Morningthorpe, Nfk g.30, contained a pair of cruciform brooches which appear to be most closely related to Reichstein's Typ West Stow Heath, a "späte" type, with half-round headplate side knobs loose on the pin axis, not cast-in-one with the brooch. Three other find-contexts have later-looking cruciform brooches: Sleaford, Lincs g.123, a cruciform brooch looking very similar to Reichstein's Typ Little Wilbraham, a "späteste" type, Morningthorpe, Nfk g.208, and a grave-group from St. John's College Cricket Ground, Cambs.

c)   With applied plates with repoussé decoration
(List 2.2;   Map 2.12)

On form B 13 c the applied decoration is a thin bronze plate carrying various forms of repoussé decoration.   This applied plate is often of the same size as the clasp-plate itself, except for never extending over or around the slit on the catch-piece. In such cases the perforations through which the clasp is sewn to the garment go through both the clasp-plate and the applied plate. In other cases the applied plate lies within the plate, between the perforations and the front edge or catch-plate slit, but I have found no cases where the applied plate is less than 1 cm. broad.

Form B 13 c may be subdivided according to the form of decoration on the applied plates, but on the majority of examples assigned to this form the applied plates are either missing (but evidenced by a broad area where something clearly has been soldered to the clasp-plate), or so corroded that the nature of the decoration is quite indeterminable.   Amongst the remainder, however, are examples with forms of geometric or spiral ornamentation, e.g. Gt. Chesterford, Ex g.135 (Fig.2.52), Islip, N'hants

(Fig.2.53), and animal ornament (though rarely legible), e.g. Wakerley, N'hants g.44/45 (Fig.2.54). The running spirals on the applied plates from Islip, N'hants illustrated here, representing at least 3 pairs of clasps from that site, are very closely paralleled in Wakerley, N'hants gg.49 and 57, and the type may be described as a Northamptonshire Type. Rarely is there room for direct decoration of the clasp-plate itself, although stamps were applied to this plate on an example from Barrington B, Cambs.

Such dating evidence as there is for form B 13 c points consistently well within the 6th. century. Two examples with animal ornament from Wakerley, N'hants gg.50/51 and 80 were associated with a type of square-headed brooch which indicates a date of burial at the earliest in the second quarter of the 6th. century (see Chapter 3). Welbeck Hill, Hu g.14 contained a B 13 c clasp plus an unusual English silver bracteate for which a similar date can be suggested (see Chapter 4). An example with an indeterminable form of ornament was found together with a florid cruciform brooch in Morningthorpe, Nfk g.16. An example with a most unusual form of spiral-decorated embossed applied plate from Nassington, N'hants g.13 (Leeds and Atkinson 1944 pl.XXIXb) was associated with a belt-mount of a distinctive "Kentish" design dating the grave to post-ca.525 (Leeds and Atkinson 1944 pl.XXIV b; Hawkes et al. 1975 pp.78-79, see also Chapter 3). Unfortunately there is no close-dating evidence for examples of the Northamptonshire Type. There are only small-long brooches and a swastika brooch in Wakerley g.57. These associations need imply no earlier date than that indicated by the other evidence.

d)   Special forms

Two examples of clasp with rectangular plates with applied decoration require separate designation as special forms. One of these is a remarkable hook piece from Woodston, Cambs (Plate 2.1). One can only infer the form of the soldered ornament on this plate from the marks this has left behind it, from which it would appear that it was wire rolled into two spirals, obviously reminiscent of Class A clasps. One may speculate that the silver or bronze wire from a broken Class A clasp may have been remounted on a simple rectangular plate rather than disposed of for scrap. There is no detailed dating-evidence for this find.

The second example is one of unknown provenance, probably from Rutland, in Rutland County Museum (Fig.2.55). Here are a pair of rectangular plates, with simple stamped ornament, and three regular, silvery discs on each, quite possibly soldering marks, with bronze staining above them. It is difficult even to guess what this may represent.

Perhaps three round buttons, reminiscent of the rivets of forms B 1 and B 8 ?

e)   With indeterminable applied ornament

For the sake of completeness it should be noted that there are a small number of examples of B 13 clasps where it is impossible to tell whether the applied ornament belongs to B 13 a, b, c, or anything else. The distribution, forms, and dates of these would make no difference whatsoever to the outlines of the forms a - d sketched above if they could be assigned amongst these.

                    * * * * * * * *

See also the postscript to form B 17.

Form B 14 - Rectangular plates with applied decoration, sewn to the garment with lugs

The rectangular plates forming the bodies of the clasps of form B 14 differ from those of forms B 7 and B 13 in that the perforations through which the clasps are to be sewn to the garment are no longer within the rectangle itself, but in two or three lugs on the back edge of the clasp-half, as on the bars of form B 12. This variant in the form of the rectangular plate seems to have a different significance for either of the two sub-groups of form B 14, a and b, described individually below. As in the case of form B 13, these two sub-groups are divided on the basis of the form of decorative items applied to the rectangular plate.

a)   With applied bars

The majority of examples of this form appear much more closely related to form B 12 than to form B 13 a, although the form obviously has something in common with both. I have recorded 5 examples of B 14 a (List 2.2), of which 4 have very much the appearance of examples of B 12, with narrow rectangular plates little wider than the bar itself, the threefold division of the bars by two ribbed areas, and one example, Wangford, Sfk (Fig.2.56), with a decorative tail or knob on the plate, as was noted on certain variants of form B 12 (cf. Figs.2.42-43). The fifth example, Bidford-on-Avon, Warwicks g.103 (Fig.2.57) has a plate which is rather more reminiscent of the proportions of B 13 a clasps. Form B 14 a is significantly different from B 12, however, in that the bar does not form the body of the clasp on these, but is in fact no more than a decorative addition to the plates which form the basis of the clasp. The bar has hardly even any function in strengthening these plates, since the detachment of the bar from the plate on three out of five examples indicates that the join of the plate and bar was the weakest point in the whole assemblage. But the evidence of numbers suggests that while B 12 was in some sense a "normal" form, B 14 a is an occasional variant of it, a copy in a significantly different form, with examples of the former outnumbering the latter by 10:1.

If this relationship between the forms correctly explains the difference in numbers between B 12 and B 14 a, then it must follow that the earliest examples of B 14 a would have been made at least slightly later than the examples of B 12. Otherwise, however, the forms are likely to have been contemporary, and the relationship cannot be used for relative dating purposes. Indeed the one example of B 14 a from a closely-datable find-context, Holywell Row, Sfk g.48, is from a context as early as any distinguishable for form B 12, containing four cruciform broches, all considered by Reichstein to be of "späte" types (Reichstein 1975 no.855). It is interesting to note that the four examples of B 14 a which most closely mirror form B 12 are all from Cambridgeshire and East Anglia.

b) With applied plates with repoussé decoration

Form B 14 b is obviously closely related to form B 13 c, the only difference being the use of attachment-lugs on the clasp-plates (Fig.2.58). The use of these lugs on the back edge of the clasp-plate is clearly an alternative to making the whole clasp broader or the decorative plate narrower, or having to perforate the decorative plate as well as the clasp-plate to sew it to the garment. This may give the clasp the appearance of slightly more graceful or careful work, or very simply save a bit of bronze, but the difference between B 13 c and B 14 b is hardly a major variant. The former is more common than the latter, the respective numbers recorded being 26:12.

The decorative plates are only preserved in any legible form on 2 examples of form B 14 b, but in accordance with the range of form B 13 c, one of these shows animal ornament (Barrington B, Cambs g.82, Fox 1923 pl.XXIX.1), and one linear ornament (Holywell Row, Sfk, Lethbridge 1931 fig.19c). Similarly the dating evidence and distribution of these clasps is entirely congruent with B 13 c (Map 2.12): Barrington B g.82 contained a florid cruciform brooch; two examples from Sleaford, Lincs gg.80 and 233 were found with cruciform brooches (the former already referred to under form B 7) of the first half of the 6th. century.

* * * * * * * * *

See also the postscript to form B 17.

Form B 15 - <u>Rectangular plates with simple or no decoration only, sewn to the garment with lugs</u>

The decoration on the clasps of this form would be defined in the same way as that on the plates of B 7 clasps, except that the two examples classified as B 15 are entirely undecorated. It is difficult to explain why a plate with simple or no decoration only should be provided with projecting lugs for sewing rather than simply be perforated. The forms of the plates of these two examples (List 2.2) are indistinguishable from the forms of plates encountered amongst B 14 b (above), and it is possible that both are examples where soldered-on decorative plates have simply disappeared without trace. One cannot simply assume that this was the case however. Another explanation would be that the clasp-plates were made for B 14 b clasps, but that the decorative plates were simply never added; the clasps would, of course, be perfectly functional despite this. The dating evidence and distribution of these clasps is quite congruent with B 14 b: the pair of square-headed brooches in Little Wilbraham, Cambs g.111 date the grave towards the middle of the 6th. century.

Form B 16 - <u>Plates with a shaped rear edge and simple or no decoration only, sewn to the garment</u>

Form B 16 introduces the third distinguishable variant in the form of the basic clasp-plates of the Anglian English Class B wrist-clasps. The two previously considered have been rectangular plates, and rectangular plates with projecting attachment-lugs on the rear edge. Form B 16 consists of clasp-plates with a shaped rear edge, that is a rear edge that is usually substantially and decoratively indented, producing a row of rounded and/or angular lobes. These unperforated decorative lobes are distinguished from the projecting perforated semi-circular or triangular sewing-lugs which have been described on previous forms. However the perforations through which these plates are sewn to the garment do usually lie quite centrally within two or more of the lobes on the shaped rear edge, which in themselves are therefore much the same as the attachment-lugs on other forms.

I have discovered only 8 examples of form B 16 (List 2.2, Map 2.13). Amongst these however the decorative range is very much the same as that of form B 7. The most common form of decoration is repoussé hemispherical bosses, e.g. Sleaford, Lincs g.154 (Fig.2.59), occurring on four examples, although three of these also carry stamped ornament. In view of the scarcity of stamped ornament on clasp-plates in the north of the wrist-clasp wearing region noted with regard to forms B 7 and B 13, it is interesting to note that one such example is from Caistor or Searby, Lincs (Fig.2.60). Two plain examples are from Fonaby, Lincs gg.1 and 16 (Cook 1981: having seen the items in

Scunthorpe Mus, I believe she is mistaken in her identification of the type in grave 1).

An example from Willoughby-on-the-Wolds, Notts g.3 is dated well within the 6th. century by association with a florid cruciform brooch. No other close-dating evidence exists for this minority form.

Form B 17 – Plates with a shaped rear edge and applied decoration, sewn to the garment

Form B 17 stands in the same relationship to form B 16 as form B 13 to B 7. A difference, however, is that the range of applied decoration added to clasp-plates with a shaped rear edge is more limited than that added to rectangular clasp-plates, and the total number of examples of form B 17 very much fewer than examples of form B 13. One problem concerning forms B 13 and B 17 is the existence of a very small number of examples on which the shaping of the plates' rear edge is so slight that it appears as no more than rilling of the edges of a rectangular plate, and it is difficult to decide whether it is more appropriate to assign the examples in question to form B 13 or form B 17. Such examples are those from Girton, Cambs g.33 and Gt. Chesterford, Ex g.66 (Fig.2.61). Neither makes any significant difference to the distribution, dating, or volume of whichever form it is assigned to, and so they are simply noted as exemplifying the slightly blurred margin between these two forms.

a)   With applied bar

Form B 17 a differs from form B 13 a only in the shaping of the clasp-plate; otherwise the forms of the bar occurring on B 17 a and B 13 a clasps are indistinguishable, and the range of simple decoration occurring on the clasp-plate itself is also the same. I have recorded 14 examples of form B 17 a (List 2.2, Map 2.13), of which 10 have undecorated clasp-plates, and two each have plates decorated with repoussé bosses or stamps respectively.

The date-range of form B 17 a appears also to be the same as B 13 a. The earliest find-contexts, possibly as early as the late 5th. century, are Bergh Apton, Nfk g.5, with a cruciform brooch corresponding fairly closely to Reichstein's "späte" Typen Corbridge, Stratford, and West Stow Heath (EAA 7 fig.66), and possibly what looks like a grave-group from Sleaford, Lincs in Derby Museum (no.399-'32), with a cruciform brooch that could as well belong to the late 5th. as the 6th. century. Finds from more certain 6th.-century contexts are Little Wilbraham, Cambs g.32 (Neville 1852 pl.7 and 12), and Sleaford, Lincs g.86, both containing more or less florid cruciform brooches.

b)   With applied tube

There is only one definite example of form B 17 b, from Spong Hill, Nfk g.46 (EAA Spong Hill vol.3, publication forthcoming). A second example which could possibly be assigned to this form is from Gt. Chesterford, Ex g.66, mentioned just above. The examples from Spong Hill were associated with a cruciform brooch which is most reminiscent of Reichstein's Typ Stratford, a "späte" type, and two Anglian equal-armed brooches (See Chapter 5). The clasps could, then, be as early as the late 5th. century.

Postscript

Here, at the end of form B 17, a postscript may be added. There are a substantial number of examples in the museums, and occasionally in the literature, of the applied decorative items involved in forms B 13, 14, and 17 being found alone, with no way of assigning them to any one of these forms, which are distinguished by the form of the basic clasp-plate. These loose items include 16 bars, 4 tubes, and 2 repoussé ornamented plates (List 2.2). None of these would make any significant difference to the dating or distribution patterns of any forms to which they could be added.

Form B 18 -   Bars cast with conjoined knobs, sewn to the garment

It is not particularly easy to find a definition of form B 18 that is both concise and expressive. But the form is nevertheless quite easily recognized and distinguished from all other forms. Form B 18 consists largely of a series of different types formed of a bar with a row of conjoined knobs alongs its rear edge. These types may appear quite closely related to examples of form B 12 where the attachment-lugs take the form of T-shaped lugs or spiggots, not perforated lugs (e.g. Fig.2.43), with the difference that the knobs here are conjoined to form a closed row, not projecting individually from the bar's rear edge. These conjoined knobs can however also take a form which approaches closely to the distinctive cast-in-one plate/bar which is the basis of forms B 19 and 20 (below). One feature of form B 18 is that the types of which it consists are frequently amongst the more splendid examples of English Class B clasps, a class which includes some very humble specimens. This richness expresses itself to the relatively imaginative design of B 18 clasps, which are frequently gilt and sometimes silver-plated, and in certain cases carry cast Style I ornament too.

<u>a</u>)   As form B 18 a I have grouped together four examples where the conjoined knobs have the common form of a triangle with a disc at its apex, i.e. ᴧᴧᴧ (List 2.2).

The ᴧ-motif occurs very widely indeed in many forms of art in Europe around this period; its range is indicated by Salin's discussion (Salin 1904 pp.158-160). The examples from Sleaford, Lincs and Londesborough, Hu g.2 (Fig.2.62) are considered similar enough to be designated the Londesborough-Sleaford Type, each with 6 conjoined knobs of very similar sizes and shapes, and with their rectangular panels containing Style I ornament on the bar. Unfortunately no close-dating evidence is available for either of these. The only one of this form with useful close-dating evidence is the example from the rich grave at Sewerby, Hu g.49, which included a developed florid cruciform brooch, of the type Leeds designated Type C2 in his study of Anglo-Saxon great square-headed brooches (Leeds 1949 nos.140-147). This grave may be dated around the middle of the 6th. century.

<u>b</u>)   Form B 18 b is a type represented by 4, possibly 5 examples (see B 18 c, below; List 2.2; Fig.2.63). This type is formed of a bar, along the rear edge of which are four conjoined roundels, on the outer two of which are two spiggots around which the clasps may be sewn to the garment, although the clasps may also be sewn through the holes between the roundels or knobs. All of these are cast bronze, the examples from Barrington A and Newnham, Cambs also being gilded. The type is restricted to Cambridgeshire and East Anglia (Map 2.14). Some close-dating evidence for the type is provided by Morningthorpe, Nfk g.208, which contained a cruciform brooch which belongs to the first half of the 6th. century.

<u>c</u>)   Form B 18 c is very similar to B 18 b, the difference being the absence of the spiggots, which were noted to be superfluous, on the two outer roundels. It is slightly more common than the above, having 6 or 7 examples (List 2.2; Map 2.14; Figs.2.64-65). Morningthorpe, Nfk g.90 contained only a fragmentary example, of which it is impossible to tell whether it had the spiggots of B 18 b or not. None of these examples is gilded. The piece from Caistor or Searby, Lincs is unusual in having 5 conjoined knobs instead of the normal 4. The slightly cheaper and simpler nature of form B 18 c relative to B 18 b may be taken as evidence that B 18 c is a derivative of B 18 b, a development that took place in East Anglia (witness the Linton Heath, Cambs example), and produced a northern group of these clasps in Lincolnshire and Humberside (Map 2.14). The northern examples are generally broader and flatter than the East Anglian examples of both B 18 b and c.

Form B 18 c probably therefore first appears later than B 18 b, but the two types may still overlap chronologically. The only possible close-dating evidence available for this form is a pair of gilt bronze saucer brooches in Linton Heath, Cambs g.76, decorated with concentric rings of linear and spiral ornament, of which all one can say at present is that they do not contradict a date some way within the 6th. century.

One rather special example to be mentioned under B 18 c is Morningthorpe, Nfk g.20 (Fig.2.66). Here the central bar area, and two rows of conjoined knobs on either side, which appear when a pair of B 18 c clasps are fastened are all represented cast on one hook-piece, and the catch-piece is a tiny undecorated bronze plate, which would almost disappear underneath the hook-piece when the pair is fastened. The example is clearly intended to reproduce the appearance of B 18 c clasps. The grave contained no closer dating evidence.

d) Form B 18 d is in many respects very similar to B 18 c, with the difference that the conjoined knobs are not roundels, but have a much more rectangular outline, giving the clasps a castellated appearance. The type is not common, represented by only two principal examples (List 2.2; Map 2.14; Fig.2.67). Both finds are East Anglian. The example from Westgarth Gardens, Bury St. Edmunds, Sfk was associated with a cruciform brooch which is most similar to Reichstein's "späte" Typen Stratford and West Stow Heath. The grave-group can therefore be dated to the last quarter of the 5th. or the first quarter of the 6th. century

One further example which can be assigned to this form is that from Swaffham, Nfk g.1 (EAA 2 fig.8). The castellated conjoined knobs appear, although without the openwork of the two previous examples, and the dot-in-circle decoration of each of these rectangular knobs links all three examples. Swaffham g.1 produced no further close-dating evidence.

e) Form B 18 e consists of a type of clasps with a prominent central rectangular area on the bar, with simple relief decoration, most often a ladder motif, and with two, lower, plain wings or lappets at either end. Most of the examples of this type have 3 conjoined knobs of triangular shape joined across the apices by a bar (Fig.2.68), or developments of this; in one case, however (St. John's College C.G., Cambs, Leeds 1945 fig.32j),), this element appears as no more than a perforated plate cast with the bar. The bronze clasps may be gilded and silver-plated.

I have recorded 7 examples of form B 18 e (List 2.2; Map 2.15). The examples from Girton, Cambs appear to be associated with a 6th.-century cruciform brooch, and the examples from the unknown find-place in Suffolk may belong to a grave-group with a square-headed brooch (Leeds 1949 no.39) which would date the grave to around the middle or into the second half of the 6th. century. Sleaford, Lincs g.205 contained a cruciform brooch assigned by Reichstein to his undated Typ Girton (Reichstein 1975 no.829).

f) Three finds represent form B 18 f (List 2.2; Map 2.15). Two rather similar examples are those from (probably) Thorpe Malsor, N'hants (Fig.2.69), and Ruskington, Lincs (Fig.2.70a). On these the bar is essentially the same as on form B 18 e, except that on the Ruskington example the uppermost lappet has been elaborated into a right-angled triangle, giving the pair of clasps a more triangular outline, and reminiscent of a pair of clasps with a gusset plate (cf. Scandinavian gusset plates, above, and English gusset plates, below). Behind the bar, however, are four roundels (cf. forms B 18 b & c), and there are three holes through which the clasps can be sewn to the garment on the rear edge between these. Both examples are gilt bronze. The Ruskington example is from a closed grave-find which included a 6th.-century cruciform brooch (Fig.2.70b).

A rather different example which may be included with this form, consisting of a bar, roundels, and open sewing-lugs, is a pair of clasps, again gilt bronze, from Kilham, Hu (VCH Yorks II p.88 fig.8.3).

g) Form B 18 g consists of 6 examples, 5 of which may be grouped as a "Midlands Type" (List 2.2; Map 2.15). On these the major part of the bar (where preserved) is decorated in essentially the same way as that on B 18 e and f clasps, and the row of conjoined knobs has essentially the same form as that on B 18 e, seen especially clearly if the Baginton, Warwicks example of B 18 g (Fig.2.71) is compared with the Sleaford, Lincs g.205 example of B 18 e (Fig.2.68). Pairs of clasps of form B 18 g, Midlands Type, however, have a basically triangular shape, with an en face mask at the apex, a broad base at the opposite end of the bar, and have the ornamental bar over the hook-piece only, the catch-piece being essentially only a row of knobs to balance those on the hook-piece when the clasp is fastened. None of the examples of the Midlands Type is from a known closely-dated context.

The one remaining example of form B 18 g, not of the Midland Type, is, however, accompanied by valuable dating evidence. This is the example from Bergh Apton, Nfk g.64 (EAA 7 pp.41-42, fig.95). These clasps could indeed be regarded as standing almost half-way between forms B 18 e and the Midlands Type; the rectangular form of the bar-plus-knobs section is a feature of the former, while the triangular appendage at the upper end of the bar (though not a mask) and the placing of the ornamental bar on the hook-piece only is a feature of the latter, and the basis on which this example is added to it. This grave also produced a square-headed brooch (EAA 7 fig.94) which dates the grave around the middle or into the second half of the 6th. century.

h) A unique example, designated B 18 h, occurs in 2 pairs of clasps from Icklingham (Leeds 1945 fig.33b). The ribbed bar on these is most reminiscent of forms B 18 b and c, as are the rounded bases on the four conjoined knobs behind this. The attachment-lugs between the conjoined knobs on the rear edge are a feature of B 18 f, while the modelling of the bar on the hook-plate only and the triangular appendage cast-in-one with one of the plates recall form B 18 g. The Icklingham clasps are cast bronze, and without a closely-dated find-context.

Form B 19 - Cast plate/bar (rectangular), sewn to the garment

Up to this point it has been possible to describe the basic part of the English Class B clasps, that is that part which is fastened to the garment and which carries the hook- or catch-element, as either a plate or a bar. The two elements do appear together in forms B 13 a, B 14 a, and B 17 a, but in these cases the essential clasp consists of the plate, and the bar is in fact no more than a decorative embellishment. Under forms B 19 and B 20, a number of clasps are collected which are basically formed of a bar and plate cast-in-one, and cannot therefore be described as consisting essentially of either one of these alone, but are designated as "cast plate/bar".

Form B 19 comprises just three examples of a rectangular cast plate/bar. Two of these, Tuddenham, Sfk, and Morningthorpe, Nfk g.96 (Fig.2.72), are obviously copies of the much more numerous form B 13 a, formed in this different way. They would be mistaken for form B 13 a if not examined carefully. The common threefold division of the bar noted on that form is found on these, and the plates of the Morningthorpe example carry stamped decoration. This grave included a cruciform brooch which indicates a date either in the late 5th. century or first half of the 6th. century.

A more individualistic example of form B 19 is provided by two identical pairs of clasps, one in the Ashmolean Museum marked Barrington A, Cambs (Ashmolean 1909.264g, Leeds 1945 fig.33a), and one in the British Museum attributed to Malton (Barrington), Cambs (BM 76.2-12.40/41). In the absence of better information one suspects that the two examples are from the same grave. These examples have spiral ornament cast in relief in rectangular panels on the bar-section, cast with a plate carrying stamped ornament and perforated for sewing. The clasps are gilt-bronze. The cast rectangular panels of decoration on the bar, and the materials used, indicate that these clasps are closely related to forms B 18 e - g. No further close-dating evidence is available.

Form B 20 - Cast plate/bar with lugs or a shaped rear edge, sewn to the garment

With forms B 14 - 17 it was found appropriate to distinguish between forms where the basic element was a rectangular plate with projecting lugs and forms where the basic element was a plate with a shaped rear edge. In the case of the cast plate/bar clasps, however, a distinction of cast plate/bar with projecting lugs and cast plate/bar with a shaped rear edge is no longer useful or significant as far as the known examples go, and in certain cases would be very difficult to make. Rather than attempt to split the material, all examples which represent either of these types are classified as a single form, B 20. Clasps of form B 20 are quite numerous: in all nearly 50 examples can be counted (List 2.2). Within their basic common form, these clasps display a marked degree of variety. In some cases the forms are very similar to form B 12, as, for instance, Holywell Row, Sfk g.58 (Lethbridge 1931 fig.15.4). Here, behind the bar, is a row of four perforated lugs. The example belongs to form B 20, not B 12, however, because the lugs are conjoined to form an indented plate-section. It is more usual, however, for the plate-section to be rather broader, with a number of unperforated decorative lobes, pointed or rounded, and the clasps in consequence much more similar in appearance to clasps of form B 17 a, e.g. the example from Ixworth, Sfk (Fig.2.73). It is not uncommon for the plate-sections to carry stamped decoration, as also occurs on form B 17 a. In certain other cases where two different forms produce clasps of such similar appearance, e.g. B 12 and B 14 a, and B 13 a and B 19, it has been possible to argue from the relative numbers of these that the latter forms are occasional copies of the former, made in a different technique from that which is "normal". But this cannot properly be done with B 20 and B 17 a. The relative numbers of the really similar examples of each, 38 (B 20) : 13 (B 17 a), show a clear majority of the cast form over the composite, but not of the same overwhelming proportions as in the other two pairs. Typologically, too, it is preferable to see forms B 20 and B 17 a as parallel, but technically different, developments, a point to be considered in more detail later.

The variety of the examples of form B 20 makes sub-classification, based for instance on the rounded and/or pointed lobes on the rear edge as suggested by Vierck 1966, inappropriate. Certain examples may, however, be picked out for special comment. Very similar examples of a distinctive type with rather restrained shaping of the rear edge, which may be called the "Morningthorpe Type", occur in two graves at Morningthorpe, Nfk gg.50 and 351, and in Little Eriswell, Sfk g.21 (Hutchinson 1966 fig.6a). A highly individualistic example belonging to this form is that from Barrington B, Cambs g.75 (Leeds 1945 fig.33c), with a bar containing rectangular panels (cf. Barrington A, Cambs, form B 19), in this case with Style I ornament, and a triangular cap, like a gusset plate, attached to the upper end of the hook-plate. This grave also contained a pair of applied saucer brooches with a markedly similar form of Style I ornament. Another pair of clasps deserving special mention is that from Kilham, Hu (VCH Yorks II p.88 fig.8.5). Here we have a cast plate/bar with four squared, projecting, perforated lugs, the clasps in consequence having a castellated shape highly reminiscent of form B 18 d, a form which one may well believe provided a model for the Kilham clasps.

The dating evidence for form B 20 reproduces a pattern that has become familiar from various sub-groups of forms B 7, B 13, and B 17. One find which could belong to the late 5th. century is Welbeck Hill, Hu g.64, which contained three cruciform brooches, a matching pair and one odd example. The latter has all the characteristics of Reichstein's "späte" Typen Stratford and West Stow Heath. One could not date the pair from Reichstein's study. The majority of closely-datable finds of form B 20 clasps seem to belong to the 6th. century. On the basis of the cruciform brooches one would assign Holywell Row, Sfk gg.58 and 79 (Lethbridge 1931 figs.15.4 and 16.9; Reichstein 1975 no.857), Little Wilbraham, Cambs g.116 (Neville 1852 pl.8.12), Wakerley, N'hants g.28, and Londesborough, Hu gg.9 and 10 (Swanton 1966 fig.6) to this period. In Welbeck Hill, Hu g.52, a form B 20 clasp was associated with an Anglian silver bracteate, dating the grave towards the middle of the 6th. century at the earliest (see Chapter 4).

Class C

As Scandinavian Class C, Class C in England consists of clasps with relatively elaborate cast ornament, zoomorphic on all recorded examples, whose forms cannot be classified as Classes A or B. While still in a considerable minority relative to Class B, Class C is markedly more numerous in England than in Scandinavia. Class C in England can again be divided into a small number of distinct forms: English form C 1 corresponds to Scandinavian form C 1, but clasps of the southern Swedish form C 2 are unknown in England, while an Anglian English form C 3 would appear to be restricted to England.

Form C 1 - Epsilon-shaped clasps

Clasps of English form C 1 are markedly similar to clasps of Scandinavian form C 1, especially the one Danish and three Norwegian examples. Besides the fundamental epsilon form, a second general similarity shared by most of these are the symmetrical profile animal heads facing into the centre of the pair of clasps. A difference typical of metalwork in the two areas is that almost all the English examples are bronze, all the Scandinavian silver, though in both cases usually gilt.

I have recorded 26 examples of form C 1 in England. Close relationships appear between certain individual examples, and a thorough study of the execution of different sections of the whole composition of these clasps reveals that a number of sub-groups or types can be distinguished, and the material is ordered according to these below. A number of as yet individualistic examples, however, remain outside these. One regrettable effect of this presentation of the material by types is to emphasize differences rather than similarities within the whole form. To correct this, and emphasize the unity of the whole form, one may point to a feature such as the use of different forms of spiral ornament in the animal necks that form the epsilon, a feature which occurs on only 7 recorded examples, but cuts right across the boundaries of the individual types, appearing in 4 of these, but being characteristic of only 2.

The Norwegian Type

Probably the most important single find in the whole English wrist-clasp corpus is a pair of clasps that are a loose find from the cemetery site of Willoughby-on-the-Wolds, Notts (fig.2.74). These clasps are almost identical with the clasps of the Norwegian group of form C 1 clasps from the grave at Ommundrød, Hedrum, Vf (Dybsand 1955 fig.8). The similarities consist of the triple-ridged animal necks, the form of the animal heads (so far as can be seen: the Willoughby-on-the-Wolds examples are, however, extremely worn), the round cover to the hook-element, and the use of the bar across the hole in the middle of either roundel around which the clasps could be sewn to the garment, a unifying feature of the three Norwegian form C 1 examples. Most of the differences are relatively minor: the Ommundrød examples are slightly larger than the Willoughby-on-the-Wolds ones (3.3 cm. long v. 3.1 cm.), and the projecting catch-element on the catch-pieces is not quite the same. More significantly, metallurgical analysis has shown the Willoughby-on-the-Wolds examples to be composed of very base silver, with a high copper content congruent with the predominance of bronze (strictly: copper alloy) as the material of English form C 1 clasps (Appendix 2.1). Analysis of the Ommundrød clasps shows them to have a much higher silver content, and to the eye, the remaining Scandinavian form C 1 clasps appear to have the same standard of purity (Appendix 2.2). The base silver content of the Willoughby-on-the-Wolds pair is entirely consistent with the use of old Roman coin as a scrap silver source in England (personal communication Dr A.M. Pollard).

Were it not for this discrepancy in material, the great similarity between finds from Willoughby-on-the-Wolds and Ommundrød, and the fact that the bar across the hole is demonstrably a Norwegian feature, would be convincing reasons for viewing the Willoughby-on-the Wolds finds as imports from Norway. Alternative explanations of the parallels are the pursuance of his craft in England by an artisan familiar with these forms in Norway and desiring to reproduce them, or the importation of an intermediary Norwegian example serving as a closely-followed model for the Willoughby-on-the-Wolds pair.

The Willoughby-on-the-Wolds examples have no closely-datable find-context, but the Ommundrød grave is well dated to Norwegian VWZ II-III, ca.475 by the current conventions. The Willoughby-on-the-Wolds clasp ought to have been made about this time too, but the unusually high degree of wear on it implies that it was in use for a long time before coming into the ground. If it was made in Norway, this would mean that its date of import to England could as well be close to 500 as to 475.

The Barrington Type

The most numerous type amongst English C 1 clasps numbers 9 examples, 6 of which are recorded as being from the cemeteries at Barrington, Cambs (e.g. Barrington A, Leeds 1945 fig.33e; Barrington B g.9, Brown III pl.LXXIX.1; Map 2.16). The remaining examples are from Lakenheath, Sfk, St. John's College C.G., Cambs, and Rothwell, N'hants. Characteristic of the type is the flat, usually undecorated area filling the V between the animal necks, and at a lower plane than these. Other common features, though not present on all of these clasps, are T-shaped spiggots as attachment-lugs and relatively simple, doubled-ridged animal necks. The one piece of close-dating evidence for an example of this type is the square-headed brooch from Barrington B g.9 (Leeds 1949 no.108). This is argued in the next chapter to be a relatively early Anglian square-headed brooch, probably manufactured before ca.530. With no signs of any marked difference in age between this and the clasps which accompanied it, they may be dated to about the same time.

The Great Chesterford Type

Four examples represent the Great Chesterford Type, named after the finest example amongst them, a silver piece from Gt. Chesterford, Ex (Plate 2.2). The other examples show a remarkably widespread distribution (List 2.2; Map 2.16). The Bifrons example is one of only three examples of wrist-clasps found south of a line from Gt. Chesterford through Marston St. Lawrence, N'hants to Bidford-on-Avon, Warwicks, the remaining two also being of form C 1, discussed below. Characteristic of this type are the confronted pair of Style I animals on the rear edge of the clasps and the second profile head modelled within the centre of the ring enclosed by the animal necks in the epsilon, and inside the profile heads on these necks.

One might hope that the examples from Londesborough, Hu would be useful for dating purposes through grave-associations, but it seems clear from the publication of this cemetery that the wrist-clasps from graves 6 and 7 have become muddled, and so the exact associations of these examples are uncertain (Swanton 1966 fig.4). However both the square-headed brooch of g.6 and the cruciform brooch of g.7 can be confidently dated to the first half of the 6th. century, which is of some value in the immediate context.

The Saxonbury-Bidford Type

A type which may derive from the above type is represented by two examples (List 2.2; Fig.2.75). Here again is found symmetrical ornament reminiscent of the Gt. Chesterford Type on the rear edge of the clasps, though it is impossible to distinguish any Style I animal features definitely relating these to that type. Both examples have spiral ornament in the animal necks. Neither is closely-datable.

A further example possibly related to these is from Haslingfield, Cambs (Fig.2.76). This has spiral ornament in the necks, and the incomplete remains of symmetrical openwork Style I animal ornament on the rear edge. It too is not closely datable.

The Central Midlands Type

Three examples (List 2.2; Map 2.16; Fig.2.77) represent a Central Midlands Type. Characteristic of these is the profile Style I animal which lies across the rear edge with a foreleg and foot filling the V between the roundels. On the Nassington example only a sunken line representing this limb remains to connect it with this type. No close dating can be offered for any of these examples.

The Mildenhall Type

Enough remains of the burnt and fragmentary form C 1 clasp from Spong Hill, Nfk urn 2007 (EAA 11 fig.140) to indicate that it was practically identical with a pair from Mildenhall, Sfk (Fig.2.78). One notes in particular the elements of the animal head, the spiral projections or lugs on the rear edge of the clasp, and the spiral ornament of the neck. No close dating can be offered here for either of these.

Unique examples

There remain three examples of form C 1 which cannot be grouped with any others within a "type". These are listed in List 2.2, and an example from West Stow, Sfk is shown in Fig.2.79. Again, no close dating can be offered for any of these.

Form C 3

Form C 3 comprises 7 recorded examples of what is clearly a single type of clasp, although minor variations exist between members of the group (List 2.2). Although there is no obvious epsilon-form to these clasps, it is possible that they are derived from the other major Class C form present in Anglian England, form C 1. The placing of the animal heads facing inwards on the outer ends of the front edge of the clasp-halves is a feature common to both. Examples of both forms are usually gilt bronze. An interesting feature on the example from Morningthorpe, Nfk g.353 (Fig.2.80) is the use of red enamel in the button on the hook-element. All the examples are of East Anglian provenance, except for one from Rothwell, N'hants. It is noteworthy that the only example of the Barrington Type of form C 1 found outside Cambridgeshire/East Anglia is also from that site.

Useful dating evidence for two of these finds places them within the 6th. century. Holywell Row, Sfk g.16 (Lethbridge 1931 fig.6.5) contained a cruciform brooch of Reichstein's "späteste" type, Typ Nassington (Reichstein 1975 no.853). Morningthorpe, Nfk g.353 contained a cruciform brooch of the same phase (see Chapter 1, Chronological Conventions).

Class C - Four individualistic examples (List 2.2)

There remain only four examples of Class C clasps from England which do not belong to forms C 1 and C 3. One of these, Morningthorpe, Nfk g.153 (Plate 2.3) in fact shows a considerable degree of affinity with the above forms, in

the style and scale of its animal ornament, and in the
heavy rounded framing of each piece. It is impossible to
put a close date on the broken cruciform brooch these
clasps were associated with. Any time from the late 5th.
or the first half of the 6th. century is possible.

A second example from Morningthorpe to be considered
here is the two pairs of clasps from g.360 (Fig.2.81).
These are gilt bronze. Their T-shaped form, without
attachment-lugs, is most reminiscent of the bars met in
forms B 4 and B 11, but no actual relationship between
these few examples can be demonstrated. This grave
contained no other useful dating evidence; the style of
animal ornament on these does not look especially early,
and a 6th.-century date can be proposed.

A third example to be described is a fine clasp-half
in gilt silver from Empingham I, Leics (Clough et al. 1975
pl.7c). No very close parallels to this piece present
themselves, but there is a degree of similarity between the
Empingham I clasp and the Scandinavian C 1 clasp from
Nygårds, Dalhem, Gotland (Nerman 1935 Taf.51, fig.541)
which is arresting. Both have an animal-mask facing to the
rear in the centre of the clasp-half; both have a
rectangular area by the hook/catch-element with raised,
heavy framing, not gilt, but decorated in niello. These
similarities could be simply coincidence, but they do allow
the possibility that the Empingham I clasp is an import
from Scandinavia, if so probably from southern Sweden or
Gotland. However there is nothing about the composition of
the Empingham I clasp that makes England a particularly
improbable place of manufacture. No contextual close-
dating evidence is available for it.

Gusset Plates

As in Norway, an artefact-type inseparable from a study of
Anglian clasps is the gusset plate, a largely decorative
mount which would have been attached over the closed-end of
the slit in the garment's sleeve which the clasps fastened,
but which may have had some utilitarian function in
protecting this from tear.

I have recorded 11 examples of these detached gusset
plates from England, of which 8 are from Cambridgeshire and
Suffolk, one each from Northamptonshire and Leicestershire,
and one of unknown provenance in the British Museum (List
2.2; Map 2.17). All have an elongated triangular form, and
the majority of them share further particular common
characteristics. These include outward-facing profile
animal heads on the corners of the base of the triangle,
with a curving beak or jaw, which usually forms an open
ring through which the plate could be sewn to the cloth.
The necks of these animals usually curve upwards to meet in

the centre of the plate, leaving a less elongated internal triangular section standing on the base of the plate. A round or square stud, sometimes with lateral wings, stands at the point where they meet (Fig.2.82). The necks are absent on a pair of examples from West Stow, Sfk (Fig.2.83) but the central stud is there. At the apex of the gusset plates of the majority form is an animal mask facing upwards; it takes, however, some imagination to see this on the West Stow examples just cited. Better examples of this form are from Mildenhall, Sfk (Fig.2.82) and Barrington A, Cambs (Leeds 1945, figs.33a and e).

The same description of the basic characteristics of this form could also be applied to the two Norwegian examples of gusset plates (see above), with the exception that the apices of the two Norwegian gusset plates carry two profile animal heads facing down towards the two at the corners of the base, not a single mask facing upwards. Other differences are that the Norwegian examples have an open base, the English a closed one, and that the two Norwegian examples are gilt silver, the English gilt bronze. The style of the profile animal heads at the base corners of the plate also differs between the two areas. Yet what truly draws attention to and emphasizes these differences is the fundamental similiarity of the form of the English and Norwegian examples.

Three English examples differ somewhat from the above, although common elements remain. These are finds from West Stow, Sfk, Rothwell, N'hants (Fig.2.84), and North Luffenham, Leics (Brown III pl.LXXIX.3). Characteristic of these is the absence of excrescent decoration outside the basically triangular lines of the gusset plate, and the filling of the inside of that plate with animal ornament in Style I. On the West Stow and Rothwell examples, however, this Style I ornament again ends in outward-facing profile heads in the lower corners of the triangle, and both of these have an upward-facing mask at the apex. The North Luffenham example may also have had the latter, now mostly broken off.

All but one of the cases where gusset plates can be confidently grouped with particular pairs of clasps involve clasps of form C 1. These are from Lakenheath, Sfk (MAA Cam 99.99), Mildenhall, Sfk (above), West Stow, Sfk (above), Barrington A, Cambs (Leeds 1945 fig.33e), and Barrington B, Cambs g.9 (Brown III pl.LXXIX.1). The clasps represent the Barrington and Mildenhall Types, and one ungrouped example. A fairly early date in the 6th. century was proposed for the assembly in Barrington B g.9 in the discussion of the Barrington Type. The one occasion where gusset plates apparently accompany clasps of another form is another find from Barrington A, Cambs (Leeds 1945 fig.33a), where they are associated with a pair of clasps of form B 19, albeit a special example of that form, as noted in the appropriate plate. With the limitations of

the evidence at present available, a date in the first
quarter of the 6th. century may be suggested for the
appearance of the gusset plate with English clasps. The
Norwegian examples were assigned to late in VWZ III, in
absolute-chronological terms about the same date as that
proposed independently here for the earliest English
examples.

In the course of the description of English Class B
clasps a few examples with cast appendages reminiscent of
gusset plates in their position and outline were mentioned.
Rarely do these have features in common with the separate
gusset plates other than these. An exception are the form
B 20 clasps from Barrington B, Cambs g.75 (Leeds 1945
fig.33c), already with so much in common with the
Barrington A form B 19 clasps just mentioned. The
triangular appendage on these is very similar to the few
separate gusset plates noted above with a smooth outline
and filled with Style I ornament. Otherwise the gusset-
plate-like appendages are of a very much simpler design,
whether in one piece (e.g. Icklingham, Sfk, Leeds 1945
fig.33b), or in two symmetrical halves on either clasp-half
(e.g. Ruskington, Lincs, Fig.2.70a). Usually these occur
with form B 18 clasps, although an example with clasps of
the similar form B 12 comes from West Stow, Sfk (Fig.2.45).
One form of clasps which in itself recalls the pair of
clasps plus gusset plate assemblage is form B 18 g, with a
triangular shape, and an animal mask at the apex. None of
these examples suggests an earlier dating for the gusset
plate than that derived from Barrington B, Cambs g.9. One
example, Bergh Apton, Nfk g.64 (form B 18 g) falls
distinctly late in the Migration Period, and it is
reasonable to suggest that these cast-in-one forms are
derivative of, and possibly successors to, the separate
gusset plates.

DISCUSSION

Three classes of clasps, and a minor adjunct, the
gusset plate, have been identified, whose range is within
an area of Anglian England to the west of the North Sea and
Scandinavia to the east. A summary of the development,
use, and significance of the Anglian English material has
not yet been made, but it seems most useful to place this
within a general review of the history of the artefact-type
as a whole.

The earliest two classes to appear are Clases A and B.
Class A would seem to have first emerged in southern
Scandinavia: Denmark and Skåne. It appears that the
source of Class B clasps can be even more narrowly
localized to the island of Gotland. It is tempting to
regard the initiation of these two separate classes as
being very closely contemporary. The earliest dated

example of Class A (Heiligenhafen, Kr. Oldenburg, Schleswig-Holstein) has been dated between 250 and the early 4th. century, and the earliest examples of Class B to the period 250-350. Several further examples of both classes are dated within the 4th. century (the late Roman Iron Age) and so one might broadly locate their beginnings at ca.300. The use of the two classes is quite similar too: early examples of both were used to fasten cuffs at the wrist, while the frequently more substantial Class B clasps were sometimes used to fasten mens' leggings by the calf or ankle too. The appearance of the two classes in two separate areas can hardly be unconnected and coincidental. Yet we have no evidence for a common source for them both, and if one area had developed the use of clasps slightly earlier than the other and subsequently exported it one would expect influence to be apparent in the form of the clasps too. But there are no known examples of Class A on Gotland, and only two Danish examples of Class B outside of Gotland certainly datable before the Migration Period. The simplest explanation of this enigma is that there are lacunae in the archaeological evidence, leaving us only an incomplete picture. An attempt to trace the origins of the clasps further back in history does not provide much greater illumination. The shirt from the Thorsberger Moor deposit provides evidence for seamed sleeves with open cuffs without wrist-clasps (Blindheim 1947 pp.23, 33-36): an advantage of open cuffs is to facilitate rolling the sleeve up; an advantage of wrist-clasps is to button the cuff close for greater warmth. The appropriate costume must have been available in southern Scandinavia and Gotland by the end of the 3rd. century. Clues as to where the idea of clasps came from may be provided by the clasps interpreted as shoulder-clasps for the brynies in the Thorsberger Moor deposit (Engelhardt 1863 pp.26-31, pl.6.4-6 and 7.8), which may stand somewhere in a line of descent between clasps worn on Roman armour (Russell Robinson 1975 pp.174ff.; Sutton Hoo 2 pp.532-535) and Anglo-Scandinavian Classes A-C. If this is the case, there still remain one or more "missing links".

During the 4th. century the range of Classes A and B is extended, and around about the beginning of the Migration Period they reached Norway. It is not possible to draw any useful picture of their northward advance in mainland Sweden. A major change in the history of the clasps occurs at about the beginning of VWZ III (ca.475). Class C clasps appear, as Class B begins to supplant Class A as the leading class across most, if not the whole, of Scandinavia. Before the end of VWZ III examples of gusset plates are found in a relatively northerly area of the Norwegian west coast. The demise of Class A in Scandinavia may have taken place at about the end of VWZ III; it certainly appears to have preceded the disappearance of clasps altogether, which may be taken as one of the signs of the close of the Migration Period.

It is somewhere in the last quarter of the 5th.
century that clasps of classes established in Scandinavia
suddenly appear in eastern England. All of the earliest
examples of English clasps dated by find-associations were
associated with cruciform brooches of, or corresponding to,
Reichstein's "späte" types, for which an approximate life-
span of ca.475-525 was proposed in the introductory
chapter. Independent support for this date is provided by
the finding of an example of the Norwegian Type of form C 1
at Willoughby-on-the-Wolds, Notts. Its Norwegian
counterpart is in a grave-assemblage dated VWZ II-III, and
therefore the form is likely to have reached England
(however that happened) not very long after ca.475.

It is in the highest degree improbable that these
classes of clasps, developed in Scandinavia, came to
eastern England other than as a result of direct
Scandinavian influence, that is, influence not channelled
via some third, intermediate area. Only two realistic
theoretical alternatives present themselves:

1) channelling of the artefact-type via the non-
Scandinavian Anglian homeland centred in Schleswig-
Holstein (see Chapter 1).

2) channelling of the artefact-type via Jutish Kent and
southern England.

Both of these possibilities are effectively ruled out by
the virtual non-occurrence of clasps in the relevant areas
(cf. Map 2.1). From the neighbourhood of the recognized
Anglian homeland, only a very few examples of Classes A and
B occur, and always on the very borders of that homeland to
the north and west, marginal areas between the Anglian
homelands and Scandinavia where the true homeland of the
clasps clearly lies. These are clasps at the extremes of
their range of use. The single example of a clasp from
what is at present West Germany (Heiligenhafen, Schleswig-
Holstein) was noted as an unusual case in more than one
respect during the discussion of Scandinavian Class A. The
other finds around the edges of the Anglian homeland are
usually from typically Danish, and not from typically
Anglian find-contexts, such as the silver hoard from
Simmersted, Magstrup, Gram, Had, or the inhumation burials
of Hjemsted, Skærbæk, Hvidinge, Tø, and Rosilde, Vindinge
s. & h., Sv (all Class A clasps). Other such finds appear
"out of place" for other reasons: the Ejsbøl Mose deposit
is by its very nature not likely to contain immediately
local material (Ørsnes 1964) and the other example of form
B 1 clasps from the south of Denmark, Galsted in Haderslev
a. (HM 4591-97) looks to contain clasp-buttons of the
typical Norwegian/North Danish cross-decorated types as
Rygh 268. They are from another inhumation burial. Clasps
have not been found in the great continental Anglian
cremation cemeteries, and since they have been recovered
from cremation graves elsewhere in England and Scandinavia,

one cannot simply explain this away through the destructive nature of the cremation rite. The argument for the transference of the clasp-habit to England via the Anglian homelands produces a very flimsy case indeed.

The second alternative, Kent, soon disappears upon consideration. The only clasps found in England south of the Thames have been three examples of form C 1, two of which are types also occurring in Anglian England (the Great Chesterford and Saxonbury-Bidford Types) and all of which have quite sufficient parallels in that area to show that they are all almost certainly imports from there. To complete the case, the examples of the Great Chesterford Type from Bifrons had been re-used as a pair of brooches, and it is possible that the same had been done with the second Bifrons pair. It is not clear what the single clasp-half from Saxonbury, ESx g.13 had been used for, being found "beneath the lower jaw" of the skeleton (Craddock 1979 p.88).

If the clasp-habit were exported from Scandinavia to Anglian England, then some at least of the forms which are common to England and Scandinavia, or on which the parallels between England and Scandinavia are the closest, must be the earliest examples of clasps in England. One must not, however, assume that all parallels between the two areas are the result of Scandinavian influence on England: once the artefact-type had been established in England it would be quite conceivable for new developments here to be re-exported to Scandinavia. The two most common forms in Scandinavia are Class A and form B 1, and these occur in a few examples in England indistinguishable from Scandinavian models. Since the histories of these in Scandinavia stretch back to the beginning of the 4th. century at least, it is clear that these reflect Scandinavian influence on England. Form C 1, too, is quite certainly an example of Scandinavian influence. The example from Willoughby-on-the-Wolds, Notts may be described as a Norwegian type, and not the Ommundrød example as an English type, because of the further examples of the hole + bar for sewing and clasp-half in Norwegian forms B 6 and C 1, and the links between the Gitlevåg C 1 clasp and the Ommundrød brooch. The transference of Class A, form B 1, and form C 1 across the North Sea introduces to England all the basic elements of clasp construction other than the bar, and the pinning-technique of Scandinavian forms B 3 and 4 and forms B 4 and 10 in England, and the gusset plates.

The similarity between the one (probable) example of form B 4 in Scandinavia (Lunde, Høyland, Ro, N) and the one full example of form B 4 from England (Sancton, Hu urn 180/1958) is a striking point of detailed formal congruency between the two areas. Both of these examples had a bronze bar bolted to an iron plate by a removable pin, sandwiching the cloth in between. Other than in this case, there is

little to link English examples with bars to Scandinavian.
The only possible Scandinavian reminiscence of the common
English tripartite division of the bar by moulding is a
form B 2 clasp-half from Stora Karlsö, Eksta, Gotland
(Nerman 1935 fig.540), but the moulding on the bar of this
piece in fact is much less fine work than Nerman's figure
indicates, and is not credible as the source of the English
forms. The broad upper bar on the Scandinavian B 2 clasps
from Kobbeå, Bornholm g.7 (Fig.2.13a) is more arrestingly
reminiscent of the cast plate/bars of English form B 20,
but this similarity is more likely to be a coincidence than
that between Scandinavian and English forms B 4. But it is
not possible to show that the parallelism within form B 4
is the result of Scandinavian influence on England rather
than vice versa. No useful dating can be made of the
Sancton example, and such weak dating evidence as there is
for the Scandinavian examples of form B 2 and 4 indicates
the 6th. century rather than the last quarter of the 5th.
The same uncertainty reigns over the gusset plates. The
marked similarity between the English and Norwegian
examples shows clearly a dependence of one area on the
other, but it is impossible to say for certain in which of
these two areas they were first developed. The best dating
evidence for these items in both areas points to the first
quarter of the 6th. century, later, it seems, than the
beginning of the clasp-habit in England, which perhaps
increases the chances of these representing reverse English
influence on Scandinavia.

The situation is made a little clearer by the
delineation of localized areas through which the
transference of the forms appears to have taken place. The
earliest dated example of Class A in England appears to be
that in Sleaford, Lincs g.155, although it by no means
follows that this is in fact the earliest known English
example. Form B 1 in England, and its derivative forms B 8
and 9, are concentrated in the Humberside and Norfolk
areas, with one example of form B 1 in northern
Cambridgeshire, and two outlying examples of English form
B 8 in Cambridgeshire and Rutland. The scarcity of
Migration Period examples of Class A in Sweden argues
against that area as a source, but otherwise Class A and
form B 1 are so widespread in Scandinavia that no localized
source for the English clasps can be defined. In the case
of form C 1, however, it has been argued that the form of
the Willoughby-on-the-Wolds example can only have come from
Norway. Although the Ommundrød grave is in Vestfold in
south-eastern Norway, the formal parallels to the clasp
make a south-western Norwegian origin for it seem more
likely. The pin-technique of Scandinavian forms B 3 and 4
and English forms B 4 and 10 is also restricted to
Humberside, Norfolk, and western Norway. The single
example of English form B 11, apparently derived from
English form B 4, is again from Norfolk. The gusset plates
link Cambridgeshire and East Anglia with western Norway,
although the two known Norwegian examples are from further

north on the west coast than any of the other parallel
items just mentioned.

One exception to this emergent pattern is the
similarity that was noted between the rather isolated Class
C examples from Empingham I, Leics and Nygårds, Dalhem,
Gotland. Otherwise there is sufficient geographical
consistency in the detailed Anglo-Scandinavian parallels to
support a theory that the clasp-habit came to England from
western Norway. The smallest area in which all the basic
elements occur, the mass transference of which could wholly
explain the forms of clasps occurring in Anglian England,
is the Norwegian coast between Vest-Agder and Møre og
Romsdal. It is quite possible that Class A, form B 1, form
B 4, form C 1, and the gusset plate, were all "exported"
from this area to eastern England in the period ca.475-500.
The close congruency of distribution of English forms B 1,
B 4, and B 8-11 suggests that both forms B 1 and B 4
arrived in the same way. Just as western Norway could be
the localized source of the clasp habit in England, it is
possible that Humberside and/or Norfolk can be identified
as the reception area. This is where English forms B 1,
B 4 and B 8-11 are concentrated. Obviously the forms could
have arrived first in either Humberside or Norfolk and have
been immediately re-exported to the other area. There are
also examples of Class A in these areas which could be very
early, although they are not demonstrably so. The
Willoughby-on-the Wolds Norwegian Type C 1 clasp falls
outside of this area, but this was extremely worn and old
by the time it came into the ground. The dating evidence
as a whole for English clasps makes it clear that even if
Humberside and Norfolk were the areas of initial use, the
clasp-habit rapidly spread into the Midlands and the rest
of East Anglia.

A problem which immediately arises is the divergent
development of clasps in England and Norway. The fact that
Classes A and C proved more popular in England and enjoyed
a longer life, producing certain later developments, is not
particularly problematic. Rather more intriguing is the
great difference between English and Scandinavian Class B,
shown by the fact that form B 1 accounts for over 96 per
cent of Scandinavian Class B clasps, but considerably less
than 1 per cent of English Class B clasps. The difference
also appears in the other 16 forms listed under Class B in
England compared with 7 in Scandinavia. The 16 English
forms all involve various permutations or commutations of
the definitive Class B elements, plate, buttons, and bar,
and could therefore all derive from forms B 1 and 4 from
Norway. If these did reach England ca.475, about the
beginning of VWZ III, then that is the period when, it has
been suggested, a major change in the Scandinavian clasps
took place, subsequent to which Class B (or form B 1)
established itself in a dominant position. The
transference of the clasp-habit to England at a time of
deep change, and before form B 1 had come to dominate in

Scandinavia, provides a remarkably neat explanation of the ability of the English clasp tradition to develop so markedly differently.

Explanations of the internal typological relationship and development of the different forms of English Class B clasps necessarily depend upon a theory explaining the origin in England. The reception of forms B 1 and 4 from Norway would provide the definitive Class B elements of plate, buttons, and bar, and the two techniques of riveting and pinning the basic clasp element to the garment. There is only one certain example of a Class B clasp in Scandinavia only sewn to the garment (form B 6), but the practice of sewing the clasps to the garment was not a particularly English development. It was presumably the normal method of fixing Class A clasps to the garment, although surviving proof of this is rare, one known example being in Sejlflod, Dk g.EQ+ER. Norwegian form C 1 clasps were sewn to the garment, and this form occurs in England. Nevertheless the common practice of sewing clasps composed of Class B elements to the garment is clearly an English development. The simple shift to sewing rather than riveting or pinning explains the development of the sewn bar and sewn plate (forms B 7, and B 11-13) direct from the putative original imported forms B 1 and B 4, and perhaps B 10. Given the ephemeral existence of form B 7 in Scandinavia, the independent development of this form from earlier forms in England and Scandinavia is on present evidence a better interpretation of this parallel between the areas than importation from Scandinavia to England. Theoretically, then, the development of English forms B 7 and B 11-13 could be contemporary. But while forms B 7 and B 13 a and b have overall the same sort of dating associations, there is rather better dating evidence for the existence of form B 12 in the last quarter of the 5th. century. This may simply reflect a greater popularity of this form then, rather than that it preceded forms B 7 and B 13, which do occur in possibly late 5th.-century contexts. The example of form B 14 a from Holywell Row, Sfk g.48 is of great importance in this context. It is clearly intended to reproduce in appearance a form B 12 clasp, and has a context as early as any B 12 example. But technically the basic clasp is formed of the plates, and the bars are only decorative embellishments to these: in this respect it is much more similar to form B 13 a. But it would be nonsensical to postulate a typological sequence B 4/B 10 -> B 12 -> B 14 a -> B 13 a, when B 13 a, by the individual developments involved (sewing the plate to the garment; use of the bar for decoration only) can be derived directly from the model of form B 4.

The earliest examples of clasps sewn to the garment through or around projecting lugs are English forms B 12 and B 14 a. There is no reason why the development in design of decorative lobes in between these functional lugs producing a shaped rear edge should not be simultaneous

106

with the development of the lugs themselves, especially as
the development of the lugs may be partly a matter of
taste, in avoiding the unsightly sewing of the clasp
around or through the body of the clasp itself. Of the
forms involved, B 16, B 17, and B 20, the dating of the
latter two indeed reproduces the picture obtained of B 7
and B 13 a and b.

Typology therefore argues against rather than for
distinctive datings of the majority of different forms of
English Class B clasps, except in that a comparison with
the Scandinavian material suggests that forms B 1, B 4, and
probably B 10 and B 11 too, are especially early amongst
the English material. Other than this, date-ranges have to
be based on the find-contexts of examples of the different
forms. It is possible that forms B 7, B 8, B 12, B 13 a,
B 13 b, B 14 a, B 16, B 17, B 19, and B 20 had all appeared
by the end of the 5th. century, and they were certainly all
present during the first quarter of the 6th. A few forms
remain which one may reasonably confidently restrict to the
6th. century: B 13 c, B 14 b, B 15, and B 18. On the
whole these show rather more elaborate ornamentation and
design than the forms which seem to appear earlier. For
the dating of form B 9 see the description of the form
above.

The use to which clasps were put seems to have been
slightly more restricted in England than Scandinavia. It is
commonly assumed that they were exclusively a female dress-
accessory, and the overwhelming majority of examples with
recorded find-contexts have clearly female grave-
assemblages, e.g. (for England) two or more brooches or
pins, festoons of beads, girdle-hangers, spindle-whorls,
etc. However there remains a sizeable proportion of the
English clasp corpus without any recorded find-context
(over one-third), and perhaps just one grave containing
wrist-clasps which otherwise appears to be male. This is
Morningthorpe, Nfk g.45. It contained a clasp-half, a
shield-boss, 5 beads, 2 knives, an iron buckle, and a pair
of tweezers. There are no distinctive signs of this being
a double or mixed burial recorded in the site notebook.
Nassington, N'hants g.23 was recorded as a male burial with
a wrist-clasp on the basis of a spear-head it contained
(Leeds and Atkinson 1944 p.108), but it also contained a
key, usually a female adjunct, and, given the circumstances
of the retrieval of material from this site, the mixing of
assemblages is not unlikely here. The situation in England
is clearly very different from Norway, where about 13 per
cent of men buried were buried with clasps of Class B.

It appears too that clasps were worn virtually
exclusively at the wrists in England, hence their usual
name here. Sufficient examples may be cited from
Mildenhall, Sfk (Fenton 1888 p.63), Holywell Row, Sfk
gg.16, 17, 46, 48, 83, and 98 (Lethbridge 1931), Bergh
Apton, Nfk gg.21, 37, 42, and 65 (EAA 7), Nassington,

N'hants gg.15, 16, 20, 23, 27B, 28, 35 and I (Leeds and Atkinson 1944), Sleaford, Lincs gg.4, 48, 51, 95, 97, 116, 123, 124/125, 134, 138, 147, 151, 158, 160, 163, 168, 176, 201, 204, 205, 207, 212, 216, 227, and 232 (Thomas 1887), and Sewerby, Hu g.49 (Vierck 1978 Ab.10.5). The point is corroborated by the fact that it is apparently unknown for more than 2 pairs of clasps to occur in a single grave. An interesting example with a substantial amount of textile still adhering has been preserved from Mildenhall, Sfk (Crowfoot 1951). However the placing of wrist-clasps on leather bracelets or cuffs is attested by Thomas at Sleaford (Thoams 1887 p.387) and Lethbridge at Holywell Row (Lethbridge 1931 pp.78-80), although none has been preserved on any example I have seen. Wood has even been reported adhering to clasps from Mildenhall, Sfk (Prigg 1888 p.68), but one wonders whether he was mistaken. Occasionally, of course, wrist-clasps may be re-used as other forms of decoration: the use of a pair as brooches at Bifrons, Kt has already been noted; in Fonaby, Lincs g.43, two pairs of clasps seem to have been strung out and worn as a form of head-dress (Cook 1981 fig.16).

The employment of clasps in England seems to consolidate the prevalent trends in their employment in Scandinavia: while they are a predominantly female item in Scandinavia, they are perhaps exclusively female in England; while they are most commonly worn at the wrists in Scandinavia, they are only worn at the wrists in England. The absence of men wearing clasps is in fact paralleled in Denmark, although with only 15 sexable Danish grave-finds with clasps recorded there is not adequate evidence to especially correlate England and Denmark in this respect. The shift in function between Scandinavia and England could in fact be explained as as divergence parallel to the divergence in development of Class B in the two areas. But there is no evidence of any parallel change of use in Scandinavia in VWZ III/IV concurrent with the significant developments in forms and preferences in England.

The shift in function is of central significance in any attempt to suggest how the clasp-habit could have crossed the North Sea. Essentially one has to weigh up the relative claims of "trade", which can take various forms, and "migration", which also can take various forms. The two are not, of course, mutually exclusive. The use and forms of clasps cannot have crossed the North Sea of their own accord, and the transference of the clasp-habit must involve people crossing the North Sea. Migration, in this context, involves the permanent settlement of people, probably from western Norway, in eastern England, while trade would involve only the movement and temporary presence of people from either area in the other. The clasps can hardly have crossed the North Sea by way of trade in the sense that a Norwegian merchant took a speculative shipment of clasps to eastern England to offer on a market where the items were unknown and could not possibly be in demand. Nor is this a case of the latest Scandinavian fashion sweeping England: the archaeological evidence generally points to considerable conservatism in womens' dress, and marked changes that do occur require special explanations. The adoption of the wearing of clasps in England requires the presence of people familiar with the fashion, and familiar with Scandinavia, Norway in particular. This could be explained as "trade" through hypothetical English "merchants" visiting Norway and learning and appreciating the practice there. This would just be sufficient to explain the parallels that exist between England and Norway, but one may doubt whether so conditional a hypothesis could adequately explain the apparent rapidity and scope of the development and extension of the range of clasps in England in about the last quarter of the 5th. century.

The arrival of Scandinavian migrants in England from about 475 could equally well explain the phenomenon. If aspects of womens' dress such as the use of wrist-clasps do indeed have the ethnic significance that some have argued for (Vierck 1978 pp.285-291) then it may be considered the best explanation. The appearance of the wrist-clasps implies the adoption of a significantly new dress-style in Anglian England, aspects of which are discussed by Vierck (Vierck 1978) in which he alludes to "östenglische-westskandinavische Trachtbeziehungen".

For the moment, however, the subject of consideration is the evidence of the clasps alone. In the assessment of the migration hypothesis the shift of function between Norway and England is a valid objection, but not an overwhelming one. The migration hypothesis nicely supplies us in England with women with a demand for this dress-accessory, and craftsmen to supply it. The minority of men wearing clasps in Norway could disappear almost without trace. The possibility of localizing areas of departure and reception for the putative migrants in western Norway on the one hand and Humberside and Norfolk on the other strengthens the case. Once established in Humberside and Norfolk, the use of wrist-clasps could diffuse in Anglian England by imitation, trade, and the small-scale movement of people that can scarcely be called "migration" in any meaningful sense, but the transfer of the habit across the North Sea cannot have taken place in that way.

Migration therefore is a good, perhaps the best, explanation of the appearance of wrist-clasps in England. It is not a popular explanation of cultural diffusion in current archaeology, but that is of no consequence. The historical significance of the clasp parallels between England and Scandinavia are further considered in a broader context in Chapter 6 of this thesis, after the detailed examination of more artefact-types.

CHAPTER 3

SQUARE-HEADED BROOCHES

A confusing excess of generic terms exists for the brooches with which this chapter is concerned: square-headed brooches, brooches with rectangular headplate, brooches with downward-biting animal heads between bow and foot, Fibeln des nordischen Typs, Fibeln mit barocken Fuss, sølvblekkspenner, and relieffspenner, none of which is entirely comprehensive or satisfactory. The common characteristics of the brooches are principally a headplate, behind which the spring or axis of the pin is fixed, of fundamentally quadrangular form, usually rectangular or trapezoid, separated by a bow from a footplate, covering the catch for the pin, of fundamentally rhomboidal form (Fig.3.1). Although no examples in fact have a truly square headplate, the English term "square-headed brooches" is clear and established enough to be normally used for this type of brooch in England, and the same term may be used for its continental counterparts. In Scandinavian archaeology, however, a distinction between "silver-sheet brooches" (sølvblekkspenner) and "relief brooches" (relieffspenner) is well established, reflecting differences in the surface decoration of the brooches, not in their essential shape. It is confusing to talk of "Scandinavian square-headed brooches" (cf. Hougen 1967) when the other two terms are so well known, and so I propose to continue to refer to Scandinavian silver-sheet and relief brooches here.

The terms "English square-headed brooches", "silver-sheet brooches", and "relief brooches", however, include a few examples of forms other than that defined by shape above, and which are not excluded from the present study. There are a few English examples of hybrids of the square-headed brooch as defined above with the florid cruciform brooch which ought to be included in any corpus of either brooch type. Some examples of both silver-sheet and relief brooches have a headplate and footplate of identical shape, usually rhomboidal, and are therefore symmetrical "equal-armed brooches". These Scandinavian variants are of little direct importance for the present study, which concentrates on those examples with a quadrangular headplate, but are of significance in assessing the history of the brooch-type in Scandinavia.

The major published study of the Anglo-Saxon square-headed brooches is Leeds's major work of 1949, A Corpus of Early Anglo-Saxon Great Square-Headed Brooches. Although of great use, and still of importance, this cannot now be considered an adequate basis of reference for further studies of these brooches. Primary significance in Leeds's classification was given to the presence or absence of the footplate bar, _alias_ the "divided" or "undivided" foot, a judgement which reflected his opinions on the sources and history of these brooches at that time, opinions he later changed without revising the corpus (Leeds 1949 pp.4, 100-115; Leeds 1957). The obvious similarity which is quickly apparent between certain features of brooches of Leeds's Groups A3, A4, and B1, casts doubt on the over-riding importance of this one feature, and Leeds did not argue his case with sufficient rigour to disperse this. Leeds's method of presenting his groupings often appears as one of authoritative pronouncement rather than methodical exposition. This provokes scepticism, and a critical study of Leeds's groupings reveals many parallels between brooches missed, e.g. the headplate upper corners of the Alfriston g.28 and Alveston Manor g.5 brooches (Leeds nos.66 and 116, pp.70-71), and selectivity in the drawing of parallels between brooches, e.g. the placing of the Woodston brooch (Leeds no.88, p.58) with Group B4 because of the triangular foot-plate inner panels and the form of the footplate lobes, which a glance through Leeds's plates shows are found far more widely. There are of course many newer, and a few older, finds to add to the corpus, and, without denigrating Leeds, the time has come for an up-to-date and more methodical survey of the brooches. Any chronology published in the late 1940s requires critical re-appraisal nowadays, and certain major anomalies with current thinking are obvious in Leeds's work: for instance his placement of the non-zoomorphic bichrome-style ornamented Group B1 amongst the earliest Anglian square-headed brooches, and his interpretation of the fish-mount on the Alveston Manor g.5 brooch (no.116) as a christian motif. It is necessary, then, to review the ordering, chronology, and background of these brooches _ab initio_. This is indeed a most appropriate time to attempt this, with such major studies of comparative material as Leigh on the Kentish and Haseloff on the continental square-headed brooches now available (Leigh 1980; Haseloff 1981). On the Scandinavian silver-sheet and relief brooches, Nissen Meyer's monograph (Nissen Meyer 1934) has proved remarkably durable over 50 years. A fresh comprehensive study may now be due, incorporating the lessons of Helgö (see below), but this is too much to attempt to present here. I have, however, included the evidence of as much as possible of the material discovered in Scandinavia in the last 50 years in this study.

A system for the analysis of relief brooches was developed and published in connection with the moulds for such brooches found at Helgö, Central Sweden (Lundström in Helgö IV). This involved the consecutive subdivision of the material according to A-, B-, and C- elements. The A-elements are the headplate, bow, and footplate which one may use to define "the square-headed brooch". The B-elements are various elements which are assembled in the composition of the A-elements. In the following analysis and classification of the Anglo-Saxon square-headed brooches something much the equivalent of the Helgö B-elements is used, namely a limited range of distinct elements or fields of ornament which are likely to occur in the composition of these brooches, e.g. the frame, second panels, upper corners, lower corners, inner panel, top knob, and lower borders of the headplate (Fig.3.1 - this figure also gives the range of compositional elements occurring on the footplates of Anglo-Saxon square-headed brooches). The compositional elements listed here add a number to the Helgö B-element range, and re-name others. The range of compositional elements given here is probably sufficient for the analysis of all the Scandinavian silver-sheet and relief brooches with quadrangular headplates, although this is a task I have not attempted.

To prevent proliferation in the names of the various compositional elements, the significance of some of the terms used is fairly elastic. Under the category "footplate lower borders", for instance, are considered both panels of ornament, as on the brooch from Holywell Row, Sfk g.11 (Leeds no.11), and small excrescent flourishes in the appropriate position, as on the brooch from Little Wilbraham, Cambs g.158 (Leeds no.104). The category "headplate frame" includes simple linear bordering ridges as on a brooch from Londesborough, Hu (Leeds no.59), a frame of masks, as on the brooch from Northampton (Leeds no.77), and certain cases where this frame of masks goes over into panels of ornament, as on the brooches of Leeds's Group B5 (Leeds nos.91-93). This is a pragmatic simplification of the system, and there are no particular pitfalls in the comparison of brooches under these conditions. Ultimately it matters little what an element is called, what matters is its similarity to elements on other brooches, and that a reader should be able to locate quickly what is referred to on a figure of a brooch. But there should be no part of the brooch which is not covered by this analytical system, and the range of B-elements used in the published Helgö analysis is deficient in this respect.

The classification of the Anglo-Saxon square-headed brooches presented here is based upon a quantification of the similarity of form between individual examples with regard to the design of these compositional elements. These elements do not, however, divide simply into two categories of "similar" and "dissimilar". It is easy to spot, for example, one degree of similarity between the headplate upper corners of the two brooches from Ipswich and Bridgham (Leeds nos.57-58), and a different degree of similarity between this element on these brooches and on the brooch from Lakenheath (Leeds no.19). In comparing the whole corpus of Anglo-Saxon square-headed brooches with one another, the distinction of three grades of positive similarity was found satisfactory:

a) <u>equivalent</u>: elements which are identical, or attempts to reproduce a single "prototype".

b) <u>related</u>: elements which are different modifications of a single "prototype".

c) <u>common</u>: elements which may be identical on different brooches, but which are characteristic of square-headed brooches in general, not of significant sub-groups. An example is the plain triple-ridged bow, found for instance on the two examples from Ipswich and Bridgham just cited, and on over 50 per cent of all Anglo-Saxon square-headed brooches.

The procedure of classification is first to establish "similarity coefficients" between all individual square-headed brooches, consisting of the number of shared "equivalent" features, as a guide to the best grouping. This is then supplemented with the evidence of the "related" features, which in fact generally confirms the clustering observed through the first stage, while allowing a few more individualistic examples to be located beside some of the clusters. No especial significance is attached to the exact value of the similarity coefficient between two brooches. In certain cases, of course, the interpretation of the similarity between features as "equivalent", "related", or "common", is a subjective one. In the following classification, for instance, the headplate upper corners on Leeds no.19 and Leeds nos.57-58 are regarded as closely related features, although one could regard them as rather unsuccessful attempts to reproduce a single model, and therefore equivalent.

There is no single correct classification of the Anglo-Saxon square-headed brooches. By virtue of all being definable as square-headed brooches all belong to one group. No two known square-headed brooches are totally identical. One could therefore ultimately subdivide the collected corpus of these brooches into as many sub-groups as there are brooches themselves. The basis of classification used here is the surface similarity of brooches in the design and association of the smaller elements available for their composition. This is not the only possible basis. Professor Sjøvold in Norway is currently working on a re-classification of most of the Scandinavian silver-sheet and relief brooches based on their shapes and the proportions between their parts (personal communication Th. Sjøvold). Leigh has put a large sample of the Anglo-Saxon brooches published by Leeds in order according to a seriation-of-motifs technique, and presents a "characterisation" of the Kentish brooches based on an investigation of apparent workshop links (Leigh 1980 pp.41-130). An analysis of the metallurgical content and composition of the Anglo-Saxon square-headed brooches, together perhaps with the use of glass, garnet, and enamel insets, might provide a different division of the material. The internal design and composition of these brooches, however, seems likely to provide richer material to work with than their shape and proportions, though this is not to deny significance to the latter. Some note has been taken of observable metallurgical features in the following classification, e.g. the use of "silver" or "bronze" for the body of the brooch, not as simple a distinction to make by eye as older literature would lead one to expect, and the presence of gilding, silver-plating, enamel, etc., but it has not proved possible to arrange for a detailed metallurgical analysis of a useful sample, let alone all, of the brooches yet. Such an analysis is certainly desirable. It would be highly valuable to compare arguments for the relationship, contemporaneity, and modes of production of various brooches with the evidence of the metallurgical composition. But the design evidence is self-standing. Other forms of evidence may supplement it, or modify the conclusions or hypotheses drawn from it, but they cannot invalidate it as evidence in itself.

A revised grouping of the Anglo-Saxon square-headed brooches should be of wider use than the immediate concerns of this thesis. To familiarize oneself with the material as a whole, there are obvious practical reasons for finding some principle of ordering the material, rather than meeting or describing similar and dissimilar brooches at random. But ordering the material is not necessarily the same as dividing it into groups. The intended usefulness of the grouping of these brooches as presented here is largely that this makes it easier to refer to the relationships between groups IV, IX, and XV (for instance), rather than citing individual brooches in every case, and thus provides a framework within which assessments of the typological and chronological history of the square-headed brooch in England can be articulated as easily as possible.

It is of the character of a grouping to imply a degree of similarity between the members of a group, and dissimilarity between these and examples outside of that group or members of other groups. While the purpose of establishing a useful grouping of the Anglo-Saxon square-headed brooches requires little special justification, deciding where to draw the line between groups is rather more problematic. The 22 groups of square-headed brooches described below include groups of markedly varying characters. In some groups all, or a considerable number, of their members share relatively high similarity coefficients with one another, providing, at least, a significantly homogeneous kernel to the other group. Other groups, group I for instance, are relatively loose and heterogeneous, with chains of brooches linked together by low similarity coefficients supplemented by related features. The phenomenon of chaining may link brooches

within the same group which have no shared equivalent
features through an intermediary brooch; this phenomenon
is, however, of interest in its own right, and a valid
basis for grouping the brooches concerned. This can give
rise to the situation that two brooches in different groups
have a higher degree of similarity to one another than two
other brooches within a single group. The decisions as to
where the divisions between formally distinguished groups
of brooches should come have been made on an ad hoc basis
rather than in accordance with any pre-ordained formula.
For instance, no advantage was seen in separating the two
very similar brooches from Alfriston, ESx, and Guildown, Sy
(Leeds nos.69-70) from the rest of group I (see below),
although they could justifiably have been called a group
within a group, and been given a separate group number.
Their relationship to the other brooches collected within
group I is analogous to the relationship between groups IV,
IX, and XV below, which could all have been collected under
a single group number, as indeed Leeds did, collecting all
of these types under his Group A3. But the separability of
these three groups is argued to reflect clear stages in the
typological and chronological development of these
brooches. The relationships amongst these brooches, and
between these brooches and brooches in other groups, can be
more clearly discussed by reference to three separate
groups rather than by using such terms as "the earliest
forms of group A3", "the middle stage of group A3", and
"the latest phase of group A3".

The differing characters of the individual groups
should be clear in the evidence which is presented for the
distinction of these groups below. Attention is also
drawn, where appropriate, to the external relationships of
these groups, when in fact they have the characters of
clusters within clusters. It is hoped therefore that this
is a system which can be followed for the classification of
future finds of Anglo-Saxon square-headed brooches. It is
partly to this end that Leeds's numbering of the corpus of
these brooches, which becomes anomalous with the
substantial revision of Leeds's classification, and has the
disadvantage that new finds of brooches have simply to be
added on to the end, out of sequence, is abandoned.
Instead, brooches are identified by their find-spot and
grave-number, if known. If no grave-number is known, and
more than one brooch is known from the same site, then the
brooch's new group number may follow the find-place, and,
if further necessary to distinguish such brooches within
the same group, an individuating letter, a, b, c ... etc.
For practical reasons, however, Leeds's figure numbers are
often cited here, as his work is such a valuable source of
illustrations. The groups are numbered I-XXII. Some of
Leeds's groups have become familiar, e.g. A4, B1, and it is
unfortunate that these known designations should be lost.
There is a good measure of agreement between the new
groupings and Leeds's, but the order of Leeds's group
numbers becomes meaningless, and it would be nonsensical to

refer to groups XIV, XVI, and XVIII below as something like Groups Bli, Blii, and Bliii. I have tried to place those groups I believe to be earliest towards the beginning of this sequence, but no great significance attaches to the exact positions of groups in this sequence. This is not a classification to last for ever. It is foreseeable that future discoveries, particularly of brooches assignable to the more heterogeneous groups, will eventually create a situation in which a formal subdivision of these groups is desirable, which would best be done by a wholesale re-assessment of the groupings rather than by establishing an apparently different class of sub-groups designated Ia, Ib, Ic, etc.

An attempt is also made here to provide a chronological outline of the sequence of production of the Anglo-Saxon square-headed brooches by assessing shared motifs on different brooches, and the development of individual compositional elements. Two or more brooches sharing an equivalent feature have to be regarded as chronologically "contiguous", or broadly contemporary in that there are no grounds for identifying one as earlier than another at least as far as this feature alone is concerned. Equivalent or identical elements, however, may theoretically be inherited unchanged from an earlier brooch-type by a successor, and further be bequeathed to yet later successors. But a reasonably circumspect effort at distinguishing "equivalent" from "related" or "common" elements leaves this concept of broad contemporaneity a useful degree of practical significance. Some examples of equivalent features which are attempts to reproduce a single prototype may differ in occurring in "fine" or "degenerate" forms. As an example may be cited the headplate inner panels on the brooches from Barrington B, Cambs g.9, and Myton, Warwicks (Leeds nos.108-109). The former may be regarded as earlier in form, but it must not therefore be assumed that the brooch on which it occurs is earlier in fact.

The occurrence of related features on different brooches is potentially a key element in determining their relative chronology. Here one must try to decide whether the two features are directly related, i.e. if one is directly descended from the other, and if so which, or if they are separate developments from a single common source. The determination of such questions is not often simple or certain. But rather than examining only individual elements in isolation, the concentration of various individual equivalent and related elements on the brooches or within groups concerned can help to clarify the picture, and lend credence to one particular interpretation of the relationship. An example may be cited of the relationship between groups V and X, below.

While this is not the basis for an especially fine relative dating of the majority of the Anglo-Saxon square-

116

headed brooches, it does, as will appear, allow the identification of certain examples as amongst the earliest, others amongst the latest, and the rest in between. It provides a simple, relative, internal typological chronology, which recommends itself by comparison with the rather inconclusive external chronology of the brooches provided by art styles and grave-associations.

Procedure

Under each group heading in turn in the following classification, a list of the brooches assigned to that group is given first, with references to published illustrations and descriptions of them. A number of plates and figures of hitherto unpublished brooches are included with this volume. A list of the equivalent elements which any of the brooches of the group share with any other brooch (in that group or not) is then given, followed, where it is felt useful, by a table of similarity coefficients drawn from these. There then follows a more open discussion of the groups, including consideration of certain related features found in the group. It would be tiresome and pedantic to discuss in full detail every discernible related feature occurring within every group. So far as possible those related features are selected which support the association of the brooches in the group, draw attention to the relationships between this group and any other, or are of chronological significance. Finally a brief survey is made of the possible sequence of forms within the group (if any), and the relative-chronological location of the group besides groups already discussed. At the end of the formal classification, the relative chronology of Anglo-Saxon square-headed brooches is summarized, on the basis of which the pattern of overseas parallels to these brooches is assessed. Thus the evidence of these brooches is added to the central enquiry of this work, the Scandinavian character of Anglian England.

Group I

Dartford, Kt	BM 1954.12-4.1. Plate 3.1
Alfriston, ESx g.28	Leeds no.66
Alfriston, ESx g.43	Leeds no.68
Alfriston, ESx [I]	Leeds no.69
Guildown, Sy g.116	Leeds no.70
Mitcham, GL g.25	Leeds no.67
Chessel Down, IoW [I]	Leeds no.79
Berinsfield, Oxon g.102	Ashmolean. Plate 3.2
Brighthampton, Oxon	Leeds no.76
Coleshill, Oxon	Leeds no.103
Fairford, Glos [I]	Leeds no.80
Hampnett, Glos	Leeds no.81
Woodston, Cambs	Leeds no.88
Kempston, Beds [I]	Leeds no.111
Alveston Manor, Warwicks g.5	Leeds no.116
North Luffenham, Leics	Leeds no.124

16 brooches. Map 3.1

Equivalent elements

Headplate frame	: Alfriston 28; Alfriston 43; Alfriston [I]; Guildown 116; Berinsfield 102; Coleshill; North Luffenham
"	: Chessel Down [I]; Fairford [I]
Heaplate upper corners	: Dartford; Alfriston 28; Berinsfield 102
"	: Alfriston 43; Alfriston [I]; Guildown 116
"	: Chessel Down [I]; Brighthampton; Fairford [I]; Hampnett
Headplate inner panel	: Alfriston [I]; Guildown 116
Footplate upper borders	: Dartford; Alfriston 28; Berinsfield 102; Brighthampton [I]; Kempston [I]; (Badby - see group II)
Footplate frame	: Alfriston 28; Berinsfield 102; (Sarre 159; Linton Heath 21; Badby; Duston; Herpes - see group II)
"	: Alfriston [I]; Guildown 116
Footplate wire frame	: Alfriston 28; Alfriston 43; (Sarre 159 - see group II)
Footplate side lobes	: Alfriston [I]; Guildown 116
Footplate inner panels	: Alfriston [I]; Guildown 116
Footplate bar	: Alfriston [I]; Guildown 116

	Alfriston 28	Berinsfield 102	Alfriston 43	Alfriston [I]	Guildown 116	Kempston [I]	Brighthampton	North Luffenham	Coleshill	Chessel Down [I]	Fairford [I]	Hampnett	Badby	Sarre 159	Linton Heath 21	Duston	Herpes
Dartford	2	2				1	1						1				
Alfriston 28		4	2	1	1	1	1	1	1				2	2	1		
Berinsfield 102			1	1	1	1	1	1	1				2	1	1		
Alfriston 43				2	2			1	1								
Alfriston [I]					7			1	1								
Guildown 116								1	1								
Kempston [I]							1										
Brighthampton										1	1	1	1				
North Luffenham									1								
Coleshill																	
Chessel Down [I]												2	1				
Fairford [I]												1					

It is clear from the above table that there is a high degree of similarity between brooches Alfriston [I] and Guildown 116, and a relatively high degree of similarity between Alfriston 28 and Berinsfield 102, but otherwise this is a particularly heterogeneous group.

Three brooches listed above as members of this group do not share any designated equivalent elements at all with other members of the group, Mitcham 25, Alveston Manor 5, and Woodston. Their place in the group is based on the features they show that are related to features on the other brooches. The Style I decorated headplate second panel on Mitcham 25 and Alfriston 28 are clearly related, and the more clearly organized animal ornament of the former suggests it to be ancestral to the latter. The footplate upper borders on Mitcham 25, a profile animal head with "nose" between the eye and the jaws, and a second, smaller, profile animal head on the end of the upper jaw, is a further related feature on this brooch, Dartford, Alfriston 28, Berinsfield 102, Brighthampton, and Kempston [I]. This element on Fairford [I] is also closely related. The same element on Alveston Manor 5 may be reckoned a related feature, although on this brooch there are two smaller profile animal heads, one on the end of each of the biting head's jaws.

The headplate upper corners on Alveston Manor 5, with a symmetrical pair of profile animal heads with necks meeting in the corner, relate this brooch to Dartford, Alfriston 28, and Berinsfield 102. The confronted masks on the headplate frame of Alveston Manor 5 may be a developed form of the frame of masks model which is seen on Dartford, from which form the examples found on Alfriston 28, Alfriston 43, Alfriston [I], Guildown 116, Berinsfield 102, Coleshill and North Luffenham seem to be derived.

In my opinion, the illustration of Woodston (Artis

1828 pl.LV.6) looks similar to Coleshill with its animal
ornament in the headplate inner panel, triangular footplate
inner panel, animal ornament framing this, and broad,
ridged footplate bar with a mask at either end. Artis's
drawing, however, is inadequate for a detailed analysis of
this brooch, which is included here with some reservations.

A number of further related features may be pointed to
which add coherence to this group. The beaded wire
footplate frame of Alfriston 28 and Alfriston 43 appears to
be copied in a cast form on Chessel Down [I]. The
footplate bars, with animals masks facing opposite
directions towards either end, on Dartford, Alfriston 28,
and Berinsfield 102 are related; as much of the footplate
bar as is preserved on North Luffenham looks similar to
those on Alfriston [I] and Guildown 116, with a broad nosed
mask facing down a bar with a raised central ridge. A
widespread related feature amongst the brooches of this
group is the inward facing mask of a generally oval outline
in the footplate side lobes of Alfriston 28, Alfriston 43,
Berinsfield 102, Chessel Down [I], Brighthampton, and
Fairford [I].

The two brooches of group I with the earliest forms
appear to be Dartford and Mitcham 25. Both of these
brooches are gilt silver, the remainder of the group being
gilt bronze. They both also have clear ornament executed
to a high quality. It is of course, questionable to assume
earliness on the basis of this alone, but it is more
probable that poorer quality workmanship in a cheaper
material will copy higher quality workmanship in a more
precious material than vice versa. Kempston [I] and
Brighthampton have the footplate upper border in openwork
as on Dartford and this version is probably earlier than
the equivalent and related filled forms on Berinsfield 102,
Alfriston 28, and Fairford [I], although this does not
necessarily give relative dates to the brooches themselves.
The headplate second panel suggests that Mitcham 25 is
earlier than Alfriston 28, while Alfriston 28 and
Berinsfield 102 cannot properly be divided chronologically.
Alveston Manor 5 belongs relatively early with these
brooches. Running scroll ornament on the headplate links
it with Dartford and Alfriston 28, and its other major
related features connect it to the same brooches. It is
difficult to separate Alfriston 43, Alfriston [I],and
Guildown 116 from Alfriston 28 and Berinsfield 102 with the
shared equivalent element of the headplate frame of masks,
and the wire footplate frame on Alfriston 28 and
Alfriston 43, but that Alfriston 28 and Berinsfield 102 are.
more similar to Dartford through the headplate upper
corners and footplate upper borders could be an earlier
sign. Coleshill and North Luffenham must be reckoned
broadly contemporary, in the sense defined above, with
Alfriston 43, Alfriston [I] and Guildown 116. The forms of
Chessel Down [I] and Fairford [I], linked by the masks in
their headplate upper corners to Brighthampton and Hampnett

may also be assigned to this later phase by the cast copy of a beaded wire frame on the former, and the simplified outline of the footplate upper borders on the latter. Brighthampton looks earlier than these with its openwork footplate upper borders, and could be placed broadly contemporary with Alfriston 28, Berinsfield 102, and Kempston [I]. Hampnett is too fragmentary to say anything further about in this respect.

The suggested relative chronology of the forms represented by the brooches of group I may be expressed diagrammatically as follows:

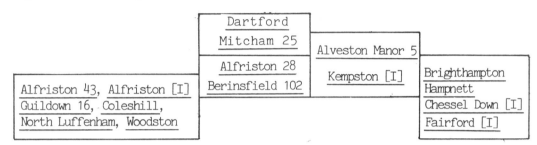

The distribution of the brooches in this group justifies its description as a Saxon group. Only Alveston Manor 5, Kempston [I], Woodston and North Luffenham lie outside areas that are indisputably Saxon, and of these Alveston Manor 5 and Kempston [I] may properly be considered marginal between the Anglian and Saxon areas. The two earliest looking examples are both from what appears to have been the early Saxon domain of Surrey, stretching into what is now West Kent. But it is interesting to note that the two "marginal" examples Alveston Manor 5 and Kempston could also be very early representatives of this group. The later examples of the group, however, fill in the distribution map in Sussex, Surrey, Oxfordshire, and Gloucestershire. Further consideration of the history of this group, its origins, and its relationship to other Anglo-Saxon square-headed brooches, is postponed to the comprehensive summary and discussion at the end of the chapter.

Group II

Sarre, Kt g.159   Leeds no.84
West Stow, Sfk [II]   Ashmolean. Fig. 3.2
Linton Heath, Cambs g.21   Leeds no.86
Badby, N'hants   Leeds no.87
Duston, N'hants   Leeds no.85
Tuxford, Notts   Leeds no.89
Herpes, Charente, France   Leeds no.83
Geneva, Switzerland (lead model)   Bonnet and Martin 1982

7 brooches + 1 lead model. Map 3.2

Equivalent elements

Headplate corners   : Sarre 159; Herpes
Headplate frame   : Sarre 159; Herpes
    "   : Linton Heath 21;
                         Duston; Geneva
Headplate second panel   : Linton Heath 21; Badby;
                         Duston; Geneva
Headplate inner panel   : Sarre 159; Herpes
Footplate upper borders   : Sarre 159; Herpes
    "   : West Stow [II]; Linton Heath
                         21; Duston
Footplate frame   : Sarre 159; Linton Heath 21;
                         Badby; Duston; Herpes;
                         (Alfriston 28, Berinsfield 102 -
                         see group I)
Footplate inner panel
frame   : Sarre 159; Herpes
       "   : Linton Heath 21;   Duston
Footplate inner panels   : Sarre 159; Herpes

Table of similarity coefficients based on the above

	Herpes	West Stow [II]	Linton Heath 21	Duston	Badby	Geneva
Sarre 159	7		1	1	1	
Herpes			1	1	1	
West Stow [II]			1	1	1	
Linton Heath 21				5	2	2
Duston					2	2
Badby						1

The high degree of similarity between the brooches from Sarre 159 and Herpes is well known. It was made clear by Leeds (1949 pp.53-56), and it is widely accepted that the Herpes brooch may be regarded as a Kentish export. Leeds also pointed out the relatively high degree of similarity between Linton Heath 21 and Duston and the lesser degree of similarity between Badby and these two brooches. Only the footplate frame is reckoned an equivalent element on these five brooches here, an equivalent element in fact shared with Alfriston 28 and Berinsfield 102 of group I, and maybe the fragmentary Dartford and Kempston [I] too, but a series of closely related features enhances the coherence of the present group. The headplate frames on Sarre 159, Herpes, Linton Heath 21, Duston and Geneva are clearly very closely related, and the headplate upper corners on Duston may be regarded as derivative of the form seen on Sarre 159 and Herpes: the outline and beaded frame of Sarre 159 are on Duston but the inset glass or garnet is replaced by a small raised plane area. Similarly the footplate side lobes of Linton Heath 21, like Sarre 159 and Herpes a framed pointed oval shape, are filled with red enamel rather than red glass or garnet. A similar pointed oval is found on Badby and Duston, the latter, however, filled with an inward-facing mask, as on some brooches of group I. The footplate bars on Herpes and Duston are related, both with a raised central ridge and a small mask at either end. Only a fragment of a sixth brooch, West Stow [II], survives, a piece of the footplate upper border, with the same transverse ribbing of the neck as Duston and a small profile animal on the end of the biting beast's lower jaw as on that brooch, suggesting that there may originally have been a high degree of similarity between these brooches generally.

The remaining brooch, Tuxford, does not share any equivalent elements with the other six. One feature which appears to be especially related to the remainder of this group is the framed plane triangular footplate inner panels whose base is some way separate from the footplate bar. These recall the footplate inner panels filled with glass or garnets on Sarre 159 and Herpes, enamel on Linton Heath 21, and animal ornament on Duston. The biting beast in the footplate upper borders has a degenerate small profile animal head on the end of either jaw as Linton Heath 21 and Duston, an element clearly related to this feature on Alveston Manor 5 of group I. A pointed oval appears in the footplate side lobe of Tuxford, as Sarre 159, Herpes, Linton Heath 21, Badby and Duston of the same group.

Group II has a remarkable amount in common with group I, especially on the footplates. Equivalent elements found in both are the footplate upper borders of Badby, Dartford, Alfriston 28, Berinsfield 102, Brighthampton, and Kempston [I], the moulded footplate frames of Sarre 159, Herpes, Linton Heath 21, Badby, Duston, Alfriston 28, and Berinsfield 102, and the wire footplate frame of Sarre 159, Alfriston 28, and Alfriston 43 (not shown on the former in Leeds, but see Brent 1866 pl.VI.1). The similarity between the footplate side lobes on Duston and a number of group I brooches has also been noted.

Sarre 159 and Herpes seem to represent the earliest forms of this group. Comparing the photographs of the two brooches in Leeds, Herpes looks the finer brooch, but no useful purpose is served by trying to divide the two chronologically. Evidence has been noted that the forms of Linton Heath 21, Duston and Geneva are derivative of the forms of Sarre 159 and Herpes, and West Stow [II] and Badby must be reckoned broadly contemporary with these. Tuxford may be assigned to a third, latest phase: in particular the footplate upper borders of Tuxford may be derivative of the Linton Heath 21/Duston form. Diagrammatically, the internal chronology of the group appears thus:

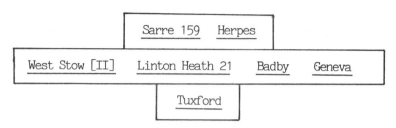

As both Sarre 159 (footplate frame and beaded wire) and Badby (footplate upper borders and frame) share two equivalent elements with Alfriston 28 in group I, both of these "phases" here must be regarded as chronologically contiguous with Alfriston 28 and Berinsfield 102 of that group. This allows one to suggest that the earliest brooches of this group Sarre 159 and Herpes are slightly later products than Dartford and Mitcham 25. Both of the former are described as gilt bronze rather than silver like the latter (Brent 1866 p.181; Delamain p.181), but the Sarre brooch has a very silvery look about it, and Leigh classifies it as a silver brooch. It appears that this group occurs first in Kent, and spreads thence to East Anglia and Northamptonshire. That one brooch and one lead model belonging to this group should find their way to the continent is remarkable. Geneva stands closest to Linton Heath 21, Duston and Badby, and on present evidence one can only suppose its source to be Anglian England. Its discovery as far away as Geneva is discussed later.

Group III

Chessel Down, IoW [III]   Leeds no.8
Tuddenham, Sfk [III]   Leeds no.10
Paglesham, Ex   C.Arch 54 (1976) pp.214-215
Linton Heath, Cambs g.9   Leeds no.9

4 brooches

Equivalent elements

Headplate frame   : Paglesham;   Linton Heath 9
Headplate inner panels   : Chessel Down [III];   Tuddenham
                             [III];   Paglesham;   Linton
                             Heath 9
Bow   : Paglesham;   Linton Heath 9
Footplate upper borders   : Chessel Down [III];   Paglesham;
                             Linton Heath 9
Footplate frame   : Paglesham; Linton Heath 9
Footplate inner panel   : Chessel Down [III];   Paglesham
        "   : Tuddenham [III];   Linton Heath 9

124

Table of similarity coefficients based on the above

	Paglesham	Linton Heath 9	Tuddenham [III]
Chessel Down [III]	3	1	1
Paglesham		5	2
Linton Heath 9			3

The one feature connecting all four members of this group is the design of the headplate inner panels, appearing in its clearest and finest form on Chessel Down [III] in a coarser form on Paglesham and Linton Heath 9, and in rather crude, low relief work on Tuddenham [III]. The footplate frame may also be regarded as a feature relating all four brooches: the presence of a tie-bar connecting the two sides of the frame where they meet by the footplate upper borders should be noted. It requires a bit of imagination to derive the form of the footplate upper borders on Paglesham from those on Chessel Down [III], but it is possible. The openwork in this element of Paglesham suggests they are an earlier form than the equivalent element on Linton Heath 9 and Tuddenham [III]. Chronologically, the forms of the brooches may be put in the order Chessel Down [III] --> Paglesham --> Linton Heath 9 --> Tuddenham.

There are a number of interesting points of contact between the brooches of this group and those of groups I and II. The profile animal head in the footplate upper borders of Chessel Down [III], with a long nose, two smaller animal heads at the end of either jaw, and two lines crossing the triangle between the jaws, appears most closely related to Linton Heath 21 and Duston of group II by the latter feature, although the nose on those two brooches is shortened and inconspicuous, and in this respect Chessel Down [III] stands closer to Alveston Manor 5 of group I. Meanwhile the masks which frame the headplate on Paglesham and Linton Heath 9 may be regarded as almost equivalent to those on Dartford of group I, although executed in a slightly simpler manner. Tuddenham [III] seems to be largely dependent in form on a model such as Linton Heath 9, and it would seem straightforward to derive the divided masks of the headplate frame on Tuddenham [III] from the same source. But in fact the form of these masks on Tuddenham shows a much closer relationship to those on another group, Leeds's Group B6, group VII below.

The earliest-looking brooch of this group was found on the Isle of Wight, the later three in eastern England north of the Thames. These are not sufficient grounds to argue

125

for an origin for the group on the island, spreading thence to East Anglia. The parallels that Chessel Down [III], Paglesham and Linton Heath 9 carry to the Saxon group I and the apparently Kentish-derived Anglian brooches of group II, imply an origin in southern England for this group, probably in Kent, and also indicate a southern origin for the form of the footplate upper borders found on Linton Heath 21 and Duston of group II, a model which further appears on Alveston Manor 5 of group I. Leigh in fact regards Chessel Down [III] as a product of his Kentish workshop (Leigh 1980 pp.81-83). The additional phenomenon of Tuddenham [III]'s relationship to group VII will be considered along with that group.

Chronologically, Chessel Down [III] may be regarded as broadly contemporary with Alveston Manor 5 of group I, and perhaps earlier than Linton Heath 21 and Duston of group II. Linton Heath 9 is probably a later product than Dartford of group I; it may therefore be broadly contemporary with Alfriston 28 and Berinsfield 102 of that group, and also Linton Heath 21 and Duston of group II. Thus Linton Heath graves 9 and 21 produce two broadly contemporary square-headed brooches betraying southern English influence.

Group IV

Holywell Row, Sfk g.11   Leeds no.11
Unknown provenance, Sfk [IV]   Leeds no.13
Rothley Temple, Leics [IV]   Leeds no.12

3 brooches

This group is unusual in that the three brooches it contains are not connected by any features that are designated "equivalent". They are rather individualistic brooches, which nevertheless may be linked together through a number of related features, occurring mostly on their footplates. Such related features also connect this group with a number of brooches outside of this group, and are of great importance in establishing the sources of this seminal Anglian group. But for the moment attention will be focussed on establishing the coherence of the group.

All three brooches have a "rampant" quadruped beast in the footplate upper borders, with the feet curled right back to the "elbow" or "knee" of the legs, and curly tails. These curling tails also characterize the "couchant" quadruped beasts which are found in the footplate lower borders of all three. The terminal lobe of all three brooches is a large mask, though of considerably different form on each brooch, except for the nose-and-eyebrows element which is almost identical on Holywell Row 11 and Rothley Temple [IV]. Similarly, the footplate frames on

Holywell Row 11 and Rothley Temple [IV] show very much the same outline: four arcs, with a mask at the top and the terminal lobe mask below, stopping at the side lobes on either side of the footplate. Both Holywell Row 11 and Suffolk [IV] have a rhomboidal setting for glass or a garnet in the centre of the footplate, and two round glass or garnet settings in the headplate inner panel. This feature also occurs on Alveston Manor 5 of group I.

All three brooches have practically symmetrical pairs of quadruped animals in the panels of the bow, those on Holywell Row 11 and Suffolk [IV] facing up to the headplate, those on Rothley Temple [IV] facing down. Both Holywell Row 11 and Rothley Temple [IV] have a stud on the central ridge of the bow, that on Holywell Row 11 having held inset glass or garnet.

The headplate inner panel of Rothley Temple [IV], a mask between two square panels, may be compared to this feature on Linton Heath 21 and Duston of group II, and indeed could be derived from the headplate inner panel of Holywell Row 11 with its mask between the garnet settings, and running scroll (as on Rothley Temple [IV]) above these. Rothley Temple [IV] could even display an intermediary form between that on Holywell Row 11 and those on the two group II brooches, but this suggestion is highly hypothetical.

Holywell Row 11 and Suffolk [IV] cannot be divided chronologically, and must be regarded as broadly contemporary. Suffolk [IV] is gilt silver; Holywell Row 11 was described by Lethbridge as gilt bronze (Lethbridge 1931 p.5), but looks to be silver, and a metallurgical analysis of these brooch would be valuable. Rothley Temple [IV] looks to be a later form. It is certainly gilt "bronze" with a relatively high copper content, and has "lost" the garnet in the stud in the bow. The posture of the animals on the bow of Holywell Row 11 and Suffolk [IV] has been reversed, and the headplate inner panel may be directly derivative of the Holywell Row 11 form.

Group V

Barrington B, Cambs g.9	Leeds no.108
Northampton, N'hants [V]	Leeds no.110
Myton, Warwicks	Leeds no.109

3 brooches

Equivalent elements

Headplate upper corners
(form)   : Barrington B 9; Myton
Headplate frame (masks)   : Barrington B 9; Northampton
                                [V]; Myton
Headplate inner panel   : Barrington B 9; Myton
Bow   : Barrington B 9; Myton
Footplate upper borders   : Barrington B 9; Myton
Footplate frame   : Barrington B 9; Myton
Footplate inner panels   : Barrington B 9; Myton

Table of similarity coefficients based on the above

	Myton	Northampton [V]
Barrington B 9	7	1
Myton		1

Only the form and disposition of the masks in the headplate frame may be counted as an equivalent feature on the very similar Barrington B 9 and Myton brooches and on Northampton [V]: the S-shaped motifs in the side-panels of the headplate frame on the latter brooch are clearly related to the decoration of the headplate upper and lower corners on Barrington B 9 and Myton [V] and the whole element may be regarded as an attempt to reproduce the same prototype. The crouching Style I animals in the headplate inner panels of all three are of identical composition, but the remainder of this panel differs on Northampton [V] from the other two, and therefore may only be reckoned a related feature.

Barrington B 9 is in most respects a finer piece of work than Myton and despite the high degree of similarity between them ought to be considered in some sense an earlier form. The raised forelegs of the animals in the headplate inner panel of Barrington B 9 have degenerated into figure-of-eight elements not immediately recognizable as legs on Myton and the outermost masks on the footplate side lobes of Barrington B 9 have been reduced almost to a meaningless block on Myton. One particularly interesting difference on Myton is the use of enamel instead of the plain gilded panel in the headplate upper corners and the small upward-facing mask in the footplate terminal lobe of Barrington B 9.

A number of features relate this group to group IV, in particular to Holywell Row 11. The crouching quadrupeds in the bow panels of Barrington B 9 and Holywell Row 11 seem to reflect the same basic model - one notes especially the position and proportions of the head, neck, and front leg, and the backward-looped foot on the hind leg (Fig.3.3). The apparently meaningless animal ornament around the headplate upper corners of <u>Barrington B 9</u> would appear to be derived from the model of the animal at this position on <u>Holywell Row 11</u> - note the curling tail, the figure-2 shaped leg, and the frond-like figures on the front leg of the latter (Fig.3.4). The masks on the footplate side lobes of <u>Barrington B 9</u> and <u>Myton</u> and <u>Holywell Row 11</u>, appear, at least, to share a common source, and the four arcs forming the footplate frame would also appear to relate <u>Holywell Row 11</u>, <u>Rothley Temple [IV]</u>, <u>Barrington B 9</u>, and <u>Myton</u>. <u>Northampton [V]</u> has the stud on the bow ridge already noted on <u>Holywell Row 11</u> and <u>Rothley Temple [IV]</u> and again a quadruped animal crouching in the panels.

Chronologically the forms of the brooches of this group form the sequence:

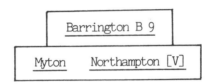

Although <u>Myton</u> is truer to the earliest-looking example of the group, <u>Barrington B 9</u>, there is no reason to regard the more deviant example <u>Northampton [V]</u> as later than this. <u>Barrington B 9</u> must be regarded as a later form of brooch than <u>Holywell Row 11</u> but the whole group may be provisionally regarded as broadly contemporary with the later-looking example of group IV, <u>Rothley Temple [IV]</u>.

<u>Group VI</u>

Cherbury Camp, Oxon	Leeds no.73
Baginton, Warwicks [VI]a	Leeds no.74
Baginton, Warwicks [VI]b	Leeds no.75
Bidford-on-Avon, Warwicks g.88	Leeds no.71
Offchurch, Warwicks	Leeds no.72
Beckford A, HW g.11	Plate 3.3

6 brooches. Map 3.3

<u>Equivalent elements</u>

Headplate frame   : Cherbury Camp; Baginton [VI]a;
                             Baginton [VI]b; Bidford-on-Avon
                             88; Offchurch

Headplate upper corners   : Baginton [VI]a; Bidford-on-Avon
                             88; Beckford A 11

Headplate panels   : Cherbury Camp; Baginton [VI]a;

```
                                Bidford-on-Avon 88; Offchurch;
                                Beckford A 11
Footplate upper borders  : Cherbury Camp;   Baginton [VI]a;
                           Baginton [VI]b; Bidford-on-Avon
                           88; Offchurch; Beckford A 11
Footplate frame          : Cherbury Camp;   Baginton [VI]a;
                           Baginton [VI]b;  Bidford-on-Avon
                           88;  Offchurch
Footplate side lobes     : Baginton [VI]a;   Baginton [VI]b;
                           Bidford-on-Avon 88
Footplate inner frame
and panels               : Cherbury Camp;   Baginton [VI]a;
                           Baginton [VI]b;  Bidford-on-Avon
                           88;  Offchurch;   Beckford A 11
Footplate bar            : Cherbury Camp;   Baginton [VI]a;
                           Baginton [VI]b; Bidford-on-Avon
                           88;  Offchurch;   Beckford A 11
```

Table of similarity coefficients based on the above

	Baginton [VI]a	Offchurch	Cherbury Camp	Baginton [VI]b	Beckford A 11
Bidford-on-Avon 88	8	6	6	6	5
Baginton [VI]a		6	6	6	6
Offchurch			6	5	4
Cherbury Camp				5	5
Baginton [VI]b					3

This group of six brooches is evidently rather more homogeneous than other groups already discussed. The coherence which is apparent in the relatively high similarity coefficients is in fact supplemented by certain related features: for instance the footplate terminal lobe, a small upward-facing mask with a broad frame in an oval lobe on Bidford-on-Avon 88, Offchurch, Beckford A 11, and Cherbury Camp. Baginton [VI]b has an oval lobe of the same proportions, but without the mask, while this piece of Baginton [VI]a is missing. An upward-facing mask in an oval footplate terminal lobe is also a feature of several brooches of group I, Duston (group II), and Barrington B 9 (group V), but beyond this general similarity, no specific close relationship with any of these other examples is clear. One may note a similar general similarity in the descending animals at the sides of the headplate second panels of Bidford-on-Avon 88, Baginton [VI]a, Offchurch, and Cherbury Camp with members of group I such as Mitcham 25, Alfriston 28 Brighthampton and Fairford [I] (cf. Leeds 1949 fig.2), but the latter brooches have symmetrical animal ornament in this field, unlike the brooches of the present group. As will be seen, a number of interesting parallels appear between headplate inner panels of this group and brooches introduced below. The headplate inner panel of Baginton [VI]b appears to be a derivative modification of the form found on the other members of this group. That form looks to be derived from the decoration of the headplate second panels of Dartford (group I), a swastika in a square panel with animal ornament below it, including a figure-2 shaped limb in exactly the same posture as on the brooches of the present group. This is also reminiscent of the decoration found on the inner panel of an individualistic silver-gilt square-headed brooch from Empingham I, Leics (Plate 3.4). The spiralling swastikas of the present group may be compared with the figures of six spirals on this Empingham brooch, below which is found a detached leg and foot, albeit in a different form on Empingham I to the brooches of group VI. One may certainly believe that this is derived from the same source as Dartford.

There can be little doubt that Bidford-on-Avon 88 represents the earliest form of this group. In all respects, the equivalent and related features it shares with the other brooches in the group are executed in a clearer and more authoritative manner. The greater degree of complexity which is particularly indicative of a prototype form is found, for instance, in the mask at the upper end of the footplate bar. Leeds set out a genealogical table for five of these brooches (Leeds 1949 p.50), and his distinction of Offchurch and Cherbury Camp and the two Baginton brooches, as representing two separate lines of descent from the model of Bidford-on-Avon 88, on the basis of the preservation or disappearance of openwork in the headplate frames and footplate upper borders, looks good. The more recently found Beckford A 11 belongs with Offchurch and Cherbury Camp. Of these three brooches, the execution of the headplate panels and footplate inner panels, and the presence of a small swelling out by the neck of the terminal lobe, indicate that Offchurch lies closer to the Bidford-on-Avon 88 model, and may, as Leeds implied, be ancestral to Cherbury Camp. In terms of shared equivalent features, Baginton [VI]a is closer to Bidford-on-Avon 88 than Baginton [VI]b is, the latter having a modified form of the headplate corners and panels, but in other respects the execution of Baginton [VI]b, as Offchurch, looks clearer and closer to Bidford-on-Avon 88: see, for instance, the footplate upper borders, inner panels, and even side lobes. It is doubtful whether there is any significant value in finer relative-chronological distinctions after Bidford-on-Avon 88, so the relative chronology of the group may be expressed as follows:

```
                    ┌─────────────────────┐
                    │  Bidford-on-Avon 88 │
                    └─────────────────────┘
┌──────────────────────────────────────────────────────────────────────┐
│ Beckford A 11   Cherbury Camp   Offchurch   Baginton [VI]a   Baginton [VI]b │
└──────────────────────────────────────────────────────────────────────┘
```

At this point, little that is useful may be said about the relationship of this group to others, beyond what has already been noted, and such discussion is therefore postponed. Attention, however, is drawn to the relatively compact western Midland distribution of the group, a geographical coherence reinforcing its formal homogeneity.

Group VII

Compton, WSx	Welch 1983 fig.129
Mitcham, GL g.116	Leeds no.100
Pewsey, Wilts g.21	Plate 3.5
Luton, Beds	Leeds no.95
Abingdon, Oxon	Leeds no.99
Fairford, Glos [VII]	Leeds no.97
Mucking, Ex urn 942	Jones 1975 pl.LXXXVIc
Haslingfield, Cambs [VII]	Leeds no.98
Market Overton, Leics [VII]	Leeds no.96

9 brooches. Map 3.4

Equivalent elements

Headplate frame	: Pewsey 21; Mitcham 116; Luton; Fairford [VII]; Mucking 942; Haslingfield [VII]; Market Overton [VII]
Headplate second panel	: Luton; Haslingfield [VII], Market Overton [VII]
Headplate inner panel	: Pewsey 21; Luton; Fairford [VII]; Haslingfield [VII]; Market Overton [VII]
Footplate upper borders	: Compton; Pewsey 21; Luton; Abingdon; Fairford [VII]; Mucking 942; Haslingfield [VII]; Market Overton [VII]
Footplate frame	: Compton; Pewsey 21; Luton; Fairford [VII]; Haslingfield [VII]; Market Overton [VII]
Footplate side lobes	: Compton; Pewsey 21; Luton; Fairford [VII]; Market Overton [VII]
Footplate terminal lobe	: Pewsey 21; Luton
Footplate inner panels	: Compton; Pewsey 21; Luton; Abingdon
Footplate bar	: Pewsey 21; Luton

Table of similarity coefficients based on the above

	Pewsey 21	Market Overton [VII]	Fairford [VII]	Haslingfield [VII]	Compton	Mucking 942	Abingdon	Mitcham 116
Luton	8	6	5	5	4	2	2	1
Pewsey 21		5	5	4	4	2	2	1
Market Overton [VII]			5	5	3	2	1	1
Fairford [VII]				4	3	2	1	1
Haslingfield [VII]					2	2	1	1
Compton						1	2	
Mucking 942							1	1

This group of nine brooches is more homogeneous than at first glance the above table would indicate. Four of its members, Compton, Mucking 942, Abingdon and Mitcham 116 are only fragmentary. There are additional related features to be brought into consideration: the headplate second panels of Fairford [VII] and Pewsey 21 look to be imaginative modifications of the form found on Luton, Haslingfield [VII] and Market Overton [VII], and the animal ornament in the footplate inner panels of Fairford [VII] is a simplified version of that found on Compton, Pewsey 21, Luton and Abingdon. The footplate inner panels of Haslingfield [VII], Market Overton [VII], and Mucking 942 may be considered related to this.

The upward-facing masks in the footplate terminal lobes of Luton, Fairford [VII] and Market Overton [VII] are a further related feature, and these, together with the side lobes of these brooches, would appear to be related to the forms on certain brooches of groups I-III, as, for instance, the raised moulded form of these masks, with a hollow on the underside, on Luton and Fairford [VII]; Alfriston 28, Berinsfield 102, Brighthampton, Guildown 116, Chessel Down [I] and Fairford [I]; Linton Heath 9, and Tuddenham [III]; and Duston. The footplate bars of Luton, Fairford [VII], Haslingfield [VII], and Market Overton [VII], with their long-nosed masks facing up into the bow and down into the terminal lobes may well be related to the bars on early examples of group I, i.e. Dartford, Alfriston 28 and Berinsfield 102. A further point of contact between this group and group I is the wire frame around the headplate, bow, and footplate of Market Overton [VII]. Such wire frames occur on the footplates of Alfriston 28 and Alfriston 43, and are copied on the headplate and footplate of Chessel Down [I]. The similarity between the masks of the headplate frame of Tuddenham [III] and brooches of this group has already been mentioned. The similarity consists of a long-nosed mask, with a double line filling in the cheeks (Fig.3.13). On the masks of the present group this double line generally curves the opposite way to that on Tuddenham [III], and there is no separate line under the eye-balls as on Tuddenham [III], except on Fairford [VII]. The headplate upper corners on Fairford [VII] and Tuddenham [III] are also remarkably similar, and it seems unnecessary to dismiss the whole similarity as coincidence (Fig.3.13). That Tuddenham [III] represents the influence of group VII on the latest-looking example of group III would appear to be the simplest explanation.

The detached pair of animal limbs in the headplate inner panel of this group must be compared with those in the lower half of the headplate inner panels of group VI. This limb in itself is common enough in Style I ornament, but its occurrence in this position and in the same proportions on the headplate inner panels of two groups of English square-headed brooches seems more than coincidence. That the present group shows only half of the typical headplate inner panel of group VI is no necessary evidence that the latter form is ancestral to this: derivation from the common source represented by Dartford, to which Empingham [I] may also be connected, is quite possible.

With its derivative form of animal ornament in the footplate inner panels and modified headplate second panel, Fairford [VII] may be said to represent a later form of this group than Luton and Abingdon. Compton also shows a slightly degenerate design in the footplate inner panels. Pewsey 21 displays a modified headplate second panel, and a generally coarser treatment of its many equivalent features with Luton. Haslingfield [VII] is also divergent from Luton and Abingdon in its footplate inner panels and lobes, and may be placed with Compton, Fairford [VII], and Pewsey 21 in a later phase. Market Overton [VII] looks to represent the latest form, with its filling in of the openwork of the headplate frame and footplate upper borders, and flattening out of the footplate lobe masks of Luton and Fairford [VII], but it nevertheless maintains a high number of features of Luton and cannot be assumed to represent a later stage than Haslingfield [VII] and Fairford [VII]. Too little of Mitcham 116 and Mucking 942 remains to suggest where they belong relative to the others. Diagrammatically, the result is:

	Luton Abingdon	Mitcham 116
Compton	Pewsey 21 Fairford [VII]	Mucking 942
Haslingfield [VII]	Market Overton [VII]	

This, together with the overall distribution of the group, suggests that the group's origins lie in the Thames Valley/ Chilterns area, origins which one would therefore describe as "Saxon" rather than "Anglian". The point is nicely supported by the finding of a mould fragment belonging to this group at Mucking, Ex (Jones 1975 pl.LXXXVIa-b). Such origins fit neatly with the group's apparently close relationship with group I, and to a lesser extent group III. The earliest forms of this group, Luton and Abingdon, may be regarded as broadly contemporary with Alfriston 28, Berinsfield 102, Brighthampton and Linton Heath 9 of those groups. Parallels exist between the later forms of group VII, e.g. Market Overton VII and Fairford VII, and later forms of groups I and III, e.g. Alfriston 43, Chessel Down [I] and Tuddenham [III], to allow these phases to be regarded as chronologically close. The link through the headplate inner panel between this group and group VI provisionally suggests that Luton and Abingdon and Bidford-on-Avon 88 may be broadly contemporary.

Group VIII

Northampton, N'hants [VIII]   Leeds no.77
Saxby, Leics   Leeds no.78

2 brooches

Equivalent elements

Headplate: upper corners; frame; inner panels
Footplate: upper borders; frame; inner panels; bar.

There is little significant difference between these two brooches: Saxby looks the slightly coarser piece of work, but it is considerably more worn.

An especially interesting features of this small group is the modelled crouching animal riveted on to the headplate upper corners of Northampton [VIII] (fig.3.14), and which evidently once existed on Saxby too, which is also to be found on Northampton [V]. These three brooches imply that this is a local Central Midlands feature.

Otherwise there is much to indicate the dependence of group VIII on the models of the Saxon group I. There are the masks of the headplate frame, with their prominent flaring nostrils, although a closer parallel to these than any known example of group I may be Linton Heath 9 of group III. The descending, symmetrical animals of the headplate second panel could be related to those on Mitcham 25 and Alfriston 28, and the latter brooch has simple scroll ornament in the headplate inner panels reminiscent of these two brooches too. The footplate upper borders of these two brooches have a biting beast with a long nose and tongue, most closely paralleled by Mitcham 25, Alveston Manor 5, Alfriston 28 and Brighthampton. The smaller profile animal heads on the ends of the jaws as on those brooches are not

to be seen here, but there is some slightly jumbled
ornament on the upper jaw, seen most clearly on
Northampton [VIII], which could be derived from the neck
and temple of the smaller profile head on Mitcham 25, and
the double line at the end of the lower jaw can be seen on
the same source.   Mitcham 25 also has flat-topped studs
riveted in the footplate side lobes as Northampton [VIII]
has, and Saxby presumably did.   It should be noted here
that Dartford also has riveted ornament on the footplate
side lobe, in this case a human mask, fixed by two rivet-
studs, like the beast on the headplate upper corners of
Northampton [V], Northampton [VIII], and Saxby, and
obviously of significance in looking for a source for this
feature in the Central Midlands.

The form of the two brooches of group VIII must be
later than Mitcham 25 of group I, and broadly contemporary
with Northampton [V].

Group IX

Lackford, Sfk urn 50/126	Leeds no.15A
Lakenheath, Sfk [IX]	Leeds no.14
Haslingfield, Cambs [IX]	Leeds no.15

3 brooches.

Equivalent elements

Headplate second panel   : Lackford 50/126; Lakenheath
                            [IX]; Haslingfield [IX]
Headplate inner panels   : Lackford 50/126; Lakenheath
                            [IX]; Haslingfield [IX]
Bow   : Lackford 50/126; Lakenheath
                            [IX]
Footplate upper borders   : Lackford 50/126; Lakenheath
                            [IX]; Haslingfield [IX]
Footplate terminal lobe   : Lakenheath [IX]; Haslingfield
                            [IX]; (Lakenheath [XV]; Linton
                            Heath 40; Barrington A 11;
                            Market Overton [XV] - see group
                            XV)
Footplate frame   : Lackford 50/126; Lakenheath
                            [IX]; Haslingfield [IX];
                            (Market Overton (Leeds no.17))
Footplate inner panel
and frame   : Lackford 50/126; Lakenheath
                            [IX];   Haslingfield [IX];
                            (Fordham (Leeds no.16); West
                            Stow (Leeds no.18))

Table of similarity coefficients based on the above

	Lakenheath [IX]	Haslingfield [IX]	Fordham, Market Overton, West Stow (Leeds nos.16-18)	Lakenheath [XV]	Linton Heath 40	Barrington A 11	Market Overton [XV]
Lackford 50/126	6	5	1				
Lakenheath [IX]		6	1			1	
Haslingfield [IX]			1			1	

   The equivalent elements show that the three brooches designated group IX form a tight little group, but with individual features in common with a much larger number of brooches. These equivalent elements shared with brooches outside of this group are in fact supplemented by further related features, but the relationship of those brooches to the present group will be considered later, when they themselves are the focus of attention.

   There is much to indicate the present group's dependence on group IV. This is the best source of the rather truncated rampant beasts in the footplate upper borders of this group. Perhaps the neatest demonstration of group IX's lineal descent from group IV may be made through the large masks of the footplate terminal lobes. The brows, noses, and eyes on Holywell Row 11, Rothley Temple [IV], Lakenheath [IX], and Haslingfield [IX] are very much the same, and all four have curling moustaches. Holywell Row 11 and Rothley Temple [IV], however, do not have the curling "ears" or hair-side pieces of Lakenheath [IX] and Haslingfield [IX], but above where these ears are on those latter brooches they have identical elements forming the tail of the couchant beast in the footplate lower borders. This integral part of the couchant beast could well have been "detached" and re-used in the composition of the group IX brooches. A profile mask in the footplate side lobes occurs on Rothley Temple [IV] as well as Lakenheath [IX] and Haslingfield [IX]. Here again the curling "beard" below the face on the latter two brooches could derive from the head of the couchant beast below the side lobe as represented on Rothley Temple [IV]. The footplate frames on these three brooches appear to be very similar to those on Holywell Row 11 and Rothley Temple [IV] while the square, plane stud in the centre of the footplate. could well be a reminiscence of garnet settings in this place, such as appear to have been on Holywell Row 11 and Suffolk [IV]. A similar stud occurs on Empingham I.

   The simpler animal ornament in the panels of the bow with the stud on the ridge of Lackford 50/126 and Lakenheath [IX] suggests that Holywell Row 11 presents an earlier form of this type of bow. Groups IX and IV, however, have rather less in common on the headplate, except for the form of the mask in the centre of the headplate on Holywell Row 11, Rothley Temple [IV], Lackford 50/178, Lakenheath [IX], and Haslingfield [IX]. It is interesting to note that the pattern of an upward-facing mask flanked by two swastikas in the headplate inner panel characteristic of his group also appears on group VI, most clearly on Bidford-on-Avon 88. The swirling swastika is, however, a common motif in Germanic art at this time, and the group IX brooches do not have the open centre to the swastika as Bidford-on-Avon 88, so there need be no particular relationship between the two groups.

Haslingfield [IX] looks to have been a plainer piece of work than the other two members of this group, but no purpose is served by seeking to divide the group chronologically. The group must follow on group IV, and there is reason to argue that they all show slightly later forms than Rothley Temple [IV].

Group X

Lackford, Sfk urn 50/178	MAA Cam 50/178B, Fig 3.5
Little Wilbraham, Cambs g.3	Leeds no.113
Little Wilbraham, Cambs g.28	Leeds no 112
Little Wilbraham, Cambs g.40	Leeds no.114
Alveston Manor, Warwicks g.89	Leeds no.121
Willoughby-on-the-Wolds, Notts g.15	Nottingham Mus, Plate 3.6
Unknown provenance [X]	Leeds no.115

7 brooches

Equivalent elements

Headplate frame	: Little Wilbraham 3; Little Wilbraham 40
Headplate lower corners	: Little Wilbraham 3; Little Wilbraham 40; Willoughby-on-the-Wolds 15; Unknown provenance [X]
Bow	: Little Wilbraham 3; Little Wilbraham 40
"	: Willoughby-on-the-Wolds 15; Unknown provenance [X]
Footplate upper borders	: Little Wilbraham 3; Little Wilbraham 28; Little Wilbraham 40; Unknown provenance [X]
Footplate side lobes	: Lackford 50/178; Willoughby-on-the-Wolds 15
"	: Little Wilbraham 3; Little Wilbraham 40
Footplate bar	: Little Wilbraham 3; Little Wilbraham 40

Table of similarity coefficients based on the above

	Unknown provenance [X]	Little Wilbraham 40	Little Wilbraham 3	Lackford 50/178
Little Wilbraham 28	1	1	1	
Willoughby-on-the-Wolds 15	2	1	1	1
Unknown provenance [X]		2	2	
Little Wilbraham 40			6	

Thus there is a relatively high degree of similarity between two brooches, Little Wilbraham 3 and Little Wilbraham 40, while the remaining members of this group are rather more loosely linked together. A number of related features, however, increase the coherence of the group. The headplate frames of Little Wilbraham 28 and Unknown provenance [X] are particularly close to one another, and the latter looks like a simplification of the former. Willoughby-on-the-Wolds 15 may be considered to share a common source with these: the side panels of the headplate on this brooch are very similar to those on Unknown provenance [X], and it has the same type of mask with a curl on either side of the forehead here, and in the centre of the upper part. The large masks of the headplate frames on these brooches must in turn be regarded as related in some way to those on Little Wilbraham 3 and Little Wilbraham 40. All the brooches of this group, other than the fragmentary Lackford 50/178, have a bow with small panels on either side of a ridge with a central stud, the only significant difference between Little Wilbraham 3 and Little Wilbraham 40, and Willoughby-on-the-Wolds 15 and Unknown provenance [X] being the different positioning of the animals within these panels.

Thus there is a relatively high degree of similarity between two brooches, Little Wilbraham 3 and Little Wilbraham 40, while the remaining members of this group are rather more loosely linked together. A number of related features, however, increase the coherence of the group. The headplate frames of Little Wilbraham 28 and Unknown provenance [X] are particularly close to one another, and the latter looks like a simplification of the former. Willoughby-on-the-Wolds 15 may be considered to share a common source with these: the side panels of the headplate on this brooch are very similar to those on Unknown provenance [X], and it has the same type of mask with a curl on either side of the forehead here, and in the centre of the upper part. The large masks of the headplate frames on these brooches must in turn be regarded as related in some way to those on Little Wilbraham 3 and Little Wilbraham 40. All the brooches of this group, other than the fragmentary Lackford 50/178, have a bow with small panels on either side of a ridge with a central stud, the only significant difference between Little Wilbraham 3 and Little Wilbraham 40, and Willoughby-on-the-Wolds 15 and Unknown provenance [X] being the different positioning of the animals within these panels.

More appears on the footplates. The footplate upper borders on Willoughby-on-the-Wolds 15 are very similar to those on the Little Wilbraham and Unknown provenance [X] brooches, but have a much more clearly modelled small profile head on the end of the upper jaw. What remains of the footplate upper borders on Lackford 50/178 shows at least a motif derived from this profile head, if not a fragment of that profile head itself. The footplate inner panels of Willoughby-on-the-Wolds 15 contain two symmetrical Style I animals very similar to those here on Little Wilbraham 28, and equally similar animals are to be found in this position on an individualistic brooch from Nassington, N'hants (Leeds no.64). The much simplified animal ornament of the footplate inner panels of Little Wilbraham 3 and Little Wilbraham 40 appears to be derivative of the same general model. The footplate bar of Willoughby-on-the-Wolds 15 has a stud on it as those of Little Wilbraham 3 and Little Wilbraham 40, although the mask at the top of this faces an opposite direction. The same stud appears on the footplate bar of Lackford 50/178, but insufficient of this remains to determine whether it can be classified as an equivalent element with Little Wilbraham 3, Little Wilbraham 40, or Willoughby-on-the-Wolds 15. One may finally note the use of large masks as the terminal lobes on all brooches of this group (except Unknown provenance [X], most of the footplate of which is missing), a feature already met on group IV.

The most divergent member of this group is Alveston Manor 89, sharing no equivalent elements with other members. It is an individualistic brooch, but a number of related features place it rather closer to this group than to any other, although many of these features also demonstrate the relationship of this to group V - Leeds indeed counted these two groups as one group, Group B8. The headplate upper corners of Willoughby-on-the-Wolds 15 and Alveston Manor 89 show indeterminate animal ornament around a pointed oval element clearly related to these parts of Barrington B 9 and Myton, as the figure-2 shaped limb used here shows. The three large masks of the upper border of the headplate frame of Alveston Manor 89 could be a substantial modification of this feature on the Willoughby-on-the-Wolds 15 model - note particularly the large, quadrangular nose - although the flaring moustache or nostrils on Alveston Manor 89 recall rather more Dartford, Alfriston 28 and Guildown 116 of group I. The ladder-like decoration of the bow panels of

Alveston Manor 89 may be compared with Little Wilbraham 28.
It is tantalizing that a significant portion of the
footplate upper borders of Alveston Manor 89 is covered up.
One can nevertheless see a crested head, and an upper jaw
in exactly the same posture as on the other brooches of
this group. At the end of this upper jaw is again a small
animal head and neck, though not identical to that on
Willoughby-on-the-Wolds 15. If a direct source for this
element on group X can be found on the brooches already
known to us, it must be the form of the more ornate and
richly formed footplate upper borders - with a crested head
and smaller profile head on the end of the upper jaw only -
on Barrington B 9 of group V. The same source could lie
behind the related footplate side lobes of
Alveston Manor 89, Little Wilbraham 3, and Little
Wilbraham 40 - an outward-facing mask with eyebrows and
nose divided down the middle, of a simpler form than on
Barrington B 9, with the inward-facing mask outside the
larger mask.

Variously, then, on different brooches, the headplate
upper corners, footplate upper borders, and footplate side
lobes, indicate the dependence of group X on at least the
earliest forms of group V, represented by Barrington B 9.
But this is not the only source which appears to influence
brooches of group X. The symmetrical animal heads and
necks around the headplate upper corners of
Little Wilbraham 28 cannot be unconnected with those on
Dartford etc., of group I - they are derived from the same
model if not from a brooch like Dartford itself, and look
to be a simpler, later form. Holywell Row 11 of group IV,
and Alveston Manor 5 of group I, seem to provide the
earliest models of the bow with stud on ridge and panels of
animal ornament; the form of Holywell Row 11 has been
shown to stand behind that of Barrington B 9, which in turn
is ancestral to the present group, and has a more complex
piece of animal ornament in the panels.

The footplate inner panels indicate that
Little Wilbraham 28 and Willoughby-on-the-Wolds 15
represent earlier forms than Little Wilbraham 3 and
Little Wilbraham 40. Willoughby-on-the-Wolds 15 also seems
to show a relatively early form of the footplate upper
border, while Little Wilbraham 28 has an earlier looking
headplate frame than Unknown provenance [X]. The relative-
chronological position of Alveston Manor 89 must be
dubious, but the execution of its headplate upper corners
and frame imply that it is a later form than Willoughby-on-
the-Wolds 15. The little that remains of Lackford 50/178
places it closer to Willoughby-on-the-Wolds 15 than any
other brooch, so it may be broadly contemporary, although
it would appear to have simpler animal ornament in the
footplate inner panels than Little Wilbraham 28 or
Willoughby-on-the-Wolds 15. The group may, then, be split

into two phases:

```
┌──────────────────────────────────────────────────────┐
│  Little Wilbraham 28   Willoughby-on-the-Wolds 15  │ Lackford 50/178 │
├──────────────────────────────────────────────────────────────────┤
│  Little Wilbraham 3  Little Wilbraham 40   Unknown provenance [X]  Alveston Manor 89 │
└──────────────────────────────────────────────────────────────────┘
```

The earliest brooches of this group appear to be slightly later forms than Barrington B 9 of group V, and later than Dartford (group I) and Holywell Row 11 (group IV). In this case it is interesting to note that Little Wilbraham 28, Little Wilbraham 40, and apparently Unknown provenance [X] of the present group carry enamel inlays, like Myton, the later example of group V. The form of the bow also implies that groups IX and X must, as a whole, be regarded as broadly contemporary. Silver-plate and enamel inlays may therefore appear to be broadly contemporary developments in craft and taste in square-headed brooches.

Group XI

Girton, Cambs [XI]   Leeds no.94
Linton Heath, Cambs g.32   Leeds no.91
Quy, Cambs   Leeds no.92
Ragley Park, Warwicks   Leeds no.93

4 brooches

Equivalent elements

Headplate frame   : Girton [XI]; Linton Heath 32;
                             Quy;   Ragley Park
Heaplate upper corners   : Girton [XI]; Linton Heath 32;
                             Quy; Ragley Park
Headplate inner panels   : Linton Heath 32; Quy; Ragley
                             Park
Bow   : Linton Heath 32; Quy; Ragley
                             Park
Footplate upper borders   : Linton Heath 32; Quy; Ragley
                             Park
Footplate frame   : Linton Heath 32; Quy; Ragley
                             Park
Footplate side lobes   : Girton [XI]; Linton Heath 32;
                             Quy; Ragley Park
Footplate terminal lobe   : Linton Heath 32; Quy; Ragley
                             Park
Footplate inner panels   : Linton Heath 32; Quy; Ragley
                             Park
Footplate bar   : Linton Heath 32; Ragley Park

142

Table of similarity coefficients based on the above

	Ragley Park	Quy	Girton [XI]
Linton Heath 32	10	9	3
Ragley Park		9	3
Quy			3

Making allowance for the fact that only fragments of Girton [XI] remain, it is obvious that this is a highly uniform group.

Brooches of this group share a number of related features with other brooches concentrated in the Cambridge area. The biting beast of the footplate upper borders has the crested head also met in groups V and X. There is the bow with a stud on the ridge and panels of zoomorphic ornament. The footplate lobes of Linton Heath 32 find a particularly close parallel in those of Linton Heath 21 of group II, a pointed oval motif filled with red enamel surrounded by a frame ending in a Style I arm or leg. Such limbs also frame the pointed motifs in the headplate upper corners of Linton Heath 32 and Ragley Park. Two interesting parallels may also be drawn between this group and the brooch from Nassington, N'hants (Leeds no.64). The masks in the headplate frames are of similar proportions and have the same form of forehead or brow. There is further an almost identical small curling motif added to the footplate lower borders of Linton Heath 32 and the Nassington brooch.

Girton [XI] and Quy are clearly coarser copies of a prototype best represented by Linton Heath 32 and Ragley Park, but no purpose is served by attempting to divide up the group chronologically. Linton Heath 32 could be regarded as broadly contemporary with the Linton Heath 21, West Stow [II], Badby, and Duston stage of group II, although if the framed and enamelled footplate lobes derive from Sarre 159 and Herpes, the Kentish source of that group, its earliest occurrences in the enamelled Cambridgeshire form should be on brooches of the same group, e.g. Linton Heath 21. The size of the masks in the headplate frame, the treatment of the bow, and the crested head of the footplate upper borders are all comparable to brooches of group X, perhaps more so to Little Wilbraham 3 and Little Wilbraham 40 of that group, and so the group may also be regarded as broadly contemporary with those brooches too. It should also be noted that the Nassington brooch (Leeds no.64) shares close parallels with both of these groups, and so this too may be provisionally placed as broadly contemporary with them.

143

Group XII

East Garston Warren, Berks   Ashmolean 1955.377.   Plate 3.7
Norton, N'hants   Leeds no.90

2 brooches

To all appearances the fragment of a square-headed
brooch, East Garston Warren, a bow with small sections of
the headplate and footplate remaining at either end, is
identical to the brooch illustrated by Leeds, Norton.

Leeds included Norton in his group B4, which is
basically group II above. Although Leeds gave more
reasons, the best reasons for doing so appear to be the
framed plane triangular footplate inner panels whose base
is some way separate from the footplate bar, and maybe too
the widening out of the footplate frame below the side- and
around the terminal lobes, which may derive from a model
such as the footplate frame and lower borders on Badby.
Other features, however, imply that this brooch draws on
models like the brooches of group V. On the headplate
frame are the rows of small masks represented almost by the
eyes alone, and the lentoid elements in the upper corners.
The bow contains animal ornament, although admittedly not
obviously derived from the group V brooches. However it is
not too imaginative to suggest that the two roundels-plus-
triangle motifs just off the end of the median ridge of the
bow of the two brooches of the present group could depend
on the two masks we find here on Barrington B 9 and Myton,
especially in the simplified form in which they occur on
the latter.

One may consequently suggest that group XII is a group
that draws evenly on the models of groups II and V, which
it must therefore follow.

Group XIII

West Stow, Sfk [XIII]   Leeds no.106
Little Wilbraham, Cambs g.158   Leeds no.104
Nassington, N'hants g.5   Leeds no.107
Ruskington, Lincs [XIII]   Leeds no.107A
Unknown provenance [XIII]   Leeds no.105

5 brooches

Equivalent elements

Headplate frame   : West Stow [XIII]; Little
                            Wilbraham 158; Nassington 5;
                            Ruskington [XIII]; Unknown
                            provenance [XIII]

Headplate upper corners : West Stow [XIII]; Little Wilbraham 158; Ruskington [XIII]; Unknown provenance [XIII]

Headplate inner panel : Little Wilbraham 158; Nassington 5

Footplate upper borders : West Stow [XIII]; Unknown provenance [XIII]

Footplate frame : Little Wilbraham 158; Nassington 5

Footplate side lobes : West Stow [XIII]; Unknown provenance [XIII]

Footplate terminal lobe : Little Wilbraham 158; Nassington 5

Footplate lower borders : Little Wilbraham 158; Nassington 5

Footplate inner panels : Nassington 5 Ruskington [XIII]

Footplate inner panel frame : Little Wilbraham 158; Ruskington [XIII]

Footplate inner panels and frame : West Stow [XIII]; Unknown provenance [XIII]

Table of similarity coefficients based on the above

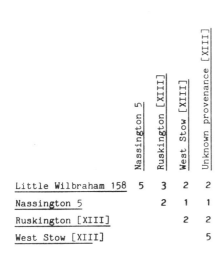

	Nassington 5	Ruskington [XIII]	West Stow [XIII]	Unknown provenance [XIII]
Little Wilbraham 158	5	3	2	2
Nassington 5		2	1	1
Ruskington [XIII]			2	2
West Stow [XIII]				5

These equivalent elements are supplemented by a number of clearly related features within the group. All brooches have an upward-facing mask surrounded by zoomorphic ornament in the headplate inner panel, only really legible on Little Wilbraham 158 and Nassington 5, which therefore appear to be the earlier forms. The pair of rampant beasts in this panel on those two brooches are presumably related to those which occur here on group V brooches, e.g. Barrington B 9, and may be interpreted as simpler and later forms.

A high degree of relationship between the brooches of this group can also be seen on the footplates. All have triangular inner panels, with related inner panel frames. The simplest explanation of the mosaic-like inner panel frames of West Stow [XIII] and Unknown provenance [XIII] is as derivatives of the panelled treatment of this element as on Nassington 5. I have unfortunately not been able to see Ruskington [XIII] myself: the photograph in Leeds is not very clear, and a number of questions concerning its relationship to the other brooches are impossible to answer from this. The mask at the head of the footplate bar and the footplate inner panel frame suggests that it is a copy of the Little Wilbraham 158 model, but the footplate lobes look to be almost entirely plain, and it is not mentioned whether these are, or have been, silvered as on Little Wilbraham 158. Otherwise the footplate lobes of West Stow [XIII] and Unknown provenance [XIII] are obviously closely related to the Little Wilbraham 158 form. Similarly the outline of the head in the footplate upper borders betrays the relationship of Little Wilbraham 158, Nassington 5, West Stow [XIII], and Unknown provenance [XIII], but the illustration of Ruskington [XIII] is insufficiently clear here to offer an opinion.

Leeds (1949 p.66) suggested that the form of the masks in the headplate frames of these brooches might be derivative of the form found on Northampton [VIII] and Saxby of group VIII, and it seems a reasonable hypothesis. Little Wilbraham 158 and Nassington 5 have a very similar curling motif added to the footplate lower borders as found on Linton Heath 32 (group XI), and another brooch from Nassington (Leeds no.64), although the other way up. The framed oval footplate lobes of this group may also be compared with those of group XI and Linton Heath 21 of group II. On the present group, however, the ends of these are cut off or indented, not pointed as on the others and the Sarre 159 model. This may indicate a slightly later development. Little Wilbraham 158 has these lobes and the triangular inner panels picked out in a bichrome style by silver plating. The rows of circles which decorate the footplate inner panel frames of Little Wilbraham 158 and Ruskington [XIII] are most likely derivative of the running scrolls found in this place on brooches such as Holywell Row 11 and Alveston Manor 5.

A rather simpler form of the headplate inner panel suggests that Nassington 5 is a slightly later form than Little Wilbraham 158, and it has in turn been suggested that Nassington 5 carries an ancestral form of the footplate inner panel design of West Stow [XIII] and Unknown provenance [XIII]. Ruskington [XIII] is derivative of Little Wilbraham 158 too, and the treatment of the headplate inner panels aligns it chronologically with West Stow [XIII] and Unknown provenance [XIII]. The group may be set out as follows:

```
                 ┌──────────────────────────────┐
                 │    Little Wilbraham 158       │
                 ├──────────────────────────────┤
                 │        Nassington 5          │
        ┌────────┴──────────────────────────────┴──────────────┐
        │ West Stow [XIII]  Unknown provenance [XIII]  Ruskington [XIII] │
        └───────────────────────────────────────────────────────┘
```

It has already been suggested that Little Wilbraham 158 is a slightly later form than Linton Heath 21 of group II, and may be later Linton Heath 32 of group XI too.

Group XIV

Londesborough, Hu g.6   Leeds no.59
"Yorkshire"   TBAA, Gloucester Congress 1846 p.100,
                                              Leeds no.59A
2 brooches. Map 3.5

Equivalent elements

Headplate   : frame
Footplate   : upper borders, frame, lobes,
                               inner panel frame.

The animal ornament in the headplate second panels of these brooches is also related, but it is not clear whether the form on either brooch is ancestral to the other.

The related features which associate these two brooches with brooches of other groups present a rather diverse pattern. The triangular footplate inner panels of this group may be compared to those of group II, as the inward-facing masks of the footplate side lobes in their pointed ovals may also be compared with Duston of that group, especially the form on "Yorkshire", with its scored hair. The headplate inner panel of Londesborough 6, an upward-facing mask flanked by two extra eyes, is remarkably similar to that on the brooch from Market Overton, Leics (Leeds no.17). The running scrolls of the footplate inner panel frames are reminiscent of Alveston Manor 5 and Holywell Row 11. These running scrolls may allow us to regard these two brooches as of an earlier form than Little Wilbraham 158 of group XIII, though not necessarily ancestral to it. Otherwise it is difficult to see how and where to place this apparently Northumbrian group relative to other Anglo-Saxon square-headed brooches already discussed.

Group XV

Lakenheath, Sfk [XV]	Leeds no.19
Tuddenham, Sfk [XV]	Leeds no.25
Barrington A, Cambs g.11	Leeds no.21
Girton, Cambs [XV]	Leeds no.24
Linton Heath, Cambs g.40	Leeds no.23
St.John's College C.G., Cambs	Leeds no.22
Nassington, N'hants [XV]	Leeds no.28
Wakerley, N'hants g.50	Kettering Mus. Plate 3.8
Wakerley, N'hants g.80	Kettering Mus. Plate 3.9
Market Overton, Leics [XV]	Leeds no.20

10 brooches. Map 3.6

Equivalent elements

Headplate frame : Lakenheath [XV]; Barrington A 11; Linton Heath 40; St John's College C.G.; Nassington [XV]; Wakerley 50; Wakerley 80; Market Overton [XV]

Headplate upper corners : Lakenheath [XV];, Barrington A 11; Linton Heath 40; St John's College C.G.; Nassington [XV]; Wakerley 50; Wakerley 80; Market Overton [XV]

Headplate second panel : Lakenheath [XV]; Tuddenham [XV]; Barrington A 11; Linton Heath 40; St John's College C.G.; Nassington [XV]; Wakerley 50; Wakerley 80; Market Overton [XV]; (Barrington A (Leeds no.27), Welbourn (Leeds no.29))

Headplate inner panel : Lakenheath [XV]; Linton Heath 40; Nassington [XV]; Wakerley 80

Headplate lower corners : Lakenheath [XV]; Wakerley 50
" : Nassington [XV]; Wakerley 80

Bow : Lakenheath [XV]; Barrington A 11

Footplate upper borders : Barrington A 11; Linton Heath 40; St John's College C.G.

Footplate side lobes : Lakenheath [XV]; Barrington A 11; Linton Heath 40; St John's College C.G.; Wakerley 50; Market Overton [XV]

Footplate terminal lobe (mask) : Lakenheath [XV]; Barrington A 11; Linton Heath 40; Market Overton [XV]

Footplate lower borders : Lakenheath [XV]; Tuddenham [XV]; Barrington A 11; Girton [XV]; Linton Heath 40; St John's College C.G.; Wakerley 50;

                              Wakerley 80; Market Overton
                              [XV]
Footplate frame   : Lakenheath [XV]; Tuddenham
                          [XV]; Barrington A 11; Girton
                          [XV]; Linton Heath 40; St
                          John's College C.G. ; Wakerley
                          50; Wakerley 80; Market
                          Overton [XV]; (Rainham,
                          (Arch.96 p.164 fig.3))
Footplate inner panel   : Tuddenham [XV]; Barrington A
                          11; Girton [XV]; Linton Heath
                          40; St John's College C.G.;
                          Wakerley 80; Market Overton
                          [XV];   (Welbourn (Leeds no.29))

Table of similarity coefficients based on the above

	Linton Heath 40	Market Overton [XV]	St.John's College C.G.	Lakenheath [XV]	Wakerley 80	Wakerley 50	Tuddenham [XV]	Nassington [XV]	Girton [XV]	Welbourn	Rainham	Barrington A [sb]
Barrington A 11	9	8	8	7	6	6	4	3	3	2	1	1
Linton Heath 40		8	8	8	7	6	4	4	3	2	1	1
Market Overton [XV]			7	8	6	5	4	3	3	2	1	1
St.John's College C.G.				6	6	6	4	3	3	2	1	1
Lakenheath [XV]					6	7	3	4	2	1	1	1
Wakerley 80						5	4	5	3	2	1	1
Wakerley 50							3	3	2	1	1	1
Tuddenham [XV]								1	3	2	1	1
Nassington [XV]										1		1
Girton [XV]										1	1	

It appears that the ten brooches recognized as members of this group were originally intended to be recognizable as reproductions, mass-produced in a sense, of a single basic prototype. The similarity coefficients adjudged to exist between individual brooches vary considerably, but this does not contradict the basic character of the group. Other than the fragmentary Girton [XV] and Nassington [XV], Tuddenham [XV] seems to be relatively weakly linked to the remainder of the group, but the majority of elements on that brooch which are not considered "equivalent" to those on other brooches are at least very closely related: for instance the simplified outline of the heads in the footplate upper borders, side lobes, and terminal lobe.

It is because they cannot be considered as attempts to reproduce the same whole prototype that the three brooches sharing significant equivalent elements with brooches of this group, Welbourn, Barrington A and Rainham, are not counted here as members of it, although Leeds added the former two to his group A3, and Evison added Rainham to it (Arch.96 pp.164-165). These three brooches are dealt with elsewhere in a more appropriate place as hybrids or individualistic forms.

The brooches of the present group are obviously closely related to those of group IX - a point made by Leeds - and as a group appear to be lineally descended from it. The profile masks of the footplate side lobes and the large terminal lobe masks are in general very similar indeed to those on Lakenheath [IX] and Haslingfield [IX] but significantly simplified: the curling beard below the side lobe profile heads has disappeared, as have the curling "ears" and side-locks of the terminal lobe masks, except on Wakerley 80, where they appear as decorative flourishes on the footplate lower borders, unconnected with the terminal lobe mask. Such items may have been lost from the damaged Lakenheath [XV]. As these ears appear to be lineally descended from the tails of the footplate lower border animals of group IV, their further reduction and disappearance could be an indication of a later stage. Some of the brooches of the present group also share with group IX the bows with a stud on the bow-ridge, and panels, though not with Style I decoration. On Linton Heath 40 and Market Overton XV, however, the bow panels of the same proportions remain, but the central stud is not there.

A feature of the brooches of group XV which recalls brooches of other groups than group IX is the crested profile heads appearing on headplate upper corners and footplate upper borders. The form of the temple, eye, and beak, on, for instance, the headplate upper corners of Lakenheath [XV], is very similar to that on the head in the footplate upper borders of the Nassington brooch (Leeds no.64); the crested head itself with this curling crest has already been met on groups V, X, and XI, of which Barrington B 9 (group V) seems to carry a particularly early form. On Lakenheath [XV], Barrington A 11, Linton Heath 40 and St. John's College C.G., however, there is a plain, stubby, element, perhaps a horn or ear, instead of this crest. Different again from the crested heads in the footplate upper borders of groups V, X and XI, is the treatment of the jaws: not wide open on this group, and sometimes with a kind of tusk crossing the upper jaw.

Leeds drew attention to the Kentish appearance of the Style I animals confronted in the headplate second panels of this group (Leeds 1949 pp.23-24, fig.2). The design and layout of these animals' bodies are indeed identical to those found on a widely-dispersed type of Kentish buckle-plate (cf. Haseloff 1981 pp.278-280), and on the headplate second panels of Sarre 159, Herpes and a Kentish brooch, Finglesham E2 (Leeds 1949 pl.S2), except for the non-appearance of the curly tail on the brooches. The compositions formed of these animals, however, are different, the group XV brooch animals being symmetrically confronted, the other examples chasing each other head-to-tail. The most plausible source for these animals on group XV brooches is presumably the early brooches of group II, although the puzzling discrepancy of the tail remains, and permits us to consider the buckle-plates as a source. Looking for parallels to the symmetrical layout of the headplate second panels, a degree of similarity is apparent between this element here and that on Mitcham 25 and Alfriston 28 in group I, with the confronted heads in the centre, and limbs in the upper corners. The influence of this Saxon group on Anglian square-headed brooches has already been noted in other instances, and it is a possibility that group XV could in this respect ultimately depend on the same source as Mitcham 25 and Alfriston 28 too.

No purpose is served by attempting to place the brooches of group XV in a chronological order amongst themselves, although it is worth noting that Wakerley 50 now provides an example with a true swastika in the footplate inner panel, presumably the original motif upon which the double-S motif of most other known examples is based. On the whole the group should be placed a little later than groups IX, X and XI, although quite probably it overlaps with later examples of the latter two.

Group XVI

Westgarth Gardens, Bury St. Edmunds,		
Sfk g.27	BSE Mus	Plate 3.10
nr. Bury St. Edmunds, Sfk	Leeds no.45	
Holywell Row, Sfk g.14	Leeds no.46	
Ipswich, Sfk [XVI]a	Leeds no.41	
Ipswich, Sfk [XVI]b	Leeds no.42	
Ipswich, Sfk [XVI]c	Leeds no.43	
Ipswich, Sfk [XVI]d	Leeds no.51	
Ipswich, Sfk [XVI]e	Leeds no.57	
Lakenheath, Sfk [XVI]	Leeds no.54	
Bergh Apton, Nfk g.64	EAA 7 fig.94	
Bridgham, Nfk	Leeds no.58	
Brooke, Nfk	Leeds no.65	
Catton, Nfk	Leeds no.52	
Crimplesham, Nfk	King's Lynn Mus	
Hunstanton, Nfk	Leeds no.44	
Kenninghall, Nfk [XVI]a	Leeds no.49	
Kenninghall, Nfk [XVI]b	Leeds no.50 ·	
Morningthorpe, Nfk g.214	Norwich Mus.	Plate 3.11
Morningthorpe, Nfk g.288	Norwich Mus	
Morningthorpe, Nfk g.359	Norwich Mus	
Spong Hill, Nfk g.24	Norwich Mus (on loan)	
	EAA Spong Hill vol.III (forthcoming)	
Great Chesterford, Ex g.2	BM 1964.7-2.11.	Plate 3.12

Ely, Cambs   MAA Cam 48.2267
Billesdon, Leics   Leeds no.48
Market Overton, Leics [XVI]   Leeds no.56
Holme Pierrepoint, Notts   Leeds no.47
Willoughby-on-the-Wolds, Notts g.46   Nottingham Mus
Laceby, Hu   Leeds no.53
Welbeck Hill, Hu g.41   Private coll. Fig.3.6
Faversham, Kt   Leeds no.55

30 brooches. Map 3.6

Equivalent elements

Headplate upper corners
(quadrangles)   : Westgarth Gardens, Bury St.
                               Edmunds 27; Ipswich [XVI]b;
                               Lakenheath [XVI]; Bergh Apton
                               64; Brooke; Crimplesham;
                               Hunstanton; Kenninghall [XVI]a;
                               Morningthorpe 214; Spong Hill
                               24; Great Chesterford 2;
                               Billesdon; Market Overton
                               [XVI]; Faversham; (see also
                               groups XVII and XXI)

Headplate lower corners
(quadrangles)   : Westgarth Gardens, Bury St.
                               Edmunds 27; Ipswich [XVI]b;
                               Crimplesham; Kenninghall
                               [XVI]a; Spong Hill 24; Great
                               Chesterford 2; Market Overton
                               [XVI]; Holme Pierrepoint;
                               Faversham; (see also group XVII)

Headplate lower corners   : Lakenheath [XVI]; Bergh Apton
                               64; Morningthorpe 214

Headplate upper corners
(angles)   : nr. Bury St. Edmunds; Ipswich
                               [XVI]a; Ipswich [XVI]c;
                               Ipswich [XVI]d; Catton;
                               Morningthorpe 359; (see also
                               group XVIII)

Headplate lower corners   : nr. Bury St. Edmunds; Ipswich
                               [XVI]a;   (see also group XVIII)
Headplate upper corners   : Ipswich [XVI]e; Bridgham
Headplate lower corners   : Ipswich [XVI]e; Bridgham
Headplate frame
(broad, plane)   : Westgarth Gardens, Bury St.
                               Edmunds 27; nr. Bury St.
                               Edmunds;   Holywell Row 14;
                               Ipswich [XVI]a; Ipswich [XVI]b;
                               Ipswich [XVI]c; Ipswich, Sfk
                               [XVI]d; Ipswich [XVI]e;
                               Lakenheath [XVI]; Bergh Apton
                               64; Bridgham; Catton;
                               Crimplesham; Hunstanton;
                               Kenninghall [XVI]a; Kenninghall

CXVIIb; Morningthorpe 214;
Morningthorpe 288; Morningthorpe
359; Spong Hill 24; Great
Chesterford 2; Ely;
Billesdon; Market Overton
CXVII; Holme Pierrepoint;
Laceby; Faversham; (Market
Overton (Leeds no.17); West
Stow (Leeds no.18); see also
groups XVII, XIX, and XXI)

Headplate inner panels : Westgarth Gardens, Bury St.
Edmunds 27; Ipswich CXVIIa;
Ipswich CXVIIb; Ipswich CXVIIc;
Morningthorpe 359;

" : nr. Bury St. Edmunds;
Holywell Row 14; Hunstanton;
Ely; Welbeck Hill 41

" : Billesdon; Holme Pierrepoint;

" : Ipswich CXVIId; Catton;
Morningthorpe 288

" : Ipswich CXVIIe; Lakenheath
CXVII; Bergh Apton 64;
Morningthorpe 214

Headplate top knob : Lakenheath CXVII;
Morningthorpe 214

Footplate upper borders : Westgarth Gardens, Bury St.
Edmunds 27; Ipswich CXVIIa;
Ipswich CXVIIb

" : nr. Bury St. Edmunds;
Hunstanton

" : Holywell Row 14; Ipswich
CXVIId; Brooke; Catton;
Crimplesham; Morningthorpe 288;
Morningthorpe 359; Market
Overton CXVII; Welbeck
Hill 41; Faversham;
(see also group XVIII)

" : Ipswich CXVIIe; Bridgham

" : Lakenheath CXVII; Bergh Apton
64; Kenninghall CXVIIa;
Morningthorpe 214; Spong Hill
24; Great Chesterford 2;
Billesdon; Holme Pierrepoint

Footplate side lobes : Westgarth Gardens, Bury St.
Edmunds 27; nr. Bury St.
Edmunds; Holywell Row 14;
Ipswich CXVIIa; Ipswich
CXVIIb; Ipswich CXVIIc;
Ipswich CXVIId; Ipswich CXVIIe;.
Lakenheath CXVII; Bergh Apton
64; Bridgham; Catton;
Crimplesham; Hunstanton;
Kenninghall CXVIIa; Kenninghall
CXVIIb; Morningthorpe 288;
Morningthorpe 359; Spong Hill
24; Great Chesterford 2; Ely;

Billesdon; Market Overton
[XVI]; Holme Pierrepoint;
Faversham; (Market Overton;
West Stow; Welbourn;
Kenninghall (Leeds nos.17, 18,
29 and 60); see also XVII,
XVIII, and Ruskington [XIII])

Footplate terminal lobe   : Westgarth Gardens, Bury St.
Edmunds 27; nr. Bury St.
Edmunds; Holywell Row 14;
Ipswich [XVI]a; Ipswich [XVI]b;
Ipswich [XVI]d; Ipswich [XVI]e;
Lakenheath [XVI]; Bergh Apton
64; Bridgham; Catton;
Crimplesham; Kenninghall
[XVI]a; Kenninghall [XVI]b;
Morningthorpe 288; Spong Hill
24; Great Chesterford 2;
Billesdon; Market Overton
[XVI]; Holme Pierrepoint;
Willoughby-on-the-Wolds 46;
Faversham; (West Stow;
Kenninghall (Leeds nos.18 and
60); see also groups XVII and
XVIII, and Ruskington [XIII])

Footplate lower borders   : Westgarth Gardens, Bury St.
Edmunds 27; Ipswich [XVI]a;
Ipswich [XVI]b; Ipswich [XVI]c;
Brooke; Hunstanton;
Morningthorpe 359; Ely

"   : Bergh Apton 64; Kenninghall
[XVI]a; Morningthorpe 214;
Great Chesterford 2; Billesdon;
Holme Pierrepoint;

"   : Lakenheath [XVI]; Spong Hill 24

Footplate inner panel
frame (I)   : Westgarth Gardens, Bury St.
Edmunds 27; nr. Bury St.
Edmunds;   Holywell Row 14;
Ipswich [XVI]a; Ipswich [XVI]b;
Ipswich [XVI]c; Brooke;
Hunstanton; Morningthorpe 359;
Ely

"   : Ipswich [XVI]e; Bergh Apton
64; Kenninghall [XVI]a;
Morningthorpe 214; Great
Chesterford 2; Billesdon;
Holme Pierrepoint

"   : Lakenheath [XVI]; Crimplesham .
"   : Ipswich [XVI]d; Catton;
Morningthorpe 288; Market
Overton [XVI]

Footplate inner panel
frame (II)   : Westgarth Gardens, Bury St.
Edmunds 27; nr. Bury St.
Edmunds; Holywell Row 14;

Ipswich [XVI]a;   Ipswich
[XVI]b;   Ipswich [XVI]c;
Ipswich [XVI]d;   Ipswich [XVI]e;
Lakenheath [XVI];   Bergh Apton
64;   Bridgham;   Brooke;   Catton;
Crimplesham;   Hunstanton;
Kenninghall [XVI]a;   Kenninghall
[XVI]b;   Morningthorpe 214;
Morningthorpe 288;
Morningthorpe 359;   Spong Hill
24;   Great Chesterford 2;   Ely;
Billesdon;   Market Overton
[XVI];   Holme Pierrepoint;
Laceby;   Welbeck Hill 41;
Faversham

Footplate inner panel
(plane)   : Ipswich [XVI]a;   Ipswich [XVI]c;
Lakenheath [XVI];   Bergh Apton
64;   Brooke;   Kenninghall
[XVI]b;   Morningthorpe 214;
Morningthorpe 359;   Ely;
Billesdon;   Welbeck Hill 41

Footplate inner panel
(faceted)   : nr. Bury St. Edmunds;   Ipswich
[XVI]e;   Hunstanton;   Faversham;
(Morningthorpe 371 - see group
XVIII)

Footplate inner panel
(openwork)   : Westgarth Gardens, Bury St.
Edmunds 27;   Holywell Row 14;
Ipswich [XVI]b;   Ipswich [XVI]d;
Bridgham;   Catton;   Crimplesham;
Kenninghall [XVI]a;
Morningthorpe 288;   Great
Chesterford 2;   Market Overton
[XVI];   Holme Pierrepoint;
Laceby

Footplate bar   : Westgarth Gardens, Bury St.
Edmunds 27;   nr. Bury St.
Edmunds;   Holywell Row 14;
Ipswich [XVI]a;   Ipswich [XVI]d;
Lakenheath [XVI];   Catton;
Crimplesham;   Morningthorpe 288;
Market Overton [XVI];   Faversham

         "   : Bergh Apton 64;   Morningthorpe
214;   Billesdon;   Holme
Pierrepoint

         "   : Kenninghall [XVI]a;   Welbeck
Hill 41

Table of similarity coefficients based on the above

	Lakenheath [XVI]	Bergh Apton 64	Morningthorpe 214	Billesdon	Holme Pierrepoint	Kenninghall [XVI]a	Great Chesterford 2	Spong Hill 24	Ipswich [XVI]e	Bridgham	nr. Bury St. Edmunds	Hunstanton	Ipswich [XVI]c	Morningthorpe 359	Westgarth Gardens, Bury St. Edmunds 27	Ipswich [XVI]a	Ipswich [XVI]b	Crimplesham	Market Overton [XVI]	Faversham	Ipswich [XVI]d	Catton	Morningthorpe 288	Holywell Row 14	Kenninghall [XVI]b	Ely	Willoughby-on-the-Wolds 46	Laceby	Welbeck Hill 41
Brooke	3	3	3	3	2	2	2	2	2	1	2	3	3	4		3	3	3	3	3	2	2	2	3	2	3		1	3
Welbeck Hill 41	2	2	2	2	1	2	1	1	2	1	2	2	2	3		1	2	1	2	3	2	2	2	2	3	2	3	1	
Laceby	2	2	2	2	3	3	3	2	2	3	2	2	2	2		3	2	3	3	2	2	3	3	3	3	2	2		
Willoughby-on-the-Wolds 46	1	1		1	1	1	1	1	1	1	1		1			1	1	1	1	1	1	1	1	1	1	1			
Ely	4	4	4	4	3	3	3	3	4	3	5	5	5	5	4	5	4	3	3	3	3	3	3	5	4				
Kenninghall [XVI]b	5	5	4	5	4	5	4	4	5	4	4	3	4	4	4	5	4	4	4	4	4	4	4	4					
Holywell Row 14	5	4	4	4	5	5	4	4	4	5	7	4	4	5	7	6	6	7	7	6	7	7	7						
Morningthorpe 288	5	4	3	4	5	5	5	4	4	5	5	3	4	5	7	6	6	7	8	6	9	9							
Catton	5	4	3	4	5	5	5	4	4	5	6	3	4	5	6	6	5	7	8	6	10								
Ipswich [XVI]d	5	4	3	4	5	5	5	4	4	5	6	3	4	5	6	6	5	7	8	6									
Faversham	6	5	4	5	6	6	6	6	5	4	6	5	3	4	7	5	6	8	8										
Market Overton [XVI]	6	5	4	3	7	7	7	6	4	5	5	4	3	4	8	5	7	9											
Crimplesham	7	5	3	5	7	7	7	6	4	5	5	4	4	4	8	5	7												
Ipswich [XVI]b	5	5	4	5	7	6	7	6	4	5	5	5	6	6	11	8													
Ipswich [XVI]a	6	5	4	5	4	4	4	5	4	8	4	8	8		9														
Westgarth Gardens, Bury St. Edmunds 27	6	5	4	5	7	7	7	6	4	5	6	4	6	6															
Morningthorpe 359	4	6	4	4	3	3	3	3	4	3	5	4	8																
Ipswich [XVI]c	4	4	4	4	3	3	3	3	4	3	5	4																	
Hunstanton	4	4	4	4	4	4	4	4	4	3	7																		
nr. Bury St. Edmunds	5	4	3	4	4	4	4	4	5	4																			
Bridgham	4	4	3	4	5	5	5	4	7																				
Ipswich [XVI]e	6	7	6	6	5	5	5	4																					
Spong Hill 24	7	6	5	6	7	6	7																						
Great Chesterford 2	6	8	6	8	10	10																							
Kenninghall [XVI]a	5	8	5	8	10																								
Holme Pierrepoint	6	9	7	10																									
Billesdon	7	10	8																										
Morningthorpe 214	9	10																											
Bergh Apton 65	9																												

This is the largest single group of square-headed brooches. It is essentially the same as Leeds's Group B1, and fairly familiar as such. Like the previous group, group XV, a characteristic of this group is that it appears to have been the original intention that all of its members should be recognised as reproductions of a single basic prototype. Certain of these brooches are very much more similar to one another than to others, of course, e.g. Lakenheath [XVI], Bergh Apton 64, and Morningthorpe 214; Kenninghall [XVI]a, Holme Pierrepoint, and Great Chesterford 2; and Westgarth Gardens, Bury St. Edmunds 27 and Ipswich [XVI]b, but certain related features recur throughout the whole group: the headplate frame and inner panels, and the footplate upper borders, inner panel frame, and framed triangular inner panel. One exception which is nevertheless allowed into the group is Brooke. Other than the upper corners, the headplate of this brooch is clearly of another model, and the moulded pointed oval footplate side lobe is totally different from the normal too. But the footplate upper borders, interlaced ribbon in the inner panel frame, and framed triangular panel unmistakably ally this brooch to the present group, and it seems reasonable to admit it as a "deviant" member, rather than leaving it unclassified.

Other than Brooke, it is interesting to note that the two least typical members of this group, Laceby and Welbeck Hill 41, are also the two most northerly examples as yet known. The remainder of the group shows a remarkably dense concentration in the East Anglian counties of Norfolk and Suffolk (Map 3.6), spreading into the more northerly Midlands. The remaining non-East Anglian members of this group - Billesdon, Market Overton [XVI], Holme Pierrepoint, Willoughby-on-the-Wolds 46, and Faversham - all have, as far as can be seen, good parallels on East Anglian brooches, and could well be imports from that area. Laceby and Welbeck Hill 41, however, may represent an attempt to reproduce the group in the Humberside area. The use of incised work rather than the usual silvering on the large round footplate side lobes may be adduced as one point at which these two brooches appear derivative of the normal model.

There are surprizingly few major points of contact between this group and groups already described. The crested profile heads in the headplate upper corners of Ipswich [XVI]e and Bridgham are clearly closely related to those which are usual in this position on group XV brooches, deriving either from the same source, or the one. being dependent on the other. It is striking how the distributions of groups XV and XVI complement one another (Map 3.6), group XV covering largely the cemeteries of Cambridgeshire and northern Northamptonshire, which group XVI does not appear to enter. One explanation for this could be that groups XV and XVI are largely contemporarary, with mutually exclusive ranges. Both make much use of a developed "bichrome style", as defined by Vierck (in Kossack and Reichstein 1977). A second point of external relationship is the additional disc on the bow of Ipswich [XVI]a and Brooke, while nr. Bury St. Edmunds, Great Chesterford 2, and Faversham have a hole in the bow which presumably held the stud fixing such a disc. A comparable disc-on-bow has already been met on Tuxford, apparently a late example of group II. Note especially the double ribbon interlace on this disc, as on the headplates and footplates of many group XVI brooches. Group XVI would therefore appear to be broadly contemporary with group XV and the latest stage of group II.

Group XVII

Finningham, Sfk	P.S.A. XXXI p.244
Ipswich, Sfk [XVII]a	Leeds no.32
Ipswich, Sfk [XVII]b	Leeds no.38
Little Eriswell, Sfk g.27	Hutchinson 1966, pl.Ib
Unknown provenance, Sfk [XVII]	Leeds no.39
Bergh Apton, Nfk g.7	EAA 7 fig 69
Burnham Norton, Nfk	Norwich Mus
Great Bircham, Nfk	King's Lynn Mus
Kenninghall, Nfk [XVII]	Leeds no.36
Merton, Nfk	Norwich Mus record. Fig.3.7
Barrington A, Cambs [XVII]	Leeds no.37
Market Overton, Leics [XVII]	Leeds no.34
Ruskington, Lincs [XVII]	Lincoln Mus
Londesborough, Hu g.4	Leeds no.35
Thornbrough, N.Yorks [XVII]	Leeds no.33

15 brooches. Map 3.7

Equivalent elements

Headplate upper corners : Ipswich [XVII]b; Little Eriswell 27; Suffolk [XVII]; Bergh Apton 7; Burnham Norton; Great Bircham; Kenninghall [XVII]; Merton; Barrington A [XVII]; Market Overton [XVII]; Ruskington [XVII]; Londesborough 4; (see also groups XVI and XXI)

Headplate lower corners : Ipswich [XVII]b; Little Eriswell 27; Suffolk [XVII]; Bergh Apton 7; Burnham Norton; Great Bircham; Kenninghall [XVII]; Merton; Barrington A [XVII]; Market Overton [XVII]; Londesborough 4; (see also group XVI)

Headplate frame
(broad, plane)   : Ipswich [XVII]a; Ipswich
                          [XVII]b; Little Eriswell 27;
                          Suffolk [XVII]; Bergh Apton 7;
                          Burnham Norton; Great Bircham;
                          Kenninghall [XVII]; Merton;
                          Barrington A [XVII]; Market
                          Overton [XVII]; Ruskington
                          [XVII]; Londesborough 4;
                          Thornbrough [XVII]; (see also
                          groups XVI, XIX, and XXI)
Headplate inner panel   : Ipswich [XVII]a; Suffolk
                          [XVII]; Burnham Norton; Great
                          Bircham; Kenninghall [XVII];
                          Londesborough 4
Bow   : Ipswich [XVII]a, Ipswich
                          [XVII]b; Burnham Norton;
                          Barrington A [XVII]; Market
                          Overton [XVII]; Thornbrough
                          [XVII]
"   : Ruskington [XVII];
                          Londesborough 4
"   : Little Eriswell 27;
                          Kenninghall [XVII]
Footplate upper borders : Ipswich [XVII]a; Burnham
                          Norton; Market Overton [XVII];
                          Londesborough 4; Thornbrough
                          [XVII]
"   : Ipswich [XVII]b; Kenninghall
                          [XVII];
                          Barrington A [XVII];
                          Ruskington [XVII]
Footplate side lobes   : Ipswich [XVII]a; Ipswich
                          [XVII]b; Little Eriswell 27;
                          Suffolk [XVII]; Bergh Apton 7;
                          Burnham Norton; Kenninghall
                          [XVII]; Merton; Barrington A
                          [XVII]; Market Overton [XVII];
                          Ruskington [XVII];
                          Londesborough 4; Thornbrough
                          [XVII]; (Market Overton;
                          Welbourn (Leeds nos.17 and 29),
                          see also groups XVI, XVIII, and
                          Ruskington [XIII])
Footplate terminal lobe : Ipswich [XVII]a; Little
                          Eriswell 27;   Suffolk [XVII];
                          Bergh Apton 7; Burnham Norton;
                          Kenninghall [XVII]; Merton;
                          Barrington A [XVII]; Market
                          Overton [XVII]; Ruskington
                          [XVII]; Londesborough 4;
                          Thornbrough [XVII]; (West Stow
                          (Leeds no.18);
                          see also groups XVI, XVIII, and
                          Ruskington [XIII])

	Market Overton [XVII]	Londesborough 4	Kenninghall [XVII]	Barrington A [XVII]	Ipswich [XVII]a	Suffolk [XVII]	Thornbrough [XVII]	Little Eriswell 27	Ipswich [XVII]b	Merton	Bergh Apton 7	Ruskington [XVII]	Great Bircham
Footplate frame	: Ipswich [XVII]a; Ipswich [XVII]b; Little Eriswell 27; Suffolk [XVII]; Bergh Apton 7; Burnham Norton; Kenninghall [XVII]; Merton; Barrington A [XVII]; Market Overton [XVII]; Ruskington [XVII]; Londesborough 4; Thornbrough [XVII]												

Footplate frame   : Ipswich [XVII]a; Ipswich [XVII]b; Little Eriswell 27; Suffolk [XVII]; Bergh Apton 7; Burnham Norton;   Kenninghall [XVII]; Merton; Barrington A [XVII]; Market Overton [XVII]; Ruskington [XVII]; Londesborough 4; Thornbrough [XVII]

Footplate inner panel : Ipswich [XVII]a; Burnham Norton;   Kenninghall [XVII]; Barrington A [XVII]; Market Overton [XVII]; Londesborough 4; Thornbrough [XVII]

Table of similarity coefficients based on the above

	Market Overton [XVII]	Londesborough 4	Kenninghall [XVII]	Barrington A [XVII]	Ipswich [XVII]a	Suffolk [XVII]	Thornbrough [XVII]	Little Eriswell 27	Ipswich [XVII]b	Merton	Bergh Apton 7	Ruskington [XVII]	Great Bircham
Burnham Norton	10	9	8	8	8	7	7	6	6	6	6	5	4
Market Overton [XVII]		9	8	8	8	7	7	6	6	6	6	5	4
Londesborough 4			8	7	7	7	6	6	5	6	6	6	4
Kenninghall [XVII]				8	6	7	5	7	6	6	6	6	4
Barrington A [XVII]					6	6	6	6	7	6	6	6	3
Ipswich [XVII]a						5	7	4	4	4	4	4	2
Suffolk [XVII]							4	6	5	6	6	5	4
Thornbrough [XVII]								4	4	4	4	4	1
Little Eriswell 27									5	6	6	5	3
Ipswich [XVII]b										5	5	5	3
Merton											6	5	3
Bergh Apton 7												5	3
Ruskington [XVII]													2

Once again this is a compact and coherent group whose character is that of brooches which were intended to be recognized as derivations or reproductions of a single basic prototype. The silhouette and outlines of the inner areas are constant, and for the most part those elements which are not equivalent on different brooches are at least related. The greatest variations that occur appear to be degenerations of the basic form, as, for instance, the rather coarse and simplified decoration of the headplate and footplate inner panels on Ipswich [XVII]b, Little Eriswell 27, Bergh Apton 7, and Ruskington [XVII]. Great Bircham has relatively low similarity coefficients because it is only a headplate fragment.

This group has a great deal in common with group XVI. They have essentially the same broad, plane headplate frame, and often the same treatment of the headplate corners; the typical use of round, silver-plated footplate lobes is identical too. Less immediately obvious points are the use of a riveted disc on the bow, noted on Ipswich [XVI]a, and probably lost from some other members of group XVI, which is most prominently seen on Merton of this group, while Little Eriswell 27, Kenninghall [XVII], Ruskington [XVII], and Londesborough 4 all have a smaller round-headed stud riveted to the bow, and all the remaining brooches except Suffolk [XVII] and Bergh Apton 7 have a rivet hole which could have taken either the larger disc or a stud. The flourishes decorating the footplate lower border on Suffolk [XVII] may be compared to those on Ipswich [XVI]a, Ipswich [XVI]b, Ipswich [XVI]c, Ipswich [XVI]d, Holywell Row 14, and Catton in group XVI. All of these perhaps share a source with the footplate lower border decorations of Little Wilbraham 158 and Nassington 5 of groups XIII. A candidate for this source might by the side-locks or ears of the footplate terminal lobe masks of group IX (see especially Wakerley 80, group XV). Finally the distribution of group XVII is very similar to that of group XVI (Maps 3.6-7), mostly in the East Anglian counties of Norfolk and Suffolk, together with the northern Midlands and Northumbria.

Group XVII must then be chronologically contingent with group XVI. None of the substantial points of contact between the two groups provides any persuasive argument that either precedes or supplants the other, and so one may only conclude that they were in broadly contemporary circulation in the same area, perhaps mostly from a single centre of mass production.

Group XVIII

Mildenhall, Sfk   Leeds no.63
Morningthorpe, Nfk g.371   Norwich Mus. Plate 3.13

2 brooches

Equivalent elements

Headplate: corners (see also group XVI);   frame; second
            panel
Footplate: upper borders (see also group XVI);   side lobes
            (see also groups XVI, XVII, Market Overton,
            Welbourn (Leeds no.17 and 29), Ruskington
            [XIII]); lower borders; inner panel frame

It is evident that these two brooches have very close links with groups XVI and XVII, particularly to the former. Leeds indeed counted the one example of the present group he knew, _Mildenhall_, in his Group B1 with the majority of the brooches of group XVI. Besides the equivalent elements, there are number of related features, for further consideration of which reference is made back to group XVI, e.g. the rectangular headplate inner panel, the disc-on-bow, and the excrescent flourishes on the footplate lower borders. Both of these brooches are from within East Anglia, where groups XVI and XVII are most densely concentrated. They can only be regarded as broadly contemporary to those groups.

Group XIX

Lakenheath, Sfk [XIX]	Hattatt 1982 fig.92
West Stow, Sfk [XIX]	Leeds no.30
Sleaford, Lincs	Leeds no.31
Willoughby-on-the-Wolds, Notts g.57	Nottingham Mus

4 brooches

Equivalent elements

Headplate frame and upper corners (outline)	: Sleaford; Willoughby-on-the-Wolds 57
Headplate inner panel	: Lakenheath [XIX]; West Stow [XIX]
Bow	: Lakenheath [XIX]; West Stow [XIX]; Sleaford; Willoughby-on-the-Wolds 57
Footplate upper borders	: Lakenheath [XIX]; West Stow [XIX]; Sleaford; Willoughby-on-the-Wolds 57
Footplate lobes	: Lakenheath [XIX]; West Stow [XIX]; Sleaford; Willoughby-on-the-Wolds 57
Footplate lower borders	: Lakenheath [XIX]; West Stow [XIX]; Sleaford; Willoughby-on-the-Wolds 57
Footplate frame	: Lakenheath [XIX]; West Stow [XIX]; Sleaford; Willoughby-on-the-Wolds 57

Table of similarity coeffients based on the above

	West Stow [XIX]	Sleaford	Willoughby-on-the-Wolds 57
Lakenheath [XIX]	6	5	5
West Stow [XIX]		5	5
Sleaford			6

This is a small and coherent group. It is interesting to note that elements on the headplate link the two East Anglian examples more closely together, and the two more northerly examples likewise, but with only four known examples, it is premature to identify northern and southern branches of the group.

A consistent pattern of relationship may be observed between the brooches of this group and those of groups IX and XV. The beaked profile heads in the headplate upper corners of Lakenheath [XIX] are very similar to those that are common in group XV and appear on Ipswich [XVI]e and Bridgham of group XVI, except that on Lakenheath [XIX] they lack the crests. The headplate inner panel of Willoughby-on-the-Wolds 57 contains a pair of swastikas, as found here amongst groups IX and XV; Willoughby-on-the-Wolds 57 stands perhaps a little closer to Lakenheath [XV], Linton Heath 40, Nassington [XV], and Wakerley 80 of the latter group, as only a plain rectangular bar divides the swastikas, not an upward-facing mask as on group IX. The bars of the footplate side lobes, silvered on the West Stow [XIX] brooch, may be derived from the bars in front of the profile masks in this position on brooches of groups IX and XV. The footplate inner panels of Lakenheath [XIX] and West Stow [XIX] are very similar to one another; this framed, plane rhombus is also found on Lakenheath [IX] and Haslingfield [IX], and West Stow (Leeds no.18). The overall impression of the relationships of group XIX suggests that the group is broadly contemporary with groups XV and XVI, and, like the former of those two, represents a later form than group IX.

Before leaving this group, one may comment upon their similarity to a group of three brooches from Norfolk, from Kenninghall, Sporle, and Spong Hill g.38, the former two of which Leeds designated as Group C1 square-headed brooches. They have nothing to contribute to a study of Anglo-Saxon square-headed brooches, and could be dismissed as brooches sui generis, but their outline is surprizingly reminiscent of group XIX brooches, especially with the lappets below the bow (cf. group XIX's projections in the footplate upper borders) and the form of the terminal lobe, which could be

reckoned an equivalent element.   I do not propose to treat
these as a separate group of square-headed brooches - they
may perhaps be a simple and contemporary copy of the form
of group XIX.

Group XX

Spong Hill, Nfk g.18   Norwich Mus (on loan)
Little Wilbraham, Cambs g.111(a)   Neville 1852 pl.2
Little Wilbraham, Cambs g.111(b)   (two examples)

3 brooches

Equivalent elements

Headplate upper corners : Spong Hill 18; Little Wilbraham
                           111a;   Little Wilbraham 111b;
                           (West Stow (Leeds no.18))
Bow   : Spong Hill 18; Little Wilbraham
                           111a; Little Wilbraham 111b
Footplate upper borders : Spong Hill 18; Little Wilbraham
                           111a; Little Wilbraham 111b
Footplate lobes   : Spong Hill 18; Little Wilbraham
                           111a; Little Wilbraham 111b
Footplate inner panel   : Spong Hill 18; Little Wilbraham
                           111b

From the above it emerges that Spong Hill 18 stands a
little closer to one of the brooches in Little Wilbraham,
Cambs g.111 than these two brooches to the third member of
the group, but the close unity of the group is obvious.

Although in plain bronze, the round plane lobes of the
footplates of these brooches clearly recall the footplate
lobes of groups XVI and XVII, which also appear on brooches
such as West Stow (Leeds no.18).   The broad area framing
the headplate defined by a line of stamps on
Little Wilbraham 111b recalls the broad plain headplate
frame of groups XVI and XVII too. Of very great interest is
the similarity between the beaked profile heads of the
footplate upper borders of the present group, and those in
this position on the brooch from Nassington, N'hants (Leeds
no.64).   As has already been pointed out, this is
essentially the same as the profile head that occurs on the
headplate upper corners of brooches of group XV and.
Ipswich [XVI]e and Bridgham of group XVI.   Other features
of the Nassington brooch, however, have already been shown
to be closely connected to features of groups X and XI, and
the brooch provisionally placed broadly contemporary to
those groups.   The present group would appear to belong in
the same horizon as groups XV, XVI, and XVII, etc., which
it was suggested, slightly overlap with groups X and XI.

The form of the Nassington brooch would appear to fall precisely into such an overlap-stage.

Group XXI - Hybrid square-headed and florid cruciform
             brooches

Little Wilbraham, Cambs [XXI]   Leeds no.142
Kempston, Beds [XXI]   Leeds no.141
Holdenby, N'hants   Leeds no.143

3 brooches

Equivalent elements

Headplate upper corners   : Little Wilbraham [XXI]; Kempston
                             [XXI]; Holdenby; (see
                             also groups XVI and XVII)
Headplate lower corners   : Kempston [XXI]; Holdenby (see
                             also groups XVI and XVII)
Headplate frame   : Little Wilbraham [XXI];
                             Kempston [XXI]; Holdenby
Bow   : Kempston [XXI]; Holdenby

    There is thus a higher demonstrable degree of
similarity between Kempston [XXI] and Holdenby than between
these brooches and the fragmentary example from a cremation
at Little Wilbraham. The silvered squares in the headplate
corners of these brooches clearly link them with groups XVI
and XVII. The form of the masks in the headplate frame
however is very similar to those already met here on
brooches of groups X, XI, and from Nassington (Leeds
no.64), adding further evidence of overlap between groups
X, XI, XVI, and XVII.

    While the headplates of these brooches connect them to
the square-headed brooch corpus, below the bow they belong
with the florid cruciform brooches. Leeds made this hybrid
feature define his Class C square-headed brooches, under
which he listed 17 examples. His brooches 127 and 128 have
already been considered with group XIX, and his brooch 129
and Group C2, have no place, as far as I can see, within a
corpus of square-headed brooches. All the features of the
headplates of Leeds's Group C2 are derived from the
cruciform brooch tradition, not that of square-headed
brooches. The three brooches listed here under group XXI
belonged to Leeds's Group C3. Leeds listed three further
brooches under that group, which may be accepted as square-
headed/cruciform brooch hybrids, although they are too
dissimilar to Little Wilbraham [XXI], Kempston [XXI], and
Holdenby to be counted as one group. For the brooch from
Ipswich (Leeds no.138), the silvered roundels in the
headplate corners may be compared with such features on

group XVI brooches Ipswich [XVI]e, Bridgham, Kenninghall XVIb, and West Stow (Leeds no.18), Welbourn (Leeds no.29), and the group XX brooches.

Group XXII

Ingarsby, Leics   Leeds no.117
Driffield, Hu   Leeds no.120
Fridaythorpe, Hu   Leeds no.119
Sewerby, Hu g.19   Sewerby Hall Mus. Hirst 1981 fig.35
Welbeck Hill, Hu g.45   Private Coll. Fig.3.8a

5 brooches. Map 3.5

Equivalent elements

Headplate inner panels   : Driffield; Sewerby 19
Bow   : Driffield; Sewerby 19
Footplate upper borders : Driffield; Sewerby 19
Footplate terminal lobe : Sewerby 19; Welbeck Hill 45
Footplate lower borders : Driffield; Welbeck Hill 45
Footplate inner panels   : Driffield; Sewerby 19

Table of similarity coefficients based on the above

	Sewerby 19	Driffield
Driffield	4	1
Sewerby 19		1

This table is drawn up here simply to show that group XXII is collected around a kernel of apparently quite similar brooches, Driffield, Sewerby 19, and a fragment, Welbeck Hill 45. The equivalent elements shared by these three are supplemented by a number of related ones. The animal ornament in the headplate second panels of Driffield and Sewerby 19 looks similar. As on Sewerby 19 and Welbeck Hill 45, an upward-facing mask can be seen in the footplate terminal lobe of Driffield, as drawn by Mortimer (Mortimer 1905 fig.828). The clearly modelled upward-facing profile head in the lower borders of Welbeck Hill 45. seems to be what was represented by Mortimer on Driffield too; Sewerby 19 has a "mask" consisting of no more than an eye here, appearing to face downwards rather than upwards.

The association of Ingarsby and Fridaythorpe with these three brooches is based upon related features. On Ingarsby there is firstly the bar running down from the headplate inner panel, across the bow, and down the footplate with small circular settings on the centre of the bow and the footplate; other circular settings on Ingarsby are illustrated as containing red glass or garnets (VCH Leics I, col.pl. opp. p.222), and Hirst notes space for such an inlay on the bow, and a "?garnet" inlay on the footplate bar of Sewerby 19 (Hirst 1981 p.271). There appears to have been a similar setting on the bow of Driffield. Fridaythorpe is similar in that a bar can be traced, although broken by masks, from the headplate inner panel, across the bow, to the footplate terminal lobe, with studs in the appropriate places. Most similar to Fridaythorpe in this respect, however, are Little Wilbraham 3 and Little Wilbraham 40 of group X. But there are further apparently related features between Fridaythorpe and the principal brooches of this group. The projecting ornament on the footplate lower borders of Fridaythorpe appear to be related to that on Welbeck Hill 45, Driffield, and Sewerby 19. The headplate and footplate inner panels of Fridaythorpe are decorated with lentoid motifs with a central groove, which appears again on the footplate side lobes of Driffield, and on the footplate side lobes of Welbeck Hill 41 of group XVI. This looks like a local Humberside characteristic, although something similar appears on the headplate inner panels of a brooch from West Stow, Sfk (Leeds no.18).

Leeds used the bar running from the headplate inner panel to the footplate terminal lobe to connect the three brooches of the present group he knew, Ingarsby, Driffield, and Fridaythorpe, to the brooches of group X in his Group B8. There are in fact further points he missed. The small profile heads on the ends of the jaws of the biting beast of the footplate upper borders of certain brooches of groups V and X appear in different forms on Ingarsby and Fridaythorpe, and may lie behind the muddled ornament here of Driffield and Sewerby 19. The headplate upper corners on Fridaythorpe appear to contain a coarse form of the symmetrical profile animal heads found on Little Wilbraham 28 of group X, and on various brooches of the Saxon group I. As Leeds further pointed out, the masks in the headplate frame of Ingarsby are very similar to those of Little Wilbraham 3 and Little Wilbraham 40, while the unclear, but probably related, scheme of animal ornament in the footplate inner panels of Ingarsby, and Driffield and Sewerby 19, bears some resemblance to that of Little Wilbraham 28 and Willoughby-on-the-Wolds 15.

We are justified, then, in regarding this group as a northern offshoot of groups V and X, Ingarsby providing rather nicely an intermediate form in the Midlands between those groups and the Humberside brooches of the present group. Ingarsby could be broadly contemporary with Little Wilbraham 3 and Little Wilbraham 40 of group X. Although the footplate lower border decoration is clearer and better on Welbeck Hill 45 than Driffield, Fridaythorpe, and <u>Sewerby 19</u>, there are no very good grounds for phasing this group any further. The special sunken lentoid motif of <u>Driffield</u> and <u>Fridaythorpe</u> implies that these brooches are chronologically contiguous with <u>Welbeck Hill 41</u> of group XVI and that the Humberside nucleus of this group as a whole may be regarded as broadly contemporary with group XVI.

⋆ ⋆ ⋆ ⋆ ⋆ ⋆ ⋆ ⋆

There remain quite a large number of Anglo-Saxon square-headed brooches which have not been given a place in any of the groups considered so far. But they can be placed in some significant order, which facilitates a survey of these brooches, which in some cases carry significant and illuminating parallels to brooches within the groups.

A possible small-brooch group

Collected here are six brooches which in various respects are intriguingly reminiscent of one another, although on detailed investigation their similar features cannot be shown to be equivalent, or even necessarily related.

East Shefford, Berks [sb]	Leeds no.82
Hornton, Oxon	Leeds no.101
Little Eriswell, Sfk g.28	Hutchinson 1966 pl.IIa
Barrington A, Cambs [sb]	Leeds no.27
Marston St. Lawrence, N'hants	Leeds no.102
Broadway, HW g.5	Cook 1958 fig.5

On the whole these brooches strike one as being relatively small, generally between 9 and 12 cm. long, although such sizes are not terribly unusual for square-headed brooches: 11-12 cm., for instance, is the average length of brooches of group XVII. Otherwise one is inclined to bring these brooches together on the basis of a number of similarities. The shape of the footplates of <u>East Shefford [sb]</u>, <u>Hornton</u>, <u>Little Eriswell 28</u>, and <u>Broadway 5</u>, with large circular lobes, and relatively short footplate upper borders with the side lobes correspondingly "high" on the footplates are very similar. <u>Hornton</u>, <u>Little Eriswell 28</u>, <u>Barrington A [sb]</u>, and <u>Broadway 5</u> all have a large upward-facing mask with strikingly rounded features in the footplate terminal lobe; the same masks recur in the side lobes of <u>Little Eriswell 28</u> and <u>Broadway 5</u>. <u>Marston St.Lawrence</u> has inward-facing masks in all three lobes, but not, apparently, with rounded features. The headplate frame of separate masks, and the

168

openwork decoration in the headplate upper corners seem to connect Hornton with Marston St.Lawrence, and a small, rounded cap over the end of the bow ridge in the headplate inner panel is found on East Shefford [sb] and Broadway 5. There is also a certain coherence in the distribution of these brooches. Nevertheless there remain very extensive differences between them. A more coherent basic group might be formed by East Shefford [sb], Hornton, Little Eriswell 28, and Broadway 5 alone.

There are a few points of contact or similarity between these six brooches and brooches of other groups. Little Eriswell 28 has a pair of swastikas in the headplate upper corners as found on certain group VI brooches, e.g. Bidford-on-Avon 88. The masks of the headplate frames of Hornton and Marston St.Lawrence look most closely related to those found amongst group I. In both cases the distribution of these groups is congruent with that of the present putative group. The confronted animal in the headplate second panels of Barrington A [sb], however, appear to be simplified form of this element found in group XV brooches. These give some indications of possible relative-chronological positions for some of these brooches, but one may not suggest a chronological range for the whole "group" on the basis of these.

Chessel Down, IoW [uc] and Empingham I, Leics
(Leeds no.6; Plate 3.4)

These two enigmatic brooches have sufficient in common to be dealt with together here, although not quite enough to require them to be formally designated as forming a group. This is, admittedly, an arbitrary decision, particularly in view of the fact that it would be defensible to attach them both to the already heterogeneous group IV. However it is sufficient to draw attention to the parallels involved here. One restraining factor is that Leigh is prepared to describe Chessel Down [uc] as "'Kentish'", while reserving judgement on the actual origins of the brooch (Leigh 1980 pp.125-126).

It is on their footplates that these two brooches appear most similar; both have essentially the same upward-facing beast with wide open jaws, above which is a triangular construction of lines, presumably representing some zoomorphic motif, in the footplate upper borders. The design of their footplate frames is very similar too, and both have framed, angular footplate side lobes. More distantly similar, both have panelled bows with sharply angled cross sections, and both have scroll ornament in their headplate inner panels. In his consideration of Chessel Down [uc], Leigh picked out the latter two points, together with the form of the footplate terminal lobe, as apparently non-Kentish features.

As has been suggested, there are a good number of parallels between these brooches and the brooches of group IV, especially Suffolk [IV]. There is the extensive scroll-work in the headplate inner panel, and the basic form of the bow. These are also found on Alveston Manor 5 of group I. Suffolk [IV] also has angular footplate side lobes and a similar footplate frame; common to all of group IV and these two brooches are upward-facing beasts in the footplate upper borders, the kind rather indiscriminately called "rampant". The plane, framed, rhomboidal footplate inner panel of Empingham I may be compared to those on group IX, the derivative of group IV, while the swastika footplate inner panel of Chessel Down [uc] may be compared to that on group XV, argued above to be a later derivative of groups IV and IX. The possibility of some indirect relationship between the headplate inner panels of Empingham I, Dartford, and the brooches of group VI, e.g. Bidford-on-Avon 88, has already been mooted in the discussion of that group.

Chronologically, the obvious berth in which to place these brooches is broadly contemporary with group IV on the one hand, and Alveston Manor 5 of group I on the other.

* * * * * * * *

There are next twelve individualistic brooches which have in common various shared equivalent and related features with groups IX, X, XV, XVI, XVII, and further minor groups. A close relationship between those groups has already been noted in the course of the above discussion, and a few of the brooches below may be regarded as genuine hybrids of the prototype forms which lie behind some of these groups. But "hybrid" and "individualistic form" are designations to be used cautiously: it may be only the chance of survival that renders certain of the brooches listed here in some way unique; one new find may attach itself to one of these brooches and create a new group; it is not, however, sensible to designate "groups" with only one member. The twelve brooches are listed here, with notes on their connections with these groups, and discussion only of particularly significant points. A more detailed treatment would give these brooches an undue prominence.

1)   Fordham, Cambs. Leeds no.16

Bow: squat, panelled type with very simple animal ornament. This seems closest to Lackford 50/128 and Lakenheath [IX] (group IX); the absence of the stud is more like group XV brooches.
Footplate: lobes: outward-facing disjointed masks, most like group X brooches, although the plane bar below the

170

terminal lobe is most like groups IX and XV; frame: the curl may be compared to Little Wilbraham 40 (group X); upper borders: the rampant beast of group IX brooches may be detected behind the scheme here; inner panel: a plane, framed, rhomboidal stud, as on group IX brooches and Lakenheath [XV].
Suggested relative date: derivative of groups IX and X; broadly contemporary with group XV.

2)   Rainham, Ex. Arch.96 p.164 fig.3

Headplate second panel: the scheme of animal ornament could depend ultimately on the same form as on Holywell Row 11 (group IV).
Bow: squat, panelled, with simple animal ornament, and central stud. Cf. groups IX and X.
Footplate: frame: the same design as group XV; inner panel: a rhomboidal stud with a series of frames, more like group IX than group XV.
Suggested relative date: with the footplate frame, and biting beasts in the footplate upper borders, close to group XV. May in some way bridge groups IX/X and XV.

3)   Lackford, Sfk [uc]. Leeds no.12A.

A fragment. Headplate second panel: confronted animals similar to those on group XV brooches.

4)   Little Wilbraham, Cambs g.6. Leeds no.26

Headplate: top knob: the same as on Willoughby-on-the-Wolds 15 (group X); upper corners: crested profile heads, very similar to those on group X brooches and Ipswich [XVI]e and Bridgham (group XVI); second panel: animal ornament very similar to that found in inner panel of Willoughby-on-the-Wolds 15 (group X).
Bow: squat, panelled, simple animal ornament. cf. Fordham above.
Footplate: lobes: outward-facing masks and plane bar below terminal mask, cf. Fordham, above; bar: stud in centre similar to Willoughby-on-the-Wolds 15, Little Wilbraham 3, and Little Wilbraham 40 (group X).
Suggested relative date: connecting groups X and XV.

5)   Nassington, N'hants. Leeds no.64

See groups X, XI, and XX.

6)   Welbourn, Lincs. Leeds no.29

Headplate: discs in upper and lower corners connect Welbourn with Ipswich [XVI]e and Bridgham (group XVI), and group XX brooches; second panel: coarse version of scheme of group XV brooches; inner panel: scroll work, compare with Lackford [uc] above.
Footplate: side lobes: as on groups XVI, XVII, etc.;

mask above terminal lobe with curling moustache as on
groups XI and XV; inner panel: as on group XV brooches.
Suggested relative date: contemporary with groups XV, XVI
and XVII - a hybrid of these major Cambridgeshire-
Northamptonshire/East Anglian-Northern Midlands groups.

7)   West Stow, Sfk [uc]. Leeds no.18

Headplate: broad, plane frame: as on groups XVI and XVII;
upper corners: discs as on group XX; inner panels:
similar to Ipswich [XVI]a, Ipswich [XVI]b, and
Ipswich [XVI]c.
Bow: squat, plain panelled, with stud on ridge. Most like
Lakenheath [XV] and Barrington A 11 (group XV).
Footplate: upper borders: rampant beasts, simplified form
of those found on group IX brooches; side lobes: profile
masks as group XV; terminal lobe: as groups XVI, XVII,
etc.; inner panel: framed rhomboidal stud, cf. Fordham
above.
Suggested relative date: derivative of group IX, and
contemporary with groups XV, XVI and XVII. A genuine
hybrid of these Cambridgeshire-Northamptonshire/East
Anglian-Northern Midlands groups.

8)   Market Overton, Leics [uc]a. Leeds no.17

Headplate: broad, plane frame: as groups XVI and XVII.
Footplate: side lobes: as groups XVI and XVII; mask
above terminal: cf. Welbourn, above; rhomboidal inner
panel with frames: cf. Rainham, above; upper borders:
outline is that of types with rampant beast here (e.g.
groups IV and IX) rather than downward-biting beast.
Suggested relative date: contemporary with groups XV, XVI
and XVII.

9)   Kenninghall, Nfk [uc]. Leeds no.60

Headplate: broad outer panels or frame may be compared to
broad, plane frame of groups XVI and XVII, although here
with the cast relief ornament.
Footplate: lobes: as on groups XVI and XVII; triangular
inner panels, and loops in inner panel frames: clearly
close to those on group XVI brooches, especially
Ipswich [XVI]d, Catton, Morningthorpe 288, Market
Overton [XVI], and Laceby.
Suggested relative date: a variant of group XVI brooches,
but not counted with that group as it is an attempt to
modify, not reproduce, the prototype. Broadly contemporary
with group XVI.

10)   Market Overton, Leics [uc]b. Leeds no.62

Headplate: broad, decorated outer panels or frame, with
lentoid motifs in upper corners, cf. Kenninghall [uc],
above; projecting rhomboids in upper corners: cf. group
XVI brooches Great Chesterford 2, Kenninghall [XVI]a,

Billesdon, and Market Overton [XVI].
Footplate: lobes: a variant of those of groups XVI and
XVII. Cf. Spong Hill 24, Laceby, and Welbeck Hill 41 of
group XVI.
Suggested relative date: as Kenninghall [uc], above,
broadly contemporary with group XVI.

11) Beckford B, HW g.74. Leigh 1980 pl.70

Headplate: broad, relief-ornamented outer panels or frame
with lentoid motifs in upper corners: cf.
Kenninghall [uc], above - the rows of simple masks in these
are similar to those on Norton (group XII), and look to be
derived from group V forms; second panel: descending
animals rather reminiscent of group VIII brooches. Note
also the descending animals here on Market Overton [uc]b,
above, inner panel: simple mask, cf. Kenninghall [uc],
above.
Footplate: upper borders: very similar to Market Overton
[uc]b, with heavy, plain frame possibly representing
temples of biting beast, and similar posture of jaws; bar:
also very similar to Market Overton [uc]b.
Suggested relative date: as Market Overton [uc]b, above.

12) Market Overton, Leics [uc]c. Leeds no.61

Headplate: broad, relief ornamented outer panels or frame
with lentoid motifs in upper corners: cf.
Kenninghall [uc], above; inner panel: upward-facing mask,
similar to that on Kenninghall [uc] and Beckford B 74
above.
Footplate: upper borders: curl and posture of jaws is
reminiscent of Beckford B 74, above; inner panel frame: a
series of running spirals, more as on group XIV brooches
than as on group XVI. Such running spirals are also seen
to the sides of the headplate, but the upper line of
decoration on the headplate is the chain of S-motifs
forming a two-ribbon interlace as in the footplate inner
panel frames of most group XVI brooches.
Suggested relative date: broadly contermproary with group
XVI.

Ruskington, Lincs and Thornbrough, N.Yorks

Ruskington, Lincs [uc]   Grantham Mus AS84. Fig.3.9
Thornbrough, N.Yorks [uc]   Leeds no.122

These two brooches, which as yet are highly
individualistic pieces within the Anglo-Saxon corpus, are
considered together here because of one significant
decorative feature they share: the use of a triple-band
interlace ornament. This is seen most clearly on the
headplate panels of Ruskington [uc], and the uppermost of
the footplate inner panels of Thornbrough [uc]. In the top
panel of the headplate of Ruskington [uc] a single band is

interlaced with itself three times, i.e.:

while in the headplate inner panel of this brooch one band which turns back on itself once is interlaced with a second band, i.e.:

On Thornbrough [uc], three separate bands are interlaced:

On both brooches the gaps lying between the cross-over points of the interlacing ribbons are filled with small single knobs. On Thornbrough [uc] this interlace appears to be part of a piece of zoomorphic ornament.

Of these two brooches it is Ruskington [uc] on which one finds the most parallels to other Anglo-Saxon square-headed brooches. In the side panels of the headplate, and around the terminal lobe, it carries a simpler double interlace band such as is often found framing the headplate and footplate inner panels of group XVI brooches. The broad panels framing the headplate of this brooch may themselves be compared to that group. There is a riveted disc on the bow of Ruskington [uc], such as has already been noted occurring amongst group XVI brooches and on the late example of group II from Tuxford, Notts. The upward-facing animal mask in the terminal lobe of Ruskington [uc] meanwhile may be compared to that on Barrington B 9 (group V) and those on Driffield, Sewerby 19, and Welbeck Hill 45 of group XXII. It is conceivable that the projection on the footplate lower borders of Ruskington [uc] are a modification of the form found on the latter three brooches too.

Thornbrough [uc] offers nothing comparable. If anything would indicate some relationship with previously described brooches one would expect it to be the masks of the headplate frame and the curious animals in the headplate upper corners. There is a certain similarity between these masks and those on group XIII brooches, with eyes and nostrils at opposite ends of the nose formed by the same kind of curl. Perhaps Thornbrough [uc] betrays some familiarity with this source, but otherwise it appears to be a very independent brooch.

It is of considerable interest that these two brooches are those which most clearly bring the Anglo-Saxon square-headed brooch corpus into contact with the milieu of

174

Salin's Style II. As Haseloff has stated in detail (Haseloff 1981 pp.581-673), basic interlacing patterns of composition underlie Style II, irrespective of whether one takes Salin's or Haseloff's definition of the style. Other, perhaps, than Thornbrough [uc], there is no sign of any interest in any more complicated forms of interlace than the simple double-band interlace on Anglian English metalwork with Style I ornament. The disc on the bow of Ruskington [uc] contains an animal with four virtually identical sections of body, each with a leg. The body sections are formed of parallel lines, forming a frame, filled up with small pellets or cross lines. Such a body is not characteristic of Style I in Anglian England, but it is characteristic of early Style II (cf. Åberg 1926 figs.246-250, 252, 288-289, and 298; Arwidsson 1942 pp.18-21). There are very similar panels of ornament on the disc on the bow of Ipswich [XVI]a, but not as zoomorphic ornament: it is therefore unclear whether these have the same Style II associations as Ruskington [uc], or are dependent on the beaded wire or filigree models which are believed to lie behind this feature of Style II, and are a probable source of inspiration for features of the decoration of the footplate of, for instance, Lakenheath [XVI]. The head and the feet of the animal on Ruskington [uc] can hardly be described as characteristically Style II, but the feet are certainly not typical of Style I either, nor is the division of the body into four virtually identical sections. Similarly one may not describe the long, beaked heads of the animals in the upper panels of the footplate of Thornbrough [uc] as Style II, but they are more reminiscent of Style II heads (cf. Salin 1904 fig.542) than Anglian English Style I animals.

It is a reasonable suggestion, therefore, that these two brooches are connected in representing late northern English production of square-headed brooches. Ruskington [uc] draws on traditions present in the square-headed brooches of groups XVI, XXII, and Tuxford (group II); to such traditions new elements drawn from metalwork in Style II are added.

Miscellaneous

There remain eight brooches, fragments of brooches, or reports of brooches, which appear to be highly individualistic, or otherwise unclassifiable. These are listed here for the sake of completeness, but are of no further signficance for the present.

East Shefford, Berks	Leeds no.123
Berinsfield, Oxon g.107	Ashmolean
Barrington A, Cambs	Leeds no.118
Barrington A, Cambs	Leeds no.125

Toddington, Beds

Newnham, N'hants
Baginton, Warwicks
Laceby, Hu

Dunno's Originals, Part IV, 1822,
figs.3-4
Leeds no.40
Coventry Mus A/1013/4
BM 1935.12-9.1

Small square-headed brooches

Finally, notice must be taken of a number of brooches from
Anglo-Saxon England which may be characterized as "small"
as distinct from "great" square-headed brooches. These are
not the "square-headed small-long brooches" described by
Leeds (Leeds 1945 p.24ff), but diminutive brooches, usually
less than 3 inches long, related to the larger series
classified above, but generally simpler and often found in
pairs. Some of these small brooches share related and even
equivalent elements with the larger ones, but no purpose
would be served by digressing into the details of these
here; they do not materially affect the distributions of
elements or patterns of relationship traced amongst the
larger brooches alone. One or two of these brooches do,
however, merit attention during the assessment of the
overseas sources of the English square-headed brooches, a
topic which is considered shortly.

Relative chronology: a summary

The principles upon which the relative chronology of the
corpus of Anglo-Saxon square-headed brooches is based here
were briefly set out in the introduction to this chapter,
and the application of them may be observed in the course
of the discussion of the groups of these brooches. This
produces a typological chronology, a suggested
chronological ordering of the forms represented by the
individual brooches. This is not necessarily the correct
order of the brooches themselves - an "early" form, for
instance, may be copied in a "late" period - although one
would not expect it to be consistently misleading. One
could attempt to assemble the observations made in the
survey of the groups into a chronological matrix of all the
individual brooches, but this is unhelpful, given the
tentative nature of the conclusions reached there: it is
easier to observe "broad contemporaneity" between brooches
than a lineal descent, and this produces a matrix of great
sideways extent, rather obscuring what interesting detail
there is in the depth of the matrix.

A form of matrix of the groups, however, may be
usefully constructed, from which it may be argued that the
Anglo-Saxon square-headed brooches can be properly divided
into three sequential but overlapping phases. The groups
themselves are not manoeuvred around as indivisible blocks

in this matrix: some of the longer-lived of these groups
can be divided into phases within themselves, and these may
be separately placed in the matrix.   In keeping with the
tentative nature of the chronological observations it seems
appropriate to construct this diagram as a honeycomb of
hexagons, indicating the possibility of overlap between
"earlier" and "later" elements, rather than having rigid
horizontal and vertical relationships implying strict
contemporaneity of precedence with the virtual certainty of
a stratigraphic matrix.

     It is clearest to begin the construction of the matrix
with groups XV - XXII, which, it has been argued above,
have all to be treated as broadly contemporary, ignoring,
here, clues for possible finer divisions within these.   The
latest form of group II brooch, Tuxford, also falls here
(see group XVI), as do many of the individualistic brooches
briefly considered above:

This line may be regarded as the nucleus of one phase of
the matrix. Ruskington uc and Thornbrough [uc] (see above)
may be placed below this line.

     It has been suggested that amongst the forms of this
phase are certain descended from group IX brooches (see
group XV), while others seem to show a degree of overlap
with brooches of groups X and XI (cf. groups XV and XXI).
To this may be added the arguments for the derivation of
group XXII from group X (cf. group XXII), and for regarding
groups IX, X, and XI as broadly contemporary (see groups X
and XI).   As a result, it seems most reasonable to place
groups IX - XI in a line above that already drawn,
representing an earlier phase than the above, though one
overlapping with it.   To this line one may also add the
phase   of   group   II   involving   Linton Heath 21,
West Stow [II], Badby, and Duston (see group XI) and
Ingarsby from group XXII.   This fits nicely with the
assignment of the latest form of group II, Tuxford, to the
lower line.

     Groups XIII and XIV may also be considered here,
though they are slightly awkward to place in the matrix.
It was suggested that group XIII emerges in a later form
than   that   represented   by   Linton Heath 21   and
Linton Heath 32 of groups II and XI, and so one could argue
for the assignment of the group to the later phase.   The·
silvering of the footplate lobes of Little Wilbraham 158
and   possible   silvering   of   the   footplate   lobes   of
Ruskington [XIII] (cf.   groups XVI, XVII, etc.) could
support this.   Alternatively the silvering of the lobes of
Little Wilbraham 158 could be regarded as an earlier
experiment in this than the group XVI and XVII brooches,

and the brooch does have other, earlier, connections (see group XIII). It would be possible to place the group between groups IX to XI and the lower line, but in order to keep the diagram as simple as possible it is permissible to assign it to the same phase as groups IX to XI, remembering that the same phase does not presuppose strict contemporaneity, and that a degree of overlap between the phases is accepted. Such few clues as group XIV provides lead it to the same niche.

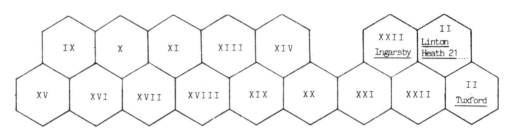

Of the groups placed in this new line, group X brooches have been argued to show forms descended from those of group V. Group V, in turn, is suggested to be broadly contemporary with group one example of IV, Rothley Temple [IV], while later than the earlier examples of this group, e.g. Holywell Row 11 and also broadly contemporary with group VIII (see group VIII). This fits quite neatly with the derivation of group IX from group IV, i.e.:

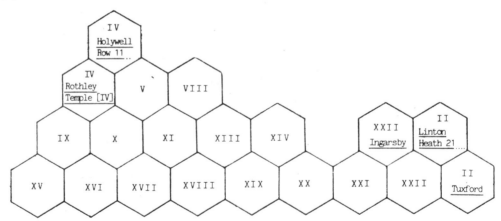

In the same line as the earlier examples of group IV, meanwhile, are to be placed the unclassified brooches from Chessel Down, IoW and Empingham I, Leics (see above), and Alveston Manor 5 from amongst the earliest brooches of group I. A line consisting of the earliest examples of group IV, Chessel Down [uc], Empingham I, and the earliest examples of group I may consequently be marked off as Phase 1 of our sequence. There are no Anglo-Saxon square-headed brooches to be placed earlier than these. It agrees nicely with this disposition of the groups that group VIII was argued to be dependent on the early brooches of group I (see group VIII).

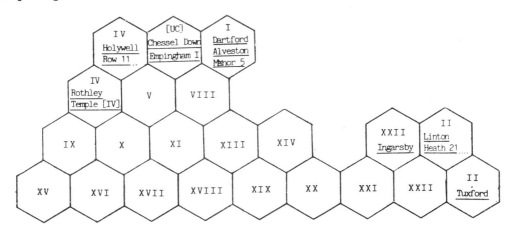

Thus the basis of three phases, early, middle and late, are distinguished, and this is probably as far as one can reasonably try to go in a formal chronological phasing of the Anglo-Saxon square-headed brooches. It remains, briefly, to fit the remaining classified brooches of this type into this pattern.

There are firm grounds for placing the earliest brooches of group II alongside the developed brooches (what may perhaps be called the "middle phase") of group I, such as Alfriston 28 (see group II). It fits the diagram most neatly to have the Alfriston 28 phase of group I immediately below the earliest forms of group I in Phase 1, in the same line as the earliest forms of group II, which therefore come immediately above the "middle" forms of group II, represented by Linton Heath 21, etc. Also to be placed on this line are groups VI and VII, and the later forms of group III (see group VII). It was suggested, however, that the earliest looking brooch of group III, Chessel Down [III], could be regarded as broadly contemporary with Alveston Manor 5 of group I, and this could therefore be assigned to Phase 1 too.

This leaves just two problems. Firstly, are the latest examples of group I (e.g. Alfriston 43, Guildown 116, Coleshill, North Luffenham, Chessel Down [I], and Fairford [I]) to be assigned to Phase 2 or Phase 3 ? It seems easiest to assign them to Phase 2, rather than stretching group I on the matrix across all three phases, a justifiable procedure considering the elasticity which has been insisted upon for the phases, although one which evades the important question of how long this Saxon group continued developing in comparison with developments in Anglian England. Finally, group XII has not yet been assigned a place. Drawing upon groups II and V, it can readily be placed in the third line of the matrix, above Phase 3, although if it is dependent on the adoption of group II models in Anglian England, its position becomes akin to that of group XIII, which sits rather awkwardly between Phases 2 and 3. It is most proper then to place

group XII alongside group XIII in this line. Our completed
diagram, then, is as follows:

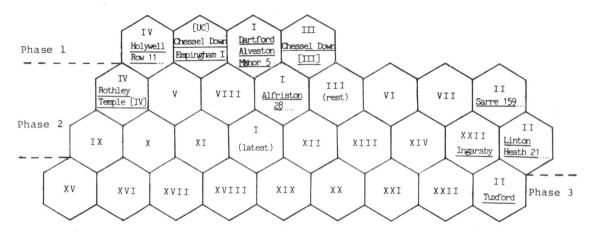

    This is an internal chronology of the Anglo-Saxon
square-headed brooches based upon a study of those brooches
alone.   It produces three basic phases:

Phase 1 - The earliest Anglo-Saxon square-headed brooches.
          Only about 9 brooches are assigned to this phase.
          Although groupable, for the most part they are
          distinctly individualistic.

Phase 2 - The middle phase, containing larger groups of
          brooches.   Certain brooches are very similar to
          others, and could be regarded as attempts to
          reproduce the same recognizable prototype.

Phase 3 - The latest phase, with a greater number of
          brooches in a smaller number of groups than Phase
          2. Here we have a phenomenon which could be
          characterized   as   "mass   production",   the
          production of large numbers of brooches
          apparently intended to be recognized, and indeed
          desired, as reproductions of a single type (e.g.
          groups XVI and XVII).   This phenomenon may be
          argued to be characteristic of the succession of
          Phase 3 to Phase 2, although group VII in Phase 2
          appears to be close to being a group of the "mass
          produced" kind.   The   most   individualistic
          brooches of Phase 3 are found in the northern
          Midlands and Northumbria.

    An external chronology of these square-headed brooches
based upon other objects with which they are found
associated in closed contemporary contexts such as graves
provides very little information at the moment. Saucer and
applied brooches are potentially the most useful artefact-
type to whose chronological sequence the suggested phasing
of the square-headed brooches could be compared, about 20
Anglo-Saxon square-headed brooches of all three phases
being associated with brooches of these types.   A
comprehensive study of the cast Anglo-Saxon saucer brooches

is currently being made by Dr Tania Dickinson, and she gave
a chronological outline for these brooches in her thesis
(Dickinson 1976). In general her chronology is that of the
dates of deposition of the brooches, and she prefers to
propose "wider" rather than "narrower" limits. There are
at least no major points of disagreement between her
chronology for the saucer brooches and mine for the square-
headed brooches. An early date is "acceptable" for the
saucer brooches in Alveston Manor, Warwicks g.5 with the
Phase 1 square-headed brooch (personal communication,
T. Dickinson). On the basis of the saucer brooches,
Dickinson accepts the burial of Berinsfield 102, a phase 2
brooch, around the middle of the 6th. century, which in her
terms covers the period 525-575 (Dickinson 1976 pp.25, 85,
and 167). Two other Phase 2 brooches, Beckford A 11 and
Bidford-on-Avon 88 (group VI) are suggested to be buried in
about the same period (op.cit. pp.167, 169). Two examples
of Phase 3 brooches, Barrington A 11 (group XV) and
Great Chesterford 2 (group XVI) are associated with very
similar forms of 5- and 6-scroll saucer brooches, which
Dickinson would see buried throughout the first half of the
6th. century (personal communication). I would venture to
suggest they could continue into the century's second half.

Otherwise, associations of square-headed brooches with
chronologically decisive, or even significant, material are
extremely scarce. Of Phase 2, Berinsfield 102 (group I)
was associated with a small shield-on-tongue buckle, a form
which occurs in Frankish graves from the 520's onwards
(Böhner 1958 p.181ff.; Ament AMII). Little Wilbraham 40
(group X) was associated with two cruciform brooches
(Reichstein 1975 no.786 Taf.112), which were not dated by
Reichstein, but are fairly safely assignable to the first
half of the 6th. century. Three Phase 3 square-headed
brooches are reliably associated with cruciform brooches:
Linton Heath 40 (group XV), Morningthorpe 371 (group
XVIII), and Little Wilbraham 111a/b (group XX). The
cruciform brooch in Linton Heath g.40 is of the florid
type, which falls relatively late in the English cruciform
brooch series, and is certainly 6th.-century, but which at
present one could only try to date more closely on the
basis of parallels on square-headed brooches, which is
scarcely admissible here. The cruciform brooch in Little
Wilbraham g.111 is not listed by Reichstein. On appearance
alone there is no obvious reason why it should be dated any
later than those with Little Wilbraham 40, a Phase 2
brooch, but this does not mean a great deal with regard to
the square-headed brooches: even if the cruciform brooches
in the two graves are closely contemporary, an overlap
between Phases 2 and 3 is allowed for; Little Wilbraham 40·
falls relatively late in Phase 2, and some connection
between Little Wilbraham 40 and Little Wilbraham 111a/b can
be traced anyway through the Nassington brooch (Leeds
no.64). The cruciform brooch in Morningthorpe, Nfk g.371
is most like the brooches of Reichstein's Typ Midlum, a
"späte" type, and Typ Little Wilbraham, a "späteste" type.

It may therefore be assigned to the first half of the 6th. century, and earlier rather than later within that half. But it could well be older than the square-headed brooch in the same grave.

It is regrettable that an attempted comparison of the internal and external chronologies of the Anglo-Saxon square-headed brooches produces no more than the negative result that the suggested phasing of these brooches runs into no major problems when their grave-associations are considered. In absolute-chronological terms, the grave-associations do no more than point us some way within the 6th. century for the more developed forms of these brooches. For reasons already given (see Chapter 1, Chronological Conventions), the demise of these brooches with Ruskington [uc] and Thornbrough [uc] and their association with Style II metalwork can be set at ca.570. Rather better dating evidence, especially for a date for the start of the Anglo-Saxon square-headed brooches comes from an assessment of their overseas connections, principally in Scandinavia, but also involving brooches found on the continent. In the present context, however, the following assessment of the overseas parallels of the Anglo-Saxon square-headed brooches is not made first and foremost for the dating evidence, although clearly the relative dates of similar objects are always of importance when those objects are being compared.

The origins and sources of the Anglian square-headed brooches

The ultimate origin of the square-headed brooch was undoubtedly Scandinavia, where the form first appears with silver-sheet brooches of VWZ I, probably towards the beginning of the 5th. century, long before the appearance of the form elsewhere. Strictly speaking, the concern of this study is limited to discovering how this brooch-form came to be so extensively used in Anglian England, but this cannot be done without thoroughly investigating its adoption in Anglo-Saxon England outside of Jutish Kent, whose square-headed brooches form a largely separate series, recently studied by Leigh (Leigh 1980). Before we can look in detail at the parallels between English, Continental, and Scandinavian square-headed brooches in an attempt to isolate lines of influence, a number of preliminary questions arise.

The first major point to consider is by what agency the brooch-form could have been diffused geographically. Of central importance in this issue is the question of how the square-headed brooches were made, a question which has been thoroughly discussed, most recently by Vierck (Vierck and Capelle 1971) and Leigh (Leigh 1980 pp.131-287), where full references can be found to the published and unpublished source material, to which may be added a crucially important contribution by Martin (Bonnet and Martin 1982). All the evidence points to the casting of the basic form (including decorative designs) of the brooch in a clay mould which could be used once only, after which the decoration of the cast form could be developed by applying further materials (e.g. garnets, gilding) or modified by tooling. For the forming of the clay mould Leigh argued in considerable depth against the use of lead models (as championed by Vierck) and for the making of each mould by the lost wax process (Leigh 1980 pp.131-178). Valid though his arguments were, they now require substantial modification in the light of the finding of what seems unmistakably to be the lead model of an Anglo-Saxon group II brooch in Geneva (Bonnet and Martin 1982). However, even the discovery of this item does not mean that lead models were invariably used in the manufacture of squre-headed brooches. The site which has produced the most voluminous remains of the manufacture of these brooches, Helgö, Uppland, Sweden, has, for instance, produced no signs of lead models, and, equally, nothing like the soapstone mould for such a brooch found at Hinna, Hetland, Rogaland, Norway (Hougen 1967 fig.37). There is thus a clear possibility of regional variation. A change in the style of production of the Anglo-Saxon brooches, broadly from individualistic items in the early phase to mass production later, has already been suggested. This could be concomitant with changes in production techniques, and one should not assume that "later" techniques should entirely exclude "earlier" techniques when adopted.

The question of how the square-headed brooches were manufactured is relevant because one means by which the basic form and individual motifs could have been dispersed is by travelling craftsmen: not necessarily continually itinerant artisans, but craftsmen who at some stage of their careers moved to practise their skill and market their wares in pastures new. These could therefore either be craftsmen travelling with their own developed repertoire of skills and motifs, or craftsmen travelling with a stock of lead models for brooches, picked up, perhaps, wherever they could. That the Geneva brooch model was imported from England, probably Anglian England, by such a craftsman seems to be a far more convincing explanation of its occurrence there than that it was locally made in order to produce a matching pair - in the local mode - to a single brooch brought by an English woman who had moved to the area (cf. Bonnet and Martin 1982). The purpose of a lead model is to produce a series of identical moulds, not a single copy of one brooch. It is interesting to note that the only two certain examples of Anglo-Saxon square-headed "brooches" on the continent, Herpes and Geneva, both belong to the one group, though they are not identical. Such evidence for craftsmen travelling widely with models for brooches qualifies the regional tags that may be given to these brooches. It forces recognition of the fact that while many of the brooches from the Herpes cemetery in

France are certainly "Kentish" in one sense (cf. Leigh 1980), this does not necessarily mean they were made in Kent.

A less commercial explanation of the dispersal of square-headed brooches is provided by various forms of migration. This could involve women alone travelling from one area to another with such brooches as part of their dress, and consequently stimulating local imitation where they arrive. At certain levels in society women might be more likely to travel in this way than men, in, for instance, marriages allying leading families, but we have no evidence for this affecting England in the appropriate period for the square-headed brooches. One may also consider migration on a larger scale: the migration of whole communities, carrying with them both a demand for and a tradition of producing these brooches. This is widely accepted as the underlying explanation of the development of square-headed brooches in Jutish-settled Kent.

Besides various possibilities as to how the square-headed brooches came to be adopted outside Scandinavia, there is also the important question of by what route these came to Anglo-Saxon, and more narrowly Anglian, England. There are three possibilities:

1)   They came direct from Scandinavia to Anglo-Saxon England.

2)   They reached Anglo-Saxon England via Jutish Kent and/ or the Isle of Wight.

3)   They reached Anglo-Saxon England via the continent.

Narrowing the focus, one may add to these the question of to what extent Anglian England derived its square-headed brooches from Saxon England.

If the relative-chronological outline suggested above for the Anglo-Saxon square-headed brooches is valid, then clearly the sources of the brooches of Phase 1 are of primary importance in investigating how these brooches came to England. Group I has its origins, as far as can be seen, in S.E. England, near Kent, but not apparently in the area which could be called Kent proper, East Kent, the area of the Kentish square-headed brooches (Leigh 1980 p.1). Leigh suggested that the brooches at the head of group I, Dartford and Mitcham 25, could be attributed to Scandinavian craftsmen working in England (1980 p.28). A study of the overseas parallels to the elements on these brooches reveals a very complex picture.

The use of outward-facing masks on the headplate frame, as on Dartford, occurs a little more frequently in Scandinavia than on the continent, though in neither area do the forms of the masks themselves approach very closely

the form on Dartford. The continental examples with this
features are all of Haseloff's Typ Langweid B (Haseloff
1981 pp.345ff.), which Haseloff regards as an essentially
Scandinavian type.   There is no inherent reason why
continental forms should not be intermediary between
Scandinavia and England, but in this case there is nothing
in particular to suggest they are.   However one of these
continental brooches, from Rheinhessen (Haseloff Taf.49)
has a symmetrical pair of animals in either headplate upper
corner, very similar to those on Dartford. Haseloff offers
only an unconvincing explanation of this motif on the
German find (p.361), not taking the English parallels into
account.   Could this be an example of continental influence
on England, English influence on the continent, or, as
Haseloff would probably argue if faced with the additional
examples, are both derived from a Scandinavian model ?
Other features on Dartford look more certainly
Scandinavian, suggesting that either of the latter two
explanations are to be preferred. The footplate bar is
definitely Scandinavian rather than continental, occurring
only once on the continent on the very Scandinavian-looking
brooch from Szolnak-Szanda, Hungary (Haseloff 1981
Taf.43.1).   For parallels to the style and scale of animal
ornament in the footplate inner panels on Dartford one
could look only to Scandinavia, e.g. the brooch from
Fonnås, Rendal, He, N (Hougen 1967 fig.23; here Fig.3.13).

The footplate upper borders on Dartford have a place
in an intriguing web of relationships between individual
brooches in England, Scandinavia, and the continent. The
key features of interest on the "biting beast" here are the
long nose, the tongue, and the single profile head on the
end of the upper jaw. The closest parallel anywhere
appears to be on the brooch from Kirchheim u. Teck,
Württemberg g.85, which Haseloff regards as a Scandinavian
export (1981 pp.289-324).   One parallel for the profile
head at the end of the jaw from within Scandinavia is a
brooch from Roses, Tingstäde, Gotland (SHM 8492; Plate
3.14). The clearly defined tongue between the jaws is of
quite widespread occurrence, and can be confidently
assigned to a South Scandinavian source (cf. Nissen Meyer
1934 fig.1; Haseloff 1981 p.422, Taf.28). The best,
perhaps the only, true parallel for the nose, however,
appears on the brooch from Fonnås referred to just above.

At this point, another early brooch of group I may be
introduced, Alveston Manor 5. This, like some other Anglo-
Saxon square-headed brooches, has a small profile head on
both of the biting beast's jaws. In this respect, it has a
remarkably close parallel in the brooch from Pompey,
Lorraine, which Haseloff regards as "Jutish" (1981 p.21ff.,
Taf.21). Interestingly, except for the nose, it is easy to
find the same basic pattern of interlacing lines in the
footplate upper borders of the Fonnås and the Pompey
brooches, but with different elements converted into
different animal parts (Fig.3.10).   Hedmark is in south-

eastern Norway, the area of Norway most likely to reflect
the forms of the southern Scandinavian region centred in
Denmark and southern Sweden. A common South Scandinavian
source can then reasonably be inferred for Dartford,
Alveston Manor 5, and the Fonnås and Pompey brooches. That
it has to be inferred, not demonstrated by direct evidence,
can be excused, as Haseloff so frequently does, on the
grounds of the "Fundknappheit" in Denmark at the
appropriate period.

Further Scandinavian features on Alveston Manor 5 are
the two circular garnet settings on the headplate inner
panel (cf. Hougen 1967 figs.20, 21, 23 etc.), and the broad
footplate inner panel frames with clear zoomorphic ornament
(cf. Hougen 1967 figs 22, 36, 39 etc.). There are not,
however, so many significant overseas parallels for a third
early brooch of group I, Mitcham 25. The footplate upper
borders of this brooch may certainly be attributed to
essentially the same South Scandinavian source. The
contrast between Dartford and Mitcham 25 in the extent of
its overseas parallels allows one to speculate that
Dartford could be an imported brooch, and Mitcham 25 an
English development from the same stream of influence.
While dealing with group I, it may be noted that the oval
footplate terminal lobe with a mask, on later brooches of
this group (e.g. Alfriston 28, Alfriston 43, Guildown 116),
is paralleled on a German brooch of unknown provenance
(Haseloff Taf.40). The motif does not occur in
Scandinavia, and may be attributed to English influence on
the continent.

One brooch from group III is assigned to Phase 1,
Chessel Down [III]. Leigh was happy to attribute this
brooch to his Kentish workshop, drawing attention to
parallels between it and the brooch from Bifrons, Kt g.63
(1980 p.81ff.). Without necessarily opposing this view, it
must be said that the case is not proven beyond doubt,
although a Kentish origin for the whole group would
certainly fit nicely with the group's distribution, on the
Isle of Wight, in Essex, and East Anglia. This would, if
correct, provide us with an example of the footplate upper
border design with a long-nosed biting beast and smaller
profile heads on the ends of the jaws in Kent. This design
otherwise leaves no impression at all on the known Kentish
square-headed brooches, which is a significant, though not
a decisive, objection to the Kentish attribution. It is
accepted that South Scandinavian influence was operative on
Kent to produce the Kentish square-headed brooches (Bakka
1958). The evidence of the group I, and perhaps the group
III, Anglo-Saxon square-headed brooches suggests that this
Scandinavian influence was effective more widely in S.E.
England. There is no good reason to suppose that it was
channelled through Kent alone.

Within Phase 1, we move further afield in England with
the early brooches of group IV, Holywell Row 11 and

Suffolk [IV], and the two comparable brooches, Chessel Down [uc] and Empingham I. Leeds (1949 pp.16-20), and Leigh (1980 pp.124-125) have discussed the "Kentishness" of the early group IV brooches, which Leeds felt was almost sufficient to attribute both of these brooches to Kent. But the similarity of these brooches to Kentish examples is only very generalized, and largely disappears in matters of detail. As on Alveston Manor 5, the circular garnet settings on the headplate inner panels of Holywell Row 11 and Suffolk [IV] have parallels in Scandinavia rather than Kent. Equally Scandinavian are the sharply angled, panelled bow of Suffolk [IV], Chessel Down [uc], and Empingham I (Holywell Row 11 is less obtrusive) (cf. Åberg 1924 figs.49, 56, and 60), and the placing of a large mask at the footplate terminal lobe, although no especially similar designs to those on Holywell Row 11 and Suffolk [IV] have been cited from Scandinavia.

The "rampant beasts" of the footplate upper borders of the group IV brooches have naturally drawn attention in the consideration of origins. "Rampant beasts" here are supposedly a Kentish characteristic, but amongst the Kentish brooches the most similar examples would appear to be those on brooches from Herpes and Milton-next-Sittingbourne (Leigh 1980 He3 and Mi 1 i-iii; Leeds 1949 pl.S3), and neither of these is a credible source of this feature of group IV brooches. A closer parallel may have been represented by the brooch from Idstedt, Schleswig-Holstein (Haseloff 1981 Taf.95) but regrettably this brooch is too fragmentary to be sure. However there is no doubt that the upward-facing animal in the footplate upper borders can be derived from a South Scandinavian source (Bakka 1958; Haseloff 1974). If no adequate models for the group IV brooches can be found in Kent, then it is reasonable to suggest these East Anglian brooches too are the subject of direct South Scandinavian influence.

Further evidence of a South Scandinavian source independent of Kent can be found on Holywell Row 11. The headplate inner panel of this brooch, with an upward-facing mask flanked by two roundels and symmetrical animal limbs may be compared to the design on a smaller brooch from Tranum, Øster Han, Hj, Dk (Fig.3.11; Haseloff 1981 Abb.29). The spiral-ornamented frame around the rhomboidal centre in the footplate inner panel on these two brooches is also comparable, a design that occurs more widely in Scandinavia (e.g. Åberg 1924 fig.64). The outward-facing masks in the footplate side lobes are also characteristically Scandinavian; one continental example. is a brooch from Niederbriesig, Rheinland, but Haseloff regards these as a particularly Scandinavian feature (1981 p.482f.). One feature on Holywell Row 11 does point us back to Kent, however. The animals in the headplate upper corners are very similar in design to those on the headplate second panel of the brooch from Herpes, Leigh's He3 (Fig.3.4). A common source is again a possible explanation of this parallel, but it warns us that lost Kentish models must be considered as well as lost Danish ones, though Kent does not suffer Denmark's Fundknappheit. In general, then, Kentish models do not adequately explain the forms of group IV, while immediate South Scandinavian origins do.

Chessel Down [uc] and Empingham I show, as Leigh says, several features that are especially characteristic of Kentish brooches, together with a number of features that would be markedly anomalous if they were Kentish (Leigh 1980 p.125). Again, it may appear that the best explanation of this phenomenon is parallel derivation from a common, South Scandinavian source. This is certainly plausible for the "rampant beasts" of the footplate upper borders. The angular footplate side lobes with linear decoration have their closest parallel on a brooch from Sarre, Kt g.4 (Leeds 1949 pl.S4), but comparable side lobes are found in Scandinavia, especially Sweden (cf. Nissen Meyer 1934 fig.25; Åberg 1924 figs.85 and 87; Helgö IV pp.186ff.). The form of the headplate frame on Chessel Down [uc] is regarded by Haseloff as a Scandinavian export (1981 p.312), with one parallel from Bornholm; a second occurrence of this form of the Zangenmuster is on a small square-headed brooch from Badwell Ash, Sfk (BSE Mus 1975.1). The swastika of the footplate inner panel of Chessel Down [uc] is also a feature of Haseloff's Typ Kirchheim u. Teck, well represented on the continent, but which Haseloff concludes is originally of south-western Scandinavian provenance (1981 p.324). A pair of small square-headed brooches from Barrington, Cambs (Haseloff 1981 Taf.41.2) are assigned to the same type by Haseloff, and could even therefore be Scandinavian exports.

In Phase 1 of the Anglo-Saxon square-headed brooches, then, a good case can be made for South Scandinavian influence being effective in southern and eastern England from the Isle of Wight to East Anglia. A "minimal" explanation of this would be the activities of travelling craftsmen, akin to Bakka's "Jutish Master" (Bakka 1958), in the whole of this area. Such activities would not be unconnected with larger-scale folk migration, since they would follow on a South Scandinavian "Jutish" settlement of Kent, the Isle of Wight, and the slightly mysterious "lands of the Meanware". There is no basis in the square-headed brooch material to postulate a more extensive Jutish settlement in Surrey, Essex, and East Anglia. Travelling craftsmen provide an adequate explanation.

Consideration of the overseas parallels also allows us to date Phase 1 reasonably satisfactorily. This can only be done by aligning the Anglo-Saxon brooches chronologically alongside the other brooches with the best parallels to them, since well-dated, direct, and undisputable ancestors to the Anglo-Saxon brooches have not been found. Firstly, however, the universal appearance of Style I on the Phase 1 brooches puts them post-475 (Haseloff's date). Two of the parallel brooches which figure significantly, Idstedt, Schleswig-Holstein (Haseloff 1981 Taf.95) and Roses, Tingstäde, Got (Plate 3.14) are largely covered by spiral ornament, and the latter has rather early-looking Style I ornament, but this by itself does not bring the Anglo-Saxon brooches especially early in the history of Style I. The form of Style I on the Phase 1 brooches is not especially early. The individual brooches which figure most prominently as parallels to the Anglo-Saxon brooches belong to the beginning of the 6th. century. The Fonnås brooch belongs to Nissen Meyer's Stadium 5, and therefore the latter half of Bakka's VWZ III, ca.500-525. The brooches from Pompey and Tranum belong to Group C of Haseloff's Jutish brooch group, dated by him to ca.500-520 (Haseloff 1981 pp.170-173). One may confidently follow Haseloff, and place Anglo-Saxon Phase 1 in the same date-range. It is not, of course, improbable that these nine brooches were produced over a shorter time than twenty years, but this is as close as we can reasonably get. One point of concern, however, is the relatively late burial dates found for Haseloff's Typ Kirchheim u. Teck, ca.580-600 (Haseloff 1981 pp.324-325; cf. Chessel Down [uc] above), which allows Haseloff to date the brooches no more closely than "first half of the 6th. century". This may imply that ca.520 is a little early for a conventional terminus ante quem for the production of Chessel Down [uc]. For the time being, however, it may be allowed to stand.

The brooches of Phase 2 are by no means simply derivative of the forms established in England in Phase 1. The overseas parallels of Phase 2 brooches indicate a complex picture of relationships, adding to the pattern already observed in Phase 1. For the sake of moderation, only the major aspects of the external relationships of Anglo-Saxon Phase 2 brooches will be examined here, not every single possibility.

The influence of Kent on Anglian square-headed brooches in Phase 2 is visible beyond doubt. The most obvious example is provided by the group II brooches, whose home in Kent has been thoroughly investigated and accepted by Leigh (1980 p.74). From its Kentish source, this becomes the most widely dispersed of the English brooch groups, one example occurring in France, and a lead model finding its way to Geneva. As an originally Kentish group it is of no great surprize that there are good Scandinavian parallels to many of the brooches' features, e.g. the footplate upper borders, inner panel frame, inner panels, and bar of Sarre 159 and Herpes. There is no need to pursue these into detail.

The few brooches of the East Anglian group IX derive many of their features from the Phase 1 East Anglian brooches of group IV (Holywell Row 11 and Suffolk [IV]), but at the same time carry a number of especially interesting parallels to Kentish brooches. The squat, panelled bow, and the plane, framed, rhomboidal footplate inner panel can both readily be derived from the group IV brooches, but both are also widespread in Kent, although the stud on the median ridge of the panelled bow occurs only once on a "Kentish" brooch, Chessel Down, IoW g.45 (three identical brooches, Arnold 1982 pl.2). Derivation from a common source is perhaps the best explanation, although nothing really like this form of panelled bow is known from Scandinavia. There are a number of comparable continental examples, of which the closest is certainly Flomborn, Kr. Worms, Rheinland-Pfalz g.71 (Haseloff 1981 pp.439-44, Taf.57.2). Haseloff, however, counts this amongst his "individual Scandinavian brooches on the continent", although accepting that the bow has a more English than Scandinavian look about it (p.443). The Scandinavian features Haseloff draws attention to are convincing enough, but there is as strong a possiblity that the brooch is from England as from Scandinavia itself. Scandinavia therefore remains a doubtful source for this feature, and the Anglian-Kentish parallelism in this respect cannot be confidently attributed to the influence of either area on the other. A further intriguing parallel between Rothley Temple [IV] (Phase 2), group IX, and Kent is provided by the profile heads of the footplate side lobes, which outside Anglian England, occur on the trio of brooches from Milton-next-Sittingbourne, Kt (Leeds 1949 pl.S3; Leigh 1980 Mi 1 i-iii), and apparently nowhere else. The examples on Rothley Temple [IV] and these Milton-next-Sittingbourne brooches are very similar (Fig.3.12), and no precedence can be determined between them. The group IX forms derive from such models. The three alternative possibilities, a common (lost) Scandinavian source, Anglian influence on Kent, or Kentish influence north, must simply remain open.

Phase 2 brooches provide evidence of further direct Scandinavian influence beyond that discovered in Phase 1. Outstanding in this regard are the brooches of group VII. The forms of the masks in the headplate frame of this group do not appear to be descended from anything already established in England, and as with the group I brooches (above), the balance of probability inclines towards a Scandinavian source. The point is greatly strengthened by a marked similarity between the masks on the group VII brooches and a brooch from Falkum, Gjerpen, Te, N (Hougen 1967 fig.20) in the filling in of the cheeks of the mask with a small double-lined element (Fig.3.13). The typical· footplate bar of the group VII brooches has a mask moulded in prominent relief at either end, of a form which has some remarkably close Scandinavian parallels, especially on two brooches from Møre og Romsdal in Norway: from Staurnes, Borgund (BMÅ 1930 no.4 pp.6-7), and Hole, Grytten (Hougen 1967 fig.18) (Fig.3.13). But comparable bars do occur more widely in Scandinavia, including southern Scandinavia, e.g. Denmark and Västergötland (Åberg 1924 figs.54 and 56). Although simple, the similarity bewteen the group VII footplate upper borders and Scandinavian examples - especially, again, the two Møre og Romsdal brooches - is arresting (Fig.3.13), and finally, as on Dartford (above), the style and scale of the animal ornament on the footplate inner panels is best referred back to examples such as the Fonnås brooch (Fig.3.13).

To some extent group VII seems to depend on forms already established in England with group I. But the parallels discussed here seem to show a connection between group VII and Scandinavia independent of that discernible on Dartford, although in many respects similar to it. The fact that many of the best Scandinavian parallels cited are Norwegian - in particular, the two brooches from Møre og Romsdal - does not in itself rule out a more southerly Scandinavian source of influence. The significant Falkum brooch from Telemark rather points this way. As with the group I brooches, this could be an example of southern Scandinavian influence direct on the Saxon areas of southern England, perhaps making its way into England along the route of the Thames.

The footplate bar on group XI brooches is rather similar to the form on the group VII brooches, but the direction of the masks is reversed, and it could be derivative. An independent Scandinavian parallel may, however, be seen in the form of the biting beast in the footplate upper borders of these brooches, which may be compared to the form found on a brooch from Å, Åfjord, ST, N (Hougen 1967 fig.53; Fig.3.15c/d). Points of similarity are the scale of the design, the form and angle of the jaws, the outlining of the elements of the design with incised lines and the ladder-motif decorating part of the head, and, more distantly, the crest-like appendage to the head. Relationship between the two, but not the dependence of one on the other, is indisputable. This form and related forms in Scandinavia seem at first to be a largely Norwegian feature (cf. Hougen 1967 figs.36, 39, 47, and 52), but a few examples allow a case to be made for the use of the form in southern Scandinavia, i.e. one brooch doubtfully attributed to Denmark (Åberg 1924 fig.68), and a couple of brooches from Gotland (e.g. Nissen Meyer 1934 fig.11). A similar Anglo-Scandinavian parallelism will be seen again when Phase 3 brooches are considered.

One of the most definite, and perhaps one of the most misleading, parallels between Anglian and Scandinavian square-headed brooches is that provided by the beasties found as decorative models riveted to the headplate upper corners of three Midlands brooches, Northampton [V] and the two group VIII brooches, and two brooches from Jæren, Rogaland, Norway (Hougen 1967 figs.35-36, here Fig.3.14). In both cases we have essentially a quadruped animal, inward-facing, with two shafts to form rivets. At first sight this would seem to form an indisputable connection between S.W. Norway and the Central Midlands, although the direction of influence would remain dubious. But there is reason to be more cautious. It was pointed out in the discussion of group VII that <u>Dartford</u> has comparable modelled ornament, a human mask, riveted to the footplate and side lobes. This implies that such riveted decoration could have been in use in South Scandinavia too, possibly also in the form of animals in the headplate upper corners. The case for a special connection between the Midlands and Jæren remains strong, but alternatives are possible.

An influential feature in Phase 2 is the form of biting beast found in the footplate upper borders of the group V brooches (see group X, above), the earliest form of which appears to be found on <u>Barrington B 9</u>. The small profile head on the end of the upper jaw has already been traced back from England to a South Scandinavian source. The posture of the jaws, and the rolled-up end to the tongue, however, have their closest parallels on continental brooches: in particular Nordendorf, Bayerisch-Schwaben g.137/1844, and Niederbriesig, Rheinland (Haseloff 1981 Taf.58-59.1). These are brooches which Haseloff classifies as "continental copies of Scandinavian patterns" (pp.465ff.), and in the course of his discussion of them he insists upon the Scandinavian chracter of their footplate upper borders (pp.470, 482-483). He does not, however, mention the rolled-up tongue, or the particuarly close English parallels. Again, it seems that three possible basic explanations for the Anglo-Continental parallel must remain open: common derivation from lost Scandinavian soruce, English influence on the continent, or continental influence on England.

From the foregoing, where it has regularly proved possible to attribute Anglo-Continental parallels to an inferrable Scandinavian source, the latter explanation might appear the least probable. In Phase 2, however, some particularly interesting parallels to continental brooches appear on the brooches of the minor Northumbrian group XIV, especially <u>Londesborough 6</u> (Leeds no.59). This may be compared to a brooch of Haseloff's originally Scandinavian Type Kirchheim u. Teck, from Worms, Rheinland-Pfalz (Haseloff 1981 Taf.42.1). There is a remarkable similarity in the footplate upper borders, and a good measure of similarity in the relatively long bow, with a small stud on the grooved median ridge. Attention may also be drawn to the extrusive decorative framing around the footplate terminal lobe of the group XIV brooches. Such framing is regarded as a particularly continental element: one example occurs on the Niederbriesig brooch referred to just above (cf. Haseloff 1981 p.485 and references). The case for some continental-Northumbrian connection thus grows, although it is not conclusive, and it would be possible to

192

derive all of these parallels independently in either area. A similar framing around the terminal lobe may evolve amongst the designs of group VI brooches, and appears on Beckford A 11 (Plate 3.3). Additionally, if there is a special relationship, influence one way or the other, it is very difficult to judge its direction.

In Phase 2, then, we see Kentish influence north on Anglian England, and the influence of the square-headed brooches of Saxon England on more northerly areas (e.g. group I to groups VI and VIII). More examples of Scandinavian influence appear, apparently independently in Kent, Saxon, and Anglian England. While in Phase 1 the source of Scandinavian influence was argued to be South Scandinavia, in Phase 2 Norwegian brooches figure more prominently amongst the parallels to English brooches, and while, with due caution, one can make a case for these parallels also having occurred in southern Scandinavia, there is no justification for any predisposition against finding Norwegian influence on England, especially Anglian England, or as indeed it may be, Anglian English influence on Norway. Finally, certain particular Anglo-Continental parallels appear amongst these brooches, but the nature of the Anglo-Continental relationship remains obscure.

The dating evidence of the overseas parallels to Anglo-Saxon Phase 2 brooches is reasonably consistent with the proposed phasing of the corpus of Anglo-Saxon brooches. Admittedly, relative to the parallels of group I Phase 1 brooches (e.g. Dartford), many of the Scandinavian brooches cited as parallels to group VII brooches are rather early. The two brooches from Møre og Romsdal, for instance, are placed by Nissen Meyer in her Stadium 3, and the majority of other parallels cited for the footplate bar to the same phase. The Falkum brooch, with the similar masks in the headplate frame, she places a little later (Nissen Meyer 1934 pp.9-14). This Stadium falls relatively early in VWZ III, but the decoration of the footplate inner panels on group VII brings the group clearly into line with Dartford and the Fonnås brooch, later in VWZ III. The internal English evidence for placing group VII in Phase 2 has already been given, but it is otherwise clearly very close to the Phase 1 brooches, a similarity which is allowed for by allowing the phases to overlap chronologically. The other parallels to Phase 2 brooches draw us steadily later. The two Rogaland brooches comparable to group VIII belong to Nissen Meyer's Stadium 5, i.e. the latter half of VWZ III. The brooch from Å, Åfjord, ST, with the similar footplate upper borders to group XI, however, is a Stadium 6 brooch, and therefore VWZ IV (post-ca.525). The continental brooches cited are of little help, especially in view of their obscure relationship to the English brooches, but both the Nordendorf brooch, and the Typ Kirchheim u. Teck brooch from Worms can be dated to the first half of the 6th. century (Haseloff 1981 pp.324-325, 473). Such evidence as there was from the grave-associations of English Phase 2 brooches indicated a burial period from about the 520s to around the middle of the 6th. century.

Overall, then, Anglo-Saxon Phase 2 can be safely located within the period 500-550. Naturally, however, one is inclined to attribute it a starting date later than that attributed to Phase 1 (500-520), though overlapping. Circa 510 may be suggested, though estimating such fine distinctions at such a distance is obviously an arbitrary exercise of rather limited significance. Further consideration of the latter end of this phase may be made in relation to its successor, Phase 3. It should be noted at this point that there is here a discrepancy between my chronology and Leigh's. Leigh would have Sarre 159 and Herpes at the latter end of the Kentish series, that is ca.560 (Leigh 1980 pp.49-50, 115-116, and 483). However, I do not find his arguments conclusive, and prefer my own reasons for dating the forms of these brooches earlier. Some supporting evidence is provided by Kentish buckle-plate type which has the same design as the headplate panels of these brooches. A recent brief survey of these buckle-plates concluded that they "were in production at latest by the second quarter of the sixth century" (Hawkes et al. 1975 pp.78-79; cf. Haseloff 1981 p.280).

In Phase 3 there is still further evidence of the apparent interchange of motifs on square-headed brooches between Anglian England and Kent, Scandinavia, and possibly the Continent too. The best example of Kentish influence on a brooch of this phase is undoubtedly the confronted beasts of the headplate second panels of the group XV brooches, which are individually of the same design as those on Sarre 159 and Herpes (group II) and the Kentish buckle-plates just referred to, although re-disposed in a different overall design. It is a little puzzling that these animals should turn up on a new group of square-headed brooches in Anglian England, not on the Anglian examples of group II. Examples of the footplate upper borders of group XV brooches meanwhile seem to stand in the same relationship to Norwegian examples as did those on group XI brooches (see above). An illustration is provided by Barrington A 11 and one of the brooches from Jæren, Rogaland with the riveted beasties on the headplate upper corners as on group VIII (Fig.3.15a/b). Here we see a projecting crest on Barrington A 11 much more like the Norwegian form than on group XI, and a similar outlining of the head. The unusual element crossing the upper jaw of the Barrington A 11 head, which one would be inclined to interpret as a tusk, could be explained through the single "jaw" crossing over itself as seen on the Rogaland brooch. The curl below this on the lower jaw of Barrington A 11 is in exactly the right place for that design to be a muddled copy or reminiscence of that on the Rogaland brooch. The footplate inner panels of group XV mostly carry a swastika motif, such as Haseloff infers to have existed in

Scandinavia, although it can be traced to England already on brooches such as Chessel Down [uc] and the small square-headed brooches from Barrington, Cambs.

Scandinavian parallels to the numerous and rather uniform brooches of groups XVI and XVII are particularly extensive. Common to those two groups are the large, round, and usually silvered footplate lobes. Similar prominent round lobes can be found on a number of Norwegian and Swedish brooches (e.g. Åberg 1924 figs.92-94; Hougen 1967 figs.74 and 77). The brooch from Jorenkjøl, Hå, Ro, N (Hougen 1967 fig.74) even has these lobes in a form of the "bichrome" style, the plain inner area being the silver of the body of the brooch, the decorated outer zone being gilt. This brooch also shares with group XVI an extensive use of two-strand interlace. Clearly these examples of parallelism can be characterized as the design of brooches in a common style, rather than the copying of individual brooches from others. It is a style that is concerned with exploiting lines and shapes, not focussing on complex ornament within the panels as earlier Style I art did. But the parallels seem a little too close for this style to be regarded as simply a common development independently in either area, out of the previous common style, dominated by Style I, without any interchange of ideas between England and Norway. A significant stylistic parallel appears between the two individualistic brooches Ruskington [uc] and Thornbrough [uc], which should be attached to the end of Phase 3, and the Jorenkjøl brooch, in the rather clumsy triple-stranded interlace in the footplate inner panel frame of the latter.

One feature of the brooches of groups XVI and XVII is the occasional appearance of a riveted disc on the bow, as also occurs on Tuxford (group II). This latter brooch in fact carries the same two-strand interlace pattern here as is seen on the disc on the bow of the Jorenkjøl brooch, and other Norwegian and Swedish brooches. However while several Scandinavian relief brooches have these apparently very similar bow-discs, there is one significant difference between these and the English examples in that they are almost invariably cast-in-one with the bow, not riveted on. The riveted disc-on-bow does make an appearance in Scandinavia with the disc-on-bow brooches, which appear to succeed directly to the relief brooches at the end of the Migration Period, and in some cases have designs very similar to those on the square-headed and relief brooches (e.g. Nerman 1969 fig.55). The disc-on-bow brooches seem to have been first developed on Gotland, and some English influence on their development is a possibility (Åberg 1924 pp.43-44). But foreign influence is not really necessary for so simple a modification as from casting-in-one to riveting-on, which anyhow seems to have been occasionally used on Scandinavian relief brooches (cf. Åberg 1924 fig.84).

The common interlaced framing of the headplate inner panel of group XVI brooches (e.g. Ipswich [XVI]a-c) has a close parallel on a brooch from Nordland, Norway (Åberg 1924 fig.76), although since this type of framing is so pervasive in this style no especial weight should be attached to this one parallel alone. The characteristic squat, T-shaped headplate inner panels with linear ornament of this group also have interesting Scandinavian parallels, e.g. a Trygsland, Bjelland, VA, N brooch (Åberg 1924 fig.62). However it is possible to spot possible earlier English sources for the feature, e.g. Rothley Temple [IV], or Duston (group II). Numerous Scandinavian parallels can be cited to the triangular footplate inner panels of this group too, but these may be argued to have already made their influence felt on English brooches through group II.

The characteristic footplate inner panel of group XVII brooches carries a motif which Haseloff has named Das grosse Tier (Haseloff 1981 p.372ff.). Haseloff demonstrates this motif to have been ultimately of South Scandinavian origin, but subsequently to have come into widespread use throughout Scandinavia and on the continent. There is one "Kentish" example of this motif, Alfriston, ESx g.47 (Welch 1983 fig.23a). This is certainly not the source of the motif on the group XVII brooches, and none of the Scandinavian or continental examples is particularly close enough to the form of the group XVII brooches to be identified as the closest source for it. In these circumstances one is inclined to regard Scandinavia as a more likely source, in line with the other parallels of this brooch group.

The curious Northumbrian-continental parallel provided by the footplate terminal lobe of group XIV is supplemented by group XXII, where this feature on Sewerby 19 and Welbeck Hill 45 appears even more persuasively similar to that on the Niederbriesig brooch (Fig.3.8). This does not help, however, in explaining the connection, if any, between the examples. A further minor but intriguing parallel between Anglian England and the continent in this phase is the footplate inner panel of Willoughby-on-the-Wolds 57 (group XIX) and those on three continental brooches (Haseloff 1981 Taf.45; Fig.3.16). This could just be coincidence, but every additional instance adds credibility to the case for the interchange of motifs between Anglian England and the continent.

The dating evidence of the parallels to Phase 3 brooches is again reasonably consistent with the relative-chronological outline proposed for the Anglo-Saxon brooches. The animals of the headplate second panel of group XV brooches belong to the second quarter of the 6th. century. The parallels to the footplate upper borders of this group, e.g. Barrington A 11, fall in Nissen Meyer's Stadia 5 and 6, that is VWZ III/IV, again allowing the dating of the group in the second quarter of the 6th.

century. All the stylistic parallels to groups XVI, XVII,
etc., belong to VWZ IV, and should be dated around the
middle of the 6th. century rather than earlier.
Das grosse Tier is certainly of earlier origin, but
continues in use on Scandinavian brooches up to this period
(e.g. Nissen Meyer 1934 fig.20, nos.93-96). Phase 3 may
therefore be assigned a starting date in the second quarter
of the 6th. century, say ca.530, and a terminal point with
Ruskington [uc] and Thornbrough [uc] at ca.570.

Thus the following chronology is proposed for the
Anglo-Saxon square-headed brooches:

Phase 1:   ca.500-520

Phase 2:   ca.510-550

Phase 3:   ca.530-570

Given the vague nature that such chronologies will
inevitably have, this outline is reasonably satisfactory
and makes sense of the material. One might wish to seek to
reduce the 20-year overlap between Phases 2 and 3 -
probably by ending Phase 2 earlier rather than beginning
Phase 3 later - but there is no real value in pursuing such
fine adjustments through estimation and guess work alone.
This gives us a period of about 70 years of square-headed
brooch production in Anglo-Saxon England. When one is
familiar with the material such a period certainly does not
appear too short, especially when one considers the
relatively few steps in motif development which lead from
Holywell Row 11 through group X to group XV, which stands
alongside group XVI, and thence to Ruskington [uc]. The
great imponderable, of course, is the question of how
quickly or slowly motifs may have developed, and how this
rate may have changed at different points in this series.
Similarly, how long would the single mass-produced types
such as group XVI have remained in production ? Is 10
years a more reasonable estimate than 20 ?

What, in summary, do the square-headed brooches
contribute to the picture of the Scandinavian character of
Anglian England at this period ? East Anglia was initially
subject in the early 6th. century to a South Scandinavian
influence of the same kind as that which was making an
impact on Kent and the continent at the same time. During
phases 2 and 3, there appears increasing and cumulative
evidence for a connection between Anglian England and
further north in Scandinavia, most probably the west coast
of Norway in particular. In certain cases one may suspect·
influence from Scandinavia on Anglian England, in other
cases we have only parallels which are evidence of a
special connection, without showing the direction in which
influence flowed. Unlike the wrist-clasps in Chapter 2, the
square-headed brooches do not suggest that this influence
was the immediate consequence of substantial migration

between these areas, and there are no other grounds to suspect that this was so. The wrist-clasps could be associated with the adoption of a new and distinctly Scandinavian female costume in Anglian England. With the adoption of the square-headed brooches in Anglo-Saxon England we see no more than the supplanting or rivalling of one brooch type (e.g. the Anglian cruciform brooch, the Saxon equal-armed brooch) by another in the function of central major brooch (cf. Vierck 1978 pp.231-253). The most plausible explanation would appear to be the activities of travelling craftsmen, like Bakka's putative "Jutish Master" and the man or men who took a lead model for group II brooches from England to Geneva. However in some cases it would appear that such craftsmens' activities and the interchange of ideas between areas would follow up contacts established by migration, i.e. the Jutes to Kent and the Isle of Wight, and the Norwegians who were suggested in the previous chapter to have migrated to Norfolk and/or Humberside in Anglian England around 475 A.D.

CHAPTER 4

BRACTEATES AND SCUTIFORM PENDANTS

I - Bracteates

The classification of the bracteates adhered to in this chapter is that which Mackeprang took from Montelius (Mackeprang 1952 p.25). In view of the enormous volume of discussion which subsequently grew up about the rectitude and other archaeologial features - e.g. dating and inter-relationship - of Montelius's "classes", it is amusing to see how casually he first introduced them as a note preceding the illustrations below the abbreviations on an unnumbered page at the end of his dissertation Från Jernaldern (Montelius 1869). As a practical rule-of-thumb, the following "definitions" of the different bracteate-types are adequate:

A - Imitations of Imperial Roman medallions or coins.
B - With full human figures, but not the horse-and-rider
    motif (cf. C).
C - A human head over a quadruped animal.
D - With ribbon-like Style I animals.

Mackeprang also resurrected Montelius's Type F, bracteates with relatively naturalistic animals, and it will be seen that this is a useful point of reference in explaining certain Anglian English developments. Montelius's Type E comprised the Vendel Period Gotlandic bracteates, and although it is not in common use, it seems to be an entirely practical form of reference for these objects.

After Mackeprang, Malmer produced an extensive and in some ways radically different study and classification of the gold bracteates (Malmer 1963 pp.76-221). Malmer demurred at Mackeprang's lack of methodicallity in his definitions of types and groups, and proposed a theoretically far more clear and rational basic classification table (pp.98-123). Yet Mackeprang remains the usual reference point for bracteate studies. The reasons are not obscure. His work was established before Malmer's reaction, and has the irreplacable merit of providing the most extensive assemblage of illustrations of bracteates available. Disputable though they may be in several points, Mackeprang's largely intuitive groupings remain largely convincing, and in certain cases apply a pragmatic common sense which is not possible with Malmer's system. The Market Overton bracteate, for instance (Mackeprang pl.7.17) must be assigned to the D-bracteates under Malmer's system, whereas it obviously is most closely related to the C-bracteates with which Mackeprang associated it. The feature which creates the anomaly, however, the lack of the head, is of course a most significant feature (discussed below).

The chronology of the bracteates is not an easy subject, and correspondingly has produced a great deal of discussion with relatively little clear progress made compared with the energy expended. Mackeprang's suggested chronology of the bracteates should be divided into the internal and external chronologies (cf. Bakka 1973 pp.54-59), which is virtually synonymous with the internal relationship between early, middle, and late forms, and their absolute-chronological dating. For the internal chronology, Mackeprang divided the bracteates into three consecutive periods (pp.66-68). These were accepted, with reservations, by Bakka (p.54), although they can scarcely function as any more than an initial reference point for the discussion of the chronology of any individual bracteate, whose dating has to be individually assessed, in the course of which assessment the defects of Mackeprang's system will inevitably appears. Mackeprang's internal and external chronologies have been almost wholly superseded by Bakka (Bakka 1973), although Bakka's quite faithful reproduction of Mackeprang's scheme in this Chronologische Übersichtstafel (p.85), indicates that he does not go as far as he might in modifying Mackeprang. Bakka's work itself is now 10 years old, and has to be re-assessed in the light of later work (see Chapter 1, Chronological Conventions).

There is little or no doubt that the earliest A-bracteates are the earliest bracteates, and these connect the bracteate series to a range of 4th.-century Roman gold medallions (Mackeprang 1942 pp.20-25). The medallion models for the bracteates can sometimes be quite definitely identified, which in certain cases provides a very precise terminus post quem for A-bracteates. Unfortunately this is of little practical value, because there appears to be a large time gap between the Roman models and the bracteate descendants; in certain cases a distance of up to 150 years looks probable (see the Undley, Sfk bracteate, below). It is not easy to date the A-bracteates, especially the earlier ones, on stylistic grounds, and easier to interpolate a date-range for the type backwards from surer dates for other forms. Type B bracteates are also a problem. Although it is probable that some of their designs are descended directly from Roman coins or medallions, Mackeprang believes they first appear later than the A-bracteates (Mackeprang 1952 pp.37-39). Bakka had very little to say about the B-bracteates, except implicitly to link them to a significant extent with the C-bracteates (cf. Bakka 1973 pp.70-74). The low, rounded relief and the general style of the figures on these bracteates certainly renders this plausible (cf. Mackeprang pls.6ff.). In fact the chronology of the B-bracteates is not of significance for this chapter, and the issue could simply be evaded on these grounds alone. Yet an opinion may be expressed on the basis of an assessment of the C-bracteates.

It is puzzling that Bakka's *Chronologische Übersichtstafel* should appear to place the first appearance of the C-bracteates substantially before VWZ III, when his survey of the grave-finds and discussion of a Fyn bracteate and the Gummersmark brooch draws attention to how they characterise that *Stufe* (pp.64-68, 71-73). It seems doubtful indeed if any C-bracteates can be argued to precede Style I, even the two bracteates which Bakka implicitly indicates to be early, by citing them as examples of Mackeprang's Period 1, i.e. from Fyn (Mackeprang pl.8.18), and "?Småland" (Mackeprang pl.9.3). If, then, early Style I may be said to be characteristic of the C-bracteates, their first appearance may be set at ca.475 (Haseloff's date), the beginning of VWZ III. It is only the head on the "?Småland" bracteate which may convincingly be used to minimize the difference between early A- and C-bracteates; the head on the Fyn example is distorted and out of proportion on the bracteate. The "?Småland":A-bracteate parallel should, I would argue, be used to bring the first appearance of the A-bracteates closer to the beginning of VWZ III rather than the first appearance of the C-bracteates back into VWZ II.

Bakka would have the C-bracteates largely supplanted by the D-bracteates at the beginning of VWZ IV. His argument is supported by limited grave-evidence and a more substantial amount of hoard-evidence. C- and D-bracteates do occur together in hoards, but that is no evidence for their contemporaneity. The evidence for the dating of the first appearance of the D-bracteates was discussed in Chapter 1, and the grounds given there for bringing this back to the early years of the 6th. century. By the very nature of the types, stylistic evidence for overlap between the C- and D-bracteates is almost impossible to find, and the grave- and hoard-evidence is not conclusive on the question of overlap. *A priori* a transitional period is more probable than an abrupt and comprehensive change, and the earlier date for the D-bracteates together with the ca.475 date for the first C-bracteates would leave us with an unconvincingly short life-span for the C-bracteates if the latter were the case. In this situation I am happiest to take Bakka's round figure of ca.475-525 for the duration of VWZ III, and thereby the C-bracteates, with a substantial period of overlap VWZ III/IV in so far as VWZ IV graves are characterized by D-bracteates. The D-bracteates appear to continue to the end of the Migration Period, that is around the 560s.

The C- and D-bracteates provide the anchorage-point to which the chronology of the A- and B-bracteates may be fixed. The earliest A-bracteates precede the earliest C-bracteates. Even if the hair-style on the head of the "?Småland" bracteate (Mackeprang pl.9.3) is very similar to

those on A-bracteates, the development in design simply in
the addition of the animal which makes this a C-bracteate
bespeaks a later stage. There is, however, no direct
evidence to tell us when to date the first appearance of
the A-bracteates. Bakka's Chronologische Übersichtstafel
implies an early date in the 5th. century, perhaps in the
first quarter. But the scarcity of truly early A-
bracteates argues against a long history before the C-
bracteates appear, and on the basis of the proposed dating
for that bracteate type, a starting point for the A-
bracteates around the middle of the 5th. century seems more
probable. Bakka would not date any A-bracteate later than
500 (pp.54-55, 85), and I see no reason to take issue on
this point. The stylistic similarities between B- and C-
bracteates, and their use of Style I, suggests that the B-
bracteates too may first appear at the start of VWZ III.
It would be easy simply to assign them the same life-span
as the C-bracteates. In view of the problem of overlap
between C- and D-bracteates considered above, it is
interesting to note that Axboe's supplement to Mackeprang's
corpus includes a grave from Várpalota, Kom. Veszprém,
Hungary, with a B-bracteate associated with three not-very-
early-looking D-bracteates (Axboe 1982 no.336c, pl.XIII).

Mackeprang's title for his monograph on the bracteates
was De nordiske Guldbrakteater, a title which was simply
translated into English by Axboe for the title of his
recent supplement to Mackeprang's work, The Scandinavian
Gold Bracteates (Axboe 1982). In what sense are the
bracteates "Scandinavian" ? The question can be answered
from two aspects, origins and distribution. Both of these
considerations in fact show that "Scandinavian" is a
qualification to be rather carefully used of these objects.
The first point to be investigated in the matter of origins
is of course the area of origin of the A-bracteates.
Mackeprang's Fig.8 shows the distribution of early A-
bracteates (those he attributes to Period 1). There are
7 examples, 2 from Blekinge, 2 from Fyn, 1 from Sjælland, 1
from Schleswig-Holstein, probably from Geltorf, just south
of the present district of Angeln (Mackeprang no.116,
pl.3.4), and one from Nord-Trøndelag. Later examples of A-
bracteates show a marked concentration further north in
Scandinavia proper (Mackeprang pp.26-33), but we have here
an indication that in the earliest bracteate period we are
hard put to insist that the origins of the bracteates are
distinctly Scandinavian as opposed to belonging partly in
the Anglian homeland. A more recently found A-bracteate of
"classical" appearance from Erin, Kr. Recklinghausen,
Nordrhein-Westfalen is published by Axboe (1982 no.325c,
pl.XI). This differs from other early bracteates in
lacking a rim, and is apparently a copy of a coin of Valens
(364-378 A.D.). Its date is uncertain. It is possible,
however, that it is a variant example of the development
under the same impulses as the early A-bracteates, but
elsewhere in northern (?Saxon) Germany, and broadly
contemporary.

The distribution and the apparent internal chronology of the C-bracteates imply an origin for them, along with Style I, in Scandinavia proper. Few early examples occur to the south in northern Germany (Mackeprang pp.39ff.). The same goes, at a later stage, for the D-bracteates, although early D-bracteates are rather more widely distributed than early C-bracteates (Mackeprang pp.56ff.). Mackeprang was also satisfied that the origin of the B-bracteates was to be localized in Denmark (p.38). The parallels between the B- and C-bracteates, mentioned above, may support this view. However the Anglian and more southerly areas of northern Germany, and the marginal areas of southern Denmark, produce a significant number of examples of various forms of B-bracteate (e.g. Mackeprang nos.109, 110, 320, 233, 323; Axboe no.325a), which one could not properly assert are later than the more common Danish examples, and which indicate that the type was of "regular" and not "chance" occurrence in these North German areas. The relative proportion of B-bracteates in northern Germany is high. They constitute some 22% of the North German finds as opposed to about 9% overall (cf. Mackeprang p.96), while the figures for A- and D-bracteates in this area are consistent with the overall pattern (7½% and 34% respectively), and that for C-bracteates rather low (about 31%).

This brief survey of origins of types indicates that the use of the term "Scandinavian" is justified with regard to the bracteates as a whole, although with certain detailed qualifications. A survey of the overall distribution of the Migration Period bracteates shows that they must impart a Scandinavian character of some sort to whatever find-context they occur in. Mackeprang recorded 623 individual examples from Scandinavia against 90 from abroad, but he included parts of what is now Schleswig-Holstein, West Germany, continental Anglian areas in a more recent period part of the kingdom of Denmark, in Scandinavia. Although Axboe in his supplement to Mackeprang's catalogue lists about the same number of additional examples from outside the current political limits of Scandinavia as from inside, the proportion of "Scandinavian" bracteates in this sense falls overall only from about 85% to 82%. The task here is to investigate what relationship between geographically non-Scandinaivan find-contexts and Scandinavia the occurrence of these objects implies.

I shall, of course, be focussing quite narrowly on one geographically non-Scandinavian find-context, Anglian England, although comparison with other such find-contexts is necessary in seeking to interpret this. Kent has produced 21 gold bracteates, 20 of Type D, and 1 of Type B. These have very recently been published and discussed thoroughly by S.C. Hawkes (Hawkes and Pollard 1981), the chronological implications of which article were considered in Chapter 1. Points concerning the Kentish finds are taken up for further discussion where relevant below. From England other than Kent, I know of, or have references to, 16 bracteates from 15 finds (Map 4.1) - that is, all examples were found singly except for one pair. These are considered below, in order according to their type, in so far as they can be classified in this way, with special attention paid to their parallels on other bracteates, and the evidence for their place of manufacture and date.

A-bracteates

Undley, Sfk	Axboe 1982 no.307d.[*]	Gold. Plate 4.1
St.Giles's Field,	Mackeprang 1952 no.307	
Oxon	pl.4.11	Gold

The Undley bracteate is a unique gold A-bracteate, with a markedly classical design and a runic legend, which may be of enormous significance both for the early history of bracteates and for runology. Its pictorial features are unparalleled to any significant degree on other A-bracteates. But a particular Roman coin and medallion type may be identified with certainty as the original source of its design. This is the VRBS ROMA type of Constantine the Great, which displays a helmeted head of the correct proportions on one side, the helmet having an appropriate brow-piece, crest, and neck-guard, and a wolf-and-twins motif, with two stars, on the other (Froehner 1878 pp.283-290; Kent 1978 no.651). On one of the medallions illustrated by Froehner the wolf-and-twins motif faces to the right, as on the bracteate, and on two to the left. The posture and design of this motif on medallions and bracteate are quite congruent: note the in-curled tail, and the ears, eyes, and nose of the wolf, and the twins seated with their arms raised (Fig.4.1). Two stars appear above the wolf-and-twins on the medallions, and two stars also appear above the wolf-and-twins and behind the helmeted head on the bracteate, although one of these is largely covered up by the applied wire spirals below the loop. A degree of modification, possibly "barbarization", appears on the bracteate, however. The helmeted figure on the Roman coins and medallions is female, though certainly not feminine in appearance, while that on the bracteate is male and bearded. The bracteate design also has transverse lines added to the brow-piece of the helmet.

According to Kent, the medallions from which this bracteate derives are datable to the years 330-353. The equivalent coins were minted between 330 and 335 at a

----

[*] I am grateful to Dr Stanley West, Director of the Suffolk Archaeological Unit, for giving me his permission and encouragement to discuss this find in advance of his own forthcoming publication of it in Frühmittelalterliche Studien.

number of western Roman mints (personal communication, A. Burnett, Department of Coins and Medals, BM, London). The individualism of the piece, and its distinct classicism, suggest that it is one of the earlier A-bracteates. The execution of the head cannot be relatively dated by style - the succession of Style I to Nydam style is not relevant here - but its clarity of line and proportions are different from the characteristically stylized human heads of most B- and C-bracteates, and the simple explanation is that it is earlier. The touch of "barbarization" of design cannot really be used for relative dating of the object amongst the A-bracteates. But further considerations suggest that it is not one of the very earliest of these bracteates. Its loop is of the type that Axboe has classified as "broad central ridge, rounded" (Axboe 1982 p.32f.). This type is of very widespread and common occurrence, but not amongst the earliest A-bracteates (cf. Mackeprang pl.3). The closest parallel to the added wire spirals below the loop appears to be on an unfortunately damaged, and now lost, B-bracteate from Heide, Schleswig-Holstein (Mackeprang no.320, pl.5.17). At the broadest the Undley bracteate can probably be dated with confidence to the period 450-480. There are reasons to believe that the latter end of this period is more probable than the earlier.

Apart from the runic legend on this bracteate, which requires special consideration, the principal evidence we have for localizing its source are its type and date, and the spirals below the loop. Axboe's study shows its type of loop and rim (beaded wire affixed to the front of the flan) to be of very widespread distribution. The other early, classical A-bracteates, however, belong to the southern Scandinavia and Schleswig-Holstein area. The closest parallel to the spirals below the loop appears to have been on another bracteate found in Schleswig-Holstein, although more distant parallels may be seen on bracteates from Öland (Mackeprang no.187, p.4.18), and Jutland (Mackeprang nos.89 and 108, pls.5.11 and 10.15), et al. On archaeological grounds alone, then, one would normally attribute the fabrication of the bracteate to the southern Scandinavia and Schleswig-Holstein area, more likely to the latter than the former.

At this point the runic text becomes a problem.[*] It reads, or appears to read:

14 13 12 11 10 9   8   7 6/5 4/3 2/1

----

[*]   I am most grateful to Bengt Odenstedt of the University of Umeå, Sweden, for a valuable discussion of these runes, and to Mr C.J.E. Ball, Keble College, Oxford, and Dr R.I. Page, Corpus Christi College, Cambridge, for the benefit of their views.

The direction of the bi-staves indicates that this should be read from right to left. The problem is wholly created by the bind-rune 3/4, which looks to be a combination of ✕ and ᛉ. ᛉ is a distinctive development of the so-called Anglo-Frisian futhorc, reflecting a sound change only known in Old English and Old Frisian (OE, OFr), that of a + nasal consonant + unvoiced spirant consonant to ō (Page 1973 pp.43-45; Campbell 1959 §§119, 121). However the rune ᛉ is unknown in Denmark and Schleswig-Holstein, the area archaeologically identified as the most probable source for the bracteate.

This has led to the suggestion that ✕ᛉ is in fact simply an error for ✕ by the bracteate die-maker, by chance producing a seriously misleading form. ✕ is a common, probably formulaic bind-rune in Scandinavia, standing perhaps for gibu auja (I give luck; cf. Krause 1966 no.127), and occurring in the sequence ✕✕✕ on a spear-shaft from Kragehul bog-find on Fyn (Krause 1966 no.27). Attributing to the runes and sound-values of the original 24-character Scandinavian futhark, the text could then be read as:

GA GA GA. M A G A. M E D U

The three initial bind-runes would be interpreted as a repeated formula: "I give luck; I give luck; I give luck". maga should probably be regarded as a weak noun related to Old Norse (ON) mǫgr, "son, young man", like OE maga, "young man", occasionally "powerful man". medu should probably be interpreted as the noun "reward", OE mēd, a feminine o-stem noun with -u still preserved as the nominative ending (Campbell 1959 §§585-588). However this seems to be a distinctly West Germanic (WGmc) word; there is no cognate noun recorded in Old Scandinavian.

But are we justified in explaining away the problem like this ? The runic text otherwise looks confidently and competently executed. The technical mode of production of bracteates is of great significance here. Axboe has argued that most if not all of the Migration Period bracteates were produced by hammering the blank gold flan into a negative matrix, i.e. the design of the bracteate was first cut into a piece of hardwood or bone, or something similarly suitable, although a positive patrix-die does exist for an English Style II bracteate (Axboe 1982 pp.11-29). The use of a matrix does not allow the ✕ᛉ bind-rune to be explained as the result of an unfortunate slip of the cutting tool: two identical unfortunate slips of the cutting tool would be required. On microscopic examination of the bracteate, I could not see any signs of the grain of the putative organic matrix die, so it cannot determined whether the disputed lines run parallel to this or not. Certainly the two disputed bi-staves taper in a manner in which none of the undisputed lines do. But it seems an extraordinary combination of factors that two identical accidents should produce what in other, not distant, contexts is a perfectly good rune form, and thus mislead and confuse us. The apparent use of the ᴏ-element as a word-divider or interpunct may be a further indicator of considerable sophistication in the use of script. If these are correctly interpreted as word-dividers then the placing of one after ᛜᛜᛜ and one after ᛗᚠᛉᚠ may be felt to weaken the case for the former sequence being a thrice-repeated formula rather than a single word. Conversely the formula interpretation may better explain why the bind-rune ᛜ occurs here, and separate runes ᛉᚠ in the following word, although it is not uncommon for inscriptions to mix bind-runes and ordinary runes.

We can in fact accept the bind rune ᛜ as genuine and maintain the bracteate's attribution to the southern Scandinavia/Schleswig-Holstein area. The rune ᛡ , if true here, must represent the sound o. It arose from a nasalized a, ã, produced from the a + nasal + voiceless spirant sequence mentioned above, but should not represent that a sound here, as ᛉ , the following sound, should represent a voiced consonant (either spirant or stop), and this is therefore not a phonetic context in which one would expect ã. The ᛡ rune is therefore apparently levelled through to represent o in all cases. In this case ᚠ probably represents æ, the sound produced by fronting of earlier Germanic a in the two known languages where a ⟩ o, OE and OFr (Campbell 1959 §§127-131). ᚠ could conceiveably still represent a while ᛡ represents o, as the nasalization of a in the relevant contexts presumably preceded the fronting of a in others, but it is not known for a fact that ã ⟩ o any substantial period of time before a ⟩ æ. Campbell has the two chronologically close together (§255). In this case a plausible reading of the text is:

G Æ G O G Æ . M Æ G Æ . M E D U

Reasonable sense can be made of such a text. As above, medu may be interpreted "reward". An alternative interpretation would be as the word "mead", OE medu, meodu. This might seem an improbable word to find on a bracteate, but it is interesting to recall the apparent confusion that arises between the element alu, believed to mean "good luck", that occurs on many bracteates, and the word for "ale", OE ealu, ON ǫl (cf. Sigrdrífumál vv.5-8), and between the related forms ealuscerwen (Beowulf 1.769) and meoduscerwen (Andreas 1.1526) in Old English verse (cf. Swanton 1978 pp.192-193). Such an interpretation would only be possible if the text were WGmc, since the form medu does not occur in the paradigm of Proto-Scandinavian *meðuR. mægæ may be regarded as the nominative singular of the feminine weak noun "kinswoman", OE mǣge with the archaic nominative -æ (Campbell §617). No such obvious interpretations present themselves for gægogæ. It could be a noun or personal name, declined and inflected in the same way as mægæ. It may be possible to associate it with the rare OE verb *gogan, "to lament", originally, probably, "to howl" (Campbell §761.7), giving a name "howler". An adequate demonstration of this point, however, would require a digression into details quite inappropriate in the immediate context. It is sufficient to note that GA. GA. GA. is not the only credible reading of runes 1-6. In the less probable event of ᚠ representing a, gagoga would be very much harder to interpret, although maga could be interpreted "kinsman". (See Appendix 4.1).

Thus a WGmc interpretation of the words of the text can be made, and has to recommend it two key points:

1.   That the rune ᚠ is West Germanic
2.   That the lexical item medu, whether meaning "reward" or "mead", is apparently peculiarly WGmc.

An attempt to relate the three words of the text to one another has not been made here, although if that could be successfully done it would greatly enhance the case for this interpretation. But it should be noted that the majority of bracteate inscriptions are single words or formulae (Krause 1966 nos.103-138). The whole significance of the words on the bracteate is likely to be an entirely different matter from their mere semantic interpretation, and we need not therefore expect to uncover a simple sentence of the subject-predicate type on this object.

The philogical implications of interpreting the text in this way, and maintaining the archaeological attribution of the bracteate to the proposed area, have been described as "sensational". First and foremost, it implies that the sound change a + nasal + voiceless spirant > ō took place in the Anglian dialect in the North German Anglian homelands by about the mid 5th. century. We otherwise know nothing about continental Anglian. There is nothing inherently improbable about this proposition though. In continental Old Saxon the nasalized ā̃ < -aŋχ- fell back to a rather than rising to ọ, but this does not significantly affect the possibility of the converse being the case in continental Anglian. Secondly, it implies that the first step(s) in the development of the distinctive Anglo-Frisian futhorc from the Scandinavian futhark were made in the Anglian homelands around Schleswig-Holstein by about the third quarter of the 5th. century, and that the Anglo-Frisian runic script was brought to England from there closely in the train of the first Anglian settlers to reach England.

The possibility that the bracteate was made in England must be considered. Such an attribution would relieve some of the tension involved in locating the sound change and concomitant development of the rune form in 5th.-century continental Anglia, although if the rune ᚷ is accepted as true, the linguistic implications are little different.

The parallels the bracteate has in southern Scandinavia/ Schleswig Holstein are so strong that it must have been made under close and immediate influence from that area, irrespective of where in actual fact it was struck. However copies of the relevant VRBS ROMA coins were in extensive circulation in the 4th. century and occur abundantly in hoard and site finds, and at least two found their way into English graves in Kent (Brent 1866 pp.161-162). This must improve the case for this being an English bracteate design. But there are no grounds for changing the dating of the object, and if the ᛈ rune form is true, then the sound change a + nasal + voiceless spirant > ọ had probably gone through by the mid 5th. century. This is early enough for it to be present in continental Anglian too, and for the rune form to have been brought to England by settlers from that area. However the case for the fabrication of the bracteate in southern Scandinavia/ Schleswig-Holstein still seems the stronger. As is shown below, gold bracteates were made in Anglian England, but it is most improbable that any were made before the 6th. century. The type of loop on the Undley bracteate is very common in Scandinavia and North-West Germany, but occurs for certain on only one other Anglian English find, a gold C-bracteate from Market Overton, Leics. That bracteate, however, is rimless, as are most other Anglian English bracteates, with the exception, perhaps, of two gold C-bracteates, from Jaywick Sands, Ex, and Chippenham, Cambs (Axboe 1982 nos.307c and 307e).*

It is therefore my opinion that the Undley bracteate was made in the area of southern Denmark/Schleswig-Holstein in the period 450-480, and subsequently brought to East Anglia. Whether the bind-rune ᛜ is regarded as genuine or an error, the runic text can be reconciled with this suggested provenance. It is not my concern here to pursue in full the philological implications of this attribution.

Turning to the second A-bracteate from Anglo-Saxon England, from St. Giles's Field, Oxford, is a great anti-climax after the Undley bracteate. This is not, strictly, an Anglian English bracteate find, and it cannot be certain that it was recovered from an authentic Anglo-Saxon find context in Oxford (see Mackeprang 1952 p.175). It deserves a brief review, however. Mackeprang regards it as a late example, lying outside the main lines of development and groups of A-bracteates (p.25 fn.1). It has significant parallels on South Scandinavian bracteates and other pendants, and an A-bracteate from Terp Hitsum, Frisia (Mackeprang no.318, pl.4.12). The applied wire ornament. below where the loop was recurs on this Frisian bracteate and a very similar A-bracteate from Sievern, Niedersachsen (Hauck 1970 Abb.6), a C-bracteate from Kjellers Mose, Ribe a., Jutland (Mackeprang pl.10.10), and a pendant from

---

* I have not been able to examine these objects myself. See below.

Darum, Ribe a. (Mackeprang pl.23.21). The closest parallel
to its stamped border is the bracteate from Terp Hitsum,
although the actual stamps are different. As Mackeprang
implies, there is no particularly close parallel to its
actual design, but the cross symbol in front of the profile
head's mouth may be compared to a cross behind the head on
an A-bracteate from Freilev, Lolland (Mackeprang pl.3.2a),
and swastikas in front of the mouth on A-bracteates from
Lingby, Randers a., Jutland, and Geltorf, Schleswig-
Holstein (Mackeprang pl.3 nos.4, 10a, and 15). It seems
most plausible to regard the St. Giles's Field, Terp
Hitsum, and Sievern A-bracteates as exports from the
southern Denmark/Schleswig-Holstein area. It could well

have reached Oxford via Kent: one recalls that the
parallels of the square-headed brooches, another form of
especially rich jewellery of the same period, of the Upper
Thames Valley also fall largely towards the South and
South-East (Chapter 3). The hair-style of the head of this
bracteate recalls that on some C-bracteates, and it may be
dated to the end of the 5th. century.

C-bracteates

Morningthorpe, Nfk g.80. Pair. Norwich Mus. Copper alloy.
    Fig.4.2a.
Jaywick Sands, Ex. Axboe 1982 no.307c. Gold. Fig.4.3.
Chippenham, Cambs. Axboe 1982 no.307e. Gold.
Longbridge, Warwicks. Mackeprang 1952 no.306; Hauck 1970
    fig.46b. Gold.
Market Overton, Leics. Mackeprang 1952 no.305. Gold.
Kirmington, Hu. Axboe 1982 no.305e. Gold.

There are 7 bracteates which may be identified as C-
bracteates from Anglian England (including the example from
Jaywick Sands, Ex), 5 of which are of gold, and one pair of
copper alloy. "Copper alloy" is the term used here rather
than the usual "bronze" because although the deep green
colour of the Morningthorpe bracteates indicate them to
have a high copper content, I suspect that analysis would
reveal the presence of a significant quantity of silver.

Four of the Anglian C-bracteates (counting the
Morningthorpe pair now as one example) have parallels to be
traced in certain "groups" of Scandinavian C-bracteates,
mostly to the bracteates of Mackeprang's West Scandinavian
group (Mackeprang pp.41-42). These are the finds from
Morningthorpe, Nfk g.80; Chippenham, Cambs; Market
Overton, Leics; and Kirmington, Hu. The examples from
Jaywick Sands, Ex, and Longbridge, Warwicks, are more
individualistic, although significant parallels to them can
still be traced on other Anglian and individual
Scandinavian and continental finds.

The examples found in England which are most similar

to bracteates of the West Scandinavian group are those from
Market Overton and Kirmington. Mackeprang included the
Market Overton bracteate in his West Scandinavian group,
and a look at his illustrations (Mackeprang pl.7 nos.5-17)
shows that the "horse" on the Market Overton bracteate
indeed has the characteristically sectioned body, forelegs,
rolled-up hindleg, and bell-shaped head of this group. The
embossed border of the central area of the Market Overton
bracteate recurs on bracteates of this group found in
Jutland, southern Norway, and northern Germany (Mackeprang
pl.7 nos.5, 7, 10, and 15). The West Scandinavian group
itself, of course, has close parallels in other groups of
C-bracteates, but it is clear that the Market Overton
bracteate is most closely related to this group. However
the Market Overton bracteate has significant pecularities,
and some interesting parallels outside of the West
Scandinavian group. Unlike all other members of the group,
the Market Overton bracteate has a bird alone above the
horse, not a head with a helmet or head-dress ending in a
bird's beak at the front. This combination of bird and
horse alone may be compared to the design of some of the
scarce F-bracteates, e.g. from Broholm, Svendborg a., Dk;
Holstein; and Nebenstedt, N. Germany (Mackeprang pl.20
nos.8, 12, and 17), which Mackeprang indicates are
themselves largely derivative of C-bracteates (pp.64-65).
Parallels to the fully outlined bird with its prominent ear
or crest are found on C-bracteates from Hjørlunde,
Frederiksborg a., Dk (Mackeprang pl.6.25) and Bolbro,
Odense a., Dk (Mackeprang pl.8.19). Thus far it may seem
probable that the Market Overton bracteate is imported from
South Scandinavia. Its loop, further, is of the type with
a rounded broad, central ridge, which is widespread in
Scandinavia and northern Germany. But it has no rim, which
it has already been suggested is a peculiarly English
characteristic. And the stamps in its border, a circle
above a double-lined chevron, appear to be very rare type
in Scandinavia (Axboe 1982 fig.47). As further evidence
for the production of gold bracteates in England is
assembled below, it will appear that we can quite happily
regard the Market Overton bracteate as of English
manufacture.

The Kirmington bracteate very clearly has the typical
horse and rider of the West Scandinavian group. It also
has the embossed inner border and is without a rim like the
Market Overton bracteate. Its loop, unfortunately, appears
to be lost. There are no significant particular and
localized parallels to it to be drawn from the Scandinavian
and continental examples of the group. Like the Market.
Overton bracteate it can be attributed to English
manufacture.

The bracteates from Morningthorpe g.80 and Chippenham
are less obviously related to the West Scandinavian group,
but on close examination distinctive links appear. The
pair of bracteates in Morningthrope g.80 are highly worn,

but a careful look reveals that the two are certainly a pair, and much of the design is reconstructable by putting the two together (Fig.4.2a). The bell-shaped head of the horse is a principal characteristic of the West Scandinavian group. It is by comparison with the same group that we can best explain the formation of the head above the beast on the Morningthorpe bracteates: a looped end to the hair-piece behind, the V-shaped mouth, and the projecting nose with short lines hanging from the end. Most comparable to the Morningthorpe bracteates in their stylization of the profile head are examples from an unknown place; Akershus, southern Norway; and Landegge, Niedersachsen (Mackeprang pl.7 nos.7, 12, and 15), bracteates which have already been cited for carrying the same bossed border as the Market Overton and Kirmington bracteates, which again appears on the Morningthorpe pair. The Morningthorpe bracteates have a broad, plain border, and no rim. This is to be regarded as an English characteristic, although interesting parallels occur on two gilt silver mounts with a D-bracteate stamp from the Netherlands (Axboe 1982 no.319a), and a gilt silver D-bracteate from Schönebeck, Sachsen-Anhalt, E.Germany (Axboe 1982 no.331a). The loop of the Morningthorpe bracteates was affixed to the back of the bracteate, which is not a Scandinavian or North German practice. So far as I know this is the only example of a bracteate in copper alloy, other than some considerably later Gotlandic E-bracteates. There can be no serious doubt that the pair is of English manufacture.

It is initially a little puzzling that Axboe describes the Chippenham bracteate as showing a "garbled C-motif", but if his illustration is turned upside down, it appears that in the normal way of portraying C-bracteates the two looped lines below a clear eye element can be interpreted as derived from the quadruped beast of the C-bracteates. The line of the front loop of this motif on the Chippenham bracteate is equally well paralleled by the forelegs of Mackeprang's Danish groups I and II, West Scandinavian group, and Danish-Swedish group (Mackeprang pp.39-42). The rear loop, however, is best compared to the looped rear leg characteristic of the West Scandinavian group, perhaps most clearly seen if the Chippenham bracteate is set beside that from Højberg, Viborg a., Dk (Mackeprang pl.7.5). The eye element, with its spiky border, very interestingly is best compared not to any C-bracteates, but to D-bracteates of Mackeprang's Jutish group I (e.g. Mackeprang pl.16 nos.1-12 etc.). From Axboe's illustration, it appears that the loop of this bracteate is lost, while the nature of the rim cannot be ascertained. The degeneracy of its design can probably be equated with English manufacture in this case, although it remains possible that it is an imported object, probably in that case from Jutland, where its parallels are centred.

The designs of the C-bracteates from Jaywick Sands and Longbridge are very much more independent. That the Jaywick Sands example has the basic design of a head over an animal is clear (Fig.4.3). No close parallels can be pointed out to the very distinctive hair-style of the head, although a marked parting of the hair can be seen on various overseas examples, e.g. a C-bracteate of Danish group II from Bjørnsholm, Ålborg a. (Mackeprang pl.7.3), and an A-bracteate from the Rheinland-Pfalz (Axboe 1982 no.334a/1). The only clear detail of the animal on the Jaywick Sands bracteate is its raised and upturned front leg, for which if any parallel could be cited it would probably be the bracteates of Mackeprang's South Swedish group II (Mackeprang pp.47-48), although this is not very persuasive. I can find no parallels to the stamps in the border of this example on other bracteates. It is of some interest, however, to compare the perpendicular strokes below the front leg of the animal on this bracteate to similar strokes along the back of the animal, below the chin of the head, and by an apparently meaningless line between the horse's head and front hoof on the Morningthorpe g.80 pair, and on an uninterpretable element of a fragmentary bracteate from Willoughby-on-the-Wolds, Notts g.33 (Axboe 1982 no.305f.). This may just be a peculiarly English feature of zoomorphic ornament on bracteates, although such strokes, more meaningfully used to denote hair, are common on the West Scandinavian group C-bracteates. The Jaywick Sands bracteate has currently gone missing, and I have been unable to discover anything about its loop. A photograph of the back of this bracteate seen in the BM suggests that it had a rim placed on the edge of the flan, but it is uncertain whether this was plain, beaded, or twisted. One is again inclined to regard the uniqueness of this bracteate's design as a sign of English manufacture: if it was imported, its region of origin cannot be located.

The Longbridge bracteate has been published and thoroughly discussed by Vierck (in Hauck 1970 pp.331-339). This bracteate is extremely worn and one could disagree with some parts of Vierck's pictorial reconstruction of it, but to produce a drawing of the object is a difficult task, and Vierck's figure is adequate and useful. It makes clear the basic design of an animal below a profile head. It is possible that the front piece of the head-dress or helmet of the profile head in fact ended in a beaked bird-element as the West Scandinavian group C-bracteates, but this cannot now be determined for certain. Many general parallels to the form of the beast on the Longbridge bracteate can be found on Scandinavian bracteates, but it is, as Vierck says, in most important respects, unique. One rather interesting and specific parallel to the use of small bosses to fill up the blank areas of the design around the horse may be cited on another individualistic C-bracteate from Kølby, Ålborg a., Jutland (Axboe 1982 no.76a). But there is little doubt that the Longbridge

bracteate is an English product.   It is stamp-linked with
other objects in the grave-group it belongs to (see Vierck
op.cit.).   It has no rim, and a suspension loop soldered to
the back and turned over to the front.

It may be argued, then, that all the English C-
bracteates so far known were probably manufactured in
Anglian England (see Map 4.1).   There is no predisposition
against recognizing the occurrence of imported C-bracteates
in this area, but the case for "local" manufacture of the
known examples seem to be the strongest.   If they are all
English derivatives of Scandinavian models, then the date
of those Scandinavian models provides only a general
terminus post quem for the dating of the English examples:
we cannot necessarily date the English examples by
regarding them as closely contemporary to those bracteates
displaying their closest parallels.   C-bracteates were
generally dated above to VWZ III, that is to ca.475-525.
The West Scandinavian group of C-bracteates, which figures
so prominently in the discussion of the English bracteates'
models, begins relatively early amongst the C-bracteates as
a whole,   but does not look to have representatives amongst
the very earliest C-bracteates, and so may be argued to
appear sometime in the last quarter of the 5th. century.
On these grounds it is improbable that the more developed
forms of the English C-bracteates, and their closest
Scandinavian parallels amongst developed C-bracteates are
to be dated earlier than the 6th. century.   Two of the
English examples are from usefully datable contexts, both
by virtue of association with cruciform brooches:
Morningthorpe, Nfk g.80, and Longbridge, Warwicks.   The
cruciform brooch in Morningthorpe g.80 (Fig.4.2b) is not
datable directly from Reichstein's study (Reichstein 1975).
But its half-round side-knobs cast-in-one with a broad
headplate, cast profile heads as lappets, and similar
profile heads in the places of the nostrils of the horse's
head terminal, indicate a 6th.-century date.   The florid
cruciform brooch from the Longbridge grave (Hauck 1970
fig.49) looks late, even amongst florid cruciform brooches,
with, for instance, its especially heavy and thick-set
headplate knobs and its rough Style I ornament.   Although I
believe Vierck's date for the grave at about the end of the
6th. century (cf. Chapter 1, Chronological Conventions) is
too late, I believe it is unlikely that the burial took
place before 550.   The bracteate is extremely worn, but it
is unlikely that its stamp-linked associated disc pendant
and silver armlet - relatively fragile things - had an
extraordinarily long working life.   We may, then, date the
English C-bracteates to at least the broad period ca.500-
550.   Production of them could indeed have gone on to the
end of the Migration Period in Anglian England.   There is
no reason why the type should not have had such a
relatively long life here, even if it is represented by so
few examples.   These examples are quite diverse, though
they nevertheless display certain common "English
characacteristics".

D-bracteates

Little Eriswell, Sfk g.27	Axboe 1982 no.307a	Silver
West Stow, Sfk	Axboe 1982 no.307b	Silver
Driffield, Hu	Axboe 1982 no.305a	Silver
	Plate 4.2	
Hornsea, Hu	Axboe 1982 no.305b	Silver

An interesting contrast between the C- and the D-bracteates recorded from Anglian England is immediately obvious here in that five out of the six examples of C-bracteates were gold, the sixth being copper alloy, while all four examples of D-bracteates are silver. Even if the Morningthorpe g.80 pair does turn out to be extremely base silver, this would not greatly weaken the contrast.

Hawkes (Hawkes and Pollard 1981 p.363) and Axboe (1982 no.307a) record Vierck's testimony that certain small silver fragments from Little Eriswell g.27 can be identified as fragments of a D-bracteate "derivative of Mackeprang 1952 Jutland group I". I did not see such fragments when I visited BSE Mus myself in June 1981, and therefore cannot discuss the find any further, but such a find would be entirely congruent as regards location (Map 4.1) and the material and design of the bracteate with the other Anglian English D-bracteates.

The bracteates from West Stow and Driffield are clearly to be associated with Mackeprang's Jutish group I. The design on the West Stow bracteate is substantially disjointed (see Axboe 1982 pl.VIII), and the loop forming a thigh in front of the Style I animal's face has become opened. The nearest parallel from Jutland itself is probably the example from Skonager, Ribe a., (Mackeprang pl.16.4). Much more similar examples are spread along the North Sea coastal area: from Sievern, Niedersachsen (Hauck 1970 Abb.2d), Burmania Terp, Frisia (Mackeprang pl.16.13), Rhenen, on the lower Rhine in the Netherlands, g.775 (Axboe 1982 no.319a), and Finglesham, Kt g.D3 (Mackeprang pl.16.9). The Rhenen examples, similar to the West Stow piece, are silver, but gilt, and used, or re-used, as some form of mount.

The Driffield bracteate is related to a separate sub-group of Jutish group I, represented by Mackeprang pl.16 nos.24-30. Of this sub-group, Mackeprang recorded four, possibly five, examples from Jutland/Denmark, three from Kent, and one from Frisia, to which can now be added an example from Hérouvillette, Normandy g.11 (Axboe no.315b). The Driffield bracteate is most similar to one of these examples in particular, that from Sarre, Kt g.IV (Plates 4.2-3). Attention is drawn especially to the design of the animal's head, the grooved, contingent lines of which the animal is formed and their density in the whole bracteate design, the embossed border, and the boss in the plain area in the centre of the bracteate.

Common to the West Stow and Driffield bracteates is the fact that they have no rim and are made of silver. The same goes for the Rhenen mounts, but these differ in being gilt, and these characteristics of the West Stow and Driffield bracteates may be taken as evidence of Anglian English manufacture. Where they derived their models from, however, is a disputable point. Ultimately the source would have been, as Mackeprang indicates, South Scandinavia, and Jutland in particular. But the closest parallels to these two finds are not South Scandinavian but from North-West Europe and Kent, for all of which the degeneracy of design is a characteristic feature contrasting them with the examples found in Scandinavia. Webster is prepared to admit this as evidence of non-Scandinavian manufacture (Webster 1977). Hawkes, however, would regard all the gold bracteates found in Kent as imports (Hawkes and Pollard 1981 p.351). She supports her case by reference to "an acute gold shortage in Kent at that time". Clearly the phrase "at that time" begs the question of when we are to date the D-bracteates under consideration (cf. Chapter 1, Chronological Conventions). In the 6th. century some gold was certainly available for the gilding of locally-produced metalwork, and it would appear that sufficient gold was obtained in Anglian England, not as wealthy an area as Kent, in the first half of the 6th. century to produce five gold bracteates there. There is, then, a case for the production of D-bracteates in 6th.-century Kent, and for the West Stow and Driffield bracteates being directly dependent on specifically Kentish models. A corollary of this argument for Kentish bracteate production is that we must regard independent production in northern Germany and even Frisia as a possibility too.

The fourth Anglian D-bracteate, from Hornsea, Hu, stands some way apart. It is worn and in poor condition, and its design is not easy to read. It can at least be affirmed that it appears to carry on Style I ornament of Haseloff's Style Phase D, identifying it as a D-bracteate. We may find some very distant reminiscence of its general design on the bracteates of Mackeprang's North Jutish-West Swedish-Norwegian group (Mackeprang pl.18 nos.1-5), but I would not argue that the Hornsea bracteate is related. Vierck drew attention to the use of Kreisaugen to denote parts of the body, and linked this to one of the above bracteates and a bracteate from Schönebeck, Sachsen-Anhalt g.15, but as he himself implies it does little more than make the designation of Hornsea as a D-bracteate more acceptable (in Hauck 1970 p.337). As a silver bracteate of unique design, without a rim, we can be sure that it is of English manufacture.

In seeking to date the Anglian English D-bracteates we now have the benefit of Hawkes's thorough and recent review of the chronology of the D-bracteates in Kent (Hawkes and Pollard 1981). Hawkes would date the bracteate from Finglesham g.D3 to which the West Stow bracteate is compared towards the 520s, and those in Sarre g.IV in the second quarter of the 6th. century, probably earlier rather than later in that quarter (op.cit. pp.342-350). Whether or not the West Stow and Driffield examples are directly derived from these models, one would not date them any earlier than the Kentish examples, which thus provide a terminus post quem in the 520s. Little Eriswell, Sfk g.27 contained a late group XVII square-headed brooch, which would indicate that the burial probably took place after 550. There is no direct dating evidence for the Hornsea bracteate, but I would date it and all the Anglian English D-bracteates between the 520s and the end of the Migration period, that is at broadest ca.520-570.

?C?D-bracteates

Willoughby-on-the-Wolds,		
Notts g.33	Axboe 1982 no.305f.	Silver
Welbeck Hill, Hu g.14	Axboe 1982 no.305c.	Silver
Welbeck Hill, Hu g.52	Axboe 1982 no.305d.	Silver

There remain these three bracteates found in Anglian England, which for different reasons cannot be satisfactorily assigned to either Types C or D. The problem with the bracteate from Willoughby-on-the-Wolds g.33 is that it is only a fragment which I have been unable to positively identify as a part of any known C- or D-bracteate design. On the contrary, just enough of this bracteate survives to suggest that its design was in fact rather individualistic. The perpendicular strokes to the two major lines of the design visible recall the Market Overton and Jaywick Sands C-bracteates, but the fact that the bracteate is silver recalls the Anglian English D-bracteates. In themselves, of course, neither of these points is conclusive in allowing a designation of the bracteate. But they are sufficient grounds to argue for Anglian English manufacture. There is also no sign of any rim, but the piece is extremely fragmentary.

Welbeck Hill, Hu is the only English site outside of Kent which has produced more than one separate bracteate finds, in graves 14 and 52. These have been published and discussed by Vierck (in Hauck 1970 pp.337-339). Both are very highly individualistic with virtually no determinative parallels on other bracteates. Vierck compares the long face on the bracteate from grave 14 to that on a bracteate from Hamfelde, Schleswig-Holstein. There appears to be a small bird depicted to the left of this on the Welbeck Hill g.14 bracteate, and the combination of bird plus face can only be paralleled on C-bracteates of Mackeprang's Danish groups I and II, East Norwegian-West Swedish group, and South and East Swedish group. It is quite unclear what the features to the other side of the face represent. It may, however, be possible to associate the sausage-shaped elements with similar depictions of the C-bracteate's animal's back, as on an example from Seierslev Klitter, Thisted a., Jutland (Mackeprang pl.10.14).

Runes occur only on A-, B-, and C-bracteates; there is no certain D-bracteate with runes. The runic text on the Welbeck Hill g.14 bracteate has been discussed by Page (Page 1973 pp.183-184). He suggests that this text, which one would normally read læw, is probably a distant copy of the repeated texts one finds on South Scandinavian bracteates such as alu and laþu.

The Welbeck Hill g.14 bracteate may evidently be considered to stand much closer to the C-bracteates than to any D-bracteate. Some may feel it should be classified as a C-bracteate. But its design is highly individualistic, and it does not show any convincing effort to reproduce the characteristic C design of a head above an animal. I prefer then to leave it relatively loosely classified. It carries distant hints of a South Scandinavian background. But as a silver bracteate with no rim it is surely of Anglian English manufacture.

The design of the bracteate from Welbeck Hill g.52 can be seen more clearly if the illustrations provided by Vierck and Axboe are turned upside down. We see the eye, temple, "nose" and lips of an animal head, with what may be interpreted as a neck or back behind, and a chin below. Below this is a simple zig-zag which could be an extremely abbreviated representation of a body or legs, which with a little imagination one could derive from the detached legs of the animal of the West Scandinavian group C-bracteates. Indeed we could see here a highly divergent derivative of the head-above-animal Type C design. Otherwise there are no obvious parallels to the form of this bracteate. For the same reasons as given for the Welbeck Hill g.14 bracteate, I believe it should be classified alongside that bracteate, and regarded as an Anglian English product.

The use of silver for all three of these bracteates, and the fact that if the Welbeck Hill bracteates are related to C-bracteates they are very extensively modified, suggest that these three should be regarded as broadly contemporary with the Anglian English D-bracteates (above). The Willoughby-on-the-Wolds example cannot be closely dated by find-context. The Welbeck Hill bracteates are from graves which did not produce much in the way of useful close-dating evidence, but both produced wrist-clasps, of forms B 13 c and B 20 respectively (cf. Chapter 2), which at least confirm that a 6th.-century date is most probable for these assemblages.

Style II bracteates

Mention must finally be made of the Style II ornamented bracteates found in England. These have recently been collected and published by Speake (Speake 1980 Ch.6). In England these bracteates are found only in Kent, with one exception from Camerton, Somerset, and there is no reason to doubt that they are a specifically Kentish type. A similar form carries interlaced ribbon but not animal ornament, and has much the same distribution, except that Vierck also records one example from Thornham, Nfk (Vierck and Capelle 1971 fig.16). I was unable to find this when I visited Norwich Castle Museum in July 1981. These might appear to be of little relevance to a study directed at the Anglian English bracteates, but a die, apparently for a Style II bracteate, has been found at Barton-on-Humber, Hu (Speake 1980 p.68). It would appear however, to have been used as a weight with a set of scales, and therefore is not proof of the production of Style II bracteates in this area, where otherwise none have been found. If Kent were producing her own D-bracteates, one would be tempted to suggest that the Style II bracteates superseded these there when Style I became obsolete, and thus we have continuity of bracteate production across this point of critical change. But this must remain just one theory amongst several possible ones, given the difference of views current on Kentish D-bracteate production; one may equally well suggest that only with the cessation of Scandinavian D-bracteate production was Kent obliged to produce her own models.

Summary

Evidence has been given here that two gold bracteates of Type A were imported to Anglo-Saxon England in the second half of the 5th. century, and that subsquently insular bracteate production began in Anglian England in the 6th. century. Of this Anglian English production we now have seven examples of Type C, four of Type D, and three not assigned to either of these types.

There is no clear and simple answer to the question of where this bracteate habit was adopted from. The two A-bracteates were almost certainly exported from the South Scandinavia/Schleswig-Holstein area, but it does not automatically follow that they were exported direct to England. A few other late A-bracteates are known from outside this area of origin: from Dokkum, Frisia (Mackeprang pl.4.12), Achersleben, Sachsen-Anhalt (Mackeprang pl.4.13), and Sievern, Niedersachsen (Hauck 1970 Abb.6). But since these are so few, the possibilities of the Undley and St Giles's Field bracteates being re-exports in any significant sense diminish.

The Anglian English C-bracteates show a predominant and consistent pattern of relationship with the C-bracteates of Mackeprang's West Scandinavian group. As that name implies, this is a rather widely distributed group, but interestingly better attested in Norway and Sweden than in Denmark, together with two examples from Niedersachsen and one from Frisia (an example from Sievern (Hauck 1970 Abb.3) can be added to Mackeprang's list of 1952; Map 4.2). Their distribution implies that the inspiration for these bracteates in Anglian England is at least as likely to have come from north or east of the Skagerrak and Kattegat as from Denmark. Of the two examples from Niedersachsen, that from Landegge (Mackeprang pl.7.15) shows a marked degeneracy of design which certainly is not intermediate between the West Scandinavian prototypes and the Anglian derivatives. Hauck (1970 pp.114, 136-142) seems to imply that the Sievern example could have been struck in northern Germany. It is more satisfactory to regard these as parallel developments to the Anglian English production rather than in some way seminal to it.

The case for a direct Kentish source for at least some of the Anglian English D-bracteates has already been put forward. Kent seems to derive its models - whatever proportion are imports or locally made - direct from southern Scandinavia, Jutland in particular. If Kent could derive its D-bracteate models direct from Jutland then so, theoretically, could Anglian England, East Anglia in particular, a pattern which would follow that proposed for the early square-headed brooches (cf. Chapter 3). But just as in the case of certain square-headed brooch elements, the Anglian English D-bracteates could equally well depend directly on Kentish sources, and thus represent Scandinavian models exported to Kent and subsequently re-exported to Anglian England, a significant pattern of re-export, such as could not be established for the A-bracteates.

We have then, apparently, a complex pattern of Scandinavian influence on Anglian England, with shifting courses of influence, arguably each associable with differential time stages: the import of A-bracteates in the latter decades of the 5th. century, the development of C-bracteate production under direct Scandinavian influence, perhaps from southern or western Norway, in the first quarter of the 6th. century, and the production of D-bracteates under direct Kentish influence around the beginning of the second quarter of the 6th. century. Further discussion of the means of diffusion along these· routes, and the significance of the contacts implied, is postponed until the evidence of a second associable artefact-type, the scutiform pendant, can be brought in too.

II - Scutiform Pendants

The similarity of the scutiform pendant to the bracteate lies in their both being types of round pendant, normally worn by women, suspended from necklets, and often made of precious metals, although unlike the bracteates the scutiform pendants are more often of silver than of gold. As we shall see, this artefact-type is to some extent similar in date-range and distribution to the bracteates, and the two types are occasionally found in association. A similar amuletic function has been claimed for both, a proposition which is examined below.

The scutiform pendants have not been badly covered in archaeological literature, although a published comprehensive or up-to-date study is wanting. Voss rather briefly considered the Danish finds he knew in conjunction with his publication of the Høstentorp hoard (Voss 1954 pp.189-190), but a number of new finds are now to be added. Magnus provides a thorough study of the Norwegian examples in connection with her publication of Krosshaugfunnet (Magnus 1975 pp.47-78). Vierck's B.Litt thesis (Vierck 1966 pp.40-61) contains the most comprehensive study of these pendants in Scandinavia and England, including a survey of the examples known to him, and a consideration of the relationship between the bracteates and the scutiform pendants. I seek here only to add more recent finds to Vierck's study, to provide, as far as is possible, a clearer and more accessible guide to the examples, and to re-assess his arguments concerning the date and significance of these objects.

Scandinavia

From Denmark, Voss noted 8 examples from the Høstentorp hoard, and 5 from elsewhere in Denmark and Bornholm. I believe the Høstentorp hoard may in fact include the remains of 9 examples (NMK df.62,95,98, and 99/33), and know of a further 8 examples from elsewhere in Denmark (List 4.1). The earliest examples seem to be from two grave-finds from northern Jutland datable to VWZ I by including silver-sheet brooches: Mejlby, Brostrup, Års, Ål (cf. Åberg 1924 fig.32), and Sejlflod, do., Fleskum, Ål g.00 (ÅHM 669/6033). Datable to VWZ II is an example from Melsted, Gudhjem, Bornholm g.8, associated with two relief brooches (Nissen Meyer 1934 no.26). The latest material in the Høstentorp hoard is decorated in early Style I, and the deposition of the hoard therefore datable to VWZ IV.

Both the examples from VWZ I are silver, that from Sejlflod being gilt. The central boss on both examples is conical. On both, the layout of the decoration takes the form of a ring or rings around the central boss, formed by stamps. The example from Melsted g.8, of VWZ II, is also silver, but on this the central boss is domed, not conical. It also has concentric rings of stamped ornament around the central boss, together with a radiate layout of stamps immediately around the boss. All the examples from the Høstentorp hoard are again silver, three being gilt. Both conical and domed central bosses occur amongst these. All but one of them are plain or principally decorated in concentric rings, but the exception (Voss 1954 fig.8.7) has a radiate decorative layout of a star cast or chased in relief. The fragment which I believe may represent a ninth scutiform pendant from the hoard (Fig.4.4) has an outer ring of ornament, embossed not stamped. The find from the latest context, Nørre Hvam, is gold, with a domed boss, and a single ring of simple stamps around it. There are two further unassociated gold examples from Hjørring amt in Denmark, from Råberg, Horns h., and Linderup Mark, Tolstrup, Borglum h. The former has a domed central boss, the latter a conical one, and both have a radiate layout of decoration. On the Råberg example this is executed in repoussé bosses rather than stamps.

Magnus listed 9 Norwegian examples of this artefact-type (Magnus 1975 p.53; List 4.1). I would make some minor modifications to her summary of the material. There must be some doubt as to whether two of her scutiform pendants really belong to this list, those from Erga, Klepp, Ro, and Hol, Inderøy, NT. The Erga disc is, as she says, "very fragmentary", and there is no evidence that it was used as a pendant. Its diameter is much larger than that of any other Norwegian scutiform pendant and the silver foil of which it consists is very thin, and must surely have originally been applied decoration on a firmer base. One cannot therefore be certain that this was a scutiform pendant, although conversely no more probable alternative suggests itself. Only a fragment of the Hol pendant remains, without the central area where the boss would have been, and so this object ought to be relegated to the status of an uncertain disc or scutiform pendant (see below). One further find might be added to Magnus's list, from Øvre Øye, Kvinnedal, VA, described by Lorange as "a round silver plate, cf. no.2299 from Krosshaug, with curved lines of single and double stamped semicircles, and a 'pin' on the middle, through which there is a hole" (Lorange 1875 p.52, nos. B86-96). Unfortunately this object seems now to be missing.

The earliest sure datings we have for Norwegian scutiform pendants are to VWZ II. This is the period to which the grave-find from Hauge, Klepp, Ro, discussed by Magnus, can be assigned on the basis of its relief brooch (Magnus 1975 pp.32-47). The find from Gjone, Hedrum, Vf is more broadly dated to VWZ I/II within the conventions used here. It contained cruciform brooches (Reichstein 1975 no.20) but Reichstein does not assist in dating these

closely. The diameter of the spirals of the Class A clasps
in the find, however, 0.9 cm., falls into a range which
appears to be restricted to VWZ I/II (see Chapter 2).   The
scutiform pendant from Hauge is gold, that from Gjone is
silver gilt.   The Hauge example, incidentally, carries a
fine example of a small model grip attached behind the
hollow of the central boss, confirming the initial
character of these pendants as model shields (Magnus 1975
fig.17b).   Both pendants carry a conical central boss, as
do all the Norwegian examples bar one (see below).   The
decorative layout of the Hauge pendant takes the form of
concentric rings of various stamps, while that of the Gjone
is "radiate", taking the form of a whirligig or curved
swastika (Magnus 1975 fig.19).

Three Norwegian examples are datable to VWZ II/III:
Mjølhus, Froland, AA; Skreros, Vegusdal, AA (C21287); and
Øvre Øye, Kvinnedal, VA.   All are from finds containing
cruciform brooches (Reichstein 1975 nos. 65, 67, and 85),
for none of which Reichstein offers a relative-
chronological dating, but which on typological grounds on
the basis of Reichstein's study one would be inclined to
assign to VWZ II/III.   The finds from Mjølhus and Skreros
both contained Class A clasps with the larger spiral
diameters which seem to be typical of this later double-
Stufe (cf. Chapter 2).   The second example from Haug 2 at
Skreros (C22140) seems to present quite a problem.   Alone
amongst the Norwegian examples it is of bronze, has a domed
central boss, and is otherwise plain.   The furnishings of
this grave, said to be that of a 6-year-old boy, appear to
include, remarkably, the scutiform pendant, a necklace, an
equal-armed and a small bow brooch, and 9 pots (Reichstein
1975 Taf.133).   This is an incongruous assemblage. Magnus
does not discuss both Skreros finds adequately (Magnus 1975
pp.56-58).   She seems to imply that the pendant could have
belonged to the same woman as pendant C21287.   The equal-
armed brooch with which the pendant appears to be
associated is datable to the RIA (see Chapter 5).   In view
of the confusion concerning this find, it is probably best
to suspend any judgement on its relative-chronological
placing.

Magnus concluded that the Norwegian examples could be
dated to the first half of the 5th. century (1975 pp.76-
78).   This may set too early a lower limit to their date-
range.   In terms of the chronological conventions used
here, this artefact-type could at its widest cover VWZ I,
II, and III, while on the other hand it is possible that
all examples could be restricted to VWZ II.   But with VWZ
III starting at ca.475 by conventional dating, Magnus's
implied terminal date of ca.450 seems too early.   The
scutiform pendant in Scandinavia is most common on either
side of the Skagerrak (Map 4.3), and this area may also be
proposed as its area of origin, sometime in VWZ I, probably
around the beginning of the 5th. century.

Obviously closely related to the scutiform pendants are a small number of disc pendants: flat pendants, without the central boss, to be worn in the same way. Two examples from Norway are from Obrestad, Hå, Ro (B4254), and Hole, Grytten, MR (Reichstein 1975 Taf.31). The former is gilt bronze, the latter silver, and the decorative scheme of both is one of concentric rings, principally composed of ornamental stamps. Both are datable to VWZ III, Obrestad by grave-association with a cruciform brooch of Reichstein's Typ Søndre Gammelsrød (Reichstein 1975 no.174), and Hole by similar asociation with a cruciform brooch of Typ Mundheim, and an early relief brooch with Style I ornament (Reichstein 1975 no.277). The famous grave group of Hol, Inderøy, NT included a fragment of either a disc or a scutiform pendant together with, inter alia, a relief brooch and a cruciform brooch of Reichstein's Typ Varhaug (Reichstein 1975 no.286, Taf.39). None of the animal ornament on the relief brooch can be identified as Style I, thereby placing that brooch in VWZ II. However the cruciform brooch is one of Reichstein's "späte" types, therefore VWZ III, and the assemblage may be designated VWZ II-III. By date and location (cf. Map 4.3) it may seem a little more likely that the Hol fragment comes from a disc rather than a scutiform pendant. The generally relatively late date of the Norwegian disc pendants suggests that they may be a derivative of the southern Norwegian scutiform pendants spreading northwards along the west coast of Norway. A period of overlap between the two forms around the beginning of VWZ III is a probability.

A single example of a Migration Period scutiform pendant from mainland Sweden has recently come to light in Önsvala, Nevishög, Sk g.18 (Larsson 1982 pp.141-43). Its appearance there is undoubtedly a sign of relationship with Denmark. This grave may be dated to the very end of the Migration Period by its late relief brooch and a pair of Husby-type brooches. The pendant appears to be plain bronze with a domed central boss.

From a nearby area on the margin of the scutiform pendants' range, Tolleby, Stenkyrka, Bo g.14, comes another disc pendant comparable to the Norwegian examples, and similar to that from Hole, Grytten, MR in particular (Fv.23 1928 fig.72). This also was found associated with cruciform brooches (Reichstein 1975 no.365, Taf.125 nos.7-8). Reichstein does not offer a dating for these, but the flattened knobs and the lappets below the bow of the example in his Taf.125.7 look to be late features, and are grounds for a date of VWZ III for this find too. Mention might also be made of the two pendants from Djurgårdsäng hoard from Västergötland (Månadsbladet 1892 pp.16-17 figs.10 and 13). The former is clearly a version of a bracteate. The second is individualistic, not obviously modelled on any bracteate, but not in any demonstrable way more closely related to the scutiform or disc pendants

either.   Vendel Period Gotland has also produced a number
of stamped disc pendants comparable to the Tolleby pendant
(Nerman 1969 figs.995-998, 2194-2195, and 2197).

The   scutiform pendant makes a quite startling re-
apperance in the Mälaren area of central Sweden in the
Viking Age.   Most examples of these have come from burials
at Birka (Arbman 1943 Taf.97).   These pendants are normally
silver, decorated with whirligigs formed of stamps or
applied granules, around a central, domed boss, and with a
strip soldered to the back with a projecting and bent-over
tongue to form the suspension loop, as on several of the
Migration Period examples.   The type in fact is distributed
rather more widely in hoards from eastern Scandinavia in
the Viking Age (cf. Johansen 1912 pp.231-232), but central
Sweden, where it occurs as a feature of womens' costume
attested in graves, appears to be its home territory.   It
would be a digression to investigate these pendants in
detail here;   probably they are a largely independent re-
invention of the type in the Viking Age.   But a single find
holds open the case for some degree of continuity between
the Migration Period and the Viking Age.   This is what
appears to be a scutiform pendant from Västbyn, Fröšn, Jä
g.4 (JLM 13804, Fig.4.5a).   This was associated with belt
hooks which clearly date the grave to the Vendel Period
(Fig.4.5b).   These finds raise questions of continuity and
significance which are best considered after the English
scutiform pendants have been introduced.

Before considering the English examples, however, two
Scandinavian finds of what may be called composite disc or
scutiform pendants may finally be noted.   These are gold
disc pendants, composite in the sense that the decoration
on their faces is applied in the form of filigree wire,
cells for garnets, etc., while the pendants previously
considered may be called "simple" in that the embossing and
stamping with which they are decorated is carried out on a
single piece of metal, and they are only composite to the
extent that the addition of a separate suspension loop,
occasional wire rims, and occasional gilding of a silver
plate may be regarded as composite.   The two Scandinavian
finds are from the hoards of Darum, do., Gjørding, Ribe,
Dk, and Sletner, Eidsten, Øf, N, the former containing one,
the latter four such pendants.   Illustrations of them are
provided by Mackeprang (1952 pl.23.21 and 28 nos.2-4).
Both hoards contained developed D-bracteates (Mackeprang
nos. 99 and 125).   A date of VWZ IV is therefore most
probable for these pendants.   Again, they may be more
usefully discussed in connection with the English material.

Enqland

In his comprehensive study of the English scutiform
and disc pendants mentioned above, Vierck did not divide or

225

order the scutiform pendants according to any formal classificational system. However the English scutiform pendants are sufficiently diverse in their dates, geographical range, and forms to render some such explicit classification of the material helpful. I would therefore distinguish between <u>simple</u> and <u>composite</u> scutiform pendants, the distinction between the two categories being that already introduced with regard to the Scandinavian scutiform and disc pendants. Similarly the differentiation of scutiform and disc pendants may be made in England exactly as in Scandinavia. Finally there is again a very small number of fragmentary finds which are uncertain disc or scutiform pendants.

I have been able to list no fewer than 90 possible examples of simple scutiform pendants from England, 24 from Kent, 1 doubtful find from the Isle of Wight, and 65 from Anglian England (List 4.2; Map 4.4). It is rather more interesting in the present context to divide and compare the Anglian and the Kentish finds than to deal with them simultaneously.

All of the Anglian English examples are basically round, except for a pair of lentoid shape from Melbourn, Cambs g.11 (Wilson 1956 pl.V). I do not have information as to what metal every example is made of, but of the 57 for which this information is available, 47 (over 80%) are of silver and the remaining 10 are of bronze. Only one of the Anglian examples is gilt, a silver pendant from Morningthorpe, Nfk g.322. The great majority of the Anglian examples have domed, not conical, central bosses, although some of these bosses are very slight. Two examples, however, from Kempston, Beds (Fig.4.6), and Sewerby, Hu g.35 (Hirst 1981 fig.40), have flattened central bosses, but with rather steep straight sides visible to suggest that they may possibly have originally had central bosses that were more conical than domed.

The decorative schemes of the Anglian English simple scutiform pendants are quite diverse, but again they can all be asigned to either or both of two basic categories, radiate or concentric. There is no very clear predominance of the one form over the other, and frequently they occur in association. Three examples carry forms of curved triskele motifs on their faces: Ruskington, Lincs g.3, Sleaford, Lincs g.95 (Fig.4.7), and Sewerby, Hu g.35. A similar curved triskele appears on the Norwegian scutiform pendant from Skreros, Vegusdal, AA (Magnus 1975 fig.21), while a similar swastika appears on the pendant from Gjone, Hedrum, Vf, and a multi-armed whirligig on that from Horr, Hå, Ro (Magnus 1975 figs.19 and 23). This does not imply a closer relationship in general of the Anglian English scutiform pendants to the Norwegian than to any ther. The use of embossed ornament is not unusual on Anglian English examples (I count some 18), and is known only on two Scandinavian examples, both Danish (from Høstentorp,

Fig.4.4, and Råberg, do., Horns, Hj). 7 of the Anglian examples are quite plain, as are 4 examples from the Høstentorp hoard, and the one example from Skåne. As far as stamped ornament goes, the range of stamps is rather restricted compared with the Scandinavian examples. Only twice are as many as three different stamps used on a single Anglian scutiform pendant (cf. Magnus 1975 fig.37), although the stamps found coincide nicely with the simpler forms found on Norwegian and Danish pendants. This difference may reflect the chronological relationship of the pendants in the two areas: most of the Scandinavian examples are datable to the 5th. century, and most of the Anglian English to the 6th.

Amongst the earliest contexts in which scutiform pendants occur in Anglian England is Holywell Row, Sfk g.11. This contained the group IV square-headed brooch Holywell Row g.11 discussed at considerable length in the previous chapter and dated there to the period 500-520. There is no reason to suppose that it should be very much older than the scutiform pendants it was found with. Other square-headed brooches associated with scutiform pendants are later: i.e. Wakerley, N'hants g.80 (a group XV brooch), and Morningthorpe, Nfk g.359 (a group XVI brooch), both of Phase 3, and unlikely to be buried much before the middle of the 6th. century. There are five finds of scutiform pendants with cruciform brooches: Mildenhall, Sfk (VCH Sfk I p.341), Morningthorpe, Nfk g.80, Sleaford, Lincs g.116, Welbeck Hill, Hu g.3, and Sewerby, Hu g.35. Of the first of these, no details are known, while the Morningthorpe example was also associated with the bronze C-bracteates described above and assigned there to the first half of the 6th. century. The brooch from Welbeck Hill, Hu g.3 has features in common with Reichstein's Typen Holywell Row and Little Wilbraham ("späte" and "späteste" respectively) and may therefore be best datable to the first quarter of the 6th. century (cf. Chapter 2, English form B 7 clasps). The brooch from Sewerby, Hu g.35 is quite similar, but does not have the lappets, and has "eyebrows" on the terminal head, a feature of the "späte" Typ Krefeld-Gellep. A contemporary dating is most probable, but Sewerby, Hu g.35 is perhaps the best contender there is for a scutiform pendant in a late 5th.-century context in Anglian England. Sleaford, Lincs g.116 contained a florid cruciform brooch and a distinctive type of form B 12 clasps which was dated in Chapter 2 to around the middle of the 6th. century.

A further substantial number of the Anglian English simple scutiform pendants are certainly from Migration Period contexts, although not very closely datable ones. Several are associated with wrist-clasps, including two with Class A clasps (Welbeck Hill, Hu g.56, Worlaby, Hu g.3A), and four with form B 7 and B 13 a clasps (Fonaby, Lincs g.1, Ruskington, Lincs g.3, Willoughby-on-the-Wolds, Notts g.58, and Worlaby, Hu g.9). These could be late

5th.-century contexts, but are much more probably 6th.-century. Other characteristically Migration Period, but not closely datable associations are small-long brooches (Sleaford, Lincs g.2), and girdle-hangers (Sleaford, Lincs g.78).

But the end of the Migration Period was not the end of the simple scutiform pendant in Anglian England. At least 8 examples are from the "late cemeteries" of the "7th. century" as identified by Hyslop (Hyslop 1963 pp.189-200) and S.C. Hawkes (Hawkes and Meaney 1970 pp.45-55), i.e. Burwell, Cambs (2 examples), Shudy Camps, Cambs (1 example), Melbourn, Cambs (3 examples), and Leighton Buzzard, Beds (2 examples). These include the pair of lentoid shape from Melbourn, Cambs g.11. The remainder are all round and silver, with domed central bosses. Again radiate and concentric decorative layouts occur, both separately and in combination, and both stamped and bossed ornament is found, although the range of stamps appear yet further restricted compared with the Migration Period examples. A ninth example which may be added to these is that from Longstone, Derbys (Fig.4.8). The wheel-like layout of the embossed ornament on this piece is comparable to the scheme of the example from Burwell, Cambs g.25 (Lethbridge 1931 fig.23.1), and Derbyshire is an area which has produced very few Migration Period finds, but many more spectacular "7th.-century" ones (Ozanne 1963), e.g. the Benty Grange barrow.

The question of the history of the simple scutiform pendant in England between the end of the Anglian English Migration Period and the period of the so-called "late cemeteries" is an intriguing one, and one which requires reference to the Kentish simple scutiform pendants to be considered properly. 15 of the 24 recorded Kentish examples are assignable to 12 grave-finds, and the remainder have no known closed context. The earliest context would appear to be that of Buckland, Dover g.35A, where the scutiform pendant was associated with a keystone garnet disc brooch of Avent's Class 3.1 (Avent 1975 no.74). Leigh reconsidered the dating of the keystone garnet disc brooches in the course of his study of the Kentish square-headed brooches, and proposed a chronological sequence Class 2 --> Class 3 --> Class 1, with Class 2 contemporary with the later Kentish square-headed brooches (Leigh 1980 pp.460-472). On these grounds, the Buckland, Dover g.35A assemblage can be dated to the later 6th. century. Buckland, Dover g.67 contained the remains of three scutiform pendants associated with a garnet pendant and a bracelet: many garnet pendants are dated to the mid 7th. century (Hawkes and Meaney 1970, as above), but this one does not have the characteristic pear- or drop-shape of these, and could be earlier. The majority of the Kentish examples from closed grave-finds are from the "late cemeteries" of Kingston Down and Sibertswold. The most spectacular of these finds is undoubtedly Kingston Down g.205, with a gold scutiform pendant associated with the famous composite brooch (Faussett 1856 pl.I), dated by Avent to the period 600-630 (Avent 1975 p.54). The association of examples with amethyst beads in Kingston Down g.59 and Sibertswold gg.18 and 86 also show us to be in the later dress phase, although there appears to be no determined absolute <u>terminus post quem</u> for the use of amethyst beads. Kingston Down g.156 and Sibertswold g.93 appear to have examples associated with remains of the chain-linked pins which may be dated to the middle or later 7th century (Hawkes and Meaney 1970, as above).

There is thus no burial evidence for the use of simple scutiform pendants in Kent before the later 6th. century, subsequent to which they appear to have continued in use down to at least the middle or later 7th. century. However the examples from Bifrons, Faversham, and Sarre are not from otherwise closely datable finds, and since these cemeteries are known to have produced earlier material, it must be considered whether these examples could be earlier, bringing the Kentish date-range into line with the Anglian. Comparing the features of the simple scutiform pendants, we find that all the Kentish examples, like all the Anglian ones, have domed central bosses, so this provides no helpful positive association between particular examples. As with the earlier Anglian simple scutiform pendants, most of the Kentish examples are silver, a few being bronze, but 8 of the 24 Kentish examples carry gilding. This may simply reflect the relative wealth of the two areas, but since 6 of these 8 gilt examples are datable to the later 6th. or 7th. centuries it could be a chronologically determinative feature. But if this were so it would imply that the two remaining gilt examples from Faversham are also of this relatively late date. None of the later Anglian examples are gilt. The design schemes of the scutiform pendants from Bifrons, Faversham, and Sarre are largely radiate, with some use of concentric ring designs, but on the whole these recall the later-dated Anglian and Kentish examples rather than the earlier. The wheel-like layout of the pendants from Burwell, Cambs and Longstone, Derbys (Fig.4.8) is seen on one of the gilt examples from Faversham (Fig.4.9) and the pendant from Sarre g.220. A cross design occurs on another example from Faversham (Fig.4.10) rather like that on the three from Spong Hill, Nfk g.11 (publication forthcoming, EAA, Spong Hill vol.3), but crosses also appear on the pieces from Buckland, Dover g.67 and Shudy Camps, Cambs g.55.

The suspension loops - where there is any evidence for them - of the Kentish simple scutiform pendants, including some examples from Faversham, are rather different from the typical early Anglian form of a strip rolled into a loop soldered across the back. More common is the tube-like loop attached to front and back, which is typical of the bracteates. This may be soldered or riveted on (Fig.4.10). Three identical pendants from Faversham (Fig.4.11) have the mark of a soldered suspension loop across the back, but so too does the example from Sarre g.220, whose design looks relatively late. Perhaps these three pendants from Faversham, with their concentric rings of rich stamped ornament, are the best candidates for Kentish scutiform pendants dated earlier in the 6th. century than Buckland, Dover g.35A, but there is no compelling reason why they should be dated early. The Kentish simple scutiform pendants from Bifrons, Faversham, and Sarre, have in general little in common in matters of special detail with the earlier Anglian scutiform pendants, and no strong case for dating them back into the first half of the 6th. century can be made.

A review of the apparent history of the simple scutiform pendants in England shows that the examples in Anglian England seem to appear first about the beginning of the 6th. century, the earliest examples perhaps showing a singificant distribution pattern in East Anglia (Holywell Row, Sfk g.11) and Humberside (Sewerby g.35, Welbeck Hill g.3). But between ca.500 and about the 560s they become widespread in Anglian England, although not, it appears, adopted to the west in the bulk of Northamptonshire and Warwickshire. So far as can be seen, the adoption of the simple scutiform pendant in Kent would appear to occur sometime in the later 6th. century, between the 560s and ca.600.

The dates of introduction are of great significance in attempting to identify the immediate sources of the simple scutiform pendants in both Anglian England and Kent. It seems possible that only in Denmark were they in use at the time when they first appear in Anglian England, although the possibly early date for Sewerby, Hu g.35, together with the fact that this triskele ornament is only paralleled on two other relatively northerly finds (from Ruskington and Sleaford, Lincs), and on Norwegian examples, leaves open the possibility of Norwegian influence on the Humberside area in the late 5th. century, a pattern which could be compared with that of the wrist-clasps (see Chapter 2). Otherwise the almost exclusive occurrence of domed central bosses, and the widespread occurrence of repoussé bossed ornament or plain simple scutiform pendants, have their parallels overwhelmingly in Denmark. The significance of the finding of an early example of these scutiform pendants with the square-headed brooch of group IV, Phase 1 which betrays direct South Scandinavian influence on East Anglia, in Holywell Row, Sfk g.11, should not be overlooked.

It is possible that only Anglian England was already using simple scutiform pendants at the period when Kent appears to adopt them. Only two South Scandinavian examples are from VWZ IV contexts, of which one was in a hoard. Certain general differences between the Kentish examples and both early and late Anglian English examples were noted above, i.e. the more common use of gilding, and

the different suspension loops, but the former can be
explained through Kent's greater wealth, and if Kent were
producing her own D-bracteates earlier in the 6th. century
(see above) this would provide a source for this form of
suspension loop.

The fate of the simple scutiform pendants in Anglian
England at the end of the Migration Period is therefore a
problem of some importance. We have numerous examples from
grave-assemblages dated up to the 560s, and then a number
from the "late cemeteries". But the received view of these
"late cemeteries" is that they are datable to the mid 7th.
century onwards, and they have further been argued to be
the cemeteries of early converted christian communities in
England (Hyslop 1963; Hawkes and Meaney 1970, as above).
It is generally appreciated that the dating of these "late
cemeteries", and thereby the characteristic dress-
accessories of the females interred there, to the mid 7th.
century at the earliest, leaves a gap in our knowledge of
Anglian womens' dress styles between the typical Migration
Period range of accessories and the finer and scarcer
adornments found in those cemeteries. Locating the end of
the Migration Period in the 560s, rather than the former,
conventional "circa 600", lengthens the obscure period.
The questions therefore arise of whether there is any
evidence for the continuity of simple scutiform pendants in
Anglian England through this gap, or whether it is
justifiable simply to infer such continuity on the basis of
the occurrence of examples both before and after.
Alternatively, could the simple scutiform pendant be re-
introduced here in the mid 7th. century, or in any other
manner receive a new lease of life at this time ?

At the theoretical level, the continuity of this
artefact-type in Anglian England seems inherently more
probable than re-introduction. The only realistic possible
sequence of events for the latter alternative would be that
the simple scutiform pendant was adopted in Kent as it died
out in Anglian England at the end of the Migration Period,
and was then re-introduced in the 7th. century. But it is
not probable that a moribund artefact-type in one area
should successfully infiltrate another. Hyslop argues that
the new dress style of the "late cemeteries" derives from
Mediterranean sources (Hyslop 1963), and comparable
scutiform pendants or bullae do occur amongst these
Mediterranean grave-assemblages (e.g. Nocera Umbra, Italy
g.107, Monumenta Antichi XXV coll.297-300, fig.158). But
the "earlier" and "later" scutiform pendants of Anglian
England are far more similar to one another than to this
Lombardic example, and a fresh introduction from this
source is not credible.

It may further be argued that the simple scutiform
pendant was especially suited to survive the changes at the
end of the Migration Period. Relative fineness,
simplicity, and elegance are the characteristics of the

dress-accessories of the later period, and the simple
silver scutiform pendants of the Migration Period, with
their stamped ornament, already fulfilled these
requirements. A second artefact-type for which a similar
case for continuity may be made is the ubiquitous annular
brooch of the Anglian English Migration Period, which re-
appears in various forms in the "late cemeteries" (cf.
Hyslop 1963 fig.12a; Leeds 1936 pl.XXVIII; and Chapter 5,
below). These brooches were always simple enough to lend
themselves to mofidication into a dress-accessory agreeable
to the new mode, in a way that types such as the florid
cruciform brooches clearly did not.

One may also query the blanket dating of the "late
cemetery" group to the mid 7th. century onwards, and
consequent creation of an effective vacuum between the end
of the Migration Period and this cultural phase. A
reasonable theoretical case can be made for the continuity
of the scutiform pendants and annular brooches through this
gap. The most detailed discussion of the absolute-dating
evidence for these cemeteries (Hawkes and Meaney 1970, as
above) indicates a general later 7th.-century date for only
some of their characteristic dress-accessories. One of
these "later" accessories is the necklace formed of silver
rings fastened with a form of slip-knot (cf. Hyslop 1963
figs.8, 9, and 17). But the occurrence of such rings in
Gilton, Kt g.27 suggests that their date-range may at least
be brought back into the early 7th. century. In this grave
they were associated with a keystone garnet disc brooch,
classified by Avent as Class 3.3, and therefore datable to
the later 6th. century, although this example was highly
worn, and presumably old, when buried (see above for
dating; Faussett 1856 pp.12-13; Avent 1975 no.97). The
grave also included a gold cross-in-ring pendant,
identified by Hawkes as a christian object, and therefore
dated to the 7th. century (Hawkes et al 1966 pp.107-108).
However some doubt must be cast on this interpretation by
the occurrence of very similar cross-in-ring pendants in
indubitably pagan 6th.-century Scandinavian contexts, i.e.
from Telemark, Norway (Mackeprang pl.28.7-8), Sjælland,
Denmark (Mackeprang pl.23.9), and Sejlflod, Dk g.FC
(Nielsen 1980 fig.19). The use of pairs of pins at the
shoulders of the dress is a feature of the later dress
style, but is also a feature of dress in Migration Period
Scandinavia, and occurs in Migration Period contexts in
England, e.g. Barrington A, Cambs g.85 (MAA Cam). In
consequence, with regard to its immediate grave-
associations alone, one may suggest that the simple
scutiform pendant from Leighton Buzzard, Beds g.57 with its
associated silver ring necklace could be dated earlier in
the 7th. century than the conventional starting-date of the
"late cemeteries". Allowing earlier starting-dates in
general for the "late cemeteries" would allow grave-groups
such as Melbourn, Cambs g.7 and pendants from Burwell,
Cambs, and Longstone, Derbys at least to reduce the gap
between the Migration Period and the later phase.

The suggestion that these "late cemeteries" are those of early christian communities has been noted. This proposition attractively deals with the phenomenon that many of these cemeteries form pairs with earlier cemeteries, which may therefore have been abandoned by communities with a new religious attitude to burial. But as both Hyslop and Hawkes concede, the character of these "late cemeteries" is not especially christian, and it is possible to explain the cemetery-shift phenomenon through the operation of other factors. The major post-Migration Period barrow burials - Asthall, Taplow, Caenby, Sutton Hoo - are a new burial phenomenon not ascribable to christianity. A more thorough characterization of the factors which may have lain behind this is attempted in Chapter 6. But the conversion of the English in the 7th. century may still be a factor in the history of the scutiform pendants. It has been suggested that the scutiform pendant becomes common again in the later phase, reflecting christian influence in the common cross designs these later examples carry. Cross designs do, of course, occur earlier (e.g. the pendants from Spong Hill, Nfk g.11, mentioned above), and like the Scandinavian cross-in-ring pendants, can hardly be christian in these cases, but it is not at all improbable that the later popularity of the design is attributable to the christian re-interpretation of this inherited feature. While arguing, then, for continuity of the simple scutiform pendant in Anglian England at some level through the later 6th. and earlier 7th. centuries, one may accept that this was followed by a period of renewed popularity in the middle and later 7th. century with christian connotations, and thus to some extent associable with influence from the south.

Like Norway and Sweden, England produces a small number of ornamented disc pendants which may be regarded as simpler derivatives of the scutiform pendants (List 4.2). Two of these are from Migration Period contexts: one associated with the C-bracteate from Longbridge, Warwicks (see above), dated to the middle or later 6th. century, and one in Sleaford, Lincs g.227 associated with clasps of form B18a, dated to the 6th. century. The remainder are all from typically "late cemetery" contexts, entirely congruent in distribution with the later scutiform pendants (Map 4.4) and generally rather crude, although the example from Wye, Kt is quite fine workmanship. The example from Burwell, Cambs in Hull Mus is rather interesting because it is of bone, with a bronze suspension loop. Alongside these should also be mentioned a series of relatively small and quite plain disc pendants, usually to be suspended through a pair of perforations by one edge, of which I have seen examples in bronze, silver, and silver-plated bronze very like the footplate lobes of square-headed brooches of groups XVI and XVII etc. I do not, regrettably, have a comprehensive list of references to these objects, but some are given at the end of List 4.2; all appear to belong to the Migration Period in the same area of England as the simple scutiform pendants.

29 examples of composite scutiform or disc pendants from England have been recorded (List 4.2). Only one of these, Willoughby-on-the-Wolds, Notts g.65, is from a presumably 6th.-century Migration Period context, being associated with annular brooches and wrist-clasps of form B 7. This piece is little different from Migration Period simple scutiform pendants, having concentric rings of stamped ornament on a round silver plate, but its central boss is a slightly convex gold stud, and so for consistency's sake it is counted here. The remaining examples show a curious polarization in their distribution (Map 4.4) to the South-East and the North-East, with 17 from Kent and 1 from Surrey, 1 each from Cambridgeshire, Buckinghamshire, Oxfordshire, and Warwickshire, and 6 from Humberside and North Yorkshire. Several of these are from the classic "late cemeteries", e.g. Kingston Down, Riseley, and Sibertswold, Kt, Acklam, Garton, and Uncleby, Hu. Of these, the example from Kingston, Kt g.96 was associated with a necklace of the amethyst beads and silver rings, while that from Sibertswold g.172 is coin-dated into the second half of the 7th. century (Hawkes and Meaney 1970 pp.47-48). A late date for some examples may also be argued on the grounds of design. The composite scutiform pendant from Coulsdon, Sy has a layout very like that of the simple scutiform pendant from Sarre, Kt g.220, which in turn was compared with the later Anglian simple scutiform pendants from Burwell, Cambs and Longstone, Derbys (above). The cross formed of applied twisted wire on the composite pendant from Milton Regis, Kt produces the same layout as that on the simple pendant from Sibertswold, Kt g.94 (Faussett 1856 pl.XI.7). That gilt bronze pair from Sibertswold is probably a copy of the gold Milton Regis model. The simple scutiform pendants from Kingston Down, Kt gg.59 and 110 have four subsidiary bosses in each quadrant around the central boss (Faussett 1856 p.53 and pl.IV.20), an arrangement that is repeated with garnet settings on certain composite scutiform pendants, e.g. Sibertswold g.172 (Faussett 1856 pl.IV.13), Compton Vernay, Warwicks, and Acklam, Hu (BM 71.12-7.1).

The use of applied twisted or filigree wire, and garnet settings in cells, sometimes with a white material, on these composite scutiform pendants, are also of potential chronological significance. Avent notes that the use of filigree with cloisonné garnet settings is a feature of his Plated Disc and Composite Brooches (Avent 1975 pp.17-20), which he dates from the very end of the 6th. through most of the first half of the 7th. centuries. The dating, then, of most of these pendants to the 7th. century is unquestionable. What remains is to seek to establish a clear starting date for the series. Other than the exceptional example from Willoughby-on-the-Wolds, Notts g.65, no example belongs by find-association to a 6th.-

century context. It may then appear justifiable to date the general appearance of this form to the end of the 6th. century. But here the parallel Scandinavian composite disc or scutiform pendants, which one would not date much later than the 560s, raise a question. Of course these need not be models for the English examples, but rather both be parallel developments in metal-working techniques that were becoming widespread in Europe (cf. Arrhenius 1971). But the use of garnet settings and filigree on one of the examples from Sletner (Mackeprang 1952 pl.28.) is remarkably similar to some English examples (e.g. Faversham, Kt, Plate 4.4). The possibility of some direct connection, and with it the dating of the beginning of the composite scutiform pendants of Kent at least back into the second half of the 6th. century, alongside the earliest Kentish simple scutiform pendants, must remain open.

Summary and Discussion

It might be helpful at this point to recapitulate the apparent developing pattern of diffusion of the scutiform pendants as far as it affects Anglian England in the pre-Viking period. The two non-Kentish A-bracteate finds are probably imports from the South Scandinavia/Schleswig-Holstein area before the end of the 5th. century. Only the Undley, Sfk example is of real interest in the present context. The C-bracteates betray a course of influence early in the 6th. century, probably more likely to have led from Norway than from Denmark. About the same time, Danish influence produces D-bracteates in Kent. The occurrence of native D-bracteates in Anglian England from about the 520s onwards is argued to be the result of Kentish influence northwards.

For the most part, Denmark seems the only plausible source for the Anglian English scutiform pendants which appear around the beginning of the 6th. century. However it may be possible to detect a trace of Norwegian influence through these items in the northern Anglian area around Humberside. Around about the end of the Migration Period, the use and production of scutiform pendants arises in Kent, and it seems most probable that the type was brought in from Anglian England. The obscuration of regional differences with the change of dress style at this time has been remarked upon, although the emphasis has been on the predominance achieved by fashions from southern Europe. (Hyslop 1963 pp.190-194). It is interesting to see an artefact-type moving south against the tide. However in view of Kent's previously strong South Scandinavian connections, the slight possibility of some South Scandinavian influence, effective in both the simple and the composite scutiform pendants of Kent, must be borne in mind.

Identifying and evaluating alternative possible modes by which the geographical range of the bracteates and scutiform pendants was expanded is a more complex problem than it was for the clasps and square-headed brooches of the last two chapters. These pendants may have had an intellectual or psychological significance quite different from that of the clasps or square-headed brooches, and the question arises of to what extent the expansion of their range implies the expansion of a particular understanding of what they meant. In his synopsis of the Anglian English bracteates and scutiform pendants, Vierck argued that they were amulets, probably with a supposedly magical power or religious character, and that their occurrence in England was evidence for the export of ideas or beliefs from Scandinavian to England:

> Anglian culture in one of its mental aspects - and with it a mode of thought of the Anglian people - derives from West Scandinavian sources.

(Vierck 1966 pp.56-61)

A very great deal has been written about the religious significance of bracteates, of which references may be made to four works: Salin 1895, Gjessing 1929, Mackeprang 1952 (pp.88-95), and Hauck 1970 plus a whole series of supplementary articles Zur Ikonologie der Goldbrakteaten (cf. FS 14 p.463 fn.1). Much of this work is highly speculative, because while enough circumstantial evidence can be found to suggest that the bracteates do have some religious or quasi-religious significance, there is little or nothing to specify clearly what that significance was. The evidence can be divided into two principal categories, runic texts and symbols. Thirty-six runic texts on bracteates were listed by Krause (Krause 1966 nos.103-138): an up-to-date tally would of course be higher, with two to add from Anglian England alone. Certain words, or sequences which may be argued to be cryptic distortions, abbreviations, or even clumsy misformations of these words, occur regularly: i.e. alu, laþu, laukar. Plausible interpretations of these words are "good fortune", "invitation", and "onion", respectively. The occurrence of the former two on an amulet intended to attract benefits to the wearer is credible. The latter might appear curious and unconvincing as part of a charm, and one wonders whether a better interpretation might be sought. However the word laukr occurs widely in later ON verse, not in its specific sense, but in a more generalized sense as "plant". It can be a glorious and dignifying plant, giving prestige and strength to its recipient, e.g. the ítrlaukr (Helgakviða Hundingsbana I v.7). An association of alu with laukr also emerges in Sigrdrífumál vv.7-8, where Sigrdrífa promises Odin first the "ǫlrúnar" (=ale- and alu-runes), and then says that laukr is to be used to neutralise a poisoned drink.

Two "symbols" which Gjessing drew attention to were the swastika and the triskele, although he was unable to provide any substantial explanation of them as symbols (Gjessing 1929 pp.167-169). These motifs are widely regarded as religious symbols in this period, although direct contemporary evidence for their meaning appears to be completely lacking. Salin regards the swastika as "prophylactic" (Salin 1895 p.92). Perhaps he had in mind its association as a disc symbol with the sun (Gelling and Davidson 1969 pp.140-145). Such an interpretation might equally be applied to the triskele. In the Viking Age the swastika is regularly regarded as a symbol of the god Thor, although again one could wish for some specific contemporary evidence that this was so (Davidson 1967 pp.137-138). One may indeed wonder whether these elements on the bracteates are indeed symbols, or simply decorative motifs. A point in support of the symbol interpretation is that they seem never to occur amongst the elements on the more certainly decorative bracteate borders. This cannot be explained away in that the borders are usually stamped and the bracteate centres embossed, as Magnus illustrates a triskele stamp from a Norwegian scutiform pendant (Magnus 1975 fig.37).

The interpretation of bracteate symbolism has been taken very much further by Hauck (Hauck 1970 et seq., see above), producing interpretations of many bracteate designs in terms of an old Germanic pagan religion, largely inferred from Norse records, but also drawing on parallels with classical and christian religious art. At best, Hauck's great study is highly subjective in his associations of material, e.g. certain B-bracteates with a church roof in Rome (p.150ff.), his characterisations of characters of Norse mythology, e.g. Ýmir as hermaphrodite (loc.cit.) and Odin as wind god (p.149), and in his ultimate interpretations, e.g. that a horse with a dripping foot symbolizes Baldr's fall (p.193). Some of his associations of the bracteates with classical motifs are stimulating, e.g. the "breath-wind motif" of Ancient Rome and the bracteates (pp.148-149). But his conclusions have won little credence, and do not add much that is certain to our knowledge of the religious significance of the bracteates.

Given the state of our evidence it is easy to be sceptical about bracteate interpretation. The texts they carry may mean nothing more profound than "Good Luck !". One may deny that their symbolism is symbolic at all, and even if it is we do not know what it means. But it would be wrong to slight the bracteates and to regard them as no more than trinkets. The fact that they were overwhelmingly of gold, especially in Migration Period Scandinavia, while gold is otherwise usually only met in the form of the gilding of silver or bronze dress-accessories, must imply that they had some special importance. It further appears, as we shall see, that the necklace as a whole was a focus for objects of an amuletic character worn about the body, and this context confirms that the bracteates had some such significance.

Less has been written about the meaning of scutiform pendants than that of bracteates, and what has appeared has been more restrained (cf. Vierck 1966 pp.56-61). There is no doubt that initially they were model shields, a point confirmed by the model shield-grips on the back of two Norwegian examples (Magnus 1975 figs.17-18). The shield has a protective function in battle; it is widely used as an image of protection in literature (e.g. Psalm 3), and model shield pendants, presumably used as protective charms, appear repeatedly in various cultures (cf. Meaney 1981 pp.149-162): the Ashmolean Museum exhibits an example in gold from Iran of the 9th. century B.C., and Etruscan examples of the 8th. century B.C. were exhibited by the National Museum, Copenhagen at Brede in 1982. These indicate that there need be no connection between the Migration Period Anglo-Scandinavian scutiform pendants and those of Viking Period Sweden.

The radiate and concentric schemes of decoration of the scutiform pendants seem only to be appropriate layouts of decoration for discs with a prominent central boss, and to interpret most of these as symbols would be implausible. The few examples carrying triskeles, swastikas, and other whirligigs should, though, have the same potential associations as these "symbols" on the bracteates, whatever those might be. No more than the metal fittings of contemporary shields survive, and there are few illustrations or descriptions of them in whole from which one could judge the extent to which the designs of the scutiform pendants reflect those on shields of the same community. However the early 5th.-century Gallehus gold horns show figures bearing shields with radiate decoration (Vierck 1978 Abb.18.1-2), and a Gotlandic picture stone from Lärbro, Tängelgarda (Davidson 1967 pl.52) shows a rider, apparently in some ritual procession, carrying a shield decorated with a whirligig, such as is also the most common scheme of the Viking Age East Scandinavian scutiform pendants.

Concerning those Viking Age scutiform pendants, there is at least broadly contemporary Scandinavian literature which can be examined for possible interpretations of the shield. It does not appear to be regularly associated with any particular divinity. However there is an important shield of later Norse mythology, Svalinn, which stands between the sun and the earth protecting the latter from the full heat of the sun (Grimnismál v.38). The whirligig design on the later shields may reflect this association, although it would not be a necessary consequence of this that the later scutiform pendants should be regarded as sun symbols. Even if this were the case, we could not force this interpretation back from the 9th. and 10th. centuries into the 5th. In general we can go no further with the scutiform pendants than to identify them as some form of protective charm, and even this amuletic character may diminish with the less shield-like disc and composite pendants of the later 6th. and 7th. centuries, although it may in England be supplanted by a christian re-interpretation. But again, lest too limited a view should be taken of the contemporary significance of the scutiform pendants, it should be remembered that the more precious materials available were regularly used for their manufacture, although less wealth was expended on them than on the bracteates.

Supplementary to the evidence for some amuletic significance to the bracteates and scutiform pendants is that which may be suggested for the necklace as a whole, in both Scandinavia and Anglian England. In both of these areas in the Migration Period it appears that the necklace was normally worn in the form of festoons between shoulder brooches or pins, not fastened behind and hanging off the neck (Vierck 1978 pp.245ff.). In Migration Period Anglian England the necklace is normally composed of beads of amber, variously coloured glass or vitreous pastes, and less commonly crystal. Where the latter does occur, it is often in the form of impressively large faceted beads. The number of beads seems to be a direct reflection of the wealth of the grave, and between one and two hundred beads are not uncommonly recovered from single burials. Interestingly, Scandinavian womens' necklaces are regularly composed of similar amber, glass, and paste beads, but virtually never crystal ones, and normally contain many fewer beads than the Anglian English examples, even in the richest graves (cf. Slomann, in Kivikoski fs. 1973 p.214). Studies by Black (P.S.A.S. XXVII 1892-93 pp.433-526) and Meaney (1981 pp.67-104) show how widely amber and crystal have been used as charms, largely for their supposed medicinal qualities, in past societies. Crystal balls were worn suspended from the waist at this time by Frankish and Kentish women, an object with no conceiveable utilitarian function which must surely be amuletic (Brown IV pp.402ff.). Rare golden neck-rings found in South Scandinavian hoards and illustrated on bracteates are commonly regarded as being of religious significance (Davidson 1967 pp.60-64, 76-82). A famous necklace in old Germanic literature is the Brísinga men (ON) or Brosinga mene (OE), which according to the ON poem Þrymskviða is owned by Freyja (Þrymskviða vv.12, 15 and 19). That a necklace should be owned by a goddess does not of course confer religious significance on all necklaces. But it has been suggested that this necklace represents the Earth's fertility, contested for by Good and Evil when the gods Heimdallr and Loki fight for it in Húsdrápa v.2, the necklace being especially associated with fertility amongst Mesopotamian fertility goddesses (personal communication, U. Dronke; cf. Schier, in Höfler fs. pp.577-588;

Encyclopaedia Britannica vol.2 1972, Babylonian and Assyrian Religion). There appears, then, to be an ancient and pervasive tradition of religious or amuletic significance attached to the non-utilitarian decoration worn around or at the neck. That the bracteates and scutiform pendants should share in this significance is entirely credible.

While it is therefore still uncertain what the original significance of the bracteates and scutiform pendants was to their makers and wearers, enough evidence can be assembled to show that it must have been far from negligible. What is now of particular interest to us is whether there is evidence that the understanding of these objects was the same in Anglian England as in Scandinavia. In the case of the bracteates, we find that the examples produced in Anglian England preserve the designs of the Scandinavian models to some extent, and in one case appear to attempt to reproduce a runic inscription. The individual and mysterious symbols, however, such as swastikas and triskeles, virtually disappear. But of most importance may be the fact that the effort to use the most precious material available in bracteate production appears to continue, with 5 C-bracteates made of gold, the D- and ?C?D-bracteates all of silver, and only one pair of C-bracteates in copper alloy. Similarly the scutiform pendants remain predominantly of silver. There is no reason why a recognizable model shield pendant should not retain its original presumably protective function wherever it occurs down into the 7th. century, although it was suggested above that the later scutiform pendants may carry some christian significance.

We may suppose, then, that the attitude towards bracteates and scutiform pendants in Anglian England was at least very similar to that in Scandinavia. How could this have come about ? If the significance of these objects was sophisticated and profound, then their diffusion may be an indication of the spreading of a system of belief from Scandinavia to England, evidence of an intimate intellectual relationship between the donors and the recipients in this act of cultural influence, which it would scarcely be acceptable to attribute to the mechanisms of commercial activity alone. It is conceiveable that these pendants had such a significance in Scandinavia, yet could be adopted as mere charms in Anglian England, but the similarity in attitude between Anglian England and Scandinavia evidenced by the materials used must to some extent contradict this. In fact, even admitting the argument for a peculiarly profound significance because of the use of gold and silver, the adoption of these objects in England can be fitted and added with reasonable comfort to the established archaeological and historical framework of the 5th. and 6th. centuries.

It was suggested tha the Undley A-bracteate was made in the southern Denmark/Schleswig-Holstein area in the period 450-480, and subsequently exported to East Anglia. Even if it were in fact made in England, its immediate background is certainly in that area and in that period. This coincides very closely with the homeland of the Angles who Bede identifies as the principal group involved in the settlement of Anglian England (cf. Chapter 1). Its date is undoubtedly two or three generations later than the first settlers to reach Anglian England, but it may nevertheless be regarded as a consequence of the Anglian settlement of England as understood by Bede.

The C-bracteates probably appear in Anglian England before the D-bracteates there, but they follow the A-bracteate(s) chronologically, and have a rather more southerly Anglian distribution, around Undley in Suffolk, than the D-bracteates (cf. Map 4.1). The bracteate wearing habit, whatever beliefs it may imply, could then have been principally established in Anglian England, initially in East Anglia, by the personal relationships between Anglian England and the southern Denmark/Schleswig-Holstein area implicit in Bede's Anglian invasion of the 5th. century. But in Chapter 2 it was argued that the occurrence of wrist-clasps in Anglian England is best explained through an influx of settlers from western Norway to Humberside and/or Norfolk around the beginning of the last quarter of the 5th. century. Congruent with this hypothesis is the slight but specific evidence for Norwegian influence in the C-bracteates and certain scutiform pendants. Thus we have evidence for migrants from two separate sources to Anglian England in the 5th. century, both liable to carry in their wake both the bracteate wearing habit, and the specific models that can be identified for the Anglian English A- and C-bracteate finds. Thus the ground was prepared for the subsequent adoption of D-bracteate models, probably from Kent, but possibly direct from South Scandinavia.

But the putative late 5th.-century migration from western Norway to Anglian England is not sufficient to explain the whole corpus of scutiform pendants from Anglian England. With regard to both form and chronology, one is drawn to consider a Danish source for the majority of these pendants as most likely, although an initial Norwegian connection could have first established a habit of wearing these things, and one recalls how rapidly the wrist-clasp wearing habit appears to have spread through Anglian England from such origins in Humberside and/or Norfolk. It would be possible, then, that the Anglian English scutiform pendants simply developed along parallel lines to the Danish in the second half of the Migration Period, and to this extent the similarities between the two areas are coincidental. However we already have evidence for direct South Scandinavian influence on East Anglian costume metalwork from very early in the 6th. century with the square-headed brooches (see Chapter 3), a pattern that exactly parallels that implied by the form and dating of the scutiform pendants. The association of the two artefact-types is emphatically illustrated by their conjunction in Holywell Row, Sfk g.11, containing the important group IV, Phase 1 square-headed brooch Holywell Row 11.

In Chapter 3, a "minimal" explanation of South Scandinavian influence on English square-headed brooches, that it was attributable to the activities of travelling craftsmen such as Bakka's "Jutish Master", was provisionally proposed. Here we must consider whether that proposition is adequate or appropriate in explaining the scutiform pendant parallels. It is not possible to claim as high a level of intellectual significance for the scutiform pendants as may be claimed for the bracteates: their inherent symbolism is less sophisticated, consisting mostly of a common "shield = protection" image, and only in rare cases do they show a possible symbolic use of triskeles, swastikas, and whirligigs. Their inherent value relative to the bracteates in the Migration Period is epitomised by the fact that most scutiform pendants are silver, most bracteates gold. If the model shield was a simple, readily explained and recognizable charm, and their use implies no more specific a system of belief than a faith in charms, and a possibly common and abiding Germanic use of the necklace as a focus for the amulets, then one can conceive of their being successfully marketed, perhaps even introduced, by the same sort of travelling craftsmen - with stocks of silver - who may have been responsible for the early forms of Anglian English square-headed brooches. It should be noted here that (unlike the bracteates) this artefact-type seems to have had its origin around the Skagerrak, and was never adopted by the continental Angles in southern Denmark/Schleswig-Holstein, although one pair of Scandinavian-type scutiform pendants found their way to Liebenau, Niedersachsen (Vierck 1978 Abb.18.12).

In assessing the nature of the relationship between Scandinavia and Anglian England as evidenced by the bracteates, one must also consider the evidence of the dispersal of the bracteates around continental Europe. A case can be made for independent bracteate production in northern Germany as well as England and Scandinavia. Nearly 60 bracteates are known from northern Germany outside of Schleswig-Holstein (Mackeprang 1952; Axboe 1982), and in the matter of numbers, Frisia, with 9 examples, and Hungary, with 8, attract attention too. To insist upon a special relationship between England and Scandinavia underlying the occurrence of so many bracteates in England virtually implies the same relationship between Scandinavia and these areas. The diffusion of an understanding of the bracteates from Scandinavia and Schleswig-Holstein through northern Germany to Frisia is not at all implausible, although the point must be stressed that Anglian England does not, on the whole, appear simply

to lie on the end of this chain of influence. It falls
beyond the scope of this study to consider in detail what
form of relationship between Scandinavia and Hungary the
Hungarian bracteate finds imply, but Hungary, and more
specifically the Lombards, clearly did have some peculiarly
intimate links with the Baltic region in the later
Migration Period (cf. Chapter 6).

We may finally consider how much of their previous
significance the bracteates and scutiform pendants may have
retained after the change in dress style at the end of the
Migration Period. The later Style II bracteates of Kent
were still produced in gold, but gold in this area
generally becomes more plentiful towards the end of the
6th. century. The model shield pendants, as stated above,
should still be equally liable to interpretation as
protective amulets, but the later composite disc and
scutiform pendants are far less obviously shield-like, and,
it has been argued, may eventually be inherited and re-
interpreted by christian communities. The continuing sense
of some religious significance attaching to the necklace
may be reflected in the eventual appearance of christian
pectoral crosses worn by women (Åberg 1926 pp.136-137).
But besides these possible changes of religious character,
the more expensive use of gold, filigree, and garnets on
the later disc and scutiform pendants, the courtly
character of Style II (Speake 1980 pp.38-40), and the more
exclusive appearance of the finer dress-accessories amongst
the later graves generally, allow one to speculate that
their function as markers of social status may have
increased too. This, together with the shift in the
geographical distribution of the richer graves producing
these later examples, is considered more fully in
Chapter 6.

CHAPTER 5

CRUCIFORM, ANGLIAN EQUAL-ARMED, AND ANNULAR BROOCHES

In this chapter, three separate brooch-types are considered which individually make useful but relatively minor contributions to the theme of the present work. Each of them contributes some new aspect to the growing picture of the Scandinavian character of early Anglian England, even if to an extent our attention ultimately becomes focussed on certain baffling and apparently as yet insoluble problems. Irrespective of the results obtained, two of these brooch-types, the cruciform and the annular brooches, demand attention because of their prominent position amongst the dress-accessories of Anglian English women; the third type, the Anglian equal-armed brooches, conversely merits attention, particularly in the current context, because their scarcity has produced neglect. This chapter should not be regarded as wholly miscellaneous in character: were any of these brooch-types studied in isolation, those apparent Anglo-Scandinavian connections observable through them might be dismissed as illusory, but their detailed investigation in the context of an Anglo-Scandinavian axis is justified by the reasonably dependable foundations for such studies established in Chapters 2 to 4. They add cumulative evidence to our picture of the Scandinavian character of Anglian England in the pre-Viking period, and the fact that they contribute specific problems, through a partial absence of ready and simple explanations of the diffusion of the particular types, need not in any way be detrimental to the case for the connection.

I - Cruciform Brooches

In 1906, in <u>The Cruciform Brooches of Norway</u>, Shetelig drew attention to certain elements on cruciform brooches apparently restricted to western Norway and England, and presented a case for these being the result of influence from the former area on the latter. This was perhaps the earliest detailed archaeological work to present a case for such a connection in the Migration Period, and certainly the earliest which still commands careful attention to-day. In 1953 the argument was briefly but effectively supplemented by Åberg in his description of the <u>Nordsjö-block</u> in <u>Den historisk relationen mellan folkvandringstid och vendeltid</u>, drawing attention to further parallels on cruciform brooches from Norway and Anglian England (Åberg 1953 p.30). More recently, the issue was briefly considered by Reichstein in <u>Die kreuzförmige Fibel</u>, the

most comprehensive study of this brooch-type to date,
although Reichstein concentrated on establishing Typen and
a chronology of the brooches, considering these to be
essential preliminaries to any consideration of inter-
regional relationships (cf. Reichstein 1975 p.107). In the
light of this substantial available literature, an
assessment of the cruciform brooches is necessary in a
consideration of the Scandinavian character of Anglian
England in the Migration Period, and best takes the form of
a constructive critical examination of Shetelig's, Åberg's,
and Reichstein's studies, with the aid of changing methods,
and further material not known to them.

Re-assessment of these works can be divided quite
neatly into two, since Shetelig and Åberg examined the
Anglo-Norwegian parallels at the level of elements or parts
of the cruciform brooches, while Reichstein's evidence for
Anglo-Scandinavian connections consisted mostly of
particular Types, i.e. similar whole compositions of these
individual parts. A review of the material thus moves
satisfactorily from the former works, the earlier, to the
latter.

Firstly, however, the cruciform brooches which are the
main subject of this section should be set in context. In
Chapter 1 it was suggested that the early cruciform
brooches of Anglian England show a special relationship
between that area and northern Germany, and Schleswig-
Holstein, which one would traditionally suppose to be the
continental homeland of the Angles, in particular.
However, this early period was one in which regional
variation amongst cruciform brooches, especially between
northern Germany and Denmark, was minimal (cf. Reichstein
1975 Karten 2-3), and one of the earlier Anglian English
finds, from Glentham, Lincs is remarkably similar to the
brooch from Mejlby in northern Jutland (Figs.1.4-5). It
was also indicated that the cruciform brooches of Kent,
which do not include such early examples as those of
Anglian England, comprise certain details which suggest a
connection with Jutland quite congruent with the accepted
Jutish character of early Kent (cf. Hawkes and Pollard 1981
pp.322-325). The parallels between Anglian England and
northern Germany extend from "ältere" brooches to "späte"
brooches, covering, perhaps, the whole 5th. century, while
those between Kent and Jutland may reflect a more limited
date-range from about the middle of the 5th. century into
the early 6th.

Shetelig believed that the earlier cruciform brooches
of England - meaning both Anglian England and Kent - showed
special features in common with Denmark, while western
Norwegian influence was a later phenomenon (Shetelig 1906
esp. pp.97-105). The most significant general criticism
that can now be made of Shetelig's study is that a greater
body of available data shows certain elements that he
considered to be decisive regional characteristics to be

less restricted in occurrence than appeared to him. With regard to the headplates of brooches, for instance, Shetelig indicated that the bending back of the headplate wings to accommodate the spring of the pin was an "Anglo-Danish" features, although occurring on one extraordinary Norwegian find, from Måge, Ullensvang, Ho (Shetelig 1906 pp.29, 101, 113-114). But in keeping with the North German parallels to the early Danish and Anglian English cruciform brooches, at least one example of this feature can also be cited from the cemetery at Borgstedt, Kr. Eckernförde, Schleswig-Holstein (Fig.5.1).

Another headplate feature which Shetelig considered to be relatively late, restricted to Norway, Sweden, and England, and to be evidence of Norwegian influence on England, is the casting of the side knobs in one with the headplate wings, rather than fixing separate side knobs to the ends of the pin axis (1906 pp.28-29). But a number of examples are now known from Jutland, e.g. from the Sejlflod cemetery to the north (gg.DD and HT, ÅHM 669/3311), and from the cemetery at Hjemsted, Skærbæk, Hvidinge, Tø to the south (g.125, HM 1004x195-196). The trefoil-headed small-long brooches of southern Norway, Jutland, and England are a distinctive type representing this particular development (cf. Chapter 1, Introduction). But excluding the Fibeln mit dreiläppige Kopfplatte, the small-long brooches with Cross Potent or Cross Pattee headplates, I know of no example of this feature in northern Germany, to the south of Hjemsted.

It was on the feet of the cruciform brooches that Shetelig and Åberg found the most substantial evidence for their proposed connection between western Norway and England, and it is these parts of the brooches that provide the most interesting parallels today, although the old presentations of the material require considerable modification. Shetelig drew attention to a series of brooches with a "square plate separating the animal-head from the end of the bow", and associated with this the provision of decorative wings, or "lappets", along the two outer edges of that plate (Shetelig 1906 pp.71-83, 104-105). The former, he claimed, was rare outside of western Norway and England, occurring only in "late" examples from Denmark, and he believed that both this and the lappets could only be considered to have developed in western Norway and subsequently to have spread thence to England as a result of direct influence.

Ancestral to the plate plus lappets below the bow was probably what Shetelig described as a "broad plate, projecting on both sides of the end of the bow", which Shetelig indicates has its origins in Schleswig and Jutland, and was subsequently "imitated" in western Norway (1906 pp.67-71). The plate plus lappets proper, however, he believed to be a specifically western Norwegian development, and consequently that this was the only source

from which England could reasonably be supposed to have
derived the feature. But this does not now agree with the
known data. The number of examples of this feature known
from Denmark, from northern Jutland in particular, has
increased considerably, due substantially to the
excavations at Lindholm Høje (Ramskou 1976 p.73) and
Sejlflod. The range of forms of the lappets known from
Jutland is very similar to that from Norway. A
straightforward and practical division of this range is
into plain, simple forms (cf. Reichstein 1975 Taff.4, 46.2
and 5, and 72.10), and downward-biting animal heads (cf.
Reichstein 1975 Taf.49.1; Shetelig 1906 fig.92). An
example of the latter from northern Jutland is from
Sejlflod (ÅHM 669/4434). Lappets are also found on a
cruciform brooch from Sahlenburg, Kr. Land Hadeln,
Niedersachsen g.25 (Böhme 1974 Taf.37.7). The up-to-date
chronology provided by Reichstein significantly affects
Shetelig's outline of the development of this feature. He
argued that its origins were in western Norway because it
occurred there on relatively small and simple brooches,
with narrow headplates, which he considered typologically
early (e.g. Shetelig 1906 fig.90). Reichstein, however,
considers the flat plate below the bow, and the lappets, to
be typologically definitely "späte" features (Reichstein
1975 p.70 Tab.4). Shetelig, as one might expect, relied
more primarily on typology than we would to-day, and the
small, simple forms he considered "early" could continue
into "late" production. None of the Norwegian brooches
with lappets need be dated earlier than VWZ III, or ca.475
by conventional dating. This means that there is little or
no chronological difference between the Norwegian examples
with this feature and the Danish, or indeed the English
(cf. Reichstein 1975 p.91 Tab.7). Even by Shetelig's
criteria of relative simplicity, an example from North
Jutland, from Ørnefenner, Thise, Børglum, Hj (Fig.5.2)
aligns itself very closely to the model in Shetelig's
fig.90.

As the range of forms of the lappets of the Danish
cruciform brooches is largely congruent with that of the
Norwegian, it follows that the similiarity between the
Danish and the English cruciform brooches in this respect
is broadly equivalent. In one case it may even be better.
A cruciform brooch from Balle Mark, Balle, Hinds, Vi
(Fig.5.3) has lappets modelling a downward-facing animal
head in the form of a half-ring, the upper part of which
contains the neck and eye, and the lower part of the jaws.
A number of Anglian English cruciform brooches show quite
similar lappets, e.g. an example from Oadby, Leics (Plate
5.1). Of course there is no necessary direct connection
between the two: they could be coincidental re-modellings
of the more common form of the downward-biting heads here,
but they underline the point that the plate plus lappets
feature was more widespread than Shetelig was aware. It
should be borne in mind that lappets below the bow may also
be found on small-long brooches, and are quite common on

these in Anglian England (Leeds 1945 pp.4-36). I know of examples of them on small-long brooches outside of Anglian England only on two brooches from northern Jutland and one from Frisia: the former are from Lindholm Høje g.1566 (Ramskou 1976 fig.257) and from Romdrup Mose, Romdrup, Fleskum, Ål (Reichstein 1975 Taf.125.15), the latter from Almenum, Frisia (Boeles 1951 pl.XXXV.6). Obviously one could not regard these as a better source for the English cruciform brooches' features than other cruciform brooches, but again they emphasize the broader distribution of this feature.

Amongst the features which Shetelig felt to be especially "Anglo-Danish" characteristics were particular forms of the nostrils of the horse's head terminal of these brooches, semi-circular and scroll-shaped nostrils, such as:

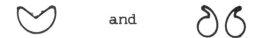

Again he gives a misleadingly restricted impression of the occurrence of these forms. The former of these is not at all unusual in Schleswig-Holstein (cf. Fig.5.1), and is known from Norway, sometimes in forms very similar to those met in Denmark and Anglian England (e.g. Reichstein 1975 Taff.13.4, 14.6, and 141.4), and sometimes in slightly divergent forms (e.g. Reichstein 1975 Taf.54.2-4). The scroll-shaped nostrils are not, as Shetelig claimed, with the exception of the Måge brooch "quite unknown in Norway or Sweden" (1906 p.103). Two examples may be cited from Vere, Vanse, VA (C22297; C22620 Reichstein 1975 Taf.19.2). A rather similar form of the nostrils is produced by circular or lentoid elements on a raised chevron-shaped background, of which examples occur from Rossøy, Steigen, No, N (Reichstein 1975 Taf.18.7) and Stentorp, Vg, S (Reichstein 1975 Taf.68.3). A further comparable form may be seen on a brooch from Veien, Norderhov, Bu, N (Reichstein 1975 Taf.139.1). In fact, I know of no more than half-a-dozen examples of this feature from Denmark, and none of these is as clearly and definitely formed as the nostrils on the Vere brooches.

The more florid horse's head terminals, and the treatment of the nostrils in particular, were the features that Åberg cited as evidence of Anglo-Norwegian contacts in the later Migration Period (Åberg 1953 p.30). Of the forms that he illustrates, the best parallels are provided by the trefoil-formed Norwegian examples of his fig.12 nos.1 and 2, as on three examples from Rogaland (Reichstein 1975 Taff.25.2, 45.1, and 46.2) and a brooch from Olde, Voss, Ho (Fig.5.4), with which may be compared a pair of brooches from Barrington B, Cambs (Reichstein 1975 Taf.91.5-6) and brooches of Reichstein's Typ Little Wilbraham (e.g.

Reichstein 1975 Taf.107.6). However the commonest form of the more florid terminal in Anglian England has an expanding spatulate element emerging from between the nostrils, which are usually scroll-shaped. Norway does provide parallels to this (e.g. Reichstein's Taff.113.7 and 8, 138.4, and 142.2), although none of these is any closer than the trefoil-like forms just noted. Slightly closer parallels to the expanding spatulate element may be provided by two Jutish brooches, from Lindholm Høje g.1558 (Ramskou 1976) and Strandelhjørn, Bevtoft, N.Rangstrup, Had (Reichstein 1975 Taf.125.12). A more restrained development of the nose parts is to prolong the nose-line of the head between the nostrils to provide a projecting knob at the bottom. This occurs on examples from Norway (e.g. Reichstein 1975 Taff.15.4-5, 17.6-7, and 23.1), Sweden (Reichstein 1975 Taff.68.3 and 73.6), Denmark (Reichstein 1975 Taf.81.6), Anglian England (Reichstein 1975 Taf.89.8), Kent (Reichstein 1975 Taf.117.2), and Frisia (Reichstein 1975 Taf.117.3), but appears to be a development that did not occur, perhaps a stage that was not reached, in northern Germany. Åberg also mentions the development of extra animal heads out of parts of the original single head terminal as a peculiarly Anglo-Norwegian feature. In the most general terms this is true, but in detail the forms developed in Anglian England and Norway are quite different. The Norwegian brooches commonly show three, highly moulded, identical masks facing at right-angles to one another (cf. Shetelig 1906 figs.92, 95, and 115), while the English brooches with any such features are usually flatter, with an upward-facing mask at either side of the nose, and an entirely different element in between (cf. Åberg 1926 fig.70.64).

The general tendency of this review of Åberg's and Shetelig's studies of the cruciform brooches has been to cast doubt on the validity of some of the parallels they drew between brooches in different areas, and more commonly to show that those parallels that do exist are found over much broader areas than they supposed. But the result of this is to recast their model of cruciform brooch history, not to destroy it. Specific forms of particular parts of cruciform brooches, i.e. cast-in-one headplate side knobs, the plate plus lappets below the bow, scroll-shaped nostrils and trefoil-formed noses at the terminal, still define a consistent Anglo-Scandinavian area covering Jutland, South Sweden, Norway, Anglian England, and to a certain extent Kent and Frisia (Map 5.1a-c). This would appear to indicate a geographical shift in the areas associated in the development of the cruciform brooches in the 5th. century. In an earlier period uniformity is apparent in the whole area covered by cruciform brooches (Reichstein 1975 p.111), but the earliest examples from northern Germany, Denmark, and Anglian England appear to be especially associated (Reichstein 1975 Karten 2-3). From some point in the second half of the 5th. century, a more northerly area of common development emerges, with northern

Germany dropping out, perhaps even ceasing to produce cruciform brooches. This commonality becomes generally apparent in VWZ III. All of the parallels shown on Map 5.1 can, of course, be simply derived from the common models available on cruciform brooches across the whole of their area of use in the earlier period. But that all of these, wherever they occur, have evolved there independently from such ancestral forms, that they imply no form of contact or interchange of designs within their area of distribution, is scarcely conceivable, especially in view of the various forms of infra-Scandinavian and Anglo-Scandinavian contact for which evidence has already been considered in this thesis. The cruciform brooches of the later 5th. century and beyond may be subsumed in that emergent pattern of Anglo-Scandinavian parallels from about the last quarter of the 5th. century onwards, and it is neither necessary nor appropriate to propose any new courses of contact to explain the parallels they show so far considered.

The distribution of Reichstein's individual Typen may be considered against this background. Reichstein in fact proposes relatively few Typen whose distribution appears to especially link Anglian England with Scandinavia. One which does this persuasively, however, is Typ Trumpington (Reichstein 1975 p.46, Taf.116.6-9). Reichstein has only four examples of this type, a pair from Skogen, Hedrum, Vf, N, one from Trumpington, Cambs, and a fragment from Hoogebeintum, Frisia. The latter in fact appears in such poor condition in Reichstein's illustration that it is not possible to judge its similarity to the other examples properly. But the similarities between the Trumpington and Skogen brooches are clear. There is a distinctive bow, with a deep median groove bordered by two slighter grooves. Below the bow is a plain plate, followed by a faceted section and transverse moulding. Most distinctive of all is the nose of the horse's head terminal: a sharp medial ridge with an incised chevron decoration above rounded nostrils with an incised diagonal cross, and a hook below which on the Trumpington brooch holds a semi-circular plate (cf. Shetelig 1906 fig.31 for a clearer illustration of this feature on the Skogen brooches). Two brooches from Northamptonshire have comparable terminals, from Islip (Fig.5.5) and Wakerley g.25 (Fig.5.6), although both of these are slightly divergent from the Trumpington/Skogen form. There are, however, discrepancies between the Trumpington and Skogen brooches, in the forms of the headplates and knobs, and the brow and eyes of the horse's head terminals. The broad spreading headplate of the Trumpington brooch is typically English (although one equivalent Danish example is from Regnemark, Kimmerslev, Ramsø, Kbh; NMK C12647), while that on the Skogen brooches is a type found over the whole cruciform brooch area (cf. Shetelig 1906 p.25). Neither of the terminal heads could be regarded as showing significant regional chracteristics. Both finds therefore are of brooches which one would readily accept as of relatively local manufacture, were it not for the occurrence of two so similar examples so far apart. It would be possible for either example to be imported from the area of the other, or to be copied from a model from that area or from a model circulating generally in the Anglo-Scandinavian area.

Reichstein's "späte" Typ Krefeld-Gellep (Reichstein 1975 p.42), distinctive with its bulging bow, and prominent brows and eyes of the terminal head, is distributed in Jutland, Schleswig-Holstein, northern Germany, Frisia, and England. This indicates that the more southerly area of common development of cruciform brooches was not entirely superseded by the northerly, exclusively Anglo-Scandinavian and Frisian zone, as we move into the last quarter of the 5th. century.

Reichstein also drew attention to the distribution of Typen Bradwell, Barrington, and Feering (1975 p.105), which interestingly appear to show types whose distribution is limited to England (Anglian England, Hampshire, and Essex) and southern Sweden (Reichstein 1975 pp.43-44). Reichstein's Typ Foldvik-Empingham, with examples from Norway, southern Sweden, and Anglian England (Reichstein 1975 p.37) may be considered along with these. Reichstein accepted the former three of these as evidence of inter-regional association, and the distribution of Typ Foldvik-Empingham should be regarded as equivalent evidence. But there must be serious doubts as to whether their evidence has the same significance as that of the distinctive Typ Trumpington. They are all relatively simple forms, as a result of which the discrepancies between the individual examples are all the more obvious, and the parallels between brooches must be particularly close to be evidence of close direct relationship. On none of the English examples of Typ Bradwell (Reichstein 1975 Taf.98.1-4) is the headplate, bow, or terminal equivalent to those on the two Swedish examples (Reichstein 1975 Taff.98.6 and 101.1). The headplates of the two Swedish examples of Typ Barrington (Reichstein 1975 Taf.101.3-4) are quite different from those on the English, which amongst themselves are not uniform (Reichstein 1975 Taf.100 nos.2, 6-8, and 10). Similar objections may be made to the groupings of Typen Feering and Foldvik-Empingham. What these brooches really have in common are certain very simple developments. They inherit the characteristic cruciform brooch headplate, a very common feature. Their bows are usually of the simplest bow brooch forms, and if otherwise are effective in dividing individual examples, not linking them. The terminals below these bows are the simple spatulate forms:

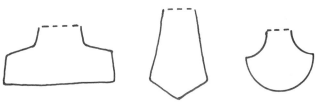

which are quite common on the small-long brooches of England and northern Germany, and the small bronze brooches of Scandinavia (cf. Åberg 1926 fig.92; Leeds 1945 pp.4-36 various figs.; Shetelig 1910 figs.23-34 and 51-62 passim). In the absence of more convincing parallels between the brooches of different areas, it seems most satisfactory to treat the relationship indicated by these "types" as evidence for a simple parallel development from the same very common features in an area of common development, and not as good evidence of the exchange of brooches, models, or ideas between those areas.

The cruciform brooches, with their potential as evidence of interregional associations in the Migration Period, merit a study less brief and sketchy than that presented here. It is regrettable that Reichstein did not make his procedure in classifying individual brooches under types more explicit: one cannot really tell whether a rigorous division of the brooches into compositional elements and a comparison of these, as done with the Anglo-Saxon square-headed brooches in Chapter 3, would produce significantly different groups and evidence of such associations than Reichstein's. There is no compelling reason to expect that to be the case, since Reichstein's descriptions of his Typen imply that they are established on such a basis. However it is not at all improbable that a more thorough, detailed investigation of the forms of the compositional elements of the cruciform brooches, looking at equivalent, related, and common features, in, say, the forms of the headplate wings, or the brows and eyes of the terminal heads, and their distribution, would produce a far more soundly based characterisation of the "areas of common development" that have been adumbrated here.

But despite the shortcomings of this short review of the cruciform brooches, one may argue that the results it suggests are satisfactorily plausible, and justify the study. A common reaction amongst Anglo-Saxon archaeologists to Shetelig's suggested West Norwegian influence on England has been to explain the parallels involved as separate, parallel developments from a common source rooted in northern Germany. But what formerly were supposedly characteristics of western Norway and England now appear to be more broadly Anglo-Scandinavian chracteristics, and the evidence of other artefact-types shows that there is no reason to discount the possibility of a direct exchange of motifs and ideas between Anglian England and Scandinavia.

The wide area of use of cruciform brooches means that they present less sharp a picture of Anglo-Scandinavian relationship than those previous artefact-types. Kent and even Frisia are associated with Anglian England and Scandinavia in the particular forms of cruciform brooches in use. The question immediately arises of whether this properly represents a shift to the north in the associations between regions using cruciform brooches, or simply the dropping out of northern Germany with a relatively early demise of cruciform brooches there. There are grounds for emphasizing the more positive aspects of the later parallels. The use of cruciform brooches in northern Germany does appear to continue into the last quarter of the 5th. century, when the Anglo-Scandinavian parallels seem to be well established, and indeed Typ Krefeld-Gellep provides a nice counterweight to the predominance of the Anglo-Scandinavian associations. Moreover the specific range of forms of the lappets below the bow, and the scroll-shaped nostrils of the terminal head, imply a definite dispersal of motifs in this Anglo-Scandinavian area, such as there is very little evidence of in the earlier stages of development before VWZ III, except, perhaps, for the inconclusive similarity between the early Glentham and Mejlby brooches. An Anglo-Scandinavian area of common development can therefore be regarded as a significant phenomenon, and one which is best affirmed from the period of VWZ III, that is about the last quarter of the 5th. century and the first quarter of the 6th., largely in agreement with the earliest evidence of direct Anglo-Scandinavian contact provided by the clasps, and perhaps the bracteates and scutiform pendants as well. The cruciform brooches, however, although they expand the survey, provide no new evidence of connections between Anglian England and Scandinavia that have not already been considered for other artefact-types. They attest the exchange of forms between brooch makers over this very large area.

II - Anglian Equal-Armed Brooches

This section is concerned with investigating the background of a particular brooch-type, of which only 8 examples are known, from East Anglia (Map 5.2):

Brandon, Sfk.	Hattatt coll.1855
Westgarth Gardens, Bury St.Edmunds,	
Sfk g.36. 2 examples	BSE Mus. Fig.5.7a-b
Holywell Row, Sfk g.16. Pair	MAA Cam. Reichstein 1975 Taf.110
Spong Hill, Nfk g.46. Pair	Norwich Mus (on loan)
	Publication forthcoming, EAA Spong Hill, vol.3
Newnham, Cambs.	MAA Cam 1892.FB. Fig.5.8

These are particular forms of the brooch-type that Roeder identified as the Griffibel (Roeder 1930 pp.43-47). Their characteristics are symmetry on the upper surface between the headplate and the footplate, which are of a basically trapezoidal form and separated by a parallel-sided bow. All the examples are of bronze, those from Brandon and Newnham also apparently having been tinned. All are of quite consistent proportions, the long base of the trapezoidal plates varying from 3.5 to 4.0 cm. in length, and the angled sides from 2.0 to 2.3 cm. The bows are between 1 and 2 cm. long. All except the two examples from Bury St. Edmunds have the plates decorated with simple and predictable forms of stamps along the three outer edges. The greatest variation between the examples is found in the form of the bow, the different forms of which are given in Fig.5.9.

Three closed grave-finds have included these brooches. Spong Hill g.46 included, inter alia, wrist-clasps of form B 17 b and a cruciform brooch, the whole assemblage probably belonging to the earlier 6th. century, though possibly to the later 5th. Holywell Row g.16 is undoubtedly a 6th.-century context, with a cruciform brooch of Reichstein's Typ Nassington (Reichstein 1975 no.853) and form C 3 clasps. The most determinative dating evidence from Westgarth Gardens, Bury St. Edmunds g.36 is a clasp-half of form B 7, a form which is mostly datable to the 6th. century, but which may have appeared before the end of the 5th. (cf. Chapter 2). The most probable dating for this brooch-type in Anglian England is that all the examples belong to the first half of the 6th. century, but it is possible that some belong to the late 5th. The paucity of examples should not lead us automatically to assume a short duration for the type: the variation of the bows could indicate occasional or low-level production over a fairly long period.

This brief survey of the brooch-type in England might give the impression that it is relatively insignificant. However an investigation of its possible sources presents us with some particularly interesting problems in the context of Anglo-Scandinavian connections in the Migration Period.

Roeder insisted that the origins of the Griffibel were quite independent of developments of the Roman Zweibelknopffibel and of the gleicharmige Fibeln which we commonly regard as Saxon. He justified the term Griffibel by suggesting that the brooch-type was actually developed from shield-grip models (Roeder 1930 pp.43-47). But a survey of possible parallels to the Anglian equal-armed brooches in northern Germany and Scandinavian, with the benefit of certain finds not known to Roeder over 50 years ago, suggests that the separation of forms might not be so clear cut. It should be pointed out here that this investigation concerns only those Griffibeln with trapezoidal head- and footplates, and not those of different shapes, and usually very different sizes, which Roeder would place in this category (cf. Roeder 1930 Taf.IX.5-6; Åberg 1953 figs.65-94).

There are two finds from Scandinavia which imply that the Scandinavian equal-armed brooches with trapezoidal plates may indeed be related in some way to the gleicharmige Fibeln of Roeder's Typus 1 (Roeder 1930 pp.59-81, Taff.X and XI.1). A grave-find from Fannerup, Ginnerup, Djurs N., Ra, Dk included two brooches, one very similar to Roeder's Typus 1 brooches, and the second very similar to that except for the addition of a triangular plate at the head of the brooch producing an appearance much more like that of the Scandinavian equal-armed brooches (Fig.5.10a-b). The assemblage, along with Roeder's Typus 1, may be dated to around the middle of the 4th. century. An early Norwegian example of the equal-armed brooch is from Tveide, Birkenes, AA (Ab. 1888 pp.160-163, fig.4). This was associated with a brooch which again is reminiscent of Roeder's Typus 1 (Ab. 1888 fig.8), but has a bow that swells slightly towards the middle, a feature of Norwegian equal-armed brooches, but not of the German gleicharmige Fibeln. A common feature of the decoration of the trapezoidal footplate of Roeder's Typus 1 brooches is the faceting of its angled sides (Roeder 1930 Textabb.29, 32-35, and 45-46), a feature also found on an equal-armed brooch from Leirol, Vang, Op, N (Fig.5.11) which was associated with beads which appear to date to the Roman Iron Age. A common feature of the plates of the Scandinavian equal-armed brooches is the single dot-in-rings motif in the centre, such as also occurs on a late Typus 1 gleicharmig Fibel from Hemmoor, Kr. Neuhaus, Niedersachsen (Roeder 1930 Textabb.42). This is not enough evidence to suggest that the Scandinavian equal-armed brooches are derivative of gleicharmige Fibeln of Roeder's Typus 1, but the development of the two forms was clearly closely linked.

The North German development of the gleicharmig Fibel which provides the closest parallels to the Anglian equal-armed brooches is Roeder's Typus 4 (Roeder 1930 pp.108-112). I know of no further examples to add to the four Roeder listed: two from Hammoor, Kr. Stormarn, Schleswig-Holstein, one from Westerwanna, Kr. Hadeln, Niedersachsen, and one from Seraing, Liège, Belgium. The type was plausibly dated by Roeder to the first half of the 5th. century. Both in date and form there are considerable discrepancies between these and the Anglian equal-armed brooches. The examples from Hammoor and Westerwanna have the bow slightly broader at the footplate end than at the headplate, a feature which Roeder takes as decisive in distinguishing gleicharmige- from Griffibeln, and all have trapezoidal plates with broader bases, and more acute basal angles, than the Anglian brooches. Nevertheless they do have the symmetrical trapezoidal plates, and on one example from Hammoor these are decorated with stamps, although not in the same pattern as the Angian English brooches. The Seraing brooch (Roeder 1930 Taf.XIII.5) has a parallel-sided bow with grooves running down the middle, a form that is also found on the pair of brooches in Holywell Row g.16.

The equal-armed brooch with trapezoidal plates has a rather richer development in Scandinavia. There are, however, no examples of this brooch proper from Denmark. From Norway, I have recorded 35 examples (List 5.1; map 5.2), some of which are pairs from single finds. The common view of these brooches in Norway is that they are characteristic of the Roman Iron Age, and not of the Migration Period (Shetelig 1910 p.84). There are positive grounds for assigning 16 of the 35 examples to the RIA. Some may be so dated by find-association, e.g. Nedre Lunde, N.Land, Op (C25200, UOÅ 1931-32 pp.238-239), found with a swastika brooch, and the example from Tveide, Birkenes, AA mentioned above. The example from Skreros, Vegusdal, AA found in Haug 2 there with the two scutiform pendants discussed in the previous chapter is very similar to the Tveide brooch, with its distinctive knobs at the four outer corners (Reichstein 1975 Taf.133), and may therefore be argued to belong to the RIA too. Several examples have the double or treble pin axis which appears to be a characteristic of RIA brooches (Åberg 1924 pp.10-11). Nevertheless this leaves a substantial number of Norwegian examples undated, and a very few from Migration Period contexts as recognized in the present work. Three examples are dated to VWZ I by association with cruciform brooches of the earliest forms: Tveitane, Brunlanes, Vf (Reichstein 1975 no.14), and two from Kvassheim, Egersund, Ro: B5293 (Reichstein 1975 no.116), and B5345 (not in Reichstein). The latest context in which a Norwegian example can be closely dated is VWZ II for the example from Løland, Vigmostad, VA, found with a cruciform brooch of Reichstein's Typ Lunde (Reichstein 1975 no.99). The example from Tjøtta, Klepp, Ro which Shetelig illustrates as a late Migration Period development of the type (Shetelig 1910 fig.67) was associated with two bird-headed pins, a characteristic Migration Period type, although not very closely datable (cf. Sjøvold 1962 pp.169-170). A shift in concentration from eastern to western Norway into the Migration Period in the distribution of these brooches may be detectable.

Amongst the forms of the Norwegian equal-armed brooches we find features considerably closer to those of the Anglian equal-armed brooches than discovered on German gleicharmige Fibeln of Roeder's Typus 4. The example from Gjevle, N.Land, Op and the two Aust-Agder finds have trapezoidal plates with broad bases more like the German brooches than the Anglian ones, but the majority are of proportions more similar to the Anglian (cf. Fig.5.11), with bases measuring from 3 to 4 cm., and angled sides from about 2 to 2.5 cm. The Migration Period example from Tjøtta, Klepp, Ro has a relatively narrow base to the trapezoidal plates, as does that from Føre, Bø, No (Sjøvold 1962 pl.17), which Sjøvold dates to the RIA (op.cit. p.77).

Some of the plates of the Norwegian examples are decorated by outlining with stamps, as the majority of the Anglian brooches, e.g. Fig.5.11. This is found on the early example from Tveide, Birkenes, AA, but also on the VWZ I example from Kvassheim, Egersund, Ro (Reichstein 1975 Taf.2.11). A more common form of decoration, however, consists of one or more dot-in-ring or concentric ring motifs, e.g. Spangereid, S.-Audnedal, VA (Fig.5.12). This form is well attested from the RIA, but occurs on VWZ I brooches from Kvassheim (B5345) and Tveitane (Reichstein 1975 Taf.4.7). The VWZ II example from Løland, Vigmostad, VA appears to have had plain head- and footplates (Fig.5.13).

One of the bow-forms found on an Anglian equal-armed brooch, that on one of the brooches from Westgarth Gardens, Bury St. Edmunds g.36 (fig.5.7b), with its sharply angled median ridge, is reminiscent of a commonly occurring form on the Norwegian brooches. The Norwegian examples tend, however, to swell in the centre, e.g. Tveide, Birkenes, and Skreros, Vegusdal, AA (Reichstein 1975 Taff.131 and 133). The examples from Spangereid, S.-Audnedal, and Løland, Vigmostad, VA (Figs.5.12-13) show this form with a series of chevrons at either end, also seen on the VWZ I brooch from Kvassheim, Egersund, Ro (Reichstein 1975 Taf.2.11) and the brooch from Indre Taule, Sæbø, Ho. Otherwise the Norwegian brooches generally have considerably longer bows thn the Anglian ones: mostly between 2.5 and 3.0 cm.

Brooches of this type are very scarce in mainland Sweden. A silver example from Skänje, Skee, Bo (SHM 16808), with three concentric ring motifs on either plate and a double pin axis, is datable to the Roman Iron Age. The only other example of which I know is from S.Åbyggeby, Hille, Gä (SHM 22776, Åberg 1953 fig.68). This is plain and simple, and has relatively narrow bases to the trapezoidal plates like the unusual Norwegian examples from Tjøtta, Klepp, Ro and Føre, Bø, No. It was found with two cruciform brooches and form B 1 clasps, datable to VWZ III (Reichstein 1975 no.370). Its relatively late date supports Shetelig's view of the Tjøtta brooches as a late and degenerate example.

As Åberg indicated in his brief consideration of the S.Åbyggeby brooches (Åberg 1953 p.62), examples of this brooch-type are also known from Migration Period Gotland. Nerman assigned five such brooches to his Period VI.1, roughly the first half of the Migration Period (Nerman 1934 figs.28-32), to which a sixth example can be added, from Ihre, Hellvi (SHM 20826:252). One of the Gotland examples shows significant similarities to the Norwegian brooches, that from Bjärs, Hejnum (Nerman 1934 fig.28) with three dot-in-concentric-ring motifs on either plate, and a long bow, swelling slightly in the middle, and lightly curved at either end (cf. Fig.5.11). Of the remaining examples, those from Havor, Hablingbo, Ihre, Hellvi, and the unknown find-spot (Nerman 1934 figs.29 and 32) have a single dot-and-rings element on either plate, but the transverse line, and the angle in the side edges of the trapezoidal plates of these remaining examples are peculiarly Gotlandic features, as is the round knob on the centre of the bow. None of the examples can be dated more closely than Nerman dates them. The Bjärs brooch suggests a degree of asociation with the Norwegian brooches at some stage, but the characters of the remaining brooches are peculiarly Gotlandic.

On purely formal grounds, Norway seems to provide the ideal source material for the Anglian equal-armed brooches. Examples from Norway have trapezoidal plates of similar sizes and proportions, and decorated in the same manner, and to a lesser extent comparable bows with sharply angled median ridges. The form of pin-fixing and catch plate found on certain later Norwegian examples (e.g. Figs.5.12-13) is exactly that found on the Anglian equal-armed brooches. Besides the formal similarities may be set the fact of their being found in twos or pairs. This is, of course, also the case with the late Swedish find from S.Åbyggeby, Hille, Gä. This however may be regarded as an example of Norwegian influence there. Åberg wrote at length on the close relationship of this area with western Norway in the "Norrlandsriket" of this period (Åberg 1953 pp.34-79). The cruciform brooch with which these brooches were found is assigned by Reichstein to his predominantly Norwegian Typ Mundheim. The only rivals to Norway for identification as the most probable source, if there is one, are northern Germany with the gleicharmige Fibeln of Roeder's Typus 4, and Gotland with her equal-armed brooches, and Norway clearly provides closer parallels to the Anglian equal-armed brooches than these.

But the chronology of the Norwegian and the Anglian equal-armed brooches is a problem. It has been demonstrated that the brooch-type continues in production into the Migration Period in Norway, but it cannot be certainly dated later than VWZ II there. One may assume a continuity of form through to the S.Åbyggeby example from a VWZ III context, and a pair from Tjøtta, Klepp, Ro could also be as late as that, but these display a development away from the forms appropriate to be sources for the Anglian equal-armed brooches. One could seek to minimize the chronological discrepancy by noting that VWZ II may be taken up to ca.475 by conventional dating, and the earliest known Anglian English examples could be from late 5th.-century contexts, but it is an unacceptable abuse of relative chronology to recast it in absolute-chronological terms in this way. It is best to face honestly the apparent facts that the comparable Norwegian examples may be dated up to about the middle of the 5th. century, and that the known Anglian equal-armed brooches may be dated at the earliest to the end of the 5th. century, and may well all be 6th.-century.

Could the Anglian equal-armed brooches have been an independent development ? If this were the case, it would be a remarkable coincidence that Anglian England should produce a form so similar to the Norwegian brooches. The Anglian equal-armed boroches are not of a design that one could expect to be produced from the apparent trends of brooch development, or assembled from the design elements available, in East Anglia at the appropriate period. These Anglian brooches are formally even more distant from the few Saxon equal-armed brooches found in England than they are from the German gleicharmige Fibeln of Roeder's Typus 4. No good case can be made for them being a curious development of the English small-long brooch series either. The form of their bows and of their pin fixings and catch plates may be paralleled amongst the small-long brooches, of course, but where occasionally small-long brooches have trapezoidal plates at the foot, these are commonly of different proportions in the relative length of the angled sides and the base, and smaller, with bases measuring an average of about 2 cm., not 3-4 cm. Moreover, trapezoidal plates at the feet of small-long brooches are never joined directly to the bow without an intervening stem as is the case on all Anglian (and Scandinavian) equal-armed brooches. No interest in symmetry between brooch head- and footplates is otherwise attestable in Anglian England in the appropriate period.

The case for independent development is therefore weak, and one may seek to propose a solution to the problem, which accepts that there is a connection between the Norwegian and the Anglian equal-armed brooches, but that there are missing links. Most simply, the links we can suggest are missing are either later-dated Norwegian finds of the appropriate form or earlier-dated Anglian examples, or both. It is not a very credible hypothesis to suggest that Denmark could have provided an intermediate post, with all relevant finds there lost in the fundknapphed, since no single true equal-armed brooch has been found there, and the fundknapphed itself is diminishing. The appearance of a new brooch-type in Anglian England as a result of direct Norwegian influence is quite an acceptable proposition. Bridging the dates for the Norwegian and Anglian series, one may suggest that this influence is datable sometime between the mid 5th. and the beginning of the 6th. centuries. Such influence would of course be most in agreement with that detectable through other artefact-types already discussed if dated to the last quarter of the 5th. or the early 6th. century. The distribution of these brooches in England interestingly reflects another parallel between East Anglia and western Norway - that provided by the gusset plates (Map 2.17). The appearance of these was dated to around the beginning of the 6th. century, and, if missing links are accepted, such a date would be quite reasonable for the appearance of the Anglian equal-armed brooch in East Anglia too.

III - Annular Brooches

Annular brooches are very simple objects. Their essential definitive form is that of a ring, with a pin attached to it at one point such that it is able to lie across the centre of the ring. This is probably the most common single type of dress-accessory known from 5th.-, 6th.-, and 7th.-century Anglian England, certainly the most common type of brooch. I have recorded details of some 700 examples from Anglian English cemeteries, and believe that this assemblage of material is far from complete. I would estimate the number countable, including those in minor museums, and those referred to in literature and otherwise lost, to approach 1,000. This may be compared with about 600 individual examples of wrist-clasp, 179 square-headed brooches, and 127 cruciform brooches listed by Reichstein, which is, however, probably no more than half the possible total currently available. Several examples of annular brooches are also known from the Upper Thames area and Kent (cf. Leeds 1945 fig.29), and even a few to the south in Hampshire and Sussex.

In a brief discussion of the annular brooches, Leeds noted seven "stages" of their "development", which he designated a - g (Leeds 1945 pp.46-49). These have been taken up by Ager in the most substantial study of any part of this material subsequently to be made, as designations for particular types of annular or quoit brooches (Ager, forthcoming*). Most of the Anglian English examples belong to stages or types d - g, and some of these appear in Ager's study, which concentrates mostly on type D, secondarily on type E. Approaching the material from an Anglian English viewpoint, however, Leeds's stages d - g are unacceptable as type-designations for a complete classification and discussion of the Anglian English annular brooches, simply because they fail to reflect the enormous range of variety of form found in this large body of material, and in the cases of stages d and g, oppose definitive elements that occur together. The general simplicity of the brooch-type draws attention to the great range of detailed variations between examples. An outline of this range in Anglian England is given here.

The shape of the rings of these brooches varies from the effectively truly circular to a distinctly elongated oval form. The latter is not particularly common. In size, the range of outer diameters for the ring most commonly falls between 3.0 and 6.5 cm., and the inner diameters between 1.5 and 5.2 cm. The great majority of

---

* I am most grateful to Mr Barry Ager for the opportunity to study his paper in draft form, and for discussing these brooches with me.

the rings are of bronze, which may occasionally be tinned, but a small number (8) of iron examples are recorded, and also 2 examples of bone (Morningthorpe, Nfk g.209; Driffield, Hu C44 g.2). Silver rings occasionally occur, but only on relatively late examples (see below). Leeds partially categorized the material according to the form of the cross-section of the ring, but implied that these divided into only three forms: flat, half-round, or oval. To these may in fact be added a half-round hollow form, faceted forms (i.e. ⌂), stepped forms (i.e. ⌐), and a grooved form (i.e. ᗯ). Leeds's categories certainly cover the great majority of examples, but are not complete. The ring is usually cast in one piece, but some 10% of the recorded examples have a ring formed of a band with two overlapping ends joined together either with a small iron rivet or by soldering. The ring may even be a composite construction assembled from more than one cast arc. The forms of decoration of the ring produce a very wide range of varieties, although including nothing particularly unusual, and generally quite congruent with the range of decorative forms already met on Class B wrist-clasps. Some rings are plain, but stamped decoration is the most common, and decoration by incised lines is common too, either all round the ring, or in bundles demarcating arcs of the ring. Cast moulded decoration of the ring includes the faceting just mentioned, and forms of the astragalus or egg-and-tongue motif. Rarer and later forms of decoration include cast Style II ornament (on a brooch from Castle Bytham, Lincs: Akerman 1855 pl.XII.2), and red glass or garnets set in cells (i.e. the Castle Bytham brooch, and one from Barrington, Cambs in the Ashmolean Museum).

A series of features associated with the pin adds yet further variety to the range of forms met with. While the most common material for the ring is bronze, the most common material recorded for the pin is iron, although a considerable number of bronze pins are known, always on bronze rings. A pair of silver annular brooches from Uncleby, Hu have silver pins; the other silver annular brooches have all lost their pins. There are two basic variants in the form of fixing the pin to the ring: it may either pass through a hole in the ring, or be hooked around the ring, in which case the ring is usually narrowed, or connected by a thin bar, at this point. This narrowed section may be bordered, in more ambitious cases with confronted animal heads (Fig.5.14). At the opposite end of the pin, it is believed that the brooches were normally to be fastened simply by the point of the pin resting on or over the ring (cf. Brown III pp.283-284). Sometimes a slot appears in the ring here, opposite the point where the pin was hinged, presumably for the easier fastening of the brooch to the material. This occurs on some 36 Anglian English examples, of which 25 also have some form of projecting edging or flanges by the slot to hold the pin-end more firmly. The majority of these are considered by Ager amongst his type D3 quoit brooches. Two brooches,

from Kenninghall, Nfk and Sleaford, Lincs g.144, have
simply a groove for the end of the pin to rest in.

There is no obvious purpose to be served in attempting
to sub-classify the annular brooches on the basis of
permutations of this wide range of variants. Such an
attempt could produce an enormous number of sub-groups or
types of very vague significance. It is sufficient for
present purposes to know the range of features that occur
within the corpus as a whole, and usually more interesting
to extract single features, or groups of closely related
features, and consider their distribution in isolation from
their associated features or compositional elements on
individual annular brooches. An example may be given of
the slot in the ring for the pin-end, either with or
without flanges, or the groove for the pin-end to rest on,
described just above. Although examples occur in most of
Anglian England, these are concentrated to the west, and in
Northamptonshire and Warwickshire in particular (Map 5.3).
The slot with flanges is a feature of quoit brooches as
defined by Ager, although he does not include all of the
Anglian English brooches carrying this feature in his type
D, as a number of them have a "narrow-band" ring of
particular proportions, which, following Leeds, is a
feature of type G. The south-westerly concentration of
this feature on Anglian English annular brooches must be
associated with the distribution of quoit brooches of
Ager's type D2, which belong largely to the Thames Valley
region in Oxfordshire and Gloucestershire. The distinction
between types D2 and D3 is that the former has the flanges
bent up on either side of the notch, and the latter has
them cast. It is Ager's view that type D2 was a model for
type D3, and he has chronological evidence consistent with
this. Certainly this is most probably the source from
which Anglian England adopted this feature on its annular
brooches, and rather more plausible than seeking to
associate this feature of annular brooches with penannular
brooch models (see below).

It is odd that there should be several significant
uncertainties concerning the date-range of so well-
represented a brooch-type. There is quite solid dating
evidence for the use of annular brooches from the last
quarter of the 5th. century up to the end of the Migration
Period according to the conventions adhered to here:
several examples have been found in association with
cruciform brooches of Reichstein's "späte" and "späteste"
forms (cf. Reichstein 1975 nos.825, 829, 861, and 870;
Leeds 1945 p.106); several examples are associated with
square-headed brooches of all three phases; there are many
examples associated with wrist-clasps from the whole range.
I know of no evidence for dating any example from Anglian
England earlier than ca.475, but this situation should not
be mistaken for positive evidence of the starting-date of
the brooch-type. However the ratio of early cruciform
brooches to annular brooches recovered from the Spong Hill

cremations, ca.33:1 (EAA 6 pp.24-25), suggests that the former define an earlier phase when the annular brooch was not present. It has already been mentioned, in the discussion of the "late cemeteries" in Chapter 4, that this brooch-type appears to survive the dress change of the second half of the 6th. century and to continue in use well into the 7th. century, to which date many of the examples from Uncleby, Hu can be assigned (Leeds 1936 pl.XXVII). Certain forms of annular brooches may be identified as distinctively "late" in Anglian England. Most of those from Uncleby just referred to are particularly small and elegant, about 3 cm. in outer diameter or less, and with very narrow bands. A characteristically "late" use of silver and garnet settings has already been noted. The occurrence of "broad-band" annular brooches in Anglian English contexts may also be regarded as a late feature: "broad-banded" is defined by Ager as where the outer diameter of the ring divided by its width produces a figure below 4.5; most brooches in this category in fact produce a quotient between 3 and 4. Typical examples are the silver, garnet-set brooch from Barrington, Cambs (Ashmolean), and a brooch from Leighton Buzzard, Beds g.32 (Hyslop 1963 fig.12). However the broad band may not be regarded as a late feature over the whole of England, as Ager dates broad-banded annular brooches of his type E, mostly from the Thames Valley or south of the Thames, from the 5th. to the 7th. centuries.

Through both the small and slender and the broad-banded types a typical uniformity between all areas of England in the accessories to the later dress style arises. It was implied in Chapter 4 that the apparent date of the demise of the old dress style, the 560s, would be an appropriate date to change the predominant form of the annular brooch in Anglian England. But examples of annular brooches of forms and proportions quite typical of the "earlier" Anglian English examples, in Monkton, Kt g.12, are from a context dated by S.C. Hawkes to ca.600 or later (Hawkes et al. 1975 pp.64-65, 76, and 80). Anglian England has produced a large number of graves with similar annular brooches and no other determinative dating evidence (e.g. Bergh Apton, Nfk gg.11 and 15, EAA 7). There is a possibility that such graves could be typical of the later 6th. century, after the demise of the characteristic Migration Period dress-accessories in about the 560s, reflecting a stage at which the distinctively later dress-accessories were either not yet developed or sufficiently widely distributed to appear in these graves. But we cannot really say at what point in the later 6th. or earlier 7th. centuries the earlier forms of the annular brooch gave way to the later forms in Anglian England, and whether the change was abrupt or gradual.

The functions of Anglian English annular brooches are of considerable significance in the present context. Various methods of actually fastening them to the material in the dress have already been referred to. There is no doubt that in Anglian England annular brooches were most commonly worn in twos or pairs, at the shoulders of the dress. At least 40 out of 65 graves at Morningthorpe, Nfk containing annular brooches contained such sets, and 25 out of 46 graves at Sleaford, Lincs. At the latter site, Thomas records the occurrence of annular brooches at the shoulders in graves 3, 19, 42, 54, 123, 124/125, 134, 144, 147, 151, 160, 177, 194, 204, 214, and 242 (Thomas 1887), and this pattern is widely repeated elsewhere. Where only single examples are recorded from individual graves, one may frequently suspect that a second example has been lost, e.g. where it is found on one shoulder as at Swaffham, Nfk gg.1 and 5 (EAA 2 fig.4), or where one remains in an otherwise empty-looking grave as at Bergh Apton, Nfk gg.15 and 55 (EAA 7). Nevertheless the occurrence of annular brooches in sets of three indicates that their use was not restricted to the shoulders (Vierck in Hauck 1970 pp.361-362): in one of the graves Vierck records, Little Eriswell, Sfk g.2, the positions of the brooches are well recorded, with one under the chin, and one on each shoulder; in Sleaford, Lincs g.205 Thomas records the finding of "two cruciform fibulae at shoulders, and one large flat annular fibula in front of chest" (Thomas 1887 p.402). Four further examples of graves containing three annular brooches from Morningthorpe, Nfk (gg.44, 114, 173, and 251) may now be added to Vierck's list, and even three graves containing four annular brooches each (gg.80, 108, and 140), although I have no information on the positions of these in the grave, for which the publication of the cemetery in EAA must be awaited. Annular brooches must then be supposed to have been used in Anglian England principally as shoulder brooches on a peplos-type dress, but also to be usable as the central brooch gathering a dress below the bosom, or fastening a shawl (Vierck 1978 pp.231-253).

The annular brooches of Anglian England are thus very simple forms, employed from some time probably before the end of the 5th. century to fasten the womens' dress in its usual positions. Ager notes a similar pattern for the employment of quoit brooches from the Thames Valley and further south. However he notes a significant number of type E broad-band annulars worn, apparently singly, relatively low on the body, by the waist, hips, or stomach. He would interpret this, however, as simply the low fastening of a cloak in front of the body. The date-range of these quoit brooches further south may be approximately contemporary with that of the Anglian English annular brooches, although there is better evidence for the dating of the earliest quoit brooches to the 5th. century.

The simplicity of the annular brooch is stressed, because it is a brooch-type that need not have a source. It would be a simple type to invent. Nevertheless there are widespread European parallels to these brooches to be considered. It was Leeds's belief that the origins of the annular brooch lay amongst the "Celtic" penannular brooches (Leeds 1936 p.3). Although partially adopted by Evison (Evison 1965 pp.47-49), this is not widely regarded as plausible nowadays. The relationship of quoit brooches to penannular brooches is firmly quashed by Ager. The western orientated Anglian annular brooches with a flanged slot for the pin-end might seem to hold open the possibility of an annular/"Celtic" penannular brooch connection, but a better source for this feature are the quoit brooches of Ager's type D2, related to the finer quoit brooches of Kent and Sussex. In general the penannular brooches found in Anglian England are smaller than the annular, with plainer hoops, square or rounded in cross-section, and usually entirely of bronze, quite unlike the annular brooches. There is also no very good case for deriving the Anglian annular brooches as a whole from earlier southern quoit brooches. Where a specific connection between the two can be made, it is geographically limited, and not a feature of the earliest-dated Anglian examples. Furthermore the southern quoit brooches consistently differ in proportions and to an extent in style of decoration from the Anglian annular brooches until a relatively late date.

Continental Europe produces a range of brooches that offer parallels to the quoit and annular brooches of England. Various ring brooches found there with slots with knobs for the pin-end have been the subject of considerable discussion recently, and two closely comparable examples are known from Kempston, Beds and Londesborough, Hu (cf. Todd 1975; Dickinson 1982). These are dated principally to the 4th. and 5th. centuries. Ager accepts these as contributory to the form of the quoit brooch in southern England, but regards the quoit brooch as the product of the combination of these with broad-band ring brooch forms already existent in Scandinavia.

There are indeed a good number of objects from later Roman Iron Age and Migration Period Scandinavia of forms extremely close to the English annular brooches, and which could provide the models that Ager suggests. It may be grossly misleading, however, to call these "annular brooches", as, for instance, Sjøvold does (Sjøvold 1962 pp.164-165), as in an English context this can give a totally false impression as to their function. For this reason I propose to use the more neutral Norwegian term ringspenner (lit. "ring-fasteners") to refer to these.

The most common Norwegian form of ringspenne consists of a plain bronze ring, round in cross-section, normally between 3 and 6 mm. thick, with an outer diameter between 3 and 4 cm. One or more tabs are usually attached to the ring. An example from the Roman Iron Age is illustrated by Shetelig (VJG fig.75) and also two examples from VWZ IV (VJG figs.319 and 357). The tabs are one key difference between these objects and the Anglian English annular

brooches; the form of the ring is another, and the
dimensions of these objects in Norway coincide only with
the lower end of the range of sizes occurring amongst the
Anglian English brooches. More similar to English annular
brooches are scarcer Norwegian ringspenner with flat rings.
Sjøvold illustrates an example from Steine, Bø, No with
inner and outer diameters of about 3 and 4 cm.
respectively, decorated with a single row of concentric
circle motifs, such as not uncommonly occur in various
forms and dispositions on Anglian English annular brooches
(Sjøvold 1962 pl.23). A fragment of a ringspenne from
Vemmestad, Lyngdal, VA (Fig.5.15) shows double semi-circle
stamps, which are very common on the English annular
brooches, and apparently the use of transverse incised
lines to sectionalize the ring. This example was
associated with a form B 1 clasp, dating it to the
Migration Period, and most probably to the Migration
Period's latter half. An example with a form of astragalus
moulding, of proportions consistent with English annular
brooches, and a ring of half-round hollow cross-section, as
on a pair of annular brooches from Newnham, Cambs, from
Sem, Lasken, VA is illustrated by Vierck (in Hauck 1970
fig.53.4, cf. fig.53.1-2). From Lunde, Vanse, VA comes an
example with a ring of a "stepped" cross-section quite
similar to that already noted on a few Anglian English
examples (Fig.5.16). This find is dated to VWZ II-III by
virtue of its combination of a Nydam-style relief brooch
with "späte" cruciform brooches (Reichstein 1975 no.105).
But quite unlike the Anglian English brooches is the fact
that the Lunde ringspenne is silver gilt. An example of
the finest forms of ringspenne found in Norway is one from
Bolstad, Evanger, Ho (Fig.5.17), with confronted animal
heads beside the point where it appears the pin would have
been hinged.

Amongst ringspenner from Denmark and Bornholm,
examples with flat rings similar to the English annular
brooches are relatively more common. A bronze example
carrying stamps and some simple incised decoration is that
from Østre Gesten Skov, Gesten, Amst, Ribe (Fig.5.18a),
from a grave which also included an iron ringspenne
(Fig.5.18b). The grave also contained pottery (Fig.5.18c)
and distinctive skittle-shaped amber beads which allow it
to be dated to the later Roman Iron Age or early Migration
Period (Norling-Christensen 1956 pp.45-47, fig.41).
Similar in size and decoration to the Ø. Gesten Skov
ringspenne is an example from Kobbeå, Bornholm g.11
(Fig.5.19) dated to the Migration Period (Klindt-Jensen
1957 pp.73-74). A pair of ringspenner were found in a
grave in Tude mark, N.Skast, Skast, Ribe, along with a
cruciform brooch of Reichstein's "späte" Typ Krefeld-Gellep
(Reichstein 1975 no.471, Taf.89.1-6), and are thereby
assignable to VWZ III. These, however, are rather small
compared to English annular brooches, with outer and inner
diameters of 3.3 and 2.5 cm. respectively, and are
decorated with incised lines running alongside the inner

and outer edges, which again is not recorded from Anglian England. Lindholm Høje g.2207 is a cremation which contained a further example of a _ringspenne_ of half-round hollow cross-section with moulded astragalus decoration, as from Newnham, Cambs and Sem, Lasken, VA, N (cf. above; Ramskou 1976 fig.391).

Swedish finds of _ringspenner_ from the Migration and Vendel Periods are illustrated by Åberg (1953 figs.56-63 and 132ff. _passim_). These variously show rings of round cross-section, faceted rings, flat and stamped rings, and rings with cast relief animal ornament. All of the Migration Period examples, however, have a cast rectangular or trapezoidal tab opposite the point where the pin is hinged. The recently published cemetery of Önsvala, Nevishög, Sk (Larsson 1982) includes two examples of some interest. Grave 18, dated to VWZ IV by its late relief brooch and Husby-type brooches, contained a _ringspenne_ with the form of a circular ring without a tab, apparently of faceted cross-section, and stamped. The proportionate diameter of the ring (about 5 cm.) to its slender width differentiates it, however, from Anglian English annular brooches. A second example was from grave 11, an early Vendel Period grave (Larsson 1982 fig.8c), carrying moulded decoration reminiscent of the astragalus pattern. A closely comparable example from Husby, Husby-Erlinghundra, Up is figured by Larsson (1982 fig.30), which again has a ring of half-round hollow cross-section, as occurs on the brooches from Cambridgeshire, Norway, and Denmark mentioned above. Larsson cites Arrhenius for a dating of the Husby _ringspenne_ to the period 530-560 (Larsson 1982 p.163).

There are thus various very close parallels in form between the Scandinavian _ringspenner_ and the Anglian English annular brooches, although they are not overwhelming in quantity. The greatest problem, however, in attempting to establish some connection between these artefact-types lies in their apparently largely different functions in the two areas. The predominant use of the annular brooches as dress fasteners, principally as shoulder brooches, has already been noted. The overwhelming majority of the _ringspenner_, however, appear to have been used on a belt, either as a buckle, or as an attachment ring for keys or a knife, etc. They are thus commonly interpreted as belt-rings or buckles in Scandinavia. Shetelig provides two figures showing their use in this way (VJG figs.313 and 352), and the _ringspenne_ in Önsvala, Nevishög, Sk g.18 appears to have been used thus (Larsson 1982 fig.12). Klindt-Jensen reports that the example from Kobbeå, Bornholm g.11 was found in this position (Klindt-Jensen 1957 p.73). Åberg describes the Swedish examples he deals with as _ringsöljor_ (ring-buckles) and the same identification is given to their similar Gotlandic successors of the Vendel Period (cf. Nerman 1975 pp.16-17). Since, then, with one exception, _ringspenner_ do not occur in matching pairs, and predominantly occur singly in graves, they must be assumed to be belt rings of some sort unless evidence to the contrary is available.

Such evidence is, rarely, to be found. The pair of ringspenner from the grave at Tude mark, Skast, Ribe a., Dk lend themselves to interpretation as paired shoulder brooches, although I was unable to find any record of their disposition in the grave in the Nationalmuseet, Copenhagen, and the costume of the woman interred here seems also to have employed three cruciform brooches. Of the two ringspenner in the grave at Ø. Gesten Skov, Gesten, Amst, Ribe, Dk, the iron example was found beside the knife in the middle of the grave, and is to be interpreted as a buckle, but the bronze example was some 50-60 cm. away from this, at one end of a spread of 124 beads, and to one side of the grave, which makes a very good case for it having been worn on the shoulders (Larsson 1982 figs.7-8). From grave II at Bjergby on Mors, Dk, a ringspenne was observed by X-ray photography, and it is claimed that it was fastened "foran på klædedragtet", "at the front, on the costume", although this was found some 20-30 cm. from a neck ring, and beside an iron knife (Albrethsen 1974 p.53). This is dated as early as the 3rd. century.

Thus we have at best three graves from South Scandinavia dated between the beginning of the Migration Period and the early Vendel Period, displaying the use of ringspenner as brooches comparable to the annular brooches of Anglian England. It seems impossible to determine whether these represent a continuous but rarely attested habit, or the chance and sporadic employment of a common type of object, normally used on the belt, in a different function. Even if the former is the case, it is scarcely credible that so few examples indicate the source of the forms and functions of the annular brooches in Agnlian England, and that this too is a matter of a South Scandinavian feature appearing in Anglian England from a date late in the 5th. century, comparable to the square-headed brooches and bracteates already discussed. The disproportion in numbers is so great that one could almost make as good a case for the derivation of the Anglian English annular brooches from Thuringia on the basis of an unusual grave-find there (Vierck in Hauck 1970 pp.355-363). In fact one of the "annular brooches" in this Thuringian grave is almost identical to those from Tude mark, Ribe a., Dk, with its apparently outlined form (Vierck op.cit. fig.53.7), and this may support the interpretation of this assemblage as Scandinavian. This barely lessens the disproportion, however. It is conversely as difficult to make a case for the occasional use of ringspenner as annular brooches in Scandinavia to be the result of Anglian English influence, a sporadic case of cultural diffusion such as may appear in the two Thuringian graves discussed by Vierck. The Ø. Gesten Skov find is too early, and the form of the Tude mark ringspenner discrepant. There would appear to be some connection between the Newnham, Cambs annular brooch pair and the Önsvala g.11 _ringspenner_, which can be shown to have been used on the shoulders, and the _ringspenner_ of similar form from Husby, Up, S, Lindholm Høje, Dk g.2207, and Sem, VA, N, but there need be none. Even if there was, the relative dates of these objects, and thus the nature of the connection, are unclear, and one (unusual) example from Anglian England, one each from Norway and northern Jutland, and two from Sweden, cannot set a pattern for the whole massive _corpora_ of annular brooches and _ringspenner_.

To this extent the results of this investigation of the annular brooches are regrettably negative. Nevertheless since we do already have evidence of a connection in material culture between Scandinavia and Anglian England in about the period that the annular brooches appear, it would be unnecessary to postulate the separate invention of this artefact-form in Scandinavia and Anglian England. The extension of its function to use as a shoulder brooch could simply be a sporadic development, and thus effectively independent, in both areas, but one that became regular in Anglian England. Against even this hypothesis is the fact that there is apparently no good evidence for the use of "annular brooches" on the belt or girdle in Anglian England. The most substantial parallels to the Anglian English annular brooches closest to hand are the annular and quoit·brooches of southern England, and the same problem of origins affects them both. But this tentative hypothesis at least takes account of the parallels to the Anglian English annular brooches that are chronologically and geographically scattered over southern Scandinavia, parallels that are sufficient in quantity to attract attention, yet insufficient, it appears, to be satisfactorily explained. The sources and history of the annular brooch in Anglian England remain largely obscure.

CHAPTER 6

SUMMARY AND DISCUSSION

A relationship and communication with the remainder of Europe set an indelible mark on Scandinavian archaeology from the later Roman period through to the Migration Period, the period with which this study has been principally concerned up to now. During the days of the late Roman Empire, Scandinavia was under substantial influence from the south, especially the area of Denmark, and the island of Sjælland in particular. This appears in a great volume of imported Roman goods there, principally bronze vessels, but also glass and silver vessels, and an amount of treasure in the form of Roman gold coin. Although the majority of these imported goods seem to have their place of origin in the west of the empire, central and eastern European routes to Scandinavia can also be identified (Brønsted 1960 pp.199-208). It is generally accepted that these Roman goods in Scandinavia reflect trade between the empire and Scandinavia, with furs, amber, and slaves believed to be Scandinavia's major exports (Brønsted 1960 p.249). Åberg would see Sjælland as the major market centre (Åberg 1956, esp.210-211), and Sjælland's pre-eminence as a find-place for imported Roman material at this period has even been associated with the emergence of a Danish kingdom there (Hedeager 1978).

Imported Roman goods of this period are also found in Norway and Sweden. In Norway they occur particularly in a series of rich, unburnt krigergraver, mostly occurring in eastern Norway. There is no great or peculiar discrepancy between the type of goods found in these, and the imports discovered in Denmark, and thus no partiuclar case for independent Norwegian contacts with the empire (Hagen 1977 pp.247-255). Imported Roman goods found in Sweden are similarly thought to have reached there mostly via Sjælland, although sporadic finds of eastern origin could presumably have crossed the Baltic direct to Sweden (Stenberger 1964 pp.379-423). It is these more northerly areas of Scandinavia that would have supplied the bulk of the furs to be traded south.

This apparently flourishing trading network of the later Roman period suffered general disruption at the start of the Migration Period. Åberg suggested that the Hunnic assaults on the Goths, ruining the central European trade routes, in particular the important route up the Elbe, were responsible (Åberg 1953 pp.23ff.). But although Sj lland appears to have lost its pre-eminence in wealth to western Scandinavia, Denmark and South Scandinavia were still subject to substantial influence from the south in the early stages of the Migration Period, from the south-west in particular. The two major early Migration Period

Scandinavian art styles are derived from such provincial, late Roman sources, the Sösdala Style (Lund Hansen 1969), and the Nydam Style (Haseloff 1981 pp.8-17). Style I is a later South Scandinavian development, but dependent in part on the Nydam Style and provincial Roman sources (Haseloff 1981 pp.18-174). A study of 5th.- and 6th.- century coin hoards of Roman solidi in Sweden and Denmark suggests that an importation of solidi to eastern Scandinavia began in the 450s, and continued into the reign of Justinian I (527-565). Initially these seem to have followed an easterly route along the Wisła, perhaps by the mediation of the Ostrogoths, although around the end of the 5th. century the route seems to shift westward to the Oder (Fagerlie 1967). It was on the models of Roman gold medallions or coins that the bracteates were initially developed, and the inception of this artefact-type has been dated to around the middle of the 5th. century (see Chapter 4).

During the Migration Period there is also evidence of the influence of northern Germany on the material culture of Scandinavia. Aspects of this have already been noted in Chapter 1, for instance the distribution of Anglian-type pottery as far north as Norway, and the occurrence of small-long brooches with Cross Potent or Cross Pattee headplates, argued to have their origin in Schleswig-Holstein, in northern Jutland and South-West Norway. While a simple correlation of this cultural influence with the expansionism of the Anglian people that saw their settlement of England seems perfectly reasonable, there is no case for any substantial migration of Angles to the area around the Skagerrak (Slomann 1961 pp.10-14).

In the later 5th. and 6th. centuries a new feature appears in Scandinavian exports and cultural influence on continental Europe. Without worrying here about the point that the origin of the bracteates does not appear to be purely Scandinavian as "Scandinavian" is defined in this work (cf. Chapter 4), from the late 5th. century onwards bracteates of all types spread out to the south and west in continental Europe, reaching what are now the areas of the U.S.S.R., Poland, Czechoslovakia, Austria, Hungary, East and West Germany, the Netherlands, and France. Scandinavian influence undoubtedly lay behind the appearance of the square-headed brooch on the continent (Haseloff 1981 pp.18-173, 281-485), although it may be argued that Haseloff underestimates the intermediary part played by England in the development of the type on the continent (cf. Chapter 3). A grave from Mühlhausen, Thuringia, discussed by Vierck (in Hauck 1970 pp.359-363) may represent a Jutish woman who had moved into that area (cf. Chapter 5: Annular Brooches). In the east, Swedish expansionism saw colonisation of the eastern side of the Baltic (Åberg 1953 pp.79-84) from about the period of VWZ III. There is evidence of contacts between the Baltic region and the area of Hungary in the period (Åberg 1953 pp.84-107). Such contacts must explain the appearance of the single continental example of a square-headed brooch with a footplate bar in Szolnok-Szanda, Hungary g.124 (cf. Haseloff 1981 pp.701-703). It may be provisionally suggested that contacts over these routes between Scandinavia and contental Europe were likely to have seen a mixture of trade, small-scale migration, exogamy, and travelling craftsmen.

A shift of focus away from the inevitably Anglo-centric viewpoint that has so far predominated in this study forces into consideration the question of whether the relationship between Scandinavia and Anglian England was any different from that between Scandinavia and continental Europe or Kent. In one regard the answer to this question must be yes, because the Anglian English culture-province in the Migration period is distinct from any other, and some of the features of this culture-province are unique parallels restricted to Anglian England and Scandinavia: the use of clasps in particular, together with the forms of square-headed brooches developed, the use of scutiform pendants in the period (except for the one example found at Liebenau, Niedersachsen), and the appearance of the Anglo-Scandinavian equal-armed brooches. But it falls subsequently to be considered whether this reflects a uniqueness in the nature of the contacts between Anglian England and Scandinavia, or peculiar conditions in Anglian England producing different reactions to the common expansionist tendencies in Scandinavian culture.

It was stressed in the introduction to this study that no single, simple, and comprehensive explanation of all the parallels between Anglian England and Scandinavia was to be expected, and the form of contacts suggested to appear through each of the artefact-types independently considered above has not been uniform. Some of these forms, for instance the South Scandinavian influence that brought the Phase 1 square-headed brooches to East Anglia, are argued to be simply geographical extensions to courses of influence that they already have been argued by others to have brought the square-headed brooches to Kent. Thus it cannot be suggested that Anglian England's contacts with Scandinavia were entirely different from those of Kent or the continent. What may be argued, however, is that Anglian England's relationship with Scandinavia was peculiar in the mixture of forms of contact between the two areas involved in it.

It is the use of clasps that is the most strikingly exclusive parallel between Anglian England and Scandinavia. It was argued at the end of Chapter 2 that a migration of folk from western Norway to the area of Norfolk and/or Humberside around the beginning of the last quarter of the 5th. century was the best hypothesis explaining the appearance of clasps in England. This particular migration would apparently be a unique course of influence between the two areas in going to Anglian England alone, and would

certainly be unique in that only in Anglian England were
the immigrants able to retain some of their character in
the success of a distinctive element of their womens'
dress. This hypothesis, however, was formed on the study
of the clasps alone, and it must now be re-assessed to see
if it makes sense in a broader archaeological and
historical context.

The essence of the migration hypothesis is that the
diffusion of the clasps implies the diffusion of a costume,
and that that is only likely to have occurred in tandem
with the movement of people who used that costume. A
sleeved woman's garment may have existed in Anglian England
before the introduction of the clasps, but that the clasps
could cross the North Sea by modes of exchange and
imitation only was thought improbable. It would render the
divergencies between the English and Scandinavian clasp
series even more extraordinary. If, however, the migration
hypothesis were true, then one might expect to find the
graves of first-generation immigrants looking like
"Norwegian" immigrants in England. But I know of no single
grave group from England which, if set as a test without
indication of provenance before an experienced eye, should
be mistaken for a find made in Norway. Especially
noticeable in this matter are certain classes of objects
through which Anglian England and Norway stand in stark and
unmitigated contrast. The pottery produced in the two
areas is vastly different, in spite of a couple of
similarities in certain features noted by Myres between
some southern English and Norwegian pots (Myres 1969 pp.48,
111). A few clasps found in Anglian England could be
imported, of Class A, form B 1, and the Willoughby-on-the-
Wolds examples of form C 1, but I am inclined to believe
that all known examples were made in England. There are
apparently no square-headed brooches, bracteates, cruciform
brooches, or Norwegian small bronze brooches imported to
Anglian England. But conversely it may be argued that if
trade were to be the preferred explanation of the parallels
on such objects between Anglian England and Scandinavia
then one might expect to find more, or at least some, such
imported objects, using "import" in Haseloff's sense
(Haseloff 1981 pp.285-287).

A comparison of details of burial rites recoverable
from Anglian England and Norway reveals some interesting
similarities, although to test the migration hypothesis
properly with this evidence would require a far more
detailed study than I have had the opportunity to
undertake, and a very thorough consideration at the
theoretical and analogical level of why and how a society's
burial rites may vary and change. The postulated
Scandinavian migration to eastern England was dated to the
beginning of the last quarter of the 5th. century, and this
appears to be the date when inhumation first established
itself as a widespread practice in Anglian England. No
single rite predominated in western Norway: both

inhumation and cremation, with various forms of grave-construction, were common in the Migration Period (Shetelig 1912 pp.69-160). Vierck has pointed out a few specific detailed parallels between burial forms in Anglian England and western Norway, i.e. the placing of both cremation and inhumation burials in stone-built cists, and cremation burials in bronze vessels (Vierck 1973 pp.29-34). Boat burial itself may be added to the parallels (Vierck 1973 pp.43ff.). A further similar detail is the lining of an inhumation grave with bark (Shetelig 1912 p.110), such as has also been observed in one grave at Welbeck Hill, Hu (personal communication, G. Taylor Esq.). But all of these instances are of details which are untypical of Anglian English graves in general. Only at Sleaford, Lincs does the use of stone "cists" for inhumations appear to have been a regular feature on the site, but Thomas unfortunately gives few useful details of what he means by "cist" in his publication, and their similarity to the Norwegian examples cannot be properly judged. Thomas indicates that the Sleaford examples were rough and crude, while the Norwegian examples are usually carefully constructed with large, flat stones set on edge (Thomas 1887; Shetelig 1912 p.110). It is of great interest and value in the present context that there is some positive evidence of Norwegian influence on Anglian English burial rites. But to attribute the adoption of inhumation in Anglian England to this hypothetical migration is to present a dubious post hoc ergo propter hoc argument. Western Scandinavia is not the only source from which inhumation could have been adopted in Anglian England, if a particular model is in fact needed. The English Angles in the later 5th. century had an inhuming Saxon population as their neighbours to the south, and whatever factors may have lead to the Saxons comprehensively adopting inhumation shortly after their settlement could later have affected the Angles. The cemetery at Sancton, Hu which was so prominent in the discussion of the earliest forms of clasps in England was predominantly a cremation cemetery.

It is not impossible to reconcile the migration hypothesis with the great abiding discrepancies between the archaeology of Anglian England and Norway in the Migration Period. The character of the migrants may have been of various forms. The lack of imported material in Anglian England is not a great problem: if the migrants were not the most successful elements of the population of Norway in the 5th. century then they may have had little to bring with them; beyond this, what metal objects were brought with them may have had to have been re-cycled for their metal content when old rather than abandoned in graves. Such a situation may be compared with the shortage of such material belonging to the earliest generations of previous settlers in England, the Jutes in Kent in particular.

But the successful introduction and rapid spread of the clasp-habit in Anglian England argues against our taking too humble a view of these postulated migrants. The most satisfactory alternative proposition appears to be that they were not numerous - hence the difficulty in finding an immigrant's grave - but influential, particularly in this one aspect of womens' costume. If this were the case, then one may argue that the immigrants' position of influence was concomitant with their social status. The evidence currently available indicates that wrist-clasps were first introduced in the Humberside and/or Norfolk area, and subsequently (rapidly) spread thence over the whole of the "Anglian province of culture". It is conceivable that it was the utilitarian attractions of a sleeved woman's garment with fastenable cuffs that caused this swift expansion of its range, but this does not seem an adequate explanation. It does not explain why the distribution of wrist-clasps in England should end so abruptly on sharply defined borders, which in the south coincide exactly with a border that is subsequently, in the later 6th. and earlier 7th. centuries, identifiable as a political border between kingdoms of the Angles to the north and Saxons to the south. We know that other cultural influences could cross this border, e.g. square-headed brooch features from the south (cf. Chapter 3). This implies that the clasps were indeed a token of a womens' costume which was a marker of group identity, and thus their function was not entirely utilitarian.

The migration hypothesis may thus be defended, although it must be conceded that being based on a single artefact-type, a female dress-accessory, its foundation is narrow, and one would wish for more supporting evidence. The migration of men from Scandinavia at this time would be difficult to detect archaeologically. Distinctive Scandinavian weapon forms are few, although any noticeable number of barbed spear-heads, arrows, or axes in Anglian English graves might be interpretable as a Scandinavian feature (Fett 1938-40). This does not however, to my knowledge, occur. But such finds are not especially numerous in Norway either, and burial practices with men may have shifted with the migration. One notes the enigmatic disappearance of men wearing clasps as the clasps' range is extended to Anglian England. The colonists may not have been in a position to expend their weapons, or the iron in them, as grave goods. There is still no disproof of the migration hypothesis here. The clasps, indeed, do not stand entirely alone as an example of Norwegian influence on Anglian England. Artefact-types which may have followed the same route at the same time are the Anglo-Scandinavian equal-armed brooches, and possibly the northern scutiform pendants with triskele motifs. The gusset plates may, however, be a later type to travel this route, in whichever direction, and likewise the influence leading to parallels on Anglian English and Norwegian square-headed brooches in the 6th. century. Norway also looks the most probable source of models for the Anglian English C-bracteates in the early 6th. century, but in this case South-East Norway rather than West. It is not a simple situation which can be inferred from this certainly fragmentary, and maybe sometimes misleading, surviving information.

The chronology of the various aspects of Scandinavian influence on Anglian England is of considerable importance in the evaluation of the migration hypothesis. That influence which is evidenced by the clasps is datable to the last quarter of the 5th. century, and early rather than later in that quarter. This is as early as any aspect of Scandinavian influence on Anglian England explicable through some form of commercial contacts, and clearly earlier than the most prominent examples of the commercial expansion or diffusion of Scandinavian culture which also occur on the continent, i.e. the square-headed brooches and the bracteates. If mercantile links had long been established between Norway and Anglian England then the proposition that the wrist-clasp was introduced by these means as a modification of a pre-existent Anglian womens' sleeved garment would be more credible. But it seems less plausible that the creation of demand for an entirely new artefact-type to fulfil an apparently hitherto unknown function should be the first result of the impact of Scandinavian craftsmen and traders on a new market, subsequent to which they noticeably influenced the form of accessories used in established functions. In general, it seems easier to cope with the objections to the migration hypothesis than to find a more satisfactory alternative explanation for the appearance of the clasps in Anglian England, and thus the migration hypothesis is supported here.

There is, of course, no particular historical evidence to support it. Bede's uncertain reference to Danai (Danes) who may have contributed to the settlement of England (HE V.9) has already been noted (Chapter 1, Introduction). As was shown there, Bede does not necessarily suggest that Danes were amongst the settlers, and even if that were the suggestion they were linked together here with some exotic names - e.g. the Huns - who can have played little or no direct part in the settlement. On the evidence reviewed above, Bede may have approximated to the truth here by accident, but we cannot claim that this statement in HE is a fragment of some valid tradition of a Scandinavian settlement. A second major influx of settlers to Anglian England in the early 6th. century, recorded in certain annals and histories (Davies 1977) attracts attention in this context. It is not, however, anywhere suggested that these immigrants were of Scandinavian origin, and their area of reception is limited to East Anglia and Mercia, with no apparent association with the Humberside area. Of limited significance though they are, the annalistic dates of this influx are also rather late for the appearance of women wearing clasps. O'Loughlin has also given evidence for the derivation of the East Anglian royal house from

Östergötland in Sweden (O'Loughlin 1964), and, on quite implausible grounds, suggests a further influx of <u>Geats</u> from the same area following this (cf. Farrell 1972 pp.29-52). Again this bears little resemblance to our archaeologically-based migration hypothesis.

It has repeatedly been stated that the Scandinavian character of Anglian England in the Migration period is not solely the result of influence from Norway, whether by means of migration or trade. Certain parallels between Anglian England and Norway could conceivably be the result of Anglian English influence on Norway: e.g. the gusset plates, and certain features of the later square-headed and relief brooches. Anglian England was also subject to quite definite and distinct influence from southern Scandinavia, principally the area around the Inner Skagerrak and Kattegat in Denmark. This emerges in the early square-headed brooches of Anglian England. The earliest bracteates here show a mixed continental Anglian and South Scandinavian character, but the early 6th.-century C-bracteates' sources look to be probably South Scandinavian. A Danish background to the bulk of Anglian England's scutiform pendants is absolutely clear. The southern Scandinavians seem to have been prolific in the dispersal of such objects towards the south and west in Europe, in Kent and West Germany in particular. It is therefore rather odd that the distribution of scutiform pendants in the Migration Period should be restricted to Anglian England outside of Scandinavia, but for one exception at Liebenau, Niedersachsen. This again must imply a peculiar relationship of Anglian England to Denmark, although does not in this case form grounds for suggesting a migration. Such a relationship might however fit the second migration discussed by Davies (Davies 1977, above) rather well ! In some details of Anglian English square-headed brooches and D-bracteates it is possible to detect Scandinavian influence on Anglian England mediated via Kent, while the later scutiform pendants appear to show Scandinavian influence on Kent via Anglian England. Anglian England and Kent also had a role to play in the diffusion of <u>Fibeln des nordischen Typs</u> on the continent. Particular channels of influence and exchange of elements within the Anglo-Scandinavian area of common development of the cruciform brooches were not investigated, but they are likely to be at least as multiplex as those listed above through which other artefact-types developed.

On Map 6.1 an attempt is made to summarise and clarify the variety of Anglo-Scandinavian contacts and relationship in the Migration Period as evidence by material considered in this study. It represents only a segment of the totality of relationships and contacts around the North Sea and involving Scandinavia at that time. Aspects of Saxon influence on England, and continental Anglian influence on England and Scandinavia could be added to the lines crossing the North Sea. The map also omits infra-

Scandinavian channels of influence, direct Scandinavian influence on continental Europe, and the complex external relationships of Frisia. The North Sea in the 5th. and 6th. centuries seems to have been a web of routes for migration, trade, and the diffusion of craftsmens' skills.

Archaeology provides circumstantial evidence for the existence of these routes. The peculiar relationship between Anglian England and western Norway implies the possibility of direct crossings of the North Sea between those areas. Our knowledge of the ships available to the Scandinavians and English at this period is very patchy (Sutton Hoo 1 pp.345-435; Ellmers 1978) but is certainly not such as to imply that any of these suggested routes was technically impossible or improbable at the time. For the direct crossing of the North Sea between western Norway and eastern England, the use of a sail would undoubtedly be an asset, and may have been available, although we do not as yet have decisive evidence for it. The sail is not, however, a <u>sine qua non</u>: rowing-boats can and could make the journey, although it may be suggested that under these conditions regular commercial contacts are less likely. One significant feature emerging from this map of routes, which run so far north in Norway, is that Scotland apparently has no connection with the network, which may be argued to enhance the case for navigation normally by coasting and relatively short sea-crossings, Humberside and Norfolk being reached from the northern Netherlands.

Historical "models" of different aspects of Anglo-Scandinavian and North Sea contacts in the Migration Period have been proposed by Åberg and Vierck, and these deserve some attention. Åberg's model emerges from his study of the historical relationships between the late Roman Period and the Migration Period, and the Migration Period and the Vendel Period (Åberg 1953; 1956). The evidence for Anglo-Scandinavian contact in the Migration Period he identified consisted of particular similarities in cruciform brooches, Style I on square-headed and relief brooches, and the occurrence of D-bracteates (Åberg 1953 pp.30-31). Åberg saw in these three archaeological periods the successive ascendencies of Sjælland, a "North Sea Block", and the Baltic region, in each case based on conditions of peace allowing the relevant area to organize and exploit long-distance trade (Åberg 1956 pp.210-211). He reckoned furs to be Scandinavia's major export commondity, and there is historical support for this from the 6th.-century Latin historian Jordanes, who mentions a northern <u>gens</u>, the <u>Suehans</u> (Swedes), as the source of <u>pelles</u> traded with the Roman world "per alias innumeras gentes" (via innumerable other peoples: Jordanes III.21). The historical event Åberg saw as creating the first watershed, between the late Roman and Migration Periods, was the assault of the Huns from the east on the Goths in the later 4th. century, breaking the so-called Gothic culture-channel (<u>kulturström</u>) in central Europe (Åberg 1953 p.23f.), while the second watershed was founded less dramatically, first upon the power of the Gepids in eastern Europe, and subsequently on the renascent strength of the Byzantine empire (Åberg 1953 pp.84-107). The key point in Åberg's views is that he saw trade as the life-blood of the North Sea block. This model is implicitly modified by my own interpretation of the material, through the addition of the postulation of a substantial movement of people: a migration from western Norway and widely-travelling craftsmen.

Before considering what sort of synthesis can or ought to be attempted between the interpretation proposed above and that of Åberg, Vierck's historical models should be introduced too. Vierck has proposed models of two aspects of Anglo-Scandinavian contact. There is firstly one to explain the parallels seen in bracteates, scutiform pendants, and clasps, and further artefact-types less thoroughly considered, in his B.Litt. thesis (Vierck 1966 pp.107-172). Vierck argued here for an indirect connection between Anglian England and Norway, thus simultaneously explaining both the similarities and the differences between the two areas. The connecting link was suggested to be the area of Schleswig-Holstein and South Scandinavia, with the characteristic Anglian English female dress style brought from that area by migration. Vierck considered the possibility of there having been two distinct groups immigrating from this broad area, a cremating group from the south, and an inhuming group from northern Jutland (Vierck 1966 pp.167-170), but did not commit himself to this hypothesis.

In an essay Zum Fernverkehr über See im 6. Jahrhundert angesichts angelsächsischer Fibelsätze in Thüringen (in Hauck 1970 pp.355-395), Vierck reviewed the evidence of exported English objects found on the continent and in Scandinavia. He noted a substantial corpus of exported Kentish material in Frankish Gaul and the Rhineland. The "English" objects found in Scandinavia, however, may be rather fewer than he suggests. In particular the disc brooches found in Scandinavia initially suggested by Arrhenius to be copied from English models (Vierck op.cit. p.371f.) are very doubtfully so. As Vierck concedes, their decoration and proportions are very different from the fairly numerous Migration Period Anglo-Saxon disc brooches. There are two further Danish examples of this Scandinavian type to be added to those noted by Vierck, from Østre Tørslev, Randers a., and Fruering, Skanderborgs a. (NMK C10077, C22889), unfortunately neither closely datable. This enhances a case for these brooches representing a scarce but native Scandinavian type. But there remain an English-looking bridle-mount found in Skåne, and the remains of two blue glass vessels of the late 6th. or early 7th. century from western Norway, and possible evidence for the influence of English metalworking styles and the presence of English craftsmen at Helgö. Vierck dated all of this English "influence" on Scandinavia post-550: in absolute terms this date could now be brought a little earlier, although the relative location of it late in the Migration Period remains. Vierck further argued that there is a significant consistency in the types in which the influence appears and in the areas associated by it: i.e. that the distribution of the relevant objects is coastal, associating Anglian England with Scandinavia, and thus coincident to a significant extent with bracteate distribution patterns. Like Åberg, he saw this dispersal of objects as a product of major trade routes principally concerned with the fur trade, but suggested that the blocking of a route from East Scandinavia towards the Mediterranean by the Avars in the mid-6th. century brought westerly trade routes into prominence.

I do not propose to make a full critical assessment of these broad historical models here, only to examine them where they touch upon England, and Anglian England in particular. It is particularly apparent how the correlation of detectable archaeological turning-points with specific historical events depends upon the accurate dating of the archaeological material. Vierck's model of increasing Scandinavian trade with the west in particular snags on the details of chronological argument. The major issue which Åberg's and Vierck's studies introduce which has not previously been considered in this work, is what part the fur trade may have played in developing a relationship and contacts between Anglian England and Scandinavia, with Norway in particular.

Denmark in the Migration Period would have been in no better position than England itself to be a significant supplier of animal pelts (cf. Brøndsted 1960 p.274), and it is further north in Scandinavia, in Norway and Sweden, that the source of traded furs would lie. There is evidence from the Migration Period of the expansion of settlement both northwards and inland in Norway, and the development of specialist hunting settlements, which may be taken as direct evidence of some expansion of Norway's fur trade (Hagen 1977 pp.265-278, and 292-294; Sjøvold 1962. esp. pp.213-240). It should be possible that it was the dynamism of the fur trade that initially set up the routes between Norway and Anglian England over the North Sea, and that consequently the tentatively identified migrants who crossed this route could have done so in order to establish this trade, and thus had a mercantile rather than a settlement-colonial character. Such a proposition might also agree happily with the suggestion that they were small in number but of considerable influence, and fit equally well with the subsequent extent of the exchange of metalworking craft ideas and motifs between England and Scandinavia.

But there are powerful reasons to doubt this proposition. Norway does seem to have expanded its hunting economy in the Migration period, and to have exported some of these products: we find precious objects coming into Norway in the Migration Period, e.g. gold to western Norway (Bøe 1921 pp.54-56, 1926 pp.83-94), and, slightly later on, English blue glass vessesls to Rogaland. But would Anglian England in the last quarter of the 5th. century want or have the wherewithal to import Norwegian furs ? Norway's Migration Period wealth of silver and gold can hardly have come from Anglian England, where such commodities appear to have been scarce. The area was agriculturally rich, especially relative to Norway, but at this time this would only be likely to attract settlers, not to produce a surplus of wealth exchangeable for luxury goods from Scandinavia. We know very little about the social and economic infrastructure of Anglian England at this time, but there is certainly no sign of emergent towns, ports, or powerful courts through which such mercantile folk could most easily hope to operate (cf. Hodges 1982, esp. Ch.2). A more attractive, but rather imaginative, alternative proposition is that the Anglian English could have shown themselves good middlemen in the North Sea trade, like the Frisians are so often reported as (but cf. Boeles 1951 pp.359ff.), trading with more plausible southerly markets. But such a proposition would rest only on a determination to attribute an essential role to the fur trade in early Anglo-Scandinavian contacts, and not on any direct archaeological or historical evidence.

To suggest that the parallels noted between Anglian England and South Scandinavia had much to do with the fur trade scarcely makes sense, since northern Scandinavia was the source of the trade, and there is no very good reason why South Scandinavia should have stood as an intermediary between Norway and Anglian England in it. In the 6th. century and later some trade in furs between Norway and Anglian England is not improbable, and may well be closely associated with the craft relationship visible in parallels on late square-headed and relief brooches. This, however, reduces the Scandinavian fur trade to a secondary and relatively insignificant role in the establishment (though not necessarily the maintenance) of Anglian England's close relationship with northern Scandinavia. Other impulses to the establishment of the relationship must be sought. The only necessary impulse to migration is that the migrants should believe that they will be in some way better off in the area that they move into. There is abundant evidence of growing population pressure on the land of western Norway in the later Roman Iron Age and Migration Period, marked partly by expansion of settlement onto agriculturally marginal land (Myhre 1978), and this, granted the accessibility of eastern England, is sufficient to explain the initial migration. Norway was not culturally isolated from the rest of Eruope, and the folk living in Norway should not have been ignorant of the activities and opportunities available in western Europe. For the supposed craftsmen's activities, all that is required are craftsmen with a marketable product and a desire to seek employment in an area that could support them to their satisfaction. The Geneva lead model of a Group II square-headed brooch may be direct evidence of one such craftsman, and we can readily accept that Anglian England, particularly in the 6th. century, fulfilled the conditions required for the attention of such artisans.

Reference to Åberg's consideration of the historical relationship between the Migration and Vendel Periods gives an opportunity here for the brief consideration of a possible historical explanation of one further major similarity between Anglian England and Scandinavia, and Anglian England and Norway in particular: the end of the Migration Period. In proposing a shift in Scandinavia's major external trade route(s) from the west to the east as the direct cause of this, Åberg may be said to propose a rather mechanical, commercial explanation of the relationship between the two periods. But while such practical matters may be of determinative significance in the _form_ of the culture of the two periods, they do not necessarily adequately explain the _character_ of the culture of the Migration and the succeeding period. If some significant change in this between the two periods is detectable, then it may lead us to a more profound conception of the nature of the critical changes that took place.

Let us first review the features that Anglian England and Scandinavia have in common in the Migration Period, as they appear in material considered in detail in this study. The two areas make use of common art styles, Style I above all, but with an additional degree of commonality between Anglian England and Norway in the use of a "bichrome style". Artefact-types that the two areas have been shown to have in common, which disappear at the end of the Migration Period, are clasps of Classes A-C, square-headed and relief brooches, A-, C-, and D-bracteates, and cruciform brooches, although the latter disappear earlier in Scandinavia than in Anglian England, particularly, it seems in Denmark. A common features of all of these artefact-types is that they belong principally to a particular form of female costume, which is consequently rather heavily decked in its richer manifestations, and certainly appears so in contrast with the fewer and finer dress-accessories of the costume of the later period in England. There appears to be a significant similarity in the disposition of these artefact-types around the dress in the two areas (Vierck 1978 pp.245-253). A significant similarity may also be seen in the burial practices of Anglian England and Scandinavia. This is not so much in the details of the relative preponderance of inhumation or cremation, or aspects of the actual construction of the grave (see above), but in the nature and volume of grave goods expended in the burial. Anglian England is especially similar to western Norway in this regard. Danish Migration Period grave furnishings are markedly less lavish, particularly in the 6th. century. The practices in Sweden and to some extent eastern Norway are harder to ascertain clearly relative to western Norway because of the predominance of cremation, but the range of female dress-accessories evidenced in Central Swedish cremation burials coincides closely with those from western Norway, and relatively few Swedish Migration Period inhumation graves are essentially of a common character with those of Norway.

In the period succeeding the Migration period, Style II and complex forms of ribbon interlace succeed Style I in Anglian England and Scandinavia. A new characteristic range of artefact-types appears in both areas. In Scandinavia these are best known from Norway and Sweden: Denmark has produced very, very few finds. A number of the new artefact-types in Anglian England and Scandinavia appear to be continuations of artefact-types present in the Migration Period, although generally modified to some degree. The one artefact-type which appears to change least across this period-division is the scutiform pendant in England. There is little general similarity between the artefact-types in this later period in England and those of the Merovingian and Vendel Periods in Norway and Sweden, other than in the art styles applied to them, and in the development of techniques such as cloisonné cell work. But it may be argued that they show a common initial shift towards simplicity and elegance of design. As an example may be cited the small early Scandinavian disc-on-bow brooches, with their clarity of line and isolated panels of ornament, apparently a radical re-design of the old relief brooches in accordance with the new taste (cf. Nerman 1969 Taff.5-10).

At the end of the Migration Period the tally of rich furnished graves in both Anglian England and Norway suddenly drops. The geographical distribution of the richer grave-finds in the later period is noticeably different from that in the earlier. If we take, for instance, the distribution of disc-on-bow brooches in Norway, it appears that the easterly and northerly fylker, Akershus, Hedmark, Oppland, Nord- and Sør-Trøndelag and Nordland, are particularly productive of these brooches (cf. Gjessing 1934 p.143), in contrast to the areas of particular density in producing such characteristic Migration Period artefacts as relief brooches, clasps, and cruciform brooches (cf. List 2.1). In Anglian England an example may be cited of the later examples of simple and composite disc and scutiform pendants, which occur largely towards and around the margins of the old "Anglian province of culture" in Cambridgeshire and Bedfordshire to the south, Derbyshire to the west and Humberside and North Yorkshire to the north (see Chaper 4, Map 4.4). Denmark, however, does not show any such falling off in the volume of grave goods deposited at the end of the Migration Period, because the comparable provision of grave goods appears to have ceased there much earlier. In central

Sweden and Gotland, by contrast, the furnishing of the majority of graves in the Vendel Period seems to be quite consistent with, and certainly no less lavish than, the habits of the Migration Period.

It is thus in Anglian England and Norway that we have the closest correspondences in changes, though not necessarily the same changes, in art styles, the range of artefact-types, and burial practices, at the end of the Migration Period. The correspondence between the two areas is sufficiently close to invite consideration of a possible common reason for the change in either area.

The end of the archaeological Migration Period in Anglian England and Scandinavia was dated in Chapter 1 to the second half of the 6th. century, approximately to the 560s. This is very broadly the period in England when the kingdoms of the English emerge from the vagaries of legend into the dim light on the margins of reliable history (cf. Stenton 1943 pp.1-95; Bede HE I.23 et seq.). The process of the conversion of the English to christianity began at the end of the 6th. century, and was clearly a process which followed on, and was connected to, the establishment, maintenance, and strengthening of the kingdoms (Mayr-Harting 1972 pp.11-113). It was this conversion which Hyslop suggested was responsible for the dress change visible in the "late cemeteries" (Hyslop 1963). But the earlier graves which characterize the culture of the later period - the "7th. century" in outdated terms - are often of an aristocratic rather than a christian nature. At Sutton Hoo we have what is generally believed to be a king's burial, and barrow burials such as Caenby, Lincs and Taplow, Bucks are conspicuously rich, the latter including in its furnishings a clear emphasis on the trappings and hospitality of the noble hall. To a large extent these conspicuously prestigious burials, especially the richest ones, may be argued to mark or dominate the edges of areas of settlement or domination, either against other areas of land or against the sea (cf. Davies and Vierck 1974 esp. fig.5). The same may be claimed for the most prominent Vendel Period burials at Vendel, Vålsgårde, Gamla Uppsala, etc., in Uppland, Sweden (although cf. Ambrosiani 1980). The elegance, wealth, and relative scarcity of the characteristic finds of the later period in England look like marks of social exclusivity. It may therefore be suggested that it was a social change that lay behind the cultural turning point between the Migration Period and the succeeding period in Anglian England, and that the conversion to christianity was itself a cultural symptom of this same social development.

A proposition concerning the nature of the historical relationship between the Migration Period and its succeeding periods, especially in England and Norway, may be formulated as follows. The Migration Period is aptly named. Its culture has in some aspects the character of

284

demonstrating wealth and power, through the decking-out of the womenfolk with conspicuous dress-accessories, whose forms appear to some extent to have been markers of group identity, and through the emphatic expenditure of grave goods in the burials of a wide section of the society. Such a culture would be particularly appropriate at a time and in areas subject to demongraphic and social flux. As this flux diminished with the progress of the 6th. century, a new social structure emerged, more stable, controlled and aristocratic, visible at the top level in the emergent kingdoms of the Engish so-called heptarchy. In this changed society it was the smaller numbers of rulers who needed to express their prestige within larger areas through burial practices, either through rich barrow burials, or later through being buried within the churches or cathedrals. This is not to suggest that, although historically unknown, the same political developments took place in Norway as in England, only that both areas show the replacement of a truly "Migration-Period" culture by the culture of a demographically settled population. Myhre notes a period of stagnation in the settlement evidence of South-West Norway after the Migration period (Myhre 1978). One might argue that the widespread use of an expressive burial rite re-emerges with a new "migration-type" culture in Viking Age Scandinavia, significantly to be rapidly abandoned by Scandinavian settlers in England.

This all-too-brief, preliminary consideration of the question of the historical relationship between these cultural periods of early medieval England and Scandinavia takes the implications of the research presented in this study beyond the simply practical issues of the lines and modes of contact between Anglian England and Scandinavia in the Migration Period, and into the problems of the relationship between the form of material culture and the psychological and social factors that may lie behind it. No research should terminate a topic, and perhaps these issues, and the proposition outlined above, would be the most rewarding line to pursue in the future. Examination of this hypothesis, however, must rest on the detailed archaeological evidence from England, Scandinavia, and northern Europe, of the post-Roman period.

CHAPTER 7

SUTTON HOO, AND THE SEVENTH AND EIGHTH CENTURIES

The main contribution of this study to our picture of the North Sea area in the early Medieval period lies in establishing that there were extensive and significant connections between Anglian England and Scandinavia in the Migration Period. This final chapter is intended to form an epilogue to the main body of the study, a chapter in which consideration is given to the question of what happened to the earlier Anglo-Scandinavian links in the centuries between the end of the Migration Period and the Viking Period. This period of something like 230 years is longer in absolute terms than the Migration Period, but a single chapter is sufficient to cover it because the relevant material from this period is much scarcer. What material there is has been the subject of recent and thorough studies, and it would be presumptuous to consider a wholesale re-evaluation of this necessary. I therefore seek here to set the results of others' up-to-date work, with due critical circumspection, within the context of my own work presented in Chapters 1-6.

Passing beyond the end of the Migration Period in Anglian England we come to a topic which hitherto has come to dominate most archaeologists' and historians' perceptions of pre-Viking Anglo-Scandinavian contacts across or around the North Sea: Sutton Hoo, and the major excavated ship burial there in particular. Since the end of the last war, a number of similarities have been observed between this grave and a series of prominent burials of the earlier Vendel period in Uppland, north of Lake Mälaren in Central Sweden. These similarities comprise both individual items from within the grave, and its whole form and composition.

Three pieces of armour from the Sutton Hoo ship burial have particularly attracted attention for appearing "Swedish" in some sense: the sword, the shield, and the helmet. At some time, each has been claimed to be a Swedish product, imported to East Anglia (cf. Bruce-Mitford 1974 pp.35-55). Such a claim has, however, now been disproved for the sword. As Bruce-Mitford pointed out (loc.cit.), the gold, cloisonné-decorated hilt and pommel of this sword have equally close parallels from both Central Sweden and continental Europe. Analysis has now shown that the cement holding the garnets in the cells of the studs that go with the sword is of a type of Frankish origin (cf. Wilson 1980 p.214). The shield and the helmet from the Sutton Hoo grave, however, have some very close parallels from Central Sweden (Bruce-Mitford op.cit.; Sutton Hoo 2 pp.91-99, 205-225), and while discrepancies between Sutton Hoo and Uppland may still be found on these items, as, for instance, in the neck- an cheek-pieces of the helmet, nothing so similar has as yet been discovered on the continent, despite Wilson's scepticism (Wilson 1980 pp.214-216). Yet it must be conceded that both the Sutton Hoo helmet and the helmets from Vendel and Valsgärde are derivative of certain forms of late Roman parade helmet, and that in some respects the Sutton Hoo helmet may be more closely related to these earlier models than to the known Swedish examples. All the techniques used in the making of the Sutton Hoo helmet, including the making of the very Swedish-looking repoussé decorative plates, can be paralleled from elsewhere in England. We cannot therefore reject Wilson's provocatively put arguments that the Sutton Hoo shield and helmet could have been made in England, and need not have been made in Sweden. But is it probable that their close similarities could be derived from some third place, a common source which we are unable actually to identify, without any Anglo-Swedish connection ? The combination of more than one such similar object may be suggested to argue against this. Bruce-Mitford's unchallenged identification of the use of a "beaded elbow" in cloisonné work as a singular parallel between the Sutton Hoo workshop and Vendel Period Uppland (Bruce-Mitford 1974 pp.40-41) may be evidence of an exchange of techniques between the craftsmen of eastern England and Vendel Period Sweden.

There can be no doubt that boat burial itself is a peculiarly Anglo-Scandinavian phenomenon (Müller-Wille 1970 pp.42ff.). Boat graves from the Roman Iron Age in northern Europe are known only from Bornholm. In the later Migration Period and in the succeeding period the practice becomes more widespread. Müller-Wille identifies 6 probable Migration Period boat burials, 5 from the Norwegian coast, and 1 from Sweden (Müller-Wille 1970 pp.43-45). The best dated of these examples is a grave from Skogøya, Steigen, No on the north-west coast of Norway which included three cruciform brooches of Reichstein's "späte" Typ Skogøya, and is thereby datable to VWZ III (Reichstein 1975 no.317). Müller-Wille notes a further 7, more doubtful, Migration Period examples from the Norwegian coast (loc.cit.). A boat grave from southern Sweden, at Augerum, Blekinge, has been studied by Arrhenius, dated by her to the transitional stage between the Migration and Vendel Periods (Arrhenius 1960). The Vendel Period boat graves of Central Sweden form a series whose starting-point Arrhenius has recently dated to ca.560 (Arrhenius 1980). Boat burial makes its earliest known appearance in eastern England in the Snape boat burial (Bruce-Mitford 1974 pp.114-140). This included a finger-ring and a claw-beaker amongst its grave-goods, which on the basis of certain continental parallels would allow the grave a date as early as the middle of the 6th. century, although Bruce-Mitford is unwilling to date the burial earlier than the first quarter of the 7th. A second boat burial is already known from Sutton Hoo (Sutton Hoo 1 pp.100-136), and it is

expected that more will be found in the forthcoming
excavations there. Boat burial therefore seems to have
been quite well-known in Scandinavia, and not improbably in
England too, by the time the famous Sutton Hoo boat burial
was made; it will be interesting to see if any further
examples at that site can be reliably dated earlier than
that grave. It appears, however, that the practice may
first flourish in the Migration Period on the west coast of
Norway. As the boat burial at Snape - and further finds at
Sutton Hoo - may be datable as early as when the practice
establishes itself in Central Sweden it may be the case
that the practice reached England from Norway rather than
Central Sweden (cf. Vierck 1973 pp.43-44). However
Vierck's attempt, in that paper, to interpret the Sutton
Hoo ship burial as West Scandinavian rests on the
contentious view that the grave contained a cremation
burial.

To put the issue in the terms used up to now in this
study, it is clear that there is at least a Scandinavian,
partially Swedish, character to the Sutton Hoo ship burial,
and an explanation must be sought for it. Bruce-Mitford
makes it clear that what we have in this grave is not a
unique and isolated deposit of material of Scandinavian
character, having descended in some sealed unit on a single
spot, but that the "Swedish element" is one which
"actively permeates the Anglo-Saxon milieu" (Bruce-Mitford
1974 p.55). Bruce-Mitford and his research team have of
course identified many more parallels between Sutton Hoo
finds and Swedish objects than those noted above, e.g.
further details of cloisonné work, the man-between-beasts
motif of the Sutton Hoo purse lid and the Torslunda, Öland
dies, the whetstone-sceptre, and the Sutton Hoo "shield-
ring" (Bruce-Mitford 1974 pp.40-46). Similar Swedish
parallels have been noted for a buckle found in Finglesham,
Kt (Hawkes et al. 1965 pp.17-23). The Sutton Hoo ship
burial thus appears as a 7th.-century representative of the
foreign connections of this post-Migration Period English
culture, foreign connections which affected England over a
broad front and which can be traced back considerably
earlier than the now-accepted date of the ship burial in
the 620s. Realization of this point puts into perspective,
and diminishes the significance of, the question of whether
the Sutton Hoo helmet and shield were made in England under
Swedish influence or made in Sweden, or whether,
conversely, the similar Swedish finds are there as a result
of English influence.

Bruce-Mitford's preferred historical explanation of
the Scandinavian character of Sutton Hoo was to suggest
that the known East Anglian royal house of the period, the
Wuffingas, was of Swedish origin, and succeeded in
establishing control over East Anglia in the mid 6th.
century (Bruce-Mitford 1974 pp.55-60). O'Loughlin, from a
study of documentary material, suggested that the Wuffing
dynasty had its origins in Östergötland (O'Loughlin 1964).

This area, however, is to the south of Uppland, the area where the Sutton Hoo ship burial's archaeological parallels are concentrated, separated from it by Lake Mälaren and the tract of Södermanland. O'Loughlin fancifully met this problem by suggesting that the Sutton Hoo finds included booty taken from the Uppland Swedes by the Gautar of -Götland before being driven out to join the Wuffingas in East Anglia. Farrell's firm criticism of the very slender bases of O'Loughlin's conclusions has already been referred to in the last chapter (Farrell 1972). The possible West Scandinavian associations of the practice of boat burial makes the Swedish dynastic explanation of the Sutton Hoo finds look rather weak. Implicit in the inclination to seek a dynastic connection to explain Sutton Hoo appears to be the assumption that the Scandinavian character of the Sutton Hoo royalty was unique to them. But we do not at present know, and may not assume, that it was necessarily different in this respect from other Anglian English royal houses at this time, or indeed from other Anglo-Saxon royal houses. We have not found the pagan burials of Northumbrian or Mercian kings from this period which might be compared with what is probably Redwald of East Anglia's grave. As far as we can tell from our historical records no Kentish king died pagan after Eormenric in ca.560 (Bede HE II.5). The supposition, then, that Sutton Hoo is the burial place of a royal house of Swedish origins in East Anglia is not a persuasive one.

A recently discovered late 7th.- or early 8th.-century helmet from York (Addyman et al. 1982) has marked similarities to the Sutton Hoo and Vendel period Swedish helmets, although it is clear that its inscribed crest is English work with an ecclesiastical character. The name in the inscription is Oshere, and Os- is a particularly common first element amongst the names of the Northumbrian royalty, although no Oshere has yet been identified in the area at the appropriate time. The helmet is a later descendant of the tradition that produced the Sutton Hoo, Vendel, and Valsgärde helmets. A fragment of a repoussé decorated plate from Caenby, Lincs (Bruce-Mitford 1974 pl.54b) may well have belonged to a similar helmet. If either the possibility or the probability of there being some direct relationship between these English finds and those of Vendel Period Sweden is accepted, then these more northerly examples strengthen the case that the channels of influence between England and Sweden operated more widely than between Uppland and Rendlesham alone. The Sutton Hoo finds should also be considered in the light of the introduction of Style II craftsmanship to Anglian England. Speake, after an extensive study of Anglo-Saxon Style II work, has recently come out in favour of a Scandinavian origin for East Anglian Style II, perhaps, he suggests, through "Swedish craftsmen actually working at the royal court of the Wuffinga dynasty" (Speake 1980 p.94). He does not, however, claim to have proved this. Speake would derive Style II in Kent initially from more westerly

Scandinavian/Jutish impulses, with Kent rapidly developing her own distinctive form of the style (Speake 1980 pp.95-96).

Unless boat burial was first practised in England, or spontaneously and independently developed there - and there is no good reason to think that it was - then its adoption in East Anglia shows the imitation of a prestigious burial form known to be practised elsewhere, and therfore implies a familiarity with Scandinavia. The evidence which has been assembled in the preceding six chapters demonstrates the probability of there being such familiarity in the later Migration period. The source of the practice in East Anglia could have been either Norway or East Scandinavia, and on the basis of the range of Anglian England's earlier contacts with Scandinavia (see Map 6.1), and the possible mid 6th.-century dates for some East Anglian boat burials, the former may be more likely. For all of the artefact parallels between Sutton Hoo and the rest of Anglian England and Vendel Period Scandinavia, and the extension of the range of Style II to Anglian England, we can postulate, along with Speake, the activities of travelling craftsmen, little different from those who have already been suggested to be responsible for a significant number of earlier correspondencies between the two areas in Migration Period metalwork. The differences would simply have been that after the changes associated with the end of the Migration Period, these craftsmen were now producing different wares for patrons of a different character in accordance with a new taste and style.

Some of the Scandinavian aspects of Sutton Hoo, and East Anglia's Style II connections, appear to show a shift in one end of the line of contact between Anglian England and Scandinavia from western Scandinavia (Denmark, south Sweden, and Norway) to eastern Scandinavia (Central Sweden and the Baltic area). This is not, of course, the earliest evidence for contacts between the craftsmen of eastern England and Central Sweden (cf. Vierck in Hauck 1970 pp.371, 375-380), but there is a definite change in that after the end of the Migration Period it is virtually exclusively in the more easterly area of Scandinavia that we can look for parallels to Anglian English artefact finds. This reflects simply the "flourishing" of the Uppland region at the transition from the Migration Period to the Vendel Period and the concomitant "decline" of western Scandinavia: a reversal of the tyngdepunktforskjutning (shift in the centre of gravity) from the Baltic side to the North Sea Block, as delineated by Åberg as the essence of the transition from the late Roman to the Migration Period (Åberg 1953). An emergent Swedish kingdom based on Uppland, together with Gotland, seem to have come to dominate the remainder of Scandinavia culturally, probably economically, and possibly politically too. The distribution of disc-on-bow brooches in Norway may indiciate a shift in wealth and power there in the

Merovingian Period, away from the South-West towards the areas bordering on Sweden (Gjessing 1934 pp.142-143; cf. Chapter 6). The Vendel period prominence of Sweden in Scandinavian archaeology does not, probably, reflect only a situation in which the folk in the west were amassing and retaining their wealth, but a genuine stagnation in Norway and Denmark, the situation which Myhre has also identified in the settlement evidence of South-West Norway (Myhre 1978 pp.261-265). It may perhaps be suggested that the social and political developments which were suggested at the end of Chapter 6 to underlie the transition from the archaeological Migration Period to its succeeding periods in England and Scandinavia in some way succeeded in England and Central Sweden but failed in Norway. Why, however, below the aristocratic level of the boat graves, Central Sweden and Gotland continue in the Vendel Period with burial habits, and sometimes burial sites, unchanged from the Migration Period, is a question that would require an answer in the light of the proposition concerning the relationship between the Migration and Vendel Periods made at the end of Chapter 6. But to seek to answer this question would involve a substantial digression at this stage; it is sufficient to acknowledge it here.

Evidence of continuing Anglo-Scandinavian contacts after the end of the Migration Period in the form of English objects found in Scandinavia is very slight. Two English blue glass squat jars, probably of Kentish manufacture, dated to the late 6th. or earlier 7th. centuries, found in South-West Norway, suggest that the North Sea route between eastern England and western Norway may have continued in being to this date (Sutton Hoo 1 pp.132-134). Even if western Norway's fortunes were declining, some volume of fur trading over this route at this date should be quite possible. But other than these, there is maybe only one other rather doubtful find of an Engish object from Merovingian or Vendel Period Scandinavia, a bronze gilt mount from Skrøppa, Breim, SFj, N (Bakka 1963 pp.55-57). This was found in association in a barrow with a 7th.-century conical brooch (cf. Gjessing 1934 pp.124-127), but it is not certain that the two belonged to a single closed context. Bakka and Wilson would prefer to date the Skrøppa disc to the 8th. or early 9th. centuries, making it more probable that it was Viking Period booty, eventually buried in a grave-mound containing an earlier burial with the conical brooch.

After the Sutton Hoo ship burial in the 7th. and 8th. centuries the archaeological evidence for direct Anglo-Scandinavian contacts fades away. There is no further evidence of Scandinavian or Scandinavian-influenced objects in England. The evidence for Scandinavia's trading relationship with North Sea areas in the 8th. century seems to be neatly encapsulated by Bendixen's recent review of sceatt- and other early coin-finds from Scandinavia in the light of recent excavations in the town of Ribe, in southern Jutland (Bendixen 1981). She shows that the 8th.-century coins have been found relatively plentifully from the south of Jutland, Schleswig-Holstein, and the East Frisian islands, but, most tellingly, all of the sceattas discovered in the Ribe excavations are Frisian, and none of them English. In Scandinavia north of Ribe only three coins have been found: a late 7th.-century Merovingian triens struck at Dorestadt from northern Jutland; a Frisian sceatt from Helgö in Uppland; and one English coin, a Northumbrian sceatt struck in ca.750-758 for Archbishop Ecgberht of York, from Ervik on the coast of Sogn og Fjordane in western Norway. But the find-context of this last coin is highly unusual: it was found in shifting sand on a sea-shore, not far from where a wide range of other antiquities of diverse dates have been found. It is quite likely that it came from a collection of antiquities lost at sea and washed up at this point (Skaare 1976 pp.42-43 and 158).

But documentary evidence of the 8th. century, when carefully read, provides persuasive contemporary witness of some form of continuing Anglo-Scandinavian contacts over the North Sea. At first sight, Bede shows no interest in or even knowledge of Scandinavia in his Historia Ecclesiastica Gentis Anglorum. Scandinavia does not appear in Bede's quite lengthy description of Britain's geographical circumstances (HE I.1), and, as has already been shown, Bede shows no certain knowledge of the presence of folk from Scandinavia at any stage amongst the settlers of England (see Chapter 6). The Scandinavians barely figure amongst the pagan Germans who were the objects of English missionary activities overseas (cf. HE V.9-11). These activities seem to have been concentrated on the Frisians and continental Saxons, although Bede does once mention the Danai (Danes) amongst the pagan Germans in connection with Ecgberht's missionary plans (HE V.9), perhaps because he knew they were subsequently briefly visited by Willibrord, probably in the South Jutland area (Alcuin VSW 9-10). But in his commentary on IV Kings XX.9 (Bede ILR I.25), he relates:

> Nam et hoc qui in insula Thyle, quae ultra Britanniam est, vel in ultimis Scytharum finibus degunt, omni aestate diebus aliquot fieri vident; quia sol caetero orbi in occasu et sub terra positus, ipsis nihilominus tota nocte supra terram appareat; et quomodo a parte occidentis ad orientem humilis redeat, manifeste videatur, donec tempore opportuno denuo toto orbi communi exortu reddatur, sicut et veterum historiae, et nostri homines aevi, qui illis de partibus adveniunt, abundantissime produnt.

(Opera Omnia, ed. J.A. Giles, vol.VIII, 1844)

... also, those who live on the island of Thyle, which
is beyond Britain, and on the extreme boundaries of
the Scythians, see this thing to happen on a number of
days every summer: that the sun, being set and placed
beneath the earth in another region, is nevertheless
visible to them above the earth all night, and the
manner in which it returns, low-down, from its
setting-place to the east is plainly seen, until at
the appropriate time it is restored once more to the
whole world in rising for all, as both the tales of
old men, and men of our own time who come from these
parts, abundantly relate.

Thyle is more likely to refer to the Shetland Islands than
Iceland, although Iceland may have been visited by Irish
peregrinati by this time, but this clear testimony of the
midnight sun must come from arctic regions, and the only
realistic source is arctic Norway. Bede's geographical
reference to the area "in ultimis Scytharum finibus" may
indeed by interpreted to support this, as he may have
confused the classical Scythia, an area by the Black Sea,
with the area of Skåne , Scedenig in Old English. We can
only conclude that in the earlier 8th. century there were
folk who visited both arctic Scandinavia and Bede's
Northumbria, perhaps like Ohthere who visited the court of
Alfred in the late 9th. century (OE Orosius I.1).

Documentary sources giving a contemporary reaction to
the first recorded Viking raids on England at the end of
the 8th. century do not suggest that these attackers were a
hitherto unknown or forgotten people. The exact meaning of
Alcuin's reference to the raid on Lindisfarne in his letter
to King Ethelred of Northumbria (Dümmler no.22; EHD I
no.193) is unclear:

> ... numquam talis terror prius apparuit in Britannia
> veluti modo a pagani gente percussi sumus, nec eius
> modi navigium fieri posse putabatur.

> ... never before has such a terror appeared in Britain
> as we have just suffered from a pagan people, nor was
> it thought possible that a "navigium" of this kind
> could be made.

navigium could mean either the journey from Scandinavia,
or, more specifically, the attack from the sea. We cannot
tell what exactly Alcuin was referring to by eius modi.
That it was not simply the appearance of unknown people
from an unexpected quarter that shocked Alcuin is indicated
by a later passage in the same letter which implies a
remarkable degree of familiarity with this pagan "gens":

> Considerate habitum, tonsuram, et mores principum et
> populi luxuriosus. Ecce tonsura, quam in barbis et in
> capillis paganis adsimilari voluistis. Nonne illorum
> terror imminet quorum tonsuram habere voluistis ?

Consider the dress, the hair-style, and the luxurious habits of the princes and people. Look at the hair-style, how you have wished to imitate the pagans in your beards and hair. Does not the terror threaten of those whose hair-style you wished to have ?

This is a clear and detailed reference to a popular vogue "paganis adsimilari", a reference that would be pointless if these "pagani" were not the Northmen and the accusation to some degree recognizably valid. Further letters of Alcuin, to Wearmouth-Jarrow and Canterbury (e.g. Dümmler nos.27 and 86), show the knowledge or expectation of extensive Scandinavian activity around the English coast, implying that the two late 8th.-century Viking raids on Dorset and Lindisfarne were not haphazard and isolated portents of the coming Viking infestation of the North Sea in the 9th. century. The Chronicle entry for 787 describing the Dorset incident and the death of the Dorchester port-reeve includes the observation, added with hindsight:

þæt wæron þa ærestan scipu Deniscra monna þe Angel cynnes lond gesohton

The verb <u>gesecan</u> may be interpreted "to attack" rather than simply "to seek, to come to", whereby the comment may read:

those were the first ships of the Danes which <u>attacked</u> the land of the English.

What was new was that the Scandinavians were no longer traders, but raiders.

There is thus no reason to suppose that the West Scandinavian-East English contacts across the North Sea were ever lost in the later 7th. and 8th. centuries, although they may have become very much attenuated, and so insignificant that Bede could ignore them in <u>HE</u>. But irrespective of the character of the continuing Anglo-Scandinavian links in this period, a different and rewarding issue to consider is that of how far Anglian English culture of the 7th. and 8th. centuries reflected the Scandinavian contacts and the Scandinavian character of Anglian England in the Migration Period.

In the 7th. century, the established Germanic culture of Anglian England was washed over by the flood-tides of Hibernian christian culture from the North-West, and Mediterranean christian culture from the South. The new religion did not favour furnished burial, and offered, albeit grudgingly and through various forms of compromise, the highest social classes who adhered to it an alternative form of prestigious burial through burial within churches or cathedrals. The monuments which christianity sought to create and bequeath to succeeding generations, churches, stone crosses, books, and manuscript art, were media in which older Germanic forms of expression had never existed, and which those forms of expression were faced with the problem of invading if they were to survive. Style II did indeed succeed in penetrating Hiberno-Saxon manuscript art, as in the Book of Durrow (cf. Speake 1980 pp.43-45).

Christianity introduced opportunities for written literary expression to England far beyond the scope of anything formerly attempted in the terse runic texts. For the most part, of course, literary activity in England was dominated by Latin ecclesiastical culture, but at some stage the ancient Germanic traditions of oral history and poetry (cf. Tacitus Germ 2) moved into written modes. It may be possible to discover in secular Anglo-Saxon poetry signs of pre-Viking period English literature displaying some inheritance from earlier Anglo-Scandinavian connections. The major work to consider in this light is Beowulf. This s an Anglo-Saxon poem of some length (3182 lines in Klaeber's edition), set in the 6th. century in Demark and southern and central Sweden. The hero of the poem, Beowulf, is identified as belonging to a people called the Geatas, the same name as ON Gautar, a folk-name which has descended to us in the place-names Öster- and Västergötland in Sweden. Other major peoples figuring prominently in the ambient of Beowulf's deeds are the Dene (Danes) and the Sweon (Swedes). Minor groups referred to, identifiable as associable with the same area, are the Heaþo-Ræmas, the Heaþo-Ream[as] of the OE poem Widsith, a name equivalent to ON Raumar, whose name survives in that of the region of Romerike in southern Norway, and the Gifðas, Widsith: Gefðas, the Gepids, a tribe once living at the mouth of the Wisła on the Baltic. The composition of Beowulf thus shows a clear knowledge of, and an expectation that the audience will be interested in, southern Scandinavia. It is not unparalleled for Germanic literature to relate tales to exotic peoples, culturally distant and geographically separated from the folk amongst whom the literature emerges, as in the Norse tales of the Goths, the Huns, and the Burgundians, but here definite historical contacts and channels via which the material of the tales would be transmitted can be identified (Dronke 1969 pp.28-34).

One of the most contentious and recurrent issues in Beowulf-studies is the question of its date. The issue of what is meant by "the date of Beowulf" is itself a complex one. In one sense, Beowulf can have only one date, the date of the manuscript of the single extant Anglo-Saxon copy of the poem, palaeographically established as ca.1000. But most discussion of the poem accepts what may be called a "single-author theory": the view that Beowulf is for the most part the composition of a single poet, composed within some definite period and committed to writing or to memory, and that if the extant copy is later than this only minor and effectively negligible alterations and interpolations will have been made in the text in the period between composition and manuscript copy. The following discussion of the poem will proceed on this basis. An argument that the date of composition of the poem is the same as that of the manuscript has recently been mounted (Kiernan in Chase ed. 1981), but this argument has been shown to be doubtful (Boyle in Chase ed. 1981), and is not the received view. The question most Old English scholars reach and seek to answer is how much earlier than the manuscript the poem may be. The most recent collection of varying views on this subject, although not presenting a complete cross-section (Chase ed. 1981), shows essentially a division of opinion into "earlier" and "later" camps. In effect these may be regarded as those who argue that Beowulf is a pre-Viking Period composition, or a Viking-Period composition, respectively.

I do not propose to offer a direct answer to this question here. It is not the present concern to argue in full the case for the single-author theory, and subsequently for a particular date of composition. What may be usefully demonstrated, however, is that much of the material of which Beowulf is composed is very much earlier than the manuscript. While the manuscript provides a terminus ante quem for the poem at ca.1000, the terminus post quem provided by the substance of the poem is at least 300 years earlier.

The poem is set in the 6th. century. It contains a reference to King Hygelac's death in a raid on Frisia, an event which can be identified with that recorded by Gregory of Tours as the raid of one Chlochilaic in 521 (HF III.3). Beowulf subsequently ruled the Geats for a long time (50 years) until his death fighting the dragon, which closes the poem. The latest sure terminus post quem in the poem, however, appears to be the poet's christianity - he knows and refers to Biblical tales - which means that the poem could at the earliest have been composed in the 7th. century, but is most unlikely to have been composed before the late 7th. century. Bede may imply that it was after Cædmon, in the period 650-679, that "others amongst the English people attempted to compose religious poems" (HE IV.24). Goffart (in Chase ed. 1981) has, however, suggested that in the details of Hygelac's raid on Frisia, Beowulf follows a recension of Gregory of Tours' Historia Francorum which could not have been known in England before the 730's. This may advance a terminus post quem from the late 7th. to the mid 8th. century, although Goffart's case would be more persuasive if he explained more fully his disbelief in a common (poetic) source lying behind both this recension and Beowulf (cf. Chase ed. 1981 p.87).

In an English context, the archaeological horizon of Beowulf reflects the later 6th. and 7th. centuries with a striking consistency. Beowulf's burial at the end of the poem is unmistakably pagan: his body is cremated and

buried in a barrow by the sea, and the grave is furnished
with splendid unburnt grave-goods. A coherent group of
pretigious burials with these features is known from late
6th.- and 7th.-century England, with better-known examples
from Broomfield, Ex and Coombe, Kt (Davidson and Webster
1967 pp.9-16). The <u>Beowulf</u>-poet had the literary and
historical sense to regard his characters as pagan from a
christian viewpoint: besides Beowulf's burial, he twice
refers to their connection with pagan fanes (11.175-188;
3069-3075[*]). It is improbable that he took the description
from Viking Age burials. This was not the normal form of
Viking burial (cf. Foote and Wilson 1970 pp.406-414).
Viking-type burial of any form is extremely rare in England
(Wilson 1976 pp.396-397), and although Scandinavians could
bury their dead with grave-goods in English churchyards,
this must have been one of the aspects of their paganism
that was particularly offensive to their English
neighbours, and quickly given up along with that paganism.

It is also material of the later 6th. and 7th.
centuries that corresponds most closely to the objects
mentioned in the poem. Parallels to helmets described in
the poem, with their boar-figures "shining above the cheek-
pieces" (11.303-305), and a "wirum bewunden wala" (11.1030-
1034), are provided by the Benty Grange helmet, helmets
depicted on Swedish helmet plates (Sutton Hoo 2 pp.205-
220), and the Sutton Hoo helmet (Bruce-Mitford 1974 pp.210-
213) of this period. At one point in the poem (1.2041)
there appears to be a reference to a ring-hilted sword
(Davidson 1962 p.125), a type of sword which first emerges
in Kent and the continent in the 6th. century, and was
popular in Sweden throughout the 7th. (Davidson 1962 pp.71-
77). There appears, too, to be a reference to barbed
spears or angons, "eoforspreotum heorohocyhtum" (11.1437-
1438), a type of spear known in 5th.-century Scandinavia,
and on the continent throughout the Migration Period, but
very scarce in England before the succeeding period
(Swanton 1974 pp.5-6; Schnurbein in Werner fs. 1974
pp.411-433). Bows and arrows are also referred to in the
course of the poem (11.2437-2438; 3114-3119), a weapon-
type well-known in Scandinavia throughout the Migration and
succeeding periods, but which on the basis of burial
evidence would appear to be scarce in Migration Period
England. References to jewellery in the poem generally
consist of far from specific references to "rings" worn on
different parts of the body. An emphasis on gold (e.g.
11.1162-1163) is noticeable in the descriptions of
jewellery. This is, of course, principally a literary
motif designed to establish a magnificent tone in the poem.
It may be reminiscent of the opulent arm- and neck-rings of
later Roman Iron Age Sweden (Stenberger 1964 pp.375, 416-
418),but once again the late 6th. and 7th. centuries are

----

[*] All line references given here are to Klaeber's 3rd.
edition of the poem.

the time when gold and gold jewellery seem to have been
most plentiful in Anglo-Saxon England.

The poem is not of the same date as the material
within it. Reference is made to a ring-hilted sword in the
ON poem Helgakviða Hjǫrvarðsonar (Davidson 1962 p.180),
which is unlikely to have been composed before the 9th.
century at the very earliest and in the form we have it is
dated by de Vries to the 12th. century (de Vries 1942
pp.57-60). As a literary motif, such images could
evidently survive for a long time. The historical setting
of Beowulf is earlier than its archaeological horizon, and
both of these are earlier than it earliest realistically
possible date of composition, the late 7th. century. But
in identifying the historical strata in Beowulf in this
way, we can show the historical stages in which material
has accreted to Old English poetic tradition and perhaps
specifically to the Beowulf legend, before that tradition
and that legend produced the poem we now have.

If we view the material contained within Beowulf in
the context of the various Anglo-Scandinavian connections
so far discussed in this book, then we can certainly reject
Franks's axiom that:

> An Alfredian or post-Alfredian date means that the
> central fable of Beowulf could have come from the lips
> of English Scandinavians and not from the wellspring
> of folk memory; it explains the poet's and audience's
> apparent acquaintance with Norse literary genres, his
> ability to manipulate Scandinavian legend and myth,
> and theirs to follow what he was doing ...
> (Chase ed. 1981 p.137)

Such a standpoint fails to comprehend the extent of the
earlier connections between England and Scandinavia. No
special pleading is required to show that all the material
found in Beowulf could have been present by the late 7th.
century - the mid 8th. century if Goffart's argument is
accepted. To estimate the date of composition of the poem
one would have to identify and date the final impulse that
catalyzed the assembly of the material into our poem. I
would not claim that the impulse had anything to do with
Scandinavian influence, only that it is entirely possible,
even probable, that the material of Beowulf is the result
of Migration Period and earlier Vendel Period Anglo-
Scandinavian connections, and that Beowulf is thereby a
reflex of these. This is good ground on which to prepare a
case for the dating of Beowulf between the late 7th. and
the early 9th. centuries, before the full force of the
Viking assaults fell on England.

A second Old English poem displaying an interest in
the same Scandinavian area as Beowulf, and to some extent
in the same characters, is Widsith. It may be possible to
localize this poem in Anglian England, as the first

digression into detail concerns the first Offa, king of the continental Angles (ll.35-44*), who is also the subject of a respectful digression in Beowulf (ll.1944-1962). The lines immediately following in Widsith (ll.45-49) contain the second digression into detail, referring to Hroðgar king of the Danes, his nephew Hroðwulf, and Heorot, all figures in the ambient of Beowulf. Later digressions of this kind mostly concern Scandinavia and the Baltic. No case has ever been made for the expressions of interest in Scandinavia in this poem reflecting the same Viking-Period Anglo-Scandinavian rapprochement as has been claimed for Beowulf. The date of Widsith indeed is quite uncertain, although Malone was satisfied that it was "composed and reduced to writing in the latter part of the seventh century" (ed. cit. pp.112-116). It appears to belong to the same school as Beowulf, likely to reflect the same wide and early culltural frame of reference.

Frank cited certain linguistic parallels between Beowulf and Old Norse in support of her case for a late dating of the poem. However the existence of a number of peculiar parallels between the "Anglian" dialect of Old English and Old Norse has long been known, parallels which appear particularly in the lexical field (Jordan 1906 pp.114-124). These comprise peculiar correspondences in words which are not Viking Age Norse loan-words in Old English. Possible forms of the relationship between different languages producing such correspondences have recently been reconsidered by Samuels (Samuels 1972), who notes three fundamental alternatives in the case of English and continental Germanic languages:

a) pre-invasion tribal connections
b) post-invasion trade and other contacts
c) pure coincidence.

In the case of the Anglian-Scandinavian parallels, there is no reason whatsoever to prefer model c, which simply denies the possibility of explaining particular similarities between sub-divisions of a larger language group, when fully reliable positive evidence for the actual relationships underlying models a and b is to be found. Our archaeological and historical evidence does not allow us to choose between them as alternatives, but either or both are plausible reflections of that context. In the case of model a it seems impossible to determine whether this intimate relationship is the result of the continental Angles' close association with a North Germanic-speaking people in Denmark (cf. Chapter 4, the Undley bracteate), or a contribution of the putative migrants from western Norway

---

*   All line reference given here are to Malone's 2nd. edition of the poem.

in the later 5th. century. Early Anglian England's contacts with Scandinavia were multi-faceted. It is by no means a far-fetched possibility that early English language and literature bear relics of the pre-Viking Scandinavian character of Anglian England.

This study was introduced with a consideration of the substance of the ethnic identity denoted by the group name _Anglii_. This name was shown to have first belonged to a Germanic group, located in the later Roman Period in or around the area of Schleswig-Holstein, a large number of whom migrated to eastern England north of the Thames from the early 5th. century onwards. Around the beginning of the last quarter of the 5th. century it has been argued that they were joined in the Humberside and/or Norfolk area by a group of immigrants from western Norway. This group may have been few, but seems to have been influential. Craft and trade contacts were subsequently maintained over the North Sea between England and Scandinavia up to at least the beginning of the 7th. century, and contacts of some form probably continued throughout the 7th. and 8th. centuries. A distinct culture group, combining features derived from the original Anglian migrants, the Scandinavian migrants, and the North Sea crafts area came to dominate an area of England north of the Stour-Avon line, an area which was known to Bede as the area of the kingdoms of the Angles. This area was thus ethnically an entity in Bede's perception, and has also been an entity in our archaeological perception, although it was not politically united within a single English kingdom until well into the 10th. century. Anglian England was not simply the creation of early Scandinavian influence, or a reflection of the area dominated by such influence. The Scandinavian background to the area was either forgotten or ignored by Bede. The people, and the material markers of their group identity in the Migration Period, seem to have been of mixed origins. However they kept the name of the non-Scandinavian, Swebian _gens_ which was a contributor to this English group. The group-name _Angle_ has a different meaning in the context of 8th.-century England from its meaning in the context of northern Germany in the 4th. century.

Thus the first Viking raiders to fall upon the English coast seem to have followed a route their forefathers had long previously established, and which had probably been maintained ever since. Alcuin shows that they were known already in England, and _Beowulf_ may give us some notion of 8th.-century visions of Scandinavia in England. What shocked Alcuin and his contemporaries was the sudden change of the Scandinavians into impious bands of menacing Vikings who could sack Lindisfarne. In this light, the hypothesis that it was virtually solely a technical improvement in the design of their ships that brought the Scandinavian raiders to English shores (cf. Loyn 1977 pp.19-30, esp. pp.23-25)

300

seems a flimsy explanation.   To account for the inception
of the Viking Age we must seek rather to explain a cultural
change in Scandinavia, a change in the attitudes and
ambitions of the Scandinavians relative to the North Sea
area.   This, however, is a task for a sequel to this study.

Appendix 2.1

Abstract from the report of Dr A.M. Pollard, Research Laboratory for Archaeology and the History of Art, Oxford University, on the analysis of the form C1 clasps from Willoughby-on-the-Wolds, Notts

XRF analysis of the uncleaned surfaces of the two clasps revealed the remains of fire-gilding, leaving traces of mercury in the amalgam ...

The body of both clasps was shown to be base silver. XRF analysis of a small clean area on the edge of each sample gave the following results:

	%Ag	%Cu	%Au	%Pb	%Sn	%Zn	%Fe
Clasp A	64	30	1.5	1.0	3	tr	tr
Clasp B	45	50	1.2	0.7	4	tr	tr

Notes:

i) The gold may be residual from the gilding.

ii) Zinc is difficult to quantify in the presence of both of both copper and gold, but "trace" implies less than 1%.

iii) Tin is likewise difficult to quantify in the presence of large amounts of silver.

Appendix 2.2

Abstract from the report of Beate Enger and Betty Dirdal, Sentralinstitutt for Industriell Forskning, on the analysis of the form C1 clasps from Ommundrød, Hedrum, Vestfold (translated from Norwegian)

The analysis was undertaken by means of I.C.P. spectrometry after dissolving the samples in nitric acid, and by means of emission spectrography directly on the metal.

The approximate constitution of the samples was as follows:

80-90%	silver
~5%	copper
0.2-0.5%	lead
0.02-0.05%	zinc
< 0.01%	iron
< 0.01%	bismuth
< 0.01%	tin

Appendix 4.1

Since this chapter was written, Bengt Odenstedt has published an article on <u>The Inscription on the Undley Bracteate and the Beginnings of English Runic Writings</u> (Umeå Papers in English, no.5, 1983). Here Odenstedt discusses the inscription in far greater linguistic detail than I do in Chapter 4, and the article must therefore supersede my own discussion in this area. Odenstedt accepts my dating and preferred provenance of the bracteate, and shows that the runic text is in harmony with this. His suggested interpretations of the text, however, are:

either a)

> [This is a] <u>she-wolf</u>. [The bracteate is a] <u>reward to</u> [my] <u>kinsman</u>.

or b)

> [This bracteate representing a] <u>she-wolf</u> [is a] <u>reward to</u> [my] <u>kinsman</u>.

I quote here an extract from Odenstedt's conclusion concerning the provenance of the bracteate:

> ... Runological considerations support (the view that it is more likely that the bracteate was manufactured in Schleswig-Holstein than in southern Jutland). The fact that none of the many Danish bracteates exhibit vowel runes of the Anglo-Frisian type speaks strongly against the assumption that the Undley bracteate is of Danish provenance. Apart from the bracteates there is unfortunately very little relevant runic material to compare Undley with, but what we do have points in the same direction. Of the few inscriptions from southern Denmark and northern Gemrany from the period 400-600 four come from southern Jutland, all dated to about 400: the Nydam spearshafts, the Frøslev wooden stick, the Strårup ring, and the Gallehus golden horn. From northern Germany we have the disc from Liebenau, Niedersachsen (early 5th. century), the fibula from Beuchte, Niedersachsen (<u>c</u>.550-600), and the fibula from Soest, Westfalen (<u>c</u>.550-600). All these inscriptions use the ordinary, continental and Scandinavian <u>futhark</u>.

> It will be noticed from this survey that there is a large area, from Liebenau, Niedersachsen, to Gallehus and Nydam, Jutland, from which no finds from the period 400-600 have so far been made. This area includes Schleswig-Holstein. It seems very likely that it was in this area that the Undley inscription

was made, probably in Schleswig-Holstein. That would explain why it contains a runic form, ᛈ , which is unknown in Denmark and in the inscriptions from Niedersachsen and Westfalen. Undley seems to show that runological practice was slightly different in this area than in the areas to the north and south. The reason for this was the differentiation of Prim. Gmc. a̲ in Prim. OE (and OFris). In Prim. Scand. and OHG there was no need for new variants of this old a̲-rune, since a̲ remained in these languages until the period of i̲-umlaut, when a̲ before i̲, j̲ became æ̲.

LIST 1.1 Small-long brooches outside England

| Find-place | Museum or Bibliographical Reference |

Schleswig-Holstein

Borgstedt, Kr. Eckernförde
9 examples

KS4026, 4041, 4044, 4231
cf. Genrich 1954 Taf.
33.1-3, 5, & 6; Leeds
1954 fig.1 c,e, & f.

Hammoor, Kr. Stormarn
KS 12084 III
Lassahn, Kr. Hzgtm. Lauenburg
Genrich 1954 Taf. 33.7
Peissen, Kr. Steinburg
KS 18231:82 92

Niedersachsen and Nordrhein-Westfalen

Krefeld-Gellep, Kr. Krefeld
Leeds 1945 fig.1 h
Liebenau, Kr. Nienburg
Böhme 1974 Taf.26.18;
3 examples
Cosack 1982 Taff. 31 & 48
Perlberg, Kr. Stade
Genrich 1954 Taf.33.8
Quelkhorn
Leeds 1945 fig.1 d

Netherlands

Almenum, Frisia
Boeles 1951 pl.XXXV.6

Denmark

Romdrup, do., Fleskum, Ål
Reichstein 1975
Taf.125.15

Sejlflod, do., Fleskum,
Ål g.Tr
ÅHM 669/1457-1458
Lindholm Høje, Lindholm,
Vennebjerg, Ål g.1566
Ramskou 1976 fig.257
Skindbjærge, Læsten,
Sønderlyng, Ra
KHM 28/79.6816

Norway

N.Fevang, Sandeherred, Vf
Reichstein 1975 Taf.24.2
Lunde, Vanse, VA
2 examples
Leeds 1945 fig.1 a-b
Sletten, Vanse, VA
B4286

Sweden

Bohuslän
Leeds 1945 fig.2b

LIST 1.2 Bucket Pendants

Find-place	Museum or Bibliographical Reference

England

Holywell Row, Sfk g.10	MAA Cam Z7105
Lackenheath, Sfk	MAA Cam 97.45
Morningthorpe, Nfk g.397	Norwich Mus
Haslingfield, Cambs	MAA Cambs Z21268
Nassington, N'hants g.I	Leeds & Atkinson 1944 fig.6
Bidford-on-Avon, Warwicks (1971) g.1	Warwicks Mus
Sleaford, Lincs g.124/125	BM 83.4-1.232
" g.158	BM 83.4-1.333
Willoughby-on-the-Wolds, Notts g.6	Nottingham Mus
" g.58	"
" g.61	"
Driffield, Hu C38 no.22	Hull Mus
" C44 no.6	"

Schleswig-Holstein

Preetz, Kr. Plön	Brandt 1960 p.31
Sörup I, Kr. Schleswig	Raddatz 1981 p.46
Thorsberger Moor, Kr. Schleswig	"

Denmark

Egebjerg, Udby, Bårse, Pr	NMK C7894-7897
Skyttemarksvej, Sct. Peders, Præstø, Pr	NMK C20515
Vimose, Allesø, Lunde, Od	NMK 22609-22610

Niedersachsen

Wehden	Meaney 1981 p.168

LIST 2.1 Scandinavian Clasps

Class A

Find-place	Museum or Bibliographical Reference

Denmark

Find-place	Museum or Bibliographical Reference
Tåstrupgård, Høje-Tåstrup, Smørum, Kbh	NMK C26672
Høstentorp, Freerslev, Ringsted, So	NMK df.35/33
Harpelev, Holme-Ostrup, Hammer, Pr	NMK C28269, 28272, 28273
Fraugde, do., Åsum, Od	NMK C8511
Rosilde, Vindinge, do., Sv	NMK C13352-13355
Alsted Vang, Alsted, Morsø Nørre, Th	NMK C1410-1411
Brodshave, Ålborg a.	NMK C11842
Sejlflod, do., Fleskum, Ål	
g.EO	ÅHM 669/3093-3094
g.EQ/ER	ÅHM 669/2165, 2184, 2216, 3000
g.FK	ÅHM 669/2077, 2126-2127
g.HY	ÅHM 669/3529
g.NR	ÅHM 669/3961
g.NT	ÅHM 669/4141, 4334
g.NV	ÅHM 669/4340, 4343, 4354
g.OO	ÅHM
g.RD	ÅHM 669/6248
Nykirke, Vejle a.	NMK C691
Simmersted, Magstrup, Gram, Had	NMK df.22 + 25/46
Hejmsted, Skærbæk, Hvidinge, Tø	
g.93	HM 1004x99
g.291	HM 1004x507
g.297	HM 1004x366
g.301	HM 1004x549-550
g.303	HM 1004x994-999, 1163
g.313	HM 1004x382-383
—	HM

Norway

Find-place	Museum or Bibliographical Reference
Storedal, Skjeberg, Øf Hg.26	C21583
Dolven, Brunlanes, Vf	C18347
Eidsten, Brunlanes, Vf	C19231-19240
Gjone, Hedrum, Vf	C20164
"	C20165
Ringdal, Hedrum, Vf	C13208
Roligheden, Hedrum, Vf	C14344
Skui, Lardal, Vf Hg.5	C11605
Uk., Lardal, Vf	C19465
Grønneborg, Tjølling, Vf	C16393
Unknown provenance, Vf	"C11234-C13000"
Ø.Sønstebø, Bø, Te	C16894
Lunde, Lunde, Te	C21648

Find-place	Museum or Bibliographical Reference
Tveiten, Mo, Te Hg.1	C32313
Hæm, Sanda, Te	C10362
Evje Nikkelverk, Evje, AA	C29610
Fossevik u.Rosseland, Evje, AA	C29487
Mjølhusmoen, Froland, AA	C30426
Skreros, Vegusdal, AA	C21287
Åtland, Bakka, VA	C8715
Helvik, Vanse, Lista, VA	C33980
Sletten, Vanse, Lista, VA	B4236
Foss, Lyngdal, VA	C21650
Vidingstad, Kvås, Lyngdal, VA	B4518
Stallemo, Øvrebo, VA	C23141
Slettebø, Bjerkreim, Ro	S5046
Kvassheim, Egersund, Ro Hg.65B	B5363
" -	B5387
Edland, Gjesdal, Ro	S5853
Øvre Mele, Hjelmeland, Ro	S2371
Dirdal, Høgsfjord, Ro	S5722
Lyse, Høle, Ro	S2718
"	S2722
Høyland, Hå, Ro	S5469
Vigrestad, Hå, Ro	C3294
Erga, Klepp, Ro	S7131
Hauge, Klepp, Ro	B2277
Reve, Klepp, Ro	S1869
Tu, Klepp, Ro	B2513
"	C21407
Næsheim, Suldal, Ro	S2848, S5372
Bryne, Time, Ro	B5607
Øvre Haugland, Imsland, Vikedal, Ro	S2532
Riskedal, Årdal, Ro Hg.3	S2587
Unknown provenance, Ro	S5543
Fosse indre, Alversund, Ho	B11475
Østebø, Etne, Ho	B7767
Mæle, Haus, Ho	?B6981
Kongshaug, Opedal, Ullensvang, Ho	B6409
Gjermo, Voss, Ho	B7607
Olde, Bordalen, Voss, Ho	B1352
Kolle, Vangen, Voss, Ho	B8791
Vele, Vangen, Voss, Ho	B11623
Skaim, Vangen, Aurland, SFj	B8552
Sande, Gloppen, SFj g.1	B6037
Nygard, Hafslo, Sfj g.II	B6110
Kjellingset, Borgund, MR	B7088
Lid, Haram, MR	B8296
Veiberg, Nordalen, MR	B7079
Flå, Øksendal, MR	T7532
Hol, Inderøy, NT	T9829
Lovik, Dverberg, No Hg.3	Ts1738-1749

	Find-place	Museum or Bibliographical Reference

Bessebostad, Trondenes, Tr — Ts4755

Sweden

Orust, Röra, Bo	SHM 1472
Djurgårdsäng, Vg	SLM
Barkälla, Väring, Vg	SHM 23796:40
Göingeholm, Häglinge, Sk	SHM 21058
Simris, Simris, Sk g.55	Stjernquist 1955 pl.XXIII.12
Sunnerbo, Annerstad, Sm	SHM 13643:5
Carlsborg, Alhelgona, Ög	SHM 15694
Bredsätra, Bredsätra, Öl g.1	SHM 18406:1

Form B 1

Denmark

Høstentorp, Freerslev, Ringsted, So	NMK df.96-97/33
Kragehul Mose, Flemløse, Båg, Od	NMK C3129, 22602
Donbæk, Gjerum, Horns, Hj	
Hg.19 g.B	NMK C14113-14115
" Hg.36 g.B	NMK C14503
Sejlflod, do., Fleskum, Ål	
g.CY	ÅHM
g.DZ	ÅHM
g.EM	ÅHM
g.ES	ÅHM
g.EX	ÅHM
g.FC	ÅHM 669/2092, 2167, 2188
g.HI	ÅHM 669/3111
g.HO	ÅHM 669/3199
g.HP	ÅHM 669/1510, 3198, 3344
g.HT	ÅHM 669/3308
g.HY	ÅHM 669/3381
g.IB	ÅHM 669/1489
g.IC	ÅHM 669/3347, 3353, 3366, 3372-76
g.IZ	ÅHM 669/1294
g.Z/AA	ÅHM 669/335
"ved Esbjerg", Ribe a.	VSM 3857
Øster Tørslev, do., Gjerlev, Ra g.7	NMK C10075
Nykirke, Vejle a.	NMK C691
Ejsbøl Mose, Haderslev a.	HM E7652, E8955
Galsted, Haderslev a.	HM 4591-4597
Melsted, Østerlars, Øster, Bornholm g.16	NMK C4790

LIST 2.1 continued

<table>
<tr><td></td><td>Find-place</td><td>Museum or Bibliographical Reference</td></tr>
</table>

Dalshøj, Ibsker, Øster,
Bornholm Hus 2   NMK C25896 △ 503

Norway: Østfold

Find-place	Reference
Østby, Rakkestad	C15597
Leikvoll, Tune	C15659
"	C15730
N.Opstad, Tune	C31072
" Hg.34	C31074

Oppland

Gamme, Gran	C347580

Vestfold

Tveitane, Brunlanes	C11228
Roligheden, Hedrum	C14345
Ommundrød, Hedrum	C29300
Ås, Sande	C29263
Fevang, Sandefjord	C7408
Lasken, Sem	C11624
Skreia, Tjølling	C18895

Telemark

Bjåland, Kviteseid	C18545
Koren, Håtveit, Mo Hg.4	C32325
Søtvet, Solum	C9442
Særen, Vinje	C17661

Aust-Agder

Verksmoen av Rosseland, Evje	C34327
Vik, Fjære	C7072-7082, 7345-7357

Vest-Agder

Gyland, Bakke	C7457-7459
Ågeland, Bjelland	B3410
"	B3663
Holmeland, Holum	C2646-2680
Stoveland, Holum Hg.7	C8920
Snartemo, Hægebostad g.II	C28026
Moi Øvre, Kvinnesdal	C28758
Vemmestad, Lyngdal	B4414
Unknown provenance, Lyngdal	C5709
Gitlevåg, Spangereid	B5060
Brastad, Vanse	C22634

	Find-place	Museum or Bibliographical Reference
Lunde, Vanse		B3203
"		B3543
Sletten, Vanse		B4234
Vere, Vanse		C22297
Løland, Vigmostad		C18297-18300

Rogaland

Kvassheim, Egersund	Hg.47a	B5343
"	Hg.65a	B5362
"	Hg.72a	B5364
"	Hg.74	B5368
"	-	B5985
"	Hg.34	B5994
"	Hg.39	B5999
Rivaland, Hjelmeland		S2547
Dirdal, Høle		S2435
Østvold, Høyland		B2717-2718
Bø, Nærbø, Hå		B4879
Obrestad, Hå		B4254
Voll, Hå		S936-937
Laland, Klepp		S1028
N.Braut, Klepp		S2451
Vatshus, Klepp		C3312
Jødestad, Riska Hg.1		S2234
Øvstebø, Sandeid		S2258
Syre, Skudenes		S9269
Unknown provenance, Suldal		S5538
Eikeland, Time		S9181
Garpestad, Time		B1781
Tegle, Time		S4311
Vestly, Time		B2546
"		S8635
Storesund, Torvestad		B5908
?Rogaland		S no number

Hordaland

Østebø, Etne	B7647
Bolstad, Evanger	B9614
Nordhus, Fjelberg	B4096
Øfsthus, Fjelberg	B3731
Hartveit, Gjerstad, Haus	B5208
Indre Arna, Haus	B566
Mele, Haus	B5742
Ytre Arna, Haus	B8649
Øvre Mjelde, Haus g.II	B8579
Løyning u.Øystese, Kvam	B6809
Li, Kvinnherad	B7907

LIST 2.1 continued

Find-place	Museum or Bibliographical Reference
Døsen, Os Hg. I g. 3	B6032
" Hg. II g. I	B6090
" Hg. II g.II	B6090
Opedal, Ullensvang	B6597
Byrkje, Voss	B6227
Gjermo, Voss	B7607
Gjerstad i Dyrvedalen, Voss	B6823
Hæve, Voss	B6473
Hæve, Voss	B6474
Mittun, Voss	B7190
Olde, Bordalen, Voss	B1352
Øvre Grane, Voss	B9373
Løn, Vossestranden	B6727

Sogn og Fjordane

Nese, Kvamsøy, Balestrand k. g.I	B8033
Evebø, Gloppen	B4590
Ugulen, Hafslo g.IV	B6109
Vik, Holmedal	B1815
Hauglum, Leikanger	B8045
Bolstad i Fortun, Luster	B3724
Flugheim, Sogndal	B7414
Kvåle, Sogndal	B6516
Nornes, Sogndal	B9688
Eikenes, Stryn	B8989

Møre og Romsdal

Giskegjerde, Giskeøy, Giske k.	B724-725

Nord-Trøndelag

Veiem, Grong	T19624
Hol, Inderøy	T10172
Dalum, Sparbu	C4821
Røkke, Stjørdal	T2569

Nordland

Ramberg, Bø	Ts2060-2065
"	Ts3065
Uteid, Hamarøy	B780-791
Hagbartsholmen, Steigen	Ts1434-1440

Unknown provenance, Norway

—	C21695
—	?B3202

LIST 2.1 continued

	Find-place	Museum or Bibliographical Reference

Sweden: Bohuslän

Tolered, Göteborg	Särlvik 1982 pp.91-92
Högen, Hjärtum	GAM 47756-47759
Unknown provenance, Kville	SHM 7678:119
Unknown provenance, Lyse	SHM 7678:117
Säms udde, Naverstad	SHM 15718:1
Trallskogen, Naverstad	SHM 15718:2
Baleröd, Skee	Särlvik 1982 pp.91-92
Hjärtums, Skee	Särlvik 1982 pp.91-92
Gisleröd, Tanum	SHM 12318
Rinnela, Ödsmål	SHM 26611:6
"	SHM 26611:9

Dalsland

Relen, Steneby	Särlvik 1982 pp.91-92
Hult, Ånimskog	SHM 7378

Västergötland

Holmagården, Friggeråker	Särlvik 1982 pp.91-92
Ingared, Hemsjö	SHM 25655
Lovsgården, Holmestad	SHM 22794
Raustad, Häggum	SHM 26214:15c:4/43
Karlsberg, Larv	SHM 22485
Rasagarden, Saleby	SHM 14416
Hanabobygge, Sjötofta	SHM 26691
Höge Jonsgården, Väne-Åsaka	Särlvik 1982 pp.91-92

Skåne

Uppåkra, Uppåkra	LUHM 28336 C40

Södermanland

Skäcklinge, Botkyrka	SHM 31097:9
"	SHM 31097:10
Alvesta, Botkyrka	SHM 30980:24
Årsta/Enskede, Brännkyrka	SSM Gf.75 A17 F9
"	SSM Gf.75 A23 F14
Vallbyhem, Eskiltuna stad	SHM Gf.502 A6 F5
Uppinge, Grödinge	SHM 26986:27
Kv. Morkullan, Huddinge	SHM Fl.31 A5 F16
"	SHM Fl.31 A8 F2
Vårberg, Huddinge	SHM Gf.4 A5
"	SHM Gf.4 A9
"	SHM Gf.8 A5
"	SHM Gf.136H A1
"	SHM Gf.136H A5
"	SHM Gf.136H A7

LIST 2.1 continued

Find-place	Museum or Bibliographical Reference
Vårberg, Huddinge	SHM Gf.136H A31
"	Dnr.5511/69 A17
"	Dnr.5511/69 A36 F95
Torp, Sorunda	SHM Gf.309 A14 F36
Vansta, Ösmo	SHM Gf.212-3 A18 F103
Vibble, Ösmo	SHM 26303:3/59
Igelsta, Östertälje	SHM Gf.23 A25 F95

Uppland

Tuna, Alsike	SHM 9404:8
"	SHM 20061:XII
Mörby, Danderyd	SHM A4
"	SHM A7
Helgö, Ekerö	SHM :43
"	SHM 26943:6360
"	SHM 28480:9068
"	SHM 27258:7173
"	SHM 28894:10299
"	SHM 27687:8139
"	SHM 29094:11035
"	SHM 27950:8757
"	SHM 28894:10778
"	SHM 28716:9992
"	SHM 28480:9609
"	SHM 26481
Väsby, Ekerö g.2	SHM 25990:2
" g.12	SHM 25990:12
" g.17	SHM 25990:17
" g.21	SHM 25990:21
Grimstaby, Fresta g.3	SHM Dnr.3988/79
" g.8	SHM Dnr.3988/79
" g.33	SHM Dnr.3988/79
" g.42	SHM Dnr.3988/79
" g.114	SHM Dnr.3988/79
" -	SHM Dnr.3988/79 F170
Hammarby, Hammarby	SHM 26843:1
Smedby, Hammarby	SSM A31
Ekilla, Husby Ärlinghundra g.1	SHM 27028:1
" g.8	SHM 27028:8
Barsbro, Järfälla	SHM 27253:503
Igelbäcken, Järfälla	SHM 26024:12
Viken, Lovö g.1	SHM 29401:1
" g.2	SHM 29401:2
" g.3	SHM 29401:3
Ljusdal, Skepptuna	SHM 27865:10
"	SHM 27865:14
Hersby, Sollentuna	SHM 22062:30
Norrbackaområdet, Solna	SHM 19915:1
"	SHM 19915:4
"	SHM 19915:7

LIST 2.1 continued

Find-place	Museum or Bibliographical Reference
Granby, Spånga	SSM Gf.158 A5 F8
Hjulsta, Spånga	SSM Gf.106A A3 F2
"	SSM Gf.106A A7 F11
Kista, Spånga	SSM Gf.163 A2 F4
"	SSM Gf.163 A10 F7
"	SSM Gf.163 A11 F6
"	SSM Gf.163 A16 F12 + 24
Kymlinge, Spånga	SSM Gf.168 A2 F61
"	SSM Gf.168 A10 F42 + 65
" g.13	SSM Gf.168
"	SSM Gf.168 A24 F41, 49
"	SSM Gf.168 A36 F4
"	SSM Gf.168 A59
"	SSM Gf.168 A63 F89
"	SSM Gf.168 A67 F92
"	SSM Gf.169 A4 F203
"	SSM Gf.169 A68 F195
Lunda, Spånga	SSM Gf.115 A27 F27
Rinkeby, Spånga	SSM Gf.175 A5 F5
"	SSM Gf.176 A2
Ärvinge, Spånga	SSM Gf.157A A46 F163
"	SSM Gf.157A A68 F178-179
Tibble, Täby	SHM 29348:5
"	SHM 29348:7
"	SHM 29348:9
"	SHM 29348:11
"	SHM 29348:12
Åkerby, Täby	SHM Gf.124 :146 F756
Unknown provenance, Täby	SHM 28019:3
Hovgårdsberg, Vendel	SHM 1033:3
"	SHM 19963:36
"	SHM 19963:49
Torsätra, Västre Ryd	SHM Gf.80 :140 F64-65
Uppgården, Västre Ryd	SHM Dnr.5620/65 :4
Ullna, Ostre Ryd	SHM 25457:33
"	SHM 25457:37

Närke

Logsjö, Edsberg g.3	SHM 13934

Västmanland

Åsen, Kolbäck	SHM 19311
Forsta, Kolbäck	VLM 29773
Stenby, Skerike	VLM
Vedbo, St. Ilian	VLM A32 F48

LIST 2.1 continued

	Find-place	Museum or Bibliographical Reference

Gästrikland

S.Åbyggeby, Hilla	SHM 22776
V.Hästbo, Torsåker	SHM 18334

Hälsingland

Hillsta, Forsa	SHM 29500:3:IV
Prästhammaran, Hassela	SHM 22142:4

Medelpad

Hovid, Alnö	SHM 22492:6b
Kvarmdal, Indal	SHM 10726:1
Gomaj, Njurunda	SHM 14276
Högom, Selanger	Sundsvall Mus
Skytteberg, Timrå	SHM 25518:II
?Rombäck, ?Torp	"SHM 20438"
Rude, Tuna	SHM 10940:2
Vattjom, Tuna	SHM 10940:21

Dalarna

Folkare, By	SHM 20811
Fornby, By	SHM 15468:4
Hjulbacka, Hedemora	SHM 20470

Jämtland

Petterskottet, Brunflo	JLM 9048
Söre, Lits	JLM 9044
Nordenberg, Lockne	JLM 9047

Gotland

Bro, Bro	SHM 21391
St. Karlsö, Eksta	SHM 8647:1
"	SHM 8647:25
"	SHM 8647:45
Käldåker, Fide	SHM 22359
Österby, Fide	SHM 16693, SHM 16693:4
Öster-Ryftes, Fole	SHM 8793
Rommunds, Gamelgarn	SHM 21781
Barshaldershed, Grötlingbo	SHM 7581:23
"	SHM 7581:34
"	SHM 19535:d
"	SHM 19766:80

	Find-place	Museum or Bibliographical Reference
Havor, Hablingbo		SHM 7785:76
"		SHM 7785:95
"		SHM 8064:116
"		SHM 8064:149
"		SHM 8064:158
"		SHM 8064:171
"		SHM 8064:185
Unknown provenance, Hablingbo		SHM 8603:6
Bjers, Hejnum		SHM 10298:153F
Ihre, Hellvi		SHM 20826:289
Lilla Bjerges, Lau		SHM 17794:VIII
"		SHM 18703:2
"	g.37	SHM 18703:31
"	g.38	SHM 18703:32
"	g.40	SHM 18703:34
"		SHM 18703:40
Kalder, Linde		SHM 11743:3
"		SHM 11743:9
"		SHM 11743:11
Etebols, Lummelunda		SHM 20163:102
Sojvide, Sjonhem 7/57		SHM 26707
" 12/57		SHM 26707
Unknown provenance, Stånga		SHM 11902:3
Gudings, Vallstena		SHM 5130
Vallstenarum, Vallstena		SHM 6595:9
"		SHM 6595:17
Bläsnungs, Vestkinde		SHM 7570:33
Hästnäs, Visby		SHM 19056:2
"		SHM 19056:3

Öland

S.Kvinneby, Stenåsa		SHM 8881
?Öland		SHM 1304:1837

Form B 2

Sjelflod, do., Fleskum, Ål, Dk g.DD		ÅHM 669/860, 872
Kobbeå, Bornholm g.7		NMK C6159
Älby, Ösmo, Sö, S		SHM 26284:47 F37
Brunflo, Brunflo, Jä, S		JLM 15700
St. Karlsö, Eksta, Got		SHM
Lilla Bjerges, Lau, Got		SHM 18703:34

Form B 3

Ugulen, Hafslo, SFj, N		B6071, B6092

LIST 2.1 continued

	Find-place	Museum or Bibliographical Reference

Form B 4

Lunde, Høyland, Ro, N   B3160

Form B 5

Sejlflod, do., Fleskum,
Ål, Dk g.DY   ÅHM 669/1168-1171

Form B 6

Lye, Time, Ro, N   S9510

Form B 7

Øvre Haugland, Time, Ro, N   S9341
Dalshøj, Ibsker, Bornholm   NMK C25896 △ 666

Class C

Form C 1

Høstentorp, Freerslev,
Ringsted, So, Dk   NMK df.100/33
Ommundrød, Hedrum, Vf, N   C29300
Gitlevåg, Spangereid, VA, N   B5060a
Mellberg, Strand, Ro, N   S7577a
Nygårds, Dalhem, Got   SHM

Form C 2

Djurgårdsäng, Vg, S   SLM 6563Vg
Grumpan, Säfvare,
Kinnefjerdings, Vg, S   SHM 14392

Gusset Plates

Giskegjerde, Giske, MR, N   B726
Dalum, Sparbu, NT, N   C4822

LIST 2.2

| | Find-place | Museum or Bibliographical Reference |

Class A

Holywell Row, Sfk g.17	MAA Cam Z7112
" g.20	MAA Cam Z7114
" g.79	MAA Cam Z7145
Little Eriswell, Sfk g.33	BSE Mus
Kenninghall, Nfk	BM 83.7-2.19
Morningthorpe, Nfk g.396	Norwich Mus
Spong Hill, Nfk g.5	Norwich Mus (on loan)
Wakerley, N'hants g.42	Kettering Mus
Alveston Manor, Warwicks g.32	Stratford Mus W60-61
Beeby, Leics	Leeds 1945 fig.33g
Burrough Hill/	
Twyford, Leics	Melton Mowbray Mus
Market Overton, Leics	RCM OS24-25
Fonaby, Lincs	Cook 1981 fig.27a
Sleaford, Lincs g.121	BM 83.4-1.220
" g.155	BM 83.4-1.323
Willoughby-on-the-Wolds,	
Notts g.57	Nottingham Mus
Welbeck Hill, Hu g.56	Private coll.
" g.57	"
Worlaby, Hu g.3A	Scunthorpe Mus
Unknown provenance	Hull Mus

Class B

Form B 1

Northwold, Nfk	BM 53.8-15.51-52
"probably Weasenham", Nfk	BM OA4946
Chippenham, Cambs	Currently at Fitzwilliam Museum, Cambridge. Personal communication C. Scull
Staxton, N.Yorks	YAJ XXXIX p.247 fig.4.2-3

Form B 4

| Castle Acre, Nfk | Norwich Mus 137.22.08 |
| Sancton, Hu urn 180.1958 | Hull Mus |

Form B 7

Westgarth Gdns.,	
Bury St. Edmunds, Sfk g.9	BSE Mus
" g.36	BSE Mus
Holywell Row, Sfk g.46	Lethbridge 1931 fig.13.C2
" g.53	" fig.17.B5

Find-place	Museum or Bibliographical Reference
Holywell Row, Sfk – (2 examples)	MAA Cam
Icklingham, Sfk g.3	Ashmolean 1909.472b
"	Ashmolean
Lackford, Sfk urn 48/2472	Lethbridge 1951 pl.20
" " 50/95A	" fig.24
" " 50/127	" fig.14
Lackenheath, Sfk (?4 examples)	BM 1910.12-22.7;
	MAA Cam 1897.46
Tuddenham, Sfk	MAA Cam Z16168B
West Stow, Sfk	Ashmolean 1909.441
Bergh Apton, Nfk g.3	EAA 7
" g.7	"
" g.9	"
" g.21	"
" g.54	
Caistor-by-Norwich, Nfk	Myres & Green 1973 p.216
Kenninghall, Nfk	Norwich Mus
Morningthorpe, Nfk g.6	Norwich Mus
" g.18	"
" g.20	"
" g.99	"
" g.108	"
" g.148	"
" g.173	"
" g.249	"
" g.251	"
" g.253	"
" g.293	"
" g.299	"
" g.358	"
" g.369	"
" g.378	"
" g.397	"
" g.415	"
Mundford, Nfk (2 examples)	Norwich Mus 165.968
Spong Hill, Nfk g.18	Norwich Mus (on loan)
" g.37	"
" g.57	"
" urn 2076	"
Swaffham, Nfk g.9	Norwich Mus
" g.16	"
Gt. Chesterford, Ex g.18	BM 1964.7-2.80-81
" g.20	BM
" g.29	BM 1964.7-2.147-148
" g.124	BM 1964.7-2.384-385
" g.160	BM
Barrington, Cambs (3 examples)	MAA Cam Z16114;
	Ashmolean 1909.276
Barrington A, Cambs (2 examples)	MAA Cam Z16126

Find-place	Museum or Bibliographical Reference
Barrington B, Cambs (4 examples)	MAA Cam Z21310, 31.851a, 23.837, g.107
Girton, Cambs	MAA Cam
Haslingfield, Cambs (3 examples)	BM 75.9-21.12; Ashmolean 1909.243, Evans Bequest
Linton Heath, Cambs (3 examples)	MAA Cam 48.1625, 1632A-B
Little Wilbraham, Cambs	MAA Cam
" g.4	
" g.5	" 48.1328
" g.32	"
" g.54	" 48.1395
" g.87	" 48.1412-1414
" g.111	"
" g.158	"
" - (2 examples)	" 48.1391, 1470
St. John's College C.G., Cambs (2 examples)	MAA Cam
Shelford, Cambs	MAA Cam
Trumpington, Cambs (3 examples)	MAA Cam Z22590, 33.625
Woodston, Cambs	Peterborough Mus L524, 525, 998, 999
Kempston, Beds	Fitch 1864 pp.270, 285
Barton Seagrave, N'hants	BM 91.3-19.21-22
Brixworth, N'hants (2 examples)	N'pton Mus
Duston, N'hants (4 examples)	N'pton Mus
Holdenby, N'hants (3 examples)	N'pton Mus Y1076-2, D66-77/1955-56
Islip, N'hants	Kettering Mus
Marston St. Lawrence, N'hants	Arch. XXXIII pl.XII
Nassington, N'hants	Leeds & Atkinson 1944
" g.20	pl.XXIXb.20
" g.28	pl.XXII.c
" g.31	pl.XXIXb.31
" g.37	pl.XXIXb.37
" group Ob	pl.XXIXb.0b
" -	Peterborough Mus L1055, 1059, 1063
Newnham, N'hants (?5 examples)	N'pton Mus
Rothwell, N'hants	Ashmolean 1927.639
Wakerley, N'hants g.1	Kettering Mus
" g.17 or 31	"
" g.21	"
" g.50/51	"
" g.57	"
" g.61	"
" g.62	"
" g.68/69	"
" g.73	"

	Find-place	Museum or Bibliographical Reference

Wakerley, N'hants g.74 Kettering Mus
"   g.84   "
Baginton, Warwicks (2 examples) Coventry Mus
              A/1013/49-50, 54-57

Churchover, Warwicks (?3
        examples) Ashmolean 1935.622;
              Warwicks Mus A1517
Glaston, Leics   RCM OS580
North Luffenham, Leics   RCM OS127
Rothley Temple, Leics   Brown III pl.LXXVIII.3
Caythorpe, Lincs (2 examples) Nottingham Mus
Fonaby, Lincs   g.44 Scunthorpe Mus
"   g.48   "
"   _ (2 examples) "
Loveden Hill, Lincs
    urn 106 ⟨47⟩ Lincoln Mus
Ruskington, Lincs (1935)
     (2 examples) Lincoln Mus
"   (1945) g.2   "
"   (1975) g.3   "
"   (1975) g.12   "
Sleaford, Lincs g.4   BM 83.4-1.30
"   g.95   BM 83.4-1.181
"   g.124/125 BM 83.4-1.231
"   g.138 BM 83.4-1.255a
"   g.143 BM 83.4-1.276
"   g.147 BM 83.4-1.295-296
"   g.151 BM OA5526
"   g.154 BM 83.4-1.318-319
"   g.155 BM 83.4-1.324
"   g.158 BM 83.4-1.330-331
"   g.160 BM 83.4-1.341-342
"   g.163 BM 83.4-1.345
"   g.176 BM 83.4-1.376-377
"   g.201 BM 83.4-1.424b
"   g.204 BM 83.4-1.429-430
"   g.207 BM 83.4-1.441-442
"   g.212 BM 83.4-1.458
"   g.216 BM 83.4-1.465
"   g.232 BM 83.4-1.504
"   -   BM 83.4-1.528c
near Welbourne, Lincs   Brown III pl.LXXVIII.1
Willoughby-on-the-Wolds, Notts
"   g.3   Nottingham Mus
"   g.6   "
"   g.8   "
"   g.10   "
"   g.12   "
"   g.13   "
"   g.17   "

LIST 2.2 continued

	Find-place	Museum or Bibliographical Reference

Willoughby-on-the-Wolds, Notts
"　　　　　　　g.23　　　　Nottingham Mus
"　　　　　　　g.32　　　　"
"　　　　　　　g.33　　　　"
"　　　　　　　g.34　　　　"
"　　　　　　　g.35　　　　"
"　　　　　　　g.50　　　　"
"　　　　　　　g.56　　　　"
"　　　　　　　g.58　　　　"
"　　　　　　　g.61　　　　"
"　　　　　　　g.62/64　　"
"　　　　　　　g.65　　　　"
"　　　　　　　g.91　　　　"
"　　　　　　　g.105　　Nottingham University Mus
"　　　　　　　g.112　　"
"　　　　　　　- (4
　　　　　　examples)　Both above museums
Driffield, Hu (?2 examples)　Hull Mus;
　　　　　　　　　　　　　Mortimer 1905 fig.852
Kilham, Hu　　　　　　　Yorks Mus 313.1/2.47
Londesborough, Hu g.6 or 7　YAJ XLI fig.4
Sewerby, Hu g.35　　　　Sewerby Hall Mus
　　"　　g.38　　　　"
　　"　　g.50　　　　"
Welbeck Hill, Hu g.3　　Private coll.
　　"　　　　g.31　　　"
　　"　　　　g.35　　　"
Staxton, N. Yorks (?6 examples)　Hull Mus 1541.42,
　　　　　　　　　　　　1556.42 (a-c)
Unknown provenance (7 examples)　Ashmolean 1909.567b;
　　　　　　　　　　　Hull Mus (3 examples)
　　　　　　　　　　　MAA Cam Z20491,
　　　　　　　　　　　　　　22.858C.A
　　　　　　　　　　　　　　(3 examples)

Form B 8

Glaston, Leics　　　　　RCM 0S580
Worlaby, Hu　　　　　　Scunthorpe Mus
Staxton, N.Yorks　　　　Hull Mus 1512.42
Girton, Cambs g.71　　　Hollingworth & O'Reilly
　　　　　　　　　　　　　　　1925 pl.II
Morningthorpe, Nfk
　　　　g.208　　　　　Norwich Mus
Sancton, Hu　　　　　　Ashmolean 1881.1316

type

LIST 2.2 continued

	Find-place	Museum or Bibliographical Reference

Form B 9

Morningthorpe, Nfk g.48	Norwich Mus
Londesborough, Hu g.10	YAJ XLI fig.4.6
near Shiptonthorpe, Hu	Hull Mus 1028.80.2

Form B 10

Sancton, Hu	Hull Mus

Form B 11

Burgh Castle, Nfk	Norwich Mus 20.39

Form B 12

Westgarth Gdns, Bury St. Edmunds, Sfk g.48	BSE Mus
Icklingham, Sfk g.9	Leeds 1945 fig.32g
" g.25	Ashmolean 1909.477
Lakenheath, Sfk	MAA Cam 97.128
Morningthorpe, Nfk g.97	Norwich Mus
" g.392	"
North Runcton, Nfk	Norwich Mus 27.956
Northwold, Nfk	BM 53.8-15.50
Spong Hill, Nfk g.29	Norwich Mus (on loan)
" g.38	"
Gt. Chesterford, Ex g.100	BM 1964.7-2.314-315
Barrington A, Cambs	MAA Cam Z16126
Barrington B, Cambs (2 examples)	MAA Cam Z16145
Girton, Cambs g.7	MAA Cam
" g.39	"
" g.45	"
" g.54	"
Linton Heath, Cambs g.30	MAA Cam 48.1551
Little Wilbraham, Cambs g.4	MAA Cam 48.1325
" g.168	MAA Cam
" g.173/174	MAA Cam 48.1466
Newnham, Cambs	MAA Cam 39.366
Woodston, Cambs	Peterborough Mus L526
"	Peterborough Mus L527
Holdenby, N'hants (2 examples)	N'pton Mus D54, 76, 77/1955-56
Islip, N'hants	Kettering Mus
Nassington, N'hants	Leeds & Atkinson 1944 pl.XXIX.0d
Newton-in-the-Willows, N'hants	Kettering Mus
Wakerley, N'hants g.57	Kettering Mus
" g.71	"
Glaston, Leics g.9	RCM

	Find-place	Museum or Bibliographical Reference
Fonaby, Lincs g.37		Scunthorpe Mus
" -		"
Kirmingham, Lincs		Scunthorpe Mus
South Elkington, Lincs g.53		Lincoln Mus
Welbeck Hill, Hu g.59		Private coll.
" -		"
Driffield, Hu barrow 11		Mortimer 1905 fig.890
Sancton, Hu		Hull Mus
Unknown provenance (3 examples)		Ashmolean (1 example 1960.722)
" (1 example)		MAA Cam Z20491

Minor types

⌈ Glaston, Leics g.2	RCM OS120
| Ruskington, Lincs	Lincoln Mus
⌊ Sleaford, Lincs	Spalding Gentlemen's Soc Mus
⌈ West Stow, Sfk	MAA Cam
⌊ Sleaford, Lincs	Leeds 1945 fig.32k
Morningthorpe, Nfk g.253	Norwich Mus

Form B 13 a

Holywell Row, Sfk g.83	MAA Cam
Icklingham, Sfk g.7	Ashmolean
" -	BSE Mus
Lakenheath, Sfk	MAA Cam 99.103
Little Eriswell, Sfk g.28	BSE Mus
Tuddenham, Sfk	MAA Cam Z16168A
West Stow, Sfk	MAA Cam
Bergh Apton, Nfk g.70	EAA 7
Brooke, Nfk	BM 70.11-5.23
Morningthorpe, Nfk g.25	Norwich Mus
" g.96	"
" g.126	"
" g.127	"
" g.133	"
" g.209	"
" g.221	"
" g.316/321	"
" g.362	"
" g.387	"
Spong Hill, Nfk g.57	Norwich Mus (on loan)
Gt. Chesterford, Ex g.124	BM 1964.7-2.386
Barrington, Cambs	Ashmolean 1909.276
Girton, Cambs g.33	MAA Cam
Haslingfield, Cambs (?6 examples)	Ashmolean 1909.243e-f; MAA Cam Z20487; BM 74.3-26.34
Little Wilbraham, Cambs g.4	MAA Cam 48.1325
" g.40	MAA Cam

Find-place	Museum or Bibliographical Reference
Woodston, Cambs (?3 examples)	Peterborough Mus L531, 532, 997, 1000
Brockhall, N'hants	N'pton Mus P6c/1936
Duston, N'hants	N'pton Mus D180a/1956-57
Holdenby, N'hants (3 examples)	N'pton Mus D46,85,87/ 1955-56
Nassington, N'hants	Leeds & Atkinson 1944
" g.I	pl.XXIX.Ib
" g.15	pl.XXIX.15
" g.23	pl.XXIXb.23
" g.31	pl.XXIXb.31
" group Oa	pl.XXIII.Oa
" group Oc	pl.XXV.Oc
Wakerley, N'hants g.70	Kettering Mus 706087
Bidford-on-Avon, Warwicks	
" g.187	Stratford Mus
" -	Arch. LXXIV pl.LVII.1f
Churchover, Warwicks (?3 examples)	Warwick Mus A1513-1516, 1521
Wasperton, Warwicks	Warwicks Mus F405 403/2
North Luffenham, Leics (2 examples)	RCM OS118, 125, 162
Caythorpe, Lincs	Nottingham Mus 99.78-79, 81, 92
Fonaby, Lincs	Scunthorpe Mus
Sleaford, Lincs g.48	BM 83.4-1.84
" g.51	BM 83.4-1.104
" g.134	BM 83.4-1.241
" g.212	BM 83.4-1.457
" g.232	BM 83.4-1.504
" -	BM 83.4-1.528c
Welton, Lincs g.2	Lincoln Museum
Willoughby-on-the-Wolds, Notts	
" g.32	Nottingham Mus
" g.33	"
" g.105	Nottingham University Mus
" - (2 examples)	Both above museums
Driffield, Hu (5 examples)	Yorks Mus 240, 242.1/ 2.47; 259-263.47; Mortimer 1905 figs.816, 852
Hornsea, Hu	Hull Mus
Sancton, Hu	Ashmolean
Sewerby, Hu g.15	Sewerby Hall Mus
Worlaby, Hu g.9	Scunthorpe Mus
Staxton, N.Yorks g.3	Hull Mus

	Find-place	Museum or Bibliographical Reference

Form B 13 b

Find-place	Museum or Bibliographical Reference
Morningthorpe, Nfk g.30	Norwich Mus
" g.208	"
St. John's College C.G., Cambs	MAA Cam
Holdenby, N'hants g.8	N'pton Mus D114a/ 1955-56
Sleaford, Lincs g.97	BM 83.4-1.193-194
" g.123	BM
" g.151	BM OA5525

Form B 13 c

Find-place	Museum or Bibliographical Reference
Westgarth Gdns, Bury St. Edmunds, Sfk g.9	BSE Mus
Lakenheath, Sfk	MAA Cam 97.129
Morningthorpe, Nfk g.16	Norwich Mus
" g.407	"
Mundford, Nfk	Norwich Mus 165.968
Gt. Chesterford, Ex g.135	BM 1964.7-2.429-430
Barrington B, Cambs	MAA Cam Z16145
Cambridge, Cambs	MAA Cam
Haslingfield, Cambs (2 examples)	BM 74.3-26.33; Ashmolean 1909.243f.
Little Wilbraham, Cambs g.158	MAA Cam
Woodston, Cambs (?4 examples)	Peterborough Mus L528, 536, 995-996
Islip, N'hants (3 examples)	N'pton Mus D120, 123a/1959-60
Nassington, N'hants g.13	Leeds & Atkinson 1944 pl.XXIX
Wakerley, N'hants g.44/45	Kettering Mus
" g.49	"
" g.50/51	"
" g.80	"
Sleaford, Lincs g.138	BM 83.4-1.256
" g.151	BM 83.4-1.304
Welton, Lincs	Lincoln Mus
Welbeck Hill, Hu g.14	Private coll.

Form B 13 d

Find-place	Museum or Bibliographical Reference
Woodston, Cambs	Peterborough Mus L530
Unknown provenance	RCM OS121

Find-place	Museum or Bibliographical Reference

Form B 13 e

Haslingfield, Cambs	BM 75.9-21.10
Little Wilbraham, Cambs g.111	MAA Cam 48.1431B
Wakerley, N'hants g.5	Kettering Mus
" g.15	"
Sleaford, Lincs g.158	BM OA5527

Form B 14 a

Holywell Row, Sfk g.48	MAA Cam
Wangford, Sfk	BM 54.9-2.35
Barrington B, Cambs	MAA Cam Z21308
Haslingfield, Cambs	BM 73.3-26.35
Bidford-on-Avon, Warwicks g.103	Stratford Mus

Form B 14 b

Holywell Row, Sfk	Lethbridge 1931 fig.19C
Gt. Chesterford, Ex g.9	BM 1964.7-2.45-46
" g.55	BM 1964.7-2.222-223
Barrington B, Cambs g.82	Fox 1923 pl.XXIX.1
Haslingfield, Cambs	Ashmolean 1909.243c
Linton Heath, Cambs g.9	MAA Cam
Woodston, Cambs	Peterborough Mus L534, 537
Wakerley, N'hants g.48	Kettering Mus
Sleaford, Lincs g.80	BM 83.4-1.145
" g.81	BM 83.4-1.150
" g.233	BM 83.4-1.512
Unknown provenance (2 examples)	Ashmolean 1909.567b; MAA Cam Z20491

Form B 15

Little Wilbraham, Cambs g.111	MAA Cam
Sleaford, Lincs g.232	BM 83.4-1.504

Form B 16

Barrington A, Cambs	MAA Cam Z16126
Duston, N'hants	N'pton Mus D195/1956-57
Baston, Lincs	Mayes & Dean 1976 fig.12.8
Caistor or Searby, Lincs	Lincoln Mus
Fonaby, Lincs g.1	Scunthorpe Mus
" g.16	Cook 1981 fig.6
Sleaford, Lincs g.154	BM 83.4-1.318-319
Willoughby-on-the-Wolds, Notts g.3	Nottingham Mus

Find-place	Museum or Bibliographical Reference

Form B 17 a

Holywell Row, Sfk g.53	Lethbridge 1931 fig.17.B5
Bergh Apton, Nfk g.5	EAA 7
" -	"
Girton, Cambs g.33 (?form B 13 a)	MAA Cam
Little Wilbraham, Cambs g.32	MAA Cam
North Luffenham, Leics	RCM OS127
Loveden Hill, Lincs S25	Lincoln Mus
Ruskington, Lincs	Lincoln Mus 35.56, ? + 65.58
Sleaford, Lincs g.86	BM 83.4-1.163
" g.151	BM OA5526
" g.216	BM 83.4-1.466a-b
" -	Derby Mus 399-'32
Worlaby, Hu	Scunthorpe Mus
Unknown provenance	MAA Cam 23.1586

Form B 17 b

Spong Hill, Nfk g.46	Norwich Mus (on loan)
Gt. Chesterford, Ex g.66 (see text)	BM 1964.7-2.244-247

Form B 17 a or b (Indeterminable)

Spong Hill, Nfk g.48	Norwich Mus (on loan)

Form B 18 a

Garton Wold, Hu	BM 76.2-12.7
Sewerby, Hu g.49	Sewerby Hall Mus
Londesborough, Hu g.2 ⎤ Londesborough-	YAJ XLI fig.4.9
Sleaford, ⎥ Sleaford Type	
Lincs g.227 ⎦	BM 83.4-1.497-498

Form B 18 b

West Stow, Sfk	Brown III pl.LXXVIII.5
Morningthorpe, Nfk g.90 (uncertain)	Norwich Mus
" g.208	"
Barrington A, Cambs	Ashmolean 1909.298
Newnham Croft, Cambs	MAA Cam 39.366

	Find-place	Museum or Bibliographical Reference

Form B 18 c

Linton Heath, Cambs g.76	MAA Cam 48.1601
"	MAA Cam 48.1613
Caistor or Searby, Lincs	Lincoln Mus
Quarrington, Lincs	BM 54.2-24.4
Driffield, Hu	Yorks Mus 241.2.47
Sewerby, Hu g.15	Sewerby Hall Mus
Unknown provenance	Hull Mus

Special form

Morningthorpe, Nfk g.20	Norwich Mus

Form B 18 d

Westgarth Gdns, Bury St. Edmunds, Sfk g.52	BSE Mus
Soham, Cambs	MAA Cam Z21363

Special form

Swaffham, Nfk g.1	Norwich Mus

Form B 18 e

Lackford, Sfk urn 48/2483	Lethbridge 1951 pl.20
Little Eriswell, Sfk g.11	BSE Mus
Unkown provenance, Sfk	MAA Cam 27.691
Girton, Cambs	MAA Cam; Fox 1923 pl.XVII.2
St. John's College C.G., Cambs (2 examples)	MAA Cam; Leeds 1945 fig.32j
Sleaford, Lincs g.205	BM83.4-1.436

Form B 18 f

Spong Hill, Nfk g.42	Norwich Mus (on loan)
?Thorpe Malsor, N'hants	Kettering Mus 1961.43/4
Ruskington, Lincs (1975) g.11	Lincoln Mus

Special form

Kilham, Hu	Yorks Mus

	Find-place	Museum or Bibliographical Reference

Form B 18 g

Bergh Apton, Nfk g.64		EAA 7
Haslingfield, Cambs	⎤	MAA Cam
Farndish, Beds		BM 1828.11-3.6
Baginton, Warwicks	⎬ Midlands Type	Coventry Mus A/1013/51-52
Churchover, Warwicks	⎪	Ashmolean 1935.621
Great Wigston, Leics	⎦	Roach Smith Coll. Ant. 2 pl.XLII

Form B 18 h

Icklingham, Sfk	Ashmolean 1909.487

Form B 19

Tuddenham, Sfk	MAA Cam Z16168C
Morningthorpe, Nfk g.96	Norwich Mus
Spong Hill, Nfk urn 1921 (?form B 13 a)	Norwich Mus
Barrington A, Cambs	Ashmolean 1909.264

Form B 20

Westgarth Gdns, Bury St. Edmunds, Sfk g.16	BSE Mus
Holywell Row, Sfk g.58	Lethbridge 1931 fig.15.4
" g.79	" fig.16.9
Ixworth, Sfk	Ashmolean 1909.444a
Little Eriswell, Sfk g.21	BSE Mus
Mildenhall, Sfk	Norwich Mus 633.76.94
West Stow, Sfk	BSE Mus K29
Bergh Apton, Nfk g.37	EAA 7
" g.65	"
Morningthorpe, Nfk g.45	Norwich Mus
" g.50	"
" g.80	"
" g.293	"
" g.303	"
" g.312	"
" g.351	"
" g.358	"
Barrington B, Cambs g.75	Leeds 1945 fig.33c
Little Wilbraham, Cambs g.68	MAA Cam
" g.116	"
" g.168	"
Newnham, Cambs	MAA Cam 39.366
Brixworth, N'hants (2 examples)	N'pton Mus D31-32/1955-56
Wakerley, N'hants g.28	Kettering Mus
Bidford-on-Avon, Warwicks g.103	Stratford Mus
Fonaby, Lincs g.43	Cook 1981 fig.16

LIST 2.2 continued

Find-place	Museum or Bibliographical
	Reference
Quarrington, Lincs	BM 54.2-24.5
Ruskington, Lincs	Lincoln Mus
Sleaford, Lincs g.168	BM 83.4-1.358-359
Welton, Lincs g.3	Lincoln Mus
Driffield, Hu C44	Mortimer 1905 pl.CIV
	fig.836
Kilham, Hu (3 examples)	Yorks Mus 308-309,
	311.1/2.47
Londesborough, Hu g.9	YAJ XLI fig.4.4-5
" g.10	YAJ XLI fig.4.6
Sancton, Hu (3 examples)	Myres & Southern 1973
Sewerby, Hu g.15	Sewerby Hall Mus
" g.16	"
" g.42	"
" g.57	"
Welbeck Hill, Hu g.6	Private coll.
" g.19	"
" g.24	"
" g.52	"
" g.59	"
" g.64	"
Staxton, N.Yorks	Hull Mus 1603.42

Detached bars, tubes, and plates

a) Bars

Eriswell, Sfk - one	MAA Cam 1894.81
Lakenheath, Sfk - two	BM OA4866, 4870-4872
Haslingfield, Cambs - four	BM 74.3-26.21-23;
	MAA Cam
Woodston, Cambs - one pair	Peterborough Mus L1000
Holdenby, N'hants - one	N'pton Mus D49A/1955-56
Glaston, Leics - two pairs	RCM OS580
Fonaby, Lincs g.5 - one	Scunthorpe Mus
Willoughby-on-the-Wolds, Notts -	
one	Nottingham Mus
Driffield, Hu - two	Hull Mus
Unknown provenance - one	Ashmolean 1909.567b

b) Tubes

Lakenheath, Sfk	BM
Duston, N'hants	N'pton Mus
Churchover, Warwicks	Warwicks Mus A1519
Driffield, Hu C38 g.28	Mortimer 1905 fig.819

	Find-place	Museum or Bibliographical Reference

c) Plates

| Islip, N'hants | | N'pton Mus D123a/1959-60 |
| Kettering Muys 74.B.12-13 |
| Alveston Manor, Warwicks | Stratford Mus |
| Sleaford, Lincs | BM 83.4-1.528A |

Class C

Form C 1

Norwegian Type

| Willoughby-on-the-Wolds, Notts | Nottingham Mus |

The Barrington Type

| Lakenheath, Sfk | MAA Cam |
| Barrington, Cambs | MAA Cam Z21313 |
| Barrington A / |
"Cambridgeshire", Cambs	Ashmolean 1909.294
	BM 1900.11-10.1
Barrington B, Cambs g.9	Brown III pl.LXXIX.1
" g.72	MAA CAM Z21309
" -	MAA Cam 34.848
" -	MAA Cam Z21299
St John's College C.G., Cambs	MAA Cam
Rothwell, N'hants	MAA Cam Z21364

The Great Chesterford Type

Spong Hill, Nfk urn 1323	EAA 6 fig.122
Great Chesterfore, Ex	BM 1964.7-2.497
Londesborough, Hu g.6 or 7	Yorks Mus 293.1/2.47
Bifrons, Kt	Maidstone Mus

The Saxonbury-Bidford Type

Bidford-upon-Avon, Warwicks	
g.200	Stratford Mus
Saxonbury, ESx g.13	Lewes Mus
Haslingfield, Cambs (see text)	Ashmolean 1909.245

The Central Midlands Type

Nassington, N'hants group F	Peterborough Mus L1053
?Thorpe Malsor, N'hants	Kettering Mus 1961.43/3
North Luffenham, Leics	RCM;
	Brown III pl.LXXVIII.7

| | Museum or Bibliographical |
| Find-place | Reference |

The Mildenhall Type

Mildenhall, Sfk   BSE Mus;
                                   Brown III pl.LXXVIII.6
Spong Hill, Nfk urn 2007   EAA 11 fig.140

Unique examples

West Stow, Sfk   MAA Cam
Fonaby, Lincs g.36   Cook 1981 fig.13
Bifrons, Kt   Maidstone Mus
                                          KAS 620.1954c

Form C 3

Holywell Row, Sfk g.16   Lethbridge 1931 fig.6.5
        "   g.98   "   fig.19.B1
Kenninghall, Nfk   BM 83.7-2.9
Morningthorpe, Nfk g.353   Norwich Mus
Linton Heath, Cambs g.39 or 44   MAA Cam 48.1564, 1576
Little Wilbraham, Cambs g.133   Neville 1852 pl.12
Rothwell, N'hants   MAA Cam 1918.208.23

Individualistic examples

Bixley, Nfk   Norfolk Archaeol. Unit
                                   Sites & Monuments Index
                                          15607
Morningthorpe, Nfk g.153   Norwich Mus
        "   g.360   "
Empingham I, Leics   RCM 1968.158

Gusset Plates

Lakenheath, Sfk   MAA Cam
Mildenhall, Sfk   BSE Mus;
                                   VCH Sfk I p.346 fig.14
West Stow, Sfk (2 examples)   MAA Cam Z20455-20456
Barrington A, Cambs   Ashmolean 1909.264
        "   Ashmolean 1909.294
Barrington B, Cambs g.9   Brown III pl.LXXIX
Haslingfield, Cambs   BM 75.9-21.9
North Luffenham, Leics   RCM;
                                   Brown III pl.LXXIX.3
Rothwell, N'hants   MAA Cam 1918.208.23
Unknown provenance   BM 99.10-7.1

LIST 4.1 Scutiform Pendants, Scandinavian

Find-place	Museum or Bibliographical Reference

Denmark

Find-place	Reference
Høstentorp, Freerslev, Ringsted, So	NMK df.62/33
"	NMK df.95/33
"	NMK df.98-99/33
	(9 examples in all)
Råberg, do., Horns, Hj	NMK MDCCXIX
Linderup Mark, Tolstrup, Borglum, Hj	NMK 15352
Mejlby, Brorstrup, Års, Ål (2 examples)	NMK C5813
Sejlflod, do., Fleskum, Ål	
g.00	ÅHM 669/1410
" g.Tr	ÅMM 669/1459
Nørre Hvam, Borbjerg, Hjerm, Rk	NMK MCCVI
Melsted, Østerlars, Øster, Bornholm g.8	NMK C2947

Norway

Find-place	Reference
Nordre Rostad, Tune, Øf	C10000
Gjone, Hedrum, Vf	C20165
Mjølhusmoen, Froland, AA	C30426d
Skreros, Vegusdal, AA Haug 2	C21287
" Haug 2	C22140
Øvre Øye, Kvinnedal, VA	B86-96
Horr, Hå, Ro	B4834
Hauge, Klepp, Ro	B2299

LIST 4.2 Scutiform and Disc Pendants, England

| | Find-place | Museum or Bibliographical Reference |

Simple Scutiform Pendants

Holywell Row, Sfk g.11 (pair)	MAA Cam
Icklingham, Sfk g.7	Ashmolean 1909.467b
Lakenheath, Sfk	MAA Cam 1906.84 (missing)
Mildenhall, Sfk	BM OA4947
" (4 examples)	VCH Sfk I p.341
West Stow, Sfk	BSE Mus K27
Morningthorpe, Nfk g.80	Norwich Mus
" g.322	"
" g.359	"
" g.369	"
Spong Hill, Nfk g.11 (3 examples)	Norwich Mus (on loan)
Weasenham, Nfk	BM 86.6-10.2
Burwell, Cambs g.25	Lethbridge 1931 fig.23.1
" –	MAA Cam 98.65
Girton, Cambs	MAA Cam
Haslingfield, Cambs	BM 74.3-26.32
Linton Heath, Cambs g.36	
(2 examples)	MAA Cam 48.1561A-B
Melbourn, Cambs g.7	P.C.A.S. XLIX pl.IV.1
" g.11	" pl.V
St. John's College C.G., Cambs	
g.8	MAA Cam
" –	"
Shudy Camps, Cambs g.55	Lethbridge 1936 fig.4F.1
Kempston, Beds	BEDFM 3848
"	BM 91.6-24.300
Leighton Buzzard, Beds g.39	Luton Mus
" –	"
Nassington, N'hants	Oundle
Wakerley, N'hants g.17	Kettering Mus
" g.80 (3	
examples)	"
Empingham II, Leics g.94	RCM
Market Overton, Leics (3	
examples)	RCM OS15
Fonaby, Lincs g.1	Scunthorpe Mus
Ruskington, Lincs g.3	Lincoln Mus
Sleaford, Lincs g.2	BM 83.4-1.17
" g.42	BM 83.4-1.77
" g.78	BM 83.4-1.138
" g.95 (2	
examples)	BM 83.4-1.179-180
" g.96	BM 83.4-1.188
" g.116	BM 83.4-1.212
" g.138	BM 83.4-1.254
" g.143 (pair)	BM 83.4-1.277-278
Worlaby, Lincs ?g.1	Scunthorpe Mus
" g.3A	"
" g.9	"

LIST 4.2 continued

Find-place	Museum or Bibliographical Reference

Willoughby-on-the-Wolds, Notts

           g.58   Nottingham Mus

Longstone, Derbys   BM 73.6-2.90

Hornsea, Hu   Hull Mus

Sewerby, Hu g.35   Sewerby Hall Mus

Welbeck Hill, Hu g.3   Private coll.

         "   g.41   "

         "   g.56   "

Bifrons, Kt   Maidstone Mus (missing)

Buckland, Dover, Kt g.35A   BM 1963.11-8.183

         "   g.67 (3

               examples) BM 1963.11-8.413A-C

Faversham, Kt (2 examples)   Ashmolean 1909.139a, 210

      "   (4 examples)   BM 81.12-12.5-7, 1150.70

      "   (1 example)   Maidstone Mus 32.1957

Kingston Down, Kt g.59   Faussett 1856 p.53

       "   g.110   "   p.60,
                                        pl.IV.20

       "   g.156   p.70-71,
                                        pl.XI.24

       "   g.205   "   pp.77-78,
                                        pl.I.2

Sarre, Kt g.220   Maidstone Mus

    "   -   "

Sibertswold, Kt g.18   Faussett 1856 pp.105-106

    "   g.86   "   pl.IV.22

    "   g.93   "   p.116

    "   g.94 (pair)   "   p.116,
                                        pl.XI.7

    "   g.124   "   p.122

Chessel Down, IoW (see text)   BM 67.7-29.85

Unkown provenance   Ashmolean

Simple Disc Pendants

Burwell, Cambs   Hull Mus

Melbourn, Cambs g.19   MAA Cam

Shudy Camps, Cambs g.32   MAA Cam

Dunstable, Beds g.C7   Beds.A.J. 1 fig.3

Longbridge, Warwicks   BM 76.5-21.2

Sleaford, Lincs g.227   BM 83.4-1.494

Wye, Kt   BM93.6-1.188

Uncertain Disc or Scutiform Pendants

Mildenhall, Sfk (2 examples)   BM OA4948-4949

Morningthorpe, Nfk   Norwich Mus

	Find-place	Museum or Bibliographical Reference

Plain Disc Pendants

Find-place	Reference
Lakenheath, Sfk	MAA Cam 97.45
St. John's College C.G., Cambs g.IX	MAA Cam
Soham, Cambs	MAA Cam
Sleaford, Lincs g.151	BM 83.4-1.307
" g.191	BM 83.4-1.396
Londesborough, Hu	Hull Mus 1615.42

Composite Disc and Scutiform Pendants

Find-place	Reference
Breach Down, Kt	BM 79.5-24.22
Faversham, Kt (3 examples)	BM 84.12-21.5-6; 1137-1138.70
" (5 examples)	Ashmolean 1909.175, 183, 188, 207
Kingston Down, Kt g.96	Faussett 1856 pl.IV.11
Milton, Kt (2 examples)	BM 1926.4-10.1-2
" (1 example)	Maidstone Mus
Riseley, Kt	Dartford Mus
Sibsertswold, Kt g.172	Faussett 1856 pl.IV.13
Wye, Kt (2 examples)	BM 93.6-1.187, 189
Farthing Down, Coulsdon, Sy	Guildford Mus
High Wycome, Bucks	BM 1942.10-7.4
Ducklington, Oxon	Ashmolean
Barrington, Cambs	MAA Cam 34.838
Compton Vernay, Warwicks	Ashmolean 1948.134
Willoughby-on-the-Wolds, Notts g.65	Nottingham Mus
Acklam, Hu (2 examples)	BM 71.12-7.1; 93.6-1.202
Garton, Hu	Hull Mus
Uncleby, Hu (2 examples)	Åberg 1926 Table VI
Womersley, N.Yorks	Åberg 1926 Table VI
Unknown provenance	Ashmolean Douglas Coll.

LIST 5.1 Scandinavian Equal-Armed Brooches

	Find-place	Museum or Bibliographical Reference

Norway

Find-place	Reference
Limestad, Vestby, Ak (pair)	C1888
Nedre Lunde, N.Land, Op	C25200
Gjevle, N.Land, Op	C23295
Leirol, Vang, Op	C10352
Eidsten, Berg, Vf	C20301
Gui, Brunlanes, Vf	C17241
Tveitane, Brunlanes, Vf	C12984
Horland, Hedrum, Vf	C15209
Nordheim, Hedrum, Vf	C19356
Skui, Lardal, Vf	C11063
Gjerla, Stokke, Vf	C22475
Reåstad, Tjølling, Vf	C18787
Valby, Tjølling, Vf	C16453
Næs, Drangedal, Te	C23263
Tveide, Birkenes, AA	C14489-14494
Skreros, Vegusdal, AA	C22140
Spangereid, S.-Audnedal, VA	C9371
Løland, Vigmostad, VA	C13692
Kvassheim, Egersund, Ro	B5290
"	B5293
"	B5303
"	B5345
"	B5348
Hå, Hå, Ro	C13525
Tjøtta, Klepp, Ro (pair)	S837
Hegreberg, Renneso, Ro	S2951
Barka, Strand, Ro	S6580
Lye, Time, Ro (2 examples)	S9510
Unknown provenance, Jæren, Ro	S5545
Indre Saule, Sæbø, Ho	B10303
Kvalstein, Borgund, MR	B8540 (missing)
Føre, Bø, No	Ts5338

Sweden

Find-place	Reference
Skänje, Skee, Bo	SHM 16808
S.Åbyggeby, Hille, Gä	SHM 22776

Gotland

Find-place	Reference
Havor, Hablingbo	SHM 7785:72
Bjärs, Hejnum	SHM 14071
Ihre, Hellvi	SHM 20826:252
Lilla Bjärges, Lau	SHM 18703:61
Meile, Visby	SHM 1358
Unknown provenance	Nerman 1935 fig.32

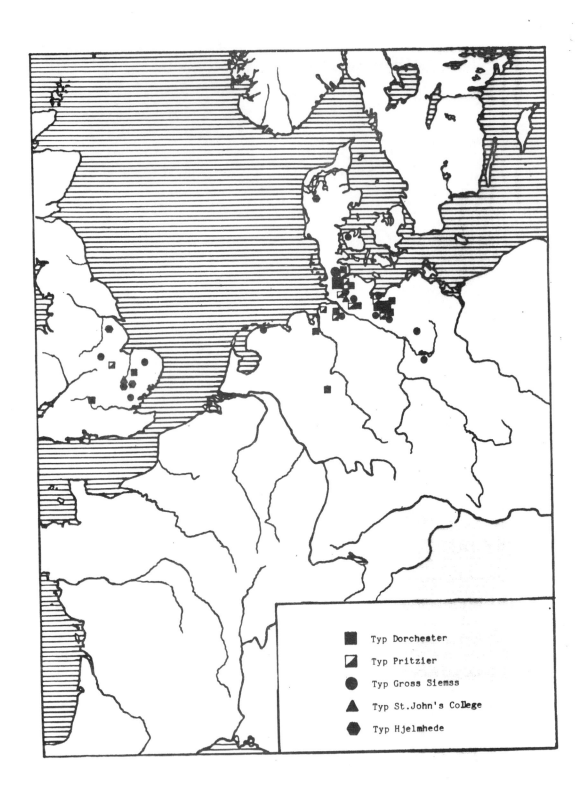

Map 1.1 Early cruciform brooch types

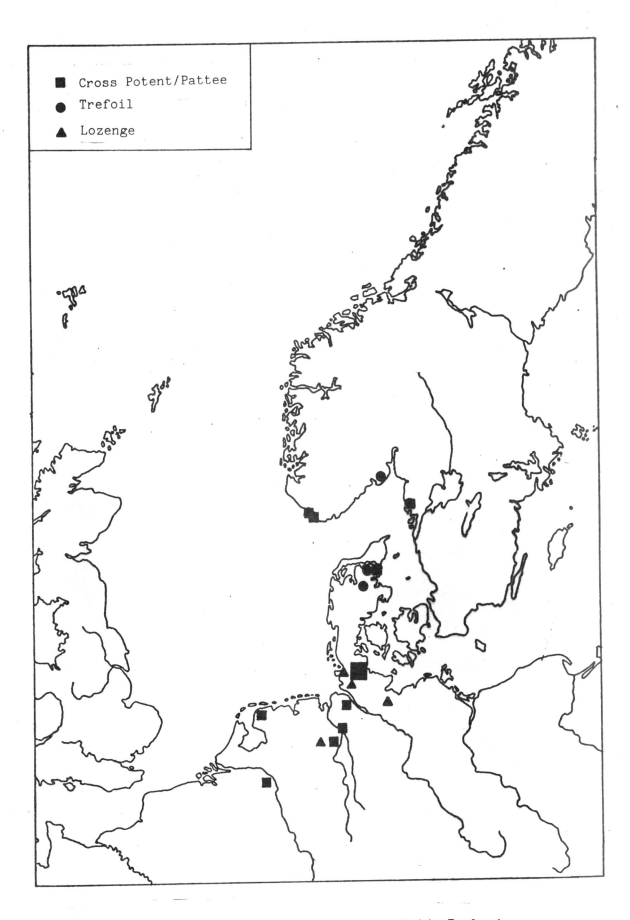

Map 1.2 Small-long brooches outside England

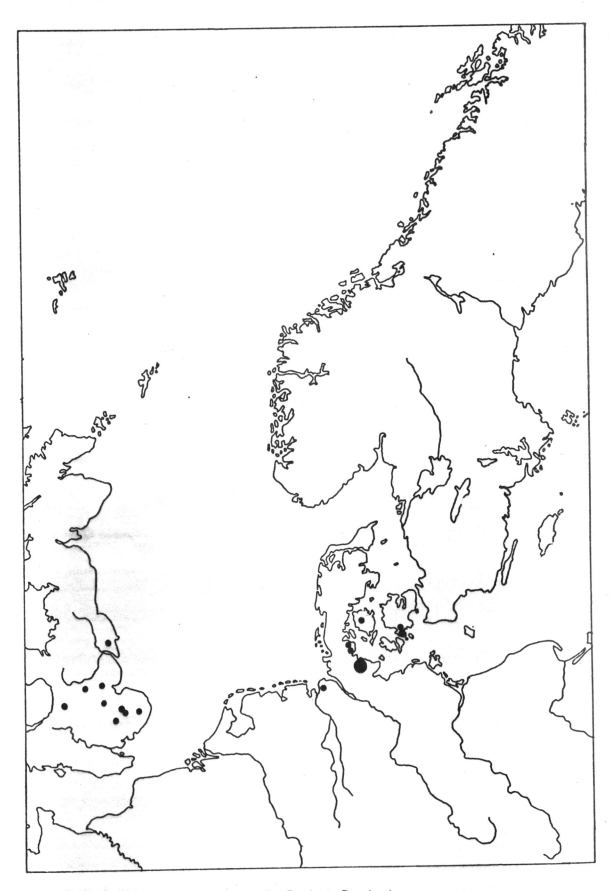

Map 1.3 Bucket Pendants

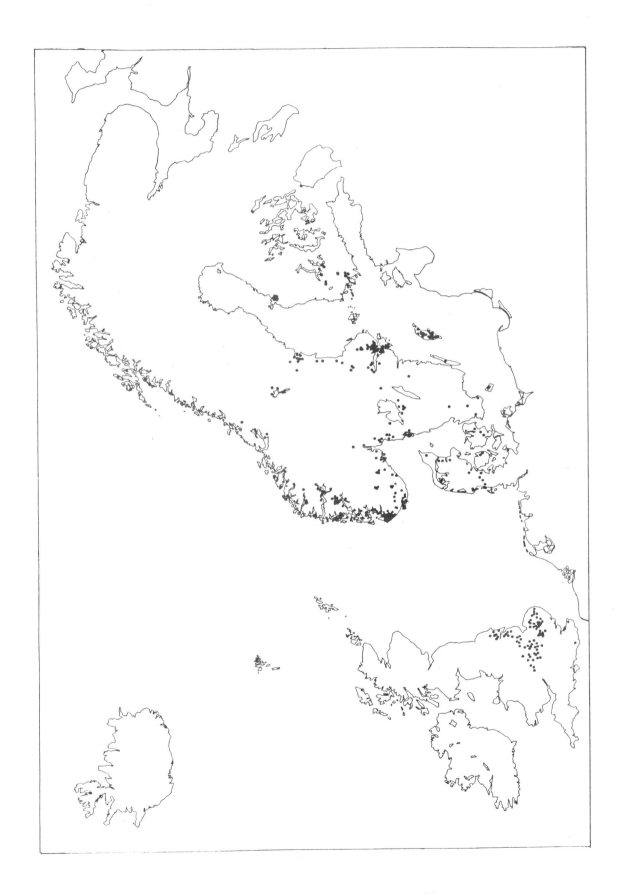

Map 2.1 English and Scandinavian Clasps

Classes A-C, Overall distribution map

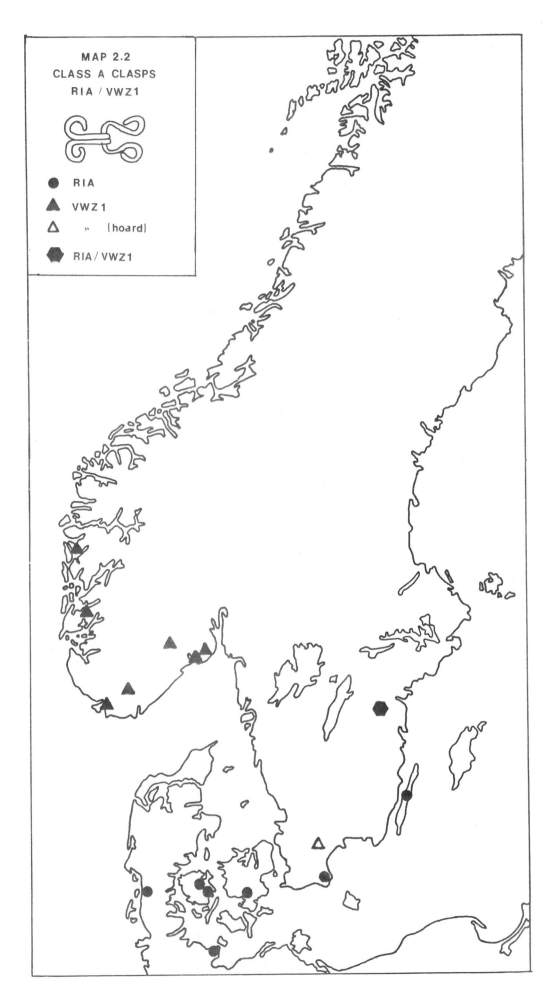

MAP 2.2
CLASS A CLASPS
RIA / VWZ1

● RIA
▲ VWZ1
△ „ (hoard)
⬣ RIA / VWZ1

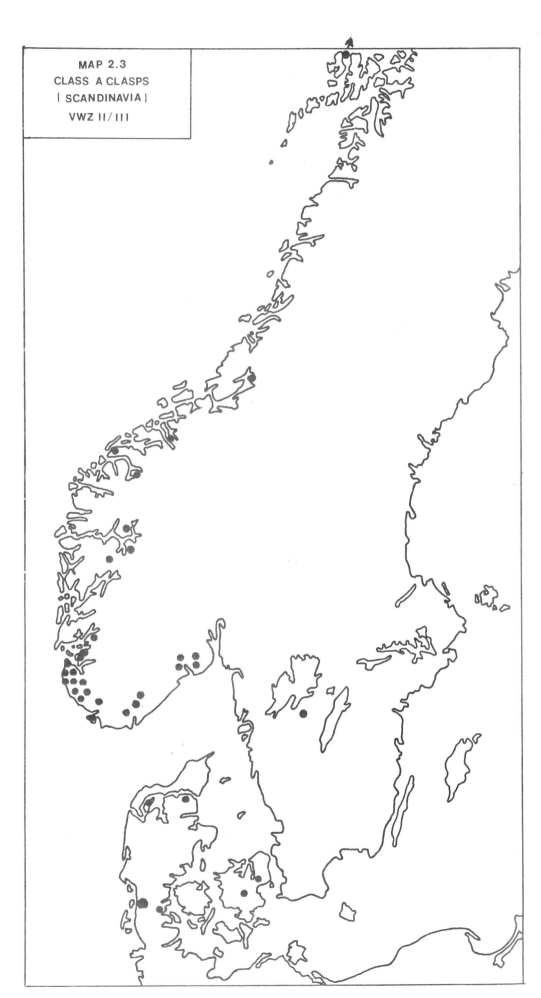

MAP 2.3
CLASS A CLASPS
[SCANDINAVIA]
VWZ II/III

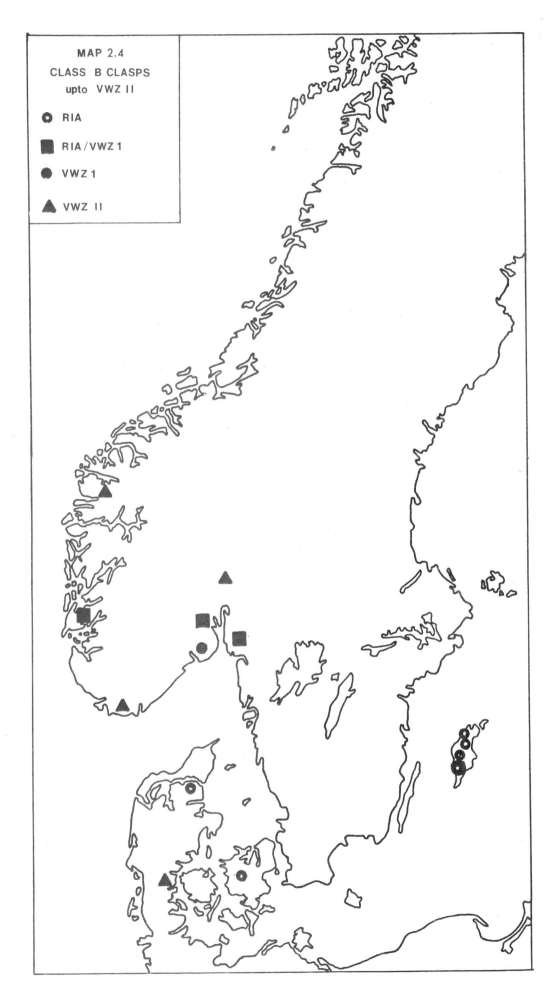

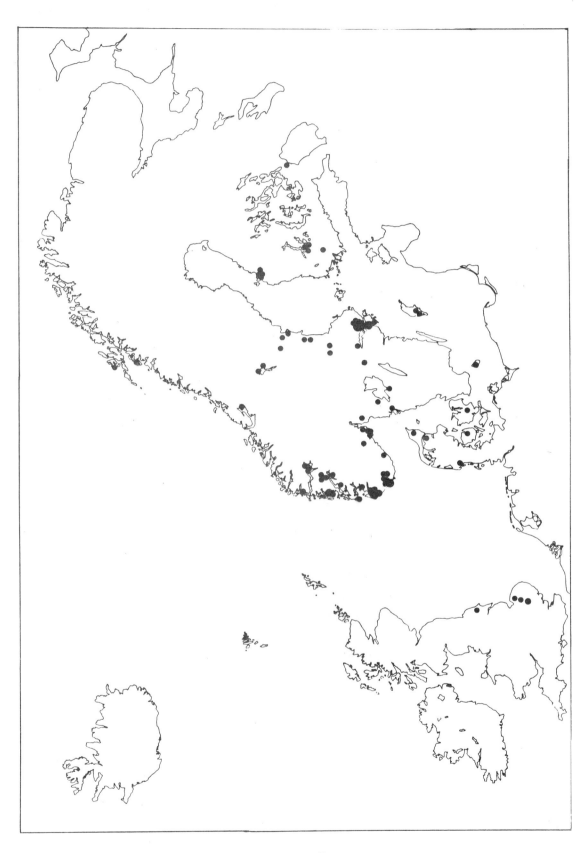

Map 2.5

Form B 1

VWZ III/IV

347

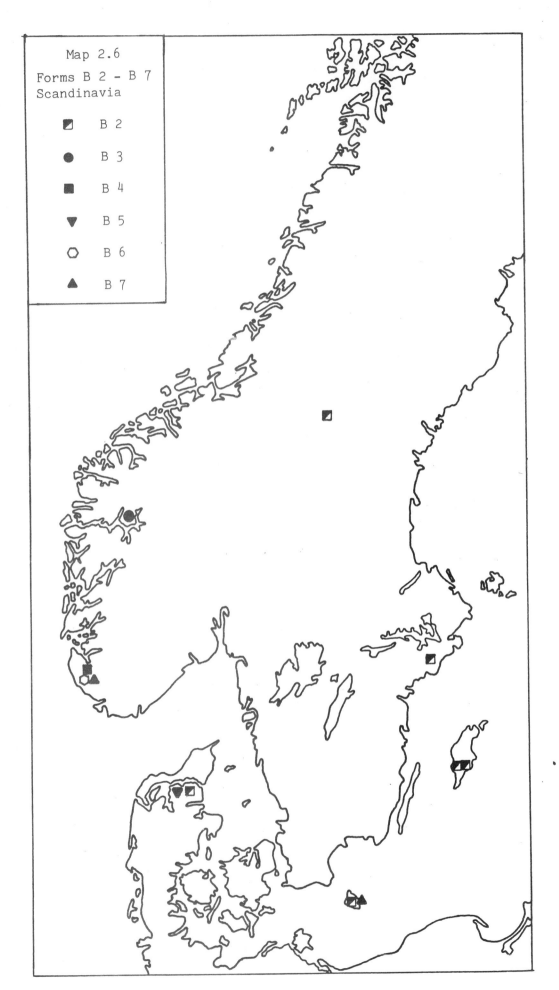

Map 2.6

Forms B 2 – B 7
Scandinavia

▨ B 2

● B 3

■ B 4

▼ B 5

⬡ B 6

▲ B 7

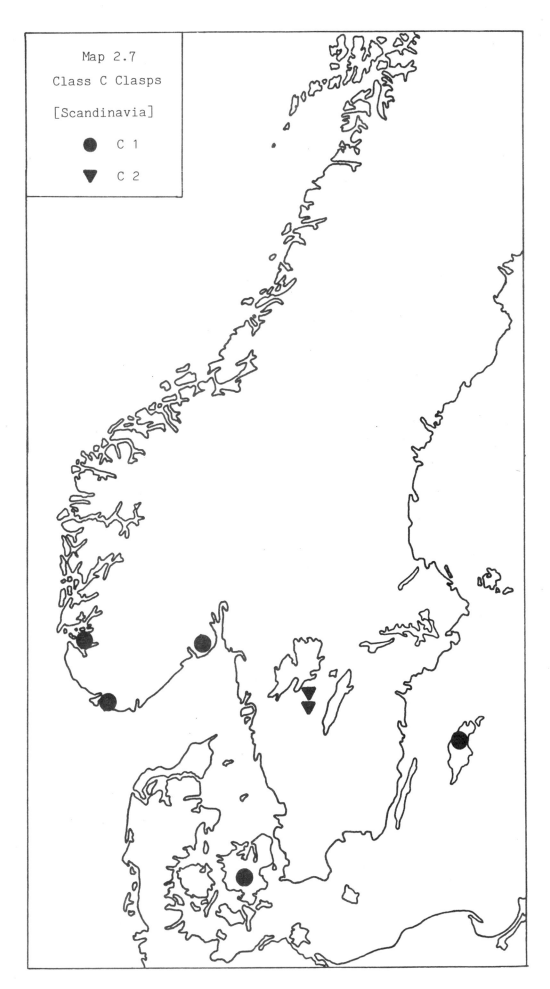

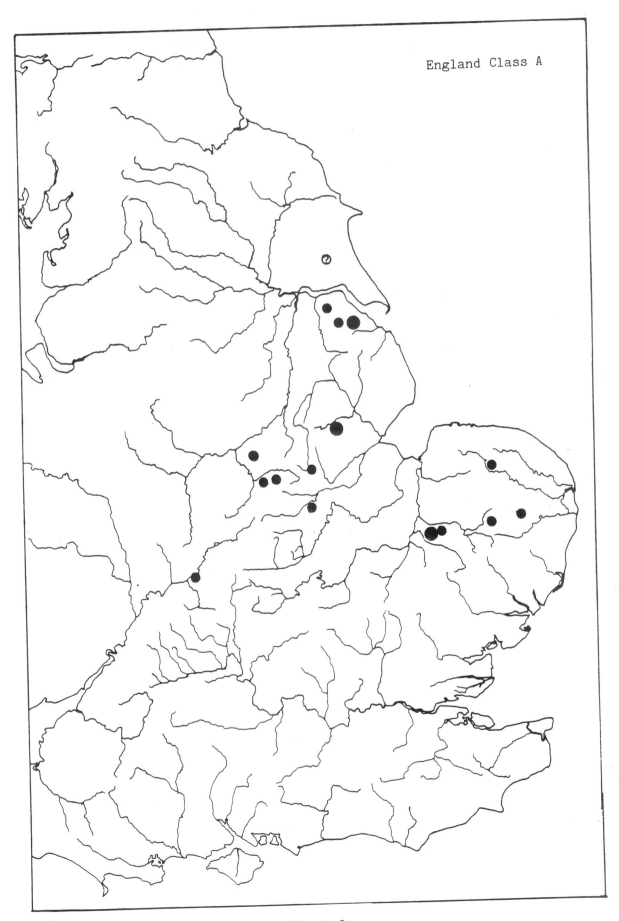

England Class A

Map 2.8

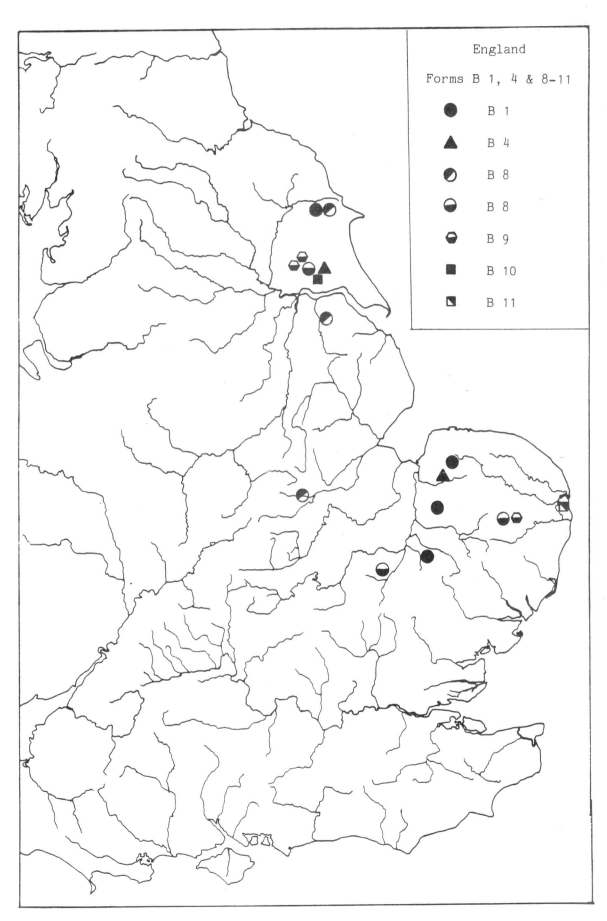

Map 2.9

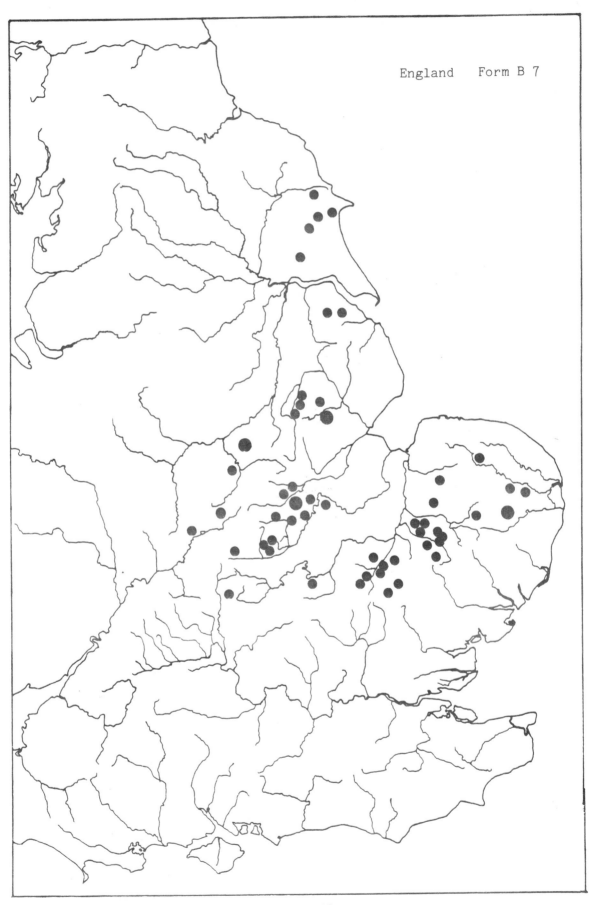

England   Form B 7

Map 2.10

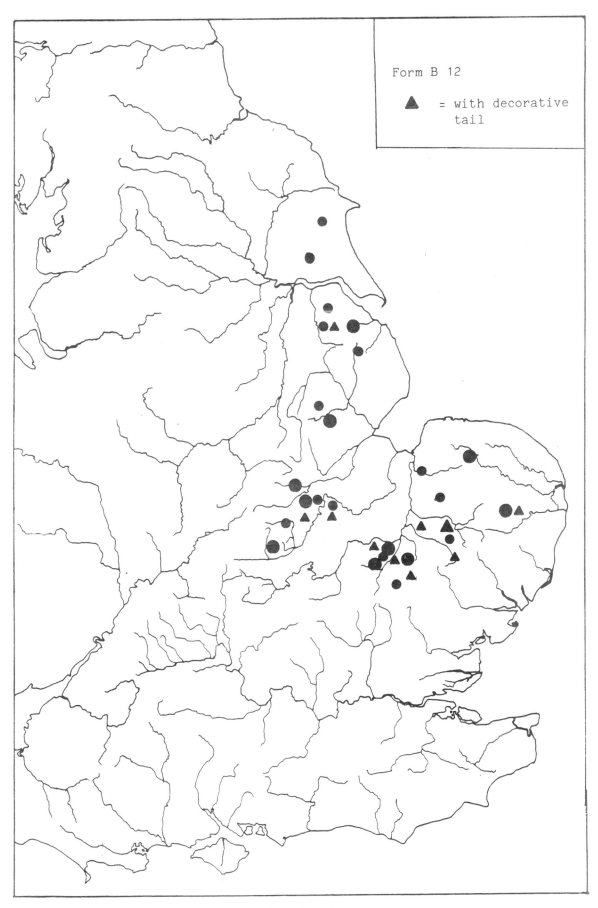

Map 2.11

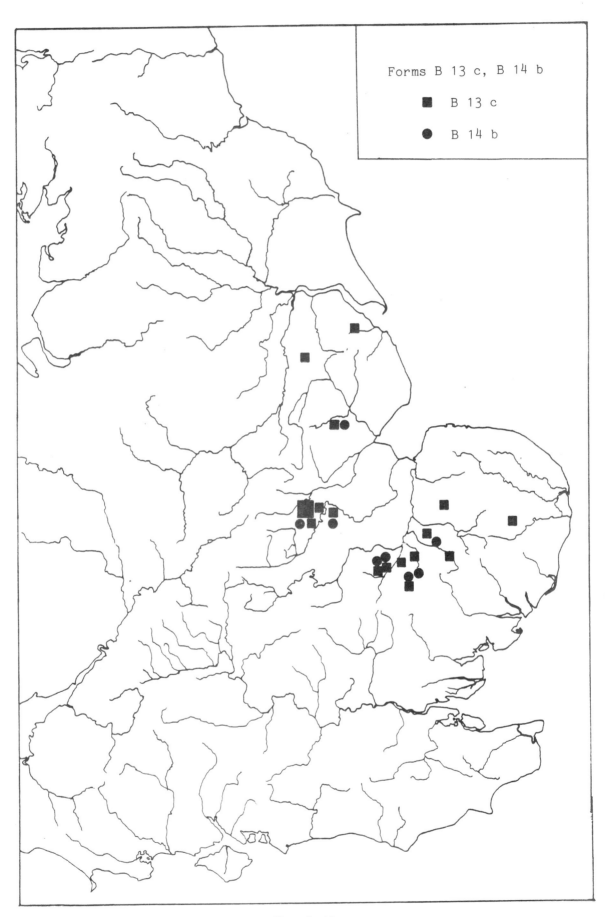

Map 2.12

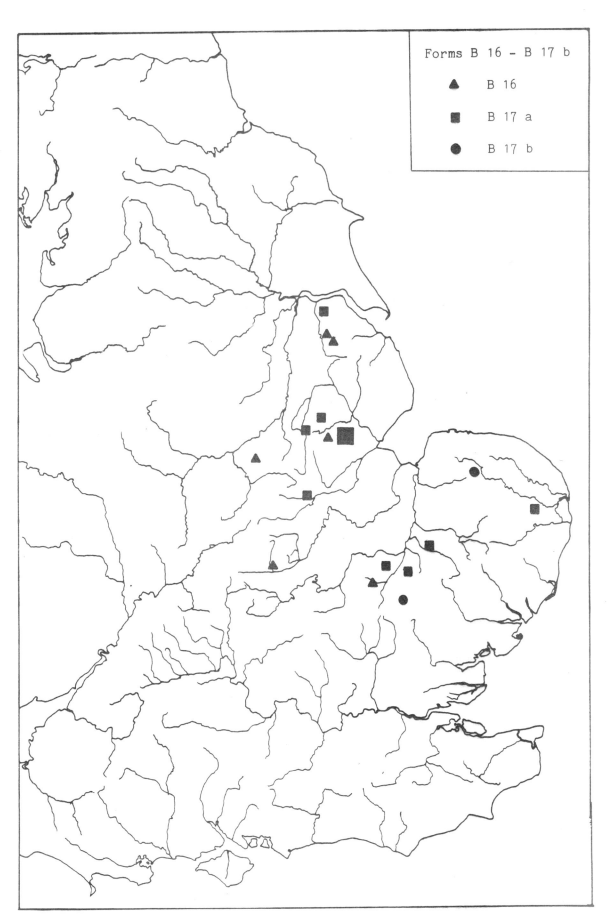

Map 2.13

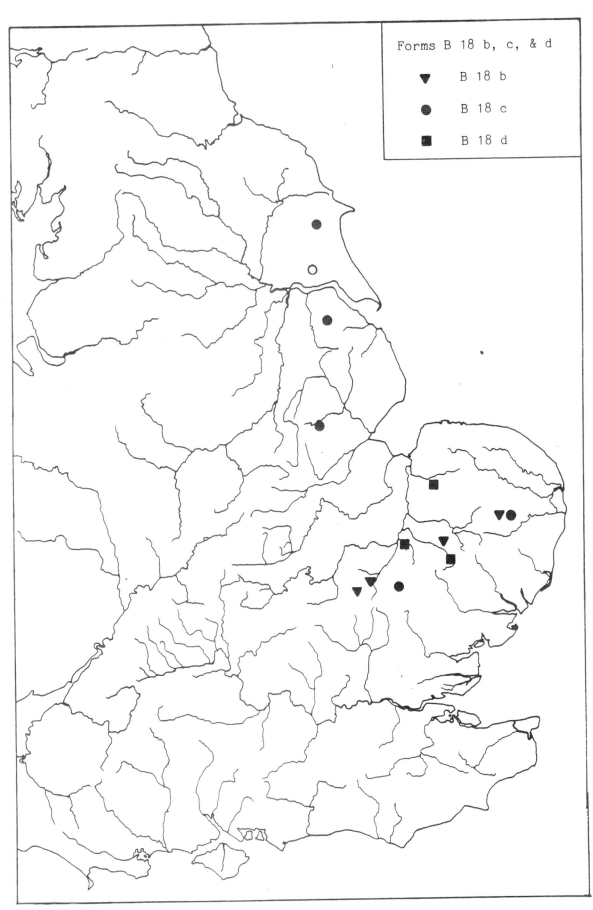

Map 2.14

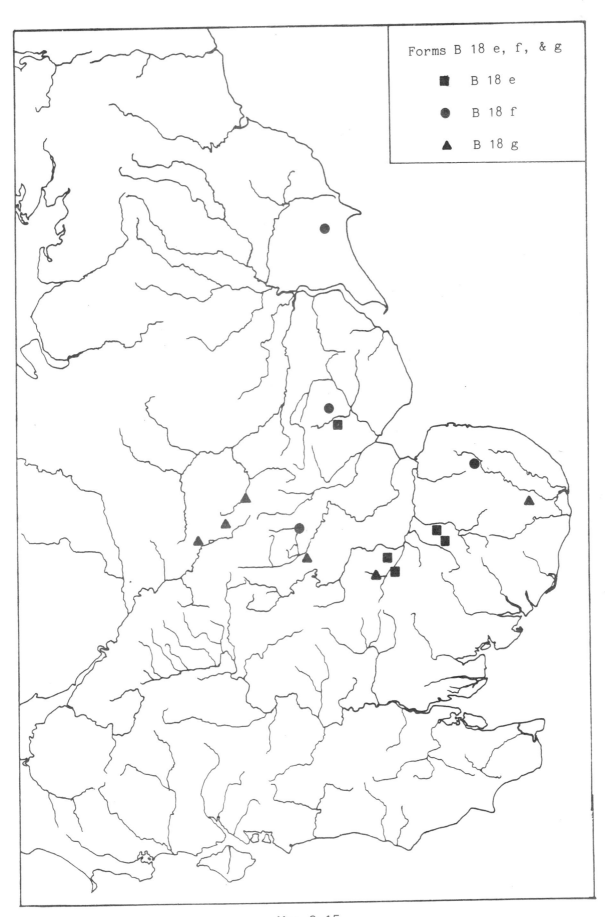

Map 2.15

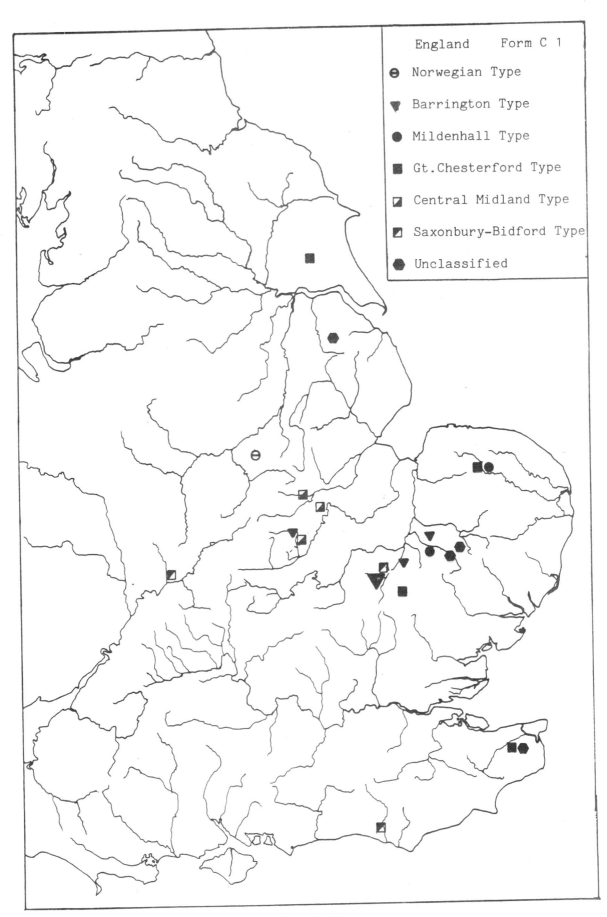

Map 2.16

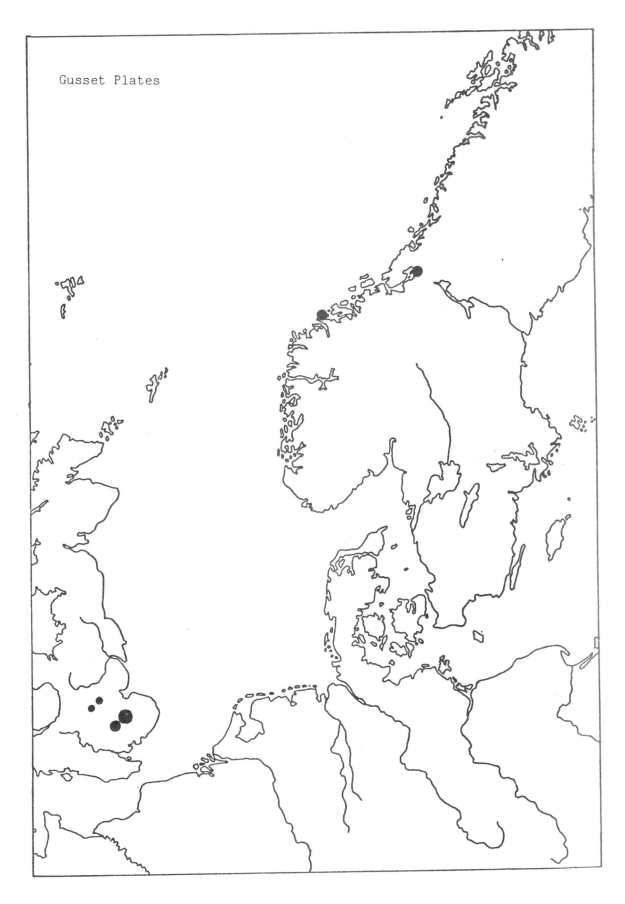

Gusset Plates

Map 2.17

359

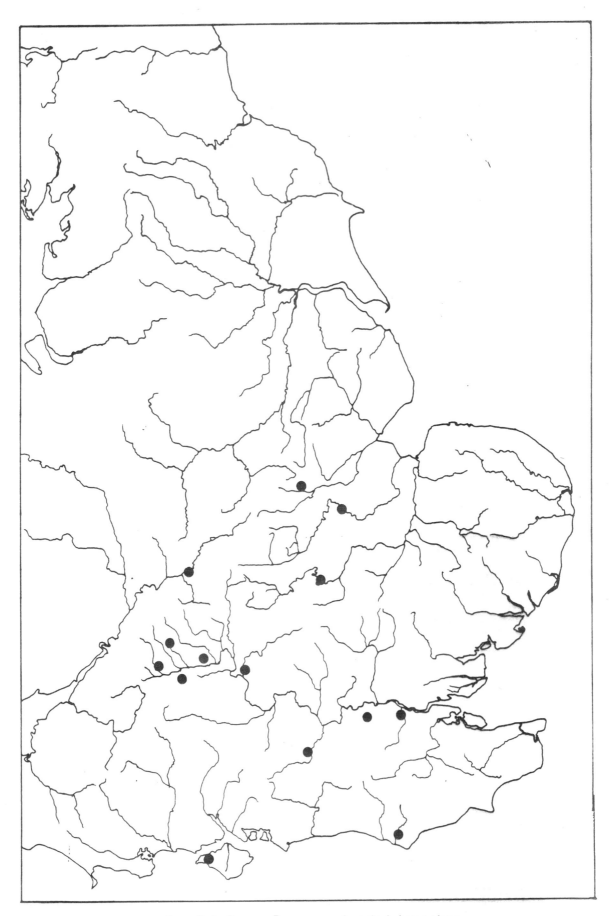

Map 3.1 Group I square-headed brooches

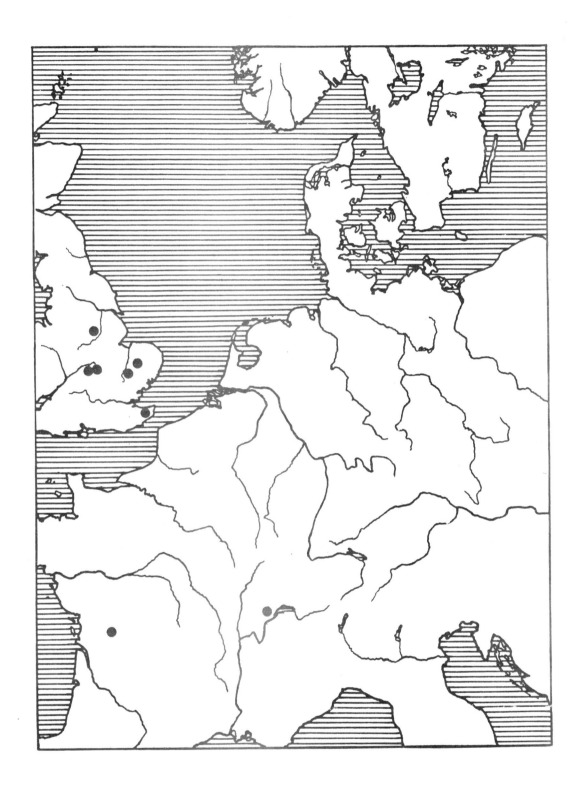

Map 3.2 Group II square-headed brooches

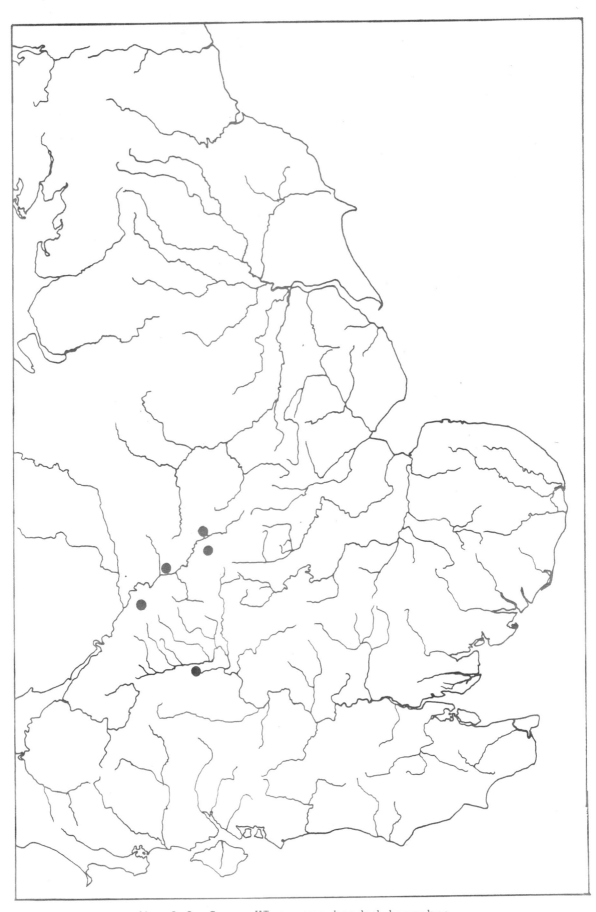

Map 3.3 Group VI square-headed brooches

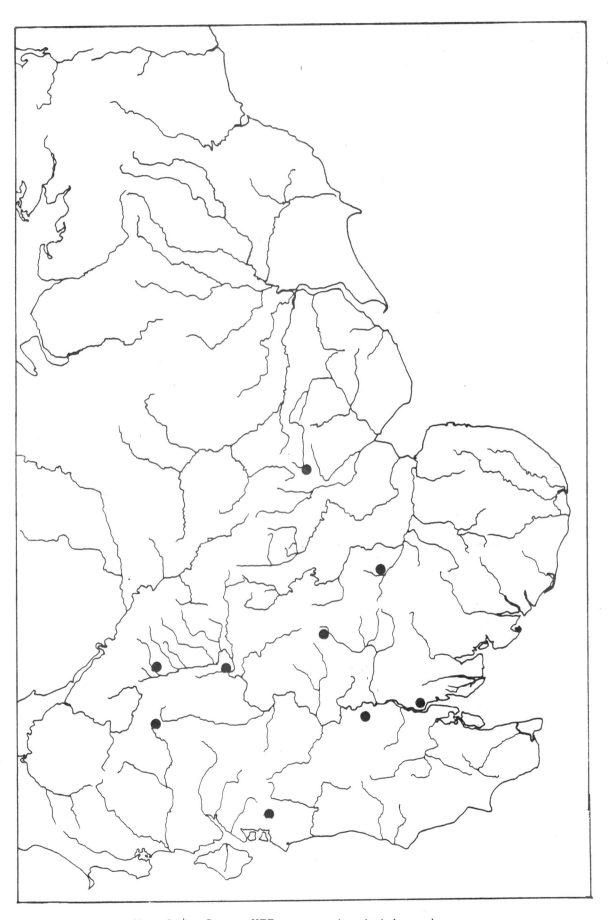

Map 3.4 Group VII square-headed brooches

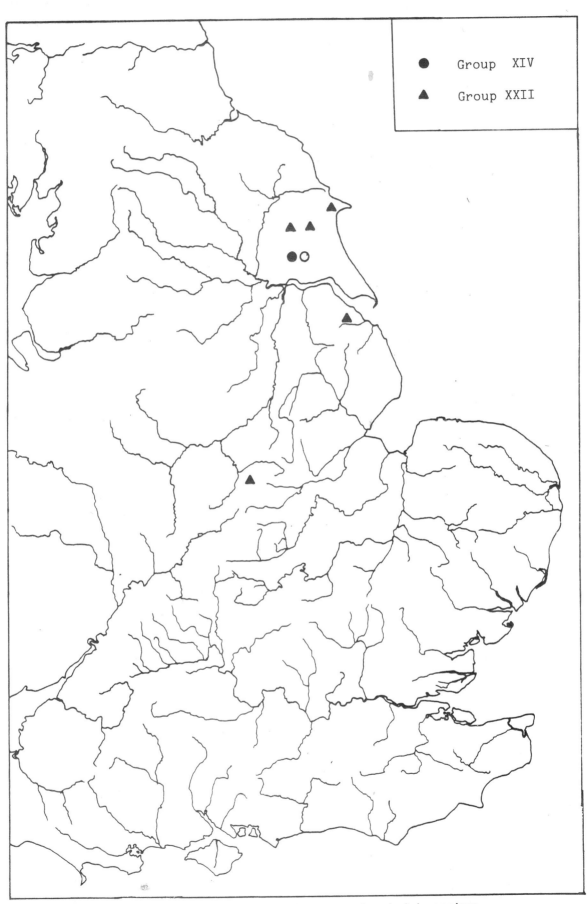

Map 3.5 Groups XIV & XXII square-headed brooches

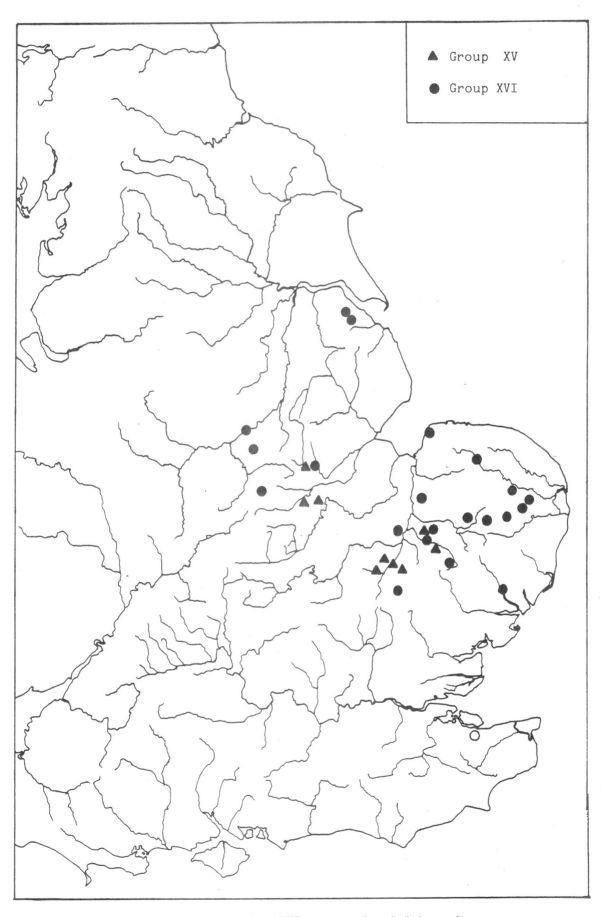

Map 3.6   Groups XV & XVI square-headed brooches

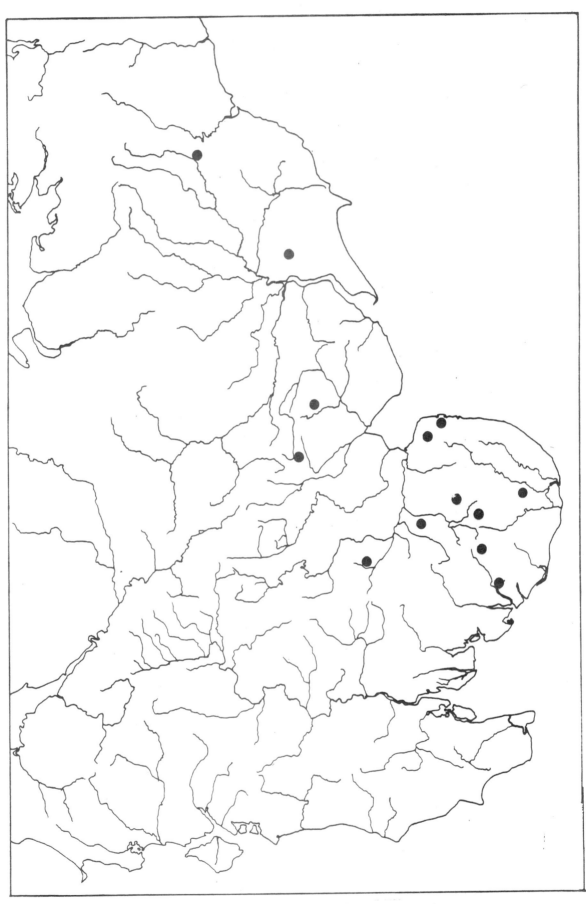

Map 3.7 Group XVII square-headed brooches

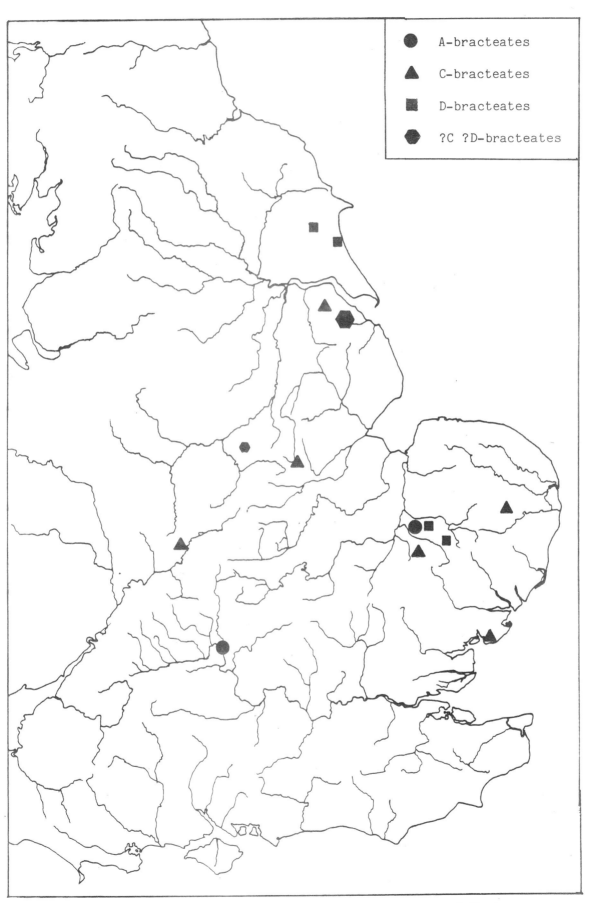

Map 4.1   Bracteate-finds in England, outside of Kent

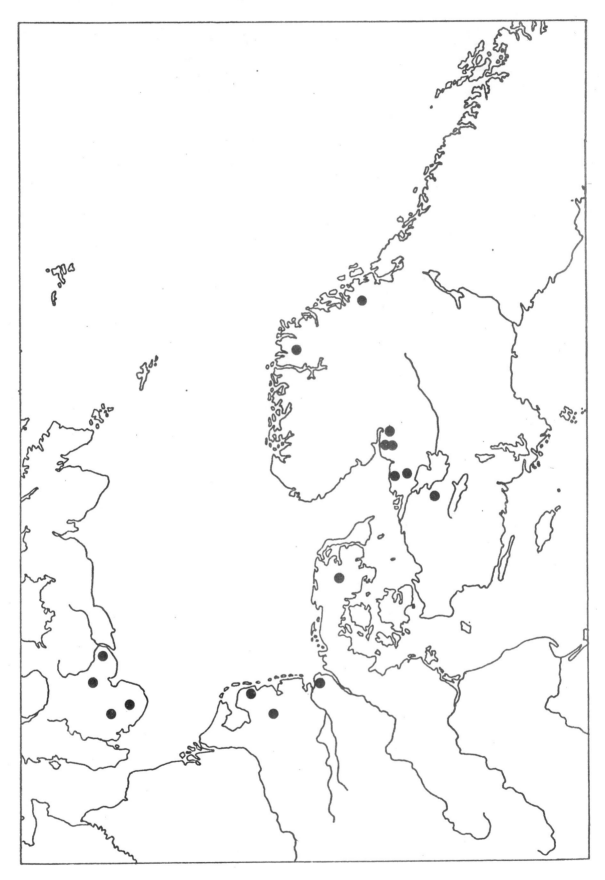

Map 4.2 C-bracteates, Mackeprang's West Scandinavian
Group, and Anglian English derivatives

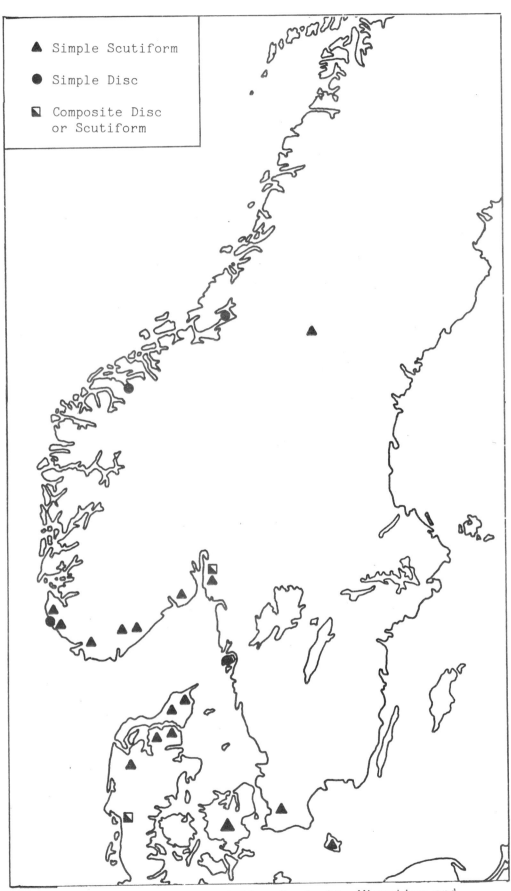

Map 4.3 Scutiform and Disc Pendants, Migration and
Vendel Periods, Scandinavia

369

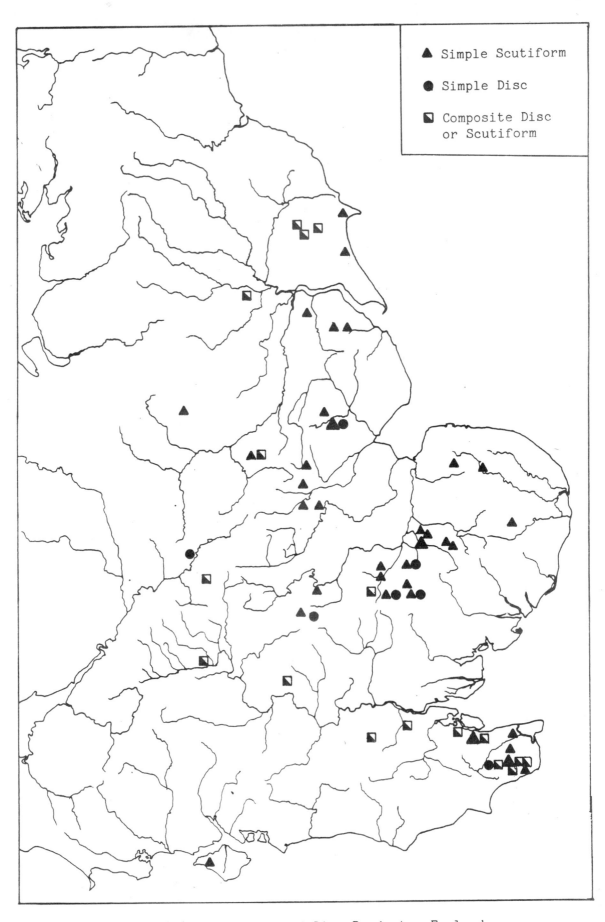

Map 4.4   Scutiform and Disc Pendants, England

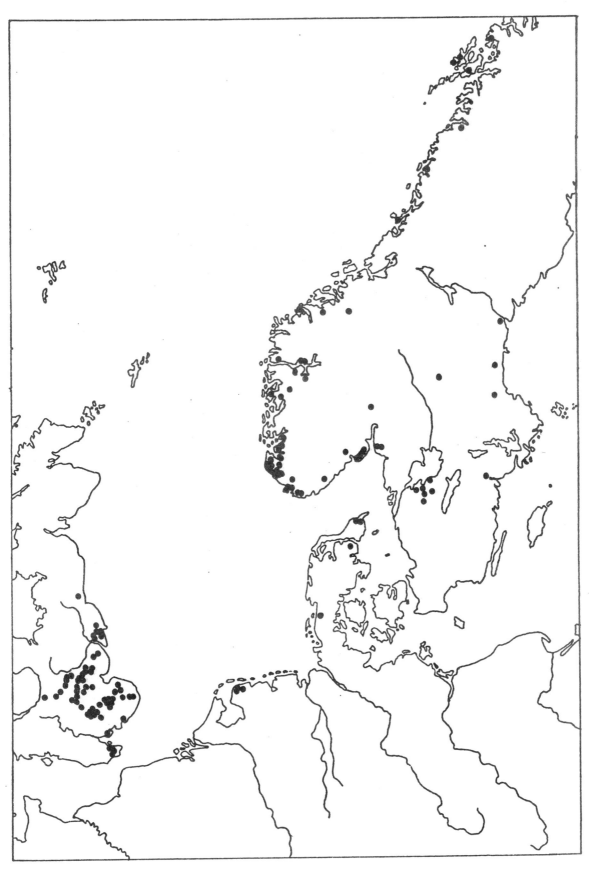

Map 5.1a Cruciform Brooches with cast side knobs

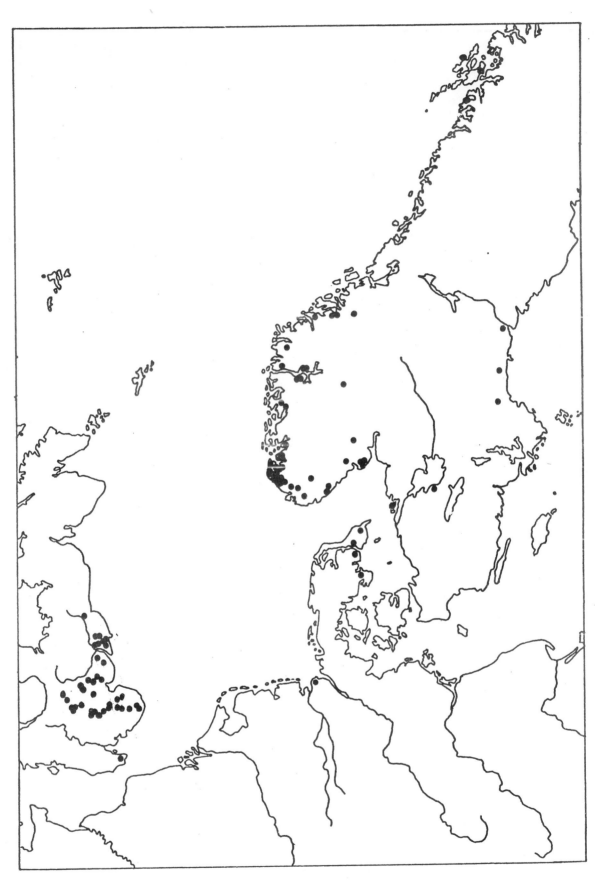

Map 5.1b Cruciform Brooches with plate plus
lappets below the bow

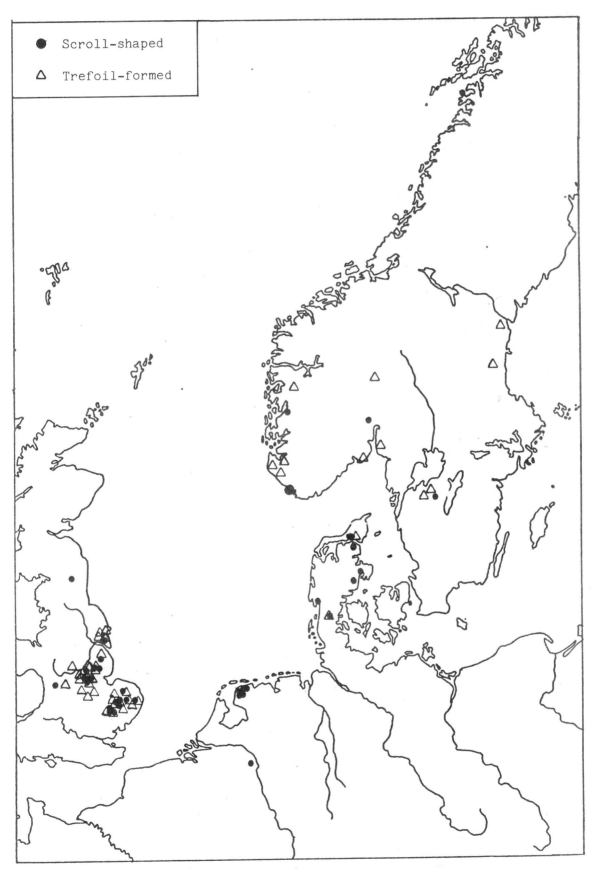

Map 5.1c Cruciform Brooches with scroll-shaped or
trefoil-formed nostrils

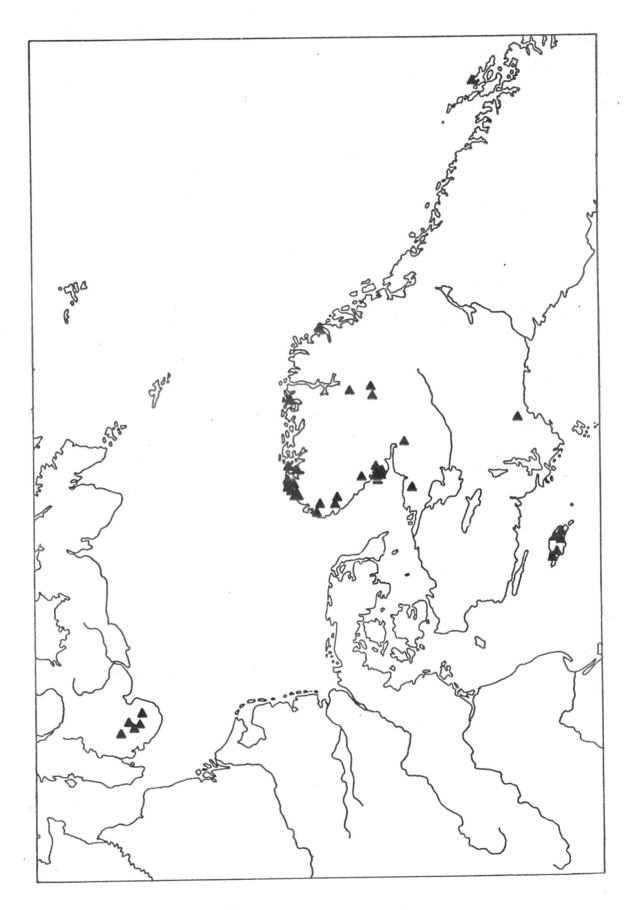

Map 5.2   Anglian and Scandinavian Equal-Armed Brooches

374

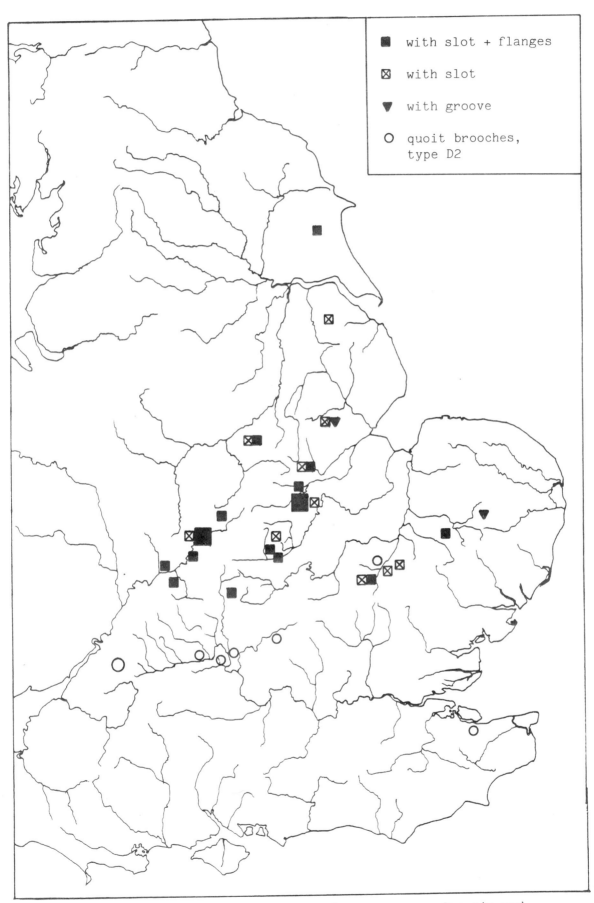

Map 5.3 Annular brooches with slot or groove for pin-end,
and quoit brooches of Ager's type D2

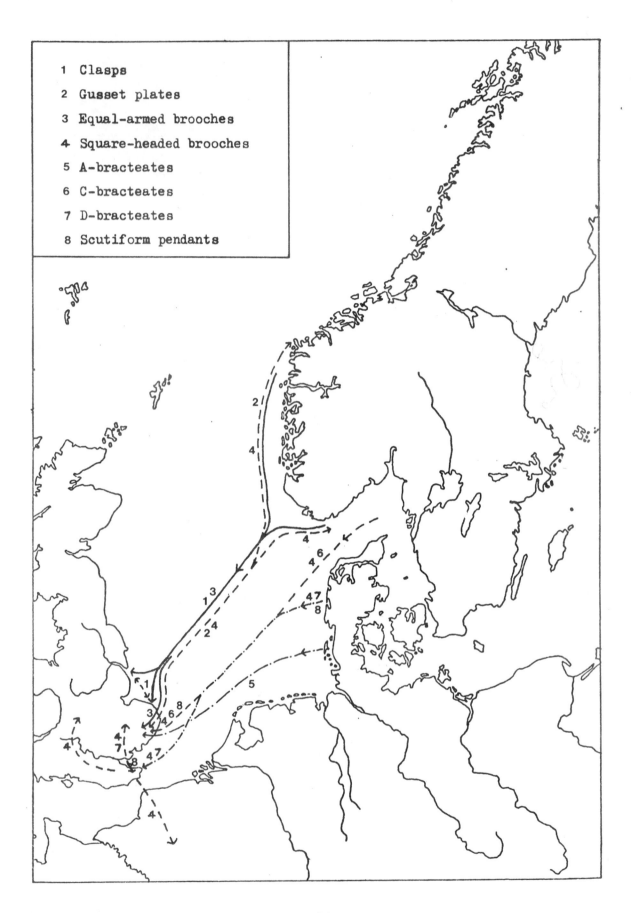

1 Clasps
2 Gusset plates
3 Equal-armed brooches
4 Square-headed brooches
5 A-bracteates
6 C-bracteates
7 D-bracteates
8 Scutiform pendants

Map 6.1

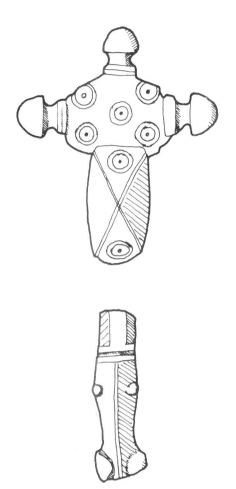

Fig.1.1
N. Møllegård,
Horne, Vennebjerg, Hj
VHM 11334

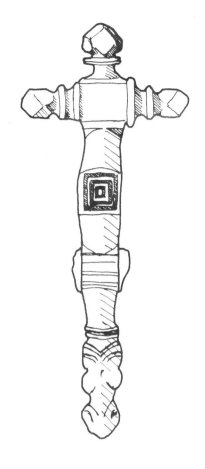

Fig.1.2
Sejlflod, Sejlflod,
Fleskum, Ål
ÅHM 669/1293

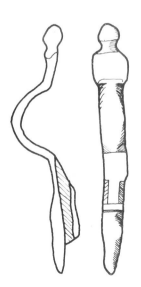

Fig.1.3
Hockwold-cum-Wilton,
Nfk
Norwich Mus 583.975

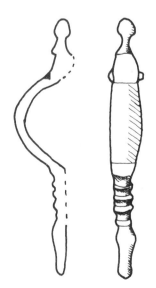

Fig.1.4
Glentham, Lincs
Lincoln Mus

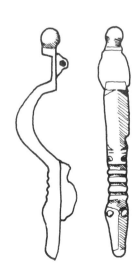

Fig.1.5
Mejlby, Ålborg a.
NMK C5814

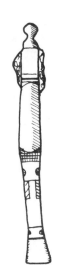

Fig.1.6
Empingham I,
Leics g.3
RCM

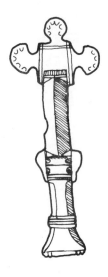

Fig.1.7
Romdrup mose, Romdrup,
Fleskum, Ål
NMK C7388

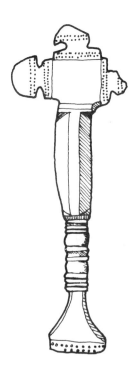

Fig.1.8
Skindbjærge, Læsten,
Sønderlyng, Ra
KHM 28/79 6816

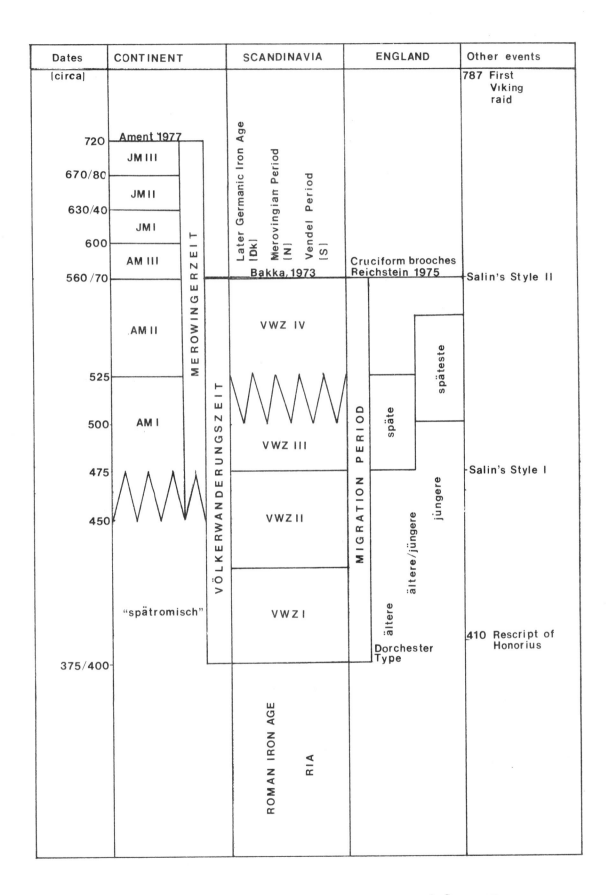

Fig.1.9   Chronological Conventions.   A Summary

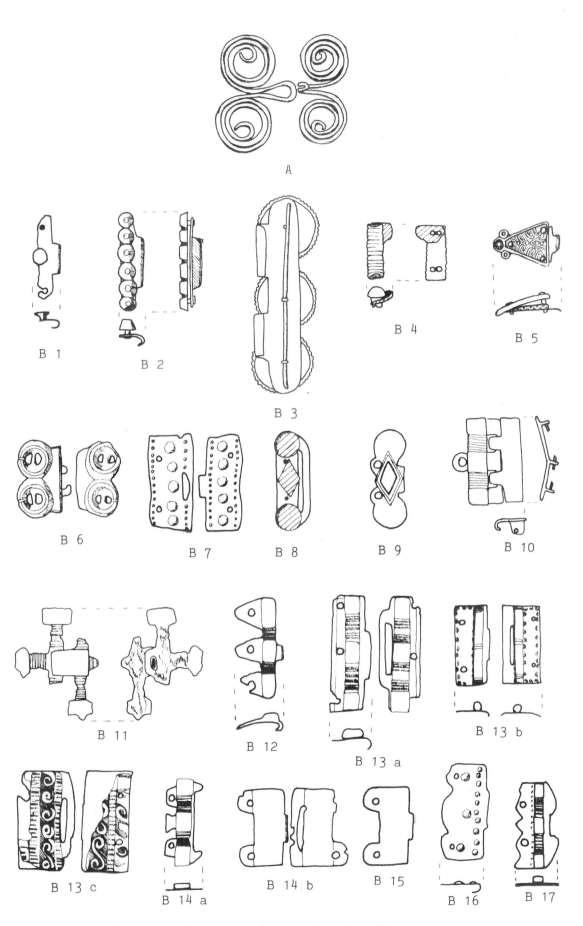

Fig.2.1 English and Scandinavian Clasps.
Summary Diagram of Classes and Forms   (see over)

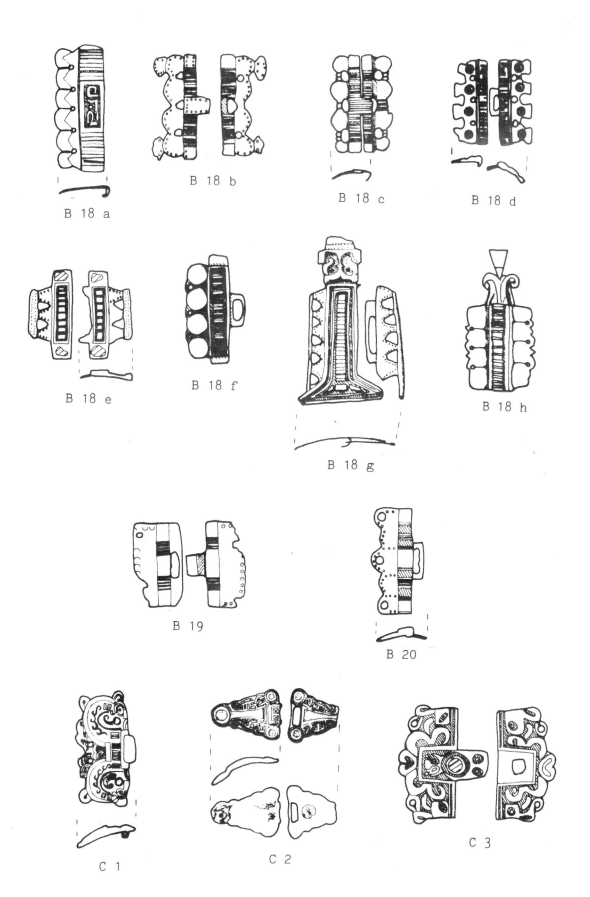

B 18 a

B 18 b

B 18 c

B 18 d

B 18 e

B 18 f

B 18 g

B 18 h

B 19

B 20

C 1

C 2

C 3

Fig.2.1 continued

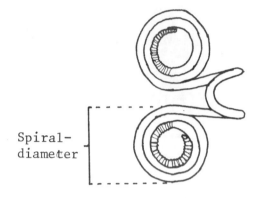

Spiral-
diameter

Fig.2.2
Kenninghall, Nfk
BM 83.7-2.19
Class A

Fig.2.3
Carlsborg, Allhelgona,
Ög, S
SHM 15694
Class A

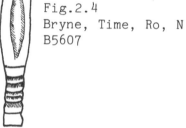

Fig.2.4
Bryne, Time, Ro, N
B5607

Fig.2.5
Holywell Row, Sfk g.17
after Lethbridge
Class A

Fig.2.6
Roligheden, Hedrum, Vf, N
C14345
Form B 1

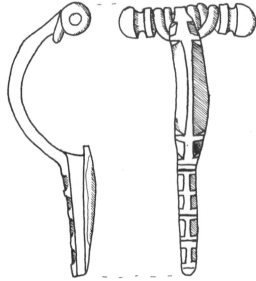

Fig.2.7
Ås, Sande, Vf, N
C29263b

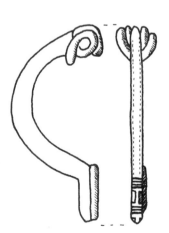

Fig.2.8
Øvstebø, Sandeid, Ro, N
S2258

Fig.2.9
N. Opstad, Tune, Øf, N
C31074
Form B 1

Fig.2.10a
Skreia, Tjølling, Vf, N
C18895
Form B 1

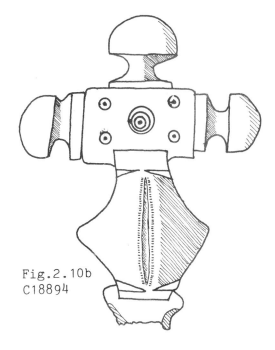

Fig.2.10b
C18894

Fig.2.11
Lunde, Vanse, VA, N
B3543
Form B 1

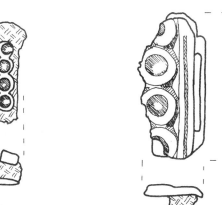

Fig.2.12
Sejlflod, Sejlflod,
Fleskum, Ålborg, Dk g.DD
ÅHM 669/860, 872
Form B 2

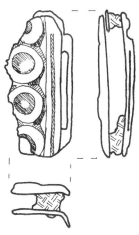

Fig.2.13a
Kobbeå, Bornholm g.7
NMK C6159
Form B 2

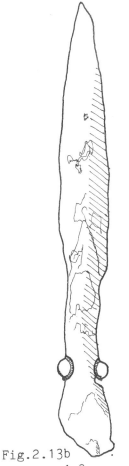

Fig.2.13b
approx. 1:3

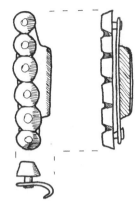

Fig.2.14
Älby, Ösmo, Sö, S
SHM 26284:47 F37
Form B 2

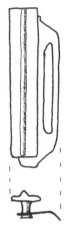

Fig.2.15
Missionshuset, Brunflo,
Jä, S
JLM 15700
Form B 2

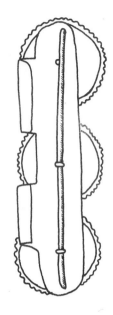

Fig.2.16
Ugulen, Hafslo, SFj, N
B6071q
Form B 3

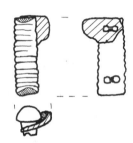

Fig.2.17
Lunde, Høyland, Ro, N
B3160
Form B 4

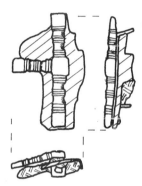

Fig.2.18
Sancton, Hu u.180/1958
Hull Mus
Form B 4

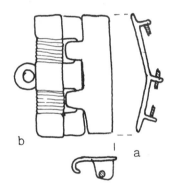

Fig.2.19
Sancton, Hu u.135/20
Hull Mus
Form B 10

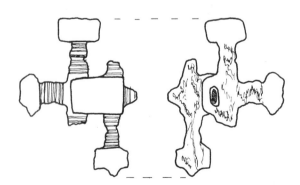

Fig.2.20
Burgh Castle, Nfk
Norwich Mus 20.39
Form B 11

Fig.2.21
Sejlflod, Sejlflod
Fleskum, Ålborg, Dk g.DY
Form B 5

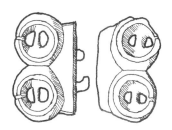

Fig.2.22a
Lye, Time, Ro, N
S9150
Form B 6

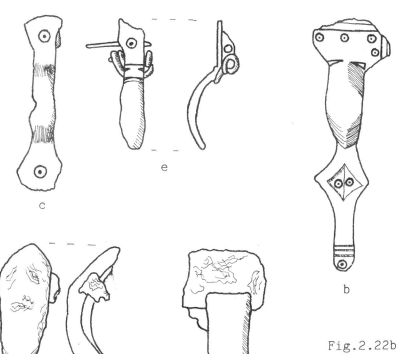

c

e

b

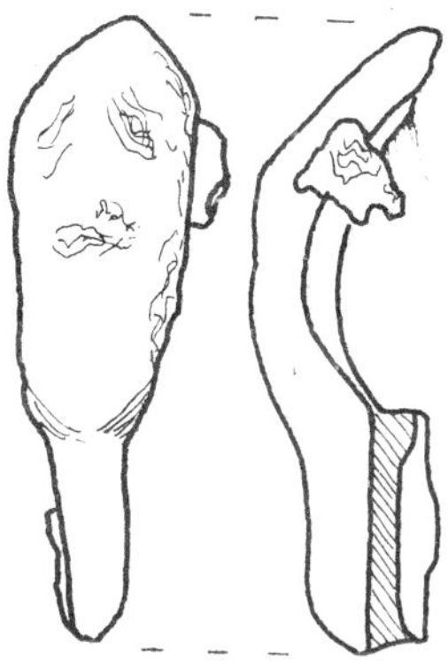

j

h

Fig.2.22b
S9150b, c, e, h, j

Fig.2.23
Gitlevåg, Spangereid,
VA
B5060a
Form C 1

Fig.2.24
Mellberg, Strand, Ro
S7577a
Form C 1

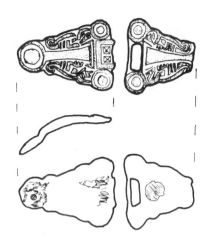

Fig.2.25
Djurgårdsäng, Vg
SLM 6563
Form C 2

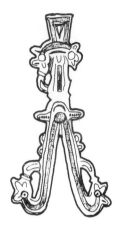

Fig.2.26
Giskegjerde, Giske,
MR
B726

Fig.2.27
Dalum, Sparbu, NT
C4822

Fig.2.28
Northwold, Nfk
BM 53.8-15.51
Form B 1

Fig.2.29
"probably Weasenham",
Nfk
BM OA4946
Form B 1

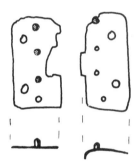

Fig.2.30
Glaston, Leics
RCM OS580
Form B 8

Fig.2.31
Staxton, N.Yorks
Hull Mus
Form B 8

Fig.2.32
Morningthorpe, Nfk
g.208
Norwich Mus
Form B 8

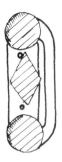

Fig.2.33
Sancton, Hu
Ashmolean 1881.1316
Form B 8

Fig.2.34
Morningthorpe, Nfk
g.48
Norwich Mus
Form B 9

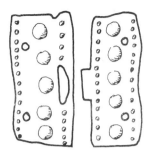

Fig.2.35
Marston St.Lawrence,
N'hants g.3
Form B 7

Fig.2.36
Sleaford, Lincs g.216
BM 83.4-1.465
Form B 7

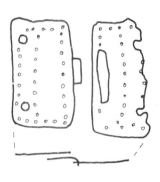

Fig.2.37
Welbeck Hill, Hu g.34
after drawing by
G. Taylor Esq.
Form B 7

Fig.2.38
Sleaford, Lincs
g.124/125
BM 83.4-1.231
Form B 7

Fig.2.39
Glaston, Leics
RCM
Form B 12

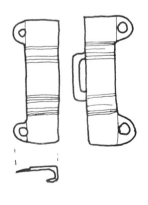

Fig.2.40
Holdenby, N'hants
N'pton Mus
D76-77/1955-56
Form B 12

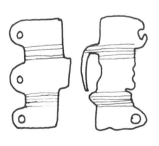

Fig.2.41
Driffield, Hu
after Mortimer
Form B 12

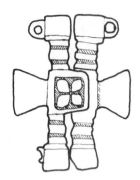

Fig.2.42
Linton Heath, Cambs
g.30
MAA Cam 48.1551
Form B 12

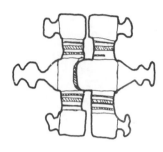

Fig.2.43
Little Wilbraham,
Cambs g.4
MAA Cam 48.1325a
Form B 12

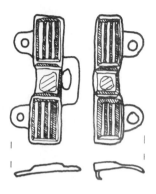

Fig.2.44
Glaston, Leics
RCM OS120
Form B 12

Fig.2.45
West Stow, Sfk
MAA Cam
Form B 12

Fig.2.46
Morningthorpe, Nfk
g.253
Norwich Mus
Form B 12

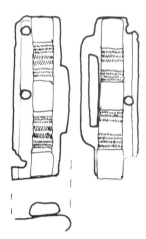

Fig.2.47
Morningthorpe, Nfk
g.25
Norwich Mus
Form B 13 a

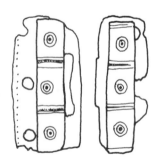

Fig.2.48
Churchover, Warwicks
Warwicks Mus
A1514, 1521
Form B 13 a

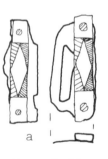

Form B 13 a

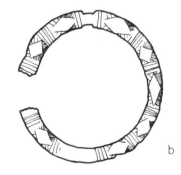

Fig.2.49a-b
Morningthorpe, Nfk
g.387
Norwich Mus

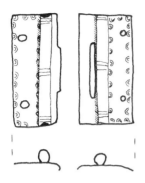

Fig.2.50
Sleaford, Lincs g.97
BM 83.4-1.193-194
Form B 13 b

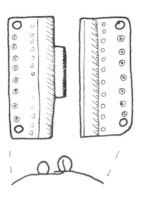

Fig.2.51
Holdenby, N'hants g.8
N'pton Mus
D114a/1955-56
Form B 13 b

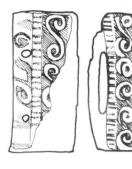

Fig.2.52
Gt. Chesterford, Ex
g.135
BM 1964.7-2.429-430
Form B 13 c

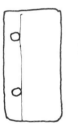

Fig.2.53
Islip, N'hants
N'pton Mus
D123a/1959-60
Form B 13 c

Fig.2.54
Wakerley, N'hants
g.44/45
Kettering Mus
690557-690558
Form B 13 c

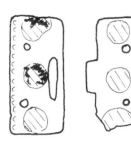

Fig.2.55
Unknown provenance
RCM OS121
Form B 13 d

Fig.2.56
Wangford, Sfk
BM 54.9-2.35
Form B 14 a

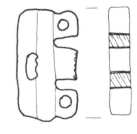

Fig.2.57
Bidford-on-Avon,
Warwicks g.103
Stratford Mus
Form B 14 a

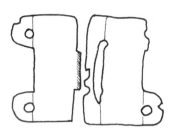

Fig.2.58
Haslingfield, Cambs
Ashmolean 1909.243c
Form B 14 b

Fig.2.59
Sleaford, Lincs g.154
BM 83.4-1.318-319
Form B 16

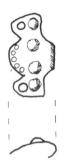

Fig.2.60
Caistor or Searby,
Lincs
Lincoln Mus
Form B 16

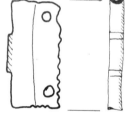

Fig.2.61
Gt. Chesterford, Ex
g.66
BM 1964.7-2.242-247

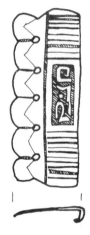

Fig.2.62
Londesborough, Hu g.2
Ashmolean 1346.1886
Form B 18 a

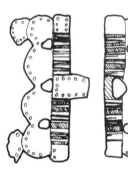

Fig.2.63
Morningthorpe, Nfk
g.208
Norwich Mus
Form B 18 b

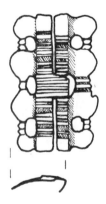

Fig.2.64
Linton Heath, Cambs
g.72
MAA Cam 48.1607
Form B 18 c

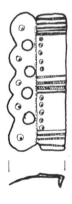

Fig.2.65
Caistor or Searby,
Lincs
Lincoln Mus
Form B 18 c

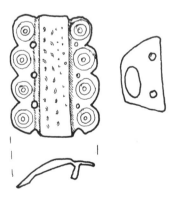

Fig.2.66
Morningthorpe, Nfk
g.20
Norwich Mus
Form B 18 c

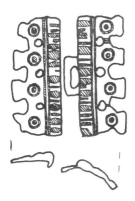

Fig.2.67
Westgarth Gardens, Bury
St. Edmunds, Sfk g.52
BSE Mus
Form B 18 d

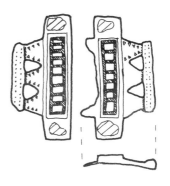

Fig.2.68
Sleaford, Lincs g.205
BM 83.4-1.436
Form B 18 e

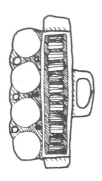

Fig.2.69
? Thorpe Malsor,
N'hants
Kettering Mus 1961.43/4
Form B 18 f

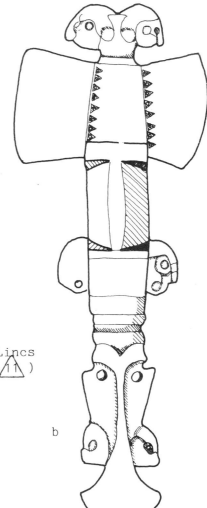

Fig.2.70a-b
Ruskington, Lincs
(1975 Level 11)
Lincoln Mus

a

Form B 18 f

b

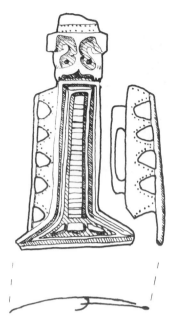

Fig.2.71
Baginton, Warwicks
Coventry Mus
A/1013/51-52
Form B 18 g

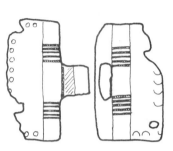

Fig.2.72
Morningthorpe, Nfk
g.96
Norwich Mus
Form B 19

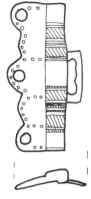

Fig.2.73
Ixworth, Sfk
Ashmolean 1909.444a
Form B 20

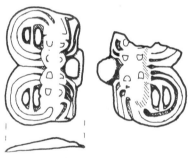

Fig.2.74
Willoughby-on-the-Wolds,
Notts
Nottingham Mus
Form C 1

Fig.2.75
Saxonbury, Sx
Lewes Mus
Form C 1

Fig.2.76
Haslingfield, Cambs
Ashmolean 1909.245
Form C 1

Fig.2.77
? Thorpe Malsor,
N'hants
Kettering Mus 1961 43/3
Form C 1

Fig.2.78
Mildenhall, Sfk
BSE Mus
Form C 1

Fig.2.79
West Stow, Sfk
MAA Cam
Form C 1

Fig.2.80
Morningthorpe, Nfk
g.353
Norwich Mus
Form C 3

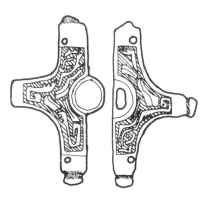

Fig.2.81
Morningthorpe, Nfk
g.360
Norwich Mus
Class C

Fig.2.82
Mildenhall, Sfk
BSE Mus

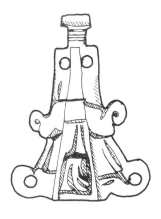

Fig.2.83
West Stow, Sfk
MAA Cam

Fig.2.84
Rothwell, N'hants
MAA Cam

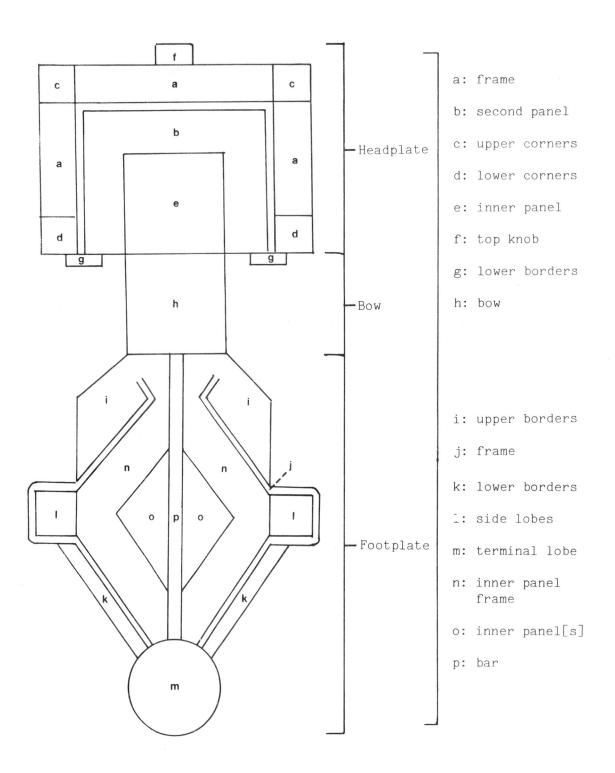

a: frame

b: second panel

c: upper corners

d: lower corners

e: inner panel

f: top knob

g: lower borders

h: bow

i: upper borders

j: frame

k: lower borders

l: side lobes

m: terminal lobe

n: inner panel frame

o: inner panel[s]

p: bar

Fig.3.1 Typical outline and elements of a square-headed
brooch

394

 Fig.3.2 West Stow [II]

Holywell Row 11    Barrington B 9

Fig.3.3 Bow panels, Holywell Row 11 and Barrington B 9

Holywell Row 11   Barrington B 9

Herpes

Fig.3.4 Headplate upper corners, Holywell Row 11, and
Barrington B 9

Headplate second panel, Herpes (Leigh 1980 He3)

(2:1)

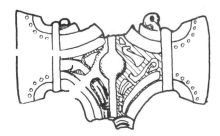

Fig.3.5 Lackford 50/178

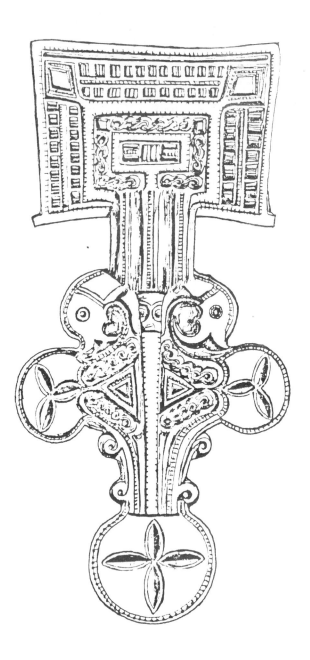

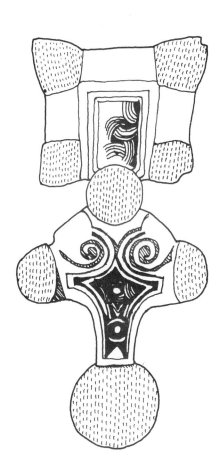

Fig.3.6 Welbeck Hill 41

Drawn by G. Taylor Esq

Fig.3.7 Merton

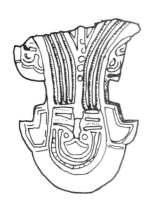

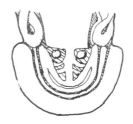

Fig.3.8a <u>Welbeck Hill</u> 45   Fig.3.8b Niederbriesig, Kr.
                                                   Ahrweiler, Rheinland
          Drawn by G. Taylor Esq   Approx. 3:2

Fig.3.9 <u>Ruskington</u> [UC]

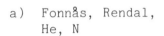

a

b

a) Fonnås, Rendal,
    He, N

b) Pompey, Lorraine
    (after Haseloff)

Fig.3.10 Footplate upper borders (not to scale)

a) Holywell Row 11

b) Tranum Klithuse, Tranum
    Hjørring a., Dk
    (after Haseloff)

Fig.3.11 Headplate inner panels (not to scale)

a) Milton-next-Sittingbourne, Kt

b) Rothley Temple [IV]

Fig.3.12 Footplate side lobes (1:1)

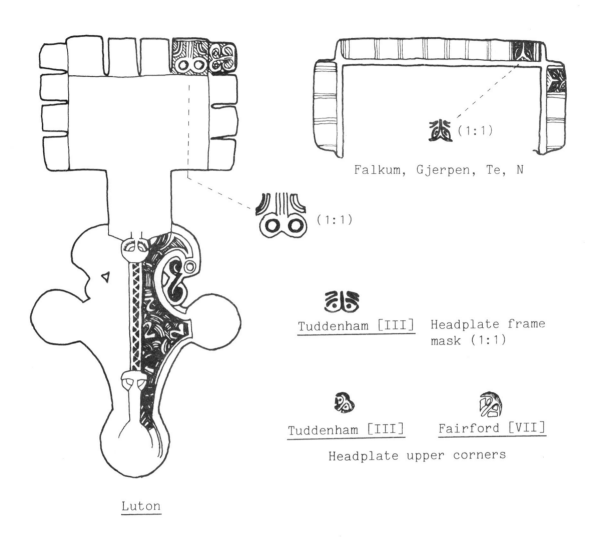

(1:1)

Falkum, Gjerpen, Te, N

(1:1)

Tuddenham [III]   Headplate frame
mask (1:1)

Tuddenham [III]   Fairford [VII]

Headplate upper corners

Luton

Fonnås, Rendal, He, N

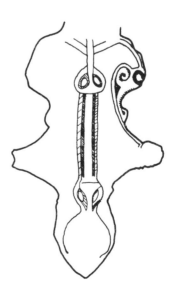

Staurnes, Borgund, MR, N

Fig.3.13

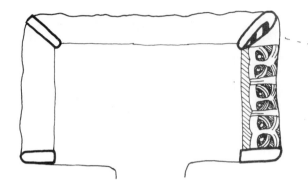

Fig.3.14a   Jæren, Ro, N
             B3045

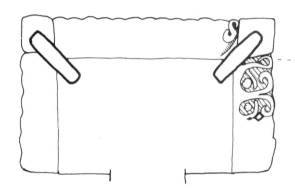
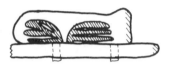

Fig.3.14b   Northampton [VIII]

a) Barrington A 11   b) Jæren, Ro, N (B3045)

c) Ragley Park   d) Å, Åfjord, ST, N

Fig.3.15a-d

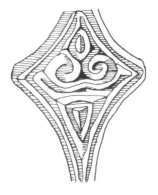

<u>Willoughby-on-the-Wolds 57</u>   Trivières, Hainault, Belgium

Fig.3.16 Footplate inner panels (approx. 2:1)

Fig.4.1
VRBS ROMA
Medallions
(after Froehner)

 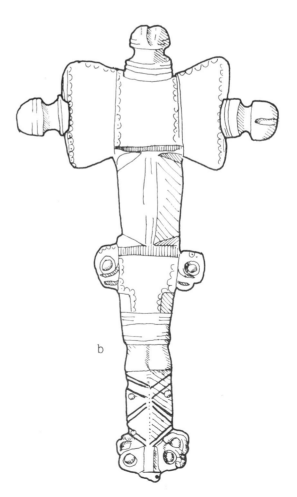

a   b

Fig.4.2a-b
Morningthorpe, Nfk
g.80
Norwich Mus

401

Fig.4.3
Jaywick Sands, Ex
(sketch)

Fig.4.4
Høstentorp, Søro a.
NMK df.62/33

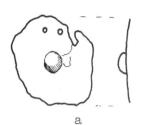

a

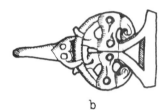

b

Fig.4.5a-b
Västbyn, Frösön, Jä
JLM 13804

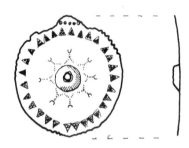

Fig.4.6
Kempston, Beds
BEDFM 3848

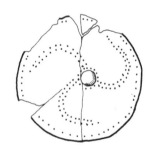

Fig.4.7
Sleaford, Lincs g.95
BM 83.4-1.179

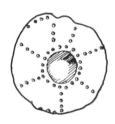

Fig.4.8
Longstone, Derbys
BM 73.6-2.90

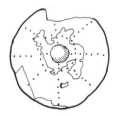

Fig.4.9
Faversham, Kt
Maidstone Mus
32.1957

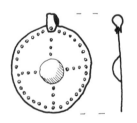

Fig.4.10
Faversham, Kt
Ashmolean 1909.139a

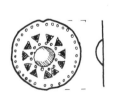

Fig.4.11
Faversham, Kt
BM 81.12-12.5-7

Fig.5.1
Borgstedt, Kr. Eckenförde,
Schleswig-Holstein
KS4026

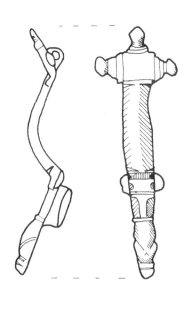

Fig.5.2
Ørnefenner, Thise,
Borglum, Hj
VHM 1981/60

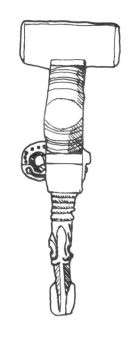

Fig.5.3
Balle mark, Balle,
Hinds, Vi
KHM 8599 rød

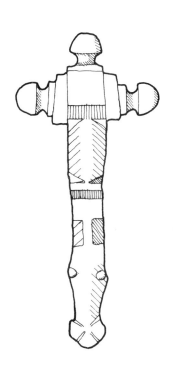

Fig.5.4
Olde, Voss, Ho
B1345

Fig.5.5
Islip, N'hants
Kettering Mus

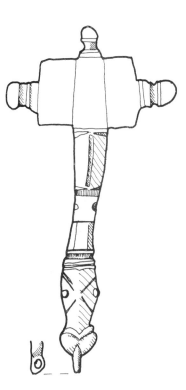

Fig.5.6
Wakerley, N'hants g.25
Kettering Mus

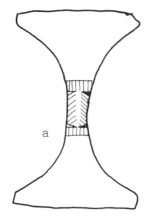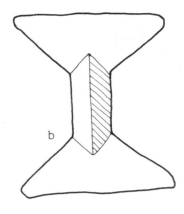

Fig.5.7a-b
Westgarth Gardens, Bury
St. Edmunds, Sfk g.36
BSE Mus

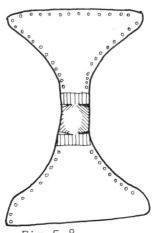

Fig.5.8
Newnham, Cambs
MAA Cam 1892.FB

Brandon, Sfk

Westgarth Gardens, Bury
St. Edmunds Sfk g.36

Holywell Row, Sfk g.16

Spong Hill, Nfk g.46

Newnham, Cambs

Fig.5.9
Anglian Equal-Armed
Brooches - Bow forms

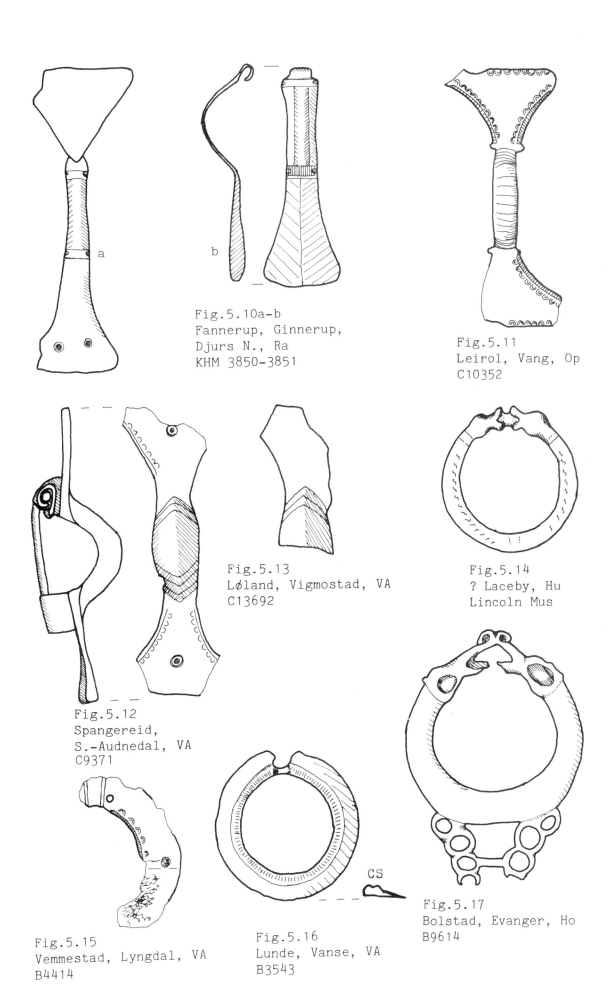

Fig.5.10a-b
Fannerup, Ginnerup,
Djurs N., Ra
KHM 3850-3851

Fig.5.11
Leirol, Vang, Op
C10352

Fig.5.12
Spangereid,
S.-Audnedal, VA
C9371

Fig.5.13
Løland, Vigmostad, VA
C13692

Fig.5.14
? Laceby, Hu
Lincoln Mus

Fig.5.15
Vemmestad, Lyngdal, VA
B4414

Fig.5.16
Lunde, Vanse, VA
B3543

CS

Fig.5.17
Bolstad, Evanger, Ho
B9614

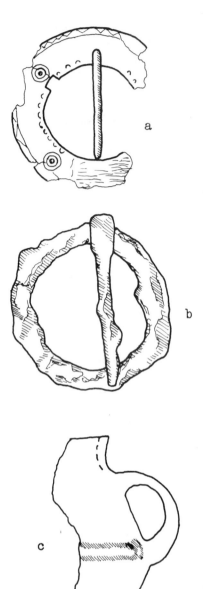

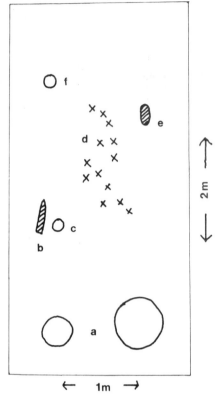

d. Grave Plan

a. Store lerkar
b. Jernkniv
c. Jernspænde
d. Perlekæde
e. Broncesmykke
f. Mindstelerkar

Fig.5.18a-d
Østre Gesten Skov
Gesten, Amst, Ribe
NMK C26940-26960

Fig.5.19
Kobbeå, Bornholm g.11
NMK C6166

406

LIST OF PLATES

Clasps

2.1 Woodston, Cambs. Form B 13 d (x 2)

2.2 Gt. Chesterford, Ex. Form C 1 (x 2)

2.3 Morningthorpe, Nfk g.153. Class C

Square-headed Brooches

3.1 <u>Dartford</u>. Group I

3.2 <u>Berinsfield 102</u>. Group I

3.3 <u>Beckford A 11</u>. Group VI. Photograph by courtesy of Dr T.M. Dickinson.

3.4 <u>Empingham I</u>

3.5 <u>Pewsey 21</u>. Group VII. Photograph by courtesy of Dr T.M. Dickinson

3.6 <u>Willoughby-on-the-Wolds 15</u>. Group X

3.7 <u>East Garston Warren</u>. Group XII

3.8 <u>Wakerley 50</u>. Group XV

3.9 <u>Wakerley 80</u>. Group XV

3.10 <u>Westgarth Gardens, Bury St.Edmunds 27</u>. Group XVI

3.11 <u>Morningthorpe 214</u>. Group XVI

3.12 <u>Great Chesterford 2</u>. Group XVI

3.13 <u>Morningthorpe 371</u>. Group XVIII

3.14 Roses, Tingstäde, Gotland

4.1 Undley, Sfk. A-bracteate (x 2)

4.2 Driffield, Hu. D-bracteate (x 2)

4.3 Sarre, Kt g.IV. D-bracteate (x 2)

4.4 Faversham, Kt. Composite Disc/Scutiform Pendants

5.1 Oadby, Leics. Cruciform Brooch with animal-head lappets below the bow

2.1

2.2

2.3

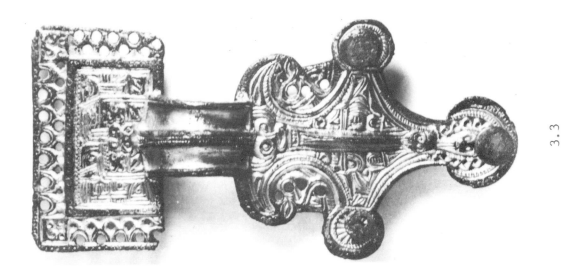

3.3

3.2 →

3.1

409

3.5

3.4

3.6

3.7

3.8

3.9

411

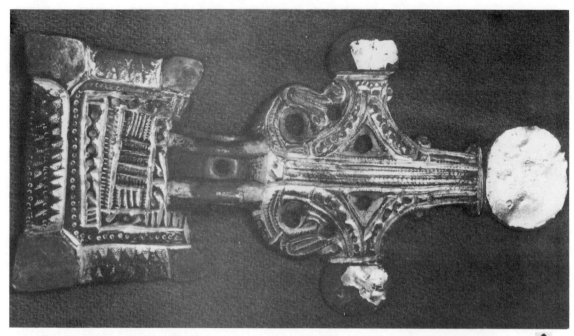

3.12 →

3.11

← 3.10

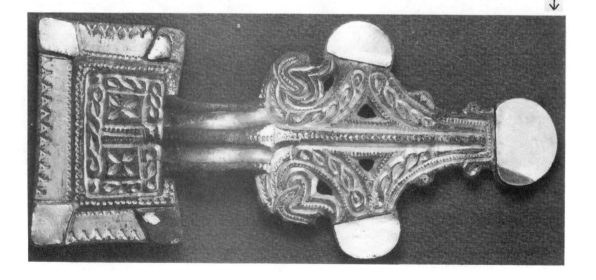

412

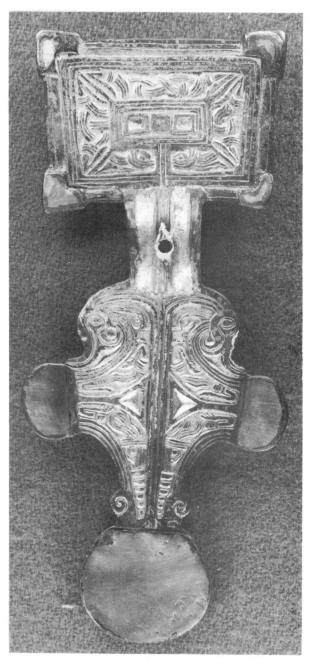

3.13

3.14

5.1

4.2

4.3

4.1

4.4

414

BIBLIOGRAPHY

ADDYMAN, P.V., PEARSON, N., and TWEDDLE, D. 1982: The Coppergate Helmet, Antiquity LVI.

AGER, B.M. forthcoming: The smaller variants of the Anglo-Saxon quoit brooch, ASSAH (4?).

AKERMAN, J.Y. 1855: Remains of Pagan Saxondom.

ALBRETHSEN, S.E. 1974: Bjerby - en jernaldergravplads på Mors, NA 1974.

ALCUIN VSW: Vita Sancti Willibrordi.

ALMGREN, B., and NERMAN, B. 1923: Die ältere Eisenzeit Gotlands.

AMBROSIANI, B. 1980: Batgravarnas bakgrund i Mälardalen. Vendeltid, Statens Historiska Museum, Stockholm.

AMBROSIANI, B., BENNETT, A., BRYNJA, E., FERENIUS, J. 1981: Projektet Mälardalens folkvandringstid. Fv 76.

AMENT, H. 1976: Chronologische Untersuchungen an fränkischen Gräberfeldern der jüngeren Merowingerzeit im Rheinland. BRGK 57.

AMENT, H. 1977: Zur archäologischen Periodisierung der Merowingerzeit. Germania LV.

Andreas in The Old English Poetic Records, ed. Krapp and Dobbie, vol.II.

ARBMAN, H. 1943: Birka. I - Die Gräber.

ARNOLD, C.J. 1982: The Anglo-Saxon Cemeteries of the Isle of Wight.

ARRHENIUS, B. 1960: Båtgraven från Augerum. Tor 6.

ARRHENIUS, B. 1971: Granatschmuck und Gemmen aus nordischen Funden des frühen Mittelalters.

ARRHENIUS, B. 1980: The Chronology of the Vendel Graves.

ARTIS, E.T. 1828: The Durobrivae of Antoninus.

ARWIDSSON, G. 1942: Vendelstile.

ASC: The Anglo-Saxon Chronicle.

AVENT, R. 1975: Anglo-Saxon Garnet Inlaid Disc and Composite Brooches.

AXBOE, M. 1982:   The Scandinavian Gold Bracteates.   _Acta Arch_ 52.

BAKKA, E. 1958:   On the beginning of Salin's Style I in England. _BMÅ_ 1958, H-a.r.3.

BAKKA, E. 1963:   Some English Decorated Metal Objects found in Norwegian Viking Graves. _ÅUB_ 1963, Hum.serie 1.

BAKKA, E. 1973:   Goldbrakteaten in norwegischen Grabfunden. Datierungsfragen. _FS_ 7.

BEDE _HE_: Historica Ecclesiastica Gentis Anglorum.

BEDE _ILR_: In Libros (Samuelis et Libros) Regum. Questionum XXX.

BENDIXEN, K. 1981:   Sceattas and Other Coin Finds. _Ribe Excavations_ 1.

Beowulf ed. Fr. Klaeber, 3rd. edn. 1950.

BLINDHEIM, C. 1946:   En detalj i eldre jernalderens drakthistorie, _SMÅ_ 1945.

BLINDHEIM, C. 1947:   Drakt og smykker, _Viking_ 11.

BOELES, P.C.J.A. 1951:   Friesland tot de Elfde Eeuw.

BÖHME, H.W. 1974:   Germanische Grabfunde des 4. bis 5. Jahrhunderts zwischen unterer Elbe und Loire.

BÖHNER, K. 1958:   Die frankische Altertümer des Trierer Landes.

BONNET, C., and MARTIN, M. 1982:   La modèle de plomb d'une fibule anglo-saxonne de Saint-Pierre à Genève. _Arch. suisse_ 1982.

BRANDT, J. 1960: Das Urnengräberfeld von Preetz in Holstein.

BRENT, J. 1866: Account of the society's researches in the Anglo-Saxon cemetery at Sarr. _Arch. Cant._ VI.

BROWN, G.B. I-V: The Arts in Early England. Vols 1-5.

BRUCE-MITFORD, R.M. 1974: Aspects of Anglo-Saxon Archaeology

BRØNSTED, J. 1960: Danmarks Oldtid. III - Jernalderen.

BULLINGER, H. 1969: Spätantike Gürtelbeschläge.

BØE, J. 1921: Norske guldfund fra folkevandringstiden.

BØE, J. 1926: Norsk gravguld fra ældre jernalder.

BØE, J. 1931: Jernalderens keramikk i Norge.

CAMERON, K. 1961: English Place-Names.

CAMPBELL, A. 1959: Old English Grammar.

CHADWICK, H.M. 1906: The Origin of the English Nation.

CHASE, C. (ed.) 1981: The Dating of Beowulf.

CLARKE, D.L. 1978: Analytical Archaeology, 2nd edn.
    revised by Bob Chapman.

CLOUGH, T.H.McK., DORNIER, A., and RUTLAND, R.A. 1975:
    Anglo-Saxon and Viking Leicestershire.

COOK, A.M. 1981: The Anglo-Saxon Cemetery at Fonaby,
    Lincolnshire.

COOK, J.M. 1958: An Anglo-Saxon Cemetery at Broadway Hill,
    Broadway, Worcestershire. Ant. J. XXXVIII.

COSACK, E. 1982: Das sächsische Gräberfeld bei Liebenau.

CRADDOCK, J. 1979: The Anglo-Saxon Cemetery at Saxonbury,
    Lewes, East Sussex, Sx.A.C. 117.

CROWFOOT, G.M. 1951: Textiles of the Saxon Period in the
    Museum of Archaeology and Ethnology. P.C.A.S. XLIV.

CRUMMY, P. et al. 1981: Aspects of Anglo-Saxon and Norman
    Colchester.

DAVIDSON, H.R.E. 1962: The Sword in Anglo-Saxon England.

DAVIDSON, H.R.E. 1967: Pagan Scandinavia.

DAVIDSON, H.R.E., and WEBSTER, L. 1967: The Anglo-Saxon
    Burial at Coombe, Kent. Med. Arch. XI.

DAVIES, W. and VIERCK, H.E.F. 1974: The Contexts of Tribal
    Hidage: Social Aggregates and Settlement Patterns.
    FS 8.

DAVIES, W. 1977: Annals and the origin of Mercia. Mercian
    Studies, ed. Dornier.

DELAMAIN, P.: Les sépultures barbares d'Herpes.

DE LANGE, E. 1909: Utgravninger i Hafslo prestegjeld. BMÅ
    1909 no.3.

DE VRIES, J. 1942: Altnordische Literaturgeschichte.

DICKINSON, T.M. 1976: The Anglo-Saxon Burial Sites of the Upper Thames Region and their Bearing on the History of Wessex, circa A.D.400-700. Oxford University D.Phil. Thesis.

DICKINSON, T.M. 1982: Fowler's Type G Penannular Brooches Reconsidered. Med. Arch. XXVI.

DRONKE, U. 1969: The Poetic Edda. Vol.I - Heroic Poems.

DÜMMLER, E. (ed.) 1873: Alcuini Epistolae.

DYBSAND, G. 1955: Et Folkevandringstids gravfunn fra Ommundrød i Hedrum, Vestfold. UOÅ 1954-55.

EHD I: English Historical Documents, vol.I, ed. Whitelock.

ELLMERS, D. 1978: Die Schiffe der Angelsachsen, Sachsen und Angelsachsen, Helms-Museum, Hamburg.

ENGELHARDT, C. 1863: Thorsbjerg Mosefund.

EVISON, V.I. 1965: The Fifth-Century Invasions South of the Thames.

EVISON, V.I. 1977: Supporting-arm brooches and equal-arm brooches in England. Studien zur Sachsenforschung I.

FAGERLIE, J. 1967: Late Roman and Byzantine Solidi found in Sweden and Denmark. ANS.NNM. 157.

FARBREGD, O. 1980: Perspektiv på Namdalens jernalder. Viking XLIII.

FARRELL, R.T. 1972: Beowulf Swedes and Geats.

FAUSSETT, B. 1856: Inventorum Sepulchrale.

FENTON, S. 1888: notes in The Anglo-Saxon Graves, Warren Hill, Mildenhall. See Prigg 1888.

FETT, P. 1938-40: Arms in Norway 400-600.

FITCH, S.E. 1864: Discovery of Saxon Remains at Kempston. AASRP 1864, Bedford Architectural Society.

FLEURY and FRANCE-LANORD, 1963: Das Grab der Arnegundis in Saint-Denis. Germania XL.

FOOTE, P.G., and WILSON, D.M., 1970: The Viking Achievement.

FOX, C.F. 1923: The Archaeology of the Cambridge region.

FROEHNER, W. 1878: Les médallions de l'empire romain.

GELLING, P., and DAVIDSON, H.R.E. 1969:   The Chariot of the Sun.

GENRICH, A. 1954: Formenkreise und Stammesgruppen in Schleswig-Holstein.

Germ: Tacitus, Germania.

GJESSING, G. 1929: De Norske Gullbrakteatene.

GJESSING, G. 1934: Studier i Norsk Merovingertid.

Grimnismál: in Edda. Die Lieder des Codex Regius ed. Neckel.

HAGEN, A. 1977: Norges Oldtid, Ny utgave.

HASELOFF, G. 1974: Salin's Style I. Med. Arch. XVIII.

HASELOFF, G. 1981: Die germanische Tierornamentik der Völkerwanderungszeit.

HATTATT, R. 1982: Ancient and Romano-British Brooches.

HAUCK, K. 1970: Goldbrakteaten aus Sievern.

HAWKES, S.C., DAVIDON, H.R.E., and HAWKES, C.F.C. 1965: The Finglesham Man. Antiquity XXXIX.

HAWKES, S.C., MERRICK, J.M., and METCALF, D.M. 1966: X-Ray Fluorescent Analysis of some Dark Age Coins and Jewellery. Archaeometry 9.

HAWKES, S.C., and MEANEY, A.L. 1970: Two Anglo-Saxon Cemeteries at Winnall, Winchester, Hampshire.

HAWKES, S.C., HOGARTH, A., and DENTON, C. 1975: The Anglo-Saxon Cemetery at Monkton, Thanet. Arch. Cant. LXXXIX.

HAWKES, S.C. 1978: Die anglo-sächsiche Invasion Britanniens. Sachsen und Angelsachsen, Helms-Museum, Hamburg.

HAWKES, S.C., and POLLARD, M. 1981: The gold bracteates from sixth-century Anglo-Saxon graves in Kent, in the light of a new find from Finglesham. FS 15.

HE: Bede, Historia Ecclesiastica Gentis Anglorum.

HEDEAGER, L. 1978: Processes towards State Formation in Early Iron Age Denmark. New Directions in Scandinavian Archaeology.

Helgakviða Hundingsbana I: in Edda. Die Lieder des Codex Regius, ed. Neckel.

HELGÖ I- :   Excavations at Helgö, Vols.I- , ed. Holmquist.

HILLS, C. 1979:   The archaeology of Anglo-Saxon England in the pagan period: a review. ASE 8.

HIRST, S. 1981:   An Anglo-Saxon Cemetery at Sewerby, East Yorkshire. Birkbeck College, London M.Phil. Thesis.

HODGES, R. 1982:   Dake Age Economics.

HÖFLER, O. fs.:   Festgabe für Otto Höfler.

HOLLINGWORTH, E.J., and O'REILLY, M.M. 1925:   The Anglo-Saxon cemetery at Girton College, Cambridge.

HOUGEN, B. 1935:   Snartemofunnene.

HOUGEN, B. 1967:   The Migration Style of Ornament in Norway, 2nd edn.

Húsdrápa: in Den norsk-islandske Skjaldedigtning (ed. Jónsson) A.I.137

HUTCHINSON, P. 1966:   The Anglo-Saxon cemetery at Little Eriswell, Suffolk. P.C.A.S. LIX.

HYSLOP, M. 1963:   Two Anglo-Saxon Cemeteries at Chamberlain's Barn, Leighton Buzzard, Bedfordshire. Arch. J. 120.

JANKUHN, H. 1979:   (with STRUWE and HINGST), Geschichte Schleswig-Holsteins. Bd.2 - Von der Bronzezeit bis zur Völkerwanderungszeit.

JOHANSEN, K.F. 1912:   Sølvskatten fra Terslev. Aarb. 1912.

JONES, M.U. 1975:   A clay piece-mould of the Migration period from Mucking, Essex. Ant. J. LV pp.407-408.

JORDAN, R. 1906:   Eigentümlichkeiten des anglischen Wortschatzes.

JORDANES: De origine actibusque Getarum.

KENT, J.P.C. 1978:   Roman Coins.

KIVIKOSKI, E. 1973:   Die Eisenzeit Finlands, Neuausgabe.

KIVIKOSKI, E. fs. 1973:   Honos Ella Kivikoski.

KLINDT-JENSEN, O. 1957:   Bornholm i folkevandringstiden og forudsætningerne i tidlig jernalder.

KOCH, U. 1977:   Das Reihengräberfeld bei Schretzheim.

KOSSACK, G., and REICHSTEIN, J. (edd.) 1977:
    Archäologische Beiträge zur Chronologie der
    Völkerwanderungszeit.

KRAUSE, W. 1966: Die Runeninschriften im älteren Futhark.

KUHN, H. 1940: Die germanischen Bügelfibeln der
    Völkerwanderungszeit in der Rheinprovinz.

LAMM, J.P. 1972: Undersökningar pa Lovö, 1958-1966.

LARSSON, L. 1982: Gräber und Siedlungsreste der jüngeren
    Eisenzeit bei Önsvala im südwestlichen Schonen,
    Schweden. Acta Arch. 52.

LEEDS, E.T. 1913: The Archaeology of the Anglo-Saxon
    Settlements.

LEEDS, E.T. 1933: The Early Saxon Penetration of the Upper
    Thames Area. Ant. J. XIII.

LEEDS, E.T. 1936: Early Anglo-Saxon Art and Archaeology.

LEEDS, E.T. and ATKINSON, R.J.C. 1944: An Anglo-Saxon
    cemetery at Nassington, Northants. Ant. J. XXIV.

LEEDS, E.T. 1945: The Distribution of the Angles and
    Saxons Archaeologically Considered.

LEEDS, E.T. 1949: A Corpus of Early Anglo-Saxon Great
    Square-Headed Brooches.

LEEDS, E.T. 1957 (ed. CHADWICK): Notes on Jutish Art in
    Kent between 450 and 575. Med. Arch. I.

LEIGH, D. 1980: The Square-Headed Brooches of Sixth-
    Century Kent. University College, Cardiff Ph.D.
    Thesis.

LETHBRIDGE, T.C. 1931: Recent excavations in Anglo-Saxon
    cemeteries in Cambridgeshire and Suffolk: a report.

LETHBRIDGE, T.C. 1936: A cemetery at Shudy Camps,
    Cambridgeshire.

LETHBRIDGE, T.C. 1951: A cemetery at Lackford, Suffolk.

LEWIS and SHORT: A Latin Dictionary, Clarendon Press,
    Oxford.

LORANGE, A. 1875: Samlingen af Norske Oldsager i Bergens
    Museum.

LOYN, H.R. 1977: The Vikings in Britain.

LUND HANSEN, U. 1969: Kvarmløsefundet. <u>Aarb.</u> 1969.

MACKEPRANG, M.B. 1943: Kulturbeziehungen im nordischen Raum des 3.-5. Jahrhunderts.

MACKEPRANG, M.B. 1952: De Nordiske Guldbrakteater.

MAGNUS, B. 1975: Krosshäugfunnet.

MALMER, M.P. 1963: Metodproblem inom järnålderns kunsthistoria.

MAYES, P. and DEAN, M.J. 1976: An Anglo-Saxon Cemetery at Baston Lincolnshire.

MAYR-HARTING, H. 1972: The Coming of Christianity to Anglo-Saxon England.

MEANEY, A.L. 1964: A Gazetteer of Early Anglo-Saxon Burial Sites.

MEANEY, A.L. 1981: Anglo-Saxon Amulets and Curing-Stones.

MONTELIUS, O. 1869: Från jernåldern.

MORTIMER, J.R. 1905: Forty Years` Researches in British and Saxon Burial Mounds of East Yorkshire.

MÜLLER-WILLE, M. 1970: Bestattung im Boot. <u>Offa</u> 25/26.

MYHRE, B. 1965: Et gravfunn fra Eikeland i Time. <u>SMÅ</u> 1965.

MYHRE, B. 1978: Agrarian Development, Settlement History, and Social Organization in South West Norway in the Iron Age. <u>New Directions in Scandinavian Archaeology</u>.

MYRES, J.N.L. 1969: Anglo-Saxon Pottery and the Settlement of England.

MYRES, J.N.L., and GREEN, B. 1973: Anglo-Saxon Cemeteries of Caistor-by-Norwich and Markshall, Norfolk.

MYRES, J.N.L., and SOUTHERN, W.H. 1973: The Anglo-Saxon cremation cemetery at Sancton, East Yorkshire.

MYRES, J.N.L. 1977: A Corpus of Anglo-Saxon Pottery of the Pagan Period.

MYRES, J.N.L. fs. 1981: Angles, Saxons, and Jutes. Essays presented to J.N.L. Myres.

MØLLERUP, O. 1960: Foreløpig meddelelse om et smedgravfunn fra Vestly i Time. <u>SMÅ</u> 1960.

NERMAN, B. 1935: Die Völkerwanderungszeit Gotlands.

NERMAN, B. 1969: Die Vendelzeit Gotlands. II - Tafeln.

NERMAN, B. 1975: Die Vendelzeit Gotlands. I - Text.

NEUMANN, H. 1982: Olgerdiget.

NEVILLE, R.C. 1852: Saxon Obsequies.

NIELSEN, J.N. 1980: En jernalderboplads og -gravplads ved Sejlflod i Østhimmerland. Ant. St. 4.

NISSEN MEYER, E. 1934: Relieffspenner i Norden.

NORLING-CHRISTENSEN, H. 1956: Haraldstedgravpladsen og ældre germanske Jærnalder i Danmark. Aarb. 1956.

OE Orosius: The Old English Orosius, ed. Bateley, EETS SS6.

O'LOUGHLIN, J.L.N. 1964: Sutton Hoo - The Evidence of the Documents. Med. Arch. 8.

OROSIUS, Paulus: Historiae adversum paganos.

OZANNE, A. 1963: The Peak Dwellers, Med. Arch. 6-7.

PAGE, R.I. 1973: An Introduction to English Runes.

PETERSEN, J. 1928: Vikingetidens Smykker.

PRIGG, H. 1888: The Anglo-Saxon Graves, Warren Hill, Mildenhall. P.Sfk.I.A.N.H. VI.

RADDATZ, K. 1962: Kaiserzeitliche Körpergräber von Heiligenhafen, Kr. Oldenburg. Offa 19.

RADDATZ, K. 1981: Sörup I.

RAMSKOU, Th. 1976: Lindholm Høje Gravpladsen.

REICHSTEIN, J. 1975: Die kreuzförmige Fibel.

ROACH SMITH, C. Coll. Ant.: Collectanea Antiqua.

ROEDER, F. 1930: Typologisch-chronologische Studien zu Metallsachen der Völkerwanderungszeit.

ROTH, H. 1973: Die Ornamentik der Langobarden in Italien.

RUSSELL ROBINSON, H. 1975: The Armour of Imperial Rome.

RYGH, O. 1885: Norske Oldsager.

SALIN, B. 1895: De nordiska guldbrakteaterna.

SALIN, B. 1904: Die altgermanische Thierornamentik.

SALWAY, P. 1981: Roman Britain.

SAMUELS, M.L. 1971: Kent and the Low Countries: some
linguistic evidence. Edinburgh Studies in English and
Scots, ed. Aitken et al.

SCHULZE, M. 1977: Die spätkaiserzeitliche Armbrustfibeln
mit fastem Nadelhalter: Gruppe Almgren VI, 2.

SHETELIG, H. 1906: The Cruciform Brooches of Norway.

SHETELIG, H. 1910: Smaa Broncespænder fra
Folkevandringstiden. Oldtiden 1910.

SHETELIG, H. 1912 (VJG): Vestlandske Graver fra
Jernalderen.

Sigrifumál: in Edda. Die Lieder des Codex Regius, ed.
Neckel.

SJØVOLD, Th. 1962: The Iron Age Settlement of Arctic
Norway. Vol. I - Early Iron Age.

SKAARE, K. 1976: Coins and Coinage in Viking Age Norway.

SLOMANN, W. 1961: Buckelurnen aus der Völkerwanderungszeit
in Norwegen. Die Kunde 12.

SOLBERG, B. 1981: Spearheads in the transition period
between the early and the late iron age in Norway.
Acta Arch. 51.

SPEAKE, G. 1980: Anglo-Saxon Animal Art and its Germanic
Background.

STENBERGER, M. 1964: Det forntida Sverige.

STENTON, F.M. 1943: Anglo-Saxon England.

STJERNQUIST, B. 1955: Simris (I).

SUTTON HOO 1-2: The Sutton Ship-Burial, ed. Bruce-Mitford,
BM Publications.

SWANTON, M.J. 1966: An Anglian Cemetery at Londesborough,
Yorks, YAJ XLI.

SWANTON, M.J. 1974: A Corpus of Pagan Anglo-Saxon Spear-
Types.

SWANTON, M. (ed.) 1978: Beowulf.

SÄRLVIK, I. 1982: Paths towards a Stratified Society.

THOMAS, G.W. 1887: Excavations in an Anglo-Saxon Cemetery

THOMAS, G.W. 1887: Excavations in an Anglo-Saxon Cemetery at Sleaford, Lincs. Arch. L.

TODD, M. 1975: The "Alamannic" brooch from Londesborough (Yorks). Ant. J. LV pp.384-388.

VCH: Victoria County History.

VIERCK, H.E.F. 1966: Some leading types of the Anglian province of culture, fifth to seventh century A.D., with their oversea connections. Oxford University B.Litt. Thesis.

VIERCK, H.E.F., and CAPELLE, T. 1971: Modeln der Merowinger- und Wikingerzeit. FS 5.

VIERCK, H.E.F. 1973: Redwalds Asche. Offa 29.

VIERCK, H.E.F. 1978: various articles in Die Menschen. Sachsen und Angelsachsen, Helms-Museum, Hamburg.

VJG: see Shetelig 1912.

VOSS, O. 1954: The Høstentorp Silver-Hoard and its Period. Acta Arch. 24.

WEBSTER, L. 1977: Brakteaten ... England. Hoops' Reallexikon der germanischen Altertumskunde. Bd.3 pp.341-342.

WELCH, M.G. 1983: Early Anglo-Saxon Sussex.

WERNER, J. 1935: Munzdatierte austrasische Grabfunde.

WERNER, J. fs. 1974: Studien zur vor- und frühgeschichtlichen Archäologie, ed. Kossack, G. and Ulbert, G.

Widsith: ed. K. Malone, 2nd. edn. 1962.

WILSON, D.M. 1956: The Initial Excavation of an Anglo-Saxon Cemetery at Melbourn, Cambridgeshire. P.C.A.S. XLIX.

WILSON, D.M. 1957: An Anglo-Saxon grave near Dartford, Kent. Arch. Cant. LXX

WILSON, D.M., and KLINDT-JENSEN, O. 1966: Viking Art.

WILSON, D.M. 1976: The Archaeology of Anglo-Saxon England.

WILSON, D.M. 1980: Sverige-England. Vendeltid, Statens Historiska Museum, Stockholm.

ØRSNES, M. 1964: The weapon find in Ejsbøl Mose at Haderslev. Acta Arch. 34.

ÅBERG, N. 1924: Den nordiska folkvandringstidens
     kronologi.

ÅBERG, N. 1926: The Anglo-Saxons in England, during the
     early centuries after the invasion.

ÅBERG, N. 1953: Den historiska relationen mellan folk-
     vandringstid och vendeltid.

ÅBERG, N. 1956: Den historiska relationen mellan
     senromersk tid och nordisk folkvandringstid.

Þrymskviða: in Edda. Die Lieder des Codex Regius, ed.
     Neckel.